$306

Funk & Wagnalls Standard Handbook of
SYNONYMS,
Antonyms, and Prepositions

Funk & Wagnalls
Standard Handbook of

SYNONYMS,
Antonyms, and Prepositions

By JAMES C. FERNALD, L.H.D.

Completely Revised Edition
By Funk & Wagnalls Editorial Staff

FUNK & WAGNALLS
A Division of Reader's Digest Books, Inc.
New York

CONTENTS

PAGE

PREFACE vii

USE THE INDEX ix

SYNONYMS, ANTONYMS, AND PREPOSITIONS 1

INDEX OF SYNONYMS 447

INDEX OF ANTONYMS 499

PREFACE TO THE NEW EDITION

In 1896 Dr. James Champlain Fernald brought out his first edition of this work. It was notably successful and so well received by careful writers and speakers that, in 1914, he produced a second edition with an augmented number of dissertations, many new synonyms, and a careful revision of the previous text. Dr. Fernald died four years after completing that revision. The passage of the years since has convinced the publishers that the style of treatment used by him in showing the divergence in meanings among words which are closely synonymous in one or another respect meets the practical needs of those who wish to be discriminatory in their use of words. Times and usages have changed to some extent within the past half century, however, and the present editors have recognized such changes. Some words are no longer as restrictive as they were; others have taken on new decisiveness. Many have acquired new synonyms.

Aside from a revision of the former text to bring it into keeping with present-day usage, this edition will be found to be richer in quantity and in treatment. A considerable number of new discussions on the discrimination among words has been added. But perhaps of greater interest and value to the reader is the more extensive treatment that has been given to discussion; many words formerly listed under the main heading, but not treated in the accompanying discussion, have been critically examined and, if their differences were not clearly evident, have been compared along with the others. Much of the material has also been rearranged, so that the word under which its synonyms are grouped is the keystone to which others are compared. Dr. Fernald's fine sense of the discrimination between words of closely parallel meanings has been carefully preserved.

USE THE INDEX

Many persons fail to find the words they are seeking in this book, because they look only at the *key-word* at the head of each article. These *key-words* are given in alphabetical order, so that if one wishes to find the word "beautiful," for instance, that will be found in the regular alphabetical order on page 87.

But under the word "beautiful" there are 17 synonyms. It is obvious that not every one of these can be made the head of a group in alphabetical order.

How can any word within the group be found? By turning to the *Index* at the back of the volume. Suppose you wish synonyms for the word "pretty." You will not find that under *P*, but by turning to the Index you will find:

"pretty, Beautiful .... 87"

That is, "pretty" is to be found under the key-word, "Beautiful," on page 87. Often one word is referred to several groups, thus:

cultivation, Agriculture 31
Education 170
Refinement 358

some different aspect or meaning of the word being treated under each of the different groups.

A

ABANDON

abdicate	desert	leave	resign
abjure	discontinue	quit	retire from
cast off	forgo	recant	retract
cease	forsake	relinquish	surrender
cede	forswear	renounce	vacate
depart from	give up	repudiate	withdraw from

Abandon is a word of wide signification, denoting the complete giving up or withdrawal from persons or things of any kind. *Abandon* implies previous association with responsibility for or control of; *forsake* implies previous association with inclination or attachment, real or assumed; a man may *abandon* or *forsake* house or friends; he *abandons* an enterprise; *forsakes* God. *Abandon* is applied to both good and evil action; a thief *abandons* his designs; a man, his principles. *Forsake,* like *abandon,* may be used either in the favorable, or unfavorable sense; *desert* is always unfavorable, involving a breach of duty, except when used of mere localities; as, "The Deserted Village."

Abdicate and *resign* apply to office, authority, or power; a monarch *abdicates,* a president or other elected or appointed officer *resigns*. It was held that Edward VIII *abdicated* his throne; that James II *deserted* it. *Cede* applies to territorial possessions; *surrender* especially to military force, and more generally to any demand, claim, passion, etc. *Quit* carries an idea of suddenness or abruptness not necessarily implied in *abandon,* and may not have the same suggestion of finality. A ruler might *cede* his territory, *desert* his followers, *abjure* or *renounce* his religion, *relinquish* his titles, *abandon* his designs, *recant* his confession. A cowardly officer *deserts* his ship; the helpless passengers *abandon* it. We *quit* business, *give up* property, *resign* office, *abandon* a habit or a trust, *cease* listening.

Relinquish commonly implies reluctance; the weary hand *relinquishes* its grasp; the creditor *relinquishes* his claim. We *discontinue* subscriptions when we *cease* to pay for them; we *give up* habits or doing something; *forgo* what we refrain from doing or *give up,* and *forswear* what we *renounce* on oath. *Repudiate,* originally to *cast off,* in this connection means to *renounce*; *retract* is to withdraw a promise or order. See **renounce; stop; surrender.**

ANTONYMS: *adopt, advocate, assert, cherish, claim, court, defend, favor, haunt, hold, keep, maintain, occupy, prosecute, protect, pursue, retain, seek, support, undertake, uphold, vindicate.*

ABATE

alleviate	diminish	lower	stop
curtail	dwindle	mitigate	subside
decline	ebb	moderate	suppress
decrease	lessen	reduce	terminate

Abate generally implies to *lessen* in some way, but may mean to *stop* or *suppress*. The storm, the fever, and the pain *abate*. Interest *declines*. Misfortunes may be *mitigated*, desires *moderated*, intense anger *abated*, population *decreased*, taxes *reduced*, pain *alleviated*. An ill-managed fortune *dwindles*; a flood *subsides*; the tide *ebbs*. We *abate* a nuisance, *terminate* a controversy, *suppress* a rebellion, *curtail* or *reduce* production when there is a surplus. See **alleviate.**

> **ANTONYMS:** *aggravate, amplify, continue, develop, enhance, enlarge, extend, foment, increase, magnify, raise, revive.*

> **PREPOSITIONS:** Abate *in* fury; abated *by* law.

ABBREVIATION

abridgment   **contraction**

An *abbreviation* is a shortening by any method; a *contraction* is a reduction of size by the drawing together of the parts. A *contraction* of a word is made by omitting certain letters or syllables and bringing together the first and last letters or elements; an *abbreviation* may be made either by omitting certain portions from the interior or by cutting off a part; a *contraction* is an *abbreviation*, but an *abbreviation* is not necessarily a *contraction*; *rec't* for receipt, *mdse.* for merchandise, and *Dr.* for debtor are *contractions*; they are also *abbreviations*; *Am.* for American is an *abbreviation*, but not a *contraction*.

Abbreviation and *contraction* are used of words and phrases; *abridgment* is used of books, paragraphs, sentences, etc., or it may denote a curtailment, as of rights or privileges. See **abridgment.**

ABET

advocate	embolden	incite	sanction
aid	encourage	instigate	support
assist	help	promote	uphold
countenance			

Abet and *instigate* are now used almost without exception in a bad sense; one may *incite* either to good or evil. One *incites* or *instigates* to action, or to increased activity or advancement of activity; one *abets* by giving sympathy, countenance, or substantial aid to the doing of that which is already projected or in process of commission. *Abet* and *instigate* apply either to persons or actions, *incite* to persons only; one *incites* a person to an action. The originator of a crime often *instigates* or *incites* others to *abet* him in it, or one may *instigate* or *incite* others to a crime in the commission of which he himself takes no active part.

A clergyman will *advocate* the claims of justice, *aid* the poor, *encourage* the despondent, *help* the needy, *support* the weak, *uphold* the constituted authorities; but he will not *incite* to a quarrel, *instigate* a riot, *abet* a crime, or *countenance* wrong-doing. To *promote* is to advance someone or something, or to *encourage*; to *embolden* is to make bold or brave by *encouraging*. See **help; support.**

ANTONYMS: *baffle, confound, counteract, denounce, deter, disapprove, disconcert, discourage, dissuade, expose, frustrate, hinder, impede, obstruct.*

ABEYANCE

adjournment	expectancy	intermission	reservation
discontinuance	expectation	interruption	suspense
dormancy	inaction	quiescence	suspension

The words in this list, except *discontinuance* which may be final or temporary, denote cessation of activity with expectation or possibility of resumption. A title to property, when in *abeyance*, is likely to be revived if a lawful owner appears; a claim or a measure is held in *abeyance* with distinct purpose of pressing it should occasion arise. *Expectancy* or *expectation*, in this connection, is *abeyance* viewed from the standpoint of one who expects to attain possession; as, an estate in *expectancy*.

Dormancy denotes a state of suspended animation like that of a hibernating animal; a law which is in *dormancy* may be again enforced, but always with a prejudice against it, because custom has held its non-enforcement to be tantamount to an unwritten repeal. *Inaction* may be habitual; as, the slothful man wastes his life in *inaction*; or it may be temporary; as, the *inaction* of an army while awaiting the moment to strike, or the *inaction* of a volcano which is not extinct. *Intermission* points to expected, or perhaps calculated, resumption, and may be frequently or regularly repeated; as, the *intermissions* of remittent fever, the *intermission* of artillery fire, or the *intermission* between sessions of a school or of a deliberative assembly.

Intermission is from within; *interruption* from without; *intermission* may be natural or voluntary; *interruption* is enforced by some disturbing cause; as, the *interruption* of a religious service by rioters. *Quiescence* is closely allied to *inaction*; but while *inaction* denotes lack of activity, *quiescence* denotes lack of disturbing symptoms of activity, as agitation, excitement, or commotion. The *reservation* of a right or claim maintains it in full force, entitling the party so reserving to press it at any time; mental *reservation* consists in holding unspoken some condition or qualification which, if uttered, would seem to change the whole character of some statement or promise.

Suspension is temporary, usually for a stated period, and is ordinarily by authority, as the *suspension* of an officer from command, under charges, or the *suspension* of a student from college; *suspension* of payment is in theory temporary, but is in fact so often final as to be closely allied to bankruptcy; *suspension* of sentence, pending good behavior, is now frequently allowed on conviction of minor offenses. *Suspense*, as compared here, is temporary cessation.

ANTONYMS: *action, enforcement, enjoyment, exercise, force, operation, possession, renewal, resuscitation, revival.*

ABHOR

abominate	detest	displease	loathe	scorn
despise	dislike	hate	nauseate	shun

Abhor is stronger than *despise*, implying a shuddering recoil, especially a moral recoil. *Detest* expresses indignation, with something of contempt. *Loathe* implies disgust, physical or moral. We *abhor* a traitor, *despise* a coward, *detest* a liar. We *dislike*, or are *displeased* by, an uncivil person. We *abhor* cruelty, *hate* tyranny. We *loathe* a reptile or a flatterer. We *abhor* Milton's heroic Satan, but we cannot *despise* him. We *scorn* what we hold in contempt; we *shun* what we *dislike* and do not want to meet; we *abominate* what we intensely *loathe*. If something disgusts us, makes us feel sick, it *nauseates* us.

To *hate*, in its strict sense, is to regard with such extreme aversion as to feel a desire to destroy or injure the object of hatred; properly employed it should be the strongest word for the expression of aversion, but it is often loosely used with no stronger meaning than to *dislike*, as well as for any other of the above words.

ANTONYMS: *admire, approve, covet, crave, desire, enjoy, esteem, like, love, relish.*

ABIDE

await	endure	remain	stop
bear	expect	reside	tarry
bide	inhabit	rest	tolerate
confront	live	sojourn	wait (for)
continue	lodge	stay	watch
dwell			

To *abide* is to *remain* continuously without limit of time unless expressed by the context: "today I must *abide* at thy house," *Luke* xix, 5. *Abide* often includes endurance; as, I can't *abide* a liar. *Lodge, sojourn, stay, tarry,* **and** *wait* always imply a limited time; *lodge,* to pass the night; *sojourn,* to remain temporarily; *live, dwell, reside,* to have a permanent home. *Stop,* in the sense of *stay* or *sojourn,* is colloquial. *Await* is to *wait for* someone or something; *bide* is to *await* expectantly, or, colloquially, to *tarry*. *Bear, tolerate,* and *endure* refer to long continued suffering, annoyance, etc. We *confront* people or problems when we meet them face to face. See **endure.**

ANTONYMS: *abandon, avoid, depart, forfeit, forfend, journey, migrate, move, proceed, reject, resist, shun.*

PREPOSITIONS: Abide *in* a place, *for* a time, *with* a person, *by* a statement.

ABOLISH

abate	eradicate	prohibit	stamp out
abrogate	exterminate	remove	subvert
annihilate	extirpate	repeal	supplant
annul	nullify	reverse	suppress
cancel	obliterate	revoke	terminate
destroy	overthrow	set aside	void
end			

Abolish, to do away with, bring absolutely to an end, especially as something hostile, hindering, or harmful, was formerly used of persons and material objects, a usage now obsolete except in poetry or highly figurative speech. *Abolish* is now used of institutions, customs, and conditions, especially those widespread and long existing; as, to *abolish* slavery, ignorance, intemperance, poverty. A building that is burned to the ground is said to be *destroyed* by fire. *Annihilate* signifies to put absolutely out of existence, with no possibility of being revived or restored. An army is *annihilated.* Some believe that the wicked will be *annihilated. Annul* is used generally of actions or agreements; a contract may be *annulled* by an action that *voids* it.

Abolish is not said of laws. There we use *repeal, abrogate, nullify,* etc.; *repeal* by the enacting body, *nullify* by revolutionary proceedings; a later statute *abrogates,* without formally *repealing,* any earlier law with which it conflicts. An appellate court may *reverse* or *set aside* the decision of an inferior court.

Cancel, as commonly used, refers to an action that invalidates or *nullifies* something; as, to *cancel* an order.

Overthrow may be used in either a good or a bad sense; *suppress* is commonly in a good, *subvert* always in a bad, sense; as, to *subvert* our liberties; to *suppress* a rebellion. The law *prohibits* what may never have existed; it *abolishes* an existing evil. We *abate* a nuisance, *terminate* a controversy. See **cancel; demolish; end** *verb*; **exterminate; overthrow; prohibit.**

ANTONYMS: *authorize, cherish, confirm, continue, enact, establish, institute, introduce, legalize, promote, reinstate, renew, repair, restore, revive, set up, support, sustain.*

ABOMINATION

abhorrence	detestation	horror	pest
abuse	disgust	iniquity	plague
annoyance	evil	loathing	shame
aversion	execration	nuisance	villainy
crime	hatred	offense	wickedness
curse			

Abomination was originally applied to anything held in religious or ceremonial *aversion* or *abhorrence*; now it is applied to any person or thing which provokes *loathing* or *disgust*. The word is oftener applied to the object of such *aversion* or *abhorrence* than to the state of mind that so regards it. Choice food may be an object of *aversion* and *disgust* to a sick person; vile food would be an *abomination*. A toad is to many an object of *disgust*; a foul sewer is an *abomination*. As applied to crimes, *abomination* is used of such as are especially brutal, shameful, or revolting; theft is an *offense*; infanticide is an *abomination*.

A *nuisance* may be simply a source of *annoyance*, or it may cause actual damage or harm. *Pest* and *plague* designate epidemic disease; *plague* also is used to denote any generally blighting occurrence, while *pest* often is used, in a milder sense, to apply to someone or something which is a great *nuisance*. See **antipathy; chagrin; fear; hatred; injury; injustice; oath; sin.**

ANTONYMS: *affection, appreciation, approval, benefit, blessing, delight, desire, enjoyment, esteem, gratification, joy, satisfaction, treat.*

ABOUND

flourish	luxuriate	prevail	stream	swell
flow	overflow	revel	swarm	teem

To *abound* signifies to *overflow*, to exist, possess, or produce in generous surplus beyond demand or need; to be abundant; luxuriant, numerous, plenteous, or plentiful, or to possess, produce, or furnish in profusion. To *teem* means to be plentifully supplied with; as, the city *teems* with people. *Luxuriate* applies to profusion in growth, as of plants; *flourish* is a general term and applies to people, conditions, vegetation, etc. To *swarm* is to congregate in large numbers crowded together: said of insects, persons, animals, and things. To *stream* is to issue forth in continuous succession, as a crowd. In this connection, to *prevail* is to extend widely; to *revel* is to indulge freely in, as in freedom. Compare **plentiful.**

> **ANTONYMS:** *be deficient, be destitute, be lacking, be wanting, fail, lack, need, want.*

ABOVE

on   over   upon

Above is the most inclusive of these prepositions. It can ordinarily be substituted for *on, upon,* or *over*; as, the boards were piled one *on* or *upon* another (one *above* another); the hawk flies *over* the wood (*above* the wood). But it will be seen that while *above* is more inclusive, it is less definite; the boards laid one *on* another are in contact, but when laid one *above* another, they may not touch. *Over* often contains an intimation, while it may be slight, of extension or motion across, while *above* may simply imply greater elevation. If we say, the mountain towers *above* the plain, we think only of its height; but if we say, the mountain towers *over* the plain, we think of the plain as in the shadow of the mountain and dominated by it. So we say the mountain is 7,000 feet *above* the sea, where it would be impossible to say 7,000 feet *over* the sea. *Upon* is practically identical with *on*, both in meaning and use, preference for the former being sometimes based on euphony. *Upon* in many connections is somewhat more formal or dignified than *on*, and is also common when motion into position is involved, *on* being then used when merely rest or support is indicated; as, he got *upon* the roof and sat *on* the ridge.

> **ANTONYMS:** See synonyms for **beneath.**

ABRIDGMENT

abbreviation   compend   epitome   summary
abstract   compendium   outline   synopsis
analysis   digest   précis

An *abridgment* gives the most important portions of a work, usually a book, substantially as they stand. An *outline* or *synopsis* is a kind of sketch closely following the plan. An *abstract* or *digest* is an independent statement of what the book contains. An *analysis* draws out the chief thoughts or arguments, whether expressed or implied. A *summary* is the most condensed statement of results or conclusions. A *précis* is a concise, brief *summary* of the ideas and points of view of a book or an article. An *abbreviation* is a shortening, usually of a single word. An *epitome, compend,* or *compendium* is a condensed view of a subject, whether derived from a previous publication or not. We may have an *abridgment* of a dictionary, but not an *analysis, abstract, digest,* or *summary.* We may have an *epitome* of religion, a *compendium* of English literature, but not an *abridgment.* An *abridgment* may also mean a curtailment, as of rights or privileges. See **abbreviation.**

ABSCOND

bolt	fly	run off
conceal oneself	hide	slip away
decamp	leave	steal away
depart	retire	steal off
disappear	retreat	take oneself off
flee	run away	withdraw

To *abscond* is to *flee* and *hide* oneself for some discreditable reason, often for the illegal taking of money. To *decamp,* literally to "break camp," march off, usually signifies to *depart* suddenly, secretly, or unceremoniously, implying danger of attack, discovery, restraint, or pursuit; a traveler might *decamp* in fear of lurking robbers or enemies, or soldiers on the discovery of a superior force; but, as good reasons for such withdrawal seldom arise, *decamp* has, on the whole, an unfavorable implication.

To *flee* implies an abrupt departure, often with the additional connotation of complete disappearance, especially when used of things. The use of *fly* as a synonym of *flee* is restricted to the present tense; as, those who *fly* may fight again; he *fled* to the hills.

All the other words of the list may have favorable meaning, the context alone determining whether the act is worthy or unworthy. To *bolt* is to start off suddenly at full sped in defiance of restraint, like a frightened or vicious horse, as a "bolt" is shot from a bow or a gun. A student *leaves* home for college; a traveler *departs* on his journey; a passer-by *disappears* in the crowd (as a hunted thief may also do); a prisoner of war may *bolt* from his guards; one may *flee* for good or bad reason.

A slave may *run away* from his master, *run off* from a plantation; a public man may *hide* from reporters, or a criminal from the police; one may *retire* or *withdraw* from observation for good reasons or bad; an army *retires* or *retreats* from an untenable position or before a superior force; one may *slip away* from a company he does not wish to break up, *slip away* or *steal away* from a sleeping invalid, whom he would not disturb, *slip away* denoting merely quietness, *steal away* adding the idea of something furtive. See **hide.**

ANTONYMS: *appear, arrive, be present, come into view emerge, hold one's ground, hold one's place, present oneself, put in an appearance, reappear, remain, stand one's ground, stay.*

ABSOLUTE

arbitrary	controlling	imperative	supreme
arrogant	despotic	imperious	tyrannical
authoritative	dictatorial	irresponsible	tyrannous
autocratic	dogmatic	lordly	unconditional
coercive	domineering	overbearing	unconditioned
compulsive	exacting	peremptory	unequivocal
compulsory	haughty	positive	unlimited

Absolute primarily signifies free from limitation by other authority; as, an *absolute* monarch. In this use, it does not necessarily carry any unfavorable sense, but as *absolute* power in human hands is generally abused, the unfavorable meaning predominates. *Arbitrary,* carrying an unfavorable connotation, means made or done at the whim or caprice of the agent. An *arbitrary* decision is one made without the guidance of those precedents and thoughtful consideration which accompany reasonable and consistent action. *Autocratic* usually refers to the assertion of the right to hold *absolute* power, as in speech or action. *Despotic, dictatorial,* and *tyrannical* refer to the actual exercise of that right. *Despotic* is commonly applied to a masterful or severe use of power, which is expressed more decidedly by *tyrannical. Irresponsible* power is not necessarily bad, but eminently dangerous; an executor or trustee should not be *irresponsible*; an *irresponsible* ruler is likely to be *tyrannical. Tyrannous* is more often used of things or qualities than of persons; as, *tyrannous* power.

Authoritative implies the right to claim authority; *imperative, peremptory,* and *positive* are used ordinarily in a good sense; as, an *authoritative* definition, an *imperative* demand, a *peremptory* command, *positive* instructions. *Imperious* signifies not only assuming a command, but determined to command and require implicit obedience. An *arrogant* demand is offensive by its tone of superiority; an *arbitrary* demand offends by its unreasonableness; an *imperious* disposition is liable to become *arbitrary* and *arrogant.* That which is *supreme* is exalted above others; as, the *supreme* court. See **authentic; dogmatic; infinite; perfect.**

> ANTONYMS: *accountable, complaisant, compliant, conditional, constitutional, contingent, docile, ductile, gentle, humble, lenient, limited, lowly, meek, mild, responsible, submissive, yielding.*

ABSOLVE

acquit	exculpate	forgive	pardon
clear	exempt	free	release
discharge	exonerate	liberate	set free

To *absolve,* in the strict sense, is to *set free* from any bond. One may be *absolved* from a promise by a breach of faith on the part of one to whom the promise was made. To *absolve* from sins is formally to remit their condemnation and penalty, regarded as a bond upon the soul. To *exonerate* is to relieve of something regarded as a load or burden. To *exempt* is more restricted in meaning; to *exempt* a person is to *free* him from some legal or other burden to which everyone else in similar circumstances is subject. To *exculpate* is to *free* from blame in some trifling matter. To *acquit* of sin or crime is to *free* from the accusation of it, pronouncing one guiltless; the innocent are rightfully *acquitted*; the guilty may be mercifully *absolved*. See **pardon** *verb*.

ANTONYMS: *accuse, bind, charge, compel, condemn, convict, impeach, inculpate, obligate, oblige.*

PREPOSITIONS: One is absolved *from* (rarely *of*) a promise. a sin, etc.

ABSORB

assimilate	drink up	imbibe	swallow up
consume	engross	suck up	take in
drink in	exhaust	swallow	take up

A fluid that is *absorbed* is taken up into the mass of the absorbing body, with which it may or may not permanently combine. Wood expands when it *absorbs* moisture, iron when it *absorbs* heat, the substance remaining perhaps otherwise substantially unchanged; quicklime, when it *absorbs* water, becomes a new substance with different qualities, hydrated or slaked lime. A substance is *consumed* which is destructively appropriated by some other substance, being, or agency, so that it ceases to exist or to be recognized as existing in its original condition; fuel is *consumed* in the fire, food in the body; *consume* is also applied to whatever is removed from the market for individual use; as, silk and woolen goods are *consumed*.

A great talker *engrosses* the conversation. A credulous person *swallows* the most preposterous statement. A busy student *imbibes* or *drinks in* knowledge; he is *absorbed* in a subject that takes his whole attention. *Imbibe* connotes drinking or breathing. A person can *imbibe* refreshing liquids or exhilarating air. *Assimilate* carries the idea of absorption, with the additional implication that the absorbed material is converted into the substance of the assimilating body. Food is *assimilated* by a living organism; a student *assimilates* knowledge.

ANTONYMS: *cast out, disgorge, disperse, dissipate, distract, eject, emit, exude, give up, put forth, radiate, send out, shoot forth, throw off, vomit.*

PREPOSITIONS: Plants absorb moisture *from* the air; the student is absorbed *in* thought; nutriment may be absorbed *into* the system *through* the skin.

ABSTINENCE

abstemiousness	continence	moderation	self-restraint
abstaining	fasting	self-control	sobriety
abstention	frugality	self-denial	temperance

Abstinence from food commonly signifies going without; *abstemiousness*, partaking moderately; *abstinence* may be for a single occasion, *abstemiousness* is habitual *moderation*. *Self-denial* is giving up what one wishes; *abstinence* may be refraining from what one does not desire. *Fasting* is *abstinence* from food for a limited time, and generally for religious reasons. *Sobriety* and *temperance* signify maintaining a quiet, even temper by moderate indulgence in some things, complete *abstinence* from others. We speak of *temperance* in eating, but of *abstinence* from vice. Total *abstinence* has come to signify the entire *abstaining* from intoxicating liquors. *Continence* denotes *self-restraint* with regard to one's desires or appetites. *Frugality* is a careful *moderation* in expenditure. See **frugality.**

ANTONYMS: *drunkenness, excess, gluttony, greed, intemperance, intoxication, reveling, revelry, self-indulgence, sensuality, wantonness.*

PREPOSITIONS: The negative side of virtue is abstinence *from* vice.

ABSTRACT

appropriate	distract	purloin	steal
detach	divert	remove	take away
discriminate	eliminate	separate	withdraw
distinguish			

The central idea of withdrawing makes *abstract* in common speech a euphemism for *appropriate* (unlawfully), *purloin, steal.* In mental processes we *discriminate* between objects by *distinguishing* their differences; we *separate* some one element from all that does not necessarily belong to it, *abstract* it, and view it alone. We may *separate* two ideas, and hold both in mind in comparison or contrast; but when we *abstract* one of them, we drop the other out of thought. The mind is *abstracted* when it is *withdrawn* from all other subjects and concentrated upon one, *diverted* when it is drawn away from what it would or should attend to by some other interest, *distracted* when the attention is divided among different subjects, so that it cannot be given properly to any. To *detach* something is to isolate it by breaking or removing all connections or bonds; one may *detach* a flower from its stem; a detached platoon is one *separated* from its company or troop.

ANTONYMS: *add, combine, complete, conjoin, fill up, increase, restore, strengthen, unite.*

PREPOSITIONS: The purse may be abstracted *from* the pocket; the substance *from* the accidents; a book *into* a compend.

ABSTRACTED

absent	distraught	indifferent	oblivious
absent-minded	heedless	listless	preoccupied
absorbed	inattentive	negligent	thoughtless
distrait			

As regards mental action, *abstracted, absorbed,* and *preoccupied* refer to the cause, *absent* or *absent-minded* to the effect. The man *absorbed* in one thing will appear *absent* in others, because his thoughts are elsewhere. The *heedless* worker may become *negligent* if he is *inattentive* to details. A *preoccupied* person may seem *listless* and *thoughtless,* but the really *listless* and *thoughtless* have not mental energy to be *preoccupied.* The *absent-minded* man is *oblivious* of ordinary matters, because his thoughts are elsewhere. One who is *preoccupied* is intensely busy in thought; one may be *absent-minded* either through intense concentration or simply through inattention, with fitful and aimless wandering of thought. *Distraught* and its French equivalent, *distrait,* carry the same meaning as *abstracted. Distrait* is often used to describe a mood or disposition; as, her *distrait* manner betrayed her preoccupation with these affairs. Compare **abstract.**

ANTONYMS: *alert, attentive, on hand, prompt, ready, thoughtful, wide-awake.*

ABSURD

anomalous	ill-considered	ludicrous	ridiculous
chimerical	ill-judged	mistaken	senseless
erroneous	inconclusive	monstrous	silly
false	incorrect	nonsensical	stupid
foolish	infatuated	paradoxical	unreasonable
ill-advised	irrational	preposterous	wild

That is *absurd* which is contrary to the first principles of reasoning; as, that a part should be greater than the whole is *absurd.* A *paradoxical* statement appears at first thought contradictory or *absurd,* while it may be really true. Anything is *irrational* when clearly contrary to sound reason, *foolish* when contrary to practical good sense, *silly* when petty and contemptible in its folly, *erroneous* when containing error that vitiates the result, *unreasonable* when there seems a perverse bias or an intent to go wrong.

Monstrous and *preposterous* refer to what is overwhelmingly *absurd. Pre posterous,* according to its etymology, denotes that which is hind side before; *monstrous* refers to something freakish or unnatural. The *ridiculous* or the *nonsensical* is worthy only to be laughed at. The lunatic's claim to be a king is *ridiculous*; sounds without meaning, as "Fe-fi-fo-fum," are *nonsensical.* See **incongruous.**

ANTONYMS: *certain, consistent, demonstrable, demonstrated, established, incontestable, incontrovertible, indisputable, indubitable, infallible, logical, rational, reasonable, sagacious, sensible, sound, substantial, true, undeniable, unquestionable, wise.*

A B U S E

aggrieve	impose on or	outrage	revile
damage	upon	persecute	ruin
defame	injure	pervert	slander
defile	malign	profane	victimize
desecrate	maltreat	prostitute	vilify
disparage	misemploy	rail at	violate
harm	misuse	ravish	vituperate
ill-treat	molest	reproach	wrong
ill-use	oppress		

Abuse covers all unreasonable or improper use or treatment by word or act. Neither *abuse* nor *misuse* necessarily implies deliberate or wilful mistreatment. One's hospitality or generosity can be *abused*; the English language can be *misused.* A tenant does not *abuse* rented property by "reasonable wear," though that may *damage* the property and *injure* its sale; he may *abuse* it by needless defacement or neglect. To *outrage* is to *abuse* so violently as to transgress all bounds; as, to *outrage* morality.

It is possible to *abuse* a man without *harming* him, as when the criminal *vituperates* the judge; or to *harm* a man without *abusing* him, as when the witness tells the truth about the criminal. *Defame, malign, rail at, revile, slander, vilify,* and *vituperate* are used always in a bad sense. One may be justly *reproached.* To *impose on* or to *victimize* one is to *injure* him by *abusing* his confidence. To *persecute* one is to *ill-treat* him for opinion's sake, commonly for religious belief; to *oppress* is generally for political or pecuniary motives. *Misemploy, misuse,* and *pervert* are commonly applied to objects rather than to persons. A dissolute youth *misemploys* his time, *misuses* his money and opportunities, *harms* his associates, *perverts* his talents, *wrongs* his parents, *ruins* himself, *abuses* every good gift of God.

ANTONYMS: *applaud, benefit, care for, cherish, conserve, consider, eulogize, extol, favor, laud, panegyrize, praise, protect, regard, respect, shield, sustain, tend, uphold, vindicate.*

ABYSS

abysm	deep	gulf	void
chasm	depth	pit	

An *abyss* (from Gr. *a-*, without, *byssos*, bottom) is primarily a bottomless gulf, unmeasurable and unfathomable; it has also come to denote any vast or interminable extent, as of interstellar space, without reference to direction. *Abyss* is figuratively used to denote what is profound and seemingly unfathomable in thought; as, an *abyss* of metaphysical disputation; an *abyss* of ignorance, degradation, or infamy. *Abysm* is an archaic or poetic equivalent of *abyss*. A *void* signifies an empty space.

A *gulf* (from Gr. *kolphos*, bay) is primarily a wide expanse of water, partly enclosed, and defined as between a bay and a sea in extent, but used with a wide range of meaning; as, the *Gulf* of Venice, the *Gulf* of Mexico. The word is then applied to any vast and deep depression on the earth's surface that seems impassable like a sea. In figurative or poetic use *gulf* is variously applied as to that which engulfs or overwhelms, as a whirlpool or vast ocean *depth* or to anything that widely and deeply separates, as in thought, feeling, character, or relations.

Pit is used with the definite article to signify the grave, the "bottomless pit," hades, gehenna, inferno, or hell, and in this sense only is a synonym of *abyss*. A *chasm* is a deep, long opening, especially in the earth's surface. In its figurative use, *chasm* emphasizes the connotation of an abrupt break; as, the *chasms* of consciousness.

> **ANTONYMS:** *canopy of heaven, dome of heaven, elevation, empyrean, firmament, height, hill, mount, mountain, summit, vault of heaven, zenith.*

ACADEMIC, ACADEMICAL

bookish	learned	Platonic	speculative
collegiate	lettered	Platonistic	theoretic
conventional	literary	scholarly	theoretical
formal	pedantic	scholastic	

Academic or *academical, collegiate, literary, learned, scholarly,* and *theoretic* or *theoretical,* all denote what pertains to an academy or a college, to learning, literature, sound scholarship, or well-considered theory. As applied to a college or university, the *academical* department is technically that which is concerned with classical, mathematical, or general literary studies as distinguished from the professional and scientific departments. In literary use, *Academic* is used of the Academy of Plato at Athens, hence of Plato or his followers, or of the *Platonic* philosophy.

Formal implies that which is done in accordance with proper and usual forms, carrying the weight and authority of what is established and recognized; as, a *formal* letter, notification, or summons (distinguished from a memorandum or from an offhand or familiar note). *Conventional* applies to conformity with conventions or usages, as of good society; *conventional* politeness may go no deeper than compliance with accepted usages. *Theoretic* and *theoretical* pertain to theory as distinguished from practice. *Academic* or *academical*, *conventional*, *formal*, and *theoretic* or *theoretical* may be used in a slightly derogatory sense. A question or discussion which is wholly or merely *academical* is one which the schools may consider, but has no bearing upon direct practical work or results. A *formal* compliment or prayer often lacks heartiness or sincerity.

A *theoretical* or *speculative* scheme is one that has not been sufficiently checked or tested by practice. *Scholarly* has only a good sense, as denoting that which pertains to or befits one worthy to be called a scholar; *scholastic* may have similar use, but sometimes refers to the intricate disputations of the medieval schoolmen; as, *scholastic* subtleties or technicalities. *Pedantic*, making a needless or concerted display of learning, is always unfavorable in meaning, while *bookish* is somewhat depreciatory, implying more connection with books than with men or with practical affairs.

ANTONYMS: *commonplace, common-sense, everyday, ignorant, illiterate, matter-of-course, matter-of-fact, obvious, ordinary, plain, practical, simple, straightforward, uninstructed, unreasoned, unstudied, untaught.*

ACCESSORY

abettor or abetter	associate	companion	henchman
accomplice	attendant	confederate	participator
ally	auxiliary	follower	partner
appendage	coadjutor	helper	retainer
assistant	colleague		

At common law, an *accessory* implies a principal, and cannot be convicted until after the conviction of the principal; the *accomplice* or *abettor* can be convicted as a principal. *Accomplice* and *abettor* have nearly the same meaning, but the former is the popular, the latter more distinctly the legal term. In law, an *abettor* (the general legal spelling) is always present, either actively or constructively, at the commission of the crime; an *accessory*, never. An *accomplice* is usually a principal; an *accessory*, never. If present, though only to stand outside and keep watch against surprise, one is an *abettor*, and not an *accessory*.

Colleague is used always in a good sense, *associate* and *coadjutor* generally so; *ally, assistant, associate, attendant, companion, helper,* either in a good or a bad sense; *abetter, accessory, accomplice, confederate*, almost always in a bad sense, but all are used for people who assist in some way. *Appendage* always denotes close connection; *auxiliary* emphasizes subordinate help. *Ally* is generally used of national and military matters, or of some other connection regarded as great and important; as, *allies* of despotism. *Colleague* is applied to civil and ecclesiastical connections; members of Congress from the same State are *colleagues*, even though they may be bitter opponents politically and personally.

An *Associate* Justice of the Supreme Court is near in rank to the Chief Justice. A surgeon's *assistant* is a physician or medical student who shares in the treatment and care of patients; a surgeon's *attendant* is one who rolls bandages and the like. *Follower, henchman, retainer* are persons especially devoted to a chief, and generally bound to him by necessity, fee, or reward. *Partner* has come to denote almost exclusively a business connection. See **appendage; auxiliary.**

> **ANTONYMS:** *adversary, antagonist, betrayer, chief, commander, enemy, foe, hinderer, instigator, leader, opponent, opposer, principal, rival.*

> **PREPOSITIONS:** An accessory *to* the crime, *before* or *after* the fact; the accessories *of* a figure *in* a painting.

ACCIDENT

adventure	contingency	hap	misadventure
calamity	disaster	happening	misfortune
casualty	fortuity	hazard	mishap
chance	fortune	incident	possibility

An *accident* is that which happens without anyone's direct intention; a *chance* that which happens without any known cause. If the direct cause of a railroad *accident* is known, we cannot call it a *chance*. We can speak of a game of *chance*, but not of a game of *accident*. An *incident* is viewed as occurring in the regular course of things, but subordinate to the main purpose, or aside from the main design.

Fortune is the result of inscrutable controlling forces, good or bad; *misfortune* is adverse *fortune*. *Fortune* and *chance* are nearly equivalent, but *chance* can be used of human effort and endeavor as *fortune* cannot be; we say "he has a *chance* of success," or "there is one *chance* in a thousand," where we could not substitute *fortune*; as personified, *Fortune* is regarded as having a fitful purpose, *Chance* as purposeless; we speak of fickle *Fortune*, blind *Chance*. The slaughter of men is an *incident* of battle; unexpected defeat, the *fortune* of war.

A *disaster* is an unforeseen and serious *misfortune* or *accident;* a *calamity* is a grievous *disaster* or a *happening* that causes great loss and distress. Since the unintended is often the undesirable, *accident* tends to signify some *calamity* or *disaster,* unless the contrary is expressed as when we say a fortunate or happy *accident.* *Hazard* risks loss for the *possibility* of profit. An *adventure* is that which may turn out ill, a *misadventure* that which does turn out ill. A slight, disturbing *accident* is a *mishap.* See **hazard; misfortune.**

ANTONYMS: *appointment, calculation, certainty, decree, fate, foreordination, intention, law, necessity, ordainment, ordinance, plan, preparation, provision, purpose.*

PREPOSITIONS: The accident *of* birth; an accident *to* the machinery.

ACQUAINTANCE

association	experience	fellowship	intimacy
attachment	familiarity	friendship	knowledge
companionship			

Acquaintance between persons supposes that each has at least actually met the other; we may know a public man by his writings or speeches, and by sight, but cannot claim *acquaintance* unless he personally knows us. There may be pleasant *acquaintance* with little *companionship;* and conversely, much *companionship* with little *acquaintance,* as between busy clerks at adjoining desks. So there may be *association* in business without *intimacy* or *friendship. Acquaintance* admits of many degrees, from a slight or passing to a familiar or intimate *acquaintance;* but *acquaintance* unmodified commonly signifies less than *familiarity* or *intimacy.* As regards persons, *familiarity* is becoming restricted to the undesirable sense, as in the proverb, "*Familiarity* breeds contempt"; hence, in personal relations, the word *intimacy,* which refers to mutual knowledge of thought and feeling, is now preferred.

Friendship includes *acquaintance* with some degree of *intimacy,* and ordinarily *companionship,* though in a wider sense *friendship* may exist between those who have never met, but know each other only by word and deed. *Acquaintance* does not involve *friendship,* for one may be well acquainted with an enemy; *attachment* implies affection. *Fellowship* involves not merely *acquaintance* and *companionship,* but sympathy as well. There may be much *friendship* without much *fellowship,* as between those whose homes or pursuits are far apart. There may be pleasant *fellowship* which does not reach the fulness of *friendship.* As regards studies, pursuits, etc., *acquaintance* is less than *familiarity,* which supposes minute *knowledge* of particulars, arising often from long *experience* or *association.* See **attachment; friendship.**

ANTONYMS: *ignorance, ignoring, inexperience, unfamiliarity.*

PREPOSITIONS: Acquaintance *with* a subject, *of* one person *with* another, *between* persons.

ACRIMONY

acerbity	enmity	severity	tartness
asperity	harshness	sharpness	unkindness
bitterness	malignity	sourness	virulence
causticity	moroseness		

Acrimony in speech or temper is like a corrosive acid; it springs from settled character or deeply rooted feeling of aversion or unkindness, and it often stings. One might speak with momentary *asperity* to his child, but not with *acrimony*, unless estrangement had begun. *Enmity* is directed against an enemy.

Acerbity is a *sharpness,* with a touch of *sourness* and *bitterness,* which may arise from momentary annoyance or habitual impatience; *asperity* is keener, harsher, and more pronounced, denoting distinct irritation or vexation; in speech *asperity* is often manifested by the tone of voice rather than by the words that are spoken.

Malignity is the extreme of settled ill intent; *virulence* is an envenomed hostility. *Virulence* of speech is a quality in language that makes the language seem as if it exuded poison. *Virulence* is outspoken; *malignity* may be covered with smooth and courteous phrases. We say intense *virulence,* deep *malignity.* *Severity* is always painful, and may be terrible, but carries ordinarily the implication, true or false, of justice. See **enmity.** Compare **morose; severe.**

ANTONYMS: *amiability, courtesy, gentleness, good nature, kindness, mildness, smoothness, sweetness.*

ACT

accomplishment	doing	exploit	performance
achievement	effect	feat	proceeding
action	execution	motion	transaction
consummation	exercise	movement	work
deed	exertion	operation	

An *act* is strictly and originally something accomplished by an *exercise* of power, in which sense it is synonymous with *deed* or *effect. Action* is a *doing. Act* is, therefore, single, individual, momentary; *action,* a complex of *acts,* or a process, state, or habit of exerting power. We speak of *action* of an acid upon a metal, not of its *act;* a virtuous *act,* but a virtuous course of *action. Act* is used, also, for the simple *exertion* of power; as, an *act* of will. In this sense an *act* does not necessarily imply an external *effect,* while an *action* does. Morally, the *act* of murder is in the determination to kill; legally, the *act* is not complete without the striking of the fatal blow. *Act* and *deed* are both used for the thing done, but *act* refers to the power put forth, *deed* to the result accomplished; as, a voluntary *act*, a bad *deed*. *Deed, achievement, exploit,* and *feat* are commonly used of great, notable, and impressive *acts*.

A *feat* exhibits strength, skill, personal power, whether mental or physical, especially the latter; as, a *feat* of arms, a *feat* of memory. An *exploit* is a conspicuous or glorious *deed*, involving valor or heroism, usually combined with strength, skill, loftiness of thought, and readiness of resource; an *achievement* is the *doing* of something great and noteworthy; an *exploit* is brilliant, but its *effect* may be transient; an *achievement* is solid, and its *effect* enduring. *Act* and *action* are both in contrast to all that is merely passive and receptive. We speak of a business *transaction*, a *work* of art, and a surgical *operation*. See exercise; motion; operation; transaction; work.

ANTONYMS: *cessation, deliberation, endurance, immobility, inaction, inactivity, inertia, passivity, quiescence, quiet, repose, rest, suffering, suspension.*

ACTIVE

agile	diligent	nimble	sprightly
alert	energetic	officious	spry
alive	expeditious	prompt	supple
brisk	industrious	quick	vigorous
bustling	lively	ready	wide-awake
busy	mobile	restless	

Active refers to both quickness and constancy of action; in the former sense it is allied with *agile, alert, brisk*, etc.; in the latter, with *busy, diligent, industrious*. The *active* enjoy employment, the *busy* are actually employed, the *diligent* and the *industrious* are habitually *busy*. *Alive* suggests vitality; *nimble*, lightness and speed; *sprightly*, gay quickness. The *restless* are *active* from inability to keep quiet; their activity may be without purpose, or out of all proportion to the purpose contemplated. The *officious* are undesirably *active* in the affairs of others. See alert; alive; busy; nimble.

ANTONYMS: *dull, heavy, idle, inactive, indolent, inert, lazy, quiescent, quiet, slow, sluggish, stupid.*

PREPOSITIONS: Active *in* work, *in* a cause, *for* an object, as *for* justice, *with* persons or instrumentalities, *about* something, as *about* other people's business.

ACUMEN

acuteness	insight	penetration	sharpness
cleverness	keenness	perspicacity	shrewdness
discernment	perception	sagacity	

Acumen is *sharpness* to some purpose, and belongs to a mind that has sound judgment and is comprehensive as well as keen. *Sharpness, acuteness,* and *insight,* however keen, and *penetration,* however deep, fall short of the meaning of *acumen,* which implies also ability to use these qualities to advantage. There are persons of keen *insight* and great *penetration* to whom these powers are practically useless. *Cleverness* is a practical aptitude for study or learning. *Insight* and *discernment* are both applied to the judgment of character; *insight* comes from deep understanding, while *discernment* is concerned with accuracy.

Sagacity is skill in using quick *perceptions* for a desired end, generally in practical affairs; *acumen* may increase with study, and applies to erudite matters. *Shrewdness* is *keenness* or *sagacity,* often with a somewhat evil bias, and ready to take advantage of duller intellects. *Perspicacity* is the power to see clearly through that which is difficult or involved; *penetration* implies a deep search. We speak of the *acuteness* of an observer or a reasoner, the *insight* and *discernment* of a student, a clergyman, or a merchant, the *sagacity* of a hound, the *keenness* of a debater, the *shrewdness* of a usurer, the *penetration, perspicacity,* and *acumen* of a philosopher. Compare **discern; sagacious.**

ANTONYMS: *bluntness, dulness, obtuseness, stupidity.*

ADAPT

accommodate	conform	put in place	set right
adjust	fit (fix)	put right	set to rights
apply	put in order	put to rights	suit
arrange			

Adapt has less reference to original structure than *fit,* and more suggestion of change than *adjust;* we *adjust* the parts of a machine without altering their structure; we *adapt* the machine to a new use by some minor changes; the eye *adapts* itself to differences of light or vision by spontaneous and unconscious changes of convexity or the dilation or contraction of the pupil; the human constitution *adapts* itself to a new climate, or the mind to a new problem. *Adapt* and *adjust* in such use are often closely synonymous, yet with a subtle difference, *adjust* referring more to the mechanism, *adapt* to the result; we *adjust* a microscope or an opera-glass, in order to *adapt* it to different eyes. We dramatize a novel in order to *adapt* it for the stage.

To *fit* is, in this connection, to make one thing or part correspond to some other, generally with the idea of antecedent shaping; as, to *fit* a garment to the form; to *fit* the key to a lock; in its application to persons it signifies to give the knowledge or training or develop the qualities needed to meet certain requirements; as, to *fit* a student for college. *Conform* (originally, to make like in form) in physical use often denotes an extensive and gradual process; as, the glacier *conforms* itself to the shape of ground on which it rests or over which it passes; in its more frequent figurative use *conform* signifies to bring into outward harmony without reference to one's personal views or feelings; as to *conform* one's conduct to the customs of society.

To *adjust* (originally, to make right) is to place one thing or part in suitable relation to some other or others, as for stability, or for suitable or harmonious action; the parts of a watch, *fitted* to each other by their original construction, must be *adjusted* by the watchmaker who assembles them; the mechanism of a typewriter must be *adjusted* for alignment; if the parts were not originally properly *fitted*, it will be found impossible to *adjust* them; *adjust* always implies some inherent fitness; this is true even in metaphorical use; differences or disputes between persons are *adjusted* when both parties agree to waive negligible matters; if the differences are fundamental, no adjustment is possible.

To *suit* is to make or to be conformable or appropriate to, accord with, befit; as, his figure *suits* the part; in a secondary sense, to *suit* is to meet the views, wishes, or tastes of, please, satisfy; as, the plan *suits* me. *Suit* is often nearly equivalent to *fit* or *adapt*, but seldom exactly corresponds to them; "the pen *suits* my hand" is comprehensive, declaring that the qualities of the pen in all respects meet the demands of my hand.

Accommodate is in some uses nearly synonymous with *adapt, adjust, conform,* or *fit*, but generally implies some concession, yielding, or sacrifice; as, to *accommodate* oneself to circumstances, *i.e.*, by giving up some things one might desire. A metallic structure must be able to *accommodate* itself to expansion or contraction of the material; the device by which the eye adapts itself to distance is called the accommodating apparatus. In the secondary uses, the idea of convenience or of concession, or of both, usually appears; we *accommodate* a friend with a loan or a traveler with lodgings; an accommodating person seeks to give comforts or conveniences to others, often at more or less sacrifice of his own. *Fix* (originally to fasten, make firm) is used colloquially in the sense of *adapt, adjust, fit, accommodate,* repair, regulate, *put in order* or in shape, fit out, equip, or in any way put in suitable or satisfactory condition. See **apply; arrange.** Compare **fit.**

> **ANTONYMS:** *confound, confuse, derange, disarrange, discompose, disjoin, disjoint, dislocate, dismember, disorder, displace, disturb, jumble, misapply, misfit, misjoin, misplace.*

ADD

adjoin	append	enlarge	make up
affix	attach	extend	subjoin
amplify	augment	increase	sum up
annex	cast up	join on	unite

To *add* is to *increase* by *adjoining* or *uniting,* in distinction from multiply, which is to *increase* by repeating. To *augment* a thing is to *increase* it by any means, but this word is seldom used directly of material objects; we do not *augment* a house, a farm, a nation, etc. We may *enlarge* a house, a farm, or an empire, *extend* influence or dominion, *augment* riches, power or influence, *attach* or *annex* a building to one that it *adjoins* or papers to the document to which they refer, *annex* a clause or a codicil, *affix* a seal or a signature, *annex* a territory, *attach* a condition to a promise. A speaker may *amplify* a discourse by a fuller treatment throughout than was originally planned, or he may *append* or *subjoin* certain supplementary remarks without changing what has gone before. We *cast up* or *sum up* an account, though *add up* and *make up* are now more usual expressions. See **amplify; append; attach.**

ANTONYMS: *abstract, deduct, diminish, dissever, lessen, reduce, remove, subtract, withdraw.*

PREPOSITION: Other items are to be added *to* the account.

ADDICTED

abandoned	devoted	given over	inclined
accustomed	disposed	given up	prone
attached	given	habituated	wedded

A person is *addicted* to that which he has allowed to gain a strong, habitual, and enduring hold upon action, inclination, or involuntary tendency, as to a habit or indulgence. A man may be *accustomed* to labor, *attached* to his profession, *devoted* to his family, *given* to study or to gluttony (in the bad sense, *given over*, or *given up*, is a stronger and more hopeless expression, as is *abandoned*). Even if *inclined* to luxury, one may become *habituated* to poverty. A man is *wedded* to that to which he has become accustomed; as one is *wedded* to science or to art. *Prone* is used only in a bad sense, and generally of natural tendencies; as, our hearts are *prone* to evil. *Abandoned* tells of the acquired viciousness of one who has given himself up to wickedness. *Addicted* may be used in a good sense; as, *addicted* to study; but more frequently it refers to bad habits; as, *addicted* to drink. *Devoted* is used chiefly in the good sense, often implying consecration; as, a mother's *devoted* affection.

ANTONYMS: *averse, disinclined, indisposed, unaccustomed.*

PREPOSITION: Addicted *to* vice.

ADDRESS *noun*

adroitness	discretion	politeness	savoir faire
courtesy	ingenuity	readiness	tact
dexterity	manners		

Address is that indefinable something which enables a man to gain his object without seeming exertion or contest, and generally with the favor and approval of those with whom he deals. It is a general power to direct to the matter in hand whatever qualities are most needed for it at the moment. It includes *adroitness* and *discretion* to know what to do or say and what to avoid; *ingenuity* to devise; *readiness* to speak or act; the *dexterity* that comes of practice; and *tact,* which is the power of the fine touch as applied to human character and feeling. *Courtesy* and *politeness* are indispensable elements of good *address. Savoir faire* stresses knowledge of the correct thing to do and how to do it. Compare **polite; speech.**

ANTONYMS: *awkwardness, boorishness, clownishness, clumsiness, fatuity, folly, ill-breeding, ill manners, rudeness, stupidity, unmannerliness, unwisdom.*

PREPOSITIONS: Address *in* dealing with opponents; the address *of* an accomplished intriguer.

ADDRESS *verb*

accost	apply to	greet	speak to
apostrophize	approach	hail	woo
appeal to	court	salute	

To *address* is slightly more formal than to *accost* or *greet,* though it may often be interchanged with them. One may *address* another at considerable length or in writing; he *accosts* orally and briefly. To *accost* is to speak first, to friend or stranger, generally with a view to opening conversation; *greet* is not so distinctly limited, since one may return another's greeting; *greet* and *hail* may imply but a passing word; greeting may be altogether silent; to *hail* is to *greet,* usually in a loud-voiced, hearty, and joyous way, as appears in the expression "*hail* fellow, well met," or to call out to someone; to *speak to* is to *address* in an ordinary tone, but colloquially it means to reprove. To *salute* is to *greet* with special token of respect, as a soldier his commander.

To *apostrophize* is to solemnly *address* some person or personified attribute apart from the audience to which one is speaking; as, a preacher may *apostrophize* virtue, the saints of old, or even the Deity. To *appeal to* or *apply to* in this sense is to *address* formally for some special purpose, *appeal* being the more urgent word. Compare **appeal.**

ANTONYMS: *avoid, cut, elude, ignore, overlook, pass, pass by, shun.*

PREPOSITIONS: Address the memorial *to* the legislature; the president addressed the people *in* an eloquent speech; he addressed an intruder *with* indignation.

ADEQUATE

able	competent	fitted	sufficient
adapted	enough	fitting	suitable
capable	equal	qualified	suited
commensurate	fit	satisfactory	

Adequate, commensurate, and *sufficient* signify *equal* to some given requirement, occasion, or work; as, a sum *sufficient* to meet expenses; an *adequate* remedy for the disease. *Commensurate* is the more precise and learned word, signifying that which exactly measures the matter in question, is proportionate to it. *Adapted, fit, fitted, suited,* and *qualified* refer to the qualities which match or suit the occasion. A clergymen may have strength *adequate* to the work of a porter; but that would not be a *fit* or *suitable* occupation for him. Work is *satisfactory* if it satisfies those for whom it is done, through it may be very poor work judged by some higher standard. *Qualified* refers to acquired abilities; *competent* to both natural and acquired; a *qualified* teacher may be no longer *competent*, by reason of ill health. *Able* and *capable* suggest general ability and reserved power; *able,* the higher word of the two, emphasizes power to act; *capable* stresses innate qualities. An *able* man will do something well in any position. A *capable* man will come up to any ordinary demand. We say an *able* orator, a *capable* accountant. See **fit.** Compare **adapt.**

> **ANTONYMS:** *disqualified, inadequate, incompetent, inferior, insufficient, poor, unequal, unfit, unqualified, unsatisfactory, unsuitable, useless, worthless.*
>
> **PREPOSITIONS:** Adequate *to* the demand, *for* the purpose.

ADHERENT

aid	ally	disciple	partisan
aider	backer	follower	supporter

An *adherent* is one who is devoted or attached to a person, party, principle, cause, or creed. One may be an *aider* and *supporter* of a party or church, while not an *adherent* to all its doctrines or claims. An *ally* is more independent still, as he may differ on every point except the specific ground of union. The *Allies* who overthrew Napoleon were united only against him. *Allies* are regarded as equals; *adherents* and *disciples* are followers. The *adherent* depends more on his individual judgment, the *disciple* is more subject to command and instruction; thus we say the *disciples* rather than the *adherents* of Christ. *Partisan* has the narrow sense of bigoted adherence to a party, right or wrong. One may be an *adherent* or *supporter* of a party and not a *partisan. Backer* is a sporting and theatrical word, usually personal in its application. Compare **follow.**

ANTONYMS: *adversary, antagonist, betrayer, deserter, enemy, hater, opponent, renegade, traitor.*

PREPOSITIONS: Adherents *to* principle; adherents *of* Luther.

ADHESIVE

cohesive	gummy	sticking	viscid
gluey	mucilaginous	sticky	viscous
glutinous			

Adhesive is the scientific, *sticking* or *sticky* the popular word. That which is *adhesive* tends to join itself, especially when heated or moistened, to the surface of any other body with which it is placed in contact; *cohesive* expresses the tendency of particles of the same substance to hold together. Polished plate glass is not *adhesive*, but such plates packed together are intensely *cohesive*. An *adhesive* plaster is in popular language a *sticking* plaster. *Sticky* expresses a more limited, and generally annoying, degree of the *adhesive* quality often caused by hot or damp weather. *Glutinous, gummy, gluey,* and *mucilaginous* are used for substances such as gum and glue; *viscid* and *viscous* are applied to semifluid substances, as pitch and tar.

ANTONYMS: *free, inadhesive, loose, separable.*

PREPOSITION: The stiff, wet clay, adhesive *to* the foot, impeded progress.

ADJACENT

abutting	bordering	coterminous	next
adjoining	close	juxtaposed	nigh
attached	conterminous	near	tangent
beside	contiguous	neighboring	

Adjacent farms may not be connected; if *adjoining*, they meet at a boundary line. *Conterminous* would imply that their dimensions were exactly equal on the common boundary. *Contiguous* may be used for either *adjacent* or *adjoining*. *Abutting* generally refers to a part of a building or estate that juts out to join the boundary of another. Buildings that are not *attached* may be *adjacent* or *adjoining*. *Near* is a relative word, places being called *near* the railroad which would elsewhere be deemed remote. *Neighboring* always implies such proximity that the inhabitants may be neighbors. *Next* views some object or person as the nearest of several or many; *nigh* is used in poetry and dialects for *near*. *Tangent* implies touching at only one point; and *juxtaposed* is placed side by side.

ANTONYMS: *detached, disconnected, disjoined, distant, remote, separate.*

PREPOSITION: The farm was adjacent *to* the village.

ADJOURN

break off	delay	procrastinate	put off
break up	dissolve	prorogue	suspend
defer	postpone	protract	

Adjourn signifies literally to *put off* to another day, hence, by extension, to *put off* to any future time. In common usage, to *adjourn* a matter is to hold it in abeyance until it may be more conveniently or suitably considered—to *defer*, or *postpone* it; in such use *defer* and *postpone* are closely equivalent to *adjourn*; to *defer* is simply to lay by or put aside temporarily; to *postpone* is strictly to put aside until "after" something else is done, known, obtained, or the like; as, to *postpone* the attack until daylight; but *postpone* is often used without such limitation; both *defer* and *postpone* imply expectation of later consideration, or action; *procrastinate* is less definite than *adjourn, defer,* or *delay*; procrastination is purposeless; one who *procrastinates* gives no assurance that he will ever act. To *protract* is to prolong to the point of boredom, as a debate.

Prorogue is a special legal or legislative term, applying only to the British Parliament or to similar colonial assemblies. A voluntary assembly may *adjourn* itself; Parliament is *prorogued* by order of the king. A parliament which is *prorogued* still exists, and may be summoned by the sovereign at any time to meet again without a new election; a parliament which is *dissolved* ceases to exist; all its unfinished business is dead; there can be no parliament until a general election is held, resulting in a new parliament, which must take up all business *de novo;* an adjournment is simply a voluntary intermission at the discretion of either or both houses. The Congress of the United States and the various State legislatures terminate their sessions only by adjournment, either to a day fixed by vote or to the time of compulsory reassembling provided by the constitution.

ANTONYMS: *act, act on, despatch, expedite, hasten, hurry, quicken, take up, urge on, urge forward.*

ADMIRE

adore	delight in	extol	respect	venerate
applaud	enjoy	honor	revere	wonder
approve	esteem	love	reverence	

In the old sense of *wonder, admire* is virtually obsolete; the word now expresses a delight and approval, in which the element of *wonder* uncousciously mingles. We *admire* beauty in nature and art, *delight in* the innocent happiness of children, *enjoy* books or society, a walk, or a dinner. We *approve* what is excellent, *applaud* heroic deeds, *esteem* the good, *love* our friends. We *honor* and *respect* noble character wherever found; we *revere* and *venerate* it in the aged. We *reverence* things, and sometimes people, that we *respect* highly; when we *revere* persons or things a feeling of tenderness is added to the *respect*. We *extol*, or praise in highest terms, God's goodness; we *adore* or worship the majesty and power of God.

ANTONYMS: *abhor, abominate, contemn, despise, detest, dislike, execrate, hate, ridicule, scorn.*

ADMISSIBLE

allowable	passable	probable	right
fair	permissible	proper	suitable
just	possible	reasonable	tolerable

Allowable and *permissible* are distinguished on the same basis as *allow* and *permit*. As between *allowable* and *admissible*, that is *allowable* which may be considered or done without active objections, opposition, or protest; that is *admissible* which may be fairly or reasonably entertained or considered; *admissible* is the stronger term; as, an *allowable* suggestion; an *admissible* hypothesis. *Admissible* and *permissible* divide along the line of theory and action; that is *admissible* which may properly be considered; that is *permissible* which may properly be done; certain evidence in a case may be *admissible*; a postponement of trial may be *permissible*; *admissible* has more of the passive, *permissible* of the active element; a statement or an excuse may be *permissible* as the act of one who makes it, *admissible* if its qualities are such that it may be received or considered. *Tolerable* is the weakest word of the series, denoting that which may be accepted or passed over with a certain degree of forbearance; as, a *tolerable* explanation; colloquially, *tolerable* signifies moderately good or agreeable, and no more; hence, just endurable. Compare **allow; justice.**

ANTONYMS: *absurd, alien, foreign, illegitimate, impertinent, inadmissible, inapposite, inapplicable, irrelevant, out of place, unallowable, unconnected, unfair, unsuitable, unwarrantable, unwarranted.*

ADORN

beautify	decorate	garnish	illustrate
bedeck	embellish	gild	ornament
deck			

To *adorn* and to *ornament* alike signify to add that which makes anything beautiful and attractive, but *ornament* is more exclusively on the material plane; as, the gateway was *ornamented* with delicate carving. *Adorn* is more lofty and spiritual, referring to a beauty which is not material. That which *adorns* not only adds beauty to its setting or background, but also is beautiful by itself; if we say, the gateway was *adorned* with beautiful carving, we imply a unity and loftiness of design such as *ornamented* cannot express.

To *decorate* something is to relieve it of dulness or monotony by adding beauty of design or color. A wall is *decorated* with paintings, a lawn with trees. To *embellish* is to brighten and enliven by adding something that is not necessary or not very closely connected with that to which it is added; to *illustrate* is to add something which will explain or throw light on, the principal matter. An author *embellishes* his narrative with fine descriptions; the artist *illustrates* it with beautiful engravings. To *garnish* something is to add to it a final touch of color or beauty. *Deck* and *bedeck* are commonly said of apparel; as, a mother *bedecks* her daughter with silk and jewels.

> **ANTONYMS:** *deface, deform, disfigure, mar, spoil.*

> **PREPOSITION:** Adorn his temples *with* a coronet.

ADVERSE

antagonistic	incompatible	opposing	unlucky
conflicting	inimical	opposite	unpropitious
contrary	opposed	unfavorable	untoward
hostile			

Adverse signifies turned toward in opposition; as, *adverse* winds that blow against the mariner's course; *adverse* circumstances that oppose one's desire or intent. *Adverse* is rarely, if ever, used of persons, but of facts, opinions, influences, tendencies, etc. We may speak of an *adverse* party, contemplated as an impersonal organization *opposite* or *antagonistic* to some other. Accordingly *adverse* carries no idea of feeling; in this it differs from *hostile* or *inimical,* and is allied with *conflicting, contrary, opposed, opposing, opposite. Antagonistic* may or may not involve *hostile* feeling; two *opposing* lawyers may be strenuous antagonists during a trial, but warm friends outside of court.

Adverse is to be sharply distinguished from *averse,* which primarily indicates opposition of feeling, however much sustained by reason. That which is *adverse* may prove to be afflictive, calamitous, fatal, hurtful, injurious, or unfortunate, and such words are sometimes given as synonyms of *adverse,* but no such elements inhere in the meaning of the word; the world's greatest exploits and careers have been triumphs over *adverse* circumstances, criticism, influences, or tendencies. Compare **enemy.** See **averse** under **reluctant.**

> **ANTONYMS:** *advanageous, aiding, assisting, auspicious, benign, contributory, cooperating, cooperative, favorable, helpful, propitious, prosperous, supporting, sustaining.*

AFFRONT

aggravate	exasperate	offend	vex
annoy	insult	provoke	wound
displease	irritate	tease	

To *affront* is to offer some defiant offense or indignity, as it were, to one's face; it is somewhat less than to *insult*. One may be *annoyed* by the well-meaning awkwardness of a servant, *irritated* by a tight shoe or a thoughtless remark, *vexed* at some careless neglect or needless misfortune, *wounded* by the ingratitude of child or friend. To *tease* is to give some slight and perhaps playful annoyance. To *aggravate* means literally to make worse; as fever *aggravates* the disease; *aggravate* in the sense of *annoy* is colloquial. To *provoke,* literally to call out or challenge, is to begin a contest; one *provokes* another to violence. Compare **pique.**

ANTONYMS: *conciliate, content, gratify, honor, please.*

AFRAID

aghast	cautious	frightened	timid
alarmed	cowardly	scared	timorous
anxious	faint-hearted	terrified	
apprehensive	fearful	terror-stricken	

Afraid is a word of wide range of meaning; it is used to indicate a slight degree of apprehension or anxiety, where nothing worthy the name of fear is involved; as, I am *afraid* we shall be late; I am *afraid* you will be disappointed; I am *afraid* the proof has not been read; in many such cases I fear would be more elegant and expressive than I am *afraid*; as, I *fear* appeal will be vain; I *fear* there may be a flaw in the title. On the other hand, *afraid* may indicate being under the power of deep, persuasive fear, due to real or imaginary cause; as, many a child is *afraid* in the dark; the superstitious are *afraid* of ghosts and goblins; the sailor is more *afraid* of fog than of storm.

Aghast, a much stronger word than *afraid,* connotes a fear manifested by certain physical signs, such as the loss of power to move or speak; one stands *aghast* at the destruction of war. A *cautious* person foresees possibilities of danger, and moves warily or seeks safeguard or protection accordingly; the *timid* or *timorous* are constitutionally and readily subject to fear, even on slight occasions, as of criticism or publicity; yet the *cautious, timid,* or *timorous* may evince dauntless courage under the influence of some strong affection, as of a mother for her child, or when moved by some high moral motive, as religion or patriotism; the *cowardly* are incapable of any high motive that can overcome the mere brute instinct of self-preservation.

Fearful is used in a double sense; objectively it signifies causing or adapted to cause fear; as, a *fearful* storm; subjectively (in the sense here considered) it signifies subject to or experiencing some degree of fear; in this sense it is nearly synonymous with *afraid*, but is a stronger and higher word; it would be unworthy of a military officer to say that he was *afraid* of defeat; to say that he was *fearful* of defeat, as in an untenable position, would involve no discredit; *fearful* in the sense of *timid* or *timorous* is now rarely, if ever, used; a *fearful* disposition would be understood as a disposition to cause fear, rather than one readily subject to fear. Compare **alarm; anxiety; fear; frighten.**

> **ANTONYMS:** *adventurous, audacious, bold, brave, calm, collected, composed, confident, cool, courageous, daring, dauntless, fearless, gallant, heroic, intrepid, reckless, undaunted, undismayed, valiant, valorous, venturesome.*

AGENT

actor	factor	means	operator	promoter
doer	instrument	mover	performer	tool

In strict philosophical usage, the prime *mover* or *doer* of an act is the *agent.* Thus we speak of man as a voluntary *agent*, a free *agent*. But in common usage, especially in business, an *agent* is not the prime *actor*, but only an *instrument* or *factor*, acting under orders or instructions. *Means* is the most general word in the class. Construed either as a singular or a plural noun, it may be used of persons, *instruments* or *tools*, or methods; as, the poor are a *means* to support the rich; books are a *means* to education; the *means* justifies the end. Compare **cause.**

> **ANTONYMS:** *chief, inventor, originator, principal.*

> **PREPOSITIONS:** An agent *of* the company *for* selling, etc.

AGGREGATE

agglomeration	collection	mass	totality
aggregation	entirety	sum	whole
amount	heap	total	

An *aggregate* is the entire number, *sum, mass*, or quantity of something. An *aggregate* of financial items as an *amount, sum*, or *total*. An *aggregate* or *aggregation* of material objects is a *collection, mass*, or *whole*; an *agglomeration* is a heterogeneous *mass*. *Collection* points rather to the differences, *mass* to the unity. We say a *collection* of minerals, a *mass* of rock. The result of multiplication is a product; the result of addition a *sum, total*, or *aggregate*. *Entirety* is the state of being complete in all parts. *Totality* is the *aggregate* of parts or individuals.

AGREE

accede	approve	comport	join
accept	assent	concur	square
accord	coincide	conform	tally
acquiesce	combine	consent	unite
admit	comply	harmonize	

Agree is the most general term of this group, signifying to have like qualities, proportions, views, or inclinations, so as to be free from jar, conflict, or contradiction in a given relation. To *concur* is to *agree* in general; to *coincide* is to *agree* in every particular. Whether in application to persons or things, *concur* tends to expression in action more than *coincide*; we may either *concur* or *coincide* in an opinion, but *concur* in a decision; views *coincide*; causes *concur*. One *accepts* another's terms, *complies* with his wishes, *admits* his statement, *approves* his plan, *conforms* to his views of doctrine or duty, *accedes* or *consents* to his proposal. *Accede* expresses the more formal agreement, *consent* the more complete. To *assent* is an act of the understanding; to *consent*, of the will. We may *concur* or *agree* with others, either in opinion or decision. Two or more persons *combine, join,* or *unite* in an undertaking.

One may silently *acquiesce* in that which does not meet his views, but which he does not care to contest. He *admits* the charge brought, or the statement made, by another—*admit* always carrying a suggestion of reluctance. *Assent* is sometimes used for a mild form of *consent*, as if agreement in the opinion assured approval of the decision. If there is exact agreement between two things, they may be said to *square* or *tally*. To *comport* is to measure up to a previously set standard; as, his actions *comport* with his reputation. Compare **harmony.**

> **ANTONYMS:** *contend, contradict, decline, demur, deny, differ, disagree, dispute, dissent, oppose, protest, refuse.*

> **PREPOSITIONS:** I agree in opinion *with* the speaker, *to* the terms proposed; persons agree *on* or *upon* a statement of principles, rules, etc.; we must agree *among* ourselves.

AGRICULTURE

agrology	farming	husbandry
agronomy	floriculture	kitchen-gardening
cultivation	gardening	market-gardening
culture	horticulture	tillage

Agriculture is the generic term, including at once the science, the art, and the process of supplying human wants by raising the products of the soil, and by the associated industries; *farming* is the practice of *agriculture* as a business; there may be theoretical *agriculture*, but not theoretical *farming*; we speak of the science of *agriculture*, the business of *farming*; scientific *agriculture* may be wholly in books; scientific *farming* is practiced upon the land; we say an *agricultural* college rather than a college of *farming*. *Farming* refers to the *cultivation* of considerable portions of land, and the raising of the coarser crops; *gardening* is the close *cultivation* of a small area for small fruits, flowers, vegetables, etc., and while it may be done upon a farm is yet a distinct industry. *Gardening* in general, *kitchen-gardening* (the *cultivation* of vegetables, etc., for the household), *market-gardening* (the raising of the same for sale), *floriculture* (the *culture* of flowers), and *horticulture* (the *culture* of fruits, flowers, or vegetables), are all departments of *agriculture*, but not strictly nor ordinarily of *farming*; *farming* is itself one department of *agriculture*.

Husbandry is a general word for any form of practical *agriculture*, but is now chiefly poetical; the term is also applied to that phase of *farming* that deals with live-stock. *Tillage* refers directly to the work bestowed upon the land, as plowing, manuring, etc.; *cultivation* refers especially to the processes that bring forward the crop; we speak of the *tillage* of the soil, the *cultivation* of corn; we also speak of land as in a state of *cultivation*, under *cultivation*, etc. *Culture* is now applied to the careful development of any product to a state of perfection, especially by care through successive generations; the choice varieties of the strawberry have been produced by wise and patient *culture*; a good crop in any year is the result of good *cultivation*. *Agronomy* is the application of scientific principles to the cultivation of land; scientific *husbandry*, specifically in the production of field crops; *agrology*, the branch of *agriculture* engaged in the study of the relation of chemicals in soils to crop production.

AIM

aspiration	end	intent	purpose
design	endeavor	intention	tendency
determination	goal	mark	
direction	inclination	object	

The *aim* is the *direction* in which one shoots, or sometimes that which is aimed at. The *mark* is that at which one shoots; the *goal,* that toward which one runs. All alike indicate the *direction* of *endeavor*. The *end* is the point at which one expects or hopes to close his labors; the *object*, that which he would grasp as the reward of his labors. *Aspiration, design, endeavor, purpose*, referring to the mental acts by which the *aim* is attained, are often used as interchangeable with *aim*. *Aspiration* applies to what are viewed as noble *aims*; *endeavor, design, intention, purpose*, indifferently to the best or worst. *Aspiration* has less of decision than the other terms; one may aspire to an *object*, and yet lack the fixedness of *purpose* by which alone it can be attained. *Purpose* is stronger than *intention*. *Design* especially denotes the adaptation of means to an *end*; *endeavor* refers to the exertions by which it is to be attained. One whose *aims* are worthy, whose *aspirations* are high, whose *designs* are wise, and whose *purposes* are steadfast, may hope to reach the *goal* of his ambition, and will surely win some *object* worthy of a life's *endeavor*. See **ambition; design; end; endeavor.**

> ANTONYMS: *aimlessness, avoidance, carelessness, heedlessness, neglect, negligence, oversight, purposelessness, thoughtlessness.*

AIR

appearance	carriage	fashion	mien	sort
bearing	demeanor	look	port	style
behavior	expression	manner	presence	way

Air is that combination of qualities which makes the entire impression we receive in a person's *presence*; as, we say he has the *air* of a scholar, or the *air* of a villain. *Appearance* refers more to the dress and other externals. We might say of a travel-soiled pedestrian, he has the *appearance* of a tramp, but the *air* of a gentleman. *Expression* and *look* especially refer to the face. *Expression* is oftenest applied to that which is habitual; as, he has a pleasant *expression* of countenance; *look* may be momentary; as, a *look* of dismay passed over his face. We may, however, speak of the *look* or *looks* as indicating all that we look at; as, he had the *look* of an adventurer; I did not like his *looks*.

Bearing is rather a lofty word; as, he has a noble *bearing*; *port* is practically identical in meaning with *bearing*, but is more exclusively a literary word. *Carriage*, too, is generally used in a good sense, to indicate the way in which a person holds himself while walking or standing; as, that lady has a good *carriage*. *Presence* refers to a person's *bearing* as it attracts or influences others. *Mien* is closely synonymous with *air* but less often used in a bad sense. We say a rakish *air* rather than a rakish *mien*. *Mien* may be used to express some prevailing feeling; as an indignant *mien*. *Demeanor* goes beyond *appearance*, including conduct, *behavior*; as, a modest demeanor. *Manner* and *style* are, in large part at least, acquired. See **behavior.**

AIRY

aerial	fairylike	joyous	lively
animated	frolicsome	light	sprightly
ethereal	gay		

Airy and *aerial* both signify of or belonging to the air, but *airy* also describes that which is breezy, seems as if made of air, or is immaterial; we speak of *airy* shapes, *airy* nothings, but *aerial* tactics. *Aerial* also connotes extreme delicacy and illusiveness. *Ethereal* describes its object as belonging to the upper air, the pure ether, and so, often, heavenly. *Sprightly*, spiritlike refers to light, free, cheerful activity of mind and body. That which is *lively* or *animated* may be agreeable or the reverse; as, an *animated* discussion; a *lively* company.

> **ANTONYMS:** *clumsy, dull, heavy, inert, ponderous, slow, sluggish, stony, wooden.*

ALACRITY

activity	briskness	promptitude	speed
agility	celerity	promptness	sprightliness
alertness	eagerness	quickness	swiftness
animation	liveliness	readiness	vivacity

Alacrity, primarily denoting *quickness*, has come to denote that cheerful and hearty willingness from which *quickness* and *promptness* naturally result; hence, a prompt response. *Alacrity* springs from some demand from without; *eagerness* is spontaneous, springing from within; *eagerness* to act may produce *alacrity* in responding to the call for action.

Alertness may be without action, as of the waiting hunter or sentinel; *readiness* is more calm and less vivid than *alertness*. *Agility, quickness, celerity, speed, swiftness,* may be without agreeable motive, as under stress of terror; *activity* may be vigorous but unwilling, as when one works fiercely under compulsion. *Agility* is light and dexterous *quickness* without reference to motive; one may climb a tree with *agility* when pursued by a mad bull; *agility* is near in meaning to *nimbleness*, but is more purposeful; it is lightness and *quickness* of movement dexterously adapted to a definite end; we speak of the *agility* of an athlete, the *nimbleness* of a dancer; *agility* commonly involves the whole body, while *nimbleness* may be limited to some portion, as the feet or the fingers.

Promptness is strictly timeliness in meeting occasion or demand, and may be eager and hearty or forced and ungracious; as, the surly *promptness* of employees in punching the time clock; the tendency is, however, to think of *promptness* as involving ready response of mind and disposition to the demand; this is still more fully expressed in *promptitude*, the state or condition from which the fact of *promptness* springs; *promptness* usually, and *promptitude* always, denotes ample or generous punctuality. Compare **active; alert; eager; nimble.**

> **ANTONYMS:** *apathy, aversion, disinclination, dislike, dulness, indifference, indolence, inertness, laziness, reluctance, repugnance, slowness, sluggishness, stupidity, unwillingness.*

ALARM

affright	dismay	fright	terror
alert	disquietude	misgiving	timidity
apprehension	dread	panic	tocsin
consternation	fear	solicitude	

Alarm, according to its derivation *all'arme,* "to arms," is an arousing to meet and repel danger, and may be quite consistent with true courage. *Tocsin* is an *alarm* or signal sounded by the bells of a belfry, or the bells that sound the *alarm.* An *alert* is a signal to prepare for an air raid or other attack; a warning against attack. *Affright* and *fright* express sudden *fear* which, for the time at least, overwhelms courage. The sentinel discovers with *alarm* the sudden approach of the enemy; the unarmed villagers view it with *affright.* *Apprehension, disquietude, dread, misgiving,* and *solicitude* are in anticipation of danger; *consternation, dismay,* and *terror* are overwhelming *fear,* generally in the actual presence of that which is terrible, though these words also may have an anticipative force. *Timidity* is a quality, habit, or condition, a readiness to be affected with *fear.* A person of great *timidity* is constantly liable to needless *alarm* and even *terror.* See **fear.**

ANTONYMS: *assurance, calmness, confidence, repose, security.*

PREPOSITIONS: Alarm was felt *in* the camp, *among* the soldiers, *at* the news.

ALERT

active	lively	prepared	vigilant
alive	nimble	prompt	watchful
brisk	on the watch	ready	wide-awake
bustling			

Alert, ready, and *wide-awake* refer to a watchful promptness for action. *Ready* suggests thoughtful preparation; the wandering Indian is *alert,* the trained soldier is *ready. Ready* and *alive* express more life and vigor than *prepared.* The gun is *prepared;* the man is *ready. Vigilant* always implies a purpose and cause for watchfulness. *Prompt* expresses readiness for appointment or demand at the required moment. The good general is *ready* for emergencies, *alert* to perceive opportunity or peril, *prompt* to seize occasion. Trade is *brisk,* healthy children are *active.* See **active; alive; nimble; vigilant.**

ANTONYMS: *drowsy, dull, heavy, inactive, slow, sluggish, stupid.*

ALIEN *noun*

emigrant   émigré   foreigner   immigrant   stranger

A naturalized citizen is not an *alien,* though a *foreigner* by birth, and perhaps a *stranger* in the place where he resides. A person of foreign birth, not naturalized, is an *alien,* though he may have been a resident in the country a large part of a lifetime, and ceased to be a *stranger* to its people or institutions. He is an *alien* in one country if his allegiance is to another. The people of any country still residing in their own land are, strictly speaking, *foreigners* to the people of all other countries, rather than *aliens;* but *alien* and *foreigner* are often used synonymously. An *emigrant* or *émigré* (one who migrates out) leaves one country to settle in another; an *immigrant* (one who migrates into) enters a foreign country to settle there.

> **ANTONYMS:** *citizen, countryman, fellow-countryman, native, native-born inhabitant, naturalized person.*

> **PREPOSITIONS:** Aliens *to* (more rarely *from*) our nation and laws; aliens *in* our land, *among* our people.

ALIEN *adj.*

conflicting	exotic	impertinent	remote
contradictory	extraneous	inapplicable	strange
contrary	extrinsic	inappropriate	unconnected
contrasted	foreign	irrelevant	unlike
distant	hostile	opposed	

Alien refers to difference of allegiance, *foreign* to difference of birth. In their figurative use, that is *foreign* which is *remote, unlike,* or *unconnected;* that is *alien* which differs in nature and can be *conflicting, hostile,* or *opposed. Extrinsic* applies to something not inherent and that cannot be included; *extraneous* is also of external origin but may be capable of assimilation. *Exotic* refers to what has been introduced from a *foreign* country; hence, sometimes, outlandish; as, *exotic* plants, *exotic* decorations. That is *impertinent* which does not pertain to the matter in hand, in which use it is closely synonymous with *irrelevant,* having no relation or application. *Impertinent* and *irrelevant* matters cannot claim consideration in a certain connection; *inappropriate* matters it would be unsuitable to consider. For *impertinent* as applied to persons see **meddlesome.** Compare **alien** *noun;* **contrast.**

> **ANTONYMS:** *akin, appropriate, apropos, essential, germane, pertinent, proper, relevant.*

> **PREPOSITIONS:** Such a purpose was alien *to* (or *from*) my thought.

ALIKE

akin	equivalent	kindred	same
analogous	homogeneous	like	similar
congruent	identical	resembling	uniform
equal			

Alike is a comprehensive word, signifying as applied to two or more objects that some or all qualities of one are the same as those of the other or others; by modifiers *alike* may be made to express more or less resemblance; as, these houses are somewhat (*i.e.*, partially) *alike*; or, these houses are exactly (*i.e.*, in all respects) *alike*. Cotton and wool are *alike* in this, that they can both be woven into cloth. Substances are *homogeneous* which are made up of elements of the *same* kind, or which are the *same* in structure. Two pieces of iron may be *homogeneous* in material, while not *alike* in size or shape.

In geometry, two triangles are said to be *congruent* when they can be laid over one another, and fit, line for line and angle for angle; they are said to be *equal* when their dimensions are exactly *alike*, although the figures may not be superposable; *congruent* figures are *equal* in every dimension; they are *equivalent* when they simply contain the *same* amount of space. *Equivalent* things are *alike* in meaning, worth, or power, but are not *identical*. To say "this is the *identical* man," is to say not merely that he is *similar* to the one I have in mind, but that he is the very *same* person. An *identical* proposition is one that says the *same* thing precisely in subject and predicate. *Similar* refers to close resemblance, which yet leaves room for question or denial of complete likeness or identity to which *identical* refers. Things are *analogous* when they are *similar* in idea, plan, use, or character, though perhaps quite unlike in appearance; as, the gills of fishes are said to be *analogous* to the lungs of terrestrial animals.

ANTONYMS: *different, dissimilar, distinct, heterogeneous, unlike.*

PREPOSITIONS: The specimens are alike *in* kind; they all look alike *to* me.

ALIVE

active	animated	existent	lively	subsisting
alert	breathing	existing	living	vital
animate	brisk	live	quick	vivacious

Alive applies to all degrees of life, from that which shows one to be barely *existing* or *existed* as a *living* thing, as when we say he is just *alive*, to that which implies the very utmost of vitality and power, as in the words "he is all *alive*," "thoroughly *alive*." *Existent* implies having being, while *existing* gives the added idea of being *alive* at the present time. The word *quick,* which began by signifying "having life," is now mostly applied to energy of life as shown in swiftness of action. *Breathing* is capable of like contrast; we say of a dying man, he is still *breathing;* or we speak of a *breathing* statue where it means having, or seeming to have, full and vigorous health, abundant life. *Animate* applies to *living* bodies as opposed to dead ones; *animated* refers to something dead that takes on new life, or something lifeless to which an appearance of life is given; as, an *animated* cartoon. *Vital* is essential to life. See **active; alert.**

> **ANTONYMS:** *dead, deceased, defunct, dispirited, dull, inanimate, lifeless, spiritless.*
>
> **PREPOSITIONS:** Alive *in* every nerve; alive *to* every noble impulse; alive *with* fervor, hope, resolve; alive *through* all his being.

ALLAY

alleviate	calm	mitigate	quiet	still
appease	compose	mollify	relieve	tranquilize
assuage	lighten	pacify	soothe	

Allay and *alleviate* have often been interchanged in usage. But, in strictness, to *allay* is to lay to rest, *quiet* or *soothe* that which is excited; to *alleviate,* on the other hand, is to *lighten* a burden, make it more bearable. We *allay* suffering by using means to *soothe* and *tranquilize* the sufferer; we *alleviate* suffering by doing something toward removal of the cause, so that there is less to suffer; we *alleviate* poverty, but do not *allay* it.

Pacify and *appease* signify to bring to peace; to *mollify* is to soften; to *calm, quiet,* or *tranquilize* is to *still; compose,* to place together, harmonize, adjust to a calm and settled condition; to *soothe* (originally to assent to, humor) is to bring to pleased quietude. To *appease* is to *allay* by satisfying demands; to *assuage* is to reduce the violence. We *allay* excitement, *appease* a ruler, *calm* agitation, *compose* our feelings or countenance, *pacify* the quarrelsome, *quiet* the boisterous or clamorous, *soothe* or *mitigate* grief or distress. See **alleviate.** Compare **calm.**

> **ANTONYMS:** *agitate, arouse, excite, fan, kindle, provoke, rouse, stir, stir up.*

ALLEGE

adduce	asseverate	claim	maintain	produce
advance	assign	declare	offer	say
affirm	aver	introduce	plead	state
assert	cite			

To *allege* is formally to *state* as true or capable of proof, but without proving. To *adduce*, literally to lead to, is to bring the evidence up to what has been *alleged*. *Adduce* is a secondary word; nothing can be *adduced* in evidence till something has been *stated* or *alleged*, which the evidence is to sustain. An *alleged* fact stands open to question or doubt. To speak of an *alleged* document, an *alleged* will, an *alleged* crime, is either to question, or at least very carefully to refrain from admitting, that the document exists, that the will is genuine, or that the crime has been committed; *alleged* simply concedes nothing and leaves the question open. To *aver* is to *declare* confidently.

To *produce* is to bring forward, as, for instance, papers or persons. *Adduce* is not used of persons; of them we say *introduce* or *produce*. When an alleged criminal is brought to trial, the counsel on either side is accustomed to *advance* a theory, and *adduce* the strongest possible evidence in its support; *produce* documents and witnesses, *cite* precedents, *assign* reasons, *introduce* suggestions, *offer* pleas. The accused will usually *assert* his innocence and *plead* not guilty. See **plead; state.**

ALLEGIANCE

devotion	fealty	loyalty	subjection
faithfulness	homage	obedience	

Allegiance is the obligation of fidelity and *obedience* that an individual owes to his government or sovereign, in return for the protection he receives. The feudal uses of *fealty* and *homage* have mostly passed away with the state of society that gave them birth; but their origin still colors their present meaning. A patriotic American feels an enthusiastic *loyalty* to the republic; he takes, on occasion, an oath of *allegiance* to the government, but his *loyalty* will lead him to do more than mere *allegiance* could demand; he pays *homage* to God alone, as the only king and lord, or to those principles of right that are spiritually supreme; he acknowledges the duty of *obedience* to all rightful authority; he resents the idea of *subjection*, submissiveness, or compulsory *obedience* to power. *Fealty* is now rare, except in elevated or poetic style. We prefer to speak of the *faithfulness* rather than the *fealty* of citizen, wife, or friend. Compare **devote; faithful.**

> **ANTONYMS:** *disaffection, disloyalty, rebellion, sedition, treason.*

> **PREPOSITIONS:** We honor the allegiance *of* the citizen *to* the government; the government has a right to allegiance *from* the citizen.

ALLEGORY

apolog	fiction	metaphor	parable
fable	illustration	myth	simile

An *allegory* is a moral or religious tale, of which the moral lesson is the substance, and in which figurative descriptions and incidents are used, making the story a prolonged *metaphor*, as "The Pilgrim's Progress." A *fable* is generally briefer, representing animals or inanimate things as the speakers and actors, and commonly conveying some lesson of practical wisdom or shrewdness, which is often stated at the end, as in "The *Fables* of Æsop." *Apolog* is a literary term for *fable*. A *parable*, as often used by Jesus in his teaching, is exclusively moral or religious, and is briefer and less adorned than an *allegory*. The *allegory*, *parable*, or *fable* tells its story as if true, leaving the reader or hearer to discover its fictitious character and learn its lesson. All these are, in strict definition, *fictions*; but the word *fiction* is now applied almost exclusively to novels or romances, to things imagined by the teller.

The *simile* carries its comparison on the surface, using expressions similar to *as* or *like*; as, blind as a bat; the *metaphor* is given directly without any note of comparison; as, a blind alley. A *myth* is sometimes traditional but usually imaginative. Any comparison, analogy, instance, example, tale, anecdote, or the like which serves to let in light upon a subject may be called an *illustration*, this word in its widest use including all the rest. See **fiction.**

ANTONYMS: *chronicle, fact, history, record.*

ALLEVIATE

abate	lessen	moderate	remove
allay	lighten	reduce	soften
assuage	mitigate	relieve	

Etymologically, to *alleviate* is to lift a burden toward oneself, and so *lighten* it for the bearer; to *relieve* is to lift it back from the bearer, nearly or quite away; to *remove* is to take it away altogether. *Alleviate* is thus less than *relieve*; *relieve*, ordinarily, less than *remove*. We *alleviate, relieve*, or *remove* the trouble; we *relieve*, not *alleviate*, the sufferer. *Assuage* is, by derivation, to sweeten; hence, to ease or pacify; *mitigate*, to make milder or less severe; *moderate*, to bring within measure; *abate*, to beat down, and so make less. We *abate* a fever; *lessen* anxiety; *moderate* passions or desires; *lighten* burdens; *mitigate* or *alleviate* pain; *reduce* inflammation; *soften, assuage*, or *moderate* grief; *allay* anxiety; we *lighten* or *mitigate* punishments; we *relieve* any suffering of body or mind that admits of help, comfort, or remedy. See **abate; allay.**

ANTONYMS: *aggravate, augment, embitter, enhance, heighten, increase, intensify, magnify, make worse.*

ALLIANCE

coalition	confederation	fusion	partnership
compact	federation	league	union
confederacy			

Alliance is, in its most common use, a connection formed by treaty between sovereign states for a specific purpose, as for mutual aid in war. *Partnership* is a mercantile word; *alliance* chiefly political or matrimonial. *Coalition* is generally used of political parties and is often a temporary *alliance*; *fusion* is often the more common word in this sense, especially if the *alliance* is formed to defeat opponents. In an *alliance* between nations there is no surrender of sovereignty, and no *union*, except for a specified time and purpose. *League* and *alliance* are used with scarcely perceptible difference of meaning, although a *league* often implies formal specifications. In a *confederacy* or *confederation* there is an attempt to unite separate states in a general government without surrender of sovereignty.

Union implies concessions which make the separate states substantially one. *Federation* is a sovereign state formed by uniting smaller states which retain their local governments. The United States is not a *confederacy* nor an *alliance*; the nation might be called a *federation*, but prefers to be styled a federal *union*.

ANTONYMS: *antagonism, discord, disunion, divorce, enmity, hostility, schism, secession, separation, war.*

PREPOSITIONS: Alliance *with* a neighboring people, *against* the common enemy, *for* offense and defense; alliance *of, between,* or *among* nations.

ALLOT

allocate	assign	divide	portion out
apply	award	give	select
appoint	destine	grant	set apart
apportion	distribute	mete out	

Allot, originally to *assign* by lot, applies to the giving of a definite thing to a certain person. A portion or extent of time is *allotted*; as, I expect to live out my *allotted* time. A definite time is *appointed*; as, the audience assembled at the *appointed* hour. *Allot* may also refer to space; as, to *allot* a plot of ground for a cemetery; but we now generally use *select, set apart,* or *assign. Allot* is not now used of persons.

Appoint may be used of time, space, or person; as, he *appointed* a day; *appoint* a new place; an officer was *appointed* to this station. *Destine* may also refer to time, place, or person, but it always has reference to what is considerably in the future; a man *destines* his son to follow his own profession. *Assign* is rarely used of time, but rather of places, persons, or things. We *assign* a work to be done and *assign* a man to do it, who, if he fails, must *assign* a reason for not doing it. That which is *allotted, appointed,* or *assigned* is more or less arbitrary; that which is *awarded* is the due requital of something the receiver has done, and he has right and claim to it; as, the medal was *awarded* for valor. We *allocate* money or property, *apportioning* it to particular purposes. See **apply; apportion; devote; give.**

> **ANTONYMS:** *appropriate, confiscate, deny, refuse, resume, retain, seize, withhold.*

> **PREPOSITIONS:** Allot *to* a company *for* a purpose.

ALLOW

admit	consent to	let	sanction	tolerate
concede	grant	permit	suffer	yield

We *allow* that which we do not attempt to hinder or prevent; we *permit* that to which we give some express authorization. When this is given verbally it is called permission; when in writing it is commonly called a permit. There are establishments that anyone will be *allowed* to visit without challenge or hindrance; there are others that no one is *allowed* to visit without a permit from the manager; there are others to which visitors are *admitted* at specified times, without a formal permit.

We *allow* a child's innocent intrusion; we *concede* a right; *grant* a request; *consent* to a sale of property; *permit* an inspection of accounts; *sanction* a marriage; *tolerate* the rudeness of a well-meaning servant; *submit* to a surgical operation; *yield* to a demand or necessity against our wish or will, or *yield* something under compulsion; as, the sheriff *yielded* the keys at the muzzle of a revolver, and *allowed* the mob to enter. *Suffer,* though used in the Bible and by Shakespeare in the sense of concession, is now becoming rare, its place being taken by *allow, permit,* or *tolerate. Allow* also implies to make allowance for; as, we *allow* an inch for the hem. Compare **permission.**

> **ANTONYMS:** *deny, disallow, disapprove, forbid, protest, refuse, reject, resist, withstand.*

> **PREPOSITIONS:** To allow one *in* such a course; allow *for* spending-money.

ALLOY

admixture	adulteration	debasement
adulterant	compound	deterioration

Alloy is commonly some *admixture* of baser with precious metal, as for giving hardness to coin; or it may be a mixture of any two or more elements, one of which is a metal. *Adulteration, debasement,* and *deterioration* always imply lessening the value of something, or the process of debasing; *admixture* is neutral, and may be good or bad; *alloy* is often good in the literal sense. An excess of *alloy* virtually amounts to *adulteration*; but *adulteration* is mostly restricted to articles used for food, drink, medicine, and kindred uses, whereas *deterioration* has a much wider range. In the figurative sense, as applied to character, etc., *alloy* is a mixture of evil with good. An *adulterant* is a substance used to make another less pure.

ALLUDE

advert	indicate	mention	refer
hint	insinuate	name	signify
imply	intimate	point	suggest

We *allude* to a person or matter slightly, perhaps by a word or phrase, as it were in passing, without direct mention. We *advert* to it when we turn toward it in reference; we *refer* to it by any clear utterance that distinctly turns the mind or attention to it; as, marginal figures *refer* to a parallel passage; we *mention* a thing by explicit word, as by *naming* it. One may *allude* to a person or thing that he does not *mention* or *name*; the speaker *adverted* to the recent disturbances and the remissness of certain public officers; though he *mentioned* no name, it was easy to see to whom he *alluded*.

One may *hint* at a thing in a friendly way, but what is *insinuated* is always unfavorable, generally both hostile and cowardly. One may *indicate* his wishes, *intimate* his plans, *imply* his opinion, *signify* his will, *suggest* a course of action. Compare **name; suggestion.**

> **PREPOSITION:** The passage evidently alludes *to* the Jewish Passover.

ALLURE

attract	captivate	decoy	entice	lure	tempt
cajole	coax	draw	inveigle	seduce	win

To *allure* is to *draw* as with a lure by some charm or some prospect of pleasure or advantage. We may *attract* others to a certain thing without intent; as, like *attracts* like. We may *allure* either to that which is evil or to that which is good and noble, by purpose and endeavor. *Lure* is rather more akin to the physical nature and is usually baleful. *Coax* suggests a kind of wily pleading; a man may be *coaxed* to that which is by no means *alluring*. *Cajole* and *decoy* carry the idea of deceiving and ensnaring, the former often by using flattery. To *inveigle* is to lead one blindly into something, to beguile. To *entice* is to *lure* skilfully and artfully. To *tempt* is to endeavor to lead someone to a course or the commission of an act that may be wrong; to *seduce* is to succeed in winning someone from good to ill. *Win* may be used in either a bad or a good sense; it succeeds in that which *allure* attempts. See **draw.**

> **ANTONYMS:** *chill, damp, deter, dissuade, drive away, repel, warn.*

> **PREPOSITIONS:** Allure *to* a course; allure *by* hopes; allure *from* evil *to* good.

ALSO

as well	in addition	likewise	too
as well as	in like manner	similarly	withal
besides			

While some distinctions between these words and phrases will appear to the careful student, yet in practice the choice between them is largely to secure euphony and avoid repetition. The words fall into two groups; *as well as, besides, in addition, too, withal* simply add a fact or thought; *also* (all so), *in like manner, likewise, similarly* affirm that what is added is like that to which it is added. *As well* follows the word or phrase to which it is joined. We can say the singers *as well as* the players, or, the players and the singers *as well.*

> **ANTONYMS:** *but, in spite of, nevertheless, notwithstanding, on the contrary, on the other hand, yet.*

AMASS

accumulate	gather	hoard	pile up
aggregate	heap up	hoard up	store up
collect			

To *amass* is to bring together materials that make a mass, a great bulk or quantity. With some occasional exceptions, *accumulate* is applied to the more gradual, *amass* to the more rapid gathering of money or materials, *amass* referring to the general result or bulk, *accumulate* to the particular process or rate of gain. We say interest is *accumulated* (or *accumulates*) rather than is *amassed*; he *accumulated* a fortune in the course of years; he rapidly *amassed* a fortune by shrewd speculations. Goods or money for immediate distribution are said to be *collected* rather than *amassed*. They may be *stored up* for a longer or shorter time; but one *hoards* always with a view of permanent retention, generally selfish. *Aggregate* is now most commonly used of numbers and amounts; as, the expenses will *aggregate* a round million.

ANTONYMS: *disperse, dissipate, divide, parcel, portion, scatter, spend, squander, waste.*

PREPOSITIONS: Amass *for* oneself, *for* a purpose, *from* a distance, *with* great labor, *by* industry.

AMATEUR

connoisseur	critic	dilettante	novice	tyro

Etymologically, the *amateur* is one who loves, the *connoisseur* one who knows. In usage, the term *amateur* is applied to one who pursues any study or art simply from the love of it; the word carries a natural implication of superficialness, though marked excellence is at times attained by *amateurs*, and in sports the term is used merely to denote one who is not a professional —one who, regardless of excellence, receives no payment for his performance. A *connoisseur* is supposed to be so thoroughly informed regarding any art or work as to be able to criticize or select intelligently and authoritatively; there are many incompetent *critics,* but there cannot, in the true sense, be an incompetent *connoisseur.* The *amateur* practices to some extent that in regard to which he may not be well informed; the *connoisseur* is well informed in regard to that which he may not practice at all. A *novice* or *tyro* may be a professional; an *amateur* never is; the *amateur* may be skilled and experienced as the *novice* or *tyro* never is. *Dilettante*, which had originally the sense of *amateur,* has to some extent come to denote one who is superficial, pretentious, and affected, whether in theory or practice.

PREPOSITION: An amateur *in* art.

AMAZEMENT

admiration	awe	confusion	surprise
astonishment	bewilderment	perplexity	wonder

Amazement and *astonishment* both express the momentary overwhelming of the mind by that which is beyond expectation. *Astonishment* especially affects the emotions, *amazement* the intellect. *Awe* is the yielding of the mind to something supremely grand in character or formidable in power, and ranges from apprehension or dread to reverent worship. *Admiration* includes delight and regard. *Surprise* lies midway between *astonishment* and *amazement,* and often refers to matters of little consequence or to such as are less startling in character. *Amazement* may be either pleasing or painful, as when induced by the grandeur of the mountains, or by the fury of the storm. We can say pleased *surprise,* but scarcely pleased *astonishment. Amazement* has in it something of *confusion* or *bewilderment;* but *confusion* and *bewilderment* may occur without *amazement,* as when a multitude of details require instant attention. *Astonishment* may be without *bewilderment* or *confusion*. *Wonder* is often pleasing, and may be continuous in view of that which surpasses our comprehension; as, the magnitude, order, and beauty of the heavens fill us with increasing *wonder*. See **perplexity.**

ANTONYMS: *anticipation, calmness, composure, coolness, expectation, indifference, preparation, self-possession, steadiness, stoicism.*

PREPOSITION: I was filled with amazement *at* such reckless daring.

AMBITION

aspiration   competition   emulation   opposition   rivalry

Ambition, literally a going around to solicit votes, has primary reference to the award or approval of others, and is the eager desire of power, fame, or something deemed great and eminent. The prizes of *aspiration* are always virtue, nobility, skill, or other high qualities. The prizes of *ambition* are commonly advancement, fame, honor, and the like. In our older literature this word is chiefly applied to inordinate and selfish desire for supremacy. However, *ambition* is now largely used of an eager and steadfast purpose to obtain something commendable in itself, viewed as a worthy prize.

There is a noble and wise or an ignoble, selfish, and harmful *ambition*. *Aspiration* is a striving for something thought to be above one, as wisdom, virtue, etc. *Emulation* is not so much to win any excellence or success for itself as to equal or surpass other persons. There is such a thing as a noble *emulation*, when those we would equal or surpass are noble, and the means we would use worthy. But, at the highest, *emulation* is inferior as a motive to *aspiration*, which seeks the high quality or character for its own sake, not with reference to another. *Competition* is the striving for something that is sought by another at the same time. *Emulation* regards the abstract, *competition* the concrete; *rivalry* is the same in essential meaning as *competition*, but differs in the nature of the objects contested for, which, in the case of *rivalry*, are usually of the nobler sort and less subject to direct gaging, measurement, and rule. We speak of *competition* in business, *emulation* in scholarship, *rivalry* in love, politics, etc.; *emulation* of excellence, success, achievement; *competition* for a prize; *rivalry* between persons or nations. *Competition* may be friendly, *rivalry* is sometimes hostile. When *opposition* is used in business language as a substitute for *competition,* it implies that the competitor is an opponent and hinderer.

ANTONYMS: *carelessness, contentment, humility, indifference, satisfaction.*

AMEND

advance	correct	meliorate	rectify
ameliorate	emend	mend	reform
better	improve	mitigate	repair
cleanse	make better	purify	

To *amend* is to change for the better by removing faults, errors, or defects, and always refers to that which at some point falls short of a standard of excellence. *Advance, better,* and *improve* may refer either to what is quite imperfect or to what has reached a high degree of excellence; we *advance* to the kingdom of God, *improve* the minds of our children, *better* the morals of the people. But for matters below the point of ordinary approval we seldom use these words; we do not speak of *bettering* a wretched alley, or *improving* a foul sewer. There we use *cleanse, purify,* or similar words. We *correct* evils, *reform* abuses, *rectify* incidental conditions of evil or error; we *ameliorate* poverty and misery, which we cannot wholly remove. We *mend* a tool, *repair* a building, *correct* proof; we *amend* character or conduct that is faulty, or a statement or law that is defective. A text, writing, or statement is *amended* by the author or some adequate authority; it is often *emended* by conjecture. A motion is *amended* by the mover or by the assembly; a constitution is *amended* by the people; the translation of an ancient text is *emended* by a critic who believes that what seems to him the better reading is what the original author had in mind in his writing. See **clean.**

ANTONYMS: *aggravate, blemish, corrupt, debase, depress, deteriorate, harm, impair, injure, mar, spoil, tarnish, vitiate.*

AMIABLE

agreeable	engaging	lovable	pleasing
attractive	gentle	lovely	sweet
benignant	good-natured	loving	winning
charming	kind	pleasant	winsome

Amiable combines the senses of *lovable* and *loving*; the *amiable* character has ready affection and kindliness for others, with the qualities that are adapted to win their love; *amiable* is a higher and stronger word than *good-natured* or *agreeable. Lovely* is often applied to externals; as, a *lovely* face. *Amiable* denotes a disposition desirous to cheer, please, and make happy. A selfish man of the world may have the art to be *agreeable*; a handsome, brilliant, and witty person may be *charming* or even *attractive,* while by no means *amiable.* The *engaging, winning,* and *winsome* add to amiability something of beauty, accomplishments, and grace. The *benignant* are calmly *kind,* as from a height and a distance.

A. *pleasant* person tries to make happy those with whom he is dealing. *Kind, good-natured* people may be coarse and rude, and so fail to be *charming* or *pleasing*; the really *amiable* are likely to avoid such faults by their earnest desire to please. The *good-natured* have an easy disposition to get along comfortably with everyone in all circumstances. A *sweet* disposition is very sure to be *amiable*, the *loving* heart bringing out all that is *lovable* and *lovely* in character. See **charming; pleasant.**

> ANTONYMS: *acrimonious, churlish, crabbed, cruel, crusty, disagreeable, dogged, gruff, hateful, ill-conditioned, ill-humored, ill-natured, ill-tempered, morose, sour, sullen, surly, unamiable, unlovely.*

AMID

amidst	amongst	betwixt	mingled with
among	between	in the midst of	surrounded by

Amid or *amidst* denotes *surrounded by*; *among* or *amongst* denotes *mingled with*. *Between* (archaic or poetic, *betwixt*) is said of two persons or objects, or of two groups of persons or objects. "Let there be no strife, I pray thee, *between* me and thee, and *between* my herdmen and thy herdmen," *Gen.* xiii, 9; the reference being to two bodies of herdmen. *Amid* denotes mere position; *among*, some active relation, as of companionship, hostility, etc. Lowell's "*Among* my Books" regards the books as companions; *amid* my books would suggest packing, storing, or some other incidental circumstance. We say *among* friends, or *among* enemies, *amidst* the woods, *amid* the shadows. *In the midst of* may have merely the local meaning; as, I found myself *in the midst of* a crowd; or it may express even closer association than *among*; as, "I found myself *in the midst of* friends" suggests their pressing up on every side, oneself the central object; so, "where two or three are met together in my name, there am I *in the midst of* them," *Matt.* xviii, 20; in which case it would be feebler to say "*among* them," impossible to say "*amid* them," not so well to say "*amidst* them."

> ANTONYMS: *afar from, away from, beyond, far from, outside, without.*

AMPLIFY

augment	dilate	expand	extend	unfold
develop	enlarge	expatiate	increase	widen

Amplify, as here compared, is now rarely used in the sense of *increase*, to add bulk, volume, or the like; it is now almost wholly applied to discourse or writing, signifying to make fuller in statement, whether with or without adding matter of importance, as by stating fully what was before only implied, or by adding illustrations to make the meaning more readily apprehended, etc. The chief difficulty of very young writers is to *amplify*, to get beyond the bare curt statement by *developing, expanding, unfolding* the thought. The chief difficulty of those who have more material and experience is to condense sufficiently. So, in the early days of our literature *amplify* was used in the favorable sense; but at present this word and most kindred words are coming to share the derogatory meaning that has long attached to *expatiate*. We may *develop* a thought, *expand* an illustration, *extend* a discussion, *expatiate* on a hobby, *dilate* on something joyous or sad, *enlarge* a volume, *unfold* a scheme, *widen* the range of treatment.

> **ANTONYMS:** *abbreviate, abridge, amputate, "boil down," condense, curtail, cut down, epitomize, reduce, retrench, summarize, sum up.*
>
> **PREPOSITIONS:** Amplify this matter *by* illustrations.

ANGER

animosity	fury	offense	rage
choler	impatience	passion	resentment
displeasure	indignation	peevishness	temper
exasperation	ire	pettishness	vexation
fretfulness	irritation	petulance	wrath

Anger is violent and vindictive emotion, which is sharp and sudden. *Resentment* (a feeling back or feeling over again) is persistent, the bitter brooding over injuries. *Exasperation,* a roughening, is a hot, superficial intensity of *anger*, demanding instant expression. *Rage* drives one beyond the bounds of prudence or discretion; *fury* is stronger yet, and sweeps one away into uncontrollable violence. *Anger* is personal and usually selfish, aroused by real or supposed wrong to oneself, and directed specifically and intensely against the person who is viewed as blameworthy. *Indignation* is impersonal and unselfish displeasure at unworthy acts, *i.e.,* at wrong as wrong. Pure *indignation* is not followed by regret, and needs no repentance; it is also more self-controlled than *anger*. *Wrath* is based on *indignation* or *anger*, but also implies a desire to chastise or to get revenge. It may, however, simply express the culmination of righteous *indignation* without malice in a pure being; as, the *wrath* of God. *Impatience, fretfulness, irritation, peevishness, pettishness, petulance,* and *vexation* are temporary and for immediate cause. *Fretfulness, pettishness,* and *peevishness* are chronic states finding in any petty matter an occasion for their exercise.

Displeasure is the mildest and most general word. *Choler* and *ire,* now rare except in poetic or highly rhetorical language, denote a still, and the latter a persistent, *anger*. *Ire* implies the expression of one's feelings in words or acts. *Temper* used alone in the sense of *anger* is colloquial, though we may correctly say a hot *temper*, a fiery *temper*, etc. *Passion*, though a word of far wider application, may, in the singular, be employed to denote *anger*; "did put me in a towering *passion*," SHAKESPEARE *Hamlet*, act v, sc. 2.

> **ANTONYMS:** *amiability, charity, forbearance, gentleness, leniency, lenity, long-suffering, love, mildness, patience, peace, peaceableness, peacefulness, self-control, self-restraint.*

> **PREPOSITIONS:** Anger *at* the insult prompted the reply; anger *toward* the offender exaggerates the offense.

ANNOUNCE

advertise	give notice (of)	proclaim	reveal
blazon	give out	promulgate	say
circulate	herald	propound	spread abroad
communicate	make known	publish	state
declare	notify	report	tell
enunciate			

To *announce* is to give intelligence of in some formal or public way. We may *announce* that which has occurred or that which is to occur, though the word is chiefly used in the anticipative sense; we *announce* a book when it is in press, a guest when he arrives. To *blazon* is to make widely known; *announce* publicly; *publish* far and wide. We *advertise* our business, *communicate* our intentions, *enunciate* our views; we *notify* an individual, *give notice* to the public. *Declare* has often an authoritative force; to *declare* war is to cause war to be, where before there may have been only hostilities; we say *declare* war, *proclaim* peace. We *propound* a question or an argument, *promulgate* the views of a sect or party, or the decision of a court, etc. We *report* an interview, *reveal* a secret, *herald* the coming of some distinguished person or great event. *Publish*, in popular usage, is becoming closely restricted to the sense of issuing through the press; we *announce* a book that is to be *published*. See **state**.

> **ANTONYMS:** *bury, conceal, cover (up), hide, hush, keep back, keep secret, secrete, suppress, withhold.*

> **PREPOSITIONS:** The event was announced *to* the family *by* telegraph.

ANSWER

rejoinder	repartee	reply	response	retort

A verbal *answer* is a return of words to something that seems to call for them, and is made to a charge as well as to a question; an *answer* may be even made to an unspoken implication or manifestation. In a wider sense, anything said or done in return for some word, action, or suggestion of another may be called an *answer*. The blow of an enraged man, the whinny of a horse, the howling of the wind, the movement of a bolt in a lock, an echo, etc., may each be an *answer* to some word or movement. A *reply* is an unfolding, and ordinarily implies thought and intelligence. A *rejoinder* is strictly an *answer* to a *reply*, though often used in the general sense of *answer*, but always with the implication of something more or less controversial or opposed, though lacking the conclusiveness implied in *answer*; an *answer*, in the full sense, to a charge, an argument, or an objection is adequate, and finally refutes and disposes of it; a *reply* or *rejoinder* may be quite inadequate, so that one may say, "This *reply* is not an *answer*"; "I am ready with an *answer*" means far more than "I am ready with a *reply*."

A *response* is accordant or harmonious, designed or adapted to carry on the thought of the words that called it forth, as the *responses* in a liturgical service, or to meet the wish of him who seeks it; as, the appeal for aid met a prompt and hearty *response*. *Response* is made to a stimulus; as, the appeal for mercy elicited an unsatisfactory *response*. *Repartee* is a prompt, witty, and commonly good-natured *answer* to some argument or attack; a *retort* may also be witty, but is severe and may be even savage in its intensity.

PREPOSITIONS: An answer *in* writing, or *by* word of mouth, *to* the question.

ANTICIPATE

apprehend	forecast	hope
divine	foretaste	look forward to
expect	foretell	predict

To *anticipate* may be either to take before in fact or to take before in thought; in the former sense it is allied with prevent; in the latter, with the synonyms above given. This is coming to be the prevalent and favorite use. We *expect* that which we have good reason to believe will happen; as, a boy *expects* to grow to manhood. We *hope* for that which we much desire and somewhat *expect*. We *apprehend* what we both *expect* and fear. *Anticipate* is commonly used now, like *foretaste*, of that which we *expect* both with confidence and pleasure. In this use it is a stronger word than *hope*, where often "the wish is father to the thought." I *hope* for a visit from my friend, though I have no word from him; I *expect* it when he writes that he is coming; and as the time draws near I *anticipate* it with pleasure.

Foretell and *predict* are often used interchangeably; *foretell* denotes knowledge of future events, but does not indicate the source of such knowledge; *predict* usually connotes reliance on past experience or on the laws of nature;

as, to *predict* a storm from the appearance of the sky. To *divine* is to know in advance by virtue of some special, unnatural, or occult ability.

> ANTONYMS: *despair of, distrust, doubt, dread, fear, recall, recollect, remember.*

ANTICIPATION

antepast	foreboding	forethought
apprehension	forecast	hope
expectancy	foresight	presentiment
expectation	foretaste	prevision

Expectation may be either of good or evil; *presentiment* almost always, *apprehension* and *foreboding* always, of evil; *anticipation* and *antepast*, commonly of good. Thus, we speak of the pleasures of *anticipation*. A *foretaste* may be of good or evil, and is more than imaginary; it is a part actually received in advance. *Foresight* and *forethought* prevent future evil and secure future good by timely looking forward, and acting upon what is foreseen. Compare **anticipate.**

> ANTONYMS: *astonishment, consummation, despair, doubt, dread, enjoyment, fear, realization, surprise, wonder.*

ANTIPATHY

abhorrence	disgust	hatred	repugnance
antagonism	dislike	hostility	repulsion
aversion	distaste	opposition	uncongeniality
detestation			

Antipathy denotes a state of mind which causes one to recoil instinctively from that toward which one is antipathetic; a person with an *antipathy* to spiders is disgusted or repelled by them, and tries to destroy them. A natural *antipathy* may give rise to *opposition* which may result in *hatred* and *hostility*. *Aversion*, literally, a turning away, is a deep and permanent *dislike*, and indicates a desire to avoid; a person with an *aversion* to spiders is not likely to frequent willingly places where spiders abound.

Antipathy, repugnance, and *uncongeniality* are instinctive; other forms of *dislike* may be acquired or cherished for cause. *Uncongeniality* is negative, a want of touch or sympathy. *Antagonism* may result from the necessity of circumstances; *opposition* may spring from conflicting views or interests; *abhorrence* and *detestation* may be the result of religious and moral training; *distaste* and *disgust* may be acquired. See **acrimony; anger; enmity; hatred.**

PREPOSITIONS: Antipathy *to* (less frequently *for* or *against*) a person or thing; antipathy *between* or *betwixt* two persons or things.

ANTIQUE

ancient	archaic	obsolete	quaint
antiquated	obsolescent	old-fashioned	superannuated

Antique refers to an *ancient, antiquated* to a discarded style. *Antique* is that which is either *ancient* in fact or *ancient* in style. We can speak of the *antique* architecture of a church just built. The difference between *antiquated* and *antique* is not in the age, for a Puritan style may be scorned as *antiquated,* while a Roman or Renaissance style may be prized as *antique.* The *antiquated* is not so much out of date as out of vogue. *Old-fashioned* may be used approvingly or contemptuously. In the latter case it becomes a synonym for *antiquated*; in the good sense it approaches the meaning of *antique,* but indicates less duration. We call a wide New England fireplace *old-fashioned*; a coin of the Cæsars, *antique.* *Quaint* combines the idea of age with a pleasing oddity; as, a *quaint* gambrel-roofed house.

Archaic suggests something that typifies an earlier, often a primitive age. *Archaic* is used especially to describe words no longer in general use, but found in special contexts, as in the Bible or in legal terminology. *Obsolete* describes that which has gone completely out of use; *obsolescent,* that which, though still in rare use, is almost *obsolete.* *Antiquated* is sometimes used of persons in a sense akin to *superannuated.* The *antiquated* person is out of style and out of sympathy with the present generation by reason of age; the *superannuated* person is incapacitated for present activities by reason of age. See **old.**

ANXIETY

anguish	disquiet	foreboding	perplexity
apprehension	disturbance	fretfulness	solicitude
care	dread	fretting	trouble
concern	fear	misgiving	worry

Anxiety is, according to its derivation, a choking *disquiet,* akin to *anguish*; *anxiety* is mental; *anguish* may be mental or physical; *anguish* is in regard to the known, *anxiety* in regard to the unknown; *anguish* is because of what has happened, *anxiety* because of what may happen. *Anxiety* refers to some future event, always suggesting hopeful possibility, and thus differing from *apprehension, fear, dread, foreboding,* all of which are generally quite despairing. In matters within our reach, *anxiety* always stirs the question whether something cannot be done, and is thus a valuable spur to doing; in this respect it is allied to *care. Foreboding, dread,* etc., commonly incapacitate for all helpful thought or endeavor. *Worry* is a more petty, restless, and manifest *anxiety; anxiety* may be quiet and silent; *worry* is communicated to all around. *Solicitude* is a milder *anxiety. Fretting* or *fretfulness* is a weak complaining without thought of accomplishing or changing anything, but merely as a relief to one's own *disquiet. Perplexity* often involves *anxiety,* but may be quite free from it. A student may be perplexed regarding a translation, yet, if he has time enough, not at all anxious regarding it.

> **ANTONYMS:** *apathy, assurance, calmness, carelessness, confidence, ease, light-heartedness, nonchalance, satisfaction, tranquillity.*

> **PREPOSITIONS:** Anxiety *for* a friend's return; anxiety *about, in regard to,* or *concerning* the future.

APATHY

calmness	insensibility	quietness	stoicism
composure	lethargy	quietude	tranquillity
immobility	passiveness	sluggishness	unconcern
impassibility	phlegm	stillness	unfeelingness
indifference			

Apathy, according to its Greek derivation, is a simple absence of feeling or emotion. There are persons to whom a certain degree of *apathy,* an innate *sluggishness* or heavy slothfulness of the emotional nature, is natural. In the *apathy* of despair, a person gives up, without resistance, to what he has fiercely struggled to avoid. While *apathy* is want of feeling, *calmness* is feeling without agitation. *Calmness* is the result of strength, courage, or trust; *apathy* is the result of dulness or weakness. *Composure* is freedom from agitation or disturbance, resulting ordinarily from perfect confidence.

Impassibility is a philosophical term applied to the Deity, as infinitely exalted above all stir of passion or emotion. *Unfeelingness,* the Old English word that should be the exact equivalent of *apathy,* really means more, a lack of the feeling one ought to have, a censurable hardness of heart. *Indifference* and *insensibility* imply absence of feeling toward certain persons or things; *apathy,* entire absence of feeling. *Indifference* is a want of interest; *insensibility* is a want of feeling; *unconcern* has reference to consequences; *immobility* is absence of motion or movement. *Stoicism* is an intentional suppression of feeling and deadening of sensibilities, while *apathy* is involuntary.

Phlegm emphasizes difficulty to arouse; *passiveness,* slowness in response. *Lethargy* is a drowsy kind of *apathy; tranquillity* implies freedom from motion or disturbance. *Quietness* or *quietude* is a state of being quiet. See **rest; stupor.** Compare **calm.**

ANTONYMS: *agitation, alarm, anxiety, care, distress, disturbance, eagerness, emotion, excitement, feeling, frenzy, fury, passion, sensibility, sensitiveness, storm, susceptibility, sympathy, turbulence, vehemence, violence.*

PREPOSITIONS: The apathy *of* monastic life; apathy *toward* good.

APIECE

distributively	individually	separately
each	respectively	severally

There is no discernible difference in sense between so much *apiece* and so much *each.* Both imply equality in distribution; the former is the more popular expression. *Distributively* is generally used of numbers and abstract relations. *Respectively* connotes regular order in distribution; *individually* emphasizes existence as a distinct personality; *separately* and *severally* emphasize apartness. The signers of a note may become jointly and *severally* responsible, that is, each liable for the entire amount, as if he had signed it alone. Witnesses are often brought *separately* into court, in order that no one may be influenced by the testimony of another. If a company of laborers demand a dollar *apiece,* that is a demand that each shall receive that sum; if they *individually* demand a dollar, each individual makes the demand.

ANTONYMS: *accumulatively, collectively, confusedly, en masse, indiscriminately, synthetically, together, unitedly.*

APOLOGY

acknowledgment	defense	plea
alibi	exculpation	pretext
apologia	excuse	vindication
confession	justification	

All these words express an answer to a charge of wrong or error that is, or might be, made. *Apology* has undergone a remarkable change from its old sense of valiant *defense*--as in Justin Martyr's *Apologies* for the Christian faith—to its present meaning of humble *confession* and concession. He who offers an *apology* admits himself, at least technically and seemingly, in the wrong; but an *apology* often also includes *defense* of an error. An *apology* is for what one has done or left undone; an *excuse* may be also for something one proposes to do or leave undone; as, an *excuse* sent beforehand for not accepting an invitation. An *excuse* for a fault is an attempt at partial *justification*; as, to allege haste as an *excuse* for carelessness.

Confession is a full *acknowledgment* of wrong, generally of a grave wrong, with or without *apology* or *excuse*. *Plea* ranges in sense from a prayer for favor or pardon to an attempt at full *vindication*. *Exculpation, justification,* and *vindication* are but synonyms for the historic, not the modern, usage of *apology*. *Apologia* is a *justification* of actions. A *pretext* suggests an ostensible reason or motive; an *alibi* is a *plea* that a person was in another place when a crime was committed. Compare **confess; defense.**

> **ANTONYMS:** *accusation, censure, charge, complaint, condemnation, imputation, injury, insult, offense, wrong.*
>
> **PREPOSITIONS:** An apology *to* the guest *for* the oversight would be fitting.

APPARENT

illusory	ostensible	probable
likely	presumable	seeming

Apparent is compared here to mean that which appears only on the surface, or which merely seems to be and may be very different from what is; as, the *apparent* motion of the sun around the earth. *Apparent* kindness casts a doubt on the reality of the kindness; *apparent* neglect implies that more care and pains may have been bestowed than we are aware of. *Presumable* implies that a thing may be taken for granted beforehand without any full knowledge of the facts. *Probable* implies that we know facts enough to make us moderately confident.

Seeming expresses great doubt of the reality; *seeming* innocence comes very near in meaning to *probable* guilt. *Apparent* indicates less assurance than *probable,* and more than *seeming.* A man's *probable* intent we believe will prove to be his real intent; his *apparent* intent may be the true one, though we have not yet evidence on which to pronounce with certainty or even with confidence; his *seeming* intent we believe to be a sham. *Likely* is a word with a wide range of usage, but always implies the belief that the thing is, or will be, true; as, it is *likely* to happen. *Illusory* connotes a misleading impression; *ostensible* implies an avowal, often in order to conceal a truth. See **evident.**

> **ANTONYMS:** *doubtful, dubious, improbable, unimaginable, unlikely.*
>
> **PREPOSITIONS:** (When *apparent* is used in the sense of evident): His guilt is apparent *in* every act *to* all observers.

APPEAL

address	call (out or upon)	refer (to)
apply (for or to)	entreat	request
ask	invoke	resort (to)
beseech		

In personal use, to *appeal* is more than to *ask*; it is to *ask* with special earnestness, and is akin to *beseech* or *entreat*; one *appeals* to another for some form of help, support, favor, or benefit; an offender may *appeal* for mercy or forgiveness. By extension to inanimate things and abstractions, to ideas, activities, emotions, etc., to *appeal* is to awaken response or sympathy; courage, sincerity, and tenderness *appeal* to some of our noblest instincts; sensationalism does not *appeal* to me:

Man is not a creature of pure reason; he must have his senses delightfully *appealed* to.   LAMB *Essays of Elia.*

Anciently, one who felt himself wronged would seize an opportunity, if possible, to *call out* to the king for redress, thus often securing reversal of the judgment of a subordinate officer. Hence comes the modern legal sense, to *appeal* (a case) from a lower authority to a higher:

I *appeal* unto Cæsar. *Acts* xxv, 11.

Figuratively, one may *appeal* to any authority believed to be decisive; as, to *appeal* to facts, statistics, history, arms, force, reason, or posterity.

To *address* or to *apply* is more formal than to *appeal*; one may *apply to* an appointing officer *for* an appointment; *apply to* the treasurer *for* funds; *apply* at the bureau of information *for* particulars; *address* a high official. We *refer* a question *to* someone; *request* a reply; *resort to* someone or something to help us out of a difficulty; *invoke* aid or protection. See **address** *verb*; **ask; plead; pray.**

ANTONYMS: *abjure, defy, deny, disavow, disclaim, refuse, repudiate.*

PREPOSITIONS: Appeal *from* a lower *to* a higher court; appeal *for* assistance.

APPEAR

look   seem

Appear and *look* refer to what manifests itself to the senses; to a semblance or probability presented directly to the mind. *Seem* applies to what is manifest to the mind on reflection but includes doubt. It suddenly *appears* to me that there is smoke in the distance; as I watch, it *looks* like a fire; from my knowledge of the locality and observation of particulars, it *seems* to me a farmhouse must be burning. Compare **apparent.**

ANTONYMS: *be; be certain, real, or true; be the fact; exist.*

PREPOSITIONS: Appear *at* the front, *among* the first, *on* or *upon* the surface, *to* the eye, *in* evidence, *in* print, *from* reports, *near* the harbor, *before* the public, *in* appropriate dress, *with* the insignia of his rank, *above* the clouds, *below* the surface, *under* the lee, *over* the sea, *through* the mist; appear *for, in behalf of,* or *against* one in court.

APPEND

add	annex	fasten	subjoin
affix	attach	fix	subscribe

To *append* (from L. *ad*, to, + *pendo*, hang) is literally to hang to, as a seal (formerly, and in some cases still, held to the document by a strip of parchment, ribbon, or the like); hence to *add* or *attach* as something accessory, subordinate, or supplemental; as, to *append* a codicil to a will. To *affix* (from L. *ad*, to, + *figo*, fasten) is to *fix, fasten,* or *attach*, to, on, or upon something already existing, of which it may or may not become an integral part; as, to *affix* a placard to a wall or a superscription to a letter; to *affix* a syllable at the beginning or end of a word (either a prefix or a suffix being called an "affix"). To *annex* (from L. *ad*, to, + *necto*, bind, tie) is either to *add* at the end, or to combine or unite something smaller or later with something larger or older; as, to *annex* a suburb to a city, or a province to an empire. To *subjoin* is also to *add* something, but refers especially to something written.

A codicil or a signature may be *affixed, annexed, appended,* or *attached*; the signature or name may also be said to be *subscribed*; a title or a superscription is *affixed* (not *annexed* or *appended*, though in some cases we may speak of it as *attached*) to a volume or a treatise; a penalty may be *affixed, annexed,* or *attached* to a prohibition; a condition may be *affixed, annexed,* or *attached* to a promise; notes or indexes are not *affixed*, but *added* or *appended* to a volume: an appendix is something *appended*. See **add; attach.**

ANTONYMS: *detach, disconnect, disengage, separate.*

APPENDAGE

accessory	addition	appurtenance	concomitant
accompaniment	adjunct	attachment	extension
addendum	appendix	auxiliary	supplement

An *appendage* is commonly a real, though not an essential or necessary part of that with which it is connected; an *adjunct* (something joined to) constitutes no real part of the thing or system to which it is joined, though perhaps a valuable *addition*; an *appurtenance* belongs subordinately to something by which it is employed, especially as an instrument to accomplish some purpose. A horse's tail is at once an ornamental *appendage* and a useful *appurtenance*; as it is an essential part, we could not call it an *adjunct*, though we might call a horseshoe an *adjunct*.

Attachment, primarily the act of attaching or the state of being attached, is extended to denote the means of attaching, as a nexus, band, or tie; as, the *attachments* of a muscle; also, to denote something appended or attached, as an *adjunct*; in machinery an *attachment* is some mechanism that can be brought into optional connection with the principal movement; as, a spiral turning *attachment* to a lathe; a phonograph *attachment* to a radio; a hemmer is a valuable *attachment* of a sewing machine.

An *extension*, as of a railroad or of a franchise, extends or carries out further something already existing. We add an *appendix* to a book, to contain names, dates, lists, etc., which would encumber the text; we add a *supplement* to supply omissions, as, for instance, to bring it up to date. An *appendix* may be called an *addendum*; but *addendum* may be used of a brief note; such notes are often grouped as *addenda*. An *addition* might be matter interwoven in the body of the work, as an index, plates, editorial notes, etc., which might be valuable *additions*, but not within the meaning of *appendix* or *supplement*. A *concomitant* is something that accompanies. As here compared, an *accessory* is something that accompanies, an *adjunct*. An *auxiliary* is often an *appendage* to another organization. Compare **accessory; attach; auxiliary.**

ANTONYMS: *main body, original, total, whole.*

PREPOSITIONS: That which is thought of as added we call an appendage *to*; that which is looked upon as an integral part is called an appendage *of*.

APPETITE

appetence	impulse	lust	propensity
craving	inclination	passion	relish
desire	liking	proclivity	thirst
disposition	longing	proneness	zest

Appetite, habitual *longing* or *desire* to gratify something, is used only of the demands of the physical system, unless otherwise expressly stated, as when we say an *appetite* for knowledge; *passion* includes all excitable impulses of our nature, as anger, fear, love, hatred, etc. *Appetite* is thus more animal than *passion*; and when we speak of *passions* and *appetites* as conjoined or contrasted, we think of the *appetites* as wholly physical and of the *passions* as, in part at least, mental or emotional. We say an *appetite* for food, a *passion* for fame. *Disposition, inclination, proneness, propensity,* and *proclivity,* all connote tendency or bent. *Zest* is an eager, often greedy *appetite*; *relish* is a keen *appetite*. *Craving* implies a very strong, unsatisfied physical or mental *desire*, especially for food, drink, or a drug. See **desire**.

ANTONYMS: *antipathy, aversion, detestation, disgust, dislike, disrelish, distaste, hatred, indifference, loathing, repugnance, repulsion.*

PREPOSITION: He had an insatiable appetite *for* the marvelous.

APPLY

adapt	allot	associate	connect	employ	refer
adjust	appropriate	attach	dedicate	exercise	use
affix	assign	conjoin	devote	fit	

To *apply* (from L. *ad*, to, + *plico*, fold), literally to fold to or upon, signifies to lay, place, or put upon for some special purpose; to bring into contact with, according to some idea of purpose, fitness, or relationship; as, to *apply* the finger to the pulse; to *apply* a poultice to a bruise or a bandage to a wound; *apply* oil to a machine; in figurative use we *apply* a principle, law, or rule to a particular case; we *apply* steam to navigation; *apply* the mind or *apply* oneself to study or to a problem; *apply* a fund to a special use; *apply* a test to a metal, or to evidence, professions, or character; *apply* an epithet or a nickname.

Apply may, in some special use, be substituted for any one of the above synonyms, but it is not always interchangeable with any one of them. Thus, a sticking plaster which is *applied* to a surface is of necessity *attached*, but the latter word is rarely used in that connection; a poultice which is *applied* is often especially so prepared that it shall not become *attached*; a postage stamp, which is *attached* or *affixed* to a letter, is not said to be *applied*; a measuring rule is *applied* to a surface, and is useful for that purpose because it is not *attached*; a whip is *applied* to a horse, but if it were *attached* to the horse it could not well be *applied*.

A placard is *affixed* to a post, but it is not said to be *applied*; a sum of money may be *allotted, applied, appropriated, dedicated,* or *devoted* to a particular use, or something may be *assigned* as a share; but *allot* carries too much of its original meaning of chance, and *dedicate* or *devote* too much of sacredness for business use; *appropriate* has a sense of official designation which is not in *apply*; money may be *applied* to a use for which it was not *appropriated*; that which is *applied* may be sometimes said to be *used, employed,* or *exercised.*

To *employ, exercise,* or *use* the mind on a problem would mean much less than to *apply* the mind to the problem; a remedy is said to be *used,* but not *applied,* internally; we *apply, adapt, adjust,* or *fit* a theory to the facts (but not the facts to the theory)—*apply* to test its correctness, *adapt, adjust,* or *fit* by any change in the theory that the facts may require; a rule, law, or principle *fits* a case to which it exactly corresponds; it *applies* to a case with which it has some inherent connection; the law against burglary does not *apply* to highway robbery; *apply* and *refer* view the same fact from opposite directions; we *apply* a rule to a case, *refer* (never *apply*) the case to the rule.

APPORTION

allot	assign	distribute	parcel (out)	ration
appoint	deal	divide	portion	share
appropriate	dispense	grant	prorate	

To *apportion* is to *distribute* by some fixed rule, which is meant to be uniform and fair; as, representatives are *apportioned* among the States according to population. To *allot* or *assign* may be to make an arbitrary division; the same is true of *distribute* or *divide*. To *dispense* is to give out freely; as, the sun *dispenses* light and heat. A thing is *appropriated* to or for a specific purpose (to which it thus becomes proper, in the original sense of being its own); money *appropriated* by Congress for one purpose cannot be expended for any other. One may *apportion* what he holds only in trust; he *shares* what is his own.

To *parcel* (*out*) or *portion* is to prepare for division, or to *divide,* into shares or lots. *Prorate* often implies authority behind the division; to *ration* is to *apportion* a fixed allowance. See *allot.*

> **ANTONYMS:** *cling to, collect, consolidate, gather together, receive, retain.*

> **PREPOSITIONS:** Apportion *to* each a fair amount; apportion the property *among* the heirs, *between* two claimants; apportion *according* to numbers, etc.

APPROXIMATION

approach	likeness	neighborhood	resemblance
contiguity	nearness	propinquity	similarity

In mathematics, *approximation* is not guesswork, not looseness, and not error. The process of *approximation* is as exact and correct at every point as that by which an absolute result is secured; the result fails of exactness only because of some inherent difficulty in the problem. The attempt to "square the circle" gives only an *approximate* result, because of the impossibility of expressing the circumference in terms of the radius. But the limits of error on either side are known, and the *approximation* has practical value. Outside of mathematics, the correct use of *approximation* (and the kindred words *approxi-*

mate and *approximately*) is to express as near an *approach* to accuracy and certainty as the conditions of human thought or action in any given case make possible. *Resemblance* and *similarity* may be but superficial and apparent; *approximation* is real. *Approach* is a relative term, indicating that one has come nearer than before in time, space, place, character, etc., though the distance may yet be considerable; an *approximation* brings one really near. *Nearness, neighborhood,* and *propinquity* are commonly used of place; *approximation,* of mathematical calculations and abstract reasoning; we speak of *approach* to the shore, *nearness* to the town, *approximation* to the truth.

ANTONYMS: *difference, distance, error, remoteness, unlikeness, variation.*

PREPOSITIONS: The approximation *of* the vegetable *to* the animal type.

ARDENT

burning	fierce	impassioned	longing
eager	fiery	inflammable	passionate
excitable	glowing	intense	sanguine
fervent	hot	keen	vehement
fervid			

Ardent is *eager* in emotion or action; as, *ardent* devotion to a cause. *Passionate* connotes capable of intense feeling; emotional. *Impassioned* can be applied to people but usually refers to utterances that show deep feeling; as, an *impassioned* entreaty. *Fervid* can be used for expressions, states of mind, or conditions; we speak of *fervid* desires, a *fervid* spirit, and *fervid* heat. *Fervent* applies chiefly to heartfelt hopes, or wishes, and includes a sense of inward steadiness; as, *fervent* gratitude or prayers. *Sanguine,* in this comparison, is *ardent* and confident; as, *sanguine* of success. *Inflammable* is easily inflamed; *excitable. Vehement* carries the idea of strong feeling, or violent or forcible action; as, a *vehement* protest, a *vehement* attack. See **eager.**

ANTONYMS: *apathetic, calm, cold, cool, dispassionate, frigid, icy, indifferent, listless, phlegmatic, platonic, stolid, stony.*

ARGUMENT

affray	controversy	dissension	scene
altercation	debate	disturbance	scrap
brawl	discussion	fracas	strife
broil	disputation	quarrel	wrangle
contention	dispute	row	wrangling

An *argument* is primarily a statement of fact tending to produce belief concerning a matter of doubt, something alleged as a reason or proof or a series of such reasons or proofs; in this sense an *argument* is wholly on one side. A *debate* is a presentation of opposing *arguments*, as by two or more contestants, in an orderly and somewhat formal manner. *Argument* may be also used for the setting forth of opposing reasons or proofs on both sides of a subject, in which case it becomes practically synonymous with *debate*. A *dispute* is an intense *debate*, commonly involving sharpness of feeling, and sometimes acrimony or anger, and being usually less methodical and orderly than a *debate*. A *discussion* is a consideration or sifting of *arguments* on both sides of a matter, and is in its best use entirely calm and fair; *discussion* involves less suggestion of opposing sides or parties than *debate*, and may be wholly conducted by a single thinker, speaker, or writer, with no recognized opponent; as, an investigator's *discussion* of a scientific problem.

Argumentation and *disputation* refer to processes of *argument* or *dispute*, usually prolonged. All these words may be intensified by adjectives, so as to express excited or hostile feeling; as, a heated *argument* or *debate*, a sharp, hot, or bitter *dispute*. A *controversy* always implies two parties, and generally strenuous opposition with excited feeling; *controversy* is often applied to *disputation* of such a character carried on in writing. *Dissension* is angry or violent difference of opinion, which may involve many persons, and on many sides of a matter. *Contention* is a strenuous effort to obtain something or to resist opposing force. In argumentative use a *contention* may be a statement or opinion which one is ready to defend strenuously and to the uttermost, but without anger or bitterness. In common use, however, *contention* signifies hot or angry *disputation* or *controversy*, in which the personal opposition and acrimony are more noticeable than the matter in *dispute*.

An *altercation* is a sharp *contention* in words, angry *controversy*, generally personal, petty, fierce, and bitter. *Altercation, affray, brawl, broil, fracas, quarrel, row, wrangle*, and *wrangling* are all words without dignity and of odious signification. When the *altercation* passes from words to blows, it becomes an *affray*. A *row* is a noisy *quarrel*, always on the verge of physical violence, which it may at any time involve. *Scrap* is a slang term, with the usual loose meaning of such words, denoting any sort of hostile encounter by word or act. *Wrangle* or *wrangling* denotes a *dispute* that is at once angry, noisy, and undignified. A *brawl* or *broil* is a rude *quarrel* by word or act or both. *Disturbance*, a word of more dignity, may likewise be by word or act; as, a disturbance about paying one's bill; a *disturbance* of the peace. A *scene* is less vigorous and pronounced than a *disturbance*, being any display of excited feeling that offends social proprieties, including any *altercation, argument, controversy, debate, discussion*, or *dispute* that has such effect. See **quarrel.** Compare **reasoning.**

ANTONYMS: *agreement, concord, concurrence, conformity, consonance, harmony, unanimity, union, unity.*

ARMS

armor   mail   weapons

Arms are implements of attack; *armor* is a defensive covering. The knight put on his *armor*; he grasped his *arms*. The word *armor* is still employed in the navy, where the distinction is clearly preserved; any vessel provided with cannon is an *armed* vessel; an *armored* ship is one covered with iron or steel plates as protection against guns and bombs, an ironclad. Anything that can be wielded in a fight may become a *weapon*, as a pitchfork or a paving stone; *arms* such as bayonets, machine guns, and cannon, are especially made and designed for use in war.

ARMY

armament   host   militia   soldiers
force   legions   multitude   soldiery
forces   military   phalanx   troops

An *army* is an organized body of men armed for war, ordinarily consider-able in numbers and independent in organization in that it is not a constituent part of any other command. Organization, unity, and independence, rather than numbers are the essentials of an *army*. We speak of the largest unit of military corps and divisions as a field *army*. We may have a small *army*, a large *army*, or a vast *army*. All the military *forces* of a nation, excluding naval and air *forces*, are called the *Army*. The *militia* comprises those citizens who are legally enrolled and drilled in military organizations other than the regular military forces. *Host* is used for any vast and orderly assemblage; as, the stars are called the heavenly *host*; the *hosts* of Midian. *Multitude* expresses number, often without order or organization; a *multitude* of armed men is not an *army*, but a mob.

Legion (from the Latin) and *phalanx* (from the Greek) are applied by a kind of poetic license to modern *forces*; the plural *legions* is preferred, in most uses, to the singular. *Military* is a general word for land *forces*; the *military* may include all the armed *soldiery* of a nation, or the term may be applied to any small detached company, as at a fort, in distinction from civilians. Any organized body of men by whom the law or will of a people is executed is a *force*; the word is a usual term for the police of any locality. *Armament* includes the warships, submarines, aircraft, etc. of a nation, as well as all the armed *forces*.

ARRAIGN

accuse   charge   impeach   prosecute
censure   cite   indict   summon

Arraign is an official word, a person accused of crime is *arraigned* when he is formally called into court, the indictment read to him, and the demand made of him to plead guilty or not guilty; in more extended use, to *arraign* is to call in question for fault in any formal, public, or official way. *Indict* and *arraign* apply strictly to criminal proceedings, and only an alleged criminal is *indicted* or *arraigned*. One is *indicted*, or *charged* with a crime, by the grand jury, and *arraigned* before the appropriate court.

One may *charge* another with any fault, great or trifling, privately or publicly, formally or informally. *Accuse* is stronger than *charge*, suggesting more of the formal and criminal; a person may *charge* a friend with unkindness or neglect; he may *accuse* a tramp of stealing.

Censure carries the idea of fault, but not of crime; it may be private and individual, or public and official. A judge, a president, or other officer of high rank may be *impeached* before the appropriate tribunal for high crimes; the veracity of a witness may be *impeached*, or called in question, by damaging evidence. A person of the highest character may be *cited* to answer as administrator, etc.

> **ANTONYMS:** *acquit, condone, discharge, excuse, exonerate, forgive, overlook, pardon, release, set free.*
>
> **PREPOSITIONS:** Arraign *at* the bar, *before* the tribunal, *of* or *for* a crime, *on* or *upon* an indictment.

◢RRANGE

adjust	compose	order	set in order
array	dispose	organize	set up
assort	form	place in order	sort
classify	group	put in order	sort out
colligate	harmonize	range	sort over
collocate	marshal	set	

To *arrange* is to place in definite order, in accordance with some plan or design; the basis of arrangement may greatly vary; we may *arrange* objects according to size or character, as books upon shelves; according to convenience or readiness for use, as a mechanic's tools; according to taste or artistic effect, as pictures or furniture, flowers in a vase, etc.; or according to rhetorical effect or logical connection, as words in a sentence, sentences in a paragraph, or arguments in a discourse. The same objects may be differently *arranged* according to the purpose in view; articles of apparel are *arranged* in a wardrobe according to space, convenience, or readiness for use; they are *arranged* upon a person according to their effect as parts of a costume.

To *assort* or *classify* is to *arrange* according to sorts or classes. *Assort* generally has reference to material qualities, as of size, color, weight, or the like; *classify*, to some mental basis of connection or sequence; goods are *assorted*;

books are *classified* in a public library; plants and animals are *classified* according to genera, species, etc.; to *assort* the specimens in a museum according to size, color, or appearance would spoil the classification; furniture is *assorted* in a warehouse, *arranged* in a room. Studies or students are not *assorted*, but *arranged* or *classified*. To *sort, sort over,* or *sort out,* is viewed as a ruder and more general process, less definite and exact than to *assort*, and quite lacking the orderly basis of *arrange*.

To *harmonize* is to *arrange* in such order or relation as to produce a harmonious effect, musical or other. To *range*, to place in a row or rows, is used primarily of large objects or those covering considerable space, as, in the use of the noun, we speak of a "range" of columns or of mountains; as used of troops, *range* refers to extended distribution as well as order and alinement.

To *array* is to draw up or *arrange* in order for battle, as an army; *array* expresses more of readiness for action on a large scale than *arrange*, and more of spectacular and cohesive formation than *range*; scouts or skirmishers may be *ranged* along the front; the main army is *arrayed* in line of battle. *Marshal* is more preparatory, and may have reference merely to the enrolment and assemblage of a force.

> False wizard, avaunt! I have *marshalled* my clan.
> CAMPBELL *Lochiel's Warning.*

The word *array* has fallen out of military use, but still, both as noun and verb, has descriptive force in literature. As applied to dress, *array* carries the idea of splendor.

> Solomon, in all his glory, was not *arrayed* like one of these. *Matt.* vi, 29.

To *form*, in this connection, is to *arrange* parts or units so that they assume a certain form or shape; as, to *form* a procession; to *form* troops in line or column; to *dispose* is to place parts or units in relative position for mutual cooperation or support on an extended scale; a modern army is *disposed* over so large an area that the different parts cannot see one another, and no "form" of the entire force is visible from any point; hence we naturally speak of the disposition rather than of the formation of the force.

To *compose* is to put together things, thoughts, parts, or elements so as to *form* an orderly whole; to *compose* may include *arranging*, but commonly involves much more; in *compose*, the thought of unity prevails; in *dispose*, the thought of distribution. In printing, to *compose* is to *arrange* (type) in proper order, as in the composing-stick—in this sense rarely used, *set* or *set up* being the technical terms; yet a typesetter is regularly called a "compositor," and the process "composition." To *colligate* is to *group* together, as facts; to *collocate* is to *arrange* side by side or in order.

ANTONYMS: *confuse, derange, disarrange, disorder, disperse, disturb, jumble, pi* or *pie* (print)*, scatter.*

ARREST

apprehend	detain	restrain	stop
capture	hold	secure	take into custody
catch	make prisoner	seize	take prisoner

The legal term *arrest* carries always the implication of a legal offense; this is true even of *arresting* for debt. To *apprehend* is to *arrest* a person by legal authority, as for some crime; to *detain* is to *take into custody* and *hold* during an inquiry; ships are *detained* for inspection; a person may be *detained* by process of law when no offense is alleged against him, as in the case of a witness who is *held* in a house of detention till a case comes to trial. An individual may have his liberty *restrained*, as in an insane asylum; an individual or corporation may be *restrained* by injunction from selling certain property. In case of an *arrest*, an officer may *secure* his prisoner by fetters, by a locked door, or other means to prevent escape. *Capture* is used of seizure by armed force; as, to *capture* a ship, a fort, etc. See **catch; hinder; restrain.**

> **ANTONYMS:** *discharge, dismiss, free, liberate, release, set free.*
>
> **PREPOSITIONS:** Arrested *for* crime, *on* suspicion, *by* the sheriff, *on, upon,* or *by virtue of* a warrant, *on* final process, *in* execution.

ASK

adjure	beg	entreat	request
appeal	beseech	implore	require
apply for	crave	petition	solicit
apply to	demand	pray	supplicate

One *asks* what he feels that he may fairly claim and reasonably expect; he *begs* for that to which he advances no claim but pity. *Demand* is a determined and often an arrogant word; one may rightfully *demand* that to which one has no claim but power. *Require* is less arrogant and obtrusive than *demand*, but is exceedingly peremptory; as, the court *requires* the attendance of witnesses. *Entreat* implies a special earnestness of asking, and *beseech*, a still added and more humble intensity; *beseech* was formerly often used as a polite intensive for *beg* or *pray*; as, I *beseech* you to tell me. To *adjure* is to *appeal* to solemnly, with the implication of enjoining as well as *requesting* something; it is often strengthened by the invocation of a sacred name; as, "By Heaven, I *adjure* thee to let me pass!"

To *importune* is to *beg* insistently and repeatedly, with the suggestion of bothersome persistency. To *implore* is to *ask* with weeping and lamentation; to *supplicate* is to *ask*, as it were, on bended knees. *Crave* and *request* are somewhat formal terms; *crave* has almost disappeared from conversation; *request* would seem distant between parent and child. *Pray* is now used chiefly of address to the Supreme Being; *petition* is used of written request to persons in authority; as, to *petition* the legislature to pass an act, or the governor to pardon an offender. See **appeal; plead; pray.**

ANTONYMS: *claim, command, deny, enforce, exact, extort, insist, refuse, reject.*

PREPOSITIONS: Ask a person *for* a thing; ask a thing *of* or *from* a person; ask *after* or *about* one's health, welfare, friends, etc.

ASSOCIATE *noun*

accomplice	colleague	consort	mate
ally	companion	fellow	partner
chum	comrade	friend	peer
coadjutor	confederate	helpmate	

Associate refers to a person with whom one is in more or less constant contact, either through vocational or social connections, or because of like interests; it is popularly used of mere friendly relations, but oftener implies some work, enterprise, or pursuit in which the associated persons unite. An *associate,* as used officially, implies one who is not fully equal in rank. We rarely speak of *associates* in crime or wrong, using *confederates* or *accomplices* instead.

Companion denotes a person who actually attends or accompanies one, whether habitually or not; a chance acquaintance at dinner may be one's *companion,* as may one's husband or wife. *Companion* gives itself with equal readiness to the good or evil sense, as also does *comrade.* One may be a *companion* in travel who would not readily become an *associate* at home. A lady advertises for a *companion*; she would not advertise for an *associate. Peer* implies equality rather than companionship; as, a jury of his *peers. Comrade* expresses more fellowship and good feeling than *companion,* and implies association in some common enterprise or vocation. *Fellow* has almost gone out of use in this connection, except in an inferior or patronizing sense. *Consort* is a word of equality and dignity, as applied especially to the marriage relation. Compare **accessory; acquaintance; friendship.**

ANTONYMS: *antagonist, enemy, foe, hinderer, opponent, opposer, rival, stranger.*

PREPOSITIONS: These were the associates *of* the leader *in* the enterprise.

ASSOCIATE *verb*

affiliate	attach	confederate	connect	join	link
ally	combine	conjoin	couple	league	unite

To *associate* (from L. *ad*, to, + *socius*, a companion, ally) is to put, bring, or come together with something else, in companionship of fact or thought; feelings, speech, manners, and morals will be influenced by the persons with whom one *associates*; things are *associated* in thought when for any reason the thought of one calls up that of the other; we *associate* a certain meaning with a word, with or without reason, rightly or wrongly (for association is far from definition); if we *attach* a certain meaning to a word, we have (or believe ourselves to have) definite reason for so doing; we *associate* a song with some scene where it was heard, or the perfume of a flower with a friend who loved it; the association of ideas is one of the most important topics in psychology. To *ally* (from L. *ad*, to, + *ligo*, bind) is to *unite* by treaty, league, or agreement, as sovereign states; hence, to *connect* by any relationship, as by marriage, likeness, origin, etc.; persons or families of prominence may be said to be *allied* by marriage. To *affiliate* (from L. *ad*, to, + *filius*, son), primarily to adopt or receive into a family, as a son or daughter, is commonly used as signifying to receive or *associate* with on friendly terms (followed by *with* or *to*—or, in certain legal or scientific use, by *on* or *upon*); as, to *affiliate* oneself *with* (or *to*) a political party; a person's character may be judged by the character of those with whom he is *affiliated*; virtue *affiliates* with virtue; we speak of *affiliated* sciences, studies, colleges, or schools. See **attach.**

ANTONYMS: *avoid, disconnect, disjoin, disrupt, dissociate, disunite, diverge, divide, divorce, estrange, part, separate, sever, sunder.*

ASSOCIATION

alliance	confederacy	familiarity	lodge
club	confederation	federation	participation
community	conjunction	fellowship	partnership
companionship	connection	fraternity	society
company	corporation	friendship	union

An *association* is an organization, usually with a serious aim, open to all of like interests and needs; as, the Young Men's Christian *Association*. *Society* suggests a more closely knit group of persons with serious aims, whose members take an active part in its work; as, the Ladies' Aid *Society*. A *club* is an organization, usually social, whose membership is obtained by invitation and election; a *club* usually has its own quarters for meeting, recreation, etc., and the word is often applied to the quarters themselves.

We speak of an *alliance* of nations, a *club* of pleasure-seekers, a *community* of Shakers, a *company* of soldiers or of friends, a *confederacy, confederation, federation,* or *union* of separate states under one general government, a *partnership* or *company* of businessmen, a *conjunction* of planets. The whole body of Freemasons constitutes a *fraternity*; one of their local organizations is called a *lodge.* A *corporation* or *company* is formed for purposes of business; an *association* or *society* (though also incorporated) is for learning, literature, benevolence, religion, etc. See **associate; acquaintance; friendship.**

ANTONYMS: disintegration, independence, isolation, separa-
tion, solitude.

PREPOSITIONS: An association *of* scholars *for* the advancement
of knowledge; association *with* the good is ennobling.

ASSUME

accept	claim	pretend	take
affect	feign	put on	usurp
appropriate	postulate	sham	
arrogate	presume	simulate	

The distinctive idea of *assume* is to take by one's own independent volition, whether well or ill, rightfully or wrongfully. One may *accept* an obligation or *assume* an authority that properly belongs to him, or he may *assume* an obligation or indebtedness that could not be required of him. He may *assume* authority or office that is his right; if he *assumes* what does not belong to him, he is said to *arrogate* or *usurp* it. A man may *usurp* the substance of power in the most unpretending way; what he *arrogates* to himself he *assumes* with a haughty and overbearing manner. One *assumes* the robes or insignia of office by putting them on, with or without right. If he *takes* to himself the credit and appearance of qualities he does not possess, he is said to *affect* or *feign*, or to *pretend* to, the character he thus *assumes*. What a debater *postulates* he openly states and *takes* for granted without proof; what he *assumes* he may take for granted without mention. A favorite trick of the sophist is quietly to *assume* as true what would at once be challanged if expressly stated. What a man *claims* he asserts his right to *take*; what he *assumes* he *takes*.

Assume, affect, feign, pretend, sham, and *simulate* all mean to *put on* a false appearance. One may *assume* a look of contentment to mask one's unhappiness. To *affect* is to assume ostentatiously, commonly for effect; as, to *affect* an English accent. To *pretend* is to profess openly something that is false; as, to *pretend* friendship. *Feign* has the same basic meaning as *pretend*, but suggests greater artfulness; one *feigns* deafness by *pretending* not to hear. To *sham* is to *feign* obviously and with a deliberate intent to deceive; the startled opossum *shams* death.

ASSURANCE

arrogance	boldness	impudence	self-confidence
assertion	confidence	presumption	self-reliance
assumption	effrontery	self-assertion	trust

Assurance may have the good sense of a high, sustained *confidence* and *trust*; as, the saint's *assurance* of heaven. *Confidence* is founded upon reasons; *assurance* is largely a matter of feeling. In the bad sense, *assurance* is a vicious courage, with belief of one's ability to outwit or defy others; the hardened criminal is remarkable for habitual *assurance*. For the calm conviction of one's own rectitude and ability, *self-confidence* is a better word than *assurance*; *self-reliance* expresses confidence in one's own resources, independently of others' aid. In the bad sense *assurance* is less gross than *impudence*, which is (according to its etymology) a shameless *boldness*. *Assurance* is in act or manner; *impudence* may be in speech. *Effrontery* is *impudence* defiantly displayed. See **effrontery; faith; impertinence; pride.**

ANTONYMS: *bashfulness, confusion, consternation, dismay, distrust, doubt, hesitancy, misgiving, shyness, timidity.*

ATTACH

add	append	combine	fix	stick
adjoin	apply	conjoin	hitch	tie
affix	associate	connect	join	unite
annex	bind	fasten	secure	

To *attach* is primarily to cause one thing to hold securely to another, as by a nail; thence the meaning is extended to include any other means of secure connection, as by a cord, etc.; a handle is *attached* to a valise, a hook to a fishing-line, a bayonet to a gun; a plant is *attached* to the ground by its roots. We commonly speak of *attaching* the less to the greater, the subordinate to the principal, the final to the preliminary, the particular to the general, the movable to the permanent, etc.; we *attach* a nozzle to a hose, a hose to a faucet or a hydrant; a barnacle *attaches* itself to a ship. In some cases we may speak of either of two objects as *attached* to the other, according to our point of view; we may say that the hilt of the sword is *attached* to the blade or the blade to the hilt; or, two or more objects may be spoken of as *attached* to each other or to one another. In official relations an officer is said to be *attached* to a regiment, a secretary to an embassy, etc. In legal use a person or property that is *attached* is viewed as *bound* and held by the bond of the law. In mental, moral, and spiritual relations we *attach* a certain meaning to a word, or significance to an action; we *attach* importance to a discovery; one may be *attached* to a party by custom, association, or self-interest, or by sympathy, principle, or patriotism; a person is *attached* to another or to others by affection.

To *fasten* is to make fast, as one object to another; as, to *fasten* a door by a bolt; to *fasten* a glove by a button; figuratively, to cause to adhere by any means or agency; as, to *fasten* a quarrel, a reproach, a nickname, etc., upon anyone. In the physical sense, *attach* and *fasten* are close *synonyms*, and often used interchangeably; that which is *attached* or *fastened* may have considerable freedom of movement, provided the connection be secure; as, a boat is *attached* or *fastened* to the wharf by a mooring-line; yet, even here, there are differences of usage; we say that a muscle is *attached* (rather than *fastened*) to a bone by a tendon; a horse is *fastened* to a post by a strap or rope; he is *attached* to the vehicle by the harness; in either case we may use the verb *hitch*, which is applied especially to a temporary fastening; we may also speak of the horse as *tied* to the post, but not to the load; a door is *attached* to the door-post by hinges; it is *fastened* at the opposite side by a bolt or lock. We may *fasten* or *attach* objects by *binding* or *tying*.

To *join* is to bring together, bring into close contact, adhesion, conjunction, or cooperation; as, to *join* hands, fortunes, forces, estates, etc.; if one building is *joined* to another the two are built against or into each other; *unite* is a close synonym for *join*, but of fuller meaning; in the physical sense things are *united* which are *joined* so as to form one concordant whole, to adhere closely together, to exist or act as one; figuratively, things are *united* which are *joined* in close and harmonious relation, as by legal, marital, social, or other tie, by interest, affection, fellowship, or the like; as, to *unite* nations by treaty, to *unite* hearts in love, to *unite* courage with fortitude; persons are *joined* or *united* in marriage, *unite* having the fuller and nobler meaning.

To *connect* is to *join* as by links or fastenings; to bring into close relation, especially by some intervening means or agency; as, two buildings are *connected* by a subway, or two oceans by a strait; thence *connect* is extended in meaning to denote numerous forms of close relationship, as by origin, derivation, significance, association of ideas, classification, causation, consequence, etc.; in the scheme of the solar system, the moon is *connected* with the earth, though it is not *attached, fastened,* or *joined* to, or *united* with it; a word is *connected* with another by derivation from the same root; two words are *connected* in meaning where each expresses some part of the meaning conveyed by the other; two thoughts, feelings, or ideas are *connected* when the one suggests the other, or when both are suggested by the same object; as the idea of food is *connected* with the sensation of hunger. *Connect* is a word of looser, less vigorous and intimate meaning than *attach, join,* or *unite*; husband and wife are *joined* or *united* (not *connected*) in marriage; their two families, or any members of either, are *connected* by that marriage; *attached* could not be used in either sense; so we speak of persons as distantly *connected* (or related), or of one as a distant connection (or relation, relative, or kinsman) of another. See **add; append; apply; associate; bind; fix.**

ANTONYMS: *alienate, detach, discard, disconnect, disjoin, dissociate, disunite, divert, divorce, remove, separate, sever.*

PREPOSITIONS: Attach *to* the document *at* the bottom *with* mucilage; attached *by* ligaments, *by* a cord, a halter, or the like; in legal usage, attach *for* a debt, etc. (anciently *of* high treason); loss or blame may attach *on* or *upon*.

ATTACHMENT

adherence	devotion	friendship	regard
adhesion	esteem	inclination	tenderness
affection	estimation	love	union
affinity			

Attachment, in the sense here considered, is a feeling that binds a person by ties of heart to another person or thing; we speak of a man's *adherence* to his purpose, his *adhesion* to his party, or to anything to which he clings tenaciously, though with no special tenderness; of his *attachment* to his church, to the old homestead, or to any persons or objects that he may hold dear. *Affection,* usually directed toward a living being, expresses more warmth of feeling; we should not speak of a mother's *attachment* to her babe, but of her *affection* or of her *devotion.* *Love* implies a more intense, less regulated feeling than *affection.* One may feel *affection* or *love* for, or *attachment* to, one's close friends. *Inclination* expresses simply a tendency, which may be good or bad, yielded to or overcome; as, an *inclination* to study; an *inclination* to drink.

Affinity is an instinctive drawing, *inclination,* liking, or friendliness founded upon some correspondence of nature; as in chemistry, *affinity* does not involve likeness, so, in spiritual relations, *affinity* may be between opposite natures or qualities, between which there is no inherent contradiction, each supplying some lack in the other; there may be *affinity* between the brave and the timid, between the martial courage of the soldier and the moral courage of the statesman, but not between courage and cowardice, nor between virtue and vice; the brave, true, and good of today have *affinity* with the brave, true, and good of all ages past. *Regard* is more distant than *affection* or *attachment,* but closer and warmer than *esteem;* we speak of high *esteem,* kind *regard.* See **acquaintance; appendage; friendship; love; union.**

ANTONYMS: *alienation, animosity, antipathy, aversion, coolness, dislike, distance, divorce, enmity, estrangement, indifference, opposition, repugnance, separation, severance.*

PREPOSITIONS: Attachment *of* a true man *to* his friends; attachment *to* a leader *for* his nobility of character; the attachments *between* two persons or things; attachment *by* muscular fibers, or *by* a rope, etc.

ATTACK *noun*

aggression	incursion	invasion	onslaught
assault	infringement	onset	trespass
encroachment	intrusion		

An *attack* is an initial move to injure, destroy, or gain an advantage. An *attack* may be by word; an *aggression* is always by deed. An *assault* is more violent than an *attack*, and may be upon the person; an *aggression* is upon rights, possessions, etc. An *invasion* of a nation's territories is an act of *aggression*; an *intrusion* upon a neighboring estate is a *trespass*; an *incursion* is a sudden *invasion*; an *encroachment* is a gradual *invasion*. *Onslaught* signifies intensely violent *assault*, as by an army or a desperado, though it is sometimes used of violent speech. *Onset* is a sudden rush at the beginning of or during an *attack*. An *infringement* violates the rights of others.

ANTONYMS: *defense, repulsion, resistance, retreat, submission, surrender.*

PREPOSITIONS: The enemy made an attack *upon* (or *on*) our works.

ATTACK *verb*

assail	besiege	combat	invade
assault	bombard	encounter	set upon
beleaguer	charge	fall upon	storm
beset			

To *attack* is to begin hostilities of any kind. A general *invades* a country by marching troops into it; he *attacks* a city by drawing up an army against it; he *assaults* it by hurling his troops directly upon its defenses. *Assail* and *assault*, though of the same original etymology, have diverged in meaning. To *assail* is to wear down one's opponent by repeated blows; as, we *assailed* the enemy with frequent raids; *assailed* by temptations. *Assault* always connotes direct physical contact, with the suggestion of an attempt to conquer by the suddenness and overpowering strength of one's attack. One may *assail* another with reproaches; he *assaults* him with a blow, a brandished weapon, etc.

To *bombard* is to *assail*, as a city or fortress, continuously and destructively with artillery shells or aerial bombs. Figuratively, it means to pester or importune; as the teacher was *bombarded* with eager questions. To *beset* is to set around, or, so to speak, to stud one's path, with menaces, attacks, or persuasions. To *besiege* and *beleaguer* are the acts of armies. To *encounter* is to meet face to face, and may be said either of the *attacking* or of the resisting force or person, or of both.

ANTONYMS: *aid, befriend, cover, defend, protect, resist, shelter, shield, support, sustain, uphold, withstand.*

PREPOSITIONS: We were attacked *by* the enemy *with* cannon and musketry.

ATTAIN

accomplish	arrive at	gain	master	reach
achieve	compass	get	obtain	secure
acquire	earn	grasp	procure	win

Attain is a lofty word, pointing to some high or desirable result; a man *attains* the mountain summit, he *attains* honor or learning as the result of strenuous and earnest labor. Even that usage of *attain* which has been thought to refer to mere progress of time carries the thought of a result desired; as, to *attain* to old age; the man desires to live to a good old age; we should not speak of his *attaining* his dotage. One may *attain* an object that will prove not worth his labor, but what he *achieves* is in itself great and splendid; as, the Greeks at Marathon *achieved* a glorious victory.

A person may *obtain* a situation by the intercession of friends; he *procures* a dinner by paying for it; he *acquires* knowledge, *masters* a language, or *wins* a scholarship by diligent study.

ANTONYMS: *abandon, fail, forfeit, give up, let go, lose, miss.*

ATTAINMENT

accomplishment   **acquirement**   **acquisition**

Attainment is the act of arriving at, gaining, or reaching something, and usually refers to achievement in some branch of the arts or sciences, or in political affairs. *Attainments* are lofty and ennobling. *Accomplishments* are showy, graceful, pleasing; *acquirements* are substantial and useful. *Acquisition* usually applies to additional money or property gained, but, especially in the plural, is often used for what is acquired by skill or endeavor; as, mental *acquisitions*. Compare **wisdom.**

ATTRIBUTE *noun*

property   **quality**

A *quality*—the "suchness" of anything, according to the German idiom—denotes what a thing really is in some respect; an *attribute* is what we conceive a thing to be in some one respect; thus, while *attribute* may, *quality* must, express something of the real nature of that to which it is ascribed; we speak of the *attributes* of God, the *qualities* of matter. Holiness is an *attribute* of God; the *attributes* of many heathen deities have been only the *qualities* of wicked men joined to superhuman power. A *property* (from L. *proprius,* one's own) is what belongs especially to one thing as its own peculiar possession, in distinction from all other things; a *quality* is inherent; a *property* may be transient. When we speak of the *qualities* or the *properties* of matter, *quality* is the more general, but *property* is the more technically correct term, and is now used by physicists in describing those *qualities* manifested by all bodies under given conditions or in certain states. Compare **characteristic; emblem.**

ANTONYMS: *being, essence, nature, substance.*

ATTRIBUTE *verb*

ascribe	associate	connect	refer
assign	charge	impute	

We may *attribute* to a person either that which belongs to him or that which we merely suppose to be his. We *attribute* to a judge a sure wisdom. We may *attribute* a wrong intent to an innocent person. We may *attribute* a result, rightly or wrongly, to a certain cause; in such case, however, *attribute* carries always a concession of uncertainty or possible error. Where we are quite sure, we *refer* a matter or indicate its relation to the cause or class to which it belongs; but we *ascribe* something to a person or thing when we simply infer that it belongs to him or it. We may *attribute* a matter in silent thought; we *ascribe* anything openly in speech or writing; King Saul said of the singing women, "They have *ascribed* unto David ten thousands, and to me they have *ascribed* but thousands." We *associate* things which may have no necessary or causal relation; as, we may *associate* the striking of a clock with the serving of dinner, though the two are not necessarily *connected*. We *charge* a person with what we deem blameworthy. *Impute,* which often includes accusation, is more definite than *ascribe*; we may *impute* good or evil, but more commonly evil.

ANTONYMS: *deny, disconnect, dissociate, separate, sever, sunder.*

PREPOSITIONS: It is uncharitable to attribute evil motives *to* (archaic *unto*) others.

AUTHENTIC

accepted	certain	original	sure
accredited	current	real	true
authoritative	genuine	received	trustworthy
authorized	legitimate	reliable	veritable

Authentic, authoritative, and *authorized* all pertain to works of man, in the strict sense; *authentic* is the strongest term, denoting that which is of undisputed origin, in agreement with all known facts, of such certainty that no one can produce valid doubt. *Authoritative,* though also a strong term, has somewhat less positiveness; it implies a weighing of evidence by one or more competent judges, and a conclusion drawn from the opinions thus formed; *author-*

ized expresses the sanction or acceptance of *authoritative* conclusion. *Authoritative* depends for its strength upon authority, but as there may be divergence of views among equally competent masters of a subject, the term suggests a possibility that further evidence may alter a conclusion.

Authentic and *genuine* are often used interchangeably, especially when applied to works of man; thus we say either a *genuine* masterpiece of da Vinci, or an *authentic* masterpiece of da Vinci, but we do not apply *authentic* to works of nature; we say a *genuine* pearl, not an *authentic* pearl. We speak of *accepted* conclusions, *certain* evidence, *current* money, a *legitimate* conclusion or *legitimate* authority, *original* manuscripts, *real* value, *received* interpretation, *reliable* information, *sure* proof, a *true* statement, a *trustworthy* witness, a *veritable* discovery, an *accredited* delegate.

ANTONYMS: *apocryphal, baseless, counterfeit, disputed. exploded, fabulous, false, fictitious, spurious, unauthorized.*

AUXILIARY

accessory	assistant	helper	promoter
aid	coadjutor	mercenary	subordinate
ally	confederate		

An *auxiliary* is a person or thing that helps in a subordinate capacity. *Allies* unite as equals; *auxiliaries* are, at least technically, inferiors or *subordinates*. Yet the *auxiliary* is more than a mere *assistant*. The word is most frequently found in the plural, and in the military sense; *auxiliaries* are troops of one nation uniting with the armies of another, and acting under its orders. *Mercenaries* serve only for pay; *auxiliaries,* often for reasons of state, policy, or patriotism as well. A *coadjutor* is a co-worker or associate, usually of equal rank; a *confederate* associates with others in a league or plot. A *promoter* is one who forwards an enterprise or an undertaking of any nature.

ANTONYMS: *antagonist, hinderer, opponent, opposer.*

AVENGE

punish	retaliate	revenge	vindicate	visit

Avenge and *revenge,* once close synonyms, are now far apart in meaning. To *avenge* is to *visit* punishment on a wrong-doer, in order to *vindicate* the righteous, or to uphold and illustrate the right by bringing suffering or destruction to the wicked. "And seeing one of them suffer wrong, he *avenged* him that was oppressed, and smote the Egyptian," *Acts* vii, 24. To *revenge* is to inflict harm or suffering upon another through personal anger and resentment at something done to ourselves. *Avenge* is unselfish; *revenge* is selfish. *Revenge,* according to present usage, could not be said of God. To *retaliate* is to give like for like, or to return evil for evil; it may be necessary for self-defense, without any idea of *revenge.* Compare **revenge.**

PREPOSITIONS: Avenge *on* or *upon* (rarely, avenge oneself *of*) a wrong-doer.

AWFUL

alarming	dread	grand	shocking
appalling	dreadful	horrible	solemn
august	exalted	imposing	stately
dire	fearful	majestic	terrible
direful	frightful	noble	terrific

In formal and literary style the sense of the first element, "awe," is carefully maintained. However, in popular use it has become a mere intensive of adverse meaning; as, an *awful* headache. A similar degeneration in meaning is seen in the words *dreadful, frightful, horrible, terrible,* etc.

Awful should not be used of things which are merely disagreeable or annoying, nor of all that are *alarming* and *terrible,* but only of such as bring a solemn awe upon the soul, as in the presence of a superior power; as, the *awful* hush before the battle. That which is *awful* arouses an oppressive, that which is *august* an admiring reverence; we speak of the *august* presence of a mighty monarch, the *awful* presence of death. We speak of an *exalted* station, a *grand* mountain, an *imposing* presence, a *majestic* cathedral, a *noble* mien, a *solemn* litany, a *stately* march, an *august* assembly, the *awful* scene of the Judgment Day.

ANTONYMS: *base, beggarly, commonplace, contemptible, despicable, humble, inferior, lowly, mean, paltry, undignified, vulgar.*

AWKWARD

boorish	gauche	maladroit	ungainly
bungling	gawky	rough	unhandy
clownish	inept	uncouth	unskilful
clumsy			

Awkward is *off-ward,* turned the wrong way; it was anciently used of a back-handed or left-handed blow in battle, of squinting eyes, etc. *Clumsy,* on the other hand, signifies benumbed, stiffened with cold; this is the original meaning of *clumsy* fingers, *clumsy* limbs. Thus, *awkward* primarily refers to action, *clumsy* to condition. A tool, a vehicle, or the human frame may be *clumsy* in shape or build, *awkward* in motion. The *clumsy* man is almost of necessity *awkward,* but the *awkward* man may not be naturally *clumsy.* The finest untrained colt is *awkward* in harness; a horse that is *clumsy* in build can never be trained out of awkwardness. An *awkward* statement has an uncomfortable, and perhaps recoiling, force; a statement that contains ill-assorted and incongruous material in ill-chosen language is *clumsy*. We speak of an *awkward* predicament, an *awkward* scrape. An *awkward* excuse commonly reflects on the one who offers it. We say the admitted facts have an *awkward* appearance. In none of these cases could *clumsy* be used. *Clumsy* is, however, applied to movements that seem as unsuitable as those of benumbed and stiffened limbs. A dancing bear is both *clumsy* and *awkward*.

Maladroit suggests tactlessness in human relations. A *maladroit* remark is one that offends or hurts. *Inept* means lacking appropriateness or aptness; an *inept* remark is one with so little bearing on the topic of conversation as to seem pointless. *Gauche*, literally left-handed, implies an unfamiliarity with social conventions and graces that makes for clumsiness. *Gauche* and *boorish* have almost the same meaning, though the latter suggests more deliberate rudeness of manner.

> **ANTONYMS:** *adroit, clever, dexterous, handy, skilful.*

> **PREPOSITIONS:** The raw recruit is awkward *in* action, *at* the business.

AXIOM

truism

Both the *axiom* and the *truism* are instantly seen to be true, and need no proof; but in an *axiom* there is progress of thought, while the *truism* simply says the same thing over again, or says what is too manifest to need saying. The *axiom* that "things which are equal to the same thing are equal to one another" unfolds in the latter part of the sentence the truth implied in the first part, which might have been overlooked if not stated. In the *truism* that "a man can do all he is capable of," the former and the latter part of the sentence are simply identical, and the mind is left just where it started. Hence the *axiom* is valuable and useful, while the *truism* is weak and flat, unless the form of statement makes it striking or racy, as "all fools are out of their wits." See **proverb**.

> **ANTONYMS:** *absurdity, contradiction, demonstration, nonsense, paradox, sophism.*

B

BABBLE

blab	chatter	gossip	palaver	prattle
blurt (out)	gabble	jabber	patter	tattle
cackle	gibber	murmur	prate	twaddle
chat				

Babble, gabble, gibber, and *jabber,* all of onomatopoetic origin, suggest inarticulate, rapid speech which is in large part unintelligible to the listener. In figurative use, *babble* is used especially of brooks and babies, *gabble* of geese, *gibber* of idiots and ghosts, and *jabber* of monkeys. A hen *cackles.* To *patter* is to repeat rapidly and as if by rote; a barker at a circus *patters* his routine. *Blab* and *blurt* (commonly *blurt out*) refer to the letting out of what the lips can no longer keep in; *blab,* of a secret; *blurt out,* of passionate feeling.

To *chat* is to talk in an easy, pleasant way, not without sense, but without special purpose. Chatting is the practice of adults, prattling that of children. To *prate* is to talk idly, presumptuously, or foolishly, but not necessarily incoherently. To *jabber* is to utter a rapid succession of unintelligible sounds, generally more noisy than chattering. To *gossip* is to talk of petty personal matters, as for pastime or mischief. To *twaddle* is to talk feeble nonsense. To *murmur* is to utter suppressed or even inarticulate sounds, suggesting the notes of a dove, or the sound of a running stream, and is used figuratively of the half-suppressed utterances of affection or pity, or of complaint, resentment, etc. See **speak.**

PREPOSITIONS: Babies babble *for* the moon; the crowd babbles *of* a hero; the sick man babbles *of* home.

BAD

abandoned	distressing	noxious	unfortunate
abominable	evil	pernicious	unhappy
baleful	false	poor	unlucky
baneful	foul	putrid	unpleasant
base	fraudulent	rascally	unprincipled
corrupt	hard	rotten	unprofitable
corrupting	hurtful	sad	untrue
decayed	ill	saddening	untrustworthy
decaying	immoral	scurvy	unwelcome
deceitful	imperfect	serious	unwholesome
deceptive	incompetent	severe	unworthy
defective	incorrect	shabby	vicious
deficient	inferior	sinful	vile
deleterious	injurious	sorrowful	villainous
depraved	lacking	sorry	wicked
detrimental	mean	troublesome	worthless
disagreeable	mischievous	unfair	wretched
dishonest	naughty		

Bad is the opposite of good in any one of its many senses, and almost any negative adjective in the language may be in some connection a synonym of *bad*. *Bad* when it refers to *disagreeable* is often *unpleasant*; when it means *wicked* it often connotes *vicious*. What is *bad* in another sense may be merely *deficient, lacking,* or just *incorrect*; as, *bad* sight, a *bad* copy. We also use *bad* to imply *unprofitable,* as, a *bad* bargain; or *unfortunate,* as, a *bad* start. A *bad* or *severe* cold is *distressing*; a *naughty* child is *troublesome*. *Bad* in such expressions as "a *bad* wound," "a *bad* pain," is a common use, verging on pleonasm; "a *severe* or *dangerous* wound," "an *intense* pain" is better usage. Do not use *bad* for *sick* or *ill*. In such expressions as "he felt *bad*," the adjective is preferred to the adverb (badly). See **pernicious.**

ANTONYMS: See synonyms for *good.*

BAFFLE

balk	counteract	frustrate	outwit
circumvent	defeat	outgeneral	thwart
contravene	foil	outmaneuver	

To *baffle* a scheme, plan, or the like is to render it ineffectual by any action or want of action, however slight, that is sufficient to spoil it for the moment, as a fox or hare may *baffle* dogs by sudden doublings or turnings. So a person may be said to be *baffled* in a scheme or plan; a shrewd witness may *baffle* a lawyer by cunning evasions. *Baffle* is especially applied to a continuous series of acts or omissions, each seemingly slight, yet sufficient for the immediate purpose.

To *foil* is to make an attempt nugatory by craft or skill, as an agile wrestler may *foil* the attempt of a heavier opponent to close with him, by slipping away from his grasp. An attack is *foiled* which is made to miss its mark. A scheme, plan, or attempt may fail because of inherent defect or weakness; it is *foiled* by a skilful antagonist. A person is also said to be *foiled* in an undertaking which is thus rendered abortive. One may be distinctly aware how and how far he is *foiled*; one who is *baffled* is left at a loss—with a sense of uncertainty whether any possible new turn may not be as effectually met.

A plan, project, or movement is *balked* when rendered impossible of accomplishment by some insuperable obstacle or hindrance less conspicuous than a block or bar; as, the advance was *balked* by a morass; the enterprise was *balked* by the apathy of those expected to engage in it. *Balk* is applied either to persons or to acts, movements, etc. *Frustrate* and *thwart* are more absolute than *baffle* or *foil,* coming close to the meaning of *defeat*. To *frustrate* is to bring to complete and final failure; that which is often *baffled* or *foiled* may yet succeed; that which is *frustrated* is definitely prevented from succeeding. To *thwart* is to *defeat* as by some force or action coming across the path; action may be *thwarted* by counter-action, as an intended movement by a counter-attack; an attempt to pass a measure in an assembly may be *thwarted* by filibustering (in which case it may also be said to be *frustrated*). *Thwart* always implies an opposer, while *frustrate* may not; a plan, scheme, or the like may be *frustrated* (not *thwarted*) by an accident; as, an attempted surprise may be *frustrated* by the accidental discharge of a gun, or *thwarted* by the vigilance of the enemy's sentinels. A person is also said to be *frustrated* or *thwarted* in his hope, plan, design, or the like.

Outwit is allied in meaning with *baffle* and *foil*, as are *outgeneral* and *outmaneuver*, but the two latter words are applied to more extensive movements and on a grander scale; Napoleon *outgeneraled* and *outmaneuvered* the Allies at Austerlitz; it would be a very inadequate statement to say that he *baffled* or *foiled* them. To *circumvent* is to *defeat* by passing around, and, as it were, attacking in flank—in common phrase "to get round" an opponent or opposition. To *contravene* is to meet by direct opposition; to *counteract* is to meet by some direct force adequate to overcome the thing opposed; as, a remedy *counteracts* a disease; a false impression may be *counteracted* by argument, explanation, or the like.

> **ANTONYMS:** *abet, advance, aid, assist, encourage, promote, prosper.*

BANISH

ban	dismiss	exile	ostracize
deport	drive out	expatriate	oust
discharge	eject	expel	transport
dislodge	evict	extradite	

To *banish* is to compel by authority to leave a place or country, either permanently or for a given time, and with or without restriction to some other place or country. To *exile* is to force to leave one's own country, with the connotation either of official expulsion or of the pressure of circumstances, or perhaps of prolonged voluntary absence. To *expatriate* is to *exile* a person, at the same time depriving him of citizenship in his own country, and often precluding his right ever to return. One may *exile* or *expatriate* oneself; James Joyce *expatriated* himself to France.

Originally *ostracize* meant to *banish* temporarily from any of several ancient Greek cities a person deemed dangerous to the state. The word now implies exclusion from recognition or acceptance by society or by a limited social group. Undesirable aliens and illegal entrants are *deported*. A person convicted of a crime may be *transported* to a penal colony. An alleged criminal may be *extradited* to a state or sovereignty claiming the right to try him for the crime with which he is charged.

> **PREPOSITIONS:** Catiline was banished *from* Rome; John the Apostle was banished *to* Patmos.

BANK

beach	bound	brink	edge	margin	shore
border	brim	coast	marge	rim	strand

Bank is a general term for the land along the edge of a watercourse; it may also denote a raised portion of the bed of a river, lake, or ocean; as, the *Banks* of Newfoundland. A *beach* is a strip or expanse of sand, which is often pebbly or full of boulders; we speak of the *beach* of a lake or ocean. *Strand* is a more poetic term for a wave-washed *shore*, especially as a place for landing or embarking; as, the keel grates on the *strand*. The whole line of a country or continent that borders the sea is a *coast*, especially when regarded as a boundary. *Shore* is any land, whether cliff, or sand, or marsh, bordering water. We do not speak of the *coast* of a river, nor of the *banks* of the ocean, though there may be *banks* by or under the sea. *Edge* is the line where land and water meet; as, the water's *edge*. *Brink* is the place from which one may fall; as, the river's *brink*; the *brink* of a precipice; the *brink* of ruin.

BANKRUPTCY

failure	insolvency	suspension of payment

These terms are all applied in a general way to the condition of one who is indebted to an amount greater than can be paid from his available assets. *Failure* is the popular term for an insolvent condition culminating in assignment of property or *suspension of payment* with or without judicial proceedings. *Insolvency* denotes the condition, which may be known to the debtor before his creditors are aware of it or any legal proceedings have been taken. *Insolvency* has limited legal use, but the leading word in law, both in England and the United States is *bankruptcy*. *Bankruptcy* may be voluntary (on the petition of the debtor) or involuntary (by legal proceedings instituted by his creditors); in either case the intent of modern laws in *bankruptcy* is to provide a humane and equitable method of distributing the property of the debtor *pro rata* among his creditors, and setting him free from further proceedings, so that he may have the opportunity again to engage in business and, if possible, to recover himself.

ANTONYMS: *credit, prosperity, solvency, soundness, standing.*

BANTER

badinage	irony	raillery	sarcasm
chaff	jeering	ridicule	satire
derision	mockery		

Banter is the touching upon some fault, weakness, or fancied secret of another in a way half to pique and half to please; *badinage* is delicate, refined *banter. Raillery* has more sharpness, but is usually good-humored and well meant. *Irony,* saying one thing that the reverse may be understood, may be either mild or bitter. All the other words have a hostile intent. *Ridicule* makes a person or thing the subject of contemptuous merriment; *derision* seeks to make the object derided seem utterly despicable—to laugh it to scorn. *Chaff* is the jesting witticism of the streets, perhaps merry, oftener malicious; *jeering* is loud, rude *ridicule*, as of a hostile crowd or mob. *Mockery* is more studied, and may include mimicry and personal violence, as well as scornful speech. A *satire* is a formal composition; a *sarcasm* may be an impromptu sentence. The *satire* shows up follies to keep people from them; the *sarcasm* hits them because they are foolish, without inquiring whether it will do good or harm; the *satire* is plainly uttered; the *sarcasm* is covert.

BARBAROUS

atrocious	cruel	pitiless	uncivilized
barbarian	inhuman	rude	uncouth
barbaric	merciless	savage	untamed
brutal			

Barbarous refers to the worst side of *barbarian* life, and to revolting acts, especially of cruelty, such as a civilized man would not be expected to do; as a *barbarous* deed. *Barbarian*, originally meaning that which differed from the accepted customs and speech of the Greeks or Romans, is still used for tribes, rulers, etc., that are in a low state of social development. *Barbaric* refers to characteristic crudeness in taste or to the want of culture, as among barbarians. *Savage* is more distinctly bloodthirsty than *barbarous*. In this sense we speak of a *savage* beast and of *barbarous* usage.

Inhuman, merciless, pitiless, cruel, all imply complete lack of human kindness and an indifference to the sufferings of others. *Uncouth* is unrefined, marked by awkwardness; *rude*, in this comparison, is primitive, *uncivilized*.

ANTONYMS: *civilized, courtly, cultured, delicate, elegant, graceful, humane, nice, polite, refined, tender, urbane.*

BARRIER

bar	breastwork	obstacle	rampart
barricade	bulwark	obstruction	restraint
block	hindrance	parapet	restriction
boundary	impediment	prohibition	

A *barrier* obstructs a passage, but is not necessarily impassable. *Barrier* is used of objects more extensive than those to which *bar* is ordinarily applied. A mountain range may be a *barrier* to exploration; but a mass of sand across the entrance to a harbor is called a *bar*. A *bar* is something that is or may be firmly fixed, ordinarily with intent to prevent entrance or egress; as, the *bars* of a prison cell; the *bars* of a woodlot. Discovered falsehood is a *bar* to confidence. *Barricade* has become practically a technical name for an improvised street fortification, and, unless in some way modified, is usually so understood

A *parapet* is a low or breast-high wall, as about the edge of a roof, terrace, etc., especially, in military use, such a wall for the protection of troops; a *rampart* is the embankment surrounding a fort, on which the *parapet* is raised; the word *rampart* is often used as including the *parapet*. *Bulwark* is a general word for any defensive wall or *rampart*; its only technical use at present is in nautical language, where it signifies the raised side of a ship above the upper deck, topped by the rail. A *breastwork* is a low, temporary, defensive work, usually about breast-high.

Obstacle can be used of material and immaterial things that stand in the way of progress; *obstruction* generally applies to a material object that blocks a passage. *Restraint* is holding back; *restriction* is holding within a prescribed limit or *boundary*; *impediment* slows down progress. See **boundary; impediment.**

> **ANTONYMS:** *admittance, entrance, opening, passage, road, thoroughfare, transit, way.*

> **PREPOSITIONS:** A barrier *to* progress, *against* invasion; a barrier *between* nations.

BASE

abject	despicable	miserable	slavish
beggarly	groveling	obsequious	sneaking
cheap	ignoble	paltry	sordid
contemptible	infamous	poor	squalid
counterfeit	low	poor-spirited	subservient
cringing	low-minded	scurvy	vile
debased	mean	servile	worthless
degraded	mean-spirited	shabby	wretched
degrading	menial		

Base is *low* in sentiment, morals, rank, or value. *Debased* or *counterfeit* coins are forged and not genuine; *sordid, squalid,* and *wretched* generally refer to *beggarly* conditions. *Subservient, slavish, servile, menial,* and *obsequious* all refer to the attitude or state of a slave or dependent subordinate; we speak of *subservient* underlings, *slavish* humility, *servile* submission, *menial* work, *obsequious* obedience. *Cringing* and *groveling* apply to a kind of shrinking, fawning approach; *mean, ignoble,* and *abject* apply to people, conditions, and conduct; as, a *mean* trick, an *ignoble* purpose, an *abject* person. *Contemptible* and *despicable* people or actions arouse scorn; *paltry* matters are trifling or *worthless*. *Vile* denotes morally *base*; *infamous* is notoriously *vile*.

BATTLE

action	combat	encounter	passage of arms
affair	conflict	engagement	skirmish
bout	contest	fight	strife

Battle is a *combat* between organized armed forces. *Conflict* is a general word which describes opponents, whether individuals or hosts, as dashed together. One continuous *conflict* between entire armies is a *battle*. Another *battle* may be fought upon the same field after a considerable interval; or a new *battle* may follow immediately, the armies meeting upon a new field. An *action* is brief and partial; a *battle* may last for days. *Engagement* is a somewhat formal expression for *battle*; as, it was the commander's purpose to avoid a general *engagement*. A protracted war, including many *battles*, may be a stubborn *contest*. *Combat*, originally a hostile *encounter* between individuals, is now used for extensive *engagements*. A *skirmish* is between small detachments or scattered troops.

An *encounter* may be either purposed or accidental, between individuals or armed forces. *Fight* is a word of less dignity than *battle*; we should not ordinarily speak of Waterloo as a *fight*, unless where the word is used in the sense of fighting; as, I was in the thick of the *fight*. A *contest* is a struggle for a common object; a *bout* is a single trial of strength; an *affair*, in this comparison, is a duel.

ANTONYMS: *armistice, concord, peace, suspension of hostilities, truce.*

PREPOSITIONS: A battle *of* giants; battle *between* armies; a battle *for* life, *against* invaders; a battle *to* the death; the battle *of* (more rarely *at*) Marathon.

BEAT

bastinado	castigate	flog	scourge	switch
batter	chastise	hit	smite	thrash
belabor	conquer	overcome	spank	vanquish
bruise	cudgel	pommel	strike	whip
buffet	defeat	pound	surpass	worst

To *beat* is to *strike* or *hit* repeatedly; as a bird *beats* the air with its wings. *Strike* or *hit* is the word for a single blow—forcible, sudden contact or impact intentional or unintentional. Others of the above words describe the manner of *beating*, as *bastinado*, to *beat* on the soles of the feet; *belabor*, to inflict a comprehensive and exhaustive beating; *cudgel*, to *beat* with a stick; *thrash*, as wheat was *beaten* out with the old hand-flail; to *pound*, originally, to *beat* with a pestle to crush to powder, is to *beat* with heavy blows; *pommel* stresses continuous blows with the fists. To *batter* and to *bruise* refer to the results of beating; that is *battered* which is broken or defaced by repeated blows on the surface; that is *bruised* which has suffered even one severe contusion. The metaphorical sense of *beat*, however, so far preponderates that one may be very badly *bruised* and *battered*, and yet not be said to be *beaten*, unless he has got the worst of the beating. To *beat* a combatant is to disable or dishearten him for further fighting. Hence *beat* becomes the synonym for every word which implies getting the advantage of another. We use words or deeds to *conquer*, but *castigate* is now generally confined to words. *Chastise* suggests corporal punishment; *flog* implies using a whip or stick to *chastise*; to *scourge* is to *flog* very severely. See **conquer; punish.**

> **ANTONYMS:** *fail, fall, get the worst of, go down, go under, surrender.*

> **PREPOSITIONS:** Beat *with* a stick *over* the head; beat *by* a trick; beat *out* of town; beat *to* the ground, *into* submission.

BEAUTIFUL

attractive	charming	exquisite	handsome
beauteous	comely	fair	lovely
bewitching	delightful	fine	picturesque
blooming	elegant	graceful	pretty
bonny			

There must be harmony and unity to constitute an object or a person really *beautiful*. Thus, we speak of a *beautiful* landscape, a *beautiful* poem. But *beautiful* implies also, in concrete objects, softness of outline and delicacy of mold. *Pretty* expresses in a far less degree that which is pleasing to a refined taste in objects that are comparatively small, slight, and dainty; as, a *pretty* bonnet; a *pretty* girl. *Handsome* implies well and harmoniously proportioned, superficially pleasing, with usually the added idea that it is made so by art, breeding, or training; as, a *handsome* horse; a *handsome* house. *Handsome* is a term far inferior to *beautiful*; we may even say a *handsome* villain.

Fair denotes what is bright, smooth, clear, and without blemish; as, a *fair* face. The word applies wholly to what is superficial; we can say "*fair*, yet false." In a specific sense, *fair* has the sense of blond, as opposed to dark or brunette. One who possesses vivacity, wit, good nature, or other pleasing qualities may be *attractive* without beauty. *Comely* denotes an aspect that is smooth, genial, and wholesome, with a certain fulness of contour and pleasing svmmetry, though falling short of the *beautiful*; as, a *comely* matron. That is *picturesque* which would make a striking picture. We speak of a *delightful* picnic, a *charming* hostess, a *graceful* pose, a *fine* day. That which is *lovely* appeals to all our senses except taste.

> **ANTONYMS:** *awkward, clumsy, deformed, disgusting, frightful, ghastly, grim, grisly, grotesque, hideous, horrid, odious, repulsive, shocking, ugly, unattractive, uncouth, ungainly, unlovely, unpleasant.*

> **PREPOSITIONS:** Beautiful *to* the eye; beautiful *in* appearance, *in* spirit; "beautiful *for* situation," *Ps.* xlviii, 2; beautiful *of* aspect, *of* its kind.

BECAUSE

| as | for | inasmuch as | since |

Because, literally *by*-cause, is the most direct and complete word for giving the reason of a thing. *Since*, originally denoting succession in time, signifies a succession in a chain of reasoning, a natural inference or result. *As* indicates something like, coordinate, parallel. *Since* is weaker than *because*; *as* is weaker than *since*; either may introduce the reason before the main statement; thus, *since* or *as* you are going, I will accompany you. Often the weaker word is the more courteous, implying less constraint; for example, *as* you request it, I will come, rather than I will come *because* you request it. *Inasmuch as* is a formal and qualified expression, implying by just so much and no more; thus, *inasmuch as* the debtor has no property, I abandon the claim. *For* is a loose connective, giving often mere suggestion or indication rather than reason or cause; as, it is morning, *for* (not *because*) the birds are singing.

> **ANTONYMS:** *although, however, nevertheless, notwithstanding, yet.*

BECOMING

appropriate	congruous	fitting	seemly
befitting	decent	graceful	suitable
beseeming	decorous	meet	worthy
comely	fit	proper	

That is *becoming* in dress which suits the complexion, figure, and other qualities of the wearer, so as to produce on the whole a pleasing effect. That is *decent* which does not offend modesty or propriety. That is *suitable* which is adapted to the age, station, situation, and other circumstances of the wearer; coarse, heavy boots are *suitable* for farmwork; a juvenile style of dress is not *suitable* for an old lady. In conduct much the same rules apply. The dignity

and gravity of a patriarch would not be *becoming* to a child; at a funeral lively, cheery sociability would not be *decorous*, while noisy hilarity would not be *decent*; sumptuous display would not be *suitable* for a poor person.

Fit applies to person, time, place, occasion, etc.; as, a *fit* person; a *fit* abode; a *fit* place. *Fitting*, or *befitting*, is somewhat more elegant, implying a nicer adaptation. *Meet*, a somewhat archaic word, expresses a moral fitness; as, *meet* for heaven. *Proper* conveys the idea of correct for the purpose; *worthy* implies *fit* in the sense of meriting; *graceful*, in this comparison, indicates having a *becoming* air. See **beautiful; fit.**

ANTONYMS: *awkward, ill-becoming, ill-fitting, improper, indecent, indecorous, unbecoming, unfit, unseemly, unsuitable.*

PREPOSITIONS: The dress was becoming *to* the wearer; such conduct was becoming *in* him.

BEGINNING

arising	fountain	initiation	outset	spring
commencement	inauguration	opening	rise	start
fount	inception	origin	source	

The Latin *commencement* is more formal than the Saxon *beginning*, as the verb commence is more formal than begin. *Commencement* is for the most part restricted to some form of action, while *beginning* has no restriction, but may be applied to action, state, material, extent, enumeration, or to whatever else may be conceived of as having a first part, point, degree, etc. The letter A is at the *beginning* (not the *commencement*) of every alphabet. If we were to speak of the *commencement* of the Pacific Railroad, we should be understood to refer to the enterprise and its initiatory act; if we were to refer to the roadway we should say, "Here is the *beginning* of the Pacific Railroad." In the great majority of cases *begin* and *beginning* are preferable to *commence* and *commencement* for simple, idiomatic English words are always accurate and expressive. "In the *beginning* was the word," John i, 1. A *commencement* is the opposite of a conclusion, *beginning* the antonym of end. An *origin* is the point from which something starts or sets out, often involving causal connection; as, the *origin* of evil; the *origin* of a nation, a government, or a family.

A *source* is that which furnishes a first and continuous supply, that which flows forth freely or may be readily recurred to; as, the *source* of a river; a *source* of knowledge; a *source* of inspiration; fertile land is a *source* (not an *origin*) of wealth. A *rise* is thought of as in an action; we say that a lake is the *source* of a certain river, or that the river takes its *rise* from the lake. Motley wrote of "The *Rise* of the Dutch Republic." *Fount, fountain,* and *spring,* used figuratively, keep close to their literal meaning. *Inauguration* refers to investment with power by installation into an office; *initiation* stresses the process of being introduced into a society or group. *Inception* is the act of *beginning* or the initial period. Compare **cause.**

ANTONYMS: See synonyms for **end.**

BEHAVIOR

action	carriage	deportment	manner
bearing	conduct	life	manners
breeding	demeanor		

Behavior is our *action* in the presence of others; *conduct* includes also that which is known only to ourselves and our Maker. *Carriage* expresses simply the manner of holding the body, especially in sitting or walking. *Bearing* refers to the bodily expression of feeling or disposition; as, a haughty *bearing*; a noble *bearing*. *Demeanor* is the bodily expression, not only of feelings, but of moral states; as, a devout *demeanor*. *Breeding*, unless with some adverse limitation, denotes that *manner* and *conduct* which result from good birth and training. *Deportment* is *behavior* as related to a set of rules; as the pupil's *deportment* was faultless. A person's *manner* may be that of a moment, or toward a single person; his *manners* are his habitual style of *behavior* toward or before others, especially in matters of etiquette and politeness; as, good *manners* are always pleasing.

PREPOSITIONS: Behavior *of* a person *to* or *toward* people, *on* or *upon* the streets, *before* a multitude, or *in* a church, *with* the godly, or *with* the worldly.

BEND

bias	deflect	influence	submit	warp
bow	deviate	mold	turn	yield
crook	diverge	persuade	twine	
curve	incline	stoop	twist	

To *bend* is to bring into a curve from a straight line; in some cases a thing is spoken of as *bent* where the parts make an angle. To *submit* or *yield* is to *bend* the mind humbly to another's wishes. To *influence* is to *bend* another's wishes toward our own; to *persuade* is to draw them quite over. To *warp* is to *bend* slightly through the whole fiber, as a board in the sun. To *crook* is to *bend* irregularly, or to make crooked like a crook.

Deflect, deviate, and *diverge* are said of any turning away; *deflect* of a turning from a fixed direction, *deviate* commonly of a slight and gradual movement, *diverge* of a more sharp and decided one. To *bias* is to cut across the texture, or *incline* to one side; in figurative use always with an unfavorable import. *Mold* is a stronger word than *bend*; we may *bend* by a superior force that which still resists the constraint; as, to *bend* a bow; we *mold* something plastic to some desired form. To *twist* is to wind strands into a single thread, to wrest, or to distort; to *twine* is to wind round something.

BENEATH

below   **under**   **underneath**

Beneath is lower in place, condition, etc., than; *below* the surface of; unworthy of; *under* the power of. *Beneath* or *below* may signify occupying a lower plane, as we speak of one marrying *below* or *beneath* his station; or, we say, he is *beneath* your notice. *Under* has also the sense of being subject to or subjected to; as, *under* tutors and governors; *under* examination. *Under* strictly implies that another object is directly upon or over in a vertical line. *Below* signifies that one object is lower than another, so as to be looked down upon from it, or hidden from view by it; as *below* (not *under* nor *beneath*) the horizon.

ANTONYMS: See synonyms for **above.**

BENEVOLENCE

almsgiving	charity	kindliness	philanthropy
altruism	generosity	kindness	sympathy
beneficence	good-will	liberality	tenderness
benignity	humanity	munificence	unselfishness
bounty	kind-heartedness		

Benevolence, according to its etymology, is the wishing or willing well to others, and suggests an inborn desire to do good. *Charity*, on the other hand, implies an instilled virtue as its motivating power. *Charity*, whether in the sense of bountiful *generosity* to the poor or in that of *kindliness* and indulgence in one's opinion of others, still retains a hint of its early meaning of brotherly love and compassion. It is now most often applied to some form of *almsgiving*, and is much more limited in meaning than *benevolence*.

Humanity in this context is a compassionate attitude toward man and beast, an attribute of a civilized, enlightened nature; we say of some act of care or *kindness*, "common *humanity* requires it." *Altruism* is devotion to the interests of others, and suggests not only an ethical principle as one's guiding motive but also the absence of any selfishness or self-interest. *Philanthropy* applies to broad schemes for human welfare, often, but not always, involving large expenditure of money, as for the endowment of hospitals, educational institutions, and the like.

Benignity suggests some occult power of blessing, such as was formerly ascribed to the stars; we may say a good man has an air of *benignity*. *Kindness* and *tenderness* are personal; *benevolence* and *charity* are general. *Kindness* extends to all sentient beings, whether men or animals, in prosperity or in distress. *Tenderness* especially goes out toward the young, feeble, and needy, or even to the dead. *Generosity* is self-forgetful *kindness* in disposition or action; it includes much besides giving; as, the *generosity* of forgiveness. *Bounty* applies to ample giving, which on a larger scale is expressed by *munificence.* *Liberality* indicates broad, genial, kindly views, whether manifested in gifts or otherwise. We speak of the *bounty* of a generous host, the *liberality* or *munificence* of the founder of a college, or of the *liberality* of a theologian toward the holders of conflicting beliefs.

> **ANTONYMS:** *barbarity, brutality, churlishness, greediness, harshness, illiberality, ill will, inhumanity, malevolence, malignity, niggardliness, selfishness, self-seeking, stinginess, unkindness.*

> **PREPOSITIONS:** Benevolence *of, on the part of,* or *from* the wealthy, *to* or *toward* the poor.

BIND

bind up	fetter	oblige	shackle
compel	fix	restrain	tether
engage	hitch	restrict	tie
fasten	moor	secure	tie up

To *bind* is primarily to draw something flexible, as a cord or bandage, closely around an object or group of objects. We *bind up* an object to close, cover, or protect it; as, to *bind up* a wound; a person is said to be *bound up* in that which engrosses his thoughts or feelings. Anything flexible may be *tied* by having the ends interlaced and drawn together so as to form a knot or bow; or any object may be *tied* by a flexible bond so interlaced; to *tie up* is to *fasten* by such a bond so as to prevent free movement or separation of parts; as, to *tie up* a dog; to *tie up* a package or an estate. An animal is *tethered,* as to a stake, by a rope or chain long enough to allow much freedom of motion, as for grazing; a vessel is *moored* by a line or cable to some fixed object. We *bind* a sheaf of wheat with a cord; we *tie* the cord in a knot; we *fasten* by any means that will make things hold together, as a board by nails, or a door by a lock. To *fetter* is to put chains on feet; to *shackle* is to encircle ankles or wrists with something fastened to something else. *Bind* and *tie* both have an extensive figurative use. A person is *tied* or *tied* down by something stronger than he is, which prevents him from escaping. One is *bound* by conscience or honor; he is *obliged* by some imperious necessity; *engaged* by his own promise; *compelled* by physical force or its moral equivalent. See **attach.**

> **ANTONYMS:** *free, loose, set free, unbind, unfasten, unloose, untie.*

PREPOSITIONS: Bind *to* a pillar, *unto* an altar, *to* a service; bind one *with* chains or *in* chains; one is bound *by* a contract; a splint is bound *upon* a limb; the arms may be bound *to* the sides or *behind* the back; bind a wreath *about, around,* or *round* the head; twigs are bound *in* or *into* fagots; for military purposes, they are bound *at* both ends and *in* the middle; one is bound *by* a contract, or bound *under* a penalty to fulfil a contract.

BITTER

acerb	acrid	harsh	sour
acetous	acrimonious	irate	stinging
acid	biting	pungent	tart
acidulated	caustic	savage	vinegarish
acidulous	cutting	sharp	virulent

Acid, sour, and *bitter* agree in being contrasted with sweet, but the two former are sharply distinguished from the latter. *Acid* or *sour* is the taste of vinegar or lemon juice; *bitter* that of quassia, quinine, or strychnine. *Acrid* is nearly allied to *bitter. Pungent* suggests the effect of pepper or snuff on the organs of taste or smell; as, a *pungent* odor. *Tart* and *acidulous* may have agreeable connotations; *acidulous* refers to a slight degree of acidity and *tart* to a pleasant acidulousness; as, the *acidulous* flavor of carbonated beverages; a pie made with *tart* apples. *Acerb* describes the taste of unripe fruit.

Caustic indicates the corroding effect of some strong chemical, as nitrate of silver. In a figurative sense, as applied to language or character, the following words are closely allied: we say a *sour* face, *sharp* words, *bitter* complaints, *caustic* wit, *cutting* irony, *biting* sarcasm, a *stinging* taunt, *harsh* judgment, a *tart* reply. *Harsh* carries the idea of intentional and severe unkindness, *bitter* of a severity that arises from real or supposed ill treatment. The *bitter* speech springs from the sore heart. *Tart* and *sharp* utterances may not proceed from an intention to wound, but merely from a wit recklessly keen; *cutting, stinging,* and *biting* speech indicates more or less of hostile intent, the last being the most deeply malicious. The *caustic* utterance is meant to burn, perhaps wholesomely, as in the satire of Juvenal or Cervantes. See **morose.**

ANTONYMS: *dulcet, honeyed, luscious, nectared, saccharine, sweet.*

BLEACH

blanch	etiolate	make white	whiten	whitewash

To *whiten* is to *make white* in general, but commonly it means to over-spread with white coloring matter. To *bleach* is to *whiten* or lighten in color, as by exposure to the sunlight or by the application of a chemical. To *blanch* is to *whiten* by removing color or that which gives color; fear *blanches* one's cheeks by removing the blood from them. *Etiolate* is the technical term applied to the *blanching* of plants; one *etiolates* celery by depriving it of light. To *whitewash* is to *whiten* superficially, as by the application of lime and water or calcimine, or, figuratively, by false approval.

ANTONYMS: *blacken, color, darken, dye, soil, stain.*

BLEAK

bare	chilling	dismal	gloomy	unsheltered
barren	chilly	dreary	lonely	waste
blank	cold	dull	piercing	wild
cheerless	cutting	exposed	stormy	windy
chill	desolate			

The chief connotations of *bleak* are coldness and exposure to the elements. *Bare* means without covering; *barren* means incapable of producing. *Bleak* may combine the meanings of the two; in the northern climate a rock, island, moor, prairie, or mountainside, which is *bare, blank, desolate, exposed, unsheltered, waste,* or *wild* is sure to be *cold* and *bleak*; but in the tropics this would not be true; the Sahara is a *desolate* waste of sand, *unsheltered* from the burning sun and swept by fierce winds, but it is not *bleak*; *bleak* is also applied to seasons, winds, etc., which are characterized by mingled chill and desolateness; in this use it is allied with such words as *chill, chilling, chilly, cold, cutting, piercing, stormy, windy.*

Dreary is independent of temperature; that which is *bleak* is commonly also *dreary,* but that which is *dreary* may not be *bleak,* as a tropical jungle in the rainy season; that which is *lonely, dismal, gloomy, cheerless* is *dreary* in any climate, at any season; so a conversation, speech, poem, or the like, may be *dreary* by dulness, monotony, and cheerlessness.

ANTONYMS: *balmy, bright, cheerful, cheery, genial, homelike, mild, sheltered, sunny, warm.*

BLEMISH

blot	deformity	flaw	speck
blur	dent	imperfection	spot
brand	disfigurement	injury	stain
crack	disgrace	reproach	stigma
daub	dishonor	smirch	taint
defacement	fault	soil	tarnish
defect			

Blemish, defect, and *flaw,* all refer to an *imperfection.* A *blemish* is anything superficial or external which spoils the appearance or mars the beauty of an object. A mole on one's face is a *blemish*, as is a *spot* on a clean dress. *Defect* refers to the lack of something without which an object is imperfect or incomplete; as, a *defect* in the orator's logic; a *defect* in the auditory organs. A *flaw* is a *defect* in structure or substance, as a crack or fissure; we may speak of a glass dish or a character without *flaws*.

In the moral sense, we speak of a *blot* or *stain* upon reputation; a *flaw* or *taint* in character. *Disfigurement* connotes *injury* to a surface. *Fault*, primarily a failing, is something that fails of an apparent intent or disappoints a natural expectation; thus a sudden dislocation or displacement of geological strata is called a *fault*. Figuratively a *blemish* comes from one's own ill-doing; a *brand* or *stigma* is inflicted by others; as, the *brand* of infamy.

BLOW

box	cuff	knock	slap
buffet	cut	lash	stripe
calamity	disaster	rap	stroke
concussion	hit	shock	thump

A *blow* is a sudden impact, as of a fist or a club; a *stroke* is a sweeping movement; as, the *stroke* of a sword, of an oar, of the arm in swimming. A *shock* is a sudden encounter with some heavy body; as, colliding railway trains meet with a *shock*; the *shock* of battle. A *slap* is given with the open hand, a *lash* with a whip, thong, or the like; we speak also of the *cut* of a whip. A *buffet* or *cuff* is given only with the hand; a *blow*, either with hand or weapon. A *cuff* is a somewhat sidelong *blow*, generally with the open hand; as, a *cuff* or *box* on the ear; a *hit* is any sudden forcible contact, intended or unintended. A *stripe* is the effect or mark of a *stroke*.

In the metaphorical sense, *blow* is used for sudden, stunning, staggering *calamity* or sorrow; *stroke*, for sweeping *disaster*, and also for sweeping achievement and success. We say a *stroke* of paralysis, or a *stroke* of genius. We speak of the *buffets* of adverse fortune. *Shock* is used of that which is at once sudden, violent, and prostrating; we speak of a *shock* of electricity, the *shock* of an amputation, a *shock* of surprise. A *hit* is something sudden and successful, whether by intention or accident, as a well-directed witticism, sarcasm, or repartee, an apt or happy remark, or a fortunate achievement; as, a capital *hit*; a lucky *hit*; the play or the player made a *hit*. Compare **beat.**

BLUFF

abrupt	coarse	impolite	rough
blunt	crusty	inconsiderate	rude
blustering	curt	open	uncivil
bold	discourteous	plain-spoken	**unmannerly**
brusk	frank		

Bluff, a word of favorable connotation, implies frankness, a rough kindliness, and an outspoken unconventionality. The *bluff* man talks and laughs loudly and freely, says and does whatever he pleases with fearless good nature, and with no thought of annoying or giving pain to others. *Blunt* suggests such frankness of manner and disregard for social conventions as to offend or irritate. The *blunt* man says things which he is perfectly aware are disagreeable.

Brusk describes a real or apparent abruptness and boorishness of manner. *Curt* suggests an *impolite* or *rude* shortness; as, a *curt* reply. *Crusty* implies a forbidding outward appearance which masks a genuinely kind heart; as, a *crusty* old man.

ANTONYMS: *bland, courteous, genial, polished, polite, refined, reserved, urbane.*

BODY

ashes	clay	dust	frame	system
cadaver	corpse	form	remains	trunk
carcass				

Body denotes the entire physical structure, living or dead, of man or animal; *form* looks upon it as a thing of shape and outline, perhaps of beauty; *frame* regards it as supported by its bony framework; *system* views it as an assemblage of many related and harmonious organs. *Body, form, frame,* and *system* may be either dead or living; *clay* and *dust* are sometimes so used in religious or poetic style, though ordinarily these words are used only of the dead. *Corpse* and *remains* are used only of the dead. *Corpse* is the plain technical word for a dead body still retaining its unity; *remains* may be used after any lapse of time; the latter is also the more refined and less ghastly term; as, friends are invited to view the *remains. Carcass* applies only to the *body* of an animal, or of a human being regarded with contempt and loathing. *Cadaver* refers chiefly to a *corpse* used for dissecting purposes in a medical laboratory.

ANTONYMS: *intellect, intelligence, mind, soul, spirit.*

BOTH

twain	two

Both refers to *two* objects previously mentioned, or had in mind, viewed or acting in connection; as, *both* men fired at once; "*two* men fired" might mean any *two*, out of any number, and without reference to any previous thought or mention. *Twain* is a nearly obsolete form of *two*. The two, or the twain, is practically equivalent to *both*; *both*, however, expresses a closer unity. We would say *both* men rushed against the enemy; the *two* men flew at each other.

ANTONYMS: *each, either, every, neither, none, no one, not any.*

BOUNDARY

barrier	confines	limit	margin
border	edge	line	term
bound	enclosure	marches	termination
bourn	frontier	marge	verge
bourne	landmark		

A *boundary* is a definitely established geographical *limit*, indicated on maps, and observed on both sides; as, the *boundary* between New York and Pennsylvania. *Border* may carry the same idea of geographical exactness as *boundary*, but is used generally to denote the region extending along a *boundary* rather than a mere *line*. *Frontier*, the part of a country which fronts on a neighboring country, can be said only of one side of a *boundary*; as Poland's Russian *frontier*, rather than the Russo-Polish *frontier*. *Frontier* is also used figuratively or literally to denote the *line* marking the farthest advance of civilization, progress, thought, etc.

A *barrier* is something that bars ingress or egress. A *barrier* may be a *boundary*, as was the Great Wall of China. *Bourn*, or *bourne*, is a poetical expression for *bound* or *boundary*. *Edge* is a sharp terminal *line*, as where the river or ocean meets the land. *Limit* is now used almost wholly in the figurative sense; as, the *limit* of discussion, of time, of jurisdiction. *Line* is a military term; as, within the *lines*, or through the *lines*, of an army. Compare **barrier; end.**

ANTONYMS: *center, citadel, estate, inside, interior, land, region, territory.*

PREPOSITIONS: The boundaries *of* an estate; the boundary *between* neighboring territories.

BRAVE

adventurous	daring	fearless	undaunted
bold	dashing	gallant	undismayed
chivalric	dauntless	heroic	valiant
chivalrous	doughty	intrepid	venturesome
courageous			

Brave implies a readiness to face danger without fear or flinching; the *brave* man does not court or seek peril, but he will not run or shrink from it. *Bold* refers either to an inherent liking for danger or a readiness to court it; the *bold* man will daringly and unhesitatingly push forward into the unknown or against odds, especially when there is something to be won. The *adventurous* man goes in quest of danger; the *bold* man stands out and faces danger or censure; the *chivalrous* man puts himself in peril for others' protection. The *daring* step out to defy danger; the *dauntless* will not flinch before anything that may come to them; the *doughty* will give and take limitless hard knocks. The *adventurous* find something romantic in dangerous enterprises; the *venturesome* may be simply heedless, reckless, or ignorant. All great explorers have been *adventurous*; children, fools, and criminals are *venturesome*.

A *dauntless* person cannot be intimidated, cowed, or discouraged; the *undaunted* person emerges from a perilous situation undefeated and unsubdued, or faces the prospect of such a situation fearlessly. The *fearless* and *intrepid* possess unshaken nerve in any place of danger. *Courageous* is more than *brave*, adding a moral element; the *courageous* man steadily encounters perils to which he may be keenly sensitive, at the call of duty; the *gallant* are *brave* in a *dashing*, showy, and splendid way; the *valiant* not only dare great dangers, but achieve great results; the *heroic* are nobly *daring* and *dauntless*, truly *chivalrous*, sublimely *courageous*. Compare **fortitude.**

ANTONYMS: *afraid, cowardly, cringing, faint-hearted, fearful, frightened, pusillanimous, shrinking, timid, timorous.*

BREAK

burst	destroy	rupture	smash
crack	fracture	sever	split
crush	rend	shatter	sunder
demolish	rive	shiver	

To *break* is to divide sharply, with severance of particles, as by a blow or strain. To *burst* is to *break* by pressure from within, as a bombshell, but it is used also for the result of violent force otherwise exerted; as, to *burst* in a door, where the door yields as if to an explosion. To *crush* is to *break* by pressure from without, as an egg shell. To *crack* is to *break* without complete severance of parts; a glass that is *cracked* may still hold together. *Fracture* has a somewhat similar sense. In a *fractured* limb, the ends of the *broken* bone may be separated, though both portions are still retained within the common muscular tissue. *Fracture* is always used of a hard, rigid substance; *rupture* is said of the breaking of a softer substance; as, a *ruptured* blood vessel. A *shattered* object is *broken* suddenly and in numerous directions; as, a vase is *shattered* by a blow, a building by an earthquake.

To *sever* is to separate, as one part from another, by cutting, tearing, etc., usually violently; to *sunder* is to wrench or tear apart with great violence; *rive* is the lofty or poetical term to express the same idea. A *shivered* glass is *broken* into numerous minute, needle-like fragments. To *smash* is to *break* thoroughly to pieces with a crashing sound by some sudden act of violence; a watch once *smashed* will scarcely be worth repair. To *split* is to cause wood to *crack* or part in the way of the grain, and is applied to any other case where a natural tendency to separation is enforced by an external cause; as, to *split* a convention or a party. To *demolish* is to beat down, as a mound, building, fortress, etc.; to *destroy* is to put beyond restoration by any process physically, mentally, or morally; to *destroy* an army is to *shatter* and scatter it so that it cannot be rallied or reassembled as a fighting force. See **rend.**

ANTONYMS: *attach, bind, fasten, join, mend, secure, solder, unite, weld.*

PREPOSITIONS: Break *to* pieces, or *in* pieces, *into* several pieces (when the object is thought of as divided rather than shattered), break *with* a friend, *from* or *away from* a suppliant; break *into* a house, *out* of prison; break *across* one's knee; break *through* a hedge; break *in upon* one's retirement; break *over* the rules; break *on* or *upon* the shore, *against* the rocks.

BRIGHT

beaming	glaring	illumined	shimmering
brilliant	gleaming	incandescent	shining
cheerful	glimmering	luminous	sparkling
cheering	glistening	lustrous	splendid
cheery	glittering	radiant	sunny
dazzling	glorious	refulgent	sunshiny
effulgent	glowing	resplendent	twinkling
flashing	illuminated	scintillating	

An object is *bright* that shines with either original or reflected light; thus the sun, the moon, and the stars are *bright*; that is *brilliant* which shines with unusual or distinctive brightness; as, one star in a constellation may be especially *brilliant*; all the stars are strikingly *brilliant* on a clear moonless night by contrast with the deep blue-black of the sky; a diamond cut so as to throw out the maximum of light is called a "brilliant." That is *radiant* from which light seems to pour forth in rays; an object which is *radiant* sends forth a steady light, while that of a *brilliant* object may be fitful. *Beaming* is applied to light which seems to be sent forth in beams, and is a milder word than *radiant*. *Gleaming* is applied to that which sends forth or reflects light in sudden flashes, as the warrior's *gleaming* sword. *Glowing* is applied to a light like that from molten metal; *dazzling* is said of the effect on the eye of the beholder, and may apply to the full splendor of the sun or to intense reflected light as from a gem, etc.; any light which the eye cannot well bear is *dazzling*; *glaring* is a kindred word, but denotes a powerful, persistent light that affects the beholder disagreeably; that which is *dazzling* may be admired, while that which is *glaring* is repellent. *Effulgent* and *refulgent* are used, with little difference of meaning, of light at once intense and pervading; *refulgent* applies especially to reflected light, shining far and wide; *resplendent* is similar to *refulgent,* but more superficial, and near to the meaning of gorgeous or magnificent.

An object is *splendid* which gives out or reflects light of especial abundance and power, and often of varied hues, impressing the beholder with mingled wonder and admiration; as, a *splendid* sunrise. That which is *luminous* sends forth distinct light, which may be greater or less in degree, emitted or reflected, though the tendency is now to use the word for light sent forth from within; a *luminous* object is thought of as self-*luminous*; the sun is a *luminous* body; the faint phosphorescence of the glow-worm makes it *luminous* in the dark. *Lustrous* is applied to that which sends forth a soft but vivid light as from a polished surface; as, *lustrous* silks. That which is *illuminated* or *illumined* is lit up by light from some source apart from itself, often by light supplied from within; we speak of a building or a city as *illuminated* when light shines out from every window on some joyous occasion; *illumined* is poetic, and oftenest used in a spiritual sense. *Sparkling* is said of light thrown out as by sparks from many points; *scintillating*, of such light in intermittent flashes. *Glistening* applies to the shining from a wet, *glittering* to that from a dry, surface; Coleridge finely chooses *glittering*, not *glistening* to describe the eye of the wasted old man in his great poem:

> By thy long gray beard and *glittering* eye,
> Now, wherefore stopp'st thou me?
> *Ancient Mariner*, pt. i, st. 1.

Glimmering and *shimmering* refer to faint, wavering, and unsteady light, that which is *shimmering* being tremulous, as from rippling waves; we speak of *shimmering* silks, that seem to change shade or hue with motion. Compare the nouns corresponding to these adjectives under **light.**

The figurative meaning of these words is largely controlled by the literal. So used, *bright* is inferior to *brilliant*; we speak of a *bright* boy, a *brilliant* genius; of a *bright* idea in common matters, a *brilliant* idea in philosophy, literature, or statesmanship; of a *brilliant* (not a *bright*) achievement; of a *dazzling* success; of *sparkling* or *scintillating* wit, of a *luminous* style, exposition, production, or sentence, of a *glaring* inconsistency or contradiction, of a *beaming* or *radiant* countenance (where *radiant* is the more vivid, *beaming* the gentler word; as, *beaming* with love, *radiant* with delight); a *bright, sunny,* or *sunshiny* face has an effect like that of a landscape lit up by pleasant sunlight, so that these words are akin to *cheerful, cheering,* and *cheery.* We speak of eyes *sparkling* with pleasure, *gleaming* with excitement, rage, or fury, *glowing* with some strong suppressed feeling as of devotion or ambition, lighting them up as by an internal fire. *Splendid* applies to that which has splendor and is akin to grand, *glorious,* magnificent, honorable, illustrious, heroic, etc.; as, a *splendid* palace, pageant, or banquet, a *splendid* achievement, career, or victory (in which latter uses it far transcends the meaning of *brilliant*).

ANTONYMS: See synonyms for **dark.**

BRUTISH

animal	brute	insensible	stupid
base	carnal	lascivious	swinish
beastly	coarse	sensual	unintellectual
bestial	ignorant	sottish	unspiritual
brutal	imbruted	stolid	vile

A *brutish* man simply follows his *animal* instincts, without special inclination to do harm; the *brutal* have always a spirit of malice and cruelty. *Brute* has no special character, except as indicating what a brute might possess; much the same is true of *animal*, except that *animal* leans more to the side of senuality, *brute* to that of force, as appears in the familiar phrase "*brute* force." Hunger is an *animal* appetite; a *brute* impulse suddenly prompts one to strike a blow in anger. *Imbruted* is degraded to a *brutish* state.

Bestial, in modern usage, implies an intensified and degrading animalism. Any supremacy of the *animal* or *brute* instincts over the intellectual and spiritual in man is *base* and *vile*. *Beastly* refers largely to the outward and visible consequences of excess; as, *beastly* drunkenness. *Carnal*, often a derogatory term, refers to the fleshly nature; *sensual* implies undue indulgence in appetites and passions; *lascivious* refers to strong sexual desires.

ANTONYMS: *elevated, enlightened, exalted, grand, great, humane, intellectual, intelligent, noble, refined.*

BURN

blaze	consume	ignite	sear
brand	cremate	incinerate	set fire to
cauterize	flame	kindle	set on fire
char	flash	scorch	singe

To *burn* is to subject to the action of fire, or of intense heat so as to effect either partial change or complete combustion; as, to *burn* wood in the fire; to *burn* one's hand on a hot stove; the sun *burns* the face. Wind, strong fertilizers, acids, and other agents can also injure as though by fire. With either a hot iron or corrosive substance, one *brands* to leave a permanent mark, *cauterizes* to prevent or destroy infection; one *sears* to do either. *Cremate* is now used specifically for *consuming* a dead body by intense heat. To *incinerate* is to reduce anything to ashes by *burning*. To *kindle* is to *set on fire*, as if with a candle; *ignite* is the more learned and scientific word for the same thing, extending even to the heating of metals to a state of incandescence without *burning*.

To *scorch* and to *singe* are superficial; we *scorch* fabrics if the iron we use is too hot, but we *singe* hair or *singe* a chicken carcass. To *char* means to *burn* the surface of or to convert into charcoal. Both *kindle* and *burn* have an extensive figurative use; as, to *kindle* strife; to *burn* with wrath, love, devotion, curiosity. Compare **light.**

> **ANTONYMS:** *cool, extinguish, put out, smother, stifle, subdue.*
>
> **PREPOSITIONS:** To burn *in* the fire; burn *with* fire; burn *to* the ground; burn *to* ashes; burn *through* the skin, or the roof; burn *into* the soil, etc.

BUSINESS

affair	concern	métier	traffic
art	craft	occupation	transaction
avocation	duty	profession	vocation
barter	employment	pursuit	work
calling	handicraft	trade	
commerce	job	trading	

A *business* is a *trade* or *profession* at which one works regularly; an *occupation* is what he happens at any time to be engaged in, and may be continuous or temporary; trout-fishing may be one's *occupation* for a time, as a relief from *business*; *business* is ordinarily for profit, while the *occupation* may be a matter of learning, philanthropy, or religion. A *profession* usually implies scholarship; as the *profession* of law. *Pursuit* is an *occupation* which one follows with ardor. An *avocation* is what calls one away from other work; a *vocation* or *calling*, that to which one is called by some special fitness or sense of duty; thus, we speak of the gospel ministry as a *vocation* or *calling*, rather than a *business*. *Trade* or *trading* is, in general, the exchanging of one thing for another; in the special sense, a *trade* is an *occupation* involving manual training and skilled labor; as, the ancient Jews held that every boy should learn a *trade*. *Trade* and *commerce* may be used as equivalents, but *trade* is capable of a more limited application; we speak of the *trade* of a village, the *commerce* of a nation.

A *transaction* is a single action, whether in *business,* diplomacy, or otherwise; *affair* has a similar, but lighter meaning; as, this little *affair*; an important *transaction.* The plural *affairs* has a distinctive meaning, including all activities where men deal with one another on any considerable scale; as, a man of *affairs.* A *job* is *work* often viewed as a single undertaking, and sometimes paid for as such.

Barter is the direct exchange of commodities; *business, trade,* and *commerce* are chiefly transacted by means of money, bills of exchange, etc.; *traffic* can be buying and selling or *barter*. *Business, occupation,* etc., may be what one does independently; *employment,* as compared here, is in the service of another. *Work* is any application of energy to secure a result, or the result thus secured; thus, we speak of the *work* of God. *Art* in the industrial sense is a system of rules and accepted methods for the accomplishment of some practical result; as, the *art* of printing; collectively, the *arts.* A *craft* is some *occupation*

---

requiring technical skill or manual dexterity, or the persons, collectively, engaged in its exercise; as, the weaver's *craft*. *Métier* is *work* or a *craft* for which one is specially suited.

> **PREPOSITIONS:** The business *of* a druggist; *in* business *with* his father; doing business *for* his father; have you business *with* me? business *in* New York; business *about, concerning,* or *in regard to* certain property.

BUSY

active	diligent	engaged	occupied
assiduous	employed	industrious	sedulous

Busy applies to an activity which may be temporary, *industrious* to a habit of life. We say a man is *busy* just now; that is, *occupied* at the moment with something that takes his full attention. It would be ridiculous or satirical to say, he is *industrious* just now. But *busy* can be used in the sense of *industrious,* as when we say he is a *busy* man; or, it may mean *engaged,* as when we say, the president is *busy* just now. *Industrious* signifies zealous or habitual application to any work or business. *Diligent* indicates also a disposition, which is ordinarily habitual, and suggests more of heartiness and volition than *industrious.* We say one is a *diligent,* rather than an *industrious,* student. *Active,* in this comparison, implies engaged in some activity or work, generally something specific. *Assiduous* application is *diligent* and unremitting; *sedulous* is painstaking and persevering. Compare **active; industry.**

> **ANTONYMS:** See synonyms for **idle.**

BUT

barely	however	notwithstanding	that
besides	just	only	though
except	merely	provided	unless
excepting	moreover	save	yet
further	nevertheless	still	

But ranges from the faintest contrast to absolute negation; as, I am willing to go, *but* (on the other hand) content to stay; he is not an honest man, *but* (on the contrary) a villain. The contrast may be with a silent thought; as, *but* let us go (it being understood that we might stay longer). In restrictive use, *except* and *excepting* are slightly more emphatic than *but*; we say, no injury *but* a scratch; or, no injury *except* some painful bruises. Such expressions as "words are *but* breath" (nothing *but*) may be referred to the restrictive use by ellipsis. So may the use of *but* in the sense of *unless;* as, "it never rains *but* it pours." To the same head must be referred the conditional use; as, "you may go, *but* with your father's consent" (*i.e., "provided* you have," "*except* that you must have,*" etc.). *But* is sometimes used to add something different; "brave *but* tender" implies that bravery and tenderness are rarely combined. For the concessive use, compare **notwithstanding** *conj*.

B Y

| **by dint of** | **by means of** | **through** | **with** |

By is followed by the agent; *through,* by the means, cause, or condition; *with,* by the instrument or by someone or something serving as agency. The road having become impassable *through* long disuse, a way was opened *by* pioneers *with* axes. *By* may also be applied to any object which is viewed as partaking of action and agency; as, the metal was corroded *by* the acid; skill is gained *by* practice. We speak of communicating *with* a person *by* letter. *Through* implies a more distant connection than *by* or *with,* and more intervening elements. Material objects are perceived *by* the mind *through* the senses. *By dint of* is by the power of; *by means of* indicates by the use of an intermediate agency.

C

CABAL

combination	confederacy	crew	gang
conclave	conspiracy	faction	junto

Cabal (from Heb. *qabbalah*, a mystic system of theosophy among the Hebrews) originally denoted something secret or occult, then a secret meeting or association of a few persons for private ends, and thence a small band or company of persons secretly associated to promote designs of their own, independent of or opposed to the public welfare; the word, already in use, received a specially opprobrious meaning as applied to a ministry of Charles II of England, a committee of the Privy Council, the forerunner of the modern Cabinet.

It happened by a whimsical coincidence that, in 1671, the cabinet consisted of five persons, the initial letters of whose names made up the word *Cabal*—Clifford, Arlington, Buckingham, Ashley, and Lauderdale. These ministers were therefore emphatically called the *Cabal*; and they soon made that appellation so infamous that it has never since their time been used except as a term of reproach.

MACAULAY *History of England.*

Hence *cabal* has come to mean a *combination* or *conspiracy* of leaders for some secret purpose viewed as unpatriotic or unworthy. The word *junto*, once current in a similar sense, has fallen almost completely out of use.

A *conspiracy* is a *combination* of persons for an evil purpose, or the act of so combining. *Conspiracy* is a distinct crime under common, and generally under statutory, law. A *faction* is more extensive than a *conspiracy*, less formal in organization, less definite in plan, but it is insubordinate and generally works for selfish ends. *Faction* and its adjective, factious, have always an unfavorable sense. A *gang* is a company of workmen, usually not organized, all doing the same work under one leader; the word is used figuratively only of *combinations* which it is meant to stigmatize as rude and mercenary; a *crew* is a body of men organized for a particular work. A *conclave* is secret, but of larger numbers, ordinarily, than a *cabal,* and may have honorable use; as, the *conclave* of cardinals. Compare **company.**

CALCULATE

account	compute	count	enumerate	number	reckon
cast	consider	deem	estimate	rate	sum up

To *calculate* is to use complicated processes, as multiplication, division, etc., to ascertain a result. *Compute* is used of more simple processes of reckoning, generally from given data; it allows more of the element of probability, which is still more strongly expressed by *estimate.* We *compute* the slain in a great war from the number known to have fallen in certain great battles; *compute* refers to the present or the past, *estimate* more frequently to the future; as, to *estimate* the cost of a proposed building. To *enumerate* is to mention item by item; as, to *enumerate* one's grievances; to *count* is to call off numbers one by one; to *number* is to *count* or to *enumerate.* To *rate* is to *estimate* by comparison, as if the object were one of a series. We *count* upon a desired future;

we do not *count* upon the undesired. Children often *reckon* on their fingers or by counters. As applied to the present, we *reckon* or *count* a thing precious or worthless. Compare **esteem** *verb*.

PREPOSITIONS: It is vain to calculate *on* or *upon* an uncertain result.

CALL

bawl	cry out	roar	shriek
bellow	ejaculate	scream	vociferate
clamor	exclaim	shout	yell

To *call* is to send out the voice in order to attract another's attention, either by word or by inarticulate utterance. Animals *call* their mates, or their young; a man *calls* his dog, his horse, etc. The sense is extended to include summons by bell, or any signal. To *shout* is to *call* or *exclaim* with the fullest volume of sustained voice; to *scream* is to utter a shriller cry; to *shriek* or to *yell* refers to that which is louder, more piercing, and wilder still. We *shout* words; in *screaming*, *shrieking*, or *yelling* there is often no attempt at articulation. To *bawl* is to utter senseless noisy cries. *Bellow* and *roar* are applied to the utterances of animals, and only contemptuously to those of persons. To *clamor* is to utter with noisy iteration; it applies also to the confused cries of a multitude. To *vociferate* is commonly applied to loud and excited speech where there is little besides the exertion of voice. In *exclaiming*, the utterance may not be strikingly, though somewhat, above the ordinary tone and pitch; we may *exclaim* by mere interjections, or by connected words, but always by some articulate utterance. To *ejaculate* is to throw out brief, disconnected, but coherent utterances of joy, regret, and especially of appeal, petition, prayer. To *cry out* is to give forth a louder and more excited utterance than in *exclaiming* or *calling*; one often *exclaims* with sudden joy as well as sorrow; if he *cries out*, it is often in grief or agony. One may *exclaim, cry out*, or *ejaculate* with no thought of others' presence; when he *calls*, it is to attract another's attention.

ANTONYMS: *be silent, be still, hark, hearken, hush, list, listen.*

CALM

balmy	imperturbable	self-possessed
bland	mild	serene
collected	pacific	smooth
composed	peaceful	still
cool	placid	tranquil
dispassionate	quiet	undisturbed
gentle	sedate	unruffled

That is *calm* which is free from disturbance or agitation; in the physical sense, free from violent motion or action; in the mental or spiritual realm, free from excited or disturbing emotion or passion. We speak of a *calm* sea, a *placid* lake, a *serene* sky, a *still* night, a *quiet* day, a *quiet* home. We speak, also, of *still* waters, *smooth* sailing, which are different modes of expressing freedom from manifest agitation. Of mental conditions, one is *calm* who triumphs over a tendency to excitement; *cool*, if he scarcely feels the tendency. One may be *calm* by the very reaction from excitement, or by the oppression of overpowering emotion, as we speak of the calmness of despair.

Mild indicates moderation, freedom from irritation or violence; *balmy* is *mild* in the sense of soothing, fragrant, refreshing, or healing like balm; *bland* is used for that which is *mild*, soft, genial, and agreeable; thus the air or the breeze may be described as *balmy* or *bland*; *bland* is also applied to *smooth* and soothing manner, speech, or the like, in the sense of *gentle*, genial, soft-spoken, or agreeable. One is *composed* who has subdued excited feeling; he is *collected* when he has every thought, feeling, or perception awake and at command. *Tranquil* refers to a present state; *placid*, to a prevailing tendency. We speak of a *tranquil* mind, a *placid* disposition. The *serene* spirit dwells as if in the clear upper air, above all storm and shadow.

ANTONYMS: *agitated, boisterous, disturbed, excited, fierce, frantic, frenzied, furious, heated, passionate, raging, roused, ruffled, stormy, turbulent, violent, wild, wrathful.*

CANCEL

abolish	delete	make void	rescind
abrogate	discharge	nullify	revoke
annul	efface	obliterate	rub off or out
blot out	eradicate	quash	scratch out
cross off or out	erase	remove	strike out
dele	expunge	repeal	vacate

Cancel, efface, erase, expunge, and *obliterate* have as their first meaning the removal of written characters or other forms of record. To *cancel* is, literally, to make cross-lines, to *cross out*; to *efface* is to *rub off*, smooth away the face, as of an inscription; to *erase* is to *scratch out*, commonly for the purpose of writing something else in the same space; to *expunge*, literally to punch dots with some sharp instrument so as to show that the words are no longer part of the writing, now means to wipe out by erasure; to *obliterate* is to cover over or *remove*, as was done by reversing the Roman stylus, and *rubbing out* with the rounded end what had been written with the point on the waxen tablet; to *eradicate* writing is to *remove* all traces, often by chemicals. What is *obliterated* is gone forever, as if it had never been. In many establishments, when a debt is *discharged* by payment, the record is *cancelled*. The figurative use of the words keeps close to the primary sense.

To *annul* is to *make void* legally; *nullify* refers especially to a deprivation of the force of what may be legal, as by lack of power to enforce; *abrogate* is to *abolish* or *annul* by authority, often by a further enactment. *Repeal* is to *annul* a law made by previous legislation; *revoke* is to *annul* something by recalling or taking back; *rescind* is to make of no effect by another enactment. We *dele* or *delete* when we *strike out* words or letters in manuscripts or print. See **abolish.**

> ANTONYMS: *approve, confirm, enact, enforce, establish, maintain, perpetuate, record, reenact, sustain, uphold, write.*

CANDID

aboveboard	honest	open	truthful
artless	impartial	simple	unbiased
fair	ingenuous	sincere	unprejudiced
frank	innocent	straightforward	unreserved
guileless	naive	transparent	unsophisticated

A *candid* statement is meant to be true to the real facts and just to all parties; a *fair* statement is really so. *Fair* is applied to conduct; *candid* is not; as, *fair* treatment, "a *fair* field, and no favor." One who is *frank* has a fearless and unconstrained truthfulness. As truth is not always agreeable or timely, *candid* and *frank* have often an objectionable sense; "to be *candid* with you," "to be perfectly *frank*," are regarded as sure preludes to something disagreeable, stated without reservation. *Artless, guileless, innocent, naive, simple,* and *unsophisticated* express the goodness which comes from want of the knowledge or thought of evil. A person who is *ingenuous* is artlessly *frank.*

Open and *unreserved* may imply unstudied truthfulness or defiant recklessness; as *open* admiration, *open* robbery. There may be *transparent* integrity or *transparent* fraud. *Impartial, unbiased,* and *unprejudiced* refer to just treatment of all, showing no favor to anyone. An *honest* man adheres to right and truth. *Sincere* applies to the feelings, as being all that one's words would imply.

> ANTONYMS: *adroit, artful, crafty, cunning, deceitful, designing, diplomatic, foxy, insincere, intriguing, knowing, maneuvering, sharp, shrewd, sly, subtle, tricky, wily.*

> PREPOSITIONS: Candid *in* debate; candid *to* or *toward* opponents; candid *with* friend or foe; to be candid *about* or *in regard to* the matter.

CAPITAL

chief city	metropolis	seat of government

The *capital* of a state or government is the *chief city* in a political sense, and usually also the *seat of government*. A *metropolis*, originally the mother or parent city or state of a Greek colony, now means the *chief city* or *capital*, or the chief center of religion or commerce, or the see of the bishop of a province. The *seat of government* is the center or city from which the government exercises authority.

CAPTIOUS

carping	critical	fretful	peevish	testy
caviling	cynical	hypercritical	petulant	touchy
censorious	faultfinding	irritable	splenetic	

Captious denotes a tendency to untimely, uncalled for, or unreasonable criticism, especially in small matters, or on petty grounds; captiousness is a fault of the spirit and disposition, and is closely synonymous with *faultfinding*; the *captious* spirit is hard to please, catches at every chance to find fault, and is on the watch for every shortcoming; hence, *captious* approaches the meaning of *fretful, irritable, peevish, petulant,* etc. *Censorious* denotes a tendency to censure for the sake of censuring and to condemn; censoriousness is less petty and more severe than captiousness; one may be *censorious* from high ideals or principles of right and duty joined with lack of appreciation, charity, tenderness, and sympathy for others; censoriousness goes with self-righteousness.

Critical, though often used invidiously, is a word of high and good meaning; as, a *critical* study of Shakespeare is worthy of respect and consideration; no important matter, as a deed, the specifications for a building, a contract, a legislative act, or the like, should be passed without *critical* examination. *Hypercritical* signifies *critical* beyond the bounds of sound reason or common sense, which recognizes the necessity of a certain amount of tolerated imperfection in all practical matters; a *hypercritical* person would reject a noble stanza for a superfluous syllable or an imperfect rime, or fix attention so strongly on the flaw as to overshadow the excellence of the whole; the *hypercritical* person may not be *captious* or ill-tempered, but merely actuated by a petty exactness of criticism.

To cavil is to pick flaws. *Caviling* is of the intellect; a cavil is not an argument, but an attack upon an argument, statement, or truth, always petty and sneering, and often insincere. *Carping* is less serious and ill-tempered than *captious,* though quite as petty, and commonly more scornful; a *carping* critic stands aloof and flings a censure or a sneer at what the *captious* person hotly blames. A *cynical* person is coldly contemptuous of most things that others admire or believe in, especially scornful of disinterestedness or moral worth; he does not become angry like the *captious,* nor severe like the *censorious,* not thinking anger or severity worth while; the *cynical* man keeps his own temper, but often seriously tries that of others.

ANTONYMS: *appreciative, approving, careless, commendatory, complimentary, considerate, easy, easy-going, encouraging, eulogistic, fair, flattering, genial, good-natured, laudatory, negligent, reasonable, thoughtful.*

CARE

anxiety	concern	oversight	trouble
attention	direction	perplexity	vigilance
bother	forethought	precaution	wariness
caution	heed	prudence	watchfulness
charge	management	solicitude	worry
circumspection			

Care concerns what we possess; *anxiety*, often, what we do not; riches bring many *cares*; poverty brings many *anxieties*. *Care* also signifies watchful *attention*, in view of possible harm; as, "This side up with *care*;" "Take *care* of yourself"; or, as a sharp warning, "Take *care!*" equivalent to the imperative, "Look out!" *Caution* has a sense of possible harm and risk only to be escaped, if at all, by careful deliberation and observation. *Care* inclines to the positive, *caution* to the negative; *care* is shown in doing, *caution* largely in not doing. *Precaution* is allied with *care*, *prudence* with *caution*; a man rides a dangerous horse with *care*; *caution* will keep him from mounting the horse; *precaution* looks to the saddle girths, bit, and bridle, and all that may make the rider secure.

Circumspection is watchful observation and calculation of possible consequences, but without the timidity implied in *caution*. *Bother* is disagreeable *care*, disliked or resented by the person compelled to exercise it. *Concern* denotes *care* which is dependent on interest, and is milder than *anxiety*; as, *concern* for the safety of a ship at sea. *Heed* implies *attention* without disquiet; it is now largely displaced by *attention* and *care*. *Solicitude* involves especially the element of desire, not expressed in *anxiety*, and of hopefulness, not implied in *care*. A parent feels constant *solicitude* for his children's welfare, *anxiety* as to dangers that threaten it, and takes *care* to guard against them.

Watchfulness recognizes the possibility of danger, *wariness* the probability. A man who is not influenced by *caution* to keep out of danger may display great *wariness* in the midst of it. *Care* has also the sense of responsibility, with possible control, as expressed in *charge, management, oversight*; as, these children are under my *care*; send the money to me in *care* of the firm. *Vigilance* implies courageous *watchfulness*, especially against evil. See **anxiety; oversight; prudence.** Compare **alarm; perplexity; vigilant.**

> **ANTONYMS:** *carelessness, disregard, heedlessness, inattention, indifference, neglect, negligence, omission, oversight, recklessness, remissness, slight.*

> **PREPOSITIONS:** Take care *of* the house, *for* the future, *about* the matter.

CARESS

coddle	cuddle	embrace	fondle	pamper
court	dandle	flatter	kiss	pet

To *caress* is less than to *embrace*; more dignified and less familiar than to *fondle*. A visitor *caresses* a friend's child; a mother *fondles* her baby. *Fondling* is always by touch; *caressing* may be also by words, or other tender and pleasing attentions. To *court*, as compared here, is to make love to; to *cuddle* refers to holding closely and affectionately, as a young child; *coddle* and *pamper* refer to indulging someone, often excessively. To *dandle* is to handle playfully.

ANTONYMS: See synonyms for **affront.**

PREPOSITIONS: Caressed *by* or *with* the hand; caressed *by* admirers.

CARICATURE

burlesque	extravaganza	mimicry	take-off
exaggeration	imitation	parody	travesty

A *caricature* is a grotesque *exaggeration* of striking features or peculiarities, generally of a person, and often satirical. A *burlesque* treats any subject in an absurd or incongruous manner. A *burlesque* is written or acted; a *caricature* is more commonly in sketch or picture. A *parody* changes the serious subject to something ludicrous, but keeps the style; a *travesty* keeps the subject, but changes the style; a *burlesque* does not hold itself to either subject or style but is content with a general resemblance to what it may imitate. A *caricature*, *parody*, or *travesty* must have an original, a *burlesque* may be an independent composition. An account of a schoolboys' quarrel after the general manner of Homer's Iliad would be a *burlesque*; the real story of the Iliad told in newspaper style would be a *travesty*. An *extravaganza* is a fantastic composition, musical, dramatic, or narrative. *Imitation* is serious; *mimicry* is either intentionally or unintentionally comical.

CAROUSAL

carnival	drinking-bout	revel	saturnalia
carouse	jollification	revelry	spree
debauch	orgy	rout	wassail

These words denote wild and careless merrymaking, in which restraint is thrown aside. All are forms of letting go, with differences in the degree of self-abandonment. *Carousal, carouse, debauch, orgy,* etc., all denote unrestrained indulgence in drunkenness or other vicious pleasure, with the accompanying degradation. The *carnival,* originally the final festival before the long privation of Lent, includes much harmless, but somewhat riotous, fun, and often reaches all degrees of unrestrained license; we may speak of a skating *carnival*, a *carnival* of debauchery, a *carnival* of slaughter. The *revel* and *revelry* may include much that is elegant and sumptuous, with enjoyment that is merely careless and unrestrained, thence extending to the wildest excess; in its best use, either *revel* or *revelry* is of a higher grade than *carnival*:

> There was a sound of *revelry* by night,
> And Belgium's capital had gathered then
> Her beauty and her chivalry.
> BYRON   *Childe Harold.*

Saturnalia, originally a feast of Saturn, is now used for excessive and wild carousal. *Wassail*, now chiefly poetic, refers to a *drinking-bout*; *spree* can mean a drinking-spell, but also a gay frolic. Compare **feast.**

ANTONYMS: *abstemiousness, abstinence, austerity, fast, privation, sobriety, temperance.*

CARRY

bear	lift	remove	sustain	transmit
bring	move	support	take	transport
convey				

A person *carries* a load only when in motion; he may *bear* a load either when in motion or at rest. The stooping Atlas *bears* the world on his shoulders; swiftly moving Time *carries* the hourglass and scythe; a person may be said either to *bear* or to *carry* a scar, since it is upon him whether in motion or at rest. If an object is to be *moved* from the place we occupy, we say *carry*; if to the place we occupy, we say *bring*. A messenger *carries* a letter to a correspondent, and *brings* an answer. *Take* is often used in this sense in place of *carry*; as, *take* that letter to the office.

We *transport* goods or passengers from place to place; messages, electricity, etc., are *transmitted* or passed on through some medium or power. To *support* is to hold up the weight of; *sustain* often implies continuous support. *Convey* presupposes delivery. *Carry* often signifies to *transport* by personal strength, without reference to the direction; as, that is more than he can *carry*. To *lift* is simply to raise from the ground, though but for an instant, with no reference to holding or moving; one may be able to *lift* what he cannot *carry*. The figurative uses of *carry* are very numerous; as, to *carry* an election, *carry* the country, *carry* (in the sense of capture) a fort, *carry* an audience, *carry* a stock of goods, etc. See **convey; keep; support.**

ANTONYMS: *drop, fall under, give up, let go, shake off, throw down, throw off.*

PREPOSITIONS: To carry coals *to* Newcastle; carry nothing *from*, or *out of*, this house; he carried these qualities *into* all he did; carry *across* the street, *over* the bridge, *through* the woods, *around* or *round* the corner, *beyond* the river; the cable was carried *under* the sea.

CATASTROPHE

| calamity | debacle | disaster | misfortune |
| cataclysm | dénouement | mischance | mishap |

A *catastrophe* is some overwhelming or disastrous convulsion in human or natural affairs; the word stresses the idea of finality; as, World War II was a *catastrophe* from which the world may never recover. Etymologically, *cataclysm* means a flood or deluge, and it is often used to denote any profound geological upheaval; figuratively it is applied to violent political or social change. In *calamity*, or *disaster*, the thought of human suffering is always present. In literature, the final event of a drama is the *catastrophe*, or *dénouement*. *Misfortune* ordinarily suggests less of suddenness and violence than *calamity* or *disaster*, and is especially applied to that which is lingering or enduring in its effects. In history, the fall of a nation, as by the outcome of a war, is a *catastrophe*, though it may not be a *calamity*. Yet such an event, if not a *calamity* to the race, will always involve much individual *disaster* and *misfortune*. Pestilence is a *calamity*; a defeat in battle, a shipwreck, or a failure in business is a *disaster*; sickness or loss of property is a *misfortune*; failure to meet a friend is a *mischance*; the breaking of a teacup is a *mishap*. A *debacle* is a sudden breakdown or collapse, as of a government.

ANTONYMS: *benefit, blessing, boon, comfort, favor, help, pleasure, privilege, prosperity, success.*

PREPOSITIONS: The catastrophe *of* a play, *of* a siege; rarely, *to* a person, etc.

CATCH

apprehend	ensnare	overtake
capture	entrap	secure
clasp	grasp	seize
clutch	grip	snatch
comprehend	gripe	take
discover	lay hold of (on, upon)	take hold of

To *catch* is to come up with or take possession of something departing, fugitive, or illusive. We *catch* a runaway horse, a flying ball, a mouse in a trap. To *capture* is to take possession of something which offers greater opposition or difficulty than is suggested by *catch*. We *clutch* with a swift, tenacious movement of the fingers; we *grasp* with a firm but incaerate closure of the whole hand; we *grip* or *gripe* with the strongest muscular closure of the whole hand possible to exert. We *clasp* in the arms. We *snatch* with a quick, sudden, and usually a surprising motion. In the figurative sense, *catch* is used of any act that brings a person or thing into our power or possession; as, to *catch* a criminal in the act; to *catch* an idea, in the sense of *apprehend* or *comprehend*. To *ensnare*, *entrap*, etc., is to *catch* in a device or situation from which escape is very difficult or dangerous. See **arrest**.

> **ANTONYMS:** *fail of, fall short of, give up, let go, lose, miss, release, restore, throw aside, throw away.*

> **PREPOSITIONS:** To catch *at* a straw; to catch a fugitive *by* the collar; to catch a ball *with* the left hand; he caught the disease *from* the patient; the thief was caught *in* the act, the bird *in* the snare.

CAUSE

actor	causation	fountain	power
agent	condition	motive	precedent
antecedent	creator	occasion	reason
author	designer	origin	source
causality	former	originator	spring

A *cause* is any event, circumstance, or force which produces an effect or result; it is also any combination of events, circumstances, etc., which contribute to the inevitable bringing about of a result. The corruption of the Imperial Government was one of the primary *causes* of the Russian Revolution. A *condition* is something that necessarily precedes a result, but does not produce it. An *antecedent* simply precedes a result, with or without any agency in producing it; as, Monday is the invariable *antecedent* of Tuesday, but not the *cause* of it. The direct antonym of *cause* is effect, while that of *antecedent* is consequent. An *occasion* is some event which brings a *cause* into action at a particular moment; gravitation and heat are the *causes* of an avalanche; the steep incline of the mountain-side is a necessary *condition*, and the shout of the traveler may be the *occasion* of its fall. *Causality* is the doctrine or principle of *causes*; *causation*, the action or working of *causes*. Compare **design; reason** *noun*.

> **ANTONYMS:** *consequence, creation, development, effect, end, event, fruit, issue, outcome, outgrowth, product, result.*

> **PREPOSITIONS:** The cause *of* the disaster; cause *for* interference.

CELEBRATE

| commemorate | keep | observe | solemnize |

To *celebrate* any event or occasion is to make some demonstration of re spect or rejoicing because of or in memory of it, or to perform such public rites or ceremonies as it properly demands. We *celebrate* the birth, *commemorate* the death of one beloved or honored. We *celebrate* a national anniversary with music and song, with firing of guns and ringing of bells; we *commemorate* by any solemn and thoughtful service, or by a monument or other enduring memorial. We *keep* the Sabbath, *observe* an anniversary; we *celebrate* or *observe* the Lord's Supper in which believers *commemorate* the sufferings and death of Christ. *Solemnize* is now restricted to religious cere monies, especially weddings.

> **ANTONYMS:** *contemn, despise, dishonor, disregard, forget, ignore, neglect, overlook, profane, violate.*

> **PREPOSITIONS:** We celebrate the day *with* appropriate ceremonies; the victory was celebrated *by* the people, *with* rejoicing.

CENTER

| core | heart | hub | middle | midst |

We speak of the *center* of a circle, the *middle* of a room, the *middle* of the street, the *midst* of a forest. The *center* is equally distant from every point of the circumference of a circle, or from the opposite boundaries on each axis of a parallelogram, etc.; the *middle* is more general and less definite. The *center* is a point; the *middle* may be a line or a space. We say at the *center*; *in* the *middle*. Center denotes any object or point around which other objects revolve or rotate, as, the sun is the *center* of the universe; or, any point to or from which lines of activity, roads, etc., radiate.

Middle is a less precise word, suggesting a general area rather than a point; as, the *middle* of the ocean. *Midst* replaces *middle* to denote a point surrounded by many persons or things, or, figuratively, problems, cares, interests, etc.; as, in the *midst* of a crowd; in the *midst* of my new and onerous duties. *Core, heart,* and *hub* are all used apart from their literal meanings to denote a place or thing situated deep inside a region, system, or the like, and supply ing to that region or system its life, energy, etc. Compare **amid.**

> **ANTONYMS:** *bound, boundary, circumference, perimeter, rim.*

CHAGRIN

confusion	discomposure	humiliation	shame
disappointment	dismay	mortification	vexation
discomfiture			

Chagrin is keen annoyance or *mortification,* as at one's failures or errors; it unites *disappointment* with some degree of *humiliation.* A rainy day may bring *disappointment;* needless failure in some enterprise brings *chagrin. Shame* involves the consciousness of fault, guilt, or impropriety; *chagrin,* of failure of judgment, or harm to reputation. A consciousness that one has displayed his own ignorance will cause him *mortification,* however worthy his intent; if there was a design to deceive, the exposure will cover him with *shame. Discomfiture* stresses the idea of defeat or frustration, as of one's schemes.

ANTONYMS: *delight, exultation, glory, rejoicing, triumph.*

PREPOSITIONS: He felt deep chagrin *at* (*because of, on account of*) failure.

CHANGE *noun*

alteration	mutation	renewing	transmutation
conversion	novelty	revolution	variation
diversity	regeneration	transformation	variety
innovation	renewal	transition	vicissitude

A *change* is a passing from one state or form to another, any act or process by which a thing becomes unlike what it was before, or the unlikeness so produced; we say a *change* was taking place, or the *change* that had taken place was manifest. *Mutation* is a more formal word for *change,* often suggesting repeated or continual *change;* as, the *mutations* of fortune. *Novelty* is a *change* to what is new, or the newness of that to which a change is made; as, he was perpetually desirous of *novelty. Revolution* is specifically and most commonly a *change* of government.

Variation is a partial *change* in form, qualities, etc., but especially in position or action; as, the *variation* of the magnetic needle or of the pulse. *Variety* is a succession of *changes* or an intermixture of different things, and is always thought of as agreeable. *Vicissitude* is sharp, sudden, or violent *change,* always thought of as surprising and often as disturbing or distressing; as, the *vicissitudes* of politics. *Transition* is *change* by passing from one place or state to another, especially in a natural, regular, or orderly way; as, the *transition* from spring to summer, or from youth to manhood. An *innovation* is a *change* that breaks in upon an established order or custom; as, an *innovation* in religion or politics. For the distinctions between the other words compare the synonyms for **change** *verb.*

ANTONYMS: *constancy, continuance, firmness, fixedness, fixity, identity, invariability, permanence, persistence, steadiness, unchangeableness, uniformity.*

PREPOSITIONS: We have made a change *for* the better; the change *from* winter to spring; the change *of* a liquid *to* or *into* a gas; a change *in* quality; a change *by* absorption or oxidation.

CHANGE *verb*

alter	exchange	shift	transmute
commute	metamorphose	substitute	turn
convert	modify	transfigure	vary
diversify	qualify	transform	veer

To *change* is distinctively to make a thing other than it has been, in some respect at least; to *exchange*, to put or take something else in its place; to *alter* is ordinarily to *change* partially, to make different in one or more particulars. To *exchange* is often to transfer ownership; as, to *exchange* city for country property. *Change* is often used in the sense of *exchange*; as, to *change* horses. To *transmute* is to *change* the qualities while the substance remains the same; as, to *transmute* the baser metals into gold. To *transform* is to *change* form or appearance, with or without deeper and more essential change; it is less absolute than *transmute*, though sometimes used for that word. *Transfigure* is to change in an exalted and glorious spiritual way; "Jesus . . . was *transfigured* before them, and his face did shine as the sun, and his raiment was white as the light." *Matt.* xxii, 1, 2.

To *metamorphose* is to make some remarkable change, ordinarily in external qualities, but often in structure, use, or chemical constitution, as of a caterpillar into a butterfly, of the stamens of a plant into petals, or of the crystalline structure of rocks, hence called "metamorphic rocks," as when a limestone is *metamorphosed* into a marble. To *vary* is to *change* from time to time, often capriciously. To *commute* is to put something easier, lighter, milder, or in some way more favorable in place of that which is *commuted*; as, to *commute* capital punishment to imprisonment for life; to *commute* daily fares on a railway to a monthly payment. To *convert* is primarily to turn about, and signifies to *change* in form, character, use, etc., through a wide range of relations; iron is *converted* into steel, joy into grief, a sinner into a saint. To *turn* is a popular word for *change* in any sense short of the meaning of *exchange*, being often equivalent to *alter, convert, transform, transmute*, etc. We *modify* or *qualify* a statement which might seem too strong; we *modify* it by some limitation, *qualify* it by some addition.

ANTONYMS: *abide, bide, continue, endure, hold, keep, persist, remain, retain, stay.*

PREPOSITIONS: To change a house dress *for* a street dress; to change *from* a caterpillar *to* or *into* a butterfly; to change clothes *with* a beggar.

CHARACTER

constitution	individuality	record	spirit
disposition	nature	reputation	temper
genius	personality	repute	temperament

Character is what one is; *reputation,* what he is thought to be; his *record* is the total of his known action or inaction. As a rule, a man's *record* will substantially express his *character;* his *reputation* may be higher or lower than his *character* or *record* will justify. *Repute* is a somewhat formal word, with the same general sense as *reputation.* One's *nature* includes all his original endowments or propensities; *character* includes both natural and acquired traits. We speak of one's physical *constitution* as strong or weak, etc., and figuratively, always with the adjective, of his mental or moral *constitution.*

Temperament includes all innate and inherent characteristics; *disposition* is *temperament* plus natural tendency. *Genius* is extraordinary mental endowment, inherent ability. *Personality* is distinctive personal *character; individuality* is individual *character* that is very strongly marked. *Spirit,* as here compared, implies mood, mental attitude. See **characteristic.**

PREPOSITIONS: The witness has a character *for* veracity; his character is *above* suspicion; the character *of* the applicant.

CHARACTERISTIC

attribute	indication	property	singularity
character	mark	quality	trace
distinction	peculiarity	sign	trait
feature			

A *characteristic* belongs to the nature or *character* of the person, thing, or class, and serves to identify an object; as, a copper-colored skin, high cheekbones, and straight, black hair are *characteristics* of the American Indian. A *sign* is manifest to an observer; a *mark* or a *characteristic* may be more difficult to discover; an insensible person may show *signs* of life, while sometimes only close examination will disclose *marks* of violence. Pallor is ordinarily a *mark* of fear; but in some brave natures it is simply a *characteristic* of intense earnestness. *Mark* is used in a good or bad sense; we speak of a *mark* of courage, the *mark* of a villain.

Distinction refers to a particular or distinguishing *mark* or *quality; feature,* to a *peculiarity* that is prominent; *singularity,* to a *characteristic* peculiar to oneself or itself. *Trait* is a distinguishing *feature* or *quality* of mind or character. Compare **attribute** *noun;* **character; trace.**

CHARMING

bewitching	delightful	enrapturing	fascinating
captivating	enchanting	entrancing	winning

That is *charming* or *bewitching* which is adapted to win others as by a magic spell. *Enchanting, enrapturing, entrancing* represent the influence as not only supernatural, but irresistible and *delightful.* That which is *fascinating* may win without delighting, drawing by some unseen power, as a serpent its prey; we can speak of horrible fascination. *Charming* applies only to what is external to oneself; *delightful* may apply to personal experiences or emotions as well; we speak of a *charming* manner, a *charming* dress, but of *delightful* anticipations. *Winning*, in this comparison, is winsome, *captivating*; as, a *winning* smile. Compare **amiable; beautiful.**

CHECK

arrest	checkmate	hinder	obstruct	slacken
baffle	counteract	impede	reduce	stay
brake	curb	inhibit	repress	stop
bridle	foil	moderate	restrain	

To *check* is to restrain movement suddenly, and partially or temporarily; as, to *check* the speed of a horse or of a railway train; to *check* the advance of an enemy; to *check* progress. It implies a retardation of motion, rather than complete stoppage; to *brake*, however, is retardation in anticipation of complete stoppage. *Check* has none of the suggestion of art, cunning, or superior skill that is in *baffle* and *foil*; an enemy's advance may be *checked* by marching up an effective force or planting cannon squarely in his front. The words *check* and *checkmate* are to be discriminated as partial and total; in the game of chess, *check* is any attack upon the king and is temporary in effect, whereas *checkmate* is final and decisive. *Checkmate* (from Pers. *shah mat*, the king is dead) is never to be used figuratively of anything less than irremediable defeat. A person or movement is *checked* if in any way *restrained*; *checkmated* if defeated beyond recovery.

A man may *curb* anger and *bridle* his tongue; barriers may *impede* or *hinder* free passage, or completely *obstruct* it. *Inhibit* and *restrain* imply drawing back again; *repress* is to press back; *restrain*, to hold in from some action. We *reduce* the volume when we *check* the flow of water. See **baffle; hinder; restrain.**

> ANTONYMS: *abet, accelerate, allow, encourage, expedite, free, hasten, hurry, indulge, instigate, let go, liberate, license, loose, loosen, quicken, rush, speed, urge forward, urge on.*

CHERISH

cheer	encourage	harbor	nurse	shelter
cling to	entertain	hold dear	nurture	treasure
comfort	foster	nourish	protect	value

To *cherish* is both to *hold dear* and to treat as dear. Mere unexpressed esteem would not be *cherishing*. In the marriage vow, "to love, honor, and *cherish*," the word *cherish* implies all that each can do by love and tenderness for the welfare and happiness of the other, as by support, protection, care in sickness, comfort in sorrow, sympathy, and help of every kind. To *nurse* is to tend the helpless or feeble, as infants, or the sick or wounded. To *nourish* is strictly to sustain and build up by food; to *nurture* includes careful mental and spiritual training, with something of love and tenderness; to *foster* is simply to maintain and care for, to bring up; a *foster* child will be *nourished,* but may not be as tenderly *nurtured* or as lovingly *cherished* as if one's own. In the figurative sense, the opinion one *cherishes* he holds, not with mere cold conviction, but with loving devotion.

As compared here, we *entertain* or *harbor* ideas when we receive them and hold them in mind; we *treasure* what we *hold dear,* and *value* what we hold in high esteem or prize.

ANTONYMS: See synonyms for **abandon.**

CHIEF

captain	commander in chief	king	prince	sachem
chieftain	head	leader	principal	
commander	headman	master	ruler	

A *chief* is either the *ruler* of a tribe or the *head* of some department of established government; as, the *chief* of police; the word is rarely, and for the most part colloquially, applied to one holding some analogous position in literary or mercantile life, etc. *Chieftain* is now mainly employed in literary, and chiefly poetic, use; it has special historic application to the *head* of a Scottish clan. A *leader* is one who is voluntarily followed, because of ability to guide or control, or as the choice of a party.

The highest officer of any considerable military force is called the *commander;* of all the forces of a nation, etc., the *commander in chief. Principal,* which is also an adjective, has important use as a noun, in the sense of a *leader;* as, the *principal* in a debate, a duel, or a crime, the *principal* of a school, etc.; also, of property, capital, or the like on which interest accrues; as, the *principal* of a loan. *Principal* is to be sharply distinguished from principle, which is never an adjective, and as a noun is wholly different in sense.

Captain is used for a person in authority, as the *leader* of a sports team, or as a courtesy title for the *master* or *commander* of a ship; or for a commissioned officer, above a lieutenant in the army, or below a rear admiral in the navy. *Master* applies to the male *head* of a school or household, or to a proficient workman or a skilled artist; as, a *master* builder, an old *master.* *Sachem* is an hereditary, tribal chief; *headman,* the chief man of a tribe or village. Compare **principal.**

ANTONYMS: *adherent, attendant, follower, minion, retainer, satellite, servant, subaltern, subordinate, underling, vassal.*

CHOICE

alternative   election   option   pick   preference   resource

A *choice* may be among many things; an *alternative* is in the strictest sense a *choice* between two things; oftener it is one of two things between which a *choice* is to be made, and either of which is the *alternative* of the other; as, the *alternative* of surrender is death; or the two things between which there is a *choice* may be called the *alternatives*. Some writers, including Mill and Gladstone, extend the meaning of *alternative* to include several particulars, Gladstone even speaking of "the fourth and last of these *alternatives*." *Option* is the right or privilege of choosing; *choice* may be either the right to choose, the act of choosing, or the thing chosen. A person of ability and readiness will commonly have many *resources*. *Pick*, from the Saxon, and *election*, from the Latin, picture the objects before one, with freedom and power to choose which he will; as, there were twelve horses, among which I could take my *pick*. A *choice, pick, election*, or *preference* is that which suits one best; an *alternative* is that to which one is restricted; a *resource*, that to which one is glad to betake oneself.

ANTONYMS: *compulsion, necessity.*

CHOOSE

cull   elect   opt   pick   pick out   prefer   select

Choose indicates an act of will; *prefer*, a state of desire and approval. Prudence or generosity may lead one to *choose* what he does not *prefer*. *Select* implies a careful consideration of the reasons for preference and choice. Among objects so nearly alike that we have no reason to *prefer* any one to another we may simply *choose* the nearest, but we could not be said to *select* it. Aside from theology, *elect* is popularly confined to the political sense; as, a free people *elect* their own rulers. *Cull*, from the Latin *colligere*, commonly means to collect, as well as to *select*. In a garden we *cull* the choicest flowers. *Pick* generally implies to *select* personally; as, to *pick* one's friends; *pick out* is to *choose* from a quantity or number; to *opt*, now rarely employed, is to *choose* between two alternatives.

ANTONYMS: *cast away, cast out, decline, disclaim, dismiss, leave, refuse, reject, repudiate, throw aside.*

PREPOSITIONS: Choose *from* or *from among* the number; choose *out of* the army; choose *between* (or *betwixt*) two, *among* many; choose *for* the purpose.

CIRCUMLOCUTION

diffuseness	prolixity	surplusage	verbiage
periphrasis	redundance	tautology	verbosity
pleonasm	redundancy	tediousness	wordiness

Circumlocution and *periphrasis* are roundabout ways of expressing thought; *circumlocution* is the more common, *periphrasis* the more technical word. Constant *circumlocution* produces an affected and heavy style; occasionally, skilful *periphrasis* conduces both to beauty and to simplicity. Etymologically, *diffuseness* is a scattering, both of words and thought; *redundancy* is an overflow; a *surplusage*, more words than needed. *Prolixity* goes into endless petty details, without selection or perspective. *Pleonasm* is the expression of an idea already plainly implied; *tautology* is the restatement in other words of an idea already stated, or a useless repetition of a word or words. *Pleonasm* may add emphasis; *tautology* is always a fault. "I saw it with my eyes" is a *pleonasm*; "all the members agreed unanimously" is *tautology*. *Verbiage* is the use of mere words without thought. *Verbosity* and *wordiness* denote an excess of words in proportion to the thought. *Tediousness* is the sure result of any of these faults of style.

> ANTONYMS: *brevity, compactness, compression, conciseness, condensation, directness, plainness, shortness, succinctness, terseness.*

CIRCUMSCRIBE

bound	delineate	enclose	mark off
confine	describe	fence	mark out
define	designate	limit	restrict

To *circumscribe* is to draw a line or figure around to mark the limits or boundary of; or, in geometry, to surround with a figure that touches at every possible point. *Bound, fence,* and *enclose,* as here compared, all refer to making a limiting line or structure around something; an island is *bounded* by water; we *fence* or *enclose* a field for cattle. We can *limit* space, time, amount, production, etc., and *confine* may also refer to several kinds of limitations or restrictions. In this comparison, *define* means to fix the limits of; *describe,* to draw a figure of; as, to *describe* a circle; and *delineate,* to outline or sketch. *Designate* is to mark out; as, to *designate* property boundaries. See **restrain.**

> ANTONYMS: *dilate, distend, enlarge, expand, fling wide, leave open, open, throw open.*

> PREPOSITIONS: Circumscribe *by* or *with* a line; circumscribe a circle *about* a polygon; circumscribe *within* narrow bounds.

CIRCUMSTANCE

accompaniment	episode	item	point
concomitant	fact	occurrence	position
detail	feature	particular	situation
event	incident		

A *circumstance* is something existing or occurring in connection with or relation to some other fact or event, modifying or throwing light upon the principal matter without affecting its essential character; an *accompaniment* is something that unites with the principal matter, though not necessary to it; as, the piano *accompaniment* to a song; a *concomitant* goes with a thing in natural connection, but in a subordinate capacity, or perhaps in contrast; as, cheerfulness is a *concomitant* of virtue.

Circumstance is not properly an *incident* unless it implies a *detail*. We say, "My decision will depend upon *circumstances*"—not "upon *incidents*." That a man wore a blue necktie would not probably be the cause, occasion, condition, or *concomitant* of his committing murder; but it might be a very important *circumstance* in identifying him as the murderer. All the *circumstances* make up the *situation*. A certain disease is the cause of a man's death; his suffering is an *incident*; that he is in his own home, that he has good medical attendance, careful nursing, etc., are consolatory *circumstances*. A person is said to be in easy *circumstances* when he is in a good *position* financially. *Facts* are actual *occurrences* or alleged *circumstances*. See **event.**

CLASS

| association | circle | clique | company | grade | rank |
| caste | clan | club | coterie | order | set |

A *class* is a number or body of persons or objects having common pursuits, purposes, attributes, or characteristics. A *caste* is hereditary; a *class* may be independent of lineage or descent; membership in a *caste* is supposed to be for life; membership in a *class* may be very transient; a religious and ceremonial sacredness attaches to the *caste*, as not to the *class*. The rich and the poor form separate *classes*; yet individuals are constantly passing from each to the other; the *classes* in a college remain the same, but their membership changes every year.

We speak of *rank* among hereditary nobility or military officers; of various *orders* of the priesthood; by accommodation, we may refer in a general way to the higher *ranks*, the lower *orders* of any society. *Grade* implies some regular scale of valuation, and some inherent qualities for which a person or thing is placed higher or lower in the scale; as, the coarser and finer *grades* of wool; a boy in the sixth *grade*. A *coterie* is a small *company* of persons of similar tastes, who meet frequently in an informal way, rather for social enjoyment than for any serious purpose.

An *association* is a body of persons united for a common purpose. *Clique* has always an unfavorable meaning. A *clique* is always fractional, implying some greater gathering of which it is a part; the *association* may break up into *cliques*. Persons unite in a *coterie* through simple liking for one another; they withdraw into a *clique* largely through aversion to outsiders. A *set*, while exclusive, is more extensive than a *clique*, and chiefly of persons who are united by common social station, etc. *Circle* is similar in meaning to *set*, but of wider application; we speak of scientific and religious as well as of social *circles*. *Clan* applies specifically to members of a Scottish household descended from the same ancestor. See **association**.

> **PREPOSITIONS:** A class *of* merchants; the senior class *at* (sometimes *of*) Harvard; the classes *in* college.

CLEAN

brush	lave	scour	sweep
cleanse	mop	scrub	wash
disinfect	purify	sponge	wipe
dust	rinse		

To *clean* is to remove dirt, impurities, or soil of any kind. *Cleanse* presupposes a worse condition to start from than *clean*. Hercules *cleansed* the Augean stables. *Cleanse* is especially applied to purifying processes where liquid is used, as in the flushing of a street, etc. We *brush* clothing if dusty, *sponge* it, or *sponge* it off, if soiled; or *sponge* off a spot. Furniture, books, etc., are *dusted*; floors are *mopped* or *scrubbed*; metallic utensils are *scoured*; a room is *swept*; soiled garments are *washed* with soap and then *rinsed* in clear water. Foul air or water is *purified*. *Cleanse* and *purify* are used extensively in a moral sense; *wash* in that sense is archaic. We *disinfect* rooms, furniture, garments, etc., to destroy disease germs. Compare **amend**; **washing.**

> **ANTONYMS:** *befoul, besmear, besmirch, bespatter, contaminate, corrupt, debase, defile, deprave, pollute, soil, spoil, stain, sully, taint, vitiate.*

> **PREPOSITIONS:** The room was cleaned *by* the attendants *with* soap and water; he cleaned *up* the mess.

CLEAR

apparent	intelligible	pellucid	transparent
definite	limpid	perspicuous	unadorned
diaphanous	lucid	plain	unambiguous
distinct	manifest	straightforward	unequivocal
evident	obvious	translucent	unmistakable
explicit			

Clear primarily refers to that which shines, and impresses the mind through the eye with a sense of luster or splendor. A substance is said to be *clear* that offers no impediment to vision—is not dim, dark, or obscure. *Transparent* refers to the medium through which a substance is seen, *clear* to the substance itself, without reference to anything to be seen through it; we speak of a stream as *clear* when we think of the water itself; we speak of it as *transparent* with reference to the ease with which we see the pebbles at the bottom.

Clear is also said of that which comes to the sense without dimness, dulness, obstruction, or obscurity, so that there is no uncertainty as to its exact form, character, or meaning, with something of the brightness or brilliancy implied in the primary meaning of the word *clear*; as, the outlines of the ship were *clear* against the sky; a *clear* view; a *clear* note, "*clear* as a bell"; a *clear*, frosty air; a *clear* sky; a *clear* statement; hence, the word is used for that which is free from any kind of obstruction; as, a *clear* field. *Lucid* and *pellucid* are used in literature to refer to a shining clearness, a transparency, as of crystal. A *transparent* body allows the forms and colors of objects beyond to be seen through it; a *translucent* body allows light to pass through, but may not permit forms and colors to be distinguished; plate glass is *transparent*, ground glass is *translucent*.

Limpid refers to a liquid clearness, or that which suggests it; as, *limpid* streams. That which is *distinct* is well defined, especially in outline, each part or object standing or seeming apart from any other, not confused, indefinite, or blurred; *distinct* enunciation enables the hearer to catch every word or vocal sound without perplexity or confusion; a *distinct* statement is free from indefiniteness or ambiguity; a *distinct* apprehension of a thought leaves the mind in no doubt or uncertainty regarding it. That is *plain*, in the sense here considered, which is, as it were, level to the thought, so that one goes straight on without difficulty or hindrance; as, *plain* language; a *plain* statement; a *clear* explanation.

Diaphanous refers to something very delicate and almost *transparent*. We speak of that which is *clear* to the eye and to the understanding as *evident*. *Perspicuous* is often equivalent to *plain*, but *plain* never wholly loses the meaning of unadorned. See **evident**.

> **ANTONYMS:** *ambiguous, cloudy, dim, dubious, foggy, indistinct, mysterious, obscure, opaque, turbid, unintelligible, vague.*

> **PREPOSITIONS:** Clear *to* the mind; clear *in* argument; clear *of* or *from* annoyances.

CLEVER

able	dexterous	intellectual	quick-witted
adroit	expert	intelligent	sharp
apt	gifted	keen	skilful
bright	happy	knowing	smart
brilliant	ingenious	quick	talented
capable			

Clever implies natural skill, ability, adroitness, whereas *intelligent* implies having or exhibiting a high degree of understanding, and *intellectual* stresses the faculty of knowing and reasoning. *Dexterous* refers to skill in manipulation; *ingenious*, to skill in devising or inventing.

Smart, indicating dashing ability, is now coming to have a suggestion of unscrupulousness, similar to that of the word *sharp*, which makes its use a doubtful compliment. The discriminating use of such words as *able, gifted, skilful, talented*, etc., is preferable to an excessive use of the word *clever*. See **skilful**. Compare **acumen; dexterity; happy; power; shrewd.**

ANTONYMS: *awkward, bungling, clumsy, dull, foolish, idiotic, ignorant, senseless, slow, stupid, thick-headed, witless.*

CLOISTER

abbey	friary	monastery	priory
convent	hermitage	nunnery	

A *cloister* is a building devoted to the secluded, religious life of monks or nuns. *Cloister, abbey, convent,* and *priory* are for either sex; a *friary* is always for men, a *nunnery* for women, a *monastery* commonly for men. A *priory* (governed by a prior or prioress) ranks next below an *abbey* (governed by an abbot or abbess). The word *monastery* lays stress upon the loneliness (Gr. *monos*, alone); *convent* emphasizes the association of its inmates (L. *convenio*, assemble). A *hermitage* was originally for a single recluse, but the word came to be applied to collections of hermits' cells.

COLLISION

clash	conflict	impact	opposition
clashing	contact	impingement	percussion
concussion	encounter	meeting	shock

Collision, the act or fact of striking violently together, is the result of motion or action, and is sudden and momentary; *contact* is a coming together, a touching; *collision* is sudden and violent *contact*. *Concussion* is often by transmitted force rather than by direct *impact*; two railway trains come into *collision*; an explosion of dynamite shatters neighboring windows by *concussion*. *Impact* is the blow given by the striking body; as, the *impact* of the cannon shot upon the target. *Impingement*, in this comparison, generally refers to sound waves striking some body sharply. An *encounter* is a sudden *meeting*, friendly or hostile; as, an *encounter* with friends or with foes; an *encounter* of wits or of combatants; the hostile meaning is becoming predominant. *Meeting* is neutral, and may be of the dearest friends or of the bitterest foes; of objects, of persons, or of opinions; of two or of a multitude.

Shock is the result of *collision* or *impact*; *concussion* often implies the effect of an *impact* on some organ of the body; *percussion* is the act of striking something sharply against something else to produce sound, as in *percussion* instruments; or a tapping against a part of the body to test sounds and vibrations, as by a doctor. In the figurative use, we speak of the *clash* of views. *Opposition* is used chiefly of persons, more rarely of opinions or interests; *conflict* is used indifferently of all.

ANTONYMS: *agreement, amity, coincidence, concert, concord, concurrence, conformity, harmony, unison, unity.*

PREPOSITIONS: Collision *of* one object *with* another, *of* or *between* opposing objects.

COMFORTABLE

agreeable	commodious	genial	satisfied
at ease	contented	pleasant	snug
at rest	convenient	reposeful	well-off
cheerful	cozy	restful	well-to-do
cheery	easy	satisfactory	

Comfortable implies providing contentment or relief. A person is *comfortable* in mind when *contented* and measurably *satisfied*. A little additional brightness makes him *cheerful*. He is *comfortable* in body when free from pain, *at ease, at rest*. He is *comfortable* in circumstances, or in *comfortable* circumstances, when things about him are generally *agreeable* and *satisfactory*, usually with the suggestion of sufficient means to secure that result.

An *easy* chair is a *comfortable* chair in which to rest. *Snug* suggests comfort and protection in small quarters; *commodious* stresses space as providing comfort; *convenient* refers to suitability to a person's needs and comfort, making work *easy*. *Cozy* always includes the idea of warmth and shelter; *genial, cheerful,* and *cheery* refer to personal disposition favorable to comfort.

ANTONYMS: *cheerless, disagreeable, discontented, dissatisfied, distressed, dreary, forlorn, miserable, uncomfortable, wretched.*

COMMIT

assign confide consign entrust relegate trust

Commit, in the sense here considered, is to give in charge, put into the care or keeping of someone or something; to *confide* or *entrust* is to *commit* especially to one's fidelity, *confide* being used chiefly of mental or spiritual, *entrust* also of material things; we *assign* a duty, *confide* a secret, *entrust* a treasure; we *commit* thoughts to writing; *commit* a paper to the flames, a body to the earth; a prisoner is *committed* to jail. *Consign* is a formal word in mercantile use; as, to *consign* goods to an agent. Religiously, we *consign* the body to the grave, *commit* the soul to God. *Relegate* is to *consign* or transfer to a particular place or class, often in order to get rid of. Compare **do.**

PREPOSITIONS: Commit *to* a friend *for* safe-keeping; in law, commit *to* prison *for* trial, *without* bail, in default *of* bail, *on* suspicion.

COMPANY

assemblage	concourse	crowd	multitude
assembly	conference	gathering	party
band	congregation	group	throng
collection	convention	host	troop
conclave	convocation	meeting	troupe

Company (from L. *cum*, with, and *panis*, bread) denotes primarily the association of those who eat at a common table, or the persons so associated, table companions, messmates, friends, and hence is widely extended to include any association of those united permanently or temporarily, for business, pleasure, festivity, travel, etc., or by sorrow, misfortune, or wrong; *company* may denote an indefinite number (ordinarily more than two), but less than a *multitude*; in the military sense a *company* is a limited and definite number of men; *company* implies more unity of feeling and purpose than *crowd*, and is a less formal and more familiar word than *assemblage* or *assembly*.

An *assemblage* may be of persons or of objects; an *assembly* is always of persons. An *assemblage* is promiscuous and unorganized; an *assembly* is organized and united in some common purpose. A *conclave* is a secret *assembly*. A *convocation* is an *assembly* called by authority for a special purpose; the term *convention* suggests less dependence upon any superior authority or summons. A *group* is small in number and distinct in outline, clearly marked off from all else in space or time. *Collection, crowd, gathering, group,* and *multitude* have the unorganized and promiscuous character of the *assemblage*; the other terms come under the general idea of *assembly*. *Congregation* is now almost exclusively religious; *meeting* is often so used, but is less restricted, as we may speak of a *meeting* of armed men. *Gathering* refers to a coming together, commonly of numbers, from far and near; as, the *gathering* of the Scottish clans.

A *band* is a *company* closely organized for a special purpose; a *party* is a *group* assembled for a common purpose. *Throng, crowd, host* and *multitude* all emphasize great numbers. Compare **cabal.**

ANTONYMS: *dispersion, loneliness, privacy, retirement, seclusion, solitude.*

COMPEL

coerce	drive	force	necessitate
constrain	exact	make	oblige

To *compel* one to an act is to secure its performance by the use of irresistible physical or moral force; figuratively, *compel* is to obtain by physical or moral force; as, to *compel* obedience. *Force* implies primarily an actual physical process, absolutely subduing all resistance. *Coerce* implies the actual or potential use of so much force as may be necessary to secure the surrender of the will; the American secessionists contended that the Federal government had no right to *coerce* a State. We can *drive* someone to an action or *drive* cattle from a field. *Constrain* implies the yielding of judgment and will, and in some cases of inclination or affection, to an overmastering power; as, "the love of Christ *constraineth* us," *2 Cor.* v. 14. *Necessitate* and *oblige* include a sense of urgency in compelling an action. *Make,* in this comparison, is a general term for all kinds of compulsion. To *exact* is to *compel* the yielding, payment, or surrender of; as, to *exact* a ransom, or to *exact* compliance. See **drive; influence; make.**

ANTONYMS: See synonyms for **hinder.**

PREPOSITIONS: The soldiers were compelled *to* desert.

COMPLAIN

croak	growl	grunt	remonstrate
find fault	grumble	murmur	repine

To *complain* is to give utterance to dissatisfaction or objection, express a sense of wrong or ill treatment. One *complains* of a real or assumed grievance; he may *murmur* through mere peevishness or ill temper; he *repines,* with vain distress, at the irrevocable or the inevitable. *Complaining* is by speech or writing; *murmuring* is commonly said of half-repressed utterance; *repining,* of the mental act alone. One may *complain* of an offense to the offender or to others; he *remonstrates* with the offender only. *Complain* has a formal and legal meaning, which the other words have not, signifying to make a formal accusation, present a specific charge; the same is true of the noun "complaint." To *croak* often connotes a foreboding of ill while *complaining*; *grumble* and *growl* both imply muttering a complaint. *Remonstrate* is used in protesting against something or urging reasons against it.

ANTONYMS: *applaud, approve, commend, eulogize, laud, praise.*

PREPOSITIONS: Complain *of* a thing *to* a person, *of* one person *to* another, *of* or *against* a person, *for* an act, *to* an officer, *before* the court, *about* a thing.

COMPLEX

abstruse	confused	intricate	mixed
complicated	conglomerate	involved	multiform
composite	entangled	manifold	obscure
compound	heterogeneous	mingled	tangled

That is *complex* which is made up of several interrelated or interacting parts; that is *compound* in which the parts are not merely connected, but fused, or otherwise combined into a single substance. In a *composite* object the different parts have less of unity than in that which is *complex* or *compound*, but maintain their distinct individuality. In a *heterogeneous* body unlike parts or particles are intermingled, often without apparent order or plan. *Conglomerate* (literally, globed together) is said of a *confused* mingling of masses or lumps of various substances. The New England pudding-stone is a *conglomerate* rock. In a *complex* object the arrangement and relation of parts may be perfectly clear; in a *complicated* mechanism the parts are so numerous, or so combined, that the mind cannot readily grasp their mutual relations; in an *intricate* arrangement the parts are so intertwined that it is difficult to follow their windings; things are *involved* which are rolled together so as not to be easily separated, either in thought or in fact; things which are *tangled* or *entangled* mutually hold and draw upon each other.

That is *intricate* which is hard to solve or follow out because of the intertwining or involvement of its parts. The conception of a material object is usually *complex,* involving form, color, size, and other elements; a clock is a *complicated* mechanism; the Gordian knot was *intricate;* the twining serpents of the Laocoon are *involved.* We speak of an *abstruse* statement, a *complex* conception, a *confused* heap, a *heterogeneous* mass, a *tangled* skein, an *intricate* problem; of *composite* architecture, an *involved* sentence; of the *complicated* or *intricate* accounts of a great business, the *entangled* accounts of an incompetent or dishonest bookkeeper.

ANTONYMS: *clear, direct, homogeneous, obvious, plain, simple, uncombined, uncompounded, uniform, unraveled.*

COMPROMISE

accommodation	arbitration	compounding	conciliation
adjustment	arrangement	concession	settlement
agreement	composition		

Compromise is mutual *concession* by those of opposing views and interests, each yielding something to the other or others; the expression "mutual *compromise,*" sometimes heard, is tautological, for *compromise* is by its very nature "mutual"; where all the *concession* is on one side, there is no *compromise* *Agreement* expresses the act or fact of agreeing, and may be free and hearty or secured with labor and difficulty. *Concession* is a yielding to another of that which one would like to retain; *concession* may be voluntary and generous, calculating and crafty, or forced and unwilling. *Adjustment* of differences is largely by treatment or explanation of matters of fact on some basis that can be mutually accepted, and may or may not involve *concession* or *compromise*; as, the *adjustment* of a loss under an insurance policy.

Accommodation is a fitting or adapting of the views or wishes of one to those of another; *arrangement* is similar in meaning; either *accommodation* or *arrangement* partakes of the nature of *compromise*, but is less formal and comprehensive in meaning; as, his creditors granted him an *accommodation*; or, he made an *arrangement* with his creditors; the decision to admit Missouri as a slave State on condition of freedom for all other territory north of the parallel of 35 degrees 30 minutes might be termed an *agreement, accommodation, adjustment,* or *arrangement*; it is historically known as the "Missouri Compromise." *Composition* and *compounding* in this sense are now somewhat rare and technical terms; the latter is chiefly used in an opprobrious sense; as, the *compounding* of a felony, by refraining, for a consideration, from bringing the guilty party to justice. *Conciliation* is a general term, signifying the overcoming of enmity or opposition by some pleasing method, action, or influence, perhaps, though not necessarily, involving *concession* or *compromise*. *Conciliation* often precedes any formal action, and is the basis that makes *agreement* possible.

Settlement is the conclusion of any matter, whether in dispute or not, by some act that is final; as, the *settlement* of an account by payment of the amount due. *Arbitration* is the most formal of these terms, signifying the reference of a disputed matter or matters, by law, treaty, or mutual *agreement*, to some outside person or persons (an "arbitrator" or "arbitrators"), whose decision shall be binding upon both the contending parties; as, the Court of *Arbitration* at the Hague. Since the readiest method of *compromise* is often by the yielding of principle for expediency, the word has come to have an opprobrious sense which is not part of its original meaning.

Temporizing is not *settlement*; it has no more virtue than *compromise*, and less stability, being a mere momentary *adjustment*, to meet the suppressed needs of the time for the time.

> ANTONYMS: *altercation, battle, contention, contest, controversy, debate, discussion, disputation, dispute, dissension, quarrel, strife, war, wrangle, wrangling.*

CONCERN

affect	impress	interest	move	touch

To *concern* is to relate to or to be connected with circumstances of any kind; to be of interest or importance to; also to occupy or engage. To *affect* is to produce some change in outward circumstances or in persons. Affairs tha *concern* us do not always *affect* future success. That which *impresses* us usually influences us deeply or *moves* us. Something that *interests* us may only *concern* part of our work or recreation, may only *touch* our life at one point, need not *affect* us at all. See **interest; pertain.**

> **PREPOSITIONS:** I am concerned *about* his affairs, *at* his misfortunes, *for* his safety; I am not concerned *with* him *in* that business; "I am not concerned *about* the matter" means "I have no anxiety in regard to it"; "I am not concerned *in* it" signifies "I have no participation in it."

CONDEMN

blame	convict	doom	reprobate	sentence
censure	denounce	reprehend	reprove	

To *condemn* is to pass judicial sentence or render judgment or decision against, with the connotation of utter unfavorableness. We may *censure* silently; we *condemn* ordinarily by open and formal utterance. *Condemn* is more final than *blame* or *censure*; a *condemned* criminal has had his trial; a *condemned* building cannot stand; a *condemned* ship cannot sail. A person is *convicted* when his guilt is made clearly manifest to others; in somewhat archaic use, a person is said to be *convicted* when guilt is brought clearly home to his own conscience (*convict* in this sense being allied with *convince*, which we see under **persuade**); in legal usage one is said to be *convicted* only by the verdict of a jury. In stating the penalty for an offense, the legal word *sentence* is now more common than *condemn*; as, he was *sentenced* to imprisonment; but it is good usage to say, he was *condemned* to imprisonment. To *denounce* is to make public or official declaration against, especially in a violent and threatening manner.

To *doom* is to *condemn* solemnly and consign to evil or destruction, or to predetermine to an evil destiny. To *reprobate* is to *condemn* or disapprove strongly; to abandon to a hopeless doom. To *reprehend* is to rebuke or criticize severely; it is used more often of things or actions than of persons; as, to *reprehend* a writer's faults. See **arraign; reprove.**

> **ANTONYMS:** *absolve, acquit, applaud, approve, exonerate, justify, pardon, praise.*

> **PREPOSITIONS:** The bandit was condemned *to* death *for* his crime.

CONDIGN

appropriate	exemplary	just	merited
deserved	fit	meet	suitable
due			

Condign, meaning well-deserved or *merited*, is applied chiefly to punishment; a *condign* sentence imposed on a criminal is one which neither falls below nor exceeds the merits of his crime. *Exemplary* views the punishment as furnishing a warning to deter others from committing a like offense; so a court may award *exemplary* damages, beyond the amount of actual injury done, as a public warning against similar acts.

That which is *due* is morally owed or owing, and is based on an obligation or duty which should not be disregarded; as, *due* respect for one's elders. *Fit* is applied to that which is adapted to the end in view; as, a *fit* instrument for one's purposes. An *appropriate* thing is so *fit* or *suitable* for the object or person with which it is associated that it seems to have been made exclusively for that purpose.

ANTONYMS: *gentle, inadequate, lenient, mild, moderate, petty, scant, scanty, slight, trifling, trivial.*

CONFESS

accept	allow	concede	grant
acknowledge	avow	disclose	own
admit	certify	endorse	recognize

To *confess* is to make known to others one's own wrong-doing; as, to *confess* a crime. In this sense *confess* is stronger than *acknowledge* or *admit*. To *acknowledge* is to make known one's knowledge of something which might hitherto have been a secret; as, she finally *acknowledged* her engagement to Jim. *Admit* implies reluctance to *grant* or *concede*; as, we finally prevailed upon him to *admit* the charge of complicity in the robbery. To *own* something, in this connection, is to *acknowledge* it as it bears some relation to oneself; as, he *owned* to a feeling of deep remorse.

We *accept* another's statement; *admit* any point made against us; *acknowledge* what we have said or done, good or bad; *avow* our individual beliefs or feelings; *certify* to facts within our knowledge; *endorse* a friend's note or statement; *grant* a request; *own* our faults or obligations; *recognize* lawful authority; *concede* a claim. Compare **apology.**

ANTONYMS: *cloak, conceal, cover, deny, disavow, disguise, disown, dissemble, dissimulate, hide, mask, repudiate, screen, secrete, veil.*

CONFIRM

assure	fix	settle	uphold
authenticate	prove	strengthen	validate
corroborate	ratify	substantiate	verify
establish	sanction	sustain	

Confirm is to add firmness or give stability to. Both *confirm* and *corroborate* presuppose something already existing to which the confirmation or corroboration is added. Testimony is *corroborated* by concurrent testimony or by circumstances; *confirmed* by *established* facts. That which is thoroughly *proved* is said to be *established*; so is that which is official and has adequate power behind it. To *assure* is to *confirm* in conviction, state confidently. The continents are *fixed*. A treaty is *ratified*; an appointment *confirmed*. An act is *sanctioned* by any person or authority that passes upon it approvingly. A statement is *substantiated*; a report *confirmed*; a controversy *settled*; the decision of a lower court *sustained* by a higher. Just government should be *upheld*.

To *verify* is to *establish* by proof the events or facts given in an account or statement. *Authenticate* is to *establish* something as true or genuine by the testimony of an expert or authority. *Validate* has the same meaning, but is used more commonly of official documents, as passports, birth certificates, etc.

> **ANTONYMS:** *abrogate, annul, cancel, destroy, overthrow, shake, shatter, unsettle, upset, weaken.*

> **PREPOSITIONS:** Confirm a statement *by* testimony; confirm a person *in* a belief.

CONGRATULATE
felicitate

Congratulate means to express one's pleasure in the success or good fortune of another. It implies that one regards the *congratulated* person as very fortunate. *Felicitate,* a more formal term, implies that one regards the other person as very happy, or that one wishes him happiness. Thus a bridegroom is *congratulated* because he is presumed to be lucky; the bride is *felicitated* because she is presumed to be happy.

> **ANTONYMS:** *condole with, console.*

> **PREPOSITIONS:** Congratulate one *on* or *upon* his success.

CONQUER

beat	master	prevail over	subject
checkmate	overcome	put down	subjugate
crush	overmaster	quell	surmount
defeat	overmatch	reduce	vanquish
discomfit	overpower	rout	win
down	overthrow	subdue	worst
humble			

To *conquer* means to gain possession of or mastery over something or some-one; to *vanquish* means to *overpower* or *subdue* someone or something; as, to *conquer* a country; to *vanquish* a foe. *Subjugate* implies utter subjection; etymologically it means to place under a yoke. To *subdue* is to *defeat* and suppress; as, to *subdue* a rebellion. To *reduce* is to force to capitulate; a fortress or a town may be *reduced*, but not an army. One *overcomes* or *surmounts* difficulties or obstacles in one's path.

To *defeat* an enemy is to gain an advantage for the time; to *vanquish* is to *win* a signal victory; to *conquer* is to *overcome* so effectually that the victory is regarded as final. An army is *defeated* when it is driven back or compelled to retire disastrously, with loss of position, military equipment, and men. A defeat is final for a battle, but not necessarily for a campaign. *Beat* is often used interchangeably with *defeat*, but carries the suggestion of greater finality. *Conquer*, in many cases, carries the idea of possession; as, to *conquer* respect, affection, peace, etc. A country is *conquered* when its armies are *defeated* and its territory is occupied by the enemy; it may be *subjected* to indemnity or to various disabilities; it is *subjugated* when it is held helplessly and continuously under military control; it is *subdued* when all resistance has died out. An army is *routed* when it is converted into a mob of fugitives. See **beat.**

ANTONYMS: *capitulate, cede, fail, fall, fly, forfeit, lose, resign, retire, retreat, submit, succumb, surrender, yield.*

CONSCIOUS

advised	aware	cognizant	sensible
apprised	certain	informed	sure
assured	certified		

To be *conscious* of something, one may see, hear, or feel it, and allow it to enter one's mind. Thus one may or may not be *conscious* of one's breathing. One is *aware* of something which one apprehends through one's own senses or about which one is told. *Cognizant* connotes absolute or certain knowledge; as, to be *cognizant* of the facts of the case. *Sensible* implies awareness through feeling or some extra-sensory perception.

One is *aware* of that which exists without him; he is *conscious* of the inner workings of his own mind. *Sensible* may be used in the exact sense of *conscious,* or it may partake of both the senses mentioned above. One may be *sensible* of his own or another's error; he is *conscious* only of his own. A person may feel *assured* or *sure* of something false or non-existent; what he is *aware* of, still more what he is *conscious* of, must be fact. *Sensible* has often a reference to the emotions where *conscious* might apply only to the intellect; to say a culprit is *sensible* of his degradation is more forcible than to say he is *conscious* of it.

ANTONYMS: *cold, dead, deaf, ignorant, insensible, unaware, unconscious.*

PREPOSITION: On the stormy sea, man is conscious *of* the limitation of human power.

CONSEQUENCE

consequent	event	outgrowth	sequel
effect	issue	result	upshot
end	outcome		

A *consequence* is that which follows an act naturally, but less directly than the *effect*. The motion of the piston is the *effect*, and the agitation of the water under the paddle wheels a *consequence* of the expansion of steam in the cylinder. The *result* is, literally, the rebound of an act, depending on many elements; the *issue* is that which flows forth directly; a *result*, that which ends a difficulty; we say the *issue* of a battle, the *result* of a campaign. A *consequent* commonly is that which follows simply in order of time, or by logical inference. The *end* is the actual *outcome* without determination of its relation to what has gone before; it is ordinarily viewed as either the necessary, natural, or logical *outcome*, any *effect, consequence,* or *result* being termed an *end*; as, the *end* of such a course must be ruin.

Effect is that which is directly produced by the action of an efficient cause; we say, "Every *effect* must have an adequate cause." In regard to human actions, *effect* commonly relates to intention; as, the shot took *effect, i.e.,* the *effect* intended. The *event* (from L. *e,* out, and *venio,* come), in this comparison, is primarily exactly the same in meaning as *outcome*; but in use it is more nearly equivalent to *upshot*, signifying the sum and substance of all *effects, consequences,* and *results* of a course of action, or the unforeseen *effect* of something beyond human control. A *sequel* is a logical *consequence*, often after an interval. See **end; event.** Compare **accident; cause; circumstance.**

CONSOLE

comfort   condole with   encourage   solace   sympathize with

To *console* is to alleviate pain or lessen loss by soothing the distress. One *condoles with* another by the expression of kindly sympathy in his trouble; he *encourages* him by the hope of some relief or deliverance; he *comforts* him by whatever act or word tends to bring mind or body to a state of rest and cheer. We *sympathize with* others, not only in sorrow, but in joy. To *solace* is give or find relief or comfort by diverting or cheering thought; as, to *solace* a child with a new book. Compare **alleviate; pity.**

ANTONYMS: *annoy, distress, disturb, grieve, hurt, sadden, trouble, wound.*

CONTAGIOUS

catching	communicable	infectious

Contagious applies to a disease or morbid condition transmitted by direct contact with the afflicted person, or with his breath, effluvia, clothing, or other objects infected by him. *Infectious* applies to all diseases transmitted by micro-organisms, specifically to those resulting from polluted water or air, or from such agents as rats, mosquitoes, fungi, etc. *Communicable* is close to *infectious* in meaning, but stresses transmission rather than the agent or means. *Catching* is a colloquial word for *contagious*.

CONTINUAL

ceaseless	invariable	regular	uninterrupted
constant	perennial	unbroken	unremitting
continuous	perpetual	unceasing	unvarying
incessant			

Continual describes that which is repeatedly renewed after each interruption or intermission; *continuous* refers to *uninterrupted* and *unbroken* continuity, that which goes on unceasingly and indefinitely. *Continual* intervention interferes with *continuous* progress. *Continual* refers to time only; *continuous*, to space and time. *Incessant* and *ceaseless* refer to activity, whereas *continuous* is generally passive; we speak of *incessant* noise, *ceaseless* labor, but a *continuous* road. *Incessant* is usually applied to something that annoys; *unceasing*, to smooth continuance; we speak of the *incessant* clatter of a typewriter, of the *unceasing* flow of a river.

Constant implies persistent uniform recurrence; *perpetual* stresses the long duration of the repetition; *perennial* refers to that which lasts or recurs for a series of years. *Regular* refers to that which recurs or returns at fixed or stated intervals.

CONTRACT

agreement	concordat	entente	pledge
arrangement	convention	indenture	promise
bargain	covenant	obligation	stipulation
cartel	engagement	pact	treaty
compact			

These words involve at least two parties, though an *engagement* or *promise* may be the act of but one. A *contract* is a formal *agreement* between two or more parties for the performance of work at a fixed rate; it is usually in writing and enforceable by law. Mutual *promises* may have the force of a *contract*. A consideration, or stipulated compensation, is essential to convert an *agree-*

ment into a *contract*. A *covenant* in law is a written *contract* under seal. *Covenant* is frequent in religious usage, as *contract* is in law and business. *Compact* is essentially the same as *contract*, and is applied to international *agreements, treaties*, etc., or to written or oral *promises* that involve mutual trust. A *convention*, as compared here, is an *agreement* that can be enforced by law.

A *bargain* is a mutual *agreement* for an exchange of values, without the formality of a *contract*. A *stipulation* is a single item in an *agreement* or *contract*. A *cartel*, although a military *agreement* between belligerent governments, as for the exchange of prisoners, treatment of wounded, etc., is also used in speaking of international *agreements* among business enterprises for the monopolistic regulation of markets for certain products. An *entente* is a friendly *agreement* between nations, generally with reference to foreign affairs; a *concordat* is an *agreement* between church and state. *Indenture* refers specifically to a *contract* between a master and an apprentice.

CONTRARY

antagonistic	different	incompatible	opposed
conflicting	discordant	incongruous	opposite
contradictory	discrepant	inconsistent	unlike
contrasted	dissimilar		

Contrary refers to what is *opposed* in nature or inclination, or *opposite* in direction. Things are *contrary* when the highest degree of each cannot exist in the same object at the same time, but where a middle term is possible, partaking of the qualities of both, as wisdom and folly, or heat and cold. Things are *contradictory* which mutually exclude each other, so that both cannot exist in the same object at the same time, as life and death.

Conflicting statements are *contradictory; contrasted* opinions express differences by comparison. *Dissimilar* and *unlike* refer to things having no resemblance. *Discordant* sounds are out of harmony; a gay tie is *incongruous* when out of harmony with the rest of the attire or unsuitable for an occasion. Things as well as feelings and facts are *incompatible* when they cannot exist together; *inconsistent* remarks contradict each other, *inconsistent* deeds are at variance with some other standard. See **alien** *adj.*; **incongruous; perverse.**

CONTRAST

compare	differentiate	discriminate	distinguish	oppose

Contrast (from L. *contra*, against, and *sto*, stand) is to set in opposition in order to show unlikeness. To *compare* (from L. *con*, together, and *par*, equal) is to place together in order to show likeness or unlikeness. We *contrast* objects that have been already *compared*. We must *compare* them, at least momentarily, even to know that they are different. We *contrast* them when we emphasize their unlikeness in a general way; we *differentiate* them when we note the difference exactly and point by point. We *distinguish* objects when we note a difference that may fall short of *contrast*; we *discriminate* them when we classify or place them by discerning their differences.

PREPOSITION: We contrast one object *with* another.

CONVERSATION

chat	communion	converse	intercourse
colloquy	confabulation	dialogue	parley
communication	conference	discourse	talk

Conversation is, etymologically, an interchange of ideas with some other person or persons. *Talk* may be wholly one-sided. Many brilliant talkers have been incapable of *conversation*. There may be *intercourse* without *conversation*, as by looks, signs, etc.; *communion* is of hearts, with or without words; *communication* is often by writing, and may be uninvited and unreciprocated. *Talk* may denote the mere utterance of words with little thought; thus, we say idle *talk*, empty *talk*, rather than idle or empty *conversation*.

Discourse is now applied chiefly to public addresses. A *conference* is more formal than a *conversation*. *Dialogue* denotes ordinarily an artificial or imaginary *conversation*, generally of two persons, but sometimes of more; or a composition in conversational form. A *colloquy* is indefinite as to number, and generally somewhat informal. A *parley* is a *conversation*, especially with an enemy, to discuss terms of a truce. *Confabulation* is familiar *conversation*; *chat*.

PREPOSITIONS: Conversation *with* friends, *between* or *among* the guests, *about* a matter.

CONVERT

disciple	neophyte	proselyte

A *convert* is a person who has come to one faith from a different belief or from unbelief. A *proselyte* is one who has been led to accept a religious system, whether with or without true faith, or a person who has been won over to a different party or opinion. A *convert* is always understood to be a believer. A *neophyte* is a new *convert*, not yet fully indoctrinated, or not admitted to full privileges. The antonyms below are condemnatory names applied to the *convert* by those whose faith he forsakes. The name *disciple* is given to the follower of a certain faith, without reference to any previous belief or allegiance.

ANTONYMS: *apostate, pervert, renegade.*

CONVEY

carry	move	shift	transmit
change	remove	transfer	transport
give	sell		

Convey, transmit, and *transport* all imply delivery at a destination; as, I will *convey* the information to your friend; air *conveys* sounds (to a listener); *carry* does not necessarily imply delivery, and often does not admit of it. *Transfer* may or may not imply delivery to another person; as, items may be *transferred* from one account to another or a word *transferred* to the following line.

In law, real estate, which cannot be *moved,* is *conveyed* by simply *transferring* title and possession. *Transport* usually refers to material; *transfer, transmit,* and *convey* may refer to immaterial objects; we *transfer* possession, *transmit* intelligence, *convey* ideas, but do not *transport* them. In the case of *convey* the figurative sense now predominates. To *shift* is to *change* the location or direction; to *move* is to *change* position or place; to *remove* generally implies to *change* from an original or settled place to a new one. See **carry.**

ANTONYMS: *cling to, hold, keep, possess, preserve, retain.*

PREPOSITIONS: Convey *to* a friend, a purchaser, etc.; convey *from* the house to the station; convey *by* express, *by* hand, etc.

CONVOKE

assemble	call together	convene	muster
call	collect	gather	summon

Convoke implies a summons to *assemble,* especially when sent to an organized body by a superior authority. A convention is *called* by some officer or officers, as by its president, its executive committee, or some eminent leaders; the delegates are *assembled* or *convened* in a certain place, at a certain hour. *Assemble* and *convene* express more independent action than *convoke.* Parliament is *convoked;* Congress *assembles.* Troops are *mustered;* witnesses and jurymen are *summoned.*

ANTONYMS: *adjourn, break up, disband, discharge, dismiss, disperse, dissolve, prorogue, scatter, separate.*

COUNSEL

admonition	dissuasion	recommendation
advice	exhortation	suggestion
caution	persuasion	warning

Counsel (L. *consulo,* consult) is mutual consultation or deliberation. *Advice* (L. *ad,* to, + *video,* see) is an opinion suggesting or urging some course of action, on the ground of real or assumed superior knowledge. *Advice* may be unsought and even unwelcome; *counsel* is supposed to be desired. Yet the two words so far approach each other that one is said to seek *advice* from a lawyer, while a lawyer who is engaged to give *advice* or to act as an advocate in a legal proceeding is called the *counsel* of the person so employing him. *Counsel* in the general sense, whether as noun or verb, is now somewhat archaic, *advice* being in more common use.

A *warning* notifies or advises in an effort to avoid possible future dangers; an *admonition* includes a gentle reproof for offenses already committed, *advice* against errors, and a *warning* against repetition of faults or oversights. *Caution* stresses the making aware that precautions are necessary to avoid danger and the need to be on guard. *Dissuasion* is *advice* against some action or course; *exhortation* is earnest and formal *advice* to do something well. *Persuasion* includes an effort to convince someone that the *advice* should be followed; *recommendation* merely makes a *suggestion* in advising a course of action.

CRIMINAL

abominable	guilty	nefarious	vile
culpable	illegal	sinful	wicked
felonious	immoral	unlawful	wrong
flagitious	iniquitous	vicious	

Every *criminal* act is *illegal* or *unlawful,* but *illegal* or *unlawful* acts may not be *criminal.* Offenses against public law are *criminal;* offenses against private rights are merely *illegal* or *unlawful.* As a general rule, all acts punishable by fine or imprisonment or both are *criminal* in ivew of the law. It is *illegal* for a man to trespass on another's land, but it is not *criminal;* the trespasser is liable to a civil suit for damages, but not to indictment, fine, or imprisonment. A *felonious* act is a *criminal* act of an aggravated kind, which is punishable by imprisonment in the penitentiary or by death. A *flagitious* crime is one that brings public odium. *Vicious* refers to the indulgence of evil appetites, habits, or passions; *vicious* acts are not necessarily *criminal,* or even *illegal;* we speak of a *vicious* horse. That which is *iniquitous, i.e.,* contrary to equity, may sometimes be done under the forms of law. Ingratitude is *sinful,* hypocrisy is *wicked,* but neither is punishable by human law; hence, neither is *criminal* or *illegal.* Compare **sin.**

ANTONYMS: *innocent, just, lawful, legal, meritorious, moral, right, virtuous.*

CRITERION

gage	proof	standard	touchstone
measure	rule	test	yardstick

A *criterion* is a *standard* believed to have special accuracy or certainty, so that other things may be "judged" by it; the meaning is often strengthened by adjectives; as, a sure or an infallible *criterion*; any fact, truth, or principle, regarded as established, may be a *criterion*. A *standard* is a *measure* of quantity, quality, or value established by law or general consent; it is general recognition and acceptance that makes a *standard*.

A *test* views a person or thing as put upon trial under fixed and approved conditions; as, a *test* for the purity or fineness of gold, for the tensile strength of a rope or wire; a chemical *test* to determine the existence or the quantity of any ingredient in a mixture; certain oaths have been at various times used as *tests* of loyalty. *Touchstone*, formerly denoting a stone supposed to indicate the fineness of gold, is now used only figuratively in the general sense of *test*.

A *gage* is a standard *measure*, or an instrument or device for measuring the amount, force, etc., of something that fluctuates, as rainfall, wind, etc. In its figurative use it partakes of the meaning of *criterion*; as, the *gage* of a man's ability is his willingness to work. *Yardstick*, literally a stick one yard long, is used figuratively to denote a *gage* for measuring some intangible attribute or quality, as honesty, virtue, bravery, or the like.

ANTONYMS: *chance, conjecture, fancy, guess, imagination, probability, possibility, supposition.*

D

DAILY

diurnal   **quotidian**

Daily is the Saxon and popular, *diurnal* the Latin and scientific term. In strict usage, *daily* is the antonym of nightly as *diurnal* is of nocturnal. *Daily* is not, however, held strictly to this use; a physician makes *daily* visits if he calls at some time within each period of twenty-four hours. *Diurnal* is more exact in all its uses; a *diurnal* flower opens or blooms only in daylight; a *diurnal* bird or animal flies or ranges only by day, in contradistinction to nocturnal flowers, birds, etc. A *diurnal* motion exactly fills an astronomical day or the time of one rotation of a planet on its axis, while a *daily* motion is much less definite. *Quotidian* means recurring or occurring every day; a *quotidian* fever is one whose paroxysms take place every day.

ANTONYMS: *nightly, nocturnal.*

DANGER

hazard   **insecurity**   **jeopardy**   **peril**   **risk**

Danger is exposure to possible evil, which may be either near and probable or remote and doubtful; *peril* is exposure to imminent and sharply threatening evil, especially to such as results from violence. An invalid may be in *danger* of pneumonia; a disarmed soldier is in *peril* of death. *Jeopardy* is nearly the same as *peril*, but involves, like *risk*, more of the element of chance or uncertainty; a man tried upon a capital charge is said to be put in *jeopardy* of life. *Insecurity* is a feeble word, but exceedingly broad, applying to the placing of a dish, or the possibilities of a life, a fortune, or a government. Compare *hazard*.

ANTONYMS: *defense, immunity, protection, safeguard, safety, security, shelter.*

DARK

black	gloomy	sable	somber
dim	murky	shadowy	swart
dismal	obscure	shady	swarthy
dusky	opaque		

Strictly, that which is *black* is absolutely destitute of color; that which is *dark* is absolutely destitute of light. In common speech, however, a coat is *black*, though not optically colorless; the night is *dark*, though the stars shine. That is *obscure, shadowy,* or *shady* from which the light is more or less cut off. *Dusky* refers to light or color and is applied to objects which appear as if viewed in fading light; human skin is said to be *swart* or *swarthy* when

quite *dark,* or even verging toward *black. Dim* refers to imperfection of out
line, from distance, darkness, mist, etc., or from some defect of vision. *Opaqu*
objects, as smoked glass, are impervious to light. *Murky* is said of that whic
is at once *dark, obscure,* and *gloomy*; as, a *murky* den; a *murky* sky. Figura
tively, *dark* is emblematic of sadness, agreeing with *somber, dismal, gloomy*
also of moral evil, as a *dark* deed. Of intellectual matter, *dark* is now rarel
used in the old sense of a *dark* saying, etc. Compare **mysterious; obscure.**

> **ANTONYMS:** *bright, brilliant, clear, crystalline, dazzling,
> gleaming, glowing, illumined, light, lucid, luminous, radiant,
> shining, transparent, white.*

DEBASE

abase	depress	dishonor	lower
bring low	discredit	humble	reduce
cast down	disgrace	humiliate	sink
degrade			

Debase, to *lower* or depreciate worth, value, purity, etc., applies to qualit
or character. The coinage is *debased* by excess of alloy; the man, by vice
Abase expresses a lowering of self-esteem or outward conditions. "Exalt hir
that is low, and *abase* him that is high." *Ezek.* xxi, 26. *Humble* suggests a los
of prestige, either in outward rank or in esteem; when one is said to *humbl*
himself, he either has or affects to have humility of heart. *Humiliate* alway
includes ignominy. To *disgrace* may be to bring shame upon others, but th
word is chiefly and increasingly applied to such moral odium as one by hi
own acts brings upon himself; the noun *disgrace* retains more of the passiv
sense than the verb; he *disgraced* himself by his conduct; he brought *disgrac*
upon his family. A sense of unworthiness *humbles*; a shameful insult *humil*
ates; imprisonment for crime *disgraces.*

Degrade may refer either to station or to character. An officer is *degrade*
by being reduced to the ranks, *disgraced* by cowardice; drunkenness *degrade*
Misfortune or injustice may *abase* or *depress*; nothing but ill-doing can *debas*
or *disgrace.* To *dishonor* a person is to deprive him of honor that should o
might be given. To *discredit* one is to injure his reputation, as for veracity o
solvency.

> **ANTONYMS:** *advance, aggrandize, dignify, elevate, exalt,
> honor, promote, raise, uplift.*

DECAY

corrupt	disintegrate	putrefy	spoil
decompose	molder	rot	

Decay connotes a gradual change from a state of soundness and health. *Rot* is a strong word, ordinarily esteemed coarse, but on occasion capable of approved emphatic use; as, "the name of the wicked shall *rot*," *Prov.* x, 7; *decay* and *decompose* are now common euphemisms. A substance is *decomposed* when resolved into its original elements by any process; it is *decayed* when resolved into its original elements by natural processes; it *decays* gradually, but may be instantly *decomposed*, as water into oxygen and hydrogen; to say that a thing is *decayed* may denote only a partial result, but to say it is *decomposed* ordinarily implies that the change is complete or nearly so.

Disintegrate suggests the breaking down of a substance so that its wholeness or the cohesiveness of its component particles is destroyed. *Putrefy* and the adjectives *putrid* and *putrescent*, and the nouns *putridity* and *putrescence*, are used almost exclusively of animal matter in a state of decomposition, the more general word *decay* being used of either animal or vegetable substances.

DECEIVER

cheat	dissembler	hypocrite	impostor	pretender

Deceiver is the most comprehensive term, including all the other words of the group. The *deceiver* seeks to give false impressions of any matter in which he has an end to gain; the *dissembler* or *hypocrite* seeks to give false impressions in regard to himself. A *hypocrite* (from Gr. *hypokrites*, one who answers on the stage, an actor, especially a mimic actor) is one who acts a false part, or assumes a character other than the real. The *dissembler* is content if he can keep some base conduct or evil purpose from being discovered; the *hypocrite* seeks not merely to cover his vices, but to gain credit for virtue. The *cheat* and *impostor* endeavor to make something out of those they may deceive. The *cheat* is the inferior and more mercenary; the *impostor* may aspire to a fortune or a throne. Compare **hypocrisy.**

DECEPTION

chicanery	dissimulation	finesse	lying
craft	double-dealing	fraud	prevarication
cunning	duplicity	guile	subterfuge
deceit	equivocation	hypocrisy	trickery
deceitfulness	fabrication	imposition	untruth
delusion	falsehood	lie	

Deceit is the habit, *deception* the act; *guile* applies to the disposition out of which *deceit* and *deception* grow, and also to their actual practice. A *lie*, *lying*, or *falsehood*, is the uttering of what one knows to be false with intent to deceive. The novel or drama is not a *lie*, because not meant to deceive; the ancient teaching that the earth was flat was not a *lie*, because not then known to be false. *Untruth* is more than lack of accuracy, implying always lack of veracity; but it is a somewhat milder and more dignified word than *lie*. *Falsehood* and *lying* are in utterance; *deceit* and *deception* may be merely in act or implication. *Deception* may be innocent, and even unintentional, as in the case of an optical illusion; *deceit* always involves injurious intent.

Craft and *cunning* have not necessarily any moral quality; they are common traits of animals, but stand rather low in the human scale. *Duplicity* is the habitual speaking or acting with intent to appear to mean what one does not. *Dissimulation* is rather a concealing of what is than a pretense of what is not. *Equivocation* is the saying or stating of one thing in order that something other and different may be understood. *Finesse* is simply an adroit and delicate management of a matter for one's own side, not necessarily involving *deceit*.

A *subterfuge* is a base means of evasion, and implies cowardice; *chicanery* is the use of petty *trickery*, especially in legal practice. *Double-dealing* invariably has the connotation of *duplicity*. *Fraud* connotes abuse of the truth in order to prevail upon someone to give up a prized possession, legal right, or the like. See **fallacy; fiction; fraud; hypocrisy; trick.**

ANTONYMS: *candor, fair dealing, frankness, guilelessness, honesty, openness, simplicity, sincerity, truth, veracity.*

DECEPTIVE

deceitful   **delusive**   **illusive**   **illusory**

Deceptive is having power or tendency to deceive or mislead. Persons are *deceitful*; things are *deceptive*. We speak of a *deceitful*, but not of a *deceptive* man. We speak, however, of *deceitful* promises, as involving personal intent to deceive. It is more accurate to say *deceptive* than *deceitful* appearances. *Delusive* refers to a belief that, though false, is accepted as true; *illusive* refers to imaginary false impressions about existing things. A very sick man may have the *delusive* idea that he is a boy; conjuror's tricks are *illusive*. *Illusory*, often used interchangeably with *illusive*, connotes tending to deceive or producing illusion. See **bad.** Compare **delusion.**

ANTONYMS: *fair, frank, genuine, honest, open, real, truthful, veracious.*

DEFENSE

apology	guard	rampart	shelter
bulwark	justification	resistance	shield
fortress	protection	safeguard	vindication

Defense implies an active repelling of some hostile power or influence; *protection*, a passive placing of something between the attacking power and the object to be protected. The guns of a fortress are its *defense*; its walls are its *protection*. The weak may speak or act in *defense* of the strong; none but the powerful can assure others of *protection*. A *defense* is ordinarily against actual attack; *protection* is against possible as well as actual dangers. We speak of *defense* against an assault, *protection* from the cold. *Vindication* is a triumphant *defense* of character and conduct against charges of error or wrong. A *safeguard* protects or guards from harm; a *shelter* covers or protects from danger or exposure; a *shield* is a device used for *protection* or *defense*. *Apology,* as compared here, is an attempt to justify or defend belief or action. See **barrier.** Compare **apology.**

ANTONYMS: *abandonment, betrayal, capitulation, desertion, flight, surrender.*

PREPOSITIONS: Defense *against* assault or assailants; in law, defense *to* an action, *from* the testimony.

DEFILE

befoul	infect	spoil	taint
contaminate	pollute	stain	tarnish
corrupt	soil	sully	vitiate

To *defile* is to make unclean that which should be pure or spotless; hence it carries the implication of desecration or profanation. *Contaminate* suggests the destruction of purity by the entry of something external; as, the reservoir was *contaminated* by sewage from the camp. *Taint* expresses the result of *contamination*; that which is *tainted* is no longer pure or wholesome. The hand may be *defiled* by a touch of pitch; swine that have been wallowing in the mud are *befouled*. *Contaminate* and *infect* refer to something evil that deeply pervades and permeates, as the human body or mind. *Pollute* is used chiefly of liquids; as, water *polluted* with sewage. *Tainted* meat is repulsive; *infected* meat contains germs of disease. A *soiled* garment may be cleansed by washing; a *stained* garment necessitates the use of a stronger agent than water alone to cleanse it; a *spoiled* garment is beyond cleansing or repair. Bright metal is *tarnished* by exposure; a fair sheet is *sullied* by a dirty hand. *Pollute* has also a reference to sacrilege; as to *pollute* a sanctuary, an altar, or an ordinance. The innocent are often *contaminated* by association with the wicked; the vicious are more and more *corrupted* by their own excesses. We speak of a *vitiated* taste or style; fraud *vitiates* a title or a contract.

ANTONYMS: *clean, cleanse, disinfect, hallow, purify, sanctify, wash.*

PREPOSITIONS: The temple was defiled *with* blood; defiled *by* sacrilegious deeds.

DEFINITION

comment	description	exposition	rendering
commentary	explanation	interpretation	translation

A *definition* is exact, an *explanation* general; a *definition* is formal, a *description* pictorial. A *definition* must include all that belongs to the object defined, and exclude all that does not; a *description* may include only some general features; an *explanation* may simply throw light upon some point of special difficulty. An *exposition* undertakes to state more fully what is compactly given or only implied in the text; as, an *exposition* of Scripture. *Interpretation* is ordinarily a statement giving the doubtful or hidden meaning of that which is recondite or perplexing; as, the *interpretation* of a dream, a riddle, or of some difficult passage. *Definition, explanation, exposition, and interpretation* are ordinarily blended in a *commentary*, which may also include *description*. A *comment* is upon a single passage; a *commentary* may be the same, but is usually understood to be a volume of *comments*. A *translation* is a *rendering* of the words of one language, or their implications, into those of another, or the language of one period into that of another; *interpretation* is sometimes used as an equivalent term.

DELEGATE

deputy	legate	proxy	representative	substitute

These words agree in designating one who acts in the place of some other or others. In strict usage the *delegate* or *deputy* is more limited in function and more closely bound by instructions than a *representative*. A single office may have a *deputy*; many persons combine to choose a *delegate* or *representative*. In the United States informal assemblies send *delegates* to nominating conventions with no legislative authority; *representatives* are legally elected to Congress and the various legislatures, with lawmaking power. A *proxy* is one person authorized to act for another. The *legate* is an ecclesiastical officer representing the Pope.

DELIBERATE

confer	debate	ponder	ruminate
consider	meditate	reflect	weigh
consult	muse		

To *deliberate* is to take careful, unhurried thought on some matter, weighing the value of each alternative offered. An individual *considers, meditates, ponders, reflects,* by himself; he *weighs* a matter in his own mind, and is sometimes said even to *debate* with himself. To *ponder* is to *consider*, but without he implication of reaching a decision, as is implied by *weigh*. *Consult* and *confer* always imply two or more persons, as does *debate*, unless expressly mited as above. *Confer* suggests the interchange of counsel, advice, or information; *consult* indicates almost exclusively seeking information. A man confers with his associates about a new investment; he *consults* his physician about is health; he may *confer* with him on matters of general interest. He *consults* dictionary, but does not *confer* with it.

Deliberate, which can be applied to a single individual, is also the word for great number, while *consult* is ordinarily limited to a few; a committee nsults; an assembly *deliberates*. *Deliberating* always carries the idea of slowess; *consulting* is compatible with haste; we can speak of a hasty consultaon, not of a hasty deliberation. *Debate* implies opposing views; *deliberate*, mply a gathering and balancing of all facts and reasons. We *consider* or eliberate with a view to action, while meditation may be quite purposeless. tymologically *ruminate* means to chew the cud, as a cow; hence the modern eaning of going over one topic or subject again and again. To *muse* is to be bsorbed in thought, with the suggestion of daydreaming or abstraction.

PREPOSITIONS: We deliberate *on* or *upon*, also *about* or *concerning* a matter: the first two are preferable.

DELICIOUS

dainty	delectable	delightful	exquisite	luscious	savory

That is *delicious* which affords a gratification at once vivid and delicate the senses, especially to those of taste and smell, as, *delicious* fruit, a licious odor; *luscious* has a kindred but more fulsome meaning, inclining ward a cloying excess of sweetness or richness. *Savory* is applied chiefly to oked food made palatable by spices and condiments. *Delightful* may be plied to the higher gratifications of sense, as *delightful* music, but is also ed for that which is mental and spiritual. *Delicious* has a limited use in this ay; as, a *delicious* bit of poetry; the word is sometimes used ironically for me pleasing absurdity; as, this is *delicious*! *Delectable* is used interchangely with *delightful* and *delicious*, though it suggests a more discriminating and fined enjoyment; as, a *delectable* morsel or story. See **pleasant.**

ANTONYMS: *acrid, bitter, loathsome, nauseous, repulsive, unpalatable, unsavory.*

DELIVER

discharge	free	ransom	release	save
emancipate	liberate	redeem	rescue	set free

To *deliver*, as compared here, is to *free* from something imposed by others, ther restraint or evil; to *liberate* is to *free* from confinement. To *emancipate* (literally, to take out of the hands of) is to *free* from legal restraint or slavery. We *free* ourselves or *set* ourselves *free* from something; someone else *sets* u *free*. To *ransom* or *redeem*, a price is always demanded. To *rescue* is t *deliver* from danger or misfortune; to *save* is to *rescue*, but it often includ the idea of preserving afterward. *Release* and *discharge* refer to persons an things.

> **ANTONYMS:** *betray, capture, confine, enslave, imprison, incarcerate, oppress.*

> **PREPOSITIONS:** Deliver *from* an enemy; deliver *to* the authorities; deliver (a speech) *at* a place, *in* a hall, *on* a platform, *before* an audience.

DELUSION

error   fallacy   hallucination   illusion   phantasm

All the words listed above agree in denoting something which appears t be true, but which is really false. *Delusion* denotes deception either by onese or by others, and may imply a deranged mind, gullibility, or the inability t distinguish between that which appears to be and that which actually is true genuine; as, *delusions* of grandeur. An *illusion* does not indicate mental di order or the inability to discern true and false, but rather ascribes reality truth to that which merely seems to be real or true. A *delusion* is a mistak conviction, an *illusion* is a mistaken perception or inference. An *illusion* ma be wholly of the senses; a *delusion* always involves some mental error. In optical *illusion* the observer sees either what does not exist or what exis otherwise than as he sees it, as when in a mirage distant springs and tre appear close at hand. We speak of the *illusions* of fancy or of hope, but the *delusions* of the insane. A *hallucination* is a false image or belief which h nothing, outside of the disordered mind, to suggest it; as, the *hallucinatio* of delirium tremens. See **deception; insanity.**

> **ANTONYMS:** *actuality, certainty, fact, reality, truth, verity.*

DEMOLISH

destroy   overthrow   overturn   raze   ruin

Demolish implies smashing or pulling to bits, with nothing left but a pi of ruins. A building, monument, or other structure is *demolished* when reduce to a shapeless mass; it is *razed* when leveled with the ground; it is *destroy* when its structural unity is gone, whether or not its component parts remai An edifice is *destroyed* by fire or earthquake; it is *demolished* by bombar ment; it is *ruined* when, by violence or neglect, it has become unfit for human habitation. See **abolish; break.**

ANTONYMS: *build, construct, create, make, repair, restore.*

DEMONSTRATION

certainty	consequence	evidence	inference
conclusion	deduction	induction	proof

Demonstration, in the strict and proper sense, is the highest form of *proof,* and gives the most absolute *certainty,* but cannot be applied outside of pure mathematics or other strictly deductive reasoning; there can be *proof* and *certainty,* however, in matters that do not admit of *demonstration.* A *conclusion* is the absolute and necessary result of the admission of certain premises; an *inference* is a probable *conclusion* toward which known facts, statements, or admissions point, but which they do not absolutely establish; sound premises, together with their necessary *conclusion,* constitute a *demonstration.* *Deduction* is reasoning from given premises to their necessary *conclusion.* *Evidence* is that which tends to show a thing to be true; in the widest sense, as including self-*evidence* or consciousness, it is the basis of all knowledge. *Proof* in the strict sense is complete, irresistible *evidence;* as, there was much *evidence* against the accused, but not amounting to *proof* of guilt. Moral *certainty* is a conviction resting on such *evidence* as puts a matter beyond reasonable doubt, while not so irresistible as *demonstration.* See **hypothesis; inference.**

DEPENDENT

conditional	contingent	relative

These four adjectives are synonymous when they define something which has its existence determined by something else. A thing is *dependent* which cannot exist or come into being by itself. Thus, everything is *dependent* save that which is original, infinite, or absolute. A *conditional* occurrence or event is one whose realization or fulfilment depends on the observance of certain conditions. An army which makes a *conditional* surrender reserves for itself certain terms, as the right to keep its officers.

Contingent implies possibility; if we say that the existence of a third major political party is *contingent* on future developments, we imply that no such party now exists, and whether or not it ever will exist depends on some uncertain event in the future. Something is *relative* which cannot be thought of apart from its relation or reference to something else, and which is inevitably affected by the flaws, fluctuations, limitations, etc., of the other thing;

as, prices for poultry are *relative* to the available supply and the current demand.

ANTONYMS: *absolute, causal, independent, infinite, original.*

DESIGN

aim	intent	plan	purpose
device	intention	project	scheme
end	object	proposal	strategy
final cause			

Design refers to the adaptation of means to an *end*, the correspondence and coordination of parts, or of separate acts, to produce a result; *intent* and *purpose* overleap all particulars, and fasten on the *end* itself. *Intention* is simply the more familiar form of the legal and philosophical *intent*. *Plan* relates to details of form, structure, and action, in themselves; *design* considers these same details all as a means to an *end*. The *plan* of a campaign may be for a series of sharp attacks, with the *design* of thus surprising and overpowering the enemy. A man comes to a fixed *intention* to kill his enemy; he forms a *plan* to entrap him into his power, with the *design* of then compassing his death; as the law cannot read the heart, it can only infer the *intent* from the evidences of *design*. The *strategy* underlying a *plan* of attack is expressed in certain tactics, limited in scope, but fitting into an over-all *design*. *Intent* denotes a straining, stretching forth toward an *object*; *purpose*, simply the placing it before oneself; hence, we speak of the *purpose* rather than the *intent* or *intention* of God. *Intention* contemplates the possibility of failure; *purpose* looks to assured success; *intent* or *intention* refers especially to the state of mind of the actor; *purpose*, to the result of the action. See **aim; cause; idea; model.**

PREPOSITIONS: The design *of* defrauding; the design *of* a building; a design *for* a statue.

DESIRE

appetence	coveting	inclination	propensity
appetite	craving	longing	urge
aspiration	hankering	proclivity	wish
concupiscence			

Desire is an earnest *longing* or wishing for something. Its range is from the highest objects to the lowest; for an object near at hand, or near in thought, and viewed as attainable; a *wish* may be for what is remote or uncertain, or even for what is recognized as impossible. *Inclination* is the mildest of these terms; it is a quiet, or even a vague or unconscious, tendency. Even when we speak of a strong or decided *inclination* we do not express the intensity of *desire.*

Craving is stronger than *hankering*; *hankering* may be the result of a fitful and capricious *appetite* which demands satisfaction; *craving* may be the imperious and reasonable demand of the whole nature. *Longing* is a reaching out with deep and persistent demand for that which is viewed as now distant but at some time attainable; as, the captive's *longing* for release. *Coveting* ordinarily denotes wrong *desire* for that which is another's. *Propensity* is a natural *inclination*, often an uncontrollable *longing*; a *proclivity* includes a former indulgence in the tendency. An *urge* is a strong *desire* that propels toward action. See **appetite.**

ANTONYMS: See synonyms for **antipathy.**

PREPOSITIONS: The desire *of* the majority; a desire *for* excellence.

DESPAIR

desperation   despondency   discouragement   hopelessness

Despair is the utter abandonment of hope. *Discouragement* is the result of so much repulse or failure as wears out courage. *Discouragements* too frequent and long continued may produce a settled *hopelessness. Hopelessness* is negative, and may result from simple apathy; it implies loss of hope, often followed by discontinuance of effort; *despondency* and *despair* are more emphatic and decided. *Despondency* is an incapacity for the present exercise of hope; it relaxes energy and effort and is always attended with sadness or distress; *despair* may produce a stony calmness, or it may lead to *desperation. Desperation* is energized *despair*, vigorous in action, reckless of consequences.

ANTONYMS: *anticipation, assurance, cheer, confidence, courage, elation, encouragement, expectancy, expectation, hope, hopefulness, trust.*

DETERMINATION

decision   resolution   resolve

Determination, as compared here, is a setting of the limits within which one must act; *resolve* is a separating of the essential act from all that might cause doubt or hesitation. *Resolve* always refers to a single act; *resolution* may have the same meaning, or it may refer to the habit of mind which readily forms and adheres to a *resolve. Decision* is literally a cutting off, or cutting short, of debate or questioning; *decision* or *determination* especially marks the beginning of action; *resolution* holds out to the end.

ANTONYMS: *doubt, faltering, fickleness, hesitancy, hesitation, indecision, instability, irresolution, vacillation, wavering.*

DEVOTE

allot	apportion	assign	dedicate	hallow
apply	appropriate	consecrate	destine	set apart

Devote (from L. *de*, from, + *voveo*, from *votum*, vow) was originally to *set apart* from oneself or from ordinary use to some sacred purpose which might be destructive. We sometimes speak of persons or things as *devoted* to death, destruction, or ruin; in common use, however, to *devote* is to *set apart* with a sacred or earnest purpose to some desirable object; as, a young man *devotes* himself to the ministry; a sum of money is *devoted* to charity; this portion of the book is *devoted* to the study of evolution. It is chiefly by the lingering touch of sacredness that *devote* differs from *apply* when the two words are used as synonyms; a person *applies* himself to study as a matter of fact and may *allot* himself certain hours for it; he *devotes* himself to study from some earnest purpose behind the fact.

Consecrate, dedicate, devote, and *hallow* are all originally words of sacred meaning; as, to *consecrate* ground for a cemetery; to *dedicate* a church to divine worship; to *devote* oneself to prayer; to *hallow* the Sabbath day. *Consecrate* and *hallow* retain their original sacredness, but *dedicate* and *devote* have drifted far away. Thus, to *dedicate* a book is for the author to preface it with a complimentary inscription bearing the name of a friend or patron. See **allot; apply.**

> **ANTONYMS:** *abuse, alienate, desecrate, misapply, misappropriate, misuse, pervert, squander, waste.*

DEVOUT

godly	moral	pious	righteous
holy	pietistic	religious	sanctimonious

Devout, in this comparison, implies *religious,* a feeling or manifestation of devotion to religion; *pious* emphasizes a reverential spirit and *religious* obligations, or duties undertaken in the name of religion; *pietistic* stresses *religious* emotionalism. *Righteous* refers to doing what is right; *moral,* to either the knowledge or practice of right action. *Godly* suggests obedience to God's commands; *holy* is set apart for the service of God; *sanctimonious* is a negative term and refers to a pretense of holiness or devotion, rather than honest and sincere observance of religious belief.

DEXTERITY

adroitness	cleverness	readiness
aptitude	expertness	skill

Dexterity (from L. *dexter*, right, right-hand) and *adroitness* (from F. *à, to,* and *droit*, right) might each be rendered "right-handedness"; but *adroitness* carries more of the idea of eluding, parrying, or checking some hostile movement, or taking advantage of another in controversy; *dexterity* conveys the idea of doing, accomplishing something readily, easily, and well, without reference to any action of others. We speak of *adroitness* in fencing, boxing, or debate; of *dexterity* in horsemanship, in the use of tools, weapons, etc. *Aptitude* (from L. *aptus*, fit, fitted) is a natural *readiness*, which by practice may be developed into *dexterity*. *Skill* is more exact to line, rule, and method than *dexterity*. *Dexterity* cannot be communicated, and oftentimes cannot even be explained by its possessor; *skill* to a very great extent can be imparted; "*skilled* workmen" in various trades are numbered by thousands. We exert power but use *skill*. See **address; power.** Compare **clever; skilful.**

> **PREPOSITIONS:** Dexterity *of* hand, *of* movement, *of* management, *with* the pen, *in* action, *in* manipulating men, *at* cards.

DICTION

expression	phrase	style	vocabulary
language	phraseology	verbiage	wording

An author's *diction* is strictly his choice and use of words, with no special reference to thought; *expression* regards the words simply as the vehicle of the thought. *Phrase* and *phraseology* apply to words or combinations of words which are somewhat technical; as, in legal *phraseology*; in military *phrase*. *Diction* is general; *wording* is limited; we speak of the *diction* of an author or of a work, the *wording* of a proposition, of a resolution, etc. The *language* of a writer or speaker may be the national speech he employs; as, the English or French *language*; or the word may denote his use of that *language*; as, the author's *language* is well (or ill) chosen.

Style includes *diction, expression,* rhetorical figures such as metaphor and simile, the effect of an author's prevailing tone of thought, of his personal traits—in short, all that makes up the clothing of thought in words; thus, we speak of a figurative *style*, a frigid or an argumentative *style*, etc., or of the *style of* Macaulay or others. An author's *vocabulary* is the range of words which he brings into his use. *Verbiage* implies wordiness, often without much sense. See **language.**

DIE

cease	decline	expire	perish
decease	depart	fade	wither

Die, to go out of life, become destitute of vital power and action, is figuratively applied to anything which has the appearance of life.

> Where the *dying* night-lamp flickers.   TENNYSON

An echo, a strain of music, a tempest, a topic, an issue, *dies. Expire* (literally, to breathe out) is a softer word for *die*; it is used figuratively of things that *cease* to exist by reaching a natural limit; as, a lease *expires*; the time has expired. To *perish* (literally, in Latin, to go through, as in English we say, "the fire goes out") is generally used of death by privation or exposure; as, "I *perish* with hunger," *Luke* xv, 17; sometimes, of death by violence. Knowledge and fame, art and empires, may be said to *perish*; the word denotes utter destruction and decay. To *decease*, or depart from this life, is a legal or rhetorical term. *Wither* and *fade* apply to the drying up of fluid and the loss of life that follows.

> **ANTONYMS:** *be born, begin, be immortal, come into being, come to life, exist, flourish, grow, live, rise again, rise from the dead, survive.*

> **PREPOSITIONS:** To die *of* fever, *by* violence; rarely, *with* the sword, famine, etc. (*Ezek.* vii, 15); to die *for* one's country; to die *at* sea, *in* one's bed, *in* agony; die *to* the world.

DIFFERENCE

contrariety	discrimination	distinction	inequality
contrast	disparity	divergence	unlikeness
disagreement	dissimilarity	diversity	variation
discrepancy	dissimilitude	inconsistency	variety

Difference is the state or quality of being unlike or the amount of such *unlikeness*. A *difference* is in the things compared; a *discrimination* is in our judgment of them; a *distinction* is in our definition or description or mental image of them. Careful *discrimination* of real *differences* results in clear *distinctions*. *Disparity* is stronger than *inequality*, implying that one thing falls far below another; as, the *disparity* of our achievements when compared with our ideals. *Dissimilarity* is between things sharply contrasted; *unlikeness* implies *difference* in things of the same species or category; there may be a *difference* between those almost alike. There is a *discrepancy* in accounts that fail to balance.

Variety involves more than two objects; so, in general, does *diversity*; *variation* is a *difference* in the condition or action of the same object at different times. *Disagreement* is not merely the lack, but the opposite, of agreement; it is a mild word for opposition and conflict; *difference* is sometimes used in the same sense. *Contrariety* is something that is opposite in nature, an *inconsistency*. *Divergence* implies deviating from a standard; *dissimilitude* stresses lack of likeness or resemblance. Compare **contrast.**

> **ANTONYMS:** *agreement, consonance, harmony, identity, likeness, resemblance, sameness, similarity, uniformity, unity.*

PREPOSITIONS: Difference *between* the old and the new; differences *among* men; a difference *in* character, *of* action, *of* style; (less frequently) a difference (controversy) *with* a person; a difference *of* one thing *from* (incorrectly *to*) another.

DIFFICULT

| arduous | hard | onerous | toilsome |
| exhausting | laborious | severe | trying |

Difficult is not used of that which merely taxes physical force; a dead lift is called *hard* rather than *difficult*; breaking stone on the road would be called *hard* rather than *difficult* work; that is *difficult* which involves skill, sagacity, or address, with or without a considerable expenditure of physical force; a geometrical problem may be *difficult* to solve, a tangled skein to unravel; a mountain *difficult* to ascend. *Hard* may be active or passive; a thing may be *hard* to do or *hard* to bear.

Arduous (from L. *arduus*, steep) signifies primarily so steep and lofty as to be *difficult* of ascent, and hence applies to that which involves great and sustained exertion and ordinarily for a lofty aim; great learning can be won only by *arduous* toil. *Hard* applies to anything that resists our endeavors, as a scarcely penetrable mass resists our physical force. Anything is *hard* that involves tax and strain whether of the physical or mental powers. *Arduous* is always active. That which is *laborious* or *toilsome* simply requires the steady application of labor or toil till accomplished; *toilsome* is the stronger word. That which is *onerous* (from L. *onus*, a burden) is mentally burdensome or oppressive. Responsibility may be *onerous* even when it involves no special exertion. We speak of a *severe* test, a *trying* experience, an *exhausting* journey.

ANTONYMS: *easy, facile, light, pleasant, slight, trifling, trivial.*

DIP

| bury | duck | immerse | sink |
| douse | immerge | plunge | submerge |

Dip is Old English, while *immerse* is Latin for the same initial act; *dip* is accordingly the more popular and commonplace, *immerse* the more elegant and dignified expression in many cases. Baptists *immerse* those they baptize. To *dip* and to *immerse* alike signify to *bury* or *submerge* some object in a liquid. *Immerse* suggests more absolute completeness of the action; one may *dip* his sleeve or *dip* a sponge in a liquid, if he but touches the edge; if he *immerses* it, he completely *sinks* it under, and covers it with the liquid. Figuratively, a person *immersed* in something is engrossed in it. *Submerge* implies that the object cannot be readily removed, if at all; as, a *submerged* wreck.

To *plunge* is to *immerse* suddenly and violently, for which *douse* and *duck* are colloquial terms. To *immerge* is to *plunge* into or under.

DIRECTION

| aim | bearing | course | inclination | tendency | way |

The *direction* of an object is the line of motion or of vision toward it, or the line in which the object is moving, considered from our own actual or mental standpoint. *Way*, literally the road or path, comes naturally to mean the *direction* of the road or path; conversationally, *way* is almost a perfect synonym of *direction*; as, which *way* did he go? or, in which *direction*? *Bearing* is the direction in which an object is seen with reference to another, and especially with reference to the points of the compass. *Course* is the *direction* of a moving object; *inclination*, that toward which a stationary object leans; *tendency*, the *direction* toward which anything stretches or reaches out; *tendency* is stronger and more active than *inclination*. See **aim; order.**

DISCERN

| behold | discriminate | espy | perceive | see |
| descry | distinguish | observe | recognize | |

What we *discern* we *see* apart from all other objects; what we *discriminate* we judge apart; what we *distinguish* we mark apart, or recognize by some special mark or manifest difference. We *discriminate* by real differences; we *distinguish* by outward signs; a police officer is readily *distinguished* from a fireman by his uniform. Objects may be dimly *discerned* at twilight, when yet we cannot clearly *distinguish* one from another. We *descry* (originally *espy*) what is difficult to discover. *Observe* implies to see and take notice; *perceive* is to know or *recognize* through any of the senses, and it generally connotes mental observation. Compare **discover; look.**

DISCOVER

ascertain	discern	expose	find	invent
descry	disclose	ferret out	find out	unearth
detect				

Of human actions or character, *discover* may be used in either the good or the bad sense, oftener in the good; *detect* is nearly always used in a bad sense; he was *detected* in a fraud; real merit is sure to be *discovered*. In scientific language, *detect* is used of delicate indications that appear in course of careful watching; as, a slight fluttering of the pulse could be *detected*. We *discover* what has existed but has not been known to us; we *invent* combinations or arrangements not before in use; Columbus *discovered* America; Morse *invented* the electric telegraph.

Find is the most general word for every means of coming to know what was not before certainly known; to *discover* by search or study, or by accident. A man *finds* in the road some stranger's purse, or *finds* his own which he is searching for. The expert *discovers* or *detects* an error in an account; the auditor *finds* the account to be correct. We *ascertain* or *find out* for a certainty by examining or experimenting; we *disclose* by uncovering, often something secret or hidden; we *expose* what we uncover and display. Compare **discern.**

ANTONYMS: See synonyms for **hide.**

DISEASE

affection	disorder	indisposition	sickness
ailment	distemper	infirmity	unhealthiness
complaint	illness	malady	unsoundness

Disease is the general term for any deviation from health, either of the whole body or organism or of any of its parts or organs, caused by a parasite or toxin, or by faulty diet; as, his body was wasted away by *disease.* When used in names of specific physical disorders, it suggests that the symptoms and causes are known; as, Addison's *disease*; skin *disease.*

Malady and *ailment* are chiefly used with reference to human beings; *ailment* does not necessarily connote seriousness; as, the common cold is often a minor *ailment. Malady*, however, nearly always refers to a deeply rooted *disease*, one that is chronic and, usually, serious; *infirmity*, though often considered as implying a general breakdown of the body through age, also implies a bodily defect, perhaps resulting from *disease*, in one who is otherwise physically sound; deafness is an *infirmity*; epilepsy is a *malady*, though often so mild in form as to be no more than an *infirmity. Distemper* is almost invariably applied to *diseases* of animals, particularly to a catarrhal *disorder* of young dogs and to an infectious throat *disease* of horses.

There is now, in England, a tendency to restrict the words *sick* and *sickness* to nausea, especially violent nausea, and to hold *ill* and *illness* as the only proper words to use in a general sense. This distinction has received but a very limited acceptance in the United States, where *sick* and *sickness* have the earlier and wider usage.

ANTONYMS: *health, robustness, soundness, strength, sturdiness, vigor.*

DISPARAGE

belittle	derogate from	dishonor	underestimate
carp at	detract from	lower	underrate
decry	discredit	minimize	undervalue
depreciate			

To *disparage* is to *belittle* subtly or insidiously, as by damaging comparison or by faint praise; it is used only of things. To *depreciate* is to represent something or someone as smaller or less important than it or he actually is. *Belittle* and *minimize* both carry the implication of depreciation. To *belittle* is to try to make something seem ridiculously small or worthless; to *minimize* is to make it seem as small as possible.

Derogate from and *detract from* both emphasize the idea of taking away or lowering. Carping critics cannot *derogate from* the merit of a truly great writer, nor can slander *detract from* his reputation.

To *decry* is to condemn or censure in some noisy, public, or conspicuous manner. A witness or a statement is *discredited*; a good name is *dishonored* by unworthy conduct; we *underestimate* in our own minds; we may *underrate* or *undervalue* in statement to others. These words are used, with few exceptions, of things such as qualities, merits, attainments, honor, virtue, etc. A man's achievements are *disparaged*, his motives *depreciated*, his professions *discredited*; he himself is calumniated, slandered, etc. See **slander.**

ANTONYMS: See synonyms for **praise.**

DISPLACE

confuse	**derange**	**disturb**	**mislay**	**remove**
crowd out	**disarrange**	**jumble**	**misplace**	**unsettle**

Objects are *displaced* when moved out of the place they have occupied; they are *misplaced* when put into a place where they should not be. One may know where to find what he has *misplaced*; what he has *mislaid* he cannot locate.

To *derange* is to put out of place one or more parts of a carefully regulated or adjusted system or organism, with a consequent confusion or upsetting of a normal condition. Inflation *deranges* the economy of a nation; one's mind is *deranged* by great sorrow. *Disarrange*, on the other hand, may imply nothing more than a slight change in an established order or system; as, some inexperienced person had *disarranged* his carefully filed papers.

Disturb implies the introduction of a force or influence that *unsettles* or *disarranges* an orderly, fixed course or plan. One's thoughts are *disturbed* by a noisy interruption; a magnetic needle is *disturbed* by the presence of iron.

ANTONYMS: *adjust, array, assort, classify, dispose, group, order, place, put in order, put in place, set in order, sort.*

DISPUTE

antagonize	**combat**	**debate**	**question**
argue	**contend**	**discuss**	**reason**
battle	**contest**	**oppose**	**wrangle**
challenge	**controvert**	**quarrel**	

To *dispute* is to *argue*, often rather heatedly, in opposition to some point. To *argue* is to offer reasons supporting or opposing some proposition; to *antagonize* is to make hostile, often by provoking to opposition. *Battle* refers either to verbal or to physical disputes; *combat*, to physical disputes only. *Discuss* implies a willingness to examine both sides of an argument; *challenge* desires an opportunity to prove one is right. To *reason* is to persuade by argument or to try to prove by explaining. Persons may *contend* either from mere ill will or self-interest, or from the highest motives; "that ye should earnestly *contend* for the faith which was once delivered to the saints," *Jude* 3. To *controvert* is to *argue* wholly on the negative side, urging consideration against an opinion, proposition, or the like. One may *argue* and *discuss* without an opponent. We may *question* or *discuss* a proposition without reference to anyone's advocacy of it, but to *contend, debate,* or *dispute* implies an opponent. A dispute may be personal, fractious, and petty; a debate is formal and orderly; if otherwise, it becomes a mere wrangle. Compare **question; reason** *verb*.

DO

accomplish	carry out	discharge	perform
achieve	carry through	effect	perpetrate
actualize	commit	execute	realize
bring about	complete	finish	transact
bring to pass	consummate	fulfil	work out

Do is the one comprehensive word which includes this whole class. We may say of the least item of daily work, "It is *done*," and of the grandest human achievement, "Well *done!*" *Finish* and *complete* signify to bring to an end what was previously begun; there is frequently the difference in usage that *finish* is applied to the fine details and is superficial, while *complete* is comprehensive, being applied to the whole ideal, plan, and execution; as, to *finish* a statue; to *complete* a scheme of philosophy. To *discharge* is to *do* what is given in charge, expected, or required; as, to *discharge* the duties of the office. To *fulfil* is to *do* or to be what has been promised, expected, hoped, or desired; as, a son *fulfils* a father's hopes.

Realize, effect, execute, and *consummate* all signify to embody in fact what was before in thought. One may *realize* that which he has done nothing to *bring about*; he may *realize* the dreams of youth by inheriting a fortune; but he cannot *effect* his early designs except by *doing* the utmost that is necessary to make them fact. *Effect* includes all that is *done* to *accomplish* the intent; *execute* refers rather to the final steps; *consummate* is limited quite sharply to the concluding act. An officer *executes* the law when he proceeds against its violators; a purchase is *consummated* when the money is paid and the property delivered. *Execute* refers more commonly to the commands of another; *effect* and *consummate*, to one's own designs; as, the commander *effected* the capture of the fort, because his officers and men promptly *executed* his commands.

Achieve—to *do* something worthy of a chief—signifies always to *perform* some great and generally some worthy exploit. *Perform* and *accomplish* both imply working toward the end; but *perform* always allows a possibility of not attaining, while *accomplish* carries the thought of full completion. As between *complete* and *accomplish*, *complete* considers rather the thing as *done*; *accomplish*, the whole process of doing it. *Commit*, as applied to actions, is used only of those that are bad, whether grave or trivial; *perpetrate* is used chiefly of aggravated crimes or, somewhat humorously, of blunders. A man may *commit* a sin, a trespass, or a murder; *perpetrate* an outrage or a felony. We *finish* a garment or a letter, *complete* an edifice or a lifework, *consummate* a bargain or a crime, *discharge* a duty, *effect* a purpose, *execute* a command, *fulfil* a promise, *perform* our daily tasks, *realize* an ideal, *accomplish* a design, *achieve* a victory. See **act; make; transact.** Compare **transaction.**

> **ANTONYMS:** *baffle, come short, defeat, destroy, fail, frustrate, mar, miscarry, miss, neglect, ruin, spoil.*

DOCILE

amenable	manageable	pliant	teachable
compliant	obedient	submissive	tractable
gentle	pliable	tame	yielding

A *docile* person responds readily to teaching, and will not resist authority. A *tractable* person is easily guided or handled, but does not have the submissive temperament of the *docile* one; a stubborn child may prove to be quite *tractable* when reasoned with. The *obedient* person complies with the commands or requests of a person or power whose authority he acknowledges.

The *amenable* person obeys or complies willingly chiefly because of an inherent desire to be agreeable or because of freedom from prejudice. The *submissive* person has surrendered his will to another's control, and accepts whatever befalls him without protest. Compare **duty.**

> **ANTONYMS:** *determined, dogged, firm, inflexible, intractable, obstinate, opinionated, resolute, self-willed, stubborn, wilful, unyielding.*

DOCTRINE

article of belief	belief	precept	teaching
article of faith	dogma	principle	tenet

Doctrine primarily signifies that which is taught; *principle*, the fundamental basis on which the *teaching* rests. A *doctrine* is reasoned out, and may be defended by reasoning; a *dogma* rests on authority, as of direct revelation, the decision of the church, etc. A *doctrine* or *dogma* is a statement of some one item of *belief*; a *creed* is a summary of *doctrines* or *dogmas*. *Dogma* has commonly, at the present day, an offensive signification, as of a *belief* arrogantly asserted. *Tenet* is simply that which is held, and is applied to a single item of *belief*; it is a neutral word, neither approving nor condemning. A *precept* relates not to *belief*, but to conduct. The *tenets* of present-day Christianity are not always in complete accordance with the *precepts* of Christ. Compare **faith; law.**

DOGMATIC

arrogant	doctrinal	magisterial	positive
authoritative	domineering	opinionated	self-opinionated
dictatorial	imperious	overbearing	systematic

Dogmatic is technically applied in a good sense to that which is formally enunciated by adequate authority; *doctrinal* to that which is stated in the form of doctrine to be taught or defended. *Dogmatic* theology, called also "dogmatics," gives definite propositions, which it holds to be delivered by authority; *systematic* theology considers the same propositions in their logical connection and order as parts of a system; a *doctrinal* statement is less absolute in its claim than a *dogmatic* treatise, and may be more partial than the term *systematic* would imply. Outside of theology, *dogmatic* has generally an offensive sense; a *dogmatic* statement is one for which the author does not trouble himself to give a reason, either because of the strength of his convictions, or because of his contempt for those whom he addresses; thus *dogmatic* is, in common use, allied with *arrogant* and kindred words.

Dictatorial has historical connotations referring to supreme powers entrusted to a single man during a time of crisis; however, it has come to suggest primarily the assumption of such powers, and now connotes an *overbearing* temper or *imperious* methods. A *magisterial* manner is one which is associated with the authority or prerogatives of a magistrate or a schoolmaster.

DOUBT *noun*

disbelief	incredulity	perplexity	suspense
distrust	indecision	question	suspicion
dubiety	irresolution	scruple	unbelief
hesitancy	misgiving	skepticism	uncertainty
hesitation			

Doubt is a lack of conviction that may refer either to matters of belief or to matters of practice. As regards belief, while *doubt* is lack of conviction, *disbelief* is conviction to the contrary; *unbelief* refers to a settled state of mind, generally accompanied with opposition of heart. *Perplexity* is active and pain ful; *doubt* may be quiescent. *Perplexity* presses toward a solution; *doubt* may be content to linger unresolved. Any improbable statement awakens *incredulity* or a question. In theological usage *unbelief* and *skepticism* have a condemnatory force, as implying wilful rejection of manifest truth. As regards practical matters, *uncertainty* applies to the unknown or undecided; *doubt* implies some negative evidence. *Suspense* regards the future, and is eager and anxious; *uncertainty* may relate to any period, and be quite indifferent.

Misgiving is ordinarily in regard to the outcome of something already done or decided; *hesitation, indecision,* and *irresolution* have reference to something that remains to be decided or done, and are due oftener to infirmity of will than to lack of knowledge. *Distrust* and *suspicion* apply especially to the motives, character, etc., of others, and are more decidedly adverse than *doubt.* *Scruple* relates to matters of conscience and duty. *Skepticism* denotes an unwillingness to believe without demonstration or positive proof. *Dubiety* expresses a lack of certainty, rather than an inability to ascertain the truth, and so is closer in meaning to *uncertainty* than to *doubt.* Compare **doubt** verb; **perplexity.**

> **ANTONYMS:** *assurance, belief, certainty, confidence, conviction, decision, determination, persuasion, resolution, resolve.*

DOUBT *verb*

distrust	mistrust	surmise	suspect

To *doubt* is to lack conviction. Incompleteness of evidence may compel one to *doubt,* or some perverse bias of mind may incline him to. *Distrust* may express simply a lack of confidence; as, I *distrust* my own judgment; or it may be nearly equivalent to *suspect;* as, I *distrusted* that man from the start. *Mistrust* and *suspect* imply that one is almost assured of positive evil; one may *distrust* himself or others; he *suspects* others. *Mistrust* is now rarely, if ever, used of persons, but only of motives, intentions, etc. *Distrust* is always serious; *mistrust* is often used playfully. Compare **fluctuate; suppose.** Compare synonyms for **doubt** noun.

> **ANTONYMS:** *believe, confide in, depend on, depend upon, rely on, rely upon, trust.*

DRAW

allure	entice	haul	induce	lure	tow
attract	hale	incline	lead	pull	tug
drag					

One object *draws* another when it moves it toward itself or in the direction of its own motion by the exertion of adequate force, whether slight or powerful.

To *attract* is to exert a force that tends to *draw*, though it may produce no actual motion; all objects are *attracted* toward the earth, though they may be sustained from falling. To *drag* is to *draw* against strong resistance; as, to *drag* a sled over bare ground, or a carriage up a steep hill. To *pull* is to exert a drawing force, whether adequate or inadequate; as, the fish *pulls* on the line; a dentist *pulls* a tooth. To *tug* is to *draw*, or try to *draw*, a resisting object with a continuous straining motion; as to *tug* at the oar. To *haul* is to *draw* somewhat slowly a heavy object; as to *haul* a seine; to *haul* logs. *Hale*, in the sense of pulling, was formerly used interchangeably with *haul*; in present usage, however, it stresses the idea of compulsion or force; as, to be *haled* to prison. One vessel *tows* another. In the figurative sense, *attract* is more nearly akin to *incline*, *draw* to *induce*. We are *attracted* by one's appearance, *drawn* to his side. Compare **allure; array; influence.**

> **ANTONYMS:** *alienate, estrange, rebuff, reject, repel, repulse.*

> **PREPOSITIONS:** To draw water *from* or *out* of the well; draw the boat *through* the water, *to* the shore; draw air *into* the lungs; draw *with* cords of love; the wagon is drawn *by* horses, *along* the road, *across* the field, *over* the stones, *through* the mud, *to* the barn.

DREAM

daydream	fantasy	phantasy	trance
fancy	hallucination	reverie	vision
fantasm	phantasm	romance	

A *dream* is strictly a train of thoughts, *fantasies*, and images passing through the mind during sleep; a *vision* may occur when one is awake, and exercising the senses and mental powers clearly; *vision* is often applied to something seen by the mind through supernatural agency, whether in sleep or wakefulness, conceived as more real and authoritative than a *dream*; a *trance* is an abnormal state which is different from normal sleep or wakefulness. A *reverie* is purposeless drifting of the mind when awake, abstract or fanciful musing; a *daydream* that which passes before the mind in such condition.

A *fancy* is a real or invented image presented to the mind. *Hallucination* is the seeming perception of non-existent objects, as in insanity or delirium. In the figurative sense, we speak of *dreams* of fortune, *visions* of glory, with little difference of meaning except that the *vision* is thought of as fuller and more vivid. We speak of a *trance* of delight when the emotion almost sweeps one away from the normal exercise of the faculties. A *fantasy* is a series of fanciful images or designs presented artistically. *Fantasm* is a mental image or a *fantasy*. Some writers prefer the spellings *phantasy* and *phantasm*.

> **ANTONYMS:** *certainty, fact, reality, realization, substance, verity.*

DRESS

apparel	clothing	habiliments	uniform
array	costume	habit	vestment
attire	garb	raiment	vesture
clothes	garments	robes	

Dress may be used, specifically, for a woman's gown, and in that sense may be either rich or shabby; but in the general sense it denotes outer *clothing* which is meant to be elegant, complete, and appropriate to some social or public occasion; as, full *dress*, court *dress*, evening *dress*, etc. *Dress* has now largely displaced *apparel* and *attire*. *Garb* denotes the *clothing* characteristic of some class, profession, or the like; as, the *garb* of a priest. *Costume* is chiefly used for that which befits an assumed character; as, a theatrical *costume*; we also speak of a national *costume*, etc.

Clothing denotes the entire covering of the body, taken as a whole; *clothes* and *garments* view it as composed of separate parts. *Clothes, clothing,* and *garments* may be used of inner or outer covering; all the other words in the list (with possible rare exceptions in the case of *raiment*) refer to the outer *garments*. *Array, raiment,* and *vesture* are archaic or poetic; so, too, is *habit*, except in technical use to denote a lady's riding *dress*. The word *vestments* is now rare, except in ecclesiastical use. *Apparel* is used when we are thinking of the articles that make up a person's outside *clothing*; *attire* often stresses the impression these make on others. We speak of strange *attire*, but wearing *apparel*.

ANTONYMS: *bareness, disarray, dishabille, exposure, nakedness, nudity, undress.*

DRIVE

compel	impel	propel	repel	resist	thrust
force	influence	push	repulse	ride	urge on

To *drive* is to move an object, or cause it to move, with some inner or outer force or violence before or away from oneself; it is the direct reverse of draw, lead, etc. A man leads a horse by the halter, *drives* it with whip and rein. One may be *driven* to a thing or from it; hence, *drive* is a synonym equally for *compel* or for *repel* or *repulse*. *Repulse* is stronger and more conclusive than *repel*; one may be *repelled* by the very aspect of the person whose favor he seeks, but is not *repulsed* except by the direct refusal or ignoring of his suit. We *drive* an automobile, but we *ride* in it and are *propelled* along the road. We *force* a lock, *compel* compliance. *Impel* implies being *driven* by an urgent inner prompting that leads to precipitate action. To *thrust* is to *push* forward suddenly, to *push* in or pierce, *forcing* a passage or entrance. We *influence* by mental power; climate *influences* growth. See **compel; influence.** Compare **banish.**

ANTONYMS: See synonyms for **draw.**

PREPOSITIONS: Drive *to* market, *to* despair; drive *from* one's presence *into* exile, *out of* the city; drive *by, with,* or *under* the lash; drive *by* or *past* beautiful estates, *along* the beach, *beside* the river, *through* the park, *across* the field, *around* the square, *to* the door, *into* the garage, *out* of the sunshine.

DRUNK

addled	exhilarated	inebriated	lush	sizzled
boozy	fuddled	intoxicated	maudlin	sottish
crapulent	full	jagged	muddled	tight
crapulous	groggy	jiggered	overcome	tipsy
drunken	half-seas-over	jingled	pie-eyed	woozy

Drunk, inebriated, intoxicated, etc., denote actual condition of someone who is under the influence of liquor; *drunken* may denote habitual condition or character, or whatever is caused or characterized by drunkenness; as, an idle, *drunken* wretch; a *drunken* sleep, speech, quarrel, brawl, or riot. *Sottish* always refers to established habit or character. *Intoxicated* is the more scientific and elegant term to denote a less offensive condition than that indicated by *drunk* or *drunken.* Figuratively, we may speak of a persecutor as *drunk* with blood; or of a person as *intoxicated* with success, ambition, glory, or the like.

Muddled, fuddled, addled, and *sottish,* all refer to a stupid, foolish state when *drunk; maudlin* implies a silly sentimental state; *crapulent,* or *crapulous,* is so *drunk* as to be sick; *tipsy* stresses unsteadiness while *drunk.*

Numerous colloquial and slang expressions might be added to the list above given. *Drunken* may immediately precede the noun which it qualifies, while *drunk* cannot; thus, the man was *drunk;* he made him *drunk;* a *drunken* man.

ANTONYMS: *abstemious, abstinent, ascetic, sober, temperate.*

DUPLICATE

copy	facsimile	likeness	reproduction
counterpart	imitation	replica	transcript

A *duplicate* is exactly like the original; a carbon *copy* of a typewritten document must be a *duplicate;* we may have an inaccurate *copy,* but never an inaccurate *duplicate.* A *copy* is as nearly like the original as the copyist has power to make it. While strictly there could be but one *duplicate,* the word is now extended to an indefinite number of exact *copies.* A *facsimile* is like the original in appearance; it may be of a different size, but it must agree in detail; a *duplicate* is the same as the original in substance and effect; a *fac-*

simile of the Declaration of Independence is not a *duplicate*. A *facsimile* of a key might be quite useless; a *duplicate* will open the lock.

A *counterpart* exactly corresponds to another object, but perhaps without design, while a *copy* is intentional. An *imitation* is always thought of as inferior to the original; as, an *imitation* of Milton. A *replica* is a *copy* of a work of art by the maker of the original. In law, a *copy* of an instrument has in itself no authority; the signatures, as well as other matters, may be copied; a *duplicate* is really an original, containing the same provisions and signed by the same persons, so that it may have in all respects the same force and effect; a *transcript* is an official *copy*, written, typed, or printed from an original, and authenticated by the signature of the proper officer and by the seal of the appropriate court. *Reproduction* is chiefly applied to living organisms; it may differ in size, material, etc., but it must be truly like the original.

ANTONYMS: *archetype, model, original, pattern, prototype.*

DUTY

| accountability | function | office | right |
| business | obligation | responsibility | righteousness |

Etymologically, *duty* is that which is owed or due; *obligation*, that to or by which one is bound; *right*, that which is correct, straight, or in the direct line of truth and goodness; *responsibility*, that for which one must answer. *Duty* and *responsibility* are thought of as to some person or persons; *right* is impersonal. One's *duty* may be to others or to himself; his *obligations* and *responsibilities* are to others. *Duty* arises from the nature of things; *obligation* and *responsibility* may be created by circumstances, as by one's own promise, or by the acceptance of a trust, etc. *Duty* stresses a moral impulse; *obligation*, a sense of compulsion. We speak of a parent's *duty*, a debtor's *obligation*; or of a child's *duty* of obedience, and a parent's *responsibility* for the child's welfare.

Right is that which accords with the moral system of the universe. *Righteousness* is *right* incarnated in action. In a more limited sense, *right* may be used of what one may rightly claim, and so be the converse of *duty*. It is the creditor's *right* to demand payment, and the debtor's *duty* to pay. *Accountability* is *responsibility* for causing something. *Function*, as compared here, implies an appropriate or special *duty* or purpose; as, it is the *function* of religion to uplift and help. *Office*, as compared here, is an expected service, a *duty* or requirement connected with a position. See **right** *noun.* Compare **business.**

E

EAGER

agog	burning	hot	keen
animated	desirous	impatient	longing
anxious	earnest	impetuous	vehement
ardent	enthusiastic	importunate	yearning
athirst	fervent	intense	zealous
avid	glowing	intent	

A person is *eager* who impatiently desires to accomplish some end; he is *earnest* with a desire that is less *impatient,* but more deep, resolute, and constant; he is *anxious* with a desire that foresees rather the pain of disappointment than the delight of attainment. One is *eager* for the gratification of any appetite or passion; he is *earnest* in conviction, purpose, or character. *Eager* usually refers to some specific and immediate satisfaction, *earnest* to something permanent and enduring; the patriotic soldier is *earnest* in his devotion to his country, *eager* for a decisive battle.

Avid connotes greediness; *athirst* implies keen *longing; yearning* is anxious *longing.* Agog is expectantly *eager; vehement, ardent,* and *burning* express forceful, fiery eagerness; *fervent,* an eagerness ready to burst into flame. An *importunate* person makes urgent, *eager* demands; he is *impetuous* who is rashly energetic and *eager. Zealous* implies immoderate eagerness, so *ardent* as to push all else aside in its pursuit.

> **ANTONYMS:** *apathetic, calm, careless, cold, cool, dispassionate, frigid, heedless, indifferent, negligent, phlegmatic, purposeless, regardless, stolid, stony, stupid, unconcerned, uninterested, unmindful, unmoved.*

> **PREPOSITIONS:** Eager *for* favor, honor, etc.; eager *in* pursuit.

EASE

easiness	expertness	facility	knack	readiness

Ease in the sense here considered denotes freedom from conscious or apparent effort, tax, or strain. *Ease* may be either of condition or of action; *facility* is always of action; *readiness* is of action or of expected action. One lives at *ease,* who has no pressing cares; one stands at *ease,* moves or speaks with *ease,* when wholly without constraint. *Facility* is always active; *readiness* may be active or passive; the speaker has *facility* of expression, *readiness* of wit; an appliance is in *readiness* for use. *Ease* of action may imply merely the possession of ample power; *facility* always implies practice and skill; any one can press down the keys of a typewriter with *ease;* only the skilled operator works the machine with *facility. Readiness* in the active sense includes much of the meaning of *ease* with the added idea of promptness or alertness. *Easi-*

ness, the state or quality of being easy, applies to the thing done, rather than to the doer. *Expertness* applies to the more mechanical processes of body and mind; we speak of the *readiness* of an orator, but of the *expertness* of a gymnast. Compare **comfortable; dexterity; power.**

> ANTONYMS: *annoyance, awkwardness, constraint, difficulty, discomfort, disquiet, irritation, perplexity, trouble, uneasiness, vexation, worry.*

EDUCATION

breeding	discipline	learning	study
cultivation	information	nurture	teaching
culture	instruction	reading	training
development	knowledge	schooling	tuition

Education (from L. *educere,* to lead or draw out) is the systematic *development* and *cultivation* of the mind and other natural powers.

> *Education* is the harmonious *development* of all our faculties.
> It begins in the nursery, and goes on at school, but does not end there. It continues through life, whether we will or not.
> JOHN LUBBOCK *The Use of Life.*

Instruction, the impartation of *knowledge* by others (from L. *instruere,* to build in or into), is but a part of *education,* often the smallest part. *Teaching* is the more familiar and less formal word for *instruction.*

Training refers not merely to the impartation of *knowledge,* but to active exercising in order to form habits. *Discipline* is systematic and rigorous *training,* with the idea of subjection to authority and perhaps of punishment. *Tuition,* the services of a teacher, is the technical term for *teaching* as the business of an instructor or as in the routine of a school; *tuition* is narrower than *teaching,* not, like the latter word, including *training.* We speak of the *teaching, training,* or *discipline,* but not of the *education* or *tuition* of a dog or a horse.

Breeding and *nurture* include *teaching* and *training,* especially as directed by and dependent upon home life and personal association; *breeding* having reference largely to manners with such qualities as are deemed distinctively characteristic of good birth; *nurture* (literally *nourishing*) having more direct reference to moral qualities, not overlooking the physical and mental. *Knowledge* and *learning* tell nothing of mental development apart from the capacity to acquire and remember, and nothing whatever of that moral development which is included in *education* in its fullest and noblest sense; *learning,* too, may be acquired by one's unaided industry, but any full *education* must be the result in great part of *instruction, training,* and personal association.

Study is emphatically what one does for himself, and in which *instruction* and *tuition* can only point the way, encourage the student to advance, and remove obstacles; vigorous, persevering *study* is one of the best elements of *training. Study* is also used in the sense of the thing studied, a subject to be mastered by *study*, a studious pursuit. *Culture* is refinement that is the result of enlightenment, or the art of developing; *cultivation* emphasizes the act of improvement and *development* by *training*; both refer to plants, etc., as well as to persons. See **knowledge; refinement; wisdom.**

ANTONYMS: *ignorance, illiteracy.*

EFFICIENT

effective   effectual   efficacious

Efficient is acting effectually or having power to produce desired results. That is *effective* which accomplishes an intended effect with emphasis, decision, and certainty; that is *effectual* which acts with such finality as to leave no more to be done. *Effective* measures will put an *effectual* stop to objectionable proceedings. That is *efficacious* which is thought of as having power, which may be active or may continue latent, to produce an *effectual* result; as, a medicine *efficacious* against fever. A person may be said to be *efficient* in general character or action; as, an *efficient* business man; he may be called *effective* in some special relation; as, an *effective* speaker; the *efficient* person is habitually energetic, industrious, sagacious, and alert; a man may be an *effective* speaker on occasion who is not *efficient* in ordinary life. *Efficacious* and *effectual* are not used of persons.

ANTONYMS: *awkward, dull, feckless, feeble, fruitless, idle, ineffective, ineffectual, inefficacious, inefficient, inoperative, negligent, powerless, remiss, unavailing, useless, vain.*

EFFRONTERY

assurance	brass	hardihood	nerve
audacity	cheek	impudence	shamelessness
boldness	gall	insolence	temerity

Effrontery adds to *audacity* and *hardihood* the special element of defiance of considerations of property, duty, and respect for others, yet not to the extent implied in *impudence* or *shamelessness. Impudence* disregards what is due to superiors: *shamelessness* defies decency. *Boldness* is forward-stepping courage, spoken of with reference to the presence and observation of others; *boldness*, in the good sense, is courage viewed from the outside; but the word is frequently used in an unfavorable sense to indicate a lack of proper sensitiveness and modesty.

Audacity, in the sense here considered, is a reckless defiance of law, decency, public opinion, or personal rights, claims, or views, approaching the meaning of *impudence* or *shamelessness*, but always carrying the thought of the personal risk that one disregards in such defiance; the merely *impudent* or shameless person may take no thought of consequences; the *audacious* person recognizes and recklessly braves them. *Hardihood* defies and disregards the rational judgment of men.

Nerve, cheek, gall, and *brass,* as considered here, are slang words, roughly equivalent in meaning to *effrontery. Nerve* carries some of the connotations of *hardihood, cheek* of *impudence, gall* of *insolence,* and *brass* of *audacity. Temerity* usually connotes scorn for danger, but may often imply merely the failure to judge one's chances of success; as, he had the *temerity* to ask his employer for a raise.

> **ANTONYMS:** *bashfulness, coyness, diffidence, modesty, sensitiveness, shrinking, shyness, timidity.*

EGOTISM

conceit	self-assertion	self-confidence	self-esteem
egoism	self-conceit	self-consciousness	vanity

Egotism denotes the desire or tendency to bring oneself, one's actions, one's thoughts, etc., to the attention of others. The egotist constantly exploits himself, or shows off. *Egoism,* on the other hand, implies preoccupation with oneself and one's needs. The egoist, though he may not specifically attempt to attract public attention to himself, is interested chiefly in himself, and in other people only as they affect himself; he has no altruistic qualities. *Egotism* is sometimes used in the sense of *egoism,* or supreme regard for oneself. *Self-assertion* is the claim by word, act, or manner of what one believes to be his due; *self-conceit* is an overestimate of one's own powers or deserts. *Conceit* is a briefer expression for *self-conceit,* with always an offensive implication; *self-conceit* is ridiculous or pitiable; *conceit* arouses resentment. There is a worthy *self-confidence* which springs from consciousness of rectitude and of power equal to demands. *Self-assertion* at times becomes a duty; but *self-conceit* is always a weakness.

Self-consciousness is the keeping of one's thoughts upon oneself, with the constant anxious question of what others will think. *Vanity* is an overweening admiration of self, craving equal admiration from others; *self-consciousness* is commonly painful to its possessor, *vanity* always a source of satisfaction, except as it fails to receive its supposed due. *Self-esteem* is more solid and better founded than *self-conceit;* but is ordinarily a weakness, and never has the worthy sense of *self-confidence. Self-love* usually denotes an abnormal regard for oneself, to the exclusion of interest in or affection for anyone else. Sometimes, however, it suggests merely that love for oneself which is an essential quality of the well-rounded personality. Compare **assurance; pride.**

ELEGANT

artistic	delicate	esthetical	fine	recherché
chaste	delicious	exquisite	nice	tasteful
dainty	esthetic	fastidious	rare	

Elegant refers to that assemblage of qualities which makes anything choice to persons of culture and refinement; it refers to the lighter, finer elements of beauty in form or motion, especially denoting that which exhibits faultless taste and perfection of finish. That which is *elegant* is made so not merely by nature, but by art and culture; a woodland dell may be beautiful or picturesque, but would not ordinarily be termed *elegant*. *Tasteful* refers to that in which the element of taste is more prominent, standing, as it were, more by itself, while in *elegant* it is blended as part of the whole. *Chaste* (primarily pure), denotes in literature and art that which is true to the higher and finer feelings and free from all excess or meretricious ornament.

Dainty and *delicate* refer to the lighter and finer elements of taste and beauty, *dainty* tending in personal use to an excessive scrupulousness which is more fully expressed by *fastidious*. *Nice* and *delicate* both refer to exact adaptation to some standard; the bar of a balance can be said to be nicely or delicately poised; as regards matters of taste and beauty, *delicate* is a higher and more discriminating word than *nice*, and is always used in a favorable sense; a *delicate* distinction is one worth observing; a *nice* distinction may be so, or may be overstrained and unduly subtle; *fine* in such use is closely similar to *delicate* and *nice*, but (though capable of an unfavorable sense) has commonly a suggestion of positive excellence or admirableness; a *fine* touch does something; *fine* perceptions are to some purpose; *delicate* is capable of the single, unfavorable sense of frail or fragile; as, a *delicate* constitution.

Rare, as here compared, suggests qualities of uncommonness and distinction in merit or excellence; as, a *rare* perception of beauty. *Recherché*, a naturalized French word, denotes that which is much sought after or carefully selected; it frequently connotes a studied elegance. *Esthetic* or *esthetical* refers to beauty or the appreciation of the beautiful, especially from the philosophic point of view. *Exquisite* denotes the utmost perfection of the *elegant* in minute details, such as attracts only the most discerning and *fastidious* tastes; we speak of an *elegant* garment, an *exquisite* lace. *Exquisite* is also applied to intense keenness of any feeling; as, *exquisite* delight; *exquisite* pain. See **beautiful; delicious; fine.**

EMBARRASS

abash	discomfit	hamper	mortify
bewilder	discompose	hinder	overawe
chagrin	disconcert	humble	rattle
confound	dishearten	humiliate	shame
confuse	fluster	impede	

Embarrass is a strong word, signifying primarily *hamper, hinder, impede.* A solitary thinker may be *confused* by some difficulty in a subject, or some mental defect; one may feel *embarrassed* in the presence of others, and because of their presence. Confusion is of the intellect, embarrassment of the feelings. A witness may be *embarrassed* by annoying personalities, so as to become *confused* in statements. The *embarrassed* speaker finds it difficult to proceed.

Any sense of inferiority *abashes,* with or without the sense of wrong. The poor are *abashed* at the splendor of wealth; the ignorant, at the learning of the wise. To *confuse* is to *bewilder* mentally, and is a milder term than *confound* which is to overwhelm the mental faculties. A pupil is *confused* by a perplexing question, a general *confounded* by overwhelming defeat. Sudden joy may *bewilder,* but will not *abash.* The true worshiper is *humbled* rather than *abashed* before God. The parent is *mortified* by the child's rudeness, the child *abashed* at the parent's reproof.

To *mortify* a person is to bring upon him a painful sense of humiliation, whether because of his own or another's fault or failure. When a person is *chagrined* he is disappointed as well as *mortified.* A hostess is *discomposed* by the tardiness of guests, a speaker *disconcerted* by a failure of memory. The mob is *overawed* by the military, the hypocrite *shamed* by exposure. See **hinder.** Compare **chagrin; impediment.**

> **ANTONYMS:** *animate, buoy, cheer, embolden, encourage, inspirit, rally, uphold.*

EMBLEM

attribute	figure	image	sign	symbol	token	type

Emblem is the English form of *emblema,* a Latin word of Greek origin, signifying a figure beaten out on a metallic vessel by blows from within; also, a figure inlaid in wood, stone, or other material as a copy of some natural object. The Greek word *symbolon* denoted a victor's wreath, a check, or any object that might be compared with, or found to correspond with another, whether there was or was not anything in the objects compared to suggest the comparison. Thus an *emblem* resembles, a *symbol* represents.

An *emblem* has some natural fitness to suggest that for which it stands; a *symbol* has been chosen or agreed upon to suggest something else, with or without natural fitness; a *sign* does actually suggest the thing with or without reason, and with or without intention or choice. A *symbol* may be also an *emblem*; thus the elements of bread and wine in the Lord's Supper are both appropriate *emblems* and his own chosen *symbols* of suffering and death. A statement of doctrine is often called a *symbol* of faith; but it is not an *emblem*. On the other hand, the same thing may be both a *sign* and a *symbol*; a letter of the alphabet is a *sign* which indicates a sound; but letters are often used as mathematical, chemical, or astronomical *symbols*.

A *token* is something given or done as a pledge or expression of feeling or intent; while the *sign* may be unintentional, the *token* is voluntary; kind looks may be *signs* of regard; a gift is a *token*; a ring, which is a natural *emblem* of eternity, and also its accepted *symbol*, is frequently given as a *token* of friendship or love. A *figure* in the sense here considered is something that represents an idea to the mind somewhat as a form is represented to the eye, as in drawing, painting, or sculpture; as representing a future reality, a *figure* may be practically the same as a *type*. An *image* is a visible representation, especially in sculpture, having or supposed to have a close resemblance to that which it represents.

A *type* in religion is a representation of a greater reality to come; we also speak of one object as the *type* of the class whose characteristics it exhibits, as in the case of animal or vegetable *types*. An *attribute* in art is some accessory used to characterize a *figure* or scene; the *attribute* is often an *emblem* or *symbol*; thus the eagle is the *attribute* of St. John as an *emblem* of lofty spiritual vision. See **sign.**

EMINENT

conspicuous	known	noticeable	remarkable
distinguished	lofty	outstanding	renowned
famous	notable	paramount	signal
illustrious	noted	prominent	supreme

Eminent is high in station, merit, or esteem, and all the words in this group include the idea of prominence because of excellence. *Prominent* men stand out from among their fellows; they are *noticeable* owing to some *outstanding* achievement. Something out of the ordinary or startlingly unusual makes persons or things *conspicuous*. *Noted* implies well-known in a particular field; as, a *noted* historian; *notable* is worthy of notice or *remarkable*. *Distinguished* signifies carrying some mark of special distinction, recognized as superior; *illustrious* is greatly *distinguished*. *Supreme* refers to what is so high that it has no rival; *paramount* is superior to all others. *Famous* and *renowned* connote widely celebrated; *signal* is *distinguished* by some special sign. We speak of an *illustrious* name, *conspicuous* bravery, an *eminent* physician, and the *supreme* sacrifice. Notorious always implies known for something bad and is therefore not a synonym for *famous*. See **high.**

ANTONYMS: *common, commonplace, inferior, low, mean, ordinary.*

EMPLOY

call	engage	hire	make use of	use	use up

In general terms it may be said that to *employ* is to devote to one's purpose, to *use* is to render subservient to one's purpose; what is *used* is viewed as more absolutely an instrument than what is *employed*; a merchant *employs* a clerk; he *uses* pen and paper; as a rule, *use* is not said of persons, except in a degrading sense; as, the conspirators *used* him as a go-between.

That which is *used* is often consumed in the *using*, or in familiar phrase *used up*; as, we *used* twenty tons of coal last winter; in such cases we could not substitute *employ*. A person may be *employed* in his own work or in that of another; in the latter case the service is always understood to be for pay. In this connection *employ* is a word of more dignity than *hire*; a general is *employed* in his country's service; a mercenary adventurer is *hired* to fight a tyrant's battles. *Hire* now implies that the one *hired* works directly and primarily for the pay, as expressed in the noun "hireling." A pastor is *called*, or when the business side of the transaction is referred to, *engaged* at a certain salary.

PREPOSITIONS: Employ *in, on, upon,* or *about* a work, business, etc., *for* a purpose, *at* a stipulated salary.

ENCOURAGE

animate	excite	inspirit	reassure
arouse	forward	instigate	stimulate
cheer	hearten	promote	urge on
countenance	impel	prompt	
embolden	inspire	rally	

To *encourage* is to *inspire* with courage, hope, confidence, or resolution; to help forward. To *animate*, in this comparison, is to move to action; to *arouse* is to awaken to action. We *countenance* that which we *encourage* a person to put into practice; we *embolden* when we make brave or bold. *Excite, inspirit* and *stimulate* all include the idea of *arousing* to quickened action, of encouraging to further effort. To *forward, promote,* or *urge on* implies to encourage to develop or to increase. In this connection, to *prompt* is to *arouse* to action and to *rally* is to *arouse* to vigorous action. When we *reassure*, we restore courage and confidence; when we *cheer* we gladden by *encouraging*. See **abet; cherish; console; help; promote.**

PREPOSITIONS: Encourage *with* aid, promises, etc.; encourage a person *in* a course of action, *to* utmost exertion (more often, with infinitive, encourage *to* hope); encouraged *by* partial success, *at* favorable indications.

END *noun*

accomplishment	conclusion	finish	purpose
achievement	consummation	fulfilment	result
bound	expiration	goal	termination
boundary	extent	limit	terminus
cessation	extremity	outcome	tip
close	finale	period	utmost
completion	finis	point	uttermost

The *end* is the terminal part of a material object that has length; the *extremity* is distinctively the terminal *point*, and may thus be but part of the *end* in the general sense of that word; the *extremity* is viewed as that which is most remote from some center, or some mean or standard position; the southern *end* of South America includes all Patagonia, the southern *extremity* or *point* is Cape Horn. *Tip* has nearly the same meaning as *extremity*, but is said of small or slight and tapering objects; as, the *tip* of the finger; *point* in such connections is said of that which is drawn out to exceeding fineness or sharpness, as the *point* of a needle, a fork, or a sword; *extremity* is said of something considerable; we do not speak of the *extremity* of a needle.

Terminus is chiefly used to designate the *end* of a line of travel or transportation: specifically, the furthermost station in any direction on a railway, or by extension the town or village where it is situated. *Termination* is the Latin and more formal word for the Saxon *end*, but is chiefly used of time, words, undertakings, or abstractions of any kind. *Expiration* signifies the coming to an *end* in the natural course of things; as, the *expiration* of a year, or of a lease; it is used of things of some consequence; we do not ordinarily speak of the *expiration* of an hour or of a day.

Limit implies some check to or restraint upon further advance, right, or privilege; as, the *limits* of an estate. A *goal* is an *end* sought or striven for, as in a race. *Completion* refers to finishing as a whole; *consummation* to such *completion* as approaches perfection. For other figurative senses of *end* and its associated words, see **aim; consequence; design;** compare the synonyms for the verb **end.** See also **boundary.**

ANTONYMS: See synonyms for **beginning.**

END *verb*

break off	close	conclude	expire	quit	terminate
cease	complete	desist	finish	stop	wind up

That *ends*, or is *ended*, of which there is no more, whether or not more was intended or needed; that is *closed, completed, concluded,* or *finished* which has come to an expected or appropriate end. A speech may be *ended* almost as soon as begun, because of the speaker's illness, or of tumult in the audience; in such a case, the speech is neither *closed, completed,* nor *finished,* nor, in the strict sense, *concluded.* An argument may be *closed* with nothing proved; when an argument is *concluded* all that is deemed necessary to prove the point has been stated.

To *finish* is to do the last thing there is to do; as, "I have *finished* my course," *2 Tim.* iv, 7. *Finish* has come to mean, not merely to *complete* in the essentials, but to perfect in all the minute details, as in the expression "to add the *finishing* touches." The enumeration is *completed*; the poem, the picture, the statue is *finished.* To *terminate* may be either to bring to an arbitrary or to an appropriate end; as, he *terminated* his remarks abruptly; the spire *terminates* in a cross. A thing *stops* that comes to rest from motion; or the motion *stops* or *ceases* when the object comes to rest; *stop* frequently signifies to bring or come to a sudden and decided cessation of motion, progress, or action of any kind. To *desist* is to *cease* from action, forbear to continue. *Expire,* to breathe a last breath, die, is now generally used in the figurative sense, meaning to come to a natural end; as, the lease *expired.* To *quit* is to *end* by giving up or going away from; it expresses voluntary termination. To *wind up* is to bring to conclusion or settlement; as, the company *wound up* its affairs.

ANTONYMS: *begin, commence, conceive, embark in, enter upon, initiate, launch, originate, start.*

ENDEAVOR

attempt	essay	striving	trial
effort	exertion	struggle	try

Endeavor is an earnest *attempt* to attain an end by a continued series of acts; an *endeavor* is sustained and enduring, and may be lifelong. *Effort* denotes the voluntary putting forth of power to attain or accomplish some specific thing; it often reaches toward a definite end; *exertion* is a putting forth of power without special reference to an object. *Attempt* is more experimental than *effort, endeavor* less strenuous but more continuous. An *effort* is a single act. We do not have a society of Christian *Attempt,* or of Christian *Effort,* but of Christian *Endeavor.* A *struggle* is a violent *effort* or strenuous *exertion.*

An *essay* is an *attempt, effort,* or *endeavor* made as a test of the powers of the one who makes it. Compare **try.**

ENDURE

abide	bear up under	put up with	sustain
afford	bear with	submit to	tolerate
allow	brook	suffer	undergo
bear	permit	support	

To *endure* is to *bear* with strain and resistance, but with conscious power; *endure* conveys a fuller suggestion of contest and conquest than *bear.* One may choose to *endure* the pain of a surgical operation rather than take anesthetics; he *permits* the thing to come which he must brace himself to *endure* when it comes.

Bear is the most general of these words; it is metaphorically to hold up or keep up a burden of care, pain, grief, annoyance, or the like, without sinking, lamenting, or repining. *Allow* and *permit* involve concession of the will; *put up with* implies forbearance or patient endurance, but may also imply reluctant withholding of opposition or interference; *tolerate,* though also used to carry the notion of patient endurance, is used more expressively to denote charitable leniency toward opinions or practices which one does not share. Whispering is *allowed* by the school-teacher who does not censure it; one *puts up with* the presence of a disagreeable visitor; one *tolerates* a religion which may differ from his own. To *afford* is to be equal to a pecuniary demand, *i.e.,* to be able to *bear* it. To *brook* is quietly to *put up with* provocation or insult. *Abide* combines the senses of await and *endure*; as I will *abide* the result. We *support,* in this comparison, that which we *bear* or *suffer* in silence; we *sustain* what we *endure* without yielding, or *bear up under*; we *undergo* something that entails suffering. See **abide; allow.** Compare **support.**

ANTONYMS: *break, break down, despair, droop, fail, faint, fall, falter, give out, give up, sink, succumb, surrender, yield.*

ENEMY

adversary   antagonist   competitor   foe   opponent   rival

An *enemy* in private life is one who is is moved by hostile feeling with active disposition to injure; but in miltary language all who fight on the opposite side are called *enemies* or collectively "the *enemy,*" where no personal animosity may be implied; *foe,* which is rather a poetical and literary word, implies active and intensely hostile spirit and purpose.

An *antagonist* is one who opposes and is opposed actively and with intensity of effort; an *opponent,* one in whom the attitude of resistance is the more prominent; a *competitor,* one who seeks the same object for which another is striving; *antagonists* in wrestling, *competitors* in business, *opponents* in debate may contend with no personal ill will; *rivals* in love, ambition, etc., rarely avoid inimical feeling. *Adversary* was formerly much used in the general sense of *antagonist* or *opponent*, but is now less common, and largely restricted to the hostile sense; an *adversary* is ordinarily one who not only opposes another in fact, but does so with hostile spirit, or perhaps out of pure malignity. Compare synonyms for **ambition.**

> **ANTONYMS:** *abettor, accessory, accomplice, ally, friend, helper, supporter.*
>
> **PREPOSITIONS:** He was the enemy *of* my friend *in* the contest.

ENMITY

acrimony	antipathy	hostility	malignity
animosity	bitterness	ill will	rancor
animus	feud	malevolence	spite
antagonism	hatred	malice	

Enmity is the state of being an enemy or the feeling and disposition characterizing an enemy. *Animosity* and *rancor* denote a feeling more active and vehement, but often less enduring and determined, than *enmity.* *Enmity* distinctly recognizes its object as an enemy, to be met or dealt with accordingly; it may or may not be concealed. *Hostility* is open *enmity* in action; the term *hostilities* between nations denotes actual armed collision. *Bitterness* is a resentful feeling arising from a belief that one has been wronged; *acrimony* is deeper and more persistent, and may arise from the crossing of one's wishes or plans by another, where no injustice or wrong is felt.

Antagonism, as between two competing authors or merchants, does not necessarily imply *enmity,* but ordinarily suggests a shade, at least, of hostile feeling. *Malice* is a disposition or intent to injure others, for the gratification of some evil passion; *malignity* is intense and violent *enmity, hatred,* or *malice. Antipathy* may carry no spirit of resentment, but is, rather, an instinctive feeling of aversion, often resulting in a desire to avoid. *Animus* is a hostile feeling or intention. A *feud* is continuous *enmity* between families or groups See **enemy; feud.** Compare synonyms for **acrimony; anger; hatred.**

> **ANTONYMS:** *agreement, alliance, amity, concord, friendship, harmony, kindliness, kindness, regard, sympathy.*

ENTERTAIN

amuse	delight	enliven	please
beguile	disport	gratify	recreate
cheer	divert	interest	

To *entertain*, in the sense here considered, is to engage and pleasantly occupy the attention; to *amuse* is to occupy the attention in an especially bright and cheerful way, often with that which excites merriment or laughter; as, he *entertained* us with an *amusing* story. To *divert* is to turn from serious thoughts or laborious pursuits to something that lightly and agreeably occupies the mind. To *recreate*, literally to re-create, is to engage mind or body in some pleasing activity that will relax and refresh, restoring strength and energy for serious work. To *beguile* is, as it were, to cheat into cheer and comfort by something that insensibly draws thought or feeling away from pain or disquiet; to relieve the tedium of. We *beguile* a weary hour, *cheer* the despondent, *divert* the preoccupied, *enliven* a dull evening or company, *gratify* our friends' wishes, *entertain*, *interest*, *please* a listening audience, indulge in fun or *disport* ourselves when merry, *recreate* when worn with toil; we *amuse* ourselves or others with whatever pleasantly passes the time without special exertion.

ANTONYMS: *annoy, bore, busy, disquiet, distract, disturb, tire, weary.*

ENTERTAINMENT

amusement	enjoyment	fun	pleasure
cheer	feast	merriment	recreation
delight	frolic	pastime	sport
diversion			

Entertainment and *recreation* imply thought and mental occupation, though in an agreeable refreshing way; they are therefore words of a high order. *Entertainment*, apart from its special senses of a public performance or a social party, and predominantly even there, is used of somewhat mirthful mental delight; *recreation* may, and usually does, combine the mental with the physical. *Amusement* and *pastime* are nearly equivalent, the latter probably the lighter word; many *diversions* may be *pastimes* which we should hardly dignify by the name of *amusements*.

Sports are almost wholly on the physical plane, though involving a certain grade of mental action; foxhunting, horse-racing, and baseball are *sports*. Certain *sports* may afford *entertainment* or *recreation* to certain persons, according to their individual tastes. *Cheer* may be very quiet, as the *cheer* of a bright fire to an aged traveler; *merriment* is with liveliness and laughter; *fun* and *frolic* are apt to be boisterous. *Amusement* is a form of *enjoyment*, but *enjoyment* may be too keen to be called *amusement*. A *feast* is the *enjoyment* of rich or plentiful food. Compare **entertain; feast.**

ANTONYMS: *ennui, fatigue, labor, lassitude, toil, weariness, work.*

ENTHUSIASM

ardor	excitement	frenzy	transport
devotion	extravagance	inspiration	vehemence
eagerness	fanaticism	intensity	warmth
earnestness	fervency	passion	zeal
ecstasy	fervor	rapture	

The old meaning of *enthusiasm* implies a pseudo *inspiration*. Later it came to mean an almost frantic *extravagance* in behalf of something supposed to be an expression of the divine will and this sense remains as the controlling one in the kindred noun *enthusiast*. *Enthusiasm* has now chiefly the meaning of an earnest and commendable *devotion*, an intense and eager interest, emotional *zeal* for a cause. Against the hindrances of the world, nothing great and good can be carried without a certain *fervor, intensity,* and *vehemence*; these joined with faith, courage, and hopefulness make *enthusiasm*. *Zeal* is consuming *earnestness*, always tending to vigorous action, though often without the hopefulness of *enthusiasm*. *Ecstasy* is overpowering exaltation; *rapture* is a serene and more enduring *ecstasy*; *transport* refers to a state of being carried out of oneself by strong emotion either sad or joyous. *Fanaticism* is excessive, unreasoning *zeal*. *Frenzy* is violent or delirious *excitement*. Compare **eager.**

ANTONYMS: *calculation, calmness, caution, coldness, deadness, dulness, indifference, lukewarmness, policy, prudence, timidity, wariness.*

ENTRANCE

access	approach	gate	introduction
accession	door	gateway	opening
adit	doorway	ingress	penetration
admission	entrée	inlet	portal
admittance	entry		

Entrance, the act of entering, refers merely to the fact of passing from without to within some enclosure; *admission* and *admittance* refer to entering by or with someone's consent, or at least to opportunity afforded by someone's act or neglect. We may effect or force an *entrance*, but not *admittance* or *admission*; those we gain, procure, obtain, secure, win. *Admittance* refers to place, *admission* refers also to position, privilege, favor, friendship, etc. An intruder may gain *admittance* to the hall of a society who would not be allowed *admission* to its membership.

Approach is a movement toward another; *access* is coming all the way to his presence, recognition, and consideration. An unworthy favorite may prevent even those who gain *admittance* to a king's audience from obtaining any real *access* to the king. *Accession*, in this connection, signifies the coming into possession, as of dignity, office, or authority, the *entrance* into a position to which one has a rightful or recognized claim; as, the *accession* of the heir to the throne on the death of the king; the beginning of a king's reign is regularly spoken of as his *accession.*

Entrance is also used figuratively for setting out upon some career, or becoming a member of some organization; as, we speak of one's *entrance* upon college life, or of *entrance* into the ministry. *Ingress* is often a narrow passage entrance, also the act of entering; in law, it often connotes permission to enter. *Inlet* is a narrow *entrance,* generally of water into the land or into a culvert. *Entrée,* adopted from the French, in this connection expresses the privilege of entering; *entry,* a formal *entrance. Penetration* implies entering by passing through some substance.

ANTONYMS: *departure, egress, ejection, exclusion, exit, expulsion, refusal, rejection, withdrawal.*

PREPOSITIONS: Entrance *into* a place, *on* or *upon* a work or course of action, *into* or *upon* office, *into* battle, *by* or *through* the door, *within* the gates, *into* or *among* the company.

EQUIVOCAL

ambiguous	enigmatical	obscure	questionable
doubtful	indefinite	perplexing	suspicious
dubious	indeterminate	precarious	uncertain
enigmatic	indistinct		

Equivocal (from L. *æquus,* equal, and *vox,* voice, word) denotes that which may equally well be understood in either of two or more ways. *Ambiguous* (from L. *ambi,* around, and *ago,* drive, lead) signifies lacking in distinctness or certainty, *obscure* or *doubtful* through indefiniteness of expression. *Ambiguous* is applied only to spoken or written statements; *equivocal* has other applications. A statement is *ambiguous* when it leaves the mind of the reader or hearer fluctuating between two meanings, which would fit the language equally well; it is *equivocal* when it would naturally be understood in one way, but is capable of a different interpretation; an *equivocal* expression is, as a rule, intentionally deceptive, while an *ambiguous* utterance may be simply the result of a want either of clear thought or of adequate expression.

That which is *enigmatical* must be guessed like a riddle; a statement may be purposely made *enigmatical* in order to provoke thought and study. That is *precarious* which is *uncertain;* that is *doubtful* which is fairly open to doubt; that is *dubious* which has become the subject of doubts so grave as scarcely to fall short of condemnation; as, a *dubious* reputation.

Questionable may be used nearly in the sense either of *dubious* or of *doubtful;* a *questionable* statement is one that must be proved before it can be accepted. To say that one's honesty is *questionable* is a mild way of saying that in the opinion of the speaker he is likely to prove dishonest. A *suspicious* character gives manifest reason to be suspected; a *suspicious* temper is inclined to suspect the motives and intentions of others, with or without reason. Compare **obscure; precarious.**

ANTONYMS: *certain, clear, distinct, evident, indisputable, indubitable, lucid, manifest, obvious, perspicuous, plain, unambiguous, unequivocal, unquestionable, unquestioned.*

ESTEEM *noun*

admiration	estimate	favor	respect
deference	estimation	regard	

Esteem for a person is a favorable opinion on the basis of worth, especially of moral worth, joined with a feeling of interest in and attraction toward the person. *Regard* for a person is the mental view or feeling that springs from a sense of his value, excellence, or superiority, with a cordial and hearty friendliness. *Regard* is more personal and less distant than *esteem*, and adds a special kindliness; *respect* is a more distant word than *esteem*. *Respect* may be wholly on one side, while *regard* is more often mutual; *respect* in the fullest sense is given to what is lofty, worthy, and honorable, or to a person of such qualities; we may pay an external *respect* to one of lofty station, regardless of personal qualities, showing *respect* for the office.

Deference, signifying respectful submission, may be wholly formal, as yielded to age, authority, or position, or it may be founded upon deepest *regard* and *esteem*. *Estimate* has more of calculation; as, my *estimate* of the man, or of his abilities, is very high. *Estimation* involves the idea of calculation or appraisal with that of *esteem* or *regard*, and is especially used of the feeling entertained by numbers of people; as, he stood high in public *estimation*. *Admiration* is often accorded to personal attractiveness, even when the person does not merit *esteem*. Compare **esteem** *verb*; **friendship; love.**

ANTONYMS: *abhorrence, antipathy, aversion, contempt, dislike, hatred, loathing, repugnance.*

ESTEEM *verb*

admire	consider	hold	respect
appreciate	deem	prize	think
calculate	estimate	regard	value

Esteem and *estimate* alike imply to set a certain mental value upon, but *esteem* is less precise and mercantile than *calculate* or *estimate*. We *esteem* a jewel precious; we *estimate* it to be worth so much money. This sense of *esteem* is now chiefly found in literary or oratorical style, and in certain conventional phrases; as, I *esteem* it an honor, a favor. In popular usage *esteem*, as said of persons, denotes a union of respect and kindly feeling and, in the highest sense, of moral approbation; as, one whom I highly *esteem*; the word may be used in a similar sense of material things or abstractions; as, one whose friendship I *esteem*; a shell greatly *esteemed* for inlaid work.

To *appreciate* anything is to be deeply or keenly sensible of or sensitive to its qualities or influence, to see its full import, be alive to its value, importance, or worth; as, to *appreciate* beauty or harmony; to *appreciate* one's services in a cause; the word is similarly, though rarely, used of persons. To *prize* is to set a high value on for something more than merely commercial reasons. One may *value* some object, as a picture, beyond all price, as a family heirloom, or may *prize* it as the gift of an *esteemed* friend; without at all *appreciating* its artistic merit or commercial value.

To *regard* (from F. *regarder*, look at, observe) is to have a certain mental view favorable or unfavorable; as, I *regard* him as a friend; or, I *regard* him as a villain; *regard* has a distinctively favorable sense as applied to institutions, proprieties, duties, etc., but does not share the use of the noun "regard" as applied to persons; we *regard* the Sabbath; we *regard* a person's feelings; we have a "regard" for the person. To *respect* is to have a deferential regard for a person or thing in recognition of worth or value. We *admire* when we recognize and *appreciate* superiority. Compare **calculate; esteem** *noun*.

ETERNAL

deathless	immortal	never-failing	undying
endless	imperishable	perennial	unending
eonian	interminable	perpetual	unfading
everlasting	infinite	timeless	unfailing
ever-living	never-ending	unceasing	without end
fadeless			

Eternal strictly signifies without beginning or end, in which sense it applies to God alone; *everlasting* applies to that which may or may not have beginning, but will never cease; *eternal* is also used in this more limited sense; *endless*, without end, in its utmost reach, is not distinguishable from *everlasting*; but *endless* is constantly used in inferior senses, especially in mechanics, as in the phrases an *endless* screw, an *endless* chain. *Everlasting* and *endless* are both used in a limited sense of protracted, indefinite, but not infinite duration; as, the *everlasting* hills; *endless* debates; so we speak of *interminable* quarrels. *Eternal* holds quite strictly to the vast and sacred meaning in which it is applied to the Divine Being and the future state. *Everlasting, endless,* and *eternal* may be applied to that which has no life; as, *everlasting* chains, *endless* night, *eternal* death; *immortal* applies to that which now has life, and is forever exempt from death; *deathless* implies not liable to die; *imperishable*. A *perennial* plant sends forth new shoots, blossoms, and fruit each year; a *perpetual* noise is *unceasing*. *Infinite* is unlimited by time or space. *Timeless* carries, perhaps, the fullest idea of *eternal*, as above and beyond time, and not to be measured by it.

EVENT

case	contingency	fortune	outcome
chance	end	incident	possibility
circumstance	episode	issue	result
consequence	fact	occurrence	sequel

Etymologically, the *event* is that which comes out, the *incident* that which falls in; *event* is thus greater and more signal than *incident*; we speak of trifling *incidents*, great *events*; *incidents* of daily life, *events* in history. *Circumstance* agrees with *incident* in denoting a matter of relatively slight importance, but implies a more direct connection with the principal matter; "circumstantial evidence" is evidence from seemingly minor matters directly connected with a case; "incidental evidence" would be some evidence that happened unexpectedly to touch it.

An *occurrence* is, etymologically, that which we run against, without thought of its origin or tendency; hence, the happening of an *event*. An *episode* is connected with the main course of *events*, like an *incident* or *circumstance*, but stands out as a single *event*, often of independent interest and importance. *Outcome* is the Saxon and *event* the Latin for expressing the same original idea. *Consequence* or *result* would express more of logical connection, and be more comprehensive.

The *end* may be simple cessation; the *event* is what has been accomplished; the *event* of a war is victory or defeat; the *end* of the war is reached when a treaty of peace is signed. Since the future is contingent, *event* comes to have the meaning of a *contingency*; as, in the *event* of his death, the policy will at once fall due. *Issue* in this connection is the final *result* or *outcome*; *sequel*, a logical *result* or *consequence*. Compare **circumstance; consequence; end** *noun*.

EVERY

all	any	both	each	either

All and *both* are collective; *any, each* and *every* are distributive. *Any* makes no selection and may not reach to the full limits of *all*; *each* and *every* make no exception or omission, and must extend to *all*; *all* sweeps in the units as part of a total, *each* and *every* proceed through the units to the total. A promise made to *all* omits none; a promise made to *any* may not reach *all*; a promise made to *every* one is so made that no individual shall fail to be aware of it: a promise made to *each* is made to the individuals personally, one by one. *Each* is thus more individual and specific than *every*; *every* classifies, *each* individualizes.

Each divides, *both* unites; if an equal sum is given to *each* of two persons, *both* (together) must receive twice the amount; *both* must be aware of what has been separately communicated to *each*; a man may fire *both* barrels of a gun by a single movement; if he fires *each* barrel, he discharges them separately. *Either* properly denotes one of two, indefinitely, to the exclusion of the other. The use of *either* in the sense of *each* or *both*, though sustained by good authority, is objectionable because ambiguous. His friends sat on *either* side of the room would naturally mean on one side or the other; if the meaning is on *both* sides, it would be better to say so. See **both.**

EVIDENT

apparent	glaring	overt	tangible
clear	indubitable	palpable	transparent
conspicuous	manifest	patent	unmistakable
discernible	obvious	perceptible	visible
distinct	open	plain	

That is *evident* of which the mind is made sure by some inference that supplements the facts of perception; that is *apparent* which clearly appears to the senses or to the mind as soon as the attention is directed toward it; the marks of a struggle were *apparent* in broken shrubbery and trampled ground, and the finding of a mutilated body and a rifled purse made it *evident* that robbery and murder had been committed.

Manifest, originally meaning from its derivation, laid hold of by the hand, now means clearly *evident* to the understanding and to the senses, especially to the sight; *manifest* is thus stronger than *evident*; that the picture was a modern copy of an ancient work was *evident*, and on comparison with the original its inferiority was *manifest*. That is *obvious* which is directly in the way, so *apparent* that it cannot be missed; as, the application of the remark was *obvious*.

Visible applies to all that can be perceived by the sense of sight, whether the noonday sun, a ship on the horizon, or a microscopic object. *Discernible* applies to that which is dimly or faintly *visible* or audible, requiring strain and effort in order to be seen or heard; as, the ship was *discernible* through the mist. *Perceptible*, that may be recognized by the senses or by signs, also means barely *visible* or audible. *Patent*, as here compared, is *open*, *obvious*. *Tangible* is *perceptible* by touch or, figuratively, by the mind. That is *conspicuous* which stands out as necessarily or strikingly to attract the attention. *Palpable* and *tangible* express more emphatically the thought of *manifest*. See **clear.**

ANTONYMS: *concealed, covert, dark, hidden, impalpable, impenetrable, imperceptible, invisible, latent, obscure, occult, secret, undiscovered, unimagined, unknown, unseen, unthought of.*

EXALT

advance	dignify	enrich
aggrandize	elevate	magnify
augment	ennoble	promote

To *exalt* is to raise to a height, as in position, condition, rank, or honor. To *aggrandize* is to make great or greater in honor, wealth, influence, or power. Both words have a certain absoluteness; the greatness or the height must be real and impressive; in this they differ from *advance* or *promote*, which are merely relative; a sergeant may be *advanced* or *promoted* to the grade of second lieutenant, but we should not speak of him as being *aggrandized* or *exalted*. See **promote**.

ANTONYMS: *abase, debase, degrade, depress, disgrace, dishonor, enfeeble, humble, humiliate, impoverish, lower, reduce, shame.*

EXAMPLE

archetype	ideal	prototype	standard
ensample	model	sample	type
exemplar	pattern	specimen	warning
exemplification	precedent		

From its original sense of *sample* or *specimen* (from L. *exemplum*) *example* derives the seemingly contradictory meanings, on the one hand of a *pattern* or *model* to be imitated, and on the other hand of a *warning*—a *sample* or *specimen* of what is to be followed, or of what is to be shunned. An *example*, however, may be more than a *sample* or *specimen* of any class; it may be an *ideal* that serves as a *model*; it may be the very *archetype* or *prototype* to which the whole class must conform, as when Christ is spoken of as being an *example* or leaving an *example* for His disciples. *Example* comes nearer to the possible freedom of the *model* than to the necessary exactness of the *pattern*; often we cannot, in a given case, exactly imitate the best *example*, but only adapt its teachings to altered circumstances.

In its application to a person or thing, *exemplar* can scarcely be distinguished from *example*; but *example* is most frequently used for an act, or course of action, for which *exemplar* is not used; as, one sets a good (or a bad) *example*. An *exemplification* is an illustrative working out in action of a principle or law, without any reference to its being copied or repeated; an *example* guides, an *exemplification* illustrates or explains. *Ensample* is the same as *example*, but is practically obsolete outside of Scriptural or theological language. *Precedent* connotes authority. See **ideal; model; precedent; sample.**

EXCESS

dissipation	luxuriance	profusion	superfluity
exorbitance	overplus	redundance	surplus
extravagance	plethora	redundancy	waste
intemperance	prodigality	superabundance	wastefulness
lavishness			

Excess is more than enough of anything, and, since this in very many cases indicates a lack either of judgment or of self-control, the word is used frequently in an unfavorable sense. Careless expenditure in *excess* of income is *extravagance*; we may have also *extravagance* of language, professions, etc. As *extravagance* is *excess* in outlay, *exorbitance* is *excess* in demands, and especially in pecuniary demands upon others.

Overplus and *superabundance* denote in the main a satisfactory, and *superfluity* an undesirable, *excess*; *lavishness* and *profusion*, a generous, bountiful, or amiable *excess*; as, a *profusion* of fair hair; *lavishness* of hospitality. *Plethora* is a state of excessive fullness. *Luxuriance* denotes such abundance, usually of growth, as to be excessively great—the acme of abundance. *Surplus* is neutral, having none of the unfavorable meaning that often attaches to *excess*; a *surplus* is that which remains over after all demands are met. *Redundance* or *redundancy* refer chiefly to literary style, denoting an *excess* of words or matter. *Excess* in the moral sense is expressed by *dissipation, prodigality, intemperance*, etc.

ANTONYMS: *dearth, defect, deficiency, destitution, economy, failure, frugality, inadequacy, insufficiency, lack, need, poverty, scantiness, shortcoming, want.*

EXECUTE

administer	dispense	enforce	mete out
carry out	do	inflict	perform

To *execute* is to follow through to the end, put into absolute and final effect; to *administer* is to conduct as one holding a trust, as a minister and not an originator; the sheriff *executes* a writ; the trustee *administers* an estate, a charity, etc.; to *enforce* is to put into effect by force, actual or potential. To *administer* the laws is the province of a court of justice; to *execute* the laws is the province of a sheriff, marshal, constable, or other executive officer; to *administer* the law is to declare or apply it; to *execute* the law is to put it in force; for this *enforce* is the more general word, *execute* the more specific. From signifying to superintend officially some application or infliction, *administer* passes by a natural transition to signify *inflict, mete out, dispense,* and blows, medicine, etc., are said to be *administered*. *Enforce* signifies also to be present and urge home by intellectual and moral force; as, to *enforce* a precept or a duty. *Perform* refers to working toward a goal which, however, may not be reached, and is used more often with reference to processes than to acts. Compare **do; kill; make.**

EXERCISE

act	application	exertion	performance
action	drill	occupation	practice
activity	employment	operation	use

Exercise, in the ordinary sense, is the easy natural *action* of any power; *exertion* is the putting of any power to strain and tax. But by qualifying adjectives we may bring *exercise* up to the full sense of *exertion*; as, violent *exercise*. *Exercise* is *action* taken at any time with a view to employing, maintaining, or increasing power, or merely for enjoyment; *practice* is systematic *exercise* with a view to the acquirement of facility and skill in some pursuit; a person takes a walk for *exercise,* or takes time for *practice* on the piano.

Practice is also used for putting into *action* and effect what one has learned or holds as a theory; as, the *practice* of law or medicine; a profession of religion is good, but the *practice* of it is better. *Drill* is systematic, rigorous, and commonly enforced *practice* under a teacher or commander, and emphasizes repetition in training or in forming habits. We speak of the *performance* of duty, the *employment* of talent by one's application to a regular *occupation.* Compare **habit.**

EXPLICIT

categorical	clear	definite	express	specific

Both *explicit* and *express* are opposed to what is merely implicit or implied. That which is *explicit* is unfolded, so that it may not be obscure, doubtful, or ambiguous; that which is *express* is uttered or stated so decidedly that it may not be forgotten nor overlooked. An *explicit* statement is too *clear* to be misunderstood; an *express* command is too emphatic to be disregarded. That is *clear* which is easily seen through or understood; that which is *definite* is exact and positive. *Specific* implies precise reference to one particular thing or to certain details among several; *categorical* refers to plain-speaking that is unconditional and admits of no qualification. See **clear.**

ANTONYMS: *ambiguous, doubtful, implicit, implied, indefinite, indeterminate, uncertain, vague.*

EXTEMPORANEOUS

extemporary	impromptu	offhand
extempore	improvised	unpremeditated

Extemporaneous, originally signifying of or from the time or occasion, has come to mean done or made with but little (if any) preparation. It is now chiefly applied to addresses of which the thought has been prepared, and only the language and incidental treatment left to the suggestion of the moment, so that an *extemporaneous* speech is understood to be any one that is not read or recited. *Impromptu* keeps its original sense, denoting something that springs from the instant, spoken on the spur of the moment as a spontaneous response to something; the *impromptu* utterance is generally brief, direct, and vigorous; the *extemporaneous* speech may chance to be prosy. *Offhand* is still more emphatic as to freedom of utterance. *Unpremeditated* is graver and more formal, denoting absolute want of preparation. *Improvised* stresses the idea that what would be required for the composition or construction was not known beforehand and so had to be devised momentarily. *Extempore,* like *extemporary,* refers to spoken thoughts, as opposed to passages read or memorized.

ANTONYMS: *elaborated, premeditated, prepared, read, recited, studied, written.*

EXTERMINATE

annihilate	eradicate	overthrow	stamp out
banish	expel	remove	uproot
destroy	extirpate	root out	wipe out

Exterminate (from L. *ex,* out, and *terminus,* a boundary) signified primarily to drive beyond the bounds or limits of a country; the word is applied to races of men or animals, and is now almost exclusively used for removal by death, extinction; individuals are now said to be *banished* or *expelled.* *Eradicate* (from L. *e,* out, and *radix,* root) is primarily applied to numbers or groups of plants which it is desired to *remove* effectually from the soil, but also to whatever has taken root and we wish to *remove;* a single tree may be *uprooted,* but it is not said to be *eradicated;* we labor to *eradicate* or *root out* noxious weeds or diseases.

To *extirpate* (from L. *ex,* out, and *stirps,* stem, stock) is not only to *destroy* the individuals of any race of plants or animals, but the very stock, so that the race can never be restored; we speak of *eradicating* a disease, of *extirpating* a cancer, *exterminating* wild beasts or hostile tribes; we seek to *eradicate* or *extirpate* all vices and evils; we *stamp out*, by vigorous action, a fire, a rebellion, an epidemic, or anything which may spread rapidly and injuriously. Compare **abolish**.

ANTONYMS: *augment, beget, breed, build up, cherish, colonize, develop, foster, increase, plant, populate, propagate, replenish, settle.*

F

FAINT

dim	fatigued	irresolute	weak
exhausted	feeble	languid	wearied
faded	half-hearted	listless	worn
faint-hearted	ill-defined	purposeless	worn down
faltering	indistinct	timid	worn out

Faint, with the general sense of lacking strength or effectiveness, covers a wide range of meaning, signifying overcome by physical weakness or exhaustion, or lacking in purpose, courage, or energy, as said of persons; or lacking definiteness or distinctness of color or sound, as said of written characters, voices, or musical notes.

A person may be *faint* when physically *wearied* or *fatigued*, or when overcome by emotion; he may be a *faint* adherent because naturally *feeble* or *purposeless*, or because *half-hearted* in the cause; he may be a *faltering* supporter because naturally *irresolute* or because *faint-hearted* and *timid* in view of perils that threaten, a *listless* worker, through want of mental energy and purpose. Written characters may be *faint, indistinct,* or *dim,* either because originally written with poor ink, or because they have become *faded* by time and exposure.

> **ANTONYMS:** *bright, brilliant, clear, conspicuous, daring, energetic, fresh, hearty, resolute, strong, sturdy, vigorous.*
>
> **PREPOSITIONS:** Faint *with* or *from* hunger; faint *in* color.

FAITH

assent	conviction	creed	persuasion
assurance	credence	doctrine	reliance
belief	credit	opinion	trust
confidence			

Faith is a union of *belief* and *trust;* it is a *belief* that is so strong that it becomes a part of one's nature. *Belief* in a person is often used with no appreciable difference from *faith.* In religion it is common to distinguish between intellectual *belief* of religious truth, as any other truth might be believed, and *belief* of the heart, or *faith.*

Belief, as an intellectual process, is the acceptance of something as true on other grounds than personal observation and experience. We give *credence* to a report, *assent* to a proposition or to a proposal. *Belief* is stronger than *credence,* which is a more formal word than *belief,* and seems to imply mere intellectual acceptance or *assent;* we speak of giving *credence* to a report, but not of giving *belief.*

Credit always includes *trust*; goods are sold on *credit*; we give one *credit* for good intentions. *Conviction* is a *belief* established by argument or evidence; *assurance* is *belief* beyond the reach of argument as it includes *confidence*; as, *assurance* of the honor of a friend. An *opinion* is a general conclusion held as probable, though without full certainty; a *persuasion* is a more confident *opinion*, involving the heart as well as the intellect. In religion, a *doctrine* is a statement of *belief* regarding a single point; a *creed* is a summary statement of *doctrines*.

Confidence is a firm dependence upon a statement as true, or upon a person as worthy. *Reliance* is *confidence* on which we act or are ready to act unquestioningly; we have a calm *reliance* upon the uniformity of nature. *Trust* is a practical and tranquil resting of the mind upon the integrity, kindness, friendship, or promises of a person; we have *trust* in parents and in God.

> **ANTONYMS:** *denial, disbelief, dissent, distrust, doubt, incredulity, infidelity, misgiving, rejection, skepticism, suspicion, unbelief.*

> **PREPOSITIONS:** Have faith *in* God; the faith *of* the gospel.

FAITHFUL

constant	loyal	steadfast	trustworthy
devoted	resolute	sure	trusty
firm	staunch	true	unwavering
incorruptible			

A person is *faithful* who will keep faith, whether with or without power to aid or serve; a person or thing is *trusty* that possesses such qualities as to justify the fullest confidence and dependence. We may speak of a *faithful* but feeble friend; we say a *trusty* agent, a *trusty* steed, a *trusty* sword. When *faithful* is used of a thing it implies *true* to fact, accurate; as, a *faithful* portrayal.

Constant stresses steadiness in devotion; *steadfast* emphasizes *unwavering*, unchanging adherence; *resolute* and *staunch* stress determination in adherence to something. *Trustworthy* is worthy to be trusted; *loyal* implies faithfulness in allegiance or adherence to a country, cause, etc. A person who is really *trustworthy* is *incorruptible*, as he cannot be corrupted or bribed.

> **ANTONYMS:** *capricious, faithless, false, fickle, unfaithful, untrue, untrustworthy, wavering.*

> **PREPOSITIONS:** Faithful *in* service, *to* duty, *to* comrade or commander; faithful *among* the faithless.

FALLACY

casuistry	paralogism	shift	special pleading
equivocation	quibble	shifting	subterfuge
evasion	quibbling	sophism	
hairsplitting	refinement	sophistry	

A *fallacy* in logic is a piece of misleading reasoning, such that the conclusion does not follow from the premises; the *fallacy* has strictly nothing to do with the truth or falsehood of the conclusion; the conclusion may be true, though the reasoning be fallacious; thus:

> All planets are inhabited;
> The earth is a planet;
> Therefore, the earth is inhabited.

This argument is a *fallacy* by fault of the major premise; that "all planets are inhabited" has never been proved, and that statement cannot, therefore, be used to prove anything else; nevertheless, the conclusion, "The earth in inhabited," happens to be true, though the argument does not prove it. Or, again:

> Time is endless;
> This hour is a portion of time;
> Therefore, this hour is endless.

Here the *fallacy* is in the unexpressed assumption that "What is true of time as a whole is true of every portion of time," which is impossible to maintain, and which leads to the manifestly false conclusion, "This hour is endless." Thus, *fallacy* is not a matter of truth or falsehood, but of the soundness or unsoundness of our reasoning; but in common use a *fallacy* is understood to be false reasoning from apparently true premises to a false conclusion. In a wider sense, *fallacy* is used of anything false, deceptive, or misleading, or some misleading quality or appearance in that with which we deal.

Sophistry is the skilful use of *fallacies* in a chain of reasoning—subtly fallacious disputation. A *sophism* is a special instance of *sophistry*; it is a *fallacy* designed to deceive. *Paralogism* is any false syllogistic reasoning, especially if the reasoner is unconscious of the *fallacy*. *Casuistry* (from L. *casus*, case) is strictly the application of the general rules of morality to particular cases; in this strict sense *casuistry* would include all practical morality, where the application of rules to cases is the very basis of right living; but *casuistry* has now become generally a word of reproach denoting *sophistry* applied to practical matters of right and wrong. In law *special pleading* has come to denote legal *casuistry*.

An *evasion* is some artifice to avoid or turn aside the force of an argument that cannot be fairly met. A *quibble* is a petty *evasion*, a trivial distinction or objection. A *subterfuge* is an attempt to escape censure by *evasion* involving inherent and conscious falsity; a *subterfuge* is more directly concerned with practical matters than a *sophism*. *Equivocation* is the use of words in one sense that may naturally be understood in another; logically an *equivocation* may be unintentional or unconscious, deceiving even him who employs it, and is thus a form of *fallacy*; but in common use *equivocation* is understood as the conscious use of misleading language with express intent to deceive, and is thus simply a disguised falsehood. *Refinement* in this sense is the drawing of over nice and unnecessary distinctions, and is often a word of reproach, suggesting shrewd and elaborate perversion of truth under logical forms. Compare **deception; delusion; equivocal.**

ANTONYMS: *argument, axiom, certainty, demonstration, evidence, fact, logic, proof, soundness, sureness, surety, truth, verity.*

FAME

celebrity	eminence	laurels	reputation
credit	glory	notoriety	repute
distinction	honor	renown	

Fame is the widely disseminated report of a person's character, deeds, or abilities, and is generally used in the favorable sense. *Reputation* and *repute* are more limited than *fame*, and may be either good or bad; *reputation* is an estimation of character; *repute* generally includes high esteem. *Notoriety* is often a dishonorable counterfeit of *fame*. *Eminence* and *distinction* may result from rank, station, or character but always include lofty superiority. *Celebrity* is limited in range; we speak of local *celebrity*, or world-wide *fame*.

Fame in its best sense may be defined as the applause of numbers; *renown*, as such applause worthily won; we speak of the conqueror's *fame*; the patriot's *renown*. *Honor* is a manifestation or an expression of great esteem which may or may not be deserved; *glory* includes praise for great achievement in according *honor*, and is high *renown*. *Laurels*, used to crown victors, are symbols of *honor* and *fame*. We can speak of an evil *fame*, but not of evil *honor*; *glory* has a more exalted and often sacred sense. See **character.**

ANTONYMS: *contempt, contumely, discredit, disgrace, dishonor, disrepute, humiliation, ignominy, infamy, oblivion, obscurity, shame.*

FANATICISM

bigotry	credulity	intolerance	superstition

Fanaticism is extravagant or even frenzied zeal; *bigotry* is obstinate and unreasoning attachment to a cause or creed; *fanaticism* and *bigotry* usually include *intolerance*, which is unwillingness to tolerate beliefs or opinions contrary to one's own; *superstition* is ignorant and irrational religious belief.

Credulity is not distinctively religious, but is a general readiness to believe without sufficient evidence, with a proneness to accept the marvelous.

Bigotry is narrow, *fanaticism* is fierce, *superstition* is ignorant, *credulity* is weak, *intolerance* is severe. *Bigotry* has not the capacity to reason fairly, *fanaticism* has not the patience, *superstition* has not the knowledge and mental discipline, *intolerance* has not the disposition. *Bigotry, fanaticism* and *superstition* are perversions of the religious sentiment.

ANTONYMS: *cynicism, free-thinking, indifference, latitudinarianism.*

FANCIFUL

| capricious | fantastic | imaginative | whimsical |
| chimerical | grotesque | visionary | |

That is *fanciful* which is guided or suggested by fancy independently of more serious considerations; the *fantastic* is the *fanciful* with the added elements of whimsicalness and extravagance; the *grotesque* includes the idea of distortion or of something incongruous. The *fanciful* swings away from the real or the ordinary lightly and pleasantly; the *fantastic,* extravagantly; the *grotesque,* ridiculously. A *fanciful* arrangement of objects is generally pleasing, a *fantastic* arrangement is striking, a *grotesque* arrangement is laughable. A *fanciful* theory or suggestion may be clearly recognized as such; a *visionary* scheme is erroneously supposed to have a basis in fact. *Chimerical* refers to *grotesque* or absurd fancies; *imaginative,* to any images in the mind, whether pleasing or unpleasant. *Whimsical* is *fanciful* regarding likes and dislikes; *capricious* suggests guidance by whims or fancies instead of reason. Compare synonyms for **dream; idea; imagination.**

ANTONYMS: *accurate, calculable, calculated, commonplace, literal, ordinary, prosaic, real, reasonable, regular, sensible, solid, sound, sure, true.*

FANCY

belief	desire	imagination	predilection
caprice	humor	inclination	supposition
conceit	idea	liking	vagary
conception	image	mood	whim

An intellectual *fancy* is a mental *image* or picture founded upon capricious or whimsical association or resemblance; *imagination* is a creation of the mind. A *conceit* is often somewhat far-fetched; a *fancy* is lighter and more airy than the common mode of thought. A *conceit* or *fancy* may be wholly unfounded, while a *conception* always has, or is believed to have, some answering reality. An intellectual *fancy* or *conceit* may be pleasing or amusing, but is never worth serious discussion; we speak of a mere *fancy*, a droll or odd *conceit*. An emotional or personal *fancy* is a capricious *liking* formed with slight reason and no exercise of judgment, and liable to fade. In a broader sense, the *fancy* signifies the faculty by which *fancies* or mental *images* are formed, associated, or combined. Some people have a *fancy* or *inclination* for mystery stories; when *inclination* connotes preference they have a *predilection* for them. *Caprice* has a suggestion of wilfulness; *whim*, of fantasy; *vagary*, of something erratic. See **imagination.** Compare **dream; idea.**

ANTONYMS: *actuality, certainty, 'fact, reality, truth, verity.*

PREPOSITIONS: To have a fancy *for* or take a fancy *to* a person or thing.

FAREWELL

adieu	congé	parting salutation
au revoir	Godspeed	valediction
auf Wiedersehen	good-by	valedictory
bon voyage	leave-taking	

Good-by is the homely and hearty, *farewell* the formal English word at parting. *Adieu*, from the French, is still more ceremonious than *farewell*; *congé*, also from the French, is a formal *leave-taking*; or when contemptuous and supercilious, equivalent to dismissal. *Valediction* is a learned word never in popular use. A *valedictory* is a public *farewell* to a company or assembly. *Au revoir* (French) and its German equivalent *auf Wiedersehen* (each, literally, "till I see you again") are often used when a meeting in the near future is expected. *Bon voyage* implies a wish for a pleasant trip, often across an ocean; *Godspeed* wishes the traveler a safe and successful journey.

PREPOSITIONS: I bade farewell *to* my comrades, or (without preposition) I bade my comrades farewell; I took a sad farewell *of* my friends.

FAVOR

benefit	civility	countenance	grace	predilection
blessing	concession	gift	kindness	preference
boon	condescension	good will	patronage	regard

A *favor* is generous service or act, a *kindness* that one is glad to receive, but cannot demand or claim, and which always indicates *good will* or *regard* on the part of the person by whom it is conferred. A *benefit* is a *favor* bestowed; something that promotes happiness or is advantageous. A *blessing* is also a *favor* conferred, but by a superior, and connotes a wish for prosperity or happiness. *Concession* is the granting of a privilege or *favor*; *condescension* is courtesy to an inferior; *patronage* is condescending *favor*. A *boon* is a good thing bestowed; a *civility* is a courteous act or speech. *Predilection* and *preference* imply predisposition in favor of something; partiality. See **friendship; gift; mercy.**

ANTONYMS: *disapproval, disfavor, dislike, harm, hostility, hurt, injury, insult, repulse.*

FEAR

affright	dismay	horror	terror
alarm	disquietude	misgiving	timidity
apprehension	dread	panic	trembling
awe	fright	scare	trepidation
consternation			

Fear is the generic term denoting an emotion excited by threatening evil with a desire to avoid or escape it; *fear* may be sudden or lingering, in view of present, or imminent, or of distant and only possible danger; in the latter sense *dread* is more often used. *Horror* (etymologically a shivering or shuddering) denotes a shuddering *fear* accompanied with abhorrence or such a shock to the feelings and sensibilities as may exist without *fear*, as when one suddenly encounters some ghastly spectacle.

Affright, fright, and *terror* are always sudden, and in actual presence of that which is terrible. *Fear* may overwhelm, or may nerve one to desperate defense; *fright* and *terror* often render one incapable of defense; *fear* may be controlled by force of will; *fright* and *terror* overwhelm the will; *terror* paralyzes; *fright* may cause one to flee, to scream, or to swoon. *Fright* is largely a matter of the nerves; *fear,* of the intellect and the imagination; *terror,* of all the faculties, bodily and mental. A *scare* is sudden *fright,* especially as due to a slight or imaginary cause.

Panic is a sudden *fear* or *fright,* affecting numbers at once; *panic* may seize vast armies or crowded audiences. In a like sense we speak of a financial *panic. Dismay* is a helpless sinking of heart in view of some overwhelming peril or sorrow. *Dismay* is more reflective, enduring, and despairing than *fright*; a horse is subject to *scare, fright,* or *terror,* but not to *dismay. Awe* is reverential *fear.* When sudden danger threatens, *alarm* is awakened. *Consternation* stresses the confusion that *fear* and *dismay* often cause; *disquietude* and *misgiving* denote a state of general uneasiness or doubt. *Dread* is a shrinking, anxious *fear* that anticipates evil; *apprehension* implies *dread* or *misgiving* concerning the future. *Trepidation* is a *dread* that connotes timid, hesitating agitation. Compare **afraid; alarm.**

ANTONYMS: See synonyms for **fortitude.**

FEAST

banquet	festival	fête	treat
entertainment	festivity	repast	

A *feast* is an occasion of abundant, social, and enjoyable eating and drinking; at the *feasts* of the Homeric heroes and the Anglo-Saxon warriors there would be song and story and other pleasures, but enormous abundance of rich food and drink was the basic feature; any abundant consumption of food, however coarse, if enjoyable to those partaking of it, may be called a *feast*; as we may speak of vultures having a *feast* upon carrion. A *repast* is a partaking of food or the food to be partaken of, without reference to quantity; we may have a slight, a hasty, a hearty, or a rich *repast*; the *repast* is thought of as satisfying need; the *feast*, as affording pleasure without reference to, and far in excess of, need.

An *entertainment* is a joyous social occasion or gathering, or the means of giving joy and pleasure at such a gathering; an *entertainment* may or may not involve the partaking of food; as, a convivial *entertainment*; a musical, or a literary, *entertainment*. A *festival* or *festivity*, for either of which the French *fête* is sometimes employed, is an occasion or season of public rejoicing, of which feasting ordinarily forms a part; the Jewish religious *festivals*, as of Passover and Pentecost, were expressly called *feasts*, as are many *festivals* of ritualistic Christian churches, as Christmas and Easter.

A *banquet* is a sumptuous *feast*, always elegant, and usually stately and splendid; the *banquet* was originally a light meal accompanied by wine-drinking, with music or other *entertainment*, following a *feast*, and often in a separate room. Hence, *banquet* properly carries the idea of grace and elegance, as *feast* does that of abundance, which may be either rude or splendid.

A *treat* is some form of *entertainment* especially provided to meet the tastes of the recipient; as, to give the children a *treat*; hence, anything that gives especial or unusual pleasure is called a *treat*; as, the music was a *treat*. In figurative use anything that affords satisfaction or delight to the intellect or the emotions may be called a *feast*; *banquet* does not lend itself so readily to figurative use. Compare **carousal.**

ANTONYMS: *abstinence, destitution, famine, fast, fasting, need, privation, want.*

FEMININE

effeminate	ladylike	womanlike
female	womanish	womanly

We apply *female* to the sex, *feminine* to the qualities, especially the finer physical or mental qualities that distinguish the *female* sex in the human family, or to the objects appropriate for or especially employed by them. A *female* voice is the voice of a woman; a *feminine* voice may belong to a man. *Womanish* denotes the undesirable; *womanly,* the admirable or lovely qualities of woman. *Womanly* tears would suggest respect and sympathy, *womanish* tears a touch of contempt. The word *effeminate* is always used reproachfully, and only of men; it implies unmanly weakness and delicacy. *Womanlike* suggests *feminine* frailties or faults of character; *ladylike,* the characteristics of a lady.

    ANTONYMS: See synonyms for **masculine.**

FETTER

bondage	custody	gyves	irons
bonds	durance	handcuffs	manacles
chains	duress	imprisonment	shackles

Fetters are primarily chains or jointed iron fastenings for the feet; *gyves* may be for the feet or wrists. *Manacles* and *handcuffs* are for the hands. A *shackle* is a metallic ring, clasp, or bracelet-like fastening for encircling and restraining a limb; commonly one of a pair, used either for hands or feet. *Bonds* may be of cord, leather, or any other substance that can bind; *chains* are of linked metal.

    Bonds, fetters, and *chains* are used in a general way for almost any form of restraint. *Gyves* is now wholly poetic, and the other words are mostly restricted to the literary style; *handcuffs* is the specific and *irons* the general term in popular usage; as, the prisoner was put in *irons. Bonds, chains,* and *shackles* are frequently used in the metaphorical sense.

FICKLE

capricious	inconstant	spasmodic	unsteady
changeable	irresolute	uncertain	vacillating
changeful	mutable	unfixed	variable
crotchety	purposeless	unreliable	versatile
fanciful	restless	unsettled	wavering
fitful	shifting	unstable	whimsical
fluctuating			

Fickle (from AS. *ficol,* deceitful, crafty) originally denoted changing with intent to deceive or betray; the word has now become softened in meaning, signifying unduly *changeable* in feeling, judgment, or purpose. Fickleness commonly involves a lack of appreciation of relative values; the *fickle* person may put the momentary enjoyment of an entertainment before the satisfaction of an enduring friendship; *fickle* characters are of short range, with little or no perspective, and as a rule have slight appreciation of what their changefulness may involve to others. The other words of this group explain themselves by reference to the meaning of the nouns *caprice, crotchet, fancy, fit, freak, spasm, whim.* The *crotchety* person is *fickle* only in so far as his eccentric notions conflict with some well-considered plan; he is likely to be pettish and ill-tempered toward all who do not appreciate his ideas at his estimate of their worth.

The words of the list given above naturally divide themselves into three groups: (1) Words denoting mere facility of change, with no reference to any known or suggested reason; as, *changeable, changeful, fluctuating, mutable, restless, shifting, vacillating, variable, varying, versatile, wavering. Versatile* lifts itself out of this group as also implying profitable and effective change— denoting abundance of power and wide adaptability; a *versatile* mind, a *versatile* genius may change its activities from mere fickleness or inconstancy of purpose, but more often changes by distinct choice and purpose in recognition of some new demand of circumstances or some new opportunity; such a mind seems able to use its full power with almost equal readiness in any field in which it chooses to act. (2) Words that denote the lack of steadiness of feeling, disposition, desire, purpose, character, or will; as, *inconstant, irresolute, purposeless, uncertain, unfixed, unreliable, unsettled, unstable, unsteady.* (3) Words denoting a tendency to change founded upon some quality or element of disposition, intellect, or character; as, *capricious, crotchety, fanciful, fickle, freakish, spasmodic, whimsical.* See **fanciful.** Compare **fluctuate.**

ANTONYMS: *changeless, constant, decided, determined, firm, fixed, immutable, invariable, resolute, settled, stable, steadfast, steady, sure, unalterable, unchanging, uniform, unwavering.*

FICTION

allegory	fabrication	invention	novel
apolog	falsehood	legend	romance
fable	figment	myth	story

Fiction is now chiefly used of a prose work in narrative form in which the characters are partly or wholly imaginary, and which is designed to portray human life. A *romance* once meant a legendary *story* of heroic deeds, and it is still used for a tale of adventure and picturesque or striking incidents. *Novel* is a general name for any continuous fictitious narrative, especially a love story; *fiction* and *novel* are often used with little difference of meaning, except that *novel* characterizes a work in which the emotional element is especially prominent.

The moral of the *fable* is expressed formally; the lesson of the *fiction*, if any, is inwrought. A *fiction* is studied: a *myth* grows up without intent. A *legend* may be true, but cannot be historically verified; a *myth* has been received as true at some time, but is now known to be false. A *fabrication* is designed to deceive; it is a less odious word than *falsehood*, but is really stronger, as a *falsehood* may be a sudden unpremeditated statement while a *fabrication* is a series of statements carefully studied and fitted together in order to deceive; the *falsehood* is all false; the *fabrication* may mingle the true with the false.

A *figment* is something imaginary which the one who utters it may or may not believe to be true; we say, "That statement is a *figment* of his imagination." The *story* may be either true or false, and covers the various senses of all the words in this group. *Apolog*, a word simply transferred from Greek into English, is the same as *fable*. See **allegory; story.**

> ANTONYMS: *certainty, fact, history, literalness, reality, truth, verity.*

FIERCE

ferocious	furious	raging	uncultivated	violent
fiery	impetuous	savage	untrained	wild

Fierce signifies having a *furious* and cruel nature, or being in a *furious* and cruel mood, more often the latter. It applies to that which is now intensely excited, or liable to intense and sudden excitement. *Ferocious* always denotes a tendency to violence or savagery; it is more distinctly bloodthirsty than *fierce*; a person may be deeply. intensely cruel, and not at all *ferocious*; a *ferocious* countenance expresses habitual ferocity; a *fierce* countenance may express habitual fierceness, or only the sudden anger of the moment. We speak of a *ferocious* animal, a *fierce* passion. A *fiery* spirit with a good disposition is quickly excitable in a good cause, but may not be *fierce* or *ferocious*. *Savage* signifies *untrained, uncultivated*. That which is *wild* is simply unrestrained; the word may imply no anger or harshness; as, *wild* delight, *wild* alarm.

> ANTONYMS: *affectionate, docile, gentle, harmless, kind, mild, patient, peaceful, submissive, sweet, tame, tender.*

FINANCIAL

bursal	fiscal	monetary	pecuniary

These words all relate to money, receipts, or expenditures. *Financial* applies especially to governmental revenues or expenditures, or to private transactions of considerable moment; we speak of a *pecuniary* reward, a *financial* enterprise; we give a needy person *pecuniary* (not *financial*) assistance. It is common to speak of the *fiscal* rather than the *financial* year. *Monetary* relates to actual money, coin, currency; as, the *monetary* system; a *monetary* transaction is one in which money is transferred. *Pecuniary* refers to that in which money is involved, but less directly; we speak of one's *pecuniary* affairs or interests, with no special reference to the handling of cash. *Bursal* and *fiscal* refer to the *financial* affairs of governments, large corporations, colleges, etc.

FINE

admirable	elegant	polished	small
beautiful	excellent	pure	smooth
choice	exquisite	refined	splendid
clarified	handsome	sensitive	subtile
clear	keen	sharp	subtle
comminuted	minute	slender	tenuous
dainty	nice	slight	thin
delicate			

Fine (from L. *finis*, end) denotes that which has been brought to a full end, finished. From this root-sense many derived meanings branch out, causing words quite remote from each other to be synonyms of *fine*. That which is truly finished, brought to an ideal end, is *excellent* of its kind, and *beautiful* if a thing that admits of beauty; as, a *fine* house, *fine* trees, a *fine* woman, a *fine* morning; if a thing that admits of the removal of impurities, it is not finished till these are removed, and hence *fine* signifies *clarified, clear, pure, refined*; as, *fine* gold. That which is finished is apt to be *polished, smooth* to the touch, minutely exact in outline.

Exquisite stresses perfection, matchless quality or beauty; *dainty* is small and *exquisite*; *delicate* is fine and light, as in texture and color, also daintily pleasing. A *slender* thread is *fine* and often *beautiful*; a *fine* edge is *thin, sharp, keen*; *slight* in figure means *small* and *thin*. *Minute* is very *fine*, very *small*; *comminuted* is reduced to *minute* particles. See **beautiful; minute.**

> **ANTONYMS:** *big, blunt, clumsy, coarse, great, heavy, huge, immense, large, rude, stout, thick.*

FIRE

blaze	burning	combustion	conflagration	flame

Fire is rapid *combustion*, accompanied always by light and heat; *combustion* being the continuous chemical combination of a substance with some element, as oxygen, evolving heat, and extending from slow processes, such as those by which the heat of the human body is maintained, to the processes producing the most intense light also, as in a blast-furnace, or on the surface of the sun. *Blaze, flame*, etc., designate the mingled light and heat of a *fire*. *Combustion* is the scientific, *burning* the popular term. A *conflagration* is an extensive *fire*. See **light.**

FIT

adapted	befitting	decorous	proper
adequate	calculated	fitted	qualified
apposite	competent	fitting	seemly
appropriate	congruous	meet	suitable
apt	contrived	pertinent	suited
becoming	decent	prepared	

Fit signifies having competence, the qualities to meet some demand, and is a word of widest range of meaning; we say of a statesman, he is thoroughly *fit* for some high task. *Fit* also has a double depreciatory use, according as it is positive or negative; we may say, he is *fit* to feed swine (meaning "only *fit*"), or, he is not *fit* to feed swine (meaning "not even *fit*" for that task). *Fit* often implies training and readiness, as of a runner for a race.

A person or thing is *adapted* for a work or purpose, when possessing natural or acquired qualities such as the work or purpose demands. *Adequate* (from L. *ad*, to, + *æquus*, equal) has a more definite idea of measuring up to a demand; as, an *adequate* supply of food or money; the strength of a machine may be *adequate* to a task, but the machine itself not *adapted* to deal with the material. *Suited* is less definite and more general than *adapted*, implying natural capacity, tendency, or taste; one who is *suited* to a work will find the work congenial, and be able and ready to acquire any qualifications he yet may lack; conversely we speak of a work as *suited* to one's character, tastes, or abilities. *Fitted* refers more especially to acquired qualifications; we might say that a student is *fitted* for college, but not *fit* or *competent* for college life and work. One is *qualified* who measures up to some fixed standard of ability or of official or legal requirements; in the latter sense we speak of *qualified* voters.

Apt, aside from its meaning of liable or likely, signifies, when applied to persons, naturally gifted, readily meeting certain work or requirements; as, an *apt* pupil. As applied to remarks, illustrations, or the like, *apt*, *apposite*, *pertinent*, *appropriate* are close synonyms; *apt* denotes more of keen, instant, and ready fitness; *apposite*, more of close and nice adjustment; *pertinent*, more of exact, comprehensive, and substantial accuracy; *appropriate* applies not only to the subject dealt with, but to the time, place, and circumstances in which the comparison is used. *Becoming*, in addition to the act itself, has something of the doer in mind. An illustration or remark may be *apt*, *apposite*, or *pertinent*, and yet not *appropriate* on a certain occasion or *becoming* in the speaker. See **adequate; becoming.** Compare **likely.**

ANTONYMS: *amiss, awkward, ill-contrived, ill-fitted, ill-fitting, ill-suited, ill-timed, improper, inadequate, inappropriate, inexpedient, misapplied, miscalculated, miscontrived, misfitted, misfitting, unfit, ungainly, unseemly, unsuitable, untimely.*

FIX

apply	decide	locate	secure
attach	determine	place	set
bind	establish	plant	settle
consolidate	fasten	root	tie

To *fix* is to make firm or secure against movement or displacement; as, t *fix* a post in the ground; to *fix* a statue upon a pedestal; figuratively, to direc or hold intently; as, to *fix* the gaze upon an object; to *fix* the attention upo a subject; also, to decide definitely, make sure, *settle, determine*; as, to *fix* th meaning of a word; to *fix* a date for adjournment; to *fix* rules of procedure or the terms of a contract, etc. Either *attach* or *fasten* is less absolute an substantial in meaning than *fix*. *Fasten* has more reference to the means o connection; if we say, the statue is *fastened* to the pedestal, we think at onc of the bolts or cement by which it is held in place. *Fix* has more referenc than *fasten* to the firmness and stability of the whole; broken bones are *fixe* (not *fastened*) in position by splints. We *bind* with something flexible, as bandage or cord.

To *fasten* the eyes or the attention refers more to the original act; to *fi* them, more to settled and persistent action; so we speak of a *fixed* gaze, or c *fixed* ideas—where *fastened* or *attached* could not be employed. To *apply* to bring together, to connect; we *apply* a rule to a given case, an antisepti to a wound, a nickname to a popular athlete. To *set* (from OE. *settan*, causa tive of *sittan*, sit) is to cause to sit, stand, or rest, as on a seat or support and is said properly of things as having some power of self-support (thu opposed to lay;—we lay a book, but *set* a dish, on the table). *Set* has refer ence to some specific end for which an object is put into a certain place, posi tion, or relation; as, to *set* a glass of water on the speaker's desk; a post ma\ be *fixed* in the ground anywhere, but is *set* with reference to some definit purpose of demarcation, support, etc.; stakes are *set* at measured distances t mark the lines of a new building, a roadway, or the like; by this idea o relative position, *set* comes close to the meaning of adjust; as, to *set* a clocl or watch, a saw, etc.

That which is *set* may or may not be *attached, fastened,* or *fixed*; the disl which is *set* in the center of the table may be removed to the side; a screw i *set* when firmly *fixed* in place. To *secure* (from L. *se,* without, + *cura,* care\ is to *fasten* effectually, so that the person *securing* may be without care o anxiety as to the object *secured*; a door may be *fastened* by a light catch easily forced open; it is *secured* by a strong lock, bolt, or bar; a surgeor *secures* an artery, as by a ligature, against hemorrhage; an object may b\ slightly *attached* to another; it is firmly *secured*. The bones of a fractured limb are *set* when brought into place, where they must then be *fixed* o\ *secured*, as by splints or a plaster cast; a prisoner is *secured*, as by fetters against escape; a commander *secures* a position for attack upon the enemy, o\

against attack by the enemy; one *secures* a loan, an inheritance, a possession, property, etc.; a debt, a mortgage, or the like, is *secured* by a legal claim upon property adequate for its payment, or when a person of adequate means becomes legally responsible for the required amount.

To *settle* is to *fix* firmly; as, to *settle* oneself in a chair; so, to *establish*, to free from agitation or disturbance, to put in order, to bring to a conclusion or settlement; also, to adjust differences; terms may be *fixed* by the party in control; they are *settled* by mutual agreement between the parties concerned. Facts are *established* by using evidence to arrive at a decision; a man's position is *established* when he is secure from sudden misfortune.

Fix in the sense of "repair" is a convenient American and British colloquialism, rooted in popular use. In the United States, especially among mechanics and artificers, to *fix* a thing is to do to or with it whatever is needed to make it answer its purpose, whether by arrangement, adjustment, repair, or otherwise; to *fix* a furnace, *fix* a clock, or the like, is to put it in complete working order by whatever process. *Up* is often added, and the expression is applied even to matters of business; as, "*Fix* that matter *up* somehow"; *i.e.*, make some kind of agreement or adjustment that may dispose of it. The best speakers, while giving the popular term a certain colloquial license, prefer wherever practicable some more discriminating word or phrase. *Fix* in the sense of "disable," "injure," or "kill," and *fix up* in the sense "dress elegantly," are slang usages. See **adapt; apply; arrange; attach; bind.** Compare **compromise; security.**

ANTONYMS: *change, detach, disarrange, displace, disturb, free, loose, loosen, set free, shake, unbolt, unfasten, unfix, unlatch, unlock, unsettle, weaken.*

FLAT

| even | level | plane |
| horizontal | plain | smooth |

That is *flat* which reveals no outstanding curves, bumps, or holes; *flat* applies to a surface only, and, in the most usual sense, to a surface that is horizontal or level in all directions; a line may be *level*, a floor is *flat*. However, a vertical surface may also be called *flat*; we speak of a *flat* wall. Anything which lies directly on or against a *flat* surface is also said to be *flat*; as, we lay *flat* on the ground.

Horizontal signifies in the direction of or parallel to the horizon. For practical purposes *level* and *horizontal* are identical, though *level*, as the more popular word, is more loosely used of that which has no specially noticeable elevations or inequalities; as, a *level* road.

Plane applies only to a surface, and is used with more mathematical exactness than *flat*. The adjective *plain*, originally the same word as *plane*, is

now rarely used except in the figurative senses, but the original sense appea
in the noun, as we speak of "a wide plain." We speak of a *horizontal* line,
flat morass, a *level* road, a *plain* country, a *plane* surface (especially in th
scientific sense). That which is *level* may not be *even*, and that which is *eve*
may not be *level*; a *level* road may be very rough; a slope may be *even*. A
even line's straightness, an *even* surface's flatness, is noticeable. That whic
is *smooth* is perfectly *even*, as if it had been polished, rubbed, or rolled; as,
smooth tennis court.

> ANTONYMS: *broken, hilly, inclined, irregular, rolling, rough,*
> *rugged, slanting, sloping, uneven.*

FLUCTUATE

hesitate	swerve	vacillate	veer
oscillate	undulate	vary	waver

To *fluctuate* (from L. *fluctus,* a wave) is to move like a wave with alterna
rise and fall. A pendulum *oscillates*; waves *fluctuate* or *undulate*; a light or
flame *wavers*; a frightened steed *swerves* from his course; a tool or weapo
swerves from the mark or line; the temperature *varies*; the wind *veers* whe
it suddenly changes its direction. That which *veers* may steadily hold the ne
direction; that which *oscillates, fluctuates, undulates,* or *wavers* retraces son
of its path. As regards mental states, he who *hesitates* sticks on the verge
decision; he who *wavers* does not stick to a decision; he who *vacillates* decid
now one way, and now another; one *vacillates* between contrasted decisions
actions; he may *waver* between decision and indecision, or between action an
inaction. Persons *hesitate, vacillate, waver*; feelings *fluctuate* or *vary*. S
shake.

> ANTONYMS: *abide, adhere, hold fast, persist, stand fast, stay,*
> *stick.*

FLUID

gas   liquid

A *fluid* is a substance that, like air or water, yields to any force that ten
to change its form; a *liquid* is a body in that state in which the particles mo
freely among themselves, but remain in one mass, keeping the same volum
but taking always the form of the containing vessel; a *liquid* is a relative
inelastic *fluid*; a gas is an elastic *fluid* that tends to distribute itself even
throughout the containing space. All *liquids* are *fluids*, but not all *fluids* a
liquids; air and all the *gases* are *fluids*, but they are not *liquids* under ordina
circumstances, though capable of being reduced to a *liquid* form by speci
means, as by cold and pressure. Water at ordinary temperatures is at once
fluid and a *liquid*.

FOLLOW

accompany	come after	go after	obey	pursue
attend	copy	heed	observe	result
chase	ensue	imitate	practice	succeed

To *follow* something is to *go after* or *come after* it, either in space or in time. A servant *follows* or *attends* his master; a victorious general may *follow* the retreating enemy merely to watch and hold him in check; he *chases* or *pursues* with intent to overtake and attack; the chase is closer and hotter than the pursuit. See **hunt.**

One event may *follow* another either with or without special connection; if it *ensues*, there is some orderly connection; as, the *ensuing* year; if it *results* from or *accompanies* another, there is some relation of effect, consequence, or inference. A clerk *observes* his employer's directions. A child *obeys* his parent's commands, *follows* or *copies* his example, *imitates* his speech and manners. The compositor *follows* copy; the incoming *succeeds* the outgoing official.

FOOD

aliment	fodder	nutriment	regimen
diet	forage	nutrition	sustenance
fare	nourishment	pabulum	viands
feed	nutrients	provender	victuals

Food, popularly, is whatever one eats, as distinguished from what one drinks. Thus, we speak of *food* and drink; of wholesome, unwholesome, or indigestible *food*. In a more exact sense, whatever serves, when taken into the digestive organs, to build up structure or supply waste is *food*; we speak of liquid *food*, plant *food*, etc. In this sense, *food* is closely synonymous with *nutriment*, *nourishment*, and *sustenance*. *Diet* refers to the quantity and quality of *food* habitually taken, with reference to the preservation of health.

Nourishment and *sustenance* apply to whatever can be introduced into the system as a means of sustaining life; an invalid takes *nourishment*. *Nutriment* and *nutrition* have more of measurable, scientific reference to the elements of various *foods*; thus, wheat is said to contain a great amount of *nutriment*. Such *food* elements as carbohydrates, proteins, etc., are known as *nutrients*.

Regimen applies to the whole ordering of life and especially to *food* taken by strict rule. *Fare* is a general word for all table supplies, good or bad; as, sumptuous *fare*, wretched *fare*. *Victuals* is a plain word for whatever may be eaten; we speak of cold *victuals*, choice *viands*, but both words are becoming rare except in literary usage. *Aliment* and *pabulum* are both used to connote *sustenance* for mind as well as body; *aliment* generally stressing that which supplies support, and *pabulum*, specifically mental food.

Feed, *fodder*, and *provender* are used only of the *food* of the lower animals, *feed* denoting anything consumed, but more commonly grain; *fodder*, hay, cornstalks, or the like, sometimes called "long *feed*"; *provender*, dry *feed*, whether grain or hay, straw, etc. *Forage* is any kind of *food* suitable for horses and cattle, either as obtained by a military force in scouring the country, especially an enemy's country, or as obtained by grazing.

FORETELL

augur	**divine**	**portend**	**prognosticate**
betoken	**forebode**	**predict**	**prophesy**
bode	**forecast**	**presage**	

To *foretell* is to make known or show beforehand that something will happen; *predict*, though with the same basic meaning, now implies a certain amount of accuracy in *foretelling*, obtained by conclusions drawn from facts. *Prophesy* differs from *predict* in that it claims divine inspiration. "Persons or things *augur*; persons only *forebode* or *presage*; things only *betoken* or *portend*." CRABB *English Synonymes*. We *augur* well for a voyage, using past good fortune and a good start as omens or indications; we *presage* success by foreknowledge of the staunchness of the ship and the skill of the captain. We *forebode* misfortune either from circumstances that *betoken* failure or from gloomy fancies for which we could not give a reason.

Portend is unfavorable in meaning (as appears also in the noun "portent" and the adjective "portentous"); dissipation among the officers and mutiny among the crew *portend* disaster. *Divine* has reference to the ancient soothsayers' arts (as in *Gen.* xliv, 5, 15) and refers rather to instinct or intuition than to reading the future. To *prognosticate* is to *foretell* from signs. Compare **sign**.

ANTONYMS: *assure, calculate, demonstrate, determine, establish, insure, make sure, prove, settle, warrant.*

FORMIDABLE

dangerous	redoubtable	terrible	tremendous

That which is *formidable* is worthy of fear if encountered or opposed; as, a *formidable* array of troops, or of evidence. *Formidable* is a word of more dignity than *dangerous*, and suggests more calm and collected power than *terrible*; *formidable* is less overwhelming than *tremendous*. A loaded gun is *dangerous*; an intrenched army is *formidable*; a bayonet charge is *terrible*; a full artillery barrage is *tremendous*. A *dangerous* man is likely to do mischief, and needs watching; a *formidable* man may not be *dangerous* if not attacked; an enraged maniac is *terrible*; the force of ocean waves in a storm and the silent pressure in the ocean depths are *tremendous*.

ANTONYMS: *contemptible, despicable, feeble, harmless, help-less, powerless, weak.*

PREPOSITIONS: Formidable *by* or *in* numbers, *in* strength; formidable *to* the enemy.

FORTIFICATION

breastwork	entrenchment	fortress	stronghold
castle	fastness	foxhole	trench
citadel	fieldworks	intrenchment	work(s)
defenses	fort	rifle pit	

Fortification is the general word for any artificial defensive *work*; a *fortress* is a *fortification* of especial size and strength; a *fortress* is regarded as permanent, and is ordinarily an independent *work*; a *fortification* may be temporary, or it may be part of a permanent system of *defenses*; we speak of the *fortifications* of a city. A *citadel* is a *fortification* within a city, or the fortified inner part of a city or *fortress,* within which a garrison may be placed to overawe the citizens, or to which the defenders may retire if the outer *works* are captured. The medieval *castle* was the fortified residence of a king or baron. *Fort* is the common military term for a permanent installation of moderate size occupied or designed to be occupied by troops, and opposed to camp, which is temporary. *Fort* is also used of harbor *defenses* on land. The *fortifications* of a city often consist of a chain of *forts.* Any defensible place, either natural or artificial, is a *fastness* or *stronghold. Entrenchment* (in military use more commonly *intrenchment*) is a very general term, which may apply to the simplest and most hastily constructed *breastworks, rifle pits,* or the like, or to a complicated system of defensive *works,* usually less substantial and permanent than *fortifications. Trench,* in modern warfare, may consist of a hastily dug shelter for one man or group of men, or a connected series of such pits, unified and deepened for semi-permanent defense or offense; the *foxhole,* also hastily dug, rarely accommodates more than one.

FORTITUDE

backbone	endurance	guts	pluck
courage	grit	heroism	resolution

Fortitude (from L. *fortis,* strong) is the strength or firmness of mind or soul to endure pain or adversity patiently and determinedly. *Fortitude* has been defined as "passive *courage,*" which is a good definition, but not complete. *Fortitude* might be termed "still *courage,*" or "enduring *courage*"; it is that quality which is able not merely to endure pain or trial, but steadily to confront dangers that cannot be actively opposed, or against which one has no adequate defense; it takes *courage* to charge a battery, *fortitude* to stand still under an enemy's fire. *Guts,* in its slang usage, is the popular expression for the literary term, *fortitude.*

Resolution is of the mind; *endurance* is partly physical; it requires *resolution* to resist temptation, *endurance* to resist hunger and cold. In this comparison, *backbone* implies determination, firmness against opposition, something so strong that it needs no support; *grit* refers to that firmness of mind and character that can carry on in the face of real difficulties; *pluck* stresses bravery or stoutheartedness in the face of odds. *Heroism* connotes the brave venturesome characteristics of a hero. See **patience.** Compare **brave.**

FORTUNATE

favored	lucky	providential
happy	prosperous	successful

A man is *fortunate* or *lucky* if advantages have come to him without or beyond his direct planning or achieving. *Lucky* is the more common and colloquial, *fortunate* the more elegant word. *Fortunate* is more naturally applied to the graver matters and often implies auspicious, as we speak of the *fortunate,* rather than the *lucky,* outcome of a great battle; *lucky* more strongly emphasizes the element of chance, as when we speak of a *lucky* hit, a *lucky* guess, or of one as "born under a *lucky* star."

A man is *successful* in any case if he achieves or gains what he seeks; he is known as a *successful* man if he has achieved or gained worthy objects of endeavor. *Favored* is used in a religious sense, implying that one is the object of divine favor. *Happy,* in this connection, signifies possessed of the means of happiness. One is said to be *happy* or *prosperous* whether his prosperity be the result of fortune or of achievement; *providential* refers to the action of a superintending Providence, and often has the sense of opportune.

ANTONYMS: *broken, crushed, fallen, ill-starred, miserable, unfortunate, unhappy, unlucky, woeful, wretched.*

FOUNDATION

base	foot	origin	substratum
basis	ground	root	substructure
bottom	groundwork		

A *foundation* is never a basement, but a substantial supporting mass on which the entire superstructure rests; in the finished building the *foundation* is usually below the surface of the ground and out of sight. *Base* and *basis* differ from *foundation,* as denoting something architecturally of less extent; we speak of the *foundation* rather than the *base* or *basis* of a skyscraper; in reference to natural objects, we speak of the *base* of a rock, cliff, or mountain; we might speak of a bed of rock as forming a good *base* for the *foundation* of building. In figurative and poetic use, the *foundation* is commonly regarded something on which to build:

> Of old hast thou laid the *foundation* of the earth.
> *Ps.* cii, 25.

A *substratum* (from L. *sub*, under, + *sterno*, spread) is something that underlies, as a natural deposit; as, a *substratum* of clay or of rock. A *substructure* (from L. *sub*, under, + *struo*, build) is something built under—perhaps forming a basement, or perhaps constructed merely for support of the building above (the superstructure); a *foundation* is a *substructure* in the latter sense.

Base and *basis*, though both ultimately derived from the same Greek word (*basis*) differ from each other in use; the *base* of a column is architecturally a part of the column, the lowest part supporting the rest. *Base* has wide use as applied to material objects; we speak of the *base* of a pyramid, the *base* of a triangle, the *base* or *base*-line of a survey, the *base* of the skull, a *base* of operations, a *base* of supply, etc. *Basis* is now rarely used literally, but has extensive figurative use, while *base* is rarely used figuratively; we speak of the *basis* of an opinion, argument, report, story, hypothesis, etc.

Ground (from OE. *grund*) is, in figurative use, akin to *basis*, but (as is usual with Old English words) more allied to practical matters than its Greek correlative; we speak of *ground* for suspicion, action, or interference, where *basis* would seem more abstract and theoretical; the *groundwork* may be the *basis* or *foundation* of anything, but is more often viewed as a fundamental and essential part. *Root* and *origin* are figurative words for *foundation*, as in "Money is the *root* of all evil."

FRAUD

artifice	**deception**	**imposture**	**treachery**
cheat	**dishonesty**	**swindle**	**treason**
cheating	**duplicity**	**swindling**	**trick**
deceit	**imposition**		

A *fraud* is an act of deliberate *deception* designed to secure something by taking unfair advantage of someone. A *deception* may be planned merely to gain some end of one's own, with no intent of harming another; *deceit* implies design to deceive; an *imposition*, to take some small advantage of another, or simply to make another ridiculous. An *imposture* is designed to obtain money, credit, or position to which one is not entitled, and may be practiced by a street beggar or by the pretender to a throne. All action that is not honest is dishonest, but the term *dishonesty* is generally applied in business, politics, etc., to deceitful practices which are not directly criminal.

Fraud includes *deceit*, but *deceit* may not reach the gravity of *fraud*; a cheat is of the nature of *fraud*, but of a petty sort; a *swindle* is more serious than a *cheat*, involving larger values and more flagrant *dishonesty*. *Fraud* commonly actionable at law; *cheating* and *swindling* are for the most part ov of the reach of legal proceedings.

Treachery is chiefly used of *dishonesty* in matters of friendship, soci relations, government, or war; *treachery* may be more harmful than *frau* but is not so gross, and is not ordinarily open to legal redress. *Treason* is specific form of *treachery* of a subject to the government to which he ow allegiance, and is definable and punishable at law. An *artifice* may be just tricky expedient to sell goods; a *trick* connotes deceit or fraud in the sellin; *duplicity* is intentional double-dealing, including bad faith. See **deception trick.**

ANTONYMS: *fairness, good faith, honesty, integrity, truth, up-rightness.*

FRIENDLY

accessible	complaisant	genial	neighborly
affable	cordial	hearty	sociable
affectionate	devoted	kind	social
amicable	favorable	kindly	tender
brotherly	fond	loving	well-disposed
companionable			

Friendly, as said of persons, signifies having the disposition of a friend; said of acts, it signifies befitting or worthy of a friend. The adjective *friend* does not reach the full significance of the nouns "friend" and "friendship" one may be *friendly* to those who are not his friends, and to be in *friend* relations often signifies little more than not to be hostile. In its applicatic to persons, *accessible* is used of public and eminent persons, who might, disposed, hold themselves at a distance from others. *Companionable* a; *sociable* refer to manner and behavior; *cordial* and *genial* express genuin kindliness of heart. We speak of a *cordial* greeting, a *favorable* reception, *neighborly* call, a *sociable* visitor, an *amicable* settlement, a *kind* interest, *friendly* regard, a *hearty* welcome.

The Saxon *friendly* is stronger than the Latin *amicable*; *amicable* sugges: formal friendship; *friendly* includes sympathetic feeling. *Fond* is common applied to an affection that becomes, or at least appears, excessive. *Affectio* ate, *devoted*, and *tender* are almost always used in a high and good sense; a an *affectionate* son; a *devoted* friend; "the *tender* mercy of our God" (*Lu* i, 78). *Affable* people are ready and willing to be *friendly*; *complaisant* peop are obliging and willing to yield to others. A *social* gathering connot *friendly* intercourse. We can trust the *well-disposed* to be favorably incline and to do *kindly* acts. Compare **friendship.**

ANTONYMS: *adverse, alienated, antagonistic, bellicose, belligerent, cold, contentious, disaffected, distant, estranged, frigid, hostile, ill-disposed, indifferent, inimical, unfriendly, unkind, warlike.*

FRIENDSHIP

affection	comity	esteem	good will
amity	consideration	favor	love
attachment	devotion	friendliness	regard

Friendship is a deep, quiet, enduring *affection,* founded upon mutual respect and *esteem. Friendship* is always mutual; there may be unreciprocated *affection* or *attachment,* unrequited *love,* or even unrecognized and unappreciated *devotion,* but never unreciprocated or unrequited *friendship;* one may have friendly feelings toward an enemy, but while there is hostility or coldness on one side there cannot be *friendship* between the two. *Friendliness* is a quality of friendly feeling, without the deep and settled *attachment* implied in the state of *friendship. Comity* is mutual kindly courtesy, with care of each other's right, and *amity* a friendly feeling and relation, not necessarily implying special *friendliness,* but just an absence of enmity; as, the *comity* of nations, or *amity* between neighboring countries.

Affection may be purely natural; *friendship* is a growth. *Friendship* is more intellectual and less emotional than *love;* it is easier to give reasons for *friendship* than for *love; friendship* is more calm and quiet, *love* more fervent, rising often to intense passion. *Friendship* implies some degree of equality, while *love* does not; we can speak of man's *love* toward God, not of his *friendship* for God. *Good will* desires the well-being of others; *favor* suggests a friendly willingness to help. We have a high *regard* for those whom we *esteem.* Compare **acquaintance; esteem; love.**

ANTONYMS: See synonyms for **battle; enmity; hatred; quarrel.**

PREPOSITIONS: The friendship *of* one person *for* or *toward* another, or the friendship *between* them.

FRIGHTEN

affright	browbeat	dismay	startle
alarm	cow	intimidate	terrify
appal	daunt	scare	terrorize

One is *frightened* by a cause of fear addressed directly and suddenly to the senses; he is *intimidated* or made afraid by threats or a show of force; the means of intimidation may act through the senses, or may appeal only to the intellect or the sensibilities. The sudden rush of an armed madman may *frighten;* the quiet leveling of a highwayman's pistol *intimidates.* A savage beast is *intimidated* by the keeper's whip. Employers may *intimidate* their employees from voting contrary to the company by threat of discharge; a mother may be *intimidated* through fear for her child.

To *browbeat* or *cow* is to bring into a state of submissive fear; to *daunt* is to give pause or check to a violent, threatening, or even a brave spirit. To *scare* is to cause sudden, unnerving fear of momentary nature; to *startle* is to surprise or shock by a sudden movement; to *terrify* is to awaken fear that is overwhelming; to *terrorize* is to reduce to a state of terror. To *appal* (from L. *ad*, to, + *paleo*, be pale) is to strike with sudden fear, dismay, and horror; one may be *appalled* at the sufferings or peril of others; he is *terrified* by danger to himself. See **alarm.** Compare **fear.**

FRUGALITY

economy	parsimony	saving	sparing
miserliness	providence	scrimping	thrift
parsimoniousness	prudence		

Frugality is a withholding of expenditure, or *sparing* of supplies or provision, to a noticeable and often to a painful degree; *parsimony* is excessive and unreasonable *saving* for the sake of *saving; scrimping* is niggardliness in providing. *Frugality* exalted into a virtue to be practiced for its own sake, instead of as a means to an end, becomes the vice of *parsimony.*

Economy is a wise and careful administration of the means at one's disposal. *Miserliness* is the denying oneself and others the ordinary comforts or even necessaries of life, for the mere sake of hoarding money. *Prudence* and *providence* look far ahead, and sacrifice the present to the future, saving as much as may be necessary for that end. *Thrift* seeks not merely to save, but to earn. *Economy* manages, *frugality* saves, *providence* plans, *thrift* at once earns and saves, with a view to wholesome and profitable expenditure at a fitting time. See **abstinence; prudence.**

ANTONYMS: *abundance, affluence, bounty, extravagance, liberality, luxury, opulence, riches, waste, wealth.*

G

GENDER
sex

Gender is a distinction in grammar that sometimes affects the form of a word; *sex* is a distinction among living things, and is also the characteristic by which most living beings are distinguished from inanimate things. While there are but two *sexes*, there are in some languages, as in English and German, three *genders*. The French language has but two *genders* and makes the names of all inanimate objects either masculine or feminine; some languages are without the distinction of *gender,* and those that maintain it are often quite arbitrary in its application. We speak of the masculine or feminine *gender,* the male or female *sex.*

GENERAL

common	familiar	normal	public
commonplace	frequent	ordinary	universal
customary	generic	popular	usual
everyday	habitual	prevalent	

General may signify pertaining equally to all of a class, race, etc., but very commonly signifies pertaining to the greater number, but not necessarily to all. *Common* signifies frequently occurring, not out of the regular course, not exceptional; hence, not above the average, not excellent or distinguished, inferior, or even low; *common* also signifies pertaining to or participated in by two or more persons or things; as, sorrow is *common* to the race. *Universal* applies to all without exception; *general* applies to all with possible or comparatively slight exceptions; *common* applies to very many without deciding whether they are even a majority.

A *common* remark is one we often hear; a *general* experience is one that comes to the majority of people; a *universal* experience is one from which no human being is exempt. It is dangerous for a debater to affirm a *universal* proposition, since that can be negatived by a single exception, while a *general* statement is not invalidated, even by adducing many exceptions. We say a *common* opinion, *common* experience, a *general* rule, *general* truth, a *universal* law. *Generic* is frequently used instead of *general* as a term referring to every member of a genus, or, in non-technical usage, of any other category; as, a mere *general* similarity between two plants proves nothing, but a *generic* likeness indicates that they belong to the same genus. See **normal; usual.**

ANTONYMS: *exceptional, infrequent, particular, rare, singular, special, specific, uncommon, unknown, unusual.*

217

GENEROUS

bountiful	free-handed	liberal	noble
disinterested	free-hearted	magnanimous	open-handed
free	handsome	munificent	open-hearted

Generous primarily signifies having the qualities worthy of noble or honorable birth; hence, *free* and abundant in giving, giving freely, heartily, and self-sacrificingly. As regards giving, *generous* refers rather to the self-sacrificing heartiness of the giver, *liberal* to the amount of the gift; a child may show himself *generous* in the gift of an apple, a millionaire makes a *liberal* donation; a *generous* gift, however, is commonly thought of as both ample and hearty. A *munificent* gift is vast in amount, whatever the motive of its bestowal.

The meaning of *handsome*, in this sense, is closely akin to that of *liberal*, when applied to a gift, remuneration, or the like; as, the president receives a *handsome* annual salary. One may be *free* with another's money; he can be *generous* only with his own. *Disinterested* suggests rather the thought of one's own self-denial; *generous*, of one's hearty interest in another's welfare or happiness. One is *magnanimous* by a greatness of soul that rises above all that is poor, mean, or weak, especially above every petty or ignoble motive or feeling pertaining to one's self, and thus above resentment of injury or insult; one is *generous* by a kindness of heart that would rejoice in the welfare rather than in the punishment of the offender.

> **ANTONYMS:** *avaricious, close, covetous, greedy, ignoble, illiberal, mean, miserly, niggardly, parsimonious, penurious, petty, rapacious, stingy.*

GENIUS

aptitude	faculty	knack	talents
bent	gift	talent	

Genius is exalted intellectual power capable of operating independently of tuition and training, and marked by an extraordinary *faculty* for original creation, invention, discovery, expression, etc. *Talent* is marked mental ability, and in a special sense, a particular and uncommon *aptitude* for some special mental work or attainment. *Genius* is higher than *talent*, more spontaneous, less dependent upon instruction, less amenable to training; *talent* is largely the capacity to learn, acquire, appropriate, adapt oneself to demand. *Gift* is applied to some ability or quality whose origin is not easily explained; as, she has the *gift* of making people happy. A *faculty* is an acquired or native quality or ability; as, he has a rare *faculty* for appreciating beauty. *Knack* means skill or dexterity in doing something, with the implication of a certain elusive quality; as, algebra problems are easy, once you get the *knack*. *Bent* refers to an inborn tendency or inclination. See **mind; power.**

ANTONYMS: *dulness, folly, imbecility, obtuseness, senselessness, stupidity.*

GET

achieve	attain	gain	procure	secure
acquire	earn	obtain	receive	win

Get is the most comprehensive of the words listed here. Unlike the others, it does not necessarily imply effort. A person *gets* whatever he comes to possess or experience, whether with or without endeavor, expectation, or desire; he *gets* a bargain, a blow, a present, etc. *Acquire* carries a strong implication of addition to what is already owned. That which is *acquired* is often regarded as an ultimate goal or as a by-product rather than as an immediate objective; as, after many years of buying stamps he *acquired* a notable collection. A person is sometimes said to *gain* and often to *acquire* what has not been an object of direct endeavor; in the pursuits of trade he incidentally *gains* some knowledge of foreign countries; he *acquires* by association with others a correct or incorrect accent.

Obtain always implies some kind of activity, desire, or intent on the part of the obtainer. *Procure* suggests effort to *obtain* something for oneself or for others. To *secure* something, in the best usage, is to *get* possession of it and to place it out of danger, as of loss. One *secures* that which is difficult to *obtain*, and places it securely under one's control; as, he *secured* the services of the best criminal lawyer in town.

A person *earns* what he gives an equivalent of labor for, though he may not *get* it. On the other hand, he may *get* what he has not *earned;* the temptation to much dishonesty is the desire to *get* a living or a fortune without *earning* it. *Win* connotes contest, with a suggestion of chance or hazard. In popular usage, a person is often said to *win* a lawsuit, but in legal phrase he is said to *gain* his suit or case. See **attain; make; reach.**

ANTONYMS: See synonyms for **abandon.**

GIFT

benefaction	bounty	endowment	gratuity
bequest	bribe	favor	largess
boon	donation	grant	present

A *gift* is in the popular, and also in the legal sense that which is voluntarily bestowed without expectation of return or compensation. *Gift* is now almost always used in the good sense, *bribe* always in the evil sense to signify payment for a dishonorable service under the semblance of a *gift*. A *benefaction* is a charitable *gift*, generally of large amount, and viewed as of enduring value, as an *endowment* for a college. A *donation* is something, perhaps of great, never of trivial value, given usually on some public ground, as to a cause or to a person representing a cause, but not necessarily of value beyond the immediate present; as, a *donation* to a pastor.

A *gratuity* is a voluntary payment, usually in money, for some extra service or attention, as a tip to a porter or waiter. A *favor* is a token or expression of friendship or good will, often an intangible one; as, "Do me the *favor* of coming to my party." *Favor* is frequently used to denote some trifling article, as a ribbon, a feather, or some knick-knack given to guests at a dance.

Largess is a grandiose or affected term for a bountiful *gratuity*, usually to be distributed among many, as among the heralds at ancient tournaments. A *present* is a *gift* of friendship, or conciliation; no one's pride is hurt by accepting what is viewed as strictly a *present*. A *boon* is a *gift* that has been desired or craved or perhaps asked, or something freely given that meets some great desire. A *grant* is commonly considerable in amount and given by public authority; as, a *grant* of public lands for a college.

> **ANTONYMS:** *compensation, earnings, guerdon, penalty, remuneration, wages.*

GIVE

afford	communicate	donate	impart
bestow	confer	furnish	present
cede	deliver	grant	supply

To *give* is primarily to transfer to another's possession or ownership without compensation; in its secondary sense in popular use, it is to put into another's possession by any means and on any terms whatever; a buyer may say "*Give* me the goods, and I will *give* you the money"; we speak of *giving* answers, information, etc., and often of *giving* what is not agreeable to the recipient, as blows, medicine, reproof; but when there is nothing in the context to indicate the contrary, *give* is always understood in its primary sense; as, this book was *given* me. *Give* thus becomes, like get, a term of such general import as to be a synonym for a wide variety of words.

Present is a more ceremonious, formal term than *give*; as, the sword of honor was *presented* to the general. *Donate* suggests a gift made to some charity or public cause. To *afford* means to *give* in the sense of produce or yield naturally or accordingly to expectation, as fruit or profits. To *grant* is to put into one's possession in some official way, or by authoritative act; as, Congress *grants* lands to a railroad corporation. To speak of *granting* a favor carries a claim or concession of superiority on the part of the one by whom the grant may be made; to *confer* has a similar sense; as, to *confer* a degree or an honor; we *grant* a request or petition, but do not *confer* it. To *impart* is to *give* of that which one still, to a greater or less degree, retains; the teacher *imparts* instruction. To *bestow* is to *give* that of which the receiver stands in especial need; we *bestow* alms.

PREPOSITIONS: We give money *to* a person *for* a thing, *for* a purpose, etc. (or without preposition, *give* a person a sum of money); we give a thing *to* or *into* one's care or keeping; the weary fugitive gave himself up *to* his pursuers.

GOOD

able	fair	pious	suitable
adequate	favorable	pleasant	thorough
admirable	fit	precious	true
advantageous	friendly	profitable	unblemished
agreeable	genial	proper	unfeigned
beneficial	genuine	ready	unimpeached
benevolent	godly	real	unsullied
capital	gracious	religious	untarnished
cheerful	gratifying	right	upright
cheering	holy	righteous	useful
companionable	honorable	satisfactory	valid
competent	humane	serious	valuable
complete	immaculate	serviceable	virtuous
considerable	kind	skilful	well-adapted
convenient	lively	social	well-disposed
dexterous	merciful	sound	well-qualified
dutiful	obliging	staunch	wholesome
excellent	perfect	sterling	worthy
expert			

Good may at some time be a synonym of almost any adjective in the language implying advantage, benefit, utility, worth, etc. *Good* almost always carries a silent connotation of the connection or purpose with reference to which it is affirmed. A horse that is *sound, kind,* and *serviceable,* whether swift, as a racer, or strong and heavy, as a dray-horse, is a *good* horse; a ship that is *staunch* and seaworthy is a *good* ship; a use of money that brings in sure and ample returns is a *good* investment; a man of high and *true* moral character is a *good* man; one of very different character, if brave and *skilful* in war, is a *good* soldier.

Beneficial, advantageous, profitable, and *useful* connote *good* because helpful in some way; *benevolent, humane, kind,* and *merciful* include the idea of kind-heartedness. *Virtuous, admirable, dutiful,* and *upright* are all used in connection with moral conduct. *Holy, godly, pious, religious, righteous* are associated with an attitude toward religion. *Able, competent, dexterous, ex-*

pert, skilful, and *well-qualified,* all convey the idea of ability. *Expert* advice is *valuable,* and a *valid* excuse is usually *satisfactory.* See **amiable; honest.**

ANTONYMS: See synonyms for **bad.**

GOVERN

command	curb	influence	mold	reign over	rule
control	direct	manage	reign	restrain	sway

Govern carries the idea of authoritative administration or some exercise of authority that is at once effective and continuous; *control* is effective, but may be momentary or occasional. One *controls* what he holds or can hold at will absolutely in check; as, a skilful horseman *controls* a spirited horse; a person *controls* his temper; we say to one who is excited, *"Control* yourself." A person *commands* another when he has, or claims, the right to make that other do his will, with power of inflicting penalty if not obeyed; he *controls* another whom he can effectually prevent from doing anything contrary to his will; he *governs* one whom he actually does cause, regularly or constantly, to obey his will; a parent may *command* a child whom he cannot *govern* or *control.* The best teachers are not greatly prone to *command,* but *govern* or *control* their pupils largely by other means. *Command* is, however, often used in the sense of securing, as well as requiring, submission or obedience, as when we speak of a *commanding* influence; a man *commands* the situation when he can shape events as he pleases; a fortress *commands* the region when no enemy can pass against its resistance. *Govern* implies the exercise of knowledge and judgment as well as power.

To *rule* is more absolute and autocratic than to *govern;* he who *rules* is empowered to lay down the laws by which a body of people are bound, and his commands must be obeyed. Hence, we speak of a tyrant or dictator as *ruling,* and of the authority placed over a democracy or republic as *governing.* To *sway* is to move by quiet but effectual influence; to *mold* is not only to influence feeling and action, but to shape character; to *manage* is to secure by skilful contrivance the doing of one's will by those whom one cannot directly *control;* a wise mother, by gentle means, *sways* the feelings and *molds* the lives of her children; to be able to *manage* servants is an important element of good housekeeping. The word *reign,* once so absolute, now simply denotes that one holds the official station of sovereign in a monarchy, with or without effective power.

ANTONYMS: *be in subjection, be subject, comply, obey, submit, yield.*

GRACEFUL

beautiful	charming	lithe	supple

That which is *graceful* is marked by elegance and harmony, with ease of action, attitude, or posture, or delicacy of form. *Graceful* commonly suggests motion or the possibility of motion, especially motion free from all strain or awkwardness. *Lithe* includes flexibility; *supple* connotes *ease*; the dancer who is *graceful* is also *lithe* and *supple*. *Graceful* applies to the perfection of motion, especially of the lighter motions, which convey no suggestion of stress or strain, and are in harmonious curves. Apart from the thought of motion, *graceful* denotes a pleasing harmony of outline, proportion, etc., with a certain degree of delicacy. We speak of a *graceful* attitude, *graceful* drapery. *Beautiful* may apply to absolute fixity; a landscape or blue sky is *beautiful*. *Graceful* commonly applies to beauty as addressed to the eye, but we often speak of a *graceful* compliment when the compliment is given with ease and charm. See **beautiful; becoming.**

ANTONYMS: See synonyms for **awkward.**

GRIEF

affliction	melancholy	sadness	trouble
anguish	mourning	sorrow	woe
distress	regret	tribulation	

Grief is acute mental pain resulting from loss, misfortune, or deep disappointment. *Grief* is more acute and less enduring than *sorrow*; *sorrow* and *grief* are for definite cause; *sadness* and *melancholy* may arise from a vague sense of want or loss, from a low state of health, or other ill-defined cause; *sadness* may be momentary; *melancholy* is more enduring, and may become chronic. *Affliction* expresses a deep heart-sorrow and is applied also to the misfortune producing such *sorrow*; *mourning* most frequently denotes *sorrow* publicly expressed, or the public expression of such *sorrow* as may reasonably be expected; as, it is common to observe thirty days of *mourning* on the death of an officer of state. *Anguish* is painful, excruciating *grief*. *Woe* is very deep, inconsolable *sorrow*.

ANTONYMS: See synonyms for **happiness.**

PREPOSITIONS: Grief *at* a loss, *for* a friend.

GROUP

bevy	flight	hatch	pack	shoal
brood	flock	herd	pride	singular
covey	gaggle	litter	set	swarm
drove	gam	lot		

Group is the general word for any gathering of a small number of objects, whether of persons, animals, or inanimate things. The individuals in a *brood* or *litter* are related to each other; those in the other *groups* may not be. *Brood* is used chiefly of fowls and birds, *litter* of certain quadrupeds which bring forth several young at a birth; we speak of a *brood* of chickens, a *litter* of puppies; *brood* is sometimes applied to a family of young children. *Bevy* is used of birds, and figuratively of any bright and lively group of women or children, but rarely of men. *Flock* is applied to birds and to some animals; *herd* is confined to the larger animals; we speak of a *bevy* of quail, a *covey* of partridges, a *flock* of blackbirds, or a *flock* of sheep, camels, goats, or lions, a *herd* of cattle, horses, buffaloes, or elephants, a *pack* of wolves, a *pack* of hounds, a *shoal* of fish, a *swarm* of bees. *Flight*, formerly used only of birds, is now used also of airplanes, as in formation. A collection of animals driven or gathered for driving is called a *drove*. Formerly, special group terms were applied to specific birds and animals; as, a *gaggle* of geese, a *gam* of whales, a *singular* of boars, a *pride* of lions; but, excepting extreme precision, most of these terms are now in disuse.

H

HABIT

custom	practice	system	use
fashion	routine	usage	wont
habitude	rule		

Habit is a tendency or inclination toward an action or condition, which **by** repetition has become easy, spontaneous, invariable, and unconscious, or **an** action or regular series of actions, or a condition so induced. *Habitude* **is** habitual relation or association. *Custom* is the uniform doing of the same **act** in the same circumstance for a definite reason; *routine* is the doing of customary acts in a regular and uniform sequence and is more mechanical than *custom*. It is the *custom* of tradesmen to open at a uniform hour, and to follow a regular *routine* of business until closing time. *Habit* always includes an involuntary tendency, natural or acquired, greatly strengthened by a frequent repetition of the act, and may be uncontrollable. *Custom* is chiefly used of the action of many; *habit,* of the action of one; we speak of the *customs* **of** society, the *habits* of an individual.

Fashion is the generally recognized *custom* in the smaller matters, especially in dress. A *rule* is prescribed either by some external authority or by one's own will; as, it is the *rule* of the house; or, I make it my invariable *rule*. *System* is the coordination of many acts or things into a unity, and is more elaborate than *routine*. *Use* and *usage* denote the manner of using something; we speak of one person's *use* of language, but of the *usage* of many; a *use* or *usage* is almost always a *habit*. Specifically, *usage* is the established *practice* of the best speakers and writers with regard to grammatical constructions, meaning of words, etc.; *use* is the *practice* of the common man.

Practice is the voluntary doing of something in a systematic way; we **do** not speak of the *practice,* but of the *habit* of going to sleep; we speak of a tradesman's *custom,* a lawyer's or a physician's *practice*. Educationally, *practice* is the voluntary and persistent attempt to make skill a *habit*; as, *practice* in penmanship. *Wont* is established *usage* or *custom,* and is now almost wholly poetic. Compare **dress.**

HAPPEN

bechance	chance	fall out	supervene
befall	come to pass	occur	take place
betide	fall		

A thing is said to *happen* when no design is manifest, or none especially thought of; it is said to *chance* when it appears to be the result of accident. An incident *happens* or *occurs*; something external or actual *happens* to **a** person; a thought or fancy *occurs* to him. *Befall* and *betide* are transitive; *happen* is intransitive; something *befalls* or *betides* a person or *happens* **to** him. *Betide* is especially used for anticipated evil, thought of as waiting and coming at its appointed time; as woe *betide* him! One event *supervenes* upon another event, one disease upon another, etc. Compare synonyms for **accident.** ["Transpire," in the sense of *happen*, is not authorized by good usage; a thing that has *happened* is properly said to *transpire* when it becomes known.]

HAPPINESS

blessedness	ecstasy	glee	pleasure
bliss	enjoyment	gratification	rapture
cheer	felicity	joy	rejoicing
comfort	gaiety	merriment	satisfaction
contentment	gladness	mirth	triumph
delight			

Happiness is the positive, agreeable experience that springs from the possession of good, the *gratification* or *satisfaction* of the desires or the relief from pain and evil. *Gratification* results from giving any mental or physical desire something that it craves; *satisfaction* is the giving such a desire all that it craves. *Comfort* may be almost wholly negative, being found in security or relief from that which pains or annoys; there is *comfort* by a warm fireside on a wintry night; the sympathy of a true friend affords *comfort* in sorrow.

Enjoyment is more positive, always implying something to be definitely and consciously delighted in; a sick person finds *comfort* in relief from pain, while he may be far from a state of *enjoyment*. *Pleasure* is still more vivid, arising from the stimulation of the senses or the mind by an agreeable activity; *satisfaction* is more tranquil than *pleasure*; when a worthy *pleasure* is past, *satisfaction* remains. As referring to a mental state, *gratification* is used to denote a mild form of *happiness* resulting from some incident not of very great importance; *satisfaction* should properly express a *happiness* deeper, more complete, and more abiding; but as some persons may find *satisfaction* in that which is very poor or unworthy, the word has come to be feeble and tame in ordinary use.

Happiness is more positive than *comfort, enjoyment,* or *satisfaction,* more serene and rational than *pleasure; pleasure* is of necessity transient; *happiness* is abiding; thus, we speak of *pleasures,* but the plural of *happiness* is scarcely used. *Happiness,* in the full sense, is mental or spiritual or both, and is viewed as resulting from some worthy *gratification* or *satisfaction;* we can speak of vicious *pleasure* or *delight,* but not of vicious *happiness. Felicity* is a more formal term than *happiness. Gladness* is *happiness* that overflows, expressing itself in countenance, voice, manner, and action.

Joy is more intense than *happiness,* deeper than *gladness,* to which it is akin, nobler and more enduring than *pleasure. Gaiety* is more superficial than *joy,* more demonstrative than *gladness,* expressing itself in *merriment* and *mirth. Rejoicing* is *happiness* or *joy,* usually of more than one person, that finds utterance in word, song, festivity, etc.; *glee* is less outward. *Delight* is vivid, overflowing *happiness* of a somewhat transient kind; *ecstasy* is a feeling of extreme or extravagant *delight* so that the one affected by it seems almost beside himself with *joy*; *rapture* is closely allied to *ecstasy*, but is more an expression of a state of joyous exaltation. *Triumph* is such *joy* as results from victory, success, achievement. *Blessedness* is at once the state and the sense of being divinely blessed; as, the *blessedness* of the righteous. *Bliss* is ecstatic, perfected *blessedness*; as, the *bliss* of heaven.

ANTONYMS: See synonyms for **grief.**

HAPPY

blessed	delighted	jolly	prosperous
blissful	delightful	jovial	rapturous
blithe	dexterous	joyful	rejoiced
blithesome	felicitous	joyous	rejoicing
bright	fortunate	lucky	smiling
buoyant	gay	merry	sprightly
cheerful	glad	mirthful	successful
cheering	jocund	pleased	sunny
cheery			

Happy, in its original sense, refers to something that comes "by good hap," a chance that brings prosperity, benefit, or success.

And grasps the skirts of *happy* chance. TENNYSON *In Memoriam.*

Here, *happy* is closely allied to *fortunate* and *lucky.* By direct reference to the divine will, it becomes almost equivalent to *blessed*, excluding all idea of chance. *Happy* is also a synonym for *dexterous, felicitous*, and associated words when it is applied to the ready skill by which favorable results, usually in minor matters, are secured; as, a *happy* wit, *happy* at retort.

In its most frequent present use, *happy* is allied to the state of one enjoying happiness, or to that which expresses happiness; as, a *happy* marriage, a *happy* face, *happy* laughter. *Cheerful* applies to the possession or expression of a moderate and tranquil happiness. A *cheery* word spontaneously gives cheer to others; a *cheering* word is more distinctly planned to cheer and encourage. *Sprightly* refers to nimbleness and to that quickness that pleases. *Gay* applies to a temporary and perhaps superficial state of happiness and an overflowing of animal spirits; we speak of a *gay* party, *gay* laughter.

That which is *jolly* is lively and *merry. Jovial* refers to a general tendency toward merriment which finds expression in smiles, laughter, and even boisterous mirth; *jovial* is often, but not necessarily associated with convivial gaiety. The *jocund* man is witty, crackling with good humor, making jokes. A *buoyant* spirit is, as it were, borne up with joy and hope. A *bright* person brings a glow of cheer and well-being to his companions; a *sunny* disposition has a constant tranquil brightness that irradiates all who come within its influence. See **fortunate.** Compare **clever; happiness.**

ANTONYMS: See synonyms for **sad.**

HARMONY

accord	concord	consistency	**uniformity**
accordance	concurrence	consonance	union
agreement	conformity	symmetry	unison
amity	congruity	unanimity	unity
concert	consent		

When tones, thoughts, or feelings, individually different, combine to form a consistent and pleasing whole, there is *harmony*. *Harmony* is deeper and more essential than *agreement*; we may have a superficial, forced, or patched-up *agreement*, but never a superficial, forced, or patched-up *harmony*. *Concord* is less full and spiritual than *harmony*. *Concord* implies more volition than *accord*; as, their views were found to be in perfect *accord*; or, by conference *concord* was secured; we do not secure *accord*, but discover it. We may speak of being in *accord* with a person on one point, but *harmony* is wider in range. *Unity* is an absolute *harmony* of parts or parties; we speak of the *unity* of a great work of art, or of a nation in time of war. *Concert* is *agreement*, as by mutual understanding, resulting in action toward a single purpose; as, *concert* of views; *concert* of action or "concerted" action.

Conformity is correspondence in form, manner, or use; the word often signifies submission to authority or necessity, and may be as far as possible from *harmony*; as, the attempt to secure *conformity* to an established religion. *Uniformity*, as of taste or opinion, suggests either an inward *agreement* to suppress individual differences or a natural lack of them. *Congruity* involves the element of suitableness; *consistency* implies the absence of conflict or contradiction in views, statements, or acts which are brought into comparison, as in the different statements of the same person or the different periods of one man's life; *unanimity* is the complete hearty *agreement* of many. *Consent* and *concurrence* refer to decision or action, but *consent* is more passive than *concurrence*; one speaks by general *consent* when no one in the assembly cares to make formal objection; a decision of the Supreme Court depends upon the *concurrence* of a majority of the judges. Compare **agree.** See **friendship; melody.**

ANTONYMS: *antagonism, battle, conflict, contention, contest, controversy, difference, disagreement, discord, disproportion, dissension, disunion, hostility, incongruity, inconsistency, opposition, schism, separation, variance, welfare.*

HARVEST

crop	increase	produce	result
fruit	ingathering	product	return
growth	proceeds	reaping	yield
harvesting			

Harvest, from the Old English, signified originally "autumn," and as that is the usual season of gathering ripened *crops* in Northern lands, the word came to its present meaning of the season of gathering ripened grain or *fruits,* whether summer or autumn, and hence a *crop* gathered or ready for gathering; also, the act or process of gathering a *crop* or *crops. Harvest* is the elegant and literary word; *crop* is the common and commercial expression; we say a man sells his *crop,* but we should not speak of his selling his *harvest;* we speak of an ample or abundant *harvest,* a good *crop. Harvest* is applied almost wholly to grain; *crop* applies to almost anything that is gathered in; we speak of the potato *crop,* not the potato *harvest;* we may say either the wheat *crop* or the wheat *harvest.*

Produce is a collective word for all that is produced in farming or gardening, and is, in modern usage, almost wholly restricted to this sense; we speak of *produce* collectively, but of a *product* or various *products;* vegetables, fruits, eggs, butter, etc., may be termed farm *produce,* or the *products* of the farm. *Product* is a word of wider application than *produce;* we speak of the *products* of manufacturing, the *products* of thought, or the *product* obtained by multiplying one number by another. The word *proceeds* is chiefly used of the *return* from an investment; we speak of the *produce* of a farm, but of the *proceeds* of the money invested in farming. The *yield* is what the land produces; we speak of the *return* from an expenditure of money or labor, but of the *yield* of corn or oats. *Harvest* has also a figurative use, such as *crop* more rarely permits; the *result* of lax enforcement of law is a *harvest* of crime.

HATRED

abhorrence	detestation	hostility	rancor
anger	dislike	ill will	repugnance
animosity	enmity	malevolence	resentment
antipathy	grudge	malice	revenge
aversion	hate	malignity	spite

Hate, or *hatred,* as applied to persons, is intense and continued *aversion,* usually with disposition to injure; *anger* is sudden and brief, *hatred* is lingering and enduring; "Her wrath became a *hate,*" TENNYSON. As applied to things, *hatred* is intense *aversion,* with desire to destroy or remove; *hatred* of evil is a righteous passion, akin to *abhorrence,* but more vehement.

Repugnance applies to that which one feels himself summoned or impelled to do or to endure, and from which he instinctively draws back. *Aversion* is the turning away of the mind or feelings from some person or thing, or from some course of action, etc. *Animosity* is an active and deep *hostility* directed toward some person. *Antipathy* is an instinctive *dislike*, emotional rather than reasoned; *detestation* knows why it dislikes; we detest a habitual liar; some people have an *antipathy* to snakes.

Malice involves the active intent to injure; in the legal sense, *malice* is the intent to injure, even though with no personal *ill will*; as, a highwayman would be said to entertain *malice* toward the unknown traveler whom he attacks. *Malice* is direct, pressing toward a result; *malignity* is deep, lingering, and venomous, though often impotent to act; *rancor* (akin to rancid) is cherished *malignity* that has soured and festered and is virulent and implacable. *Spite* is petty *malice* that delights to inflict stinging pain; *grudge* is deeper than *spite;* it is sinister and bitter. *Grudge, resentment,* and *revenge* are all retaliatory, *grudge* being the disposition, *revenge* the determination to repay real or supposed offense with injury; *revenge* may denote also the retaliatory act; *resentment* always holds itself to be justifiable, but looks less certainly to action than *grudge* or *revenge*. *Malevolence* burns with a desire to cause evil to others. Simple goodness may arouse the *hatred* of the wicked; they will be moved to *revenge* only by what they deem an injury or affront. See **abomination; anger; antipathy; enmity.**

ANTONYMS: See synonyms for **friendship; love.**

HAVE

| be in possession (of) | hold | own |
| be possessed of | occupy | possess |

Have is the most general word, and is applied to whatever belongs to or is connected with someone; a man *has* a head or a headache, a fortune or an opinion, a friend or an enemy; he *has* time, or *has* need; he may be said to *have* what is his own, what he has borrowed, what has been entrusted to him, or what he has stolen. To *possess* a thing is to *have* the ownership with control and enjoyment of it. To *hold* is to *have* in one's hand, or securely in one's control; a man *holds* his friend's coat for a moment, or he *holds* a struggling horse; he *holds* a promissory note, or *holds* an office.

To *own* is to *have* the right of property in; to *possess* is to *have* that right in actual exercise; to *occupy* is to *have* possession and use, with some degree of permanency, with or without ownership. A man *occupies* his own house or a room in a hotel; a man may *own* a farm of which he is not in possession because a tenant *occupies* it and is determined to *hold* it; the proprietor *owns* the property, but the tenant *is in possession*. To *be in possession* differs from *possess* in that to *possess* denotes both right and fact, while to *be in possession* denotes simply the fact with no affirmation as to the right. To *have* reason is to be endowed with the faculty; to *be in possession of* one's reason denotes that the faculty is in actual present exercise.

HAZARD

accident	chance	danger	jeopardy	risk
casualty	contingency	fortuity	peril	venture

Hazard, like all the other words discussed in this paragraph, indicates the absence of control over events. *Hazard* is the incurring of a possibility of loss or harm for the possibility of benefit; *danger* may have no compensating alternative. In *hazard* the possibilities of gain or loss are nearly balanced; in *risk* the possibility of loss is the chief thought; the foolhardy take great *risks*; in *chance* and *venture* the hope of good predominates; we speak of *a* merchant's *venture*, but of an insurance company's *risk*; one may be driven by circumstances to run a *risk*; he freely seeks a *venture*; we speak of the *chance* of winning, the *hazard* or *risk* of losing. *Accidents* are incalculable; *casualties* may be to a certain extent anticipated; death and wounds are *casualties* of battle, certain to happen to some, but uncertain as to whom or how many. A *contingency* is simply an indeterminable future event, which may or may not be attended with *danger* or *risk*. *Fortuity* is a chance occurrence; *chance*. See **accident; danger.**

> ANTONYMS: *assurance, certainty, necessity, plan, protection, safeguard, safety, security, surety.*

HEALTHY

hale	hygienic	sanitary	vigorous
healthful	salubrious	sound	well
hearty	salutary	strong	wholesome

Healthy is most correctly used to signify possessing or enjoying health or its results; as, a *healthy* person; a *healthy* condition. *Healthful* signifies promotive of health, tending or adapted to confer, preserve, or promote health; as a *healthful* climate. *Wholesome* food in a *healthful* climate helps to make a *healthy* man. With *healthful* are ranged the words *hygienic, salubrious, salutary, sanitary,* and *wholesome,* while the other words are associated with *healthy. Salubrious* is always used in the physical sense, and is chiefly applied to air or climate. *Salutary* is now chiefly used in the moral sense; as, a *salutary* lesson.

> ANTONYMS: *delicate, diseased, emaciated, exhausted, failing, fainting, fragile, frail, ill, sick, unhealthy, unsound, wasted, weak, worn.*

HELP

abet	encourage	befriend	second	succor	sustain
aid	cooperate	foster	stand by	support	uphold
assist					

Help expresses greater dependence and deeper need than *aid*. In extremity we say "God *help* me!" rather than "God *aid* me!" In time of danger we cry "*help! help!*" rather than "*aid! aid!*" To *aid* is to *second* another's own exertions. We can speak of *helping* the helpless, but not of *aiding* them. *Help* includes *aid*, but *aid* may fall short of the meaning of *help*. In law to *aid* or *abet* makes one a principal. Compare synonyms for **accessory.**

To *cooperate* is to *aid* as an equal; to *assist* implies a subordinate and secondary relation. One *assists* a fallen friend to rise; he *cooperates* with him in *helping* others. We *stand by* someone in trouble, ready to *help. Encourage* refers to mental aid, as *uphold* now usually does; *succor* and *support*, oftenest to material assistance. We *encourage* the timid or despondent, *succor* the endangered, *support* the weak, *uphold* those who else might be shaken or cast down. See **abet; promote.**

> ANTONYMS: *counteract, discourage, hinder, oppose, resist, thwart, withstand.*

> PREPOSITIONS: Help *in* an enterprise *with* money; help *to* success, *against* the enemy.

HERETIC

apostate	dissenter	nonconformist	renegade	sectarian
deserter	heresiarch	pervert	schismatic	traitor

Etymologically, a *heretic* is one who takes or chooses his own belief, instead of the belief of his church; hence, a *heretic* is one who denies commonly accepted views, or who holds opinions contrary to the recognized standard or tenets of any established religious, philosophical, or other system, school, or party; the religious sense of the word is the predominant one; a *schismatic* is primarily one who separates from or produces a split or rent in the church. A *heretic* differs in doctrine from the religious body with which he is connected; a *schismatic* differs in doctrine or practice, or in both. A *heretic* may be reticent, or even silent; a *schismatic* introduces divisions. A *heresiarch* is the author of a heresy or the leader of a heretical party, and is thus at once a *heretic* and a *schismatic*. An *apostate* is one who forsakes a faith that he formerly professed.

A *pervert* is one who is regarded as "perverted" from a true to a false faith; the same person is often called a *pervert* by those whom he leaves and a "convert" by those whom he joins. With advancing ideas of religious liberty, the odious sense once attached to these words is largely modified, and *heretic* is often used playfully. A *sectarian* is a member of any religious denomination; originally, and especially in England, it applied opprobriously to any member of a heretical group.

Dissenter and *nonconformist* are terms specifically applied to English subjects who hold themselves aloof from the Church of England. A *deserter* is one who forsakes duty or allegiance; a soldier who becomes a *deserter* may simply abscond, or he may "desert to the enemy"—one of the most unpardonable of military offenses; a *renegade* may be a *deserter* in either sense, though the latter is the prevailing one; in the ancient struggles against the Moslem powers a Christian who joined the Turks or Moors was distinctively called a *renegade*. A *traitor* is one who basely betrays his associates in religious, civil, or military life. Compare **treason** under **fraud.**

HIDE

bury	cover	ensconce	mask	secrete
cloak	disguise	entomb	overwhelm	suppress
conceal	dissemble	inter	screen	veil

Hide is the general term, including all the rest, signifying to put out of sight or beyond ready observation or approach; a thing may be *hidden* by intention, by accident, or by the imperfection of the faculties of the one from whom it is *hidden*; in their games, children *hide* the slipper, or *hide* themselves from each other; a man unconsciously *hides* a picture from another by standing before it, or *hides* a thing from himself by laying something else over it. Even an unconscious object may *hide* another; as, a cloud *hides* the sun, or a building *hides* some part of the prospect by intervening between it and the observer's position. As an act of persons, to *conceal* is more often intentional; one may *hide* his face in anger, grief, or abstraction; he *conceals* his face when he fears recognition. A house is *hidden* by foliage; the bird's nest is artfully *concealed*.

Secrete is a stronger word than *conceal*, and is used chiefly of such material objects as may be separated from the person, or from their ordinary surroundings, and put in unlooked-for places; a man *conceals* a scar on his face, but does not *secrete* it; a thief *secretes* stolen goods; an officer may also be said to *secrete* himself to watch the thief. A thing is *covered* by putting something over or around it, whether by accident or design; it is *screened* by putting something before it, always with some purpose of protection from observation, inconvenience, attack, censure, etc. In the figurative use, a person may *hide* honorable feelings; he *conceals* an evil or hostile intent.

Anything which is effectually *covered* and *hidden* under any mass or accumulation is *buried*. Money is *buried* in the ground; a body is *buried* in the sea; a paper is *buried* under other documents. Whatever is *buried* is *hidden* or *concealed*; but there are many ways of *hiding* or *concealing* a thing without *burying* it. So a person may be *covered* with wraps, and not *buried* under them. *Bury* may be used of any object, *entomb* and *inter* only of a dead body. Figuratively, one may be said to be *buried* in business, in study, etc. *Ensconce* formerly meant to hide safely; in present usage it means to settle snugly or comfortably; as, he *ensconced* himself in the chair. See **dip; palliate.**

ANTONYMS: *admit, advertise, avow, betray, confess, disclose,
discover, disinter, divulge, exhibit, exhume, expose, lay bare,
lay open, make known, manifest, promulgate, publish, raise,
reveal, show, tell, uncover, unmask, unveil.*

HIGH

elevated	exalted	noble	steep	towering
eminent	lofty	proud	tall	uplifted

High is a relative term signifying greatly raised above any object, base, or
surface, in comparison with what is usual or with some standard; a table is
high if it exceeds thirty inches; a hill is not *high* at a hundred feet. Deep,
while an antonym of *high* in usage, may apply to the very same distance
simply measured in an opposite direction, *high* applying to vertical distance
measured from below upward, and deep to vertical distance measured from
above downward; as, a deep valley nestling between *high* mountains.

That is *tall* whose height is greatly in excess of its breadth or diameter,
and whose actual height is great for an object of its kind; as, a *tall* tree; a
tall man; *tall* grass. That is *lofty* which is imposing or majestic in height;
we term a spire *tall* with reference to its altitude, or *lofty* with reference to its
majestic appearance. That is *elevated* which is raised somewhat above its
surroundings; that is *eminent* which is far above them; as, an *elevated* plat-
form; an *eminent* promontory. In the figurative sense, *elevated* is less than
eminent, and this less than *exalted*; we speak of *high, lofty*, or *elevated*
thoughts, aims, etc., in the good sense, but sometimes of *high* feelings, looks,
words, etc., in the invidious sense of haughty or arrogant. A *high* ambition
may be merely selfish; a *lofty* ambition is worthy and *noble*. *Towering*, in the
literal sense, compares with *lofty* and majestic; but in the figurative sense, its
use is superlative, as, a *towering* passion; a *towering* ambition. See **steep.**

ANTONYMS: *base, deep, degraded, depressed, dwarfed, inferior, low, mean, short, stunted.*

HINDER

arrest	clog	encumber	obstruct	resist
baffle	counteract	foil	oppose	retard
balk	defer	frustrate	postpone	stay
bar	delay	hamper	prevent	stop
block	deter	impede	prolong	thwart
check	embarrass	interrupt		

To *hinder* is to keep from action, progress, motion, or growth, or to make
such action, progress, motion, or growth later in beginning or completion than
it would otherwise have been. An action is *prevented* by anything that comes

in before it to make it impossible; it is *hindered* by anything that keeps it from either beginning or ending as soon as it otherwise would, or as expected or intended. An action that is *hindered* does not take place at the appointed or appropriate time; that which is *prevented* does not take place at all; to *hinder* a thing long enough may amount to *preventing* it. A railroad train may be *hindered* by a snowstorm from arriving on time; it may by special order be *prevented* from starting.

To *impede* is to place a block or obstacle in the way of something, which renders progress or movement difficult or even impossible. To *block* is to *obstruct* so effectively as to *prevent* all passage for the time being; as, the entrance to the driveway was completely *blocked* by the snow. *Bar* is closely akin in meaning to *block,* with a strong suggestion of prohibition; as, a heavy guard *barred* all persons from entering the castle. To *stop* is to bring movement to an end, or a moving object to enforced rest. To *arrest* is to cause to *stop* suddenly. To *retard* is simply to make slow by any means whatever. To *obstruct* is to *hinder,* or possibly to *prevent* advance or passage by putting something in the way; to *oppose* or *resist* is to *hinder,* or possibly to *prevent* by directly contrary or hostile action, *resist* being the stronger term and having more suggestion of physical force; *obstructed* roads *hinder* the march of an enemy, though there may be no force strong enough to *oppose* it; one *opposes* a measure, a motion, an amendment, or the like; it is a criminal offense to *resist* an officer in the discharge of his duty; the physical system may *resist* the attack of disease or the action of a remedy. See **adjourn; protract.** Compare **impediment.**

ANTONYMS: See synonyms for **quicken.**

PREPOSITIONS: Hinder one *in* his progress, *from* acting promptly, *by* opposition.

HISTORY

account	biography	muniment	record
annals	chronicle	narration	register
archives	memoir	narrative	story
autobiography	memorial	recital	

History is a systematic *record* of past events; it is often regarded as an interpretation of events in the light of their effect on later times. *Annals* and *chronicles* relate events with little regard to their relative importance, and with complete subserviency to their succession in time. *Annals* are yearly records; *chronicles* follow the order of time. Both necessarily lack emphasis, selection, and perspective. *Archives* are public *records,* which may be *annals,* or *chronicles,* or deeds of property, etc. A *memoir* is a recollection of some incident in one's life; a group of such recollections constitutes one's *memoirs.* *Memoirs* generally record the lives of individuals or facts pertaining to indi-

vidual lives. A *biography* is a written *account* of one person's life and actions;
an *autobiography* is a *biography* written by the person whose life it records.
Annals, archives, chronicles, biographies, and *records* furnish the materials of
history. History recounts events with careful attention to their importance,
their mutual relations, their causes and consequences, selecting and grouping
events on the ground of interest or importance. *History* is usually applied to
such an *account* of events affecting communities and nations, though sometimes we speak of the *history* of a single eminent life. See **record.**

ANTONYMS: See synonyms for **fiction.**

HOBO

bo	floater	sundowner	tramp	vagrant
bum	professional	swagman	trombo	willie
drifter	stiff	tourist	vagabond	

The word *hobo* has two, somewhat contradictory meanings; a *hobo* is a
migratory worker, and in this sense is also called a *drifter* or a *floater*; a *hobo*
is also a professional *tramp.* A *tramp,* the most inclusive of all these terms,
is a non-working wanderer, a tramper from place to place. A professional
tramp, or *professional,* scorns to work, preferring to live by begging or petty
stealing. *Tourist* is the ironical, self-coined term of the *professional.* A *trombo*
is a *tramp* pugilist. A *willie* is a *professional* who carries a bedroll. *Bo* is short
for *hobo,* but also means a boy *tramp.*

Swagman and *sundowner* are terms of the Australian bush for a *tramp* who
carries a swag or a pack, and turns up at sundown asking for food and shelter.
A *vagabond* is a homeless wanderer. In modern usage the word is a true
synonym for *tramp;* in old English law, a *vagabond* was any idle disorderly
person, not necessarily wandering. *Vagrant* is almost identical with the modern
meaning of *vagabond.*

HOLE

aperture	concavity	fissure	perforation
bore	crack	gap	pipe
breach	crater	gorge	pore
burrow	defile	hold	ravine
cave	dell	hollow	rent
cavern	den	indentation	slit
cavity	dent	mine	tube
cell	depression	notch	tunnel
chasm	depth	opening	vale
cleft	excavation	orifice	valley

A *hole* is an *opening* in a solid body or compact substance; it may extend entirely through the body, or only partly through it, forming a *cavity,* and may be of any shape, provided the transverse axes are not greatly unequal, as illustrated in the proverb of "fitting round men into square *holes.*" A *hole* is generally thought of as open at one or both surfaces of the body containing it, though we speak of the *holes* in a cheese, or the *holes* in worm-eaten wood, which extend at random within the substance; a *hole* in the ground, in the trunk or branch of a tree, or the like, either found existing or purposely excavated, is often used for the home or hiding-place of an animal, and may be a *burrow* or *den*; from the use of such resorts by the inferior animals as foxes, rats, or the like, the word *hole* has an opprobrious meaning as applied to human habitations or resorts; as, the Black *Hole* of Calcutta; a rum-*hole.*

A *cavity* is a hollow space within a body, which may be open externally or completely enclosed; as, the *cavity* of the mouth; the *cavity* of the skull; *concavity* usually denotes the state of being concave, but may denote a concave surface or *cavity.* An *opening* very long in proportion to its width is more commonly called a *crack, fissure, slit,* or the like, or on the surface of the earth such an opening is designated as a *chasm, gorge,* or *ravine.* A *defile* is a long mountain pass so narrow that it can be marched through only in file, as in single file. A *rent* in a garment is made by tearing; a *slit,* by cutting. A small space wholly enclosed is called a *cell*; a biological *cell* is commonly filled with protoplasm.

A *tube* is a long, hollow, cylindrical body, as of wood, rubber, metal, or glass, for the passage of liquids or gases; a similar formation in the body of a plant or animal is likewise called a *tube*; as, the bronchial *tubes*; a *pipe* is a long, conducting passage, commonly, but not necessarily cylindrical; as, a drain*pipe*; a *pipe*-line for oil, etc.; the metallic *tubes* of a wind instrument are called *pipes*; as, the *pipes* of an organ. For the most part the difference between *tube* and *pipe* is simply a matter of usage. The minute *orifices* or perforations of the sweat glands through the skin are called *pores.* An *orifice* is an *opening* into a cavity, as the mouth of a *hole, tube,* or *pipe.*

In nautical use, the *hold* is the *cavity* of a ship below the deck, used for storage of cargo. A *crater* is an *opening* of a volcano, at or near the summit, through which eruptions occur. A *bore, excavation, mine, perforation,* or *tunnel* is artificially made; as, the *bore* of a cannon, the *excavation* for the foundation of a new building; a *mine* run by an enemy under a fortress; the *tunnel* under the Simplon; a *perforation* may be extensive, as of a shot through armor, or minute, as of a needle point through paper, rubber, or the like. A *dent* or *indentation* is a depression on the surface of a solid, as if beaten in. A *notch* is sharply cut, as with a knife or saw, generally in the edge or convex surface of an object; a *notch* in a mountain chain is named from its shape as viewed from a distance, when it seems to be sharply cut into the contour of the range.

Aperture is a very general word, applying to an *opening* of almost any shape or size through the surface of a solid body, affording ingress or egress, or permitting the passage of light, sound, etc.; *aperture* is much used in science of a measurable *opening* or interval; as, the *aperture* of a lens; the *aperture* of a microscope or of a telescope. The noun *hollow* denotes a shallow *concavity* or sunken space, usually round or oval, on the outer surface of a solid, as of the earth. A *cleft* is an *opening* or separation made, or seeming as if made, by splitting or cleaving. A *breach* is an *opening* roughly broken, generally from the top or edge down through a wall or other object, as by a battering-ram or cannon; a *gap* may be between portions that never were joined; as, a *gap* in a mountain range. Compare **break; rend.**

> ANTONYMS: *convexity, elevation, eminence, excrescence, height, hill, hillock, knoll, lump, mound, mount, mountain, peak, projection, prominence, protuberance, rampart, rising, swelling.*

HOLY

blessed	devoted	hallowed	sacred	spiritual
consecrated	divine	religious	saintly	

Holy, as the strongest of the adjectives here compared, suggests some attribute in the thing or person it describes which makes that thing or person worthy of veneration; it is the one adjective applied directly to the Supreme Being or to any of the members of the Trinity. It is also used to describe persons, places, or objects deserving the highest reverence; as, the *Holy* Family; the *Holy* Land; the *Holy* Bible. In general, non-religious contexts, *holy* is used to distinguish something from that which is commonplace, worldly, or transitory; as, he felt a *holy* love for her.

Sacred denotes something which has been consecrated to worship or to the uses of religion, or which is devoted entirely to such uses. That which is *sacred* may be made so by institution, decree, or association; that which is *holy* is so by its own nature, possessing absolute moral purity and perfection. God is *holy*; *His* commands are *sacred*. As opposed to profane, sacred implies a *religious* or Biblical connection. The Bible is *sacred* literature; Bach's B Minor Mass is *sacred* music. In general use, *sacred* describes anything which is treasured as something special, and kept apart from vulgar uses.

Divine, in its oldest and highest sense, describes a god or deity, or something which originates from or is associated with a deity. The *divine* right of kings supposedly came from God. However, *divine* has been used with great looseness, as applying to anything eminent or admirable—eloquence, music, poetry, or the like.

Blessed, consecrated, and *hallowed* stress the idea of having been devoted to religious uses, and therefore of being worthy of the highest veneration. See **perfect; pure.**

ANTONYMS: *abominable, common, cursed, impure, polluted, profane, secular, unconsecrated, unhallowed, unholy, unsanctified, wicked, worldly.*

HOME

abode	dwelling	habitation	hearthstone	ingleside
domicile	fireside	hearth	house	residence

Home, from the Old English, denoting originally a *dwelling,* came to mean an endeared *dwelling* as the scene of domestic love and happy and cherished family life, a sense to which there is an increasing tendency to restrict the word—desirably so, since we have other words to denote the mere dwelling-place; we say "The wretched tenement could not be called *home,*" or "The humble cabin was dear to him as the *home* of his childhood."

Abode, dwelling, and *habitation* are used with little difference of meaning to denote the place where one is staying; *abode* and *habitation* belong to the poetic or elevated style. Even *dwelling* is not used in familiar speech; a person says "my *house,*" "my *home,*" or more formally "my *residence.*"

Abode and *domicile* stress the contrasting ideas of transience and permanence, respectively. An *abode* is merely a place where one happens to be staying; a *domicile* is the place where one plans to stay permanently and to which one returns after any absence. A *residence* is a handsome, distinguished *home.* The idea expressed in *habitation* is that of a fixed location in which one lives, rather than an impermanent, transient *home,* as of a gypsy or nomad.

HONEST

candid	genuine	just	true
equitable	good	scrupulous	trustworthy
fair	honorable	sincere	trusty
faithful	ingenuous	straightforward	upright
frank			

One who is *honest* in the ordinary sense acts or is always disposed to act with careful regard for the rights of others, especially in matters of business or property; one who is *honorable* scrupulously observes the dictates of a personal honor that is higher than any demands of mercantile law or public opinion, and will do nothing unworthy of his own inherent nobility of soul. The *honest* man does not steal, cheat, or defraud; the *honorable* man will not take an unfair advantage that would be allowed him; he will make a sacrifice which no one could require of him, when his own sense of right demands it. One who is *honest* in the highest and fullest sense is scrupulously careful to adhere to all known truth and right even in thought. In this sense *honest* differs from *honorable* as having regard rather to absolute truth and right than to even the highest personal honor.

Sincere connotes strict adherence to the truth, with a strong implication of genuineness. The *upright* man maintains high moral principles; the *scrupulous* man is careful to obey the rules of moral conduct not only with regard to the ultimate ends, but in the small details. *Equitable* connotes impartial and *just*; *straightforward* stresses honesty and frankness of manner and conduct. See **candid**. Compare **justice.**

> ANTONYMS: *deceitful, dishonest, disingenuous, faithless, false, fraudulent, hypocritical, lying, mendacious, perfidious, traitorous, treacherous, unfaithful, unscrupulous, untrue.*

HUMANE

altruistic	compassionate	humanitarian	pitying
benevolent	forgiving	kind	sympathetic
benignant	gentle	kind-hearted	tender
charitable	gracious	merciful	tender-hearted
clement	human	philanthropic	

Humane denotes what may rightly be expected of mankind at its best in the treatment of sentient beings; a *humane* enterprise or endeavor is one that is intended to prevent or relieve suffering. The *humane* man is kindly and *sympathetic* and will not needlessly inflict pain upon the meanest thing that lives; a *merciful* man is disposed to withold or mitigate the suffering even of the guilty.

Human denotes what pertains to mankind, with no suggestion as to its being good or evil; as, the *human* race; *human* qualities; we speak of *human* achievements, virtues, or excellences, *human* follies, vices, or crimes. The *compassionate* man sympathizes with and desires to relieve actual suffering, while one who is *humane* tries to forestall and prevent the suffering which he sees to be possible. The *altruistic* person is devoted to the interests and welfare of others. *Altruistic* and *humanitarian* are close in meaning, but *humanitarian* connotes more the idea of *philanthropic*. A *charitable* person is *merciful* in judging others, or generous in giving to those in need; a *clement* person is lenient and disposed to spare offenders; he who is *kind* and *gracious*, especially to subordinates, is *benignant*. Compare **mercy; pity.**

> ANTONYMS: See synonyms for **barbarous.**

HUMBLE

compliant	lowly	soft	unostentatious
deferential	meek	submissive	unpretentious
demure	mild	unassuming	yielding
gentle	modest		

Humble and *lowly* referred originally to position or station; *humble* signifies on or near the ground; as, a *humble* cottage; *lowly* signifies lying or being low; as, a *lowly* abode; a *lowly* flower; hence, all that is below the average or recognized standard of means, position, authority, etc., is *humble* or *lowly*; thus *humble* and *lowly* came to include all that is *compliant, deferential, submissive, unpretentious, unostentatious, meek,* and *yielding*; a *humble* apology expresses either great sense of demerit or special deference toward the person offended; the former courteous phrase for closing a letter was "Your *humble* servant." The *humble* man is free from pride in himself or in his accomplishments; in the religious sense, the *humble* man ascribes to God all credit for his achievements. The *modest* man likewise takes no credit for himself or his actions; but, unlike the *humble* man, he does not necessarily have a deep conviction of his inferiority. *Lowly* expresses less of abasement than *humble*, and more of *gentle* resignation.

One who is *gentle* is free from sternness or rudeness—kindly, peaceful, calm, and *mild*; we speak of *gentle* words; a *gentle* hand; a *gentle* touch; one who is *meek* as at once *gentle*, patient, and peaceable, and disposed to be *submissive* and *yielding* under injury and provocation, rather than resistant. The *meek* person exhibits patience under all afflictions, and a *gentle*, equable temper, so much so that the word has taken on connotations of spiritlessness. The comic-strip character, Caspar Milquetoast, exhibits meekness in its highest degree; on the other hand, one may be timid, weak, and outwardly *gentle* and *submissive*, but by no means *meek*, as has often been proved by some sudden change of fortune. Meekness is of the spirit. *Demure* relates to demeanor and appearance; it is generally used of women; one who is *demure* has the mien and air of modesty, gentleness, and meekness, but there is always in the word the suggestion of latent feelings or qualities that may be quite different from the controlled appearance. Compare **modesty.**

ANTONYMS: *arrogant, assuming, **bold,** choleric, **contentious,** fierce, fiery, furious, haughty, **high-spirited,** impertinent, impudent, **lofty, obstinate,** presuming, presumptuous, **proud,** raging, resentful, revengeful, self-asserting, **stubborn, vengeful,** vindictive, wilful, wrathful.*

HUNT

chase	hunting	inquisition	pursuit	search

A *hunt* may be either the act of pursuing or the act of seeking, or a combination of the two. A *chase* or *pursuit* is after that which is fleeing or departing; a *search* is for that which is hidden or lost; a *hunt* may be for that which is either hidden or fleeing; a *search* is a minute and careful seeking, and is especially applied to a locality; we make a *search* of or through a house, for an object, in which connection it would be colloquial to say a *hunt*.

Hunt never quite loses its association with field sports, where it includes both *search* and *chase*; the *search* till the game is hunted out, and the *chase* till it is hunted down. Figuratively, we speak of literary *pursuits*, or of the *pursuit* of knowledge; a *search* for reasons; *hunt* and *pursuit*, in figurative use, incline to the unfavorable sense of *inquisition*, but with more aggressiveness; as, a *hunt* for heresy, the *pursuit* of heresy by the Holy Office.

HYPOCRISY

affectation	formalism	pretense	sanctimony
cant	pharisaism	sanctimoniousness	sham
dissimulation	pietism		

Hypocrisy is the false *pretense* of moral excellence, a simulation of greater virtue than one possesses, either as a cover for actual wrong or for the sake of the credit and advantage attaching to virtue. *Cant* (from L. *cantus*, a song), primarily the singsong iteration of the language of any party, school, or sect, as compared here, denotes pretentious use of religious phraseology, without corresponding feeling or character; *sanctimoniousness* or *sanctimony* is the assumption of a saintly manner without a saintly character. As *cant* is *hypocrisy* in utterance, so *sanctimoniousness* is *hypocrisy* in appearance, as in looks, tones, etc.

Pretense (from L. *prætendo*) primarily signifies the holding something forward as having certain rights or claims, whether truly or falsely; in the good sense, it is now rarely used except with a negative; as, there can be no *pretense* that this is due; a false *pretense* implies the possibility of a true *pretense*; but, alone and unlimited, *pretense* commonly signifies the offering of something for what it is not.

Pietism, originally a word of good import, is now chiefly used for an exaggerated show of piety; *formalism* is an exaggerated devotion to forms, rites, and ceremonies, without corresponding earnestness of heart; a *sham* shamefully disappoints expectation or falsifies appearance; *pharisaism* is a self-righteous, censorious attitude or spirit, assumed by the Pharisees of old. *Dissimulation* conceals or disguises what one really is or feels. *Affectation* is in matters of intellect, taste, etc., much what *hypocrisy* is in morals and religion; *affectation* might be termed petty *hypocrisy*. Compare **deception; pretense.**

> **ANTONYMS:** *candor, frankness, genuineness, honesty, ingenuousness, openness, sincerity, transparency, truth, truthfulness.*

HYPOTHESIS

conjecture	scheme	supposition	system
guess	speculation	surmise	theory
law			

A *hypothesis* is a statement of what is deemed possibly true, assumed and reasoned upon as if certainly true, with a view of reaching truth not yet surely known; especially, in the sciences, a *hypothesis* is a comprehensive tentative explanation of certain phenomena, which is meant to include all other facts of the same class, and which is assumed as true till there has been opportunity to bring all related facts or further evidence into comparison; if the *hypothesis* explains all the facts, it is regarded as verified; till then it is regarded as a working *hypothesis*, that is, one that may answer for present practical purposes. A *hypothesis* may be termed a comprehensive *guess*.

A *guess* is a swift conclusion from as much data as is at hand, and held as probable or tentative, while one confessedly lacks material for absolute certainty. A *conjecture* is more methodical than a *guess*, while a *supposition* is still slower and more settled; a *conjecture*, like a *guess*, is preliminary and tentative; a *supposition* is more nearly final; a *surmise* is more floating and visionary, and often sinister; as, a *surmise* that a stranger may be a pickpocket.

Theory is a *hypothesis* into which more known facts fit; as it contains evidence, it is more likely to be true than a *hypothesis*; a machine may be perfect in *theory*. *Scheme* is applied to proposed action, and in the sense of a somewhat visionary plan. A *speculation* may be wholly of the brain, resting upon no facts worthy of consideration; *system* is the highest of these terms, having the most assurance and fixity; a *system* unites many facts, phenomena, or doctrines into an orderly and consistent whole; we speak of a *system* of theology, of the Copernican *system* of the universe. The word *law* partakes of more certainty; it involves some proof and remains true under the given conditions. No *law*, however, is inevitable; new facts may either disprove or modify it to the point in which it slips back to the status of *theory*. See **system.**

ANTONYMS: *certainty, demonstration, discovery, evidence, fact, proof.*

I

IDEA

apprehension	design	impression	plan
archetype	fancy	judgment	purpose
belief	fantasy	model	sentiment
conceit	ideal	notion	supposition
concept	image	opinion	theory
conception	imagination	pattern	thought

Idea is in Greek a *form* or an *image*. The word signified in early philosophical use the *archetype* or primal *image* which the Platonic philosophy supposed to be the *model* or *pattern* that existing objects imperfectly embody. This sense has nearly disappeared from the word *idea,* and has been largely appropriated by *ideal,* the perfect type, though something of the original meaning still appears when in theological or philosophical language we speak of the *ideas* of God. The present popular use of *idea* generally signifies any product of mental *apprehension* or *imagination;* this coincides with the primitive sense at but a single point—that an *idea* is mental as opposed to anything substantial or physical; thus, almost any mental product, as a *belief, conception, design, opinion,* etc., may now be called an *idea.*

Concept, conception, and *notion,* as here compared, imply a general *idea* of what should be, but *concept* suggests an *idea* typical of a class, whereas *conception* often applies to an individual *idea* and suggests both the power of thinking and the act of thinking. *Conceit* is a far-fetched, often theoretical, *notion; impression* connotes an *idea* or *opinion,* the result of an outside stimulus. *Design, plan, pattern,* in this comparison, all refer to *images* in mind as proposed methods. See **fancy; ideal; imagination.**

ANTONYMS: *actuality, fact, reality, substance.*

IDEAL

archetype	model	pattern	standard
example	original	prototype	

An *ideal* is that which is conceived or taken as the highest type of excellence or ultimate object of attainment. The *archetype* is the primal form, actual or imaginary, according to which any existing thing is constructed; the *prototype* has or has had actual existence; in the derived sense, as in metrology, a *prototype* may not be the original form, but one having equal authority with that as a *standard.* An *ideal* may be primal, or may be slowly developed even from failures and by negations; an *ideal* is meant to be perfect, not merely the thing that has been attained or is to be attained, but the best conceivable thing that could by possibility be attained. The artist's *ideal* is his own mental image, of which his finished work is but an imperfect expression.

The *orginal* is the first specimen, good or bad; the *original* of a master is superior to all copies. The *standard* may be below the *ideal*. The *ideal* is imaginary, and ordinarily unattainable; the *standard* is concrete, and ordinarily attainable, being a measure to which all else of its kind must conform; as, the *standard* of weights and measures, of corn, or of cotton. See **example; idea.**

> **ANTONYMS:** *accomplishment, achievement, act, action, attainment, development, doing, embodiment, execution, fact, incarnation, performance, practice, reality, realization.*

IDIOCY

fatuity	foolishness	incapacity	senselessness
folly	imbecility	moronity	stupidity

Idiocy is a state of mental deficiency amounting almost to total absence of understanding, caused by congenital nondevelopment or abnormality of the brain tissue. *Idiocy* is the lowest grade of mental deficiency. *Imbecility* is one step up from *idiocy* in the scale of mental capacity and intelligence, but incapacitates the individual for earning a living or other serious duties of life. *Moronity* is the least severe of the mental deficiencies, but the individual still needs care and guardianship in the common walks of life. *Incapacity*, or lack of legal qualification for certain acts, such as necessarily results from *imbecility*, may also result from other causes, as from age, sex, etc.; as, the *incapacity* of a minor to make a contract.

Folly and *foolishness* denote a want of mental and often of moral balance. *Fatuity* signifies conceited and excessive *foolishness* or *folly*. *Stupidity* is dullness and slowness of mental action which may range all the way from lack of normal readiness to *imbecility*. Compare **insanity; stupidity.**

> **ANTONYMS:** *acuteness, astuteness, brilliancy, capacity, common sense, intelligence, sagacity, sense, soundness, wisdom.*

IDLE

inactive	lazy	sluggish	unoccupied
indolent	leisure	trifling	vacant
inert	slothful	unemployed	vain

Idle in all uses rests upon its root meaning, as derived from the Old English *idel*, which signifies *vain*, empty, useless. *Idle* thus denotes not primarily the absence of action, but *vain* action—the absence of useful, effective action; the *idle* schoolboy may be very actively whittling his desk or tormenting his neighbors. Doing nothing whatever is the secondary meaning of *idle*. One may be temporarily *idle* of necessity; if he is habitually *idle*, it is his own fault. *Lazy* signifies indisposed to exertion, averse to labor; idleness is in fact; laziness is in disposition or inclination. A *lazy* person may chance to be employed in useful work, but he acts without energy or impetus. We speak figuratively of a *lazy* stream.

The *inert* person seems like dead matter (characterized by inertia), powerless to move; the *sluggish* moves heavily and laboriously; the most active person may sometimes find the bodily or mental powers *sluggish.* *Slothful* and *indolent* belong in the moral realm, denoting self-indulgent aversion to exertion; the *indolent* man loves to be inactive. We need *leisure* hours for rest and relaxation; *idle* hours may be ill-spent; *vacant* hours are those in which we have no appointments or employment. Compare **vacant; vain.**

> **ANTONYMS:** *active, busy, diligent, employed, industrious, occupied, working.*

IGNORANT

ill-informed	unenlightened	unlearned	untaught
illiterate	uninformed	unlettered	untutored
uneducated	uninstructed	unskilled	

Ignorant signifies destitute of education or knowledge, or lacking knowledge or information; it is thus a relative term. The most learned man is still *ignorant* of many things; persons are spoken of as *ignorant* who have not the knowledge that has become generally diffused in the world; the *ignorant* savage may be well instructed in matters of the field and the chase, and is thus more properly *untutored* than *ignorant.* *Illiterate* is *ignorant* of letters and unable to read; hence, without the knowledge that comes through reading.

Unlettered is similar in meaning to *illiterate,* but less absolute; the *unlettered* man may have acquired the art of reading and writing and some elementary knowledge; the *uneducated* man has never taken any systematic course of training. *Ignorance* is relative; *illiteracy* is absolute; we have statistics of *illiteracy*; no statistics of *ignorance* are possible. *Uninformed* refers to lack of definite information or data; *uninstructed, untaught, untutored* refer to lack of teaching or schooling; *unenlightened* connotes lack of clarity as well as lack of information.

> **ANTONYMS:** *educated, instructed, learned, sage, skilled, trained, well-informed, wise.*

IMAGINATION

fancy	fantasy	phantasy

Imagination is the act or power of imaging or of reimaging objects of perception or thought, of combining the products of knowledge in modified, new, or ideal forms—the creative or constructive power of the mind; while *fancy* is the act or power of forming pleasing, graceful, whimsical, or odd mental images, or of combining them with little regard to rational processes of construction, *imagination* in its lower form. Both *fancy* and *imagination* recombine and modify mental images; either may work with the other's materials; *imagination* may glorify the tiniest flower; *fancy* may play around a mountain or a star.

Phantasy is visionary *imagination; fantasy*, originally the faculty of reproducing mental images, now generally denotes a whimsical or erratic *fancy*. *Fantasy* (often loosely called *imagination*) appears in dreaming, reverie, somnambulism, and intoxication. *Fantasy* in ordinary usage simply denotes capricious or extravagant *fancy*, as appears in the adjective *fantastic*.

Imagination can transcend the work of *fancy*, and endow an image drawn from the external world with some spiritual truth. *Fancy* flits about the surface, and is airy and playful, sometimes petty and sometimes false; *imagination* goes to the heart of things, and is deep, earnest, serious, and creative. *Fancy* sets off, variegates, and decorates; *imagination* transforms and exalts. *Fancy* delights and entertains; *imagination* moves and thrills. *Imagination* is not only poetic or literary, but scientific, philosophical, and practical. Science, philosophy, and mechanical invention have little use for *fancy*, but the creative, penetrative power of *imagination* is to them the condition of all advance and success. See **fancy; idea.**

IMMEDIATELY

at once	instanter	presently	straightway
directly	instantly	right away	this instant
forthwith	now	right off	without delay

Immediately primarily signifies without the intervention of anything as a medium, hence without the intervention of any, even the briefest, interval or lapse of time. *Directly*, which once meant with no intervening time, now means after some little while; *presently* no longer means in this very present, but before very long. Even *immediately* is sliding from its instantaneousness, so that we substitute *at once, instantly, without delay, this instant*, etc., when we would make promptness emphatic. *Right away* and *right off* are vigorous American idioms.

   ANTONYMS: *after a while, by and by, hereafter, in the future, sometime.*

IMMINENT
   impending   threatening

Imminent, from the Latin, with the sense of projecting over, signifies liable to happen at once, as some calamity, dangerous and close at hand. *Impending* also from the Latin, with the sense of hanging over, is closely akin to *imminent,* but somewhat less emphatic. *Imminent* is more immediate, *impending* more remote, *threatening* more contingent. An *impending* evil includes the idea that there are ominous signs that something is almost sure to happen at some uncertain time, perhaps very near; an *imminent* peril is one liable to befall at any moment; a *threatening* peril may be near or remote, but always with hope that it may be averted.

> **ANTONYMS:** *chimerical, contingent, doubtful, improbable, problematical, unexpected, unlikely.*

IMPATIENCE

fretfulness	peevishness	petulance
irritation	pettishness	vexation

Impatience is lack of patience, or intolerance of opposition or control; unwillingness to brook delay. *Irritation, petulance,* and *vexation* express the slighter forms of anger which are temporary and for immediate cause. *Fretfulness, pettishness,* and *peevishness* are chronic states finding in any petty manner an occasion for expressing coarseness or slight ill-temper. See **anger; hatred.** Compare **acrimony.**

> **ANTONYMS:** *amiability, benignity, forbearance, gentleness, leniency, lenity, mildness, patience, peace, peaceableness, peacefulness, self-control, self-restraint.*

IMPEDIMENT

bar	difficulty	hindrance	obstruction
barrier	encumbrance	obstacle	snag
clog			

An *impediment* may be either what one finds in his way or what he carries with him; *impedimenta* was the Latin name for the baggage of a soldier or of an army. The tendency is to view an *impediment* as something constant or, at least for a time, continuous; as, an *impediment* in one's speech. An *impediment* is primarily something that checks the foot or in any way makes advance slow or difficult; an *obstacle* is something that stands across the way, an *obstruction* something that is built or placed across the way. An *obstruction* is always an *obstacle,* but an *obstacle* may not always be properly termed an *obstruction;* boxes and bales placed on the sidewalk are *obstructions* to travel; an ice floe is an *obstacle* to navigation, and may become an *obstruction* if it closes an inlet or channel.

A *hindrance* (kindred with *hind, behind*) is anything that holds one back or hinders, or makes one come behind or short of his purpose. *Difficulty* implies something hard to overcome. That which rests upon one as a burden in an *encumbrance.* A *difficulty* or a *hindrance* may be either within one or without; a speaker may find *difficulty* in expressing himself, or *difficulty* in holding the attention of restless children. An *encumbrance* is always what one carries with him; *obstacles* and *obstructions* bar or impede progress. To a marching soldier the steepness of a mountain path is a *difficulty,* loose stones are *impediments,* a fence is an *obstruction,* a cliff or a boulder across the way is an *obstacle.* A *bar* prevents entering or leaving, but a *barrier* is erected to stop progress or attack; a *clog* checks or slows down motion. A knapsack is an *encumbrance.* See **barrier.**

ANTONYMS: *advantage, aid, assistance, benefit, help, relief, succor.*

IMPERTINENCE

assurance	impudence	intrusiveness	presumption
boldness	incivility	officiousness	rudeness
effrontery	insolence	pertness	sauciness
forwardness			

Impertinence primarily denotes what does not pertain or belong to the occasion or the person, and hence comes to signify interference by word or act inconsistent with the age or position of the interferer or of the person interfered with; especially, forward, presumptuous, or meddlesome speech. What would be arrogance in a superior becomes *impertinence* or *impudence* in an inferior. *Impertinence* has less of intent and determination than *impudence.* We speak of thoughtless *impertinence,* shameless *impudence.*

Insolence is literally that which is against custom, *i.e.,* the violation of customary respect and courtesy. *Officiousness* is thrusting upon others unasked and undesired service, and is often as well-meant as it is annoying. *Rudeness* is the behavior that might be expected from a thoroughly uncultured person, and may be either deliberate and insulting or unintentional and even unconscious. *Incivility* implies lack of courtesy. *Pertness* and *sauciness* connote lack of respect, whereas *effrontery, forwardness,* and *presumption* all include the idea of overboldness or shameless *boldness.* See **pertness.** Compare **assurance; effrontery.**

ANTONYMS: *bashfulness, coyness, diffidence, humility, lowliness, meekness, modesty, submissiveness.*

IMPORTANT

consequential	determinative	influential	relevant
considerable	determining	material	serious
critical	essential	momentous	significant
deciding	grave	powerful	substantial
decisive	great	prominent	weighty

That is *important* which imports or means much with reference to some desired result; *important* is thus a stronger word than *considerable*. *Momentous* is stronger still, signifying of such weight or consequence as to make other matters seem trivial by comparison. The Old English *weighty* is less emphatic than *momentous*, more substantial than *important*; *weighty* applies to statements or decisions which have power by and of themselves, with less reference to an effect upon the result than *important* matters; many *weighty* reasons may be overmatched by one *momentous* consideration.

That which is *essential*, or *material*, is so involved in the essence, or subject-matter of what is in hand that it cannot be separated from it in fact or thought; *material* adheres closely to the matter as existing; as, a *material* difference; *material* evidence; or a *material* witness; *essential* starts at the existing essence, as the *essential* properties of matter, but goes on to a result to be secured; as, an *essential* condition of success. That which is *determinative* tends to determine or fix a result; that which is *determining* does fix it. That which is *decisive* or *deciding* forces decision. That which is *critical* may determine the result at a crisis; as, a *critical* moment; a *critical* issue. That which is *relevant* has real and necessary relation to the matter in hand.

To say that any matter is *considerable* implies that it is not to be overlooked, is worthy to be considered, but may very possibly be surpassed. *Indispensable*, *necessary*, and *supreme* reach far beyond what is *considerable*, *important* or *momentous* to that which is absolutely controlling, and are thus closely allied with *essential*. Compare **necessary**.

> **ANTONYMS:** *feeble, flimsy, frivolous, idle, immaterial, inconsequential, inconsiderable, indifferent, insignificant, light, mean, minor, needless, negligible, non-essential, paltry, petty, secondary, slight, trifling, trivial, unimportant, uninfluential, unnecessary, useless, worthless.*

IMPRACTICABLE

> impossible　　　　impractical　　　　intractable

That which is *impossible* cannot be done at all; that which is *impracticable* is theoretically possible, but cannot be done under existing conditions because it is unreasonably difficult of performance. *Impractical*, which strictly means unpractical, not practical, is coming into frequent popular use as the equivalent of *impracticable*, but the difference should be maintained; an *impractical* man lacks practical judgment or efficiency; an *impracticable* man is difficult to deal with; an *impractical* scheme lacks practical fitness, is theoretic or visionary; an *impracticable* scheme has some inherent difficulties that would ensure its failure in action. That which is *intractable* is not easy to work or treat; an *intractable* person is unreasonable. Compare **obstinate; perverse.**

> **ANTONYMS:** *easy, feasible, possible, practicable.*

IMPRUDENT

careless	impolitic	injudicious	thriftless
foolhardy	improvident	rash	unthinking
heedless	incautious	reckless	unthrifty
ill-advised	inconsiderate	short-sighted	venturesome
ill-judged	indiscreet	thoughtless	venturous

Imprudent is used of a lack of provision against future danger, loss, or harm, or of a lack of discretion. *Improvident* is used chiefly of lack of provision for future need, supply, support, etc. Each word has also acquired a positive meaning; *improvident* referring to *careless* or *reckless* waste of present resources without thought of future need; *imprudent*, to *thoughtless* or *reckless* disregard of possible or probable future dangers. A *reckless* youth is utterly heedless of consequences; a *foolhardy* one is foolishly *reckless*. A *rash* word or act is imprudently hasty; an *incautious* move is unwary. *Short-sighted* implies a marked lack of foresight. A *venturous* person is very likely to take chances and is ready to take risks; a *venturesome* person is inclined to venture. *Inconsiderate* and *unthinking* emphasize thoughtlessness of the wishes or feelings of others; *ill-judged* and *injudicious* include lack of judgment.

ANTONYMS: See synonyms for **shrewd.**

INABILITY

disability	impotence	incapability

Inability is the state of being unable; it implies in general the lack of physical, mental, or moral power to achieve a purpose, but is tending to become used for the lack of means, health, education, or equipment to do a certain thing; as, *inability* to pay, *inability* to arise or read, etc. *Disability*, however, implies the loss of some physical or mental power or capacity previously possessed. A crippled condition is a *disability*. We speak of the *disabilities* of war veterans; loss of sight is a grave *disability*. In the legal sense, *disability* means disqualification, as the *disability* to vote, inherit, hold office, etc., for various specific reasons. *Impotence* is *inability* caused by lack of power; *incapability* connotes *inability* due to lack of capacity, fitness, ability, etc.

ANTONYMS: *ability, capability, power.*

INCONGRUOUS

absurd	discrepant	incommensurable	mismatched
conflicting	ill-matched	incompatible	mismated
contradictory	inapposite	inconsistent	repugnant
contrary	inappropriate	inharmonious	unsuitable
discordant	incoherent	irreconcilable	

Two or more things that do not fit well together, are *unsuitable*, or are not adapted to each other, are said to be *incongruous*; a thing is said to be *incongruous* that is not adapted to the time, place, or occasion; the term is also applied to a thing made up of ill-assorted parts or *inharmonious* elements. *Discordant* is applied to all things that jar in association, like musical notes that are not in accord; *inharmonious* has the same original sense, but is a milder term. *Incompatible* primarily signifies unable to sympathize or feel alike; *inconsistent* means unable to stand together, or at variance. Things are *incompatible* which cannot exist together in harmonious relations, and whose action when associated tends to ultimate extinction of one by the other. *Inconsistent* applies to what cannot be made to agree in thought, or with some standard of truth or right; slavery and freedom are *inconsistent* with each other in theory, and *incompatible* in fact.

That which is *incoherent* lacks coherence or cohesion or the capacity to coalesce; the word may be used of material substances; as, *incoherent* volcanic ashes; or it may be used of thought or argument which lacks logical cohesion. It is most often applied to speech, as of one under excitement, delirium, or intoxication. *Incongruous* applies to relations, *unsuitable* to purpose or use; two colors are *incongruous* which cannot be agreeably associated; either may be *unsuitable* for a person, a room, or an occasion. *Incommensurable* is a mathematical term, applying to two or more quantities that have no common measure or aliquot part. When something is very *incongruous* it often becomes *absurd*. *Mismatched* or *mismated* persons or things are unsuitably coupled. *Discrepant* statements disagree; *conflicting* statements are in opposition; only one of two *contradictory* statements can be true.

ANTONYMS: *accordant, agreeing, compatible, consistent, harmonious, suitable.*

PREPOSITION: The illustrations were incongruous *with* the theme.

INDUSTRY

application	diligence	labor	perseverance
assiduity	effort	pains	persistence
attention	exertion	patience	sedulousness
constancy	intentness		

Industry is the quality, action, or habit of earnest, steady, and continued *attention* or devotion to any useful or productive work or task, manual or mental. *Assiduity* (from L. *ad*, to, and *sedeo*, sit), as the etymology suggests, sits down to a task until it is done. *Diligence* (from L. *diligo*, love, choose) invests more effort and exertion, with love of work or deep interest in its accomplishment; *application* (from L. *ad*, to, and *plico*, fold) bends to its work and concentrates upon it with utmost intensity; hence, *application* can hardly be as unremitting as *assiduity*. *Constancy* is a steady devotion of heart and principle. *Patience* works on in spite of annoyances; *perseverance* over-comes hindrances and difficulties; *persistence* strives relentlessly against opposition; *persistence* has very frequently an unfavorable meaning, implying that one persists in spite of considerations that should induce him to desist. *Industry* is *diligence* applied to some avocation, business, or profession. *Labor* and *pains* refer to the *exertions* of the *worker* and the tax upon him, while *assiduity, perseverance,* etc., refer to his continuance in the work.

> ANTONYMS: *changeableness, fickleness, idleness, inattention, inconstancy, indolence, neglect, negligence, remissness, sloth.*

INFERENCE
conclusion   consequence   deduction   induction   judgment

An *inference* is a reasoned *conclusion* or opinion drawn from evidence or premises. An *induction* is of the nature of an *inference*, but while an *inference* may be partial and hasty, an *induction* is careful, and aims to be complete.

Deduction is reasoning from the general to the particular; *induction* is reasoning from the particular to the general. *Deduction* proceeds from a general principle through an admitted instance to a *conclusion*. *Induction*, on the other hand, proceeds from a number of collated instances, through some attribute common to them all, to a general principle. The proof of an *induction* is by using its *conclusion* as the premise of a new *deduction*. Thus what is ordinarily known as scientific *induction* is a constant interchange of *induction* and *deduction*. In *deduction*, if the general rule is true and the special case falls under the rule, the *conclusion* is certain; *induction* can ordinarily give no more than a probable *conclusion*, because we can never be sure that we have collated all instances. A *consequence* follows something else as a result; a *judgment*, which carries more weight than the other words of this group, is arrived at only after due consideration of all available evidence. Compare **demonstration; hypothesis.**

INFINITE

absolute	illimitable	limitless	unconditioned
boundless	immeasurable	measureless	unfathomable
countless	innumerable	numberless	unlimited
eternal	interminable	unbounded	unmeasured

Infinite signifies without bounds or limits in any way, and is applied to space, time, quantity, or number. *Countless, innumerable,* and *numberless* are in common usage vaguely employed to denote what is difficult or practically impossible to count or number; as, *countless* leaves, the *countless* sands on the seashore, *numberless* battles, *innumerable* delays. So, too, *boundless, illimitable, limitless, measureless,* and *unlimited* are loosely used in reference to what has no apparent or readily determinable limits in space or time; as, we speak of the *boundless* ocean. *Eternal* means without beginning or end of time. *Infinite* space is without bounds, not only in fact, but in thought; *infinite* time is truly *eternal* in the early and literary sense; but the new physics has contradicted these concepts. In modern mathematics and science *infinite* means that an end or limit cannot be determined, not that there is no end or limit. Compare synonyms for **eternal.**

> ANTONYMS: *bounded, brief, circumscribed, evanescent, finite, limited, little, measurable, moderate, narrow, restricted, shallow, short, small, transient, transitory.*

INFLUENCE

actuate	draw	impel	induce	move	stir
compel	drive	incite	instigate	persuade	sway
dispose	excite	incline	lead	prompt	urge

To *influence* is to affect, modify, or act upon by physical, mental, or moral power, especially in some gentle, subtle, and gradual way; as, vegetation is *influenced* by light; everyone is *influenced* to some extent by public opinion; *influence* is chiefly used of power acting from without, though it may be used of motives regarded as forces acting upon the will. *Actuate* refers solely to mental or moral power *impelling* one from within. One may *influence*, but cannot directly *actuate* another; but one may be *actuated* to cruelty by hatred which another's misrepresentation has aroused.

Prompt and *stir* are words of mere suggestion toward some course of action; *dispose, draw, incline, influence,* and *lead* refer to the use of means to awaken in another a purpose or disposition to act. To *excite* is to arouse one from lethargy or indifference to action. To *persuade* is to appeal to someone's feelings or desires rather than to his reason. *Incite* and *instigate*, to spur or goad one to action, differ in the fact that *incite* may be to good, while *instigate* is always to evil. To *urge* and *impel* signify to produce strong excitation toward some act. We are *urged* from without, *impelled* from within. *Drive* and *compel* imply irresistible influence accomplishing its object. One may be *driven* either by his own passions or by external force or urgency; one is *compelled* only by some external power; as, the owner was *compelled* by his misfortunes to sell his estate. See **compel; drive.** Compare **abet.**

> ANTONYMS: *deter, discourage, dissuade, hinder, impede, inhibit, prevent, restrain, retard.*

INGENUITY

acuteness	dexterity	invention	readiness
cleverness	genius	inventiveness	skill
cunning	ingeniousness		

Ingenuity is inferior to *genius*, being rather mechanical than creative, and is shown in devising expedients, overcoming difficulties, inventing appliances, adapting means to ends. *Dexterity* is chiefly of the hand; *cleverness* may be either of the hand or of the mind, but chiefly of the latter. *Acuteness* is mental keenness; *skill* is *cleverness* or *dexterity*; *readiness* is the state or quality of being ready to act immediately. *Ingeniousness* refers to inventive *skill*; *invention*, to the act or process of originating; *inventiveness*, to the ability to invent. See **address** *noun*.

> ANTONYMS: *awkwardness, clumsiness, dulness, stupidity, unskilfulness.*

INHERENT

congenital	indispensable	innate	inwrought
essential	indwelling	inseparable	native
immanent	infixed	internal	natural
inborn	ingrained	intrinsic	subjective
inbred	inhering		

Inherent signifies permanently united as an element or original quality, naturally existent or incorporated in something so as to have become an integral part. *Immanent* is a philosophic word, to denote that which dwells in or pervades any substance or spirit without necessarily being a part of it, and without reference to any working out. That which is *inherent* is an *inseparable* part of that in which it inheres, and is usually thought of with reference to some out-working or effect; as, an *inherent* difficulty. Frequently *intrinsic* and *inherent* can be interchanged, but *inherent* applies to qualities, while *intrinsic* applies to essence, so that to speak of *intrinsic* excellence conveys higher praise than if we say *inherent* excellence.

Inherent and *intrinsic* may be said of persons or things; *congenital, inborn, inbred, innate* apply to living beings. *Congenital* is frequent in medical and legal use with special application to defects; as, *congenital* idiocy. *Innate* and *inborn* are almost identical, but *innate* is preferred in philosophic use, as when we speak of *innate* ideas; that which is *inborn, congenital,* or *innate* may be original with the individual, but that which is *inbred* is inherited. *Ingrained* signifies dyed in the grain, and denotes that which is deeply wrought into substance or character.

Essential describes a part of something's essence, which is inseparably involved in the very nature of the thing's being; as, truth is an *essential* element of morality. *Native*, in this sense, is closely akin to *innate* and *inborn,* meaning born with one, not acquired, as *native* wit.

> ANTONYMS: *accidental, casual, external, extrinsic, fortuitous, incidental, outward, subsidiary, superadded, superficial, superfluous, superimposed, supplemental, transient, unconnected.*

INJURY

blemish	evil	injustice	outrage
damage	harm	loss	prejudice
detriment	hurt	mischief	wrong
disadvantage	impairment		

Injury signifies primarily something done contrary to law or right; hence, something contrary to some standard of right or good; whatever reduces the value, utility, beauty, or desirableness of anything is an *injury* to that thing; of persons, whatever is so done as to operate adversely to one in his person, rights, property, or reputation is an *injury*; the word is especially used of whatever mars the integrity of the body or causes pain; as, when rescued from the wreck his *injuries* were found to be very slight. *Injury* is the general term including all the rest.

Damage is that which occasions *loss* to the possessor; hence, any impairment of value, often with the suggestion of fault on the part of the one causing it; *damage* reduces value, utility, or beauty; *detriment* is similar in meaning, but far milder. *Detriment* may affect value only; *damage* always affects real worth or utility; as a rule, the slightest use of an article by a purchaser operates to its *detriment* if again offered for sale, though the article may have received not the slightest *damage*. *Damage* is partial; *loss* is properly absolute as far as it is predicated at all; the *loss* of a ship implies that it is gone beyond recovery; the *loss* of the rudder is a *damage* to the ship; but since the *loss* of a part still leaves a part, we may speak of a partial or a total *loss*.

Evil commonly suggests suffering or sin, or both; as, the *evils* of poverty, the social *evil*. *Harm* is closely synonymous with *injury*; it may apply to body, mind, or estate, but always affects real worth, while *injury* may concern only estimated value. A *hurt* is an *injury* that causes pain, physical or mental; a slight *hurt* may be no real *harm*. *Mischief* is disarrangement, trouble, or *harm* usually caused by some voluntary agent, with or without injurious intent; a child's thoughtless sport may do great *mischief*; *wrong* is harm done with *evil* intent. An *outrage* combines insult and *injury*. Compare synonyms for blemish; criminal; injustice.

> **ANTONYMS:** *advantage, amelioration, benefit, blessing, boon, help, improvement, remedy, service, utility.*

> **PREPOSITIONS:** The injury *of* the cause; an injury *to* the structure; injury *by* fire, *by* or *from* collision, interference, etc.

INJUSTICE

grievance	injury	unfairness	wrong
iniquity	tort	unrighteousness	

Injustice is a violation or denial of justice, an act or omission that is contrary to equity or justice; as, the *injustice* of unequal taxes. In legal usage, a *wrong* involves *injury* to person, property, or reputation, as the result of evil intent; *injustice* applies to civil damage or loss, not necessarily involving *injury* to person or property, as by misrepresentation of goods which does not amount to a legal warranty. In popular usage, *injustice* may involve no direct *injury* to person, property, interest, or character, and no harmful intent, while *wrong* always involves both; one who attributes another's truly generous act to a selfish motive does him an *injustice*. *Iniquity*, in the original sense, is a want of or a deviation from equity; but it is now applied in the widest sense to any form of wickedness.

Tort, an almost exclusively legal term, is any private or civil *wrong* or *injury*, except breach of contract. *Grievance* refers to any condition that, in the opinion of the injured party, constitutes a *wrong* or gives cause for complaint; it is used in a general rather than a legal sense. Compare synonyms for **criminal; sin.**

> ANTONYMS: *equity, fairness, fair play, faithfulness, honesty, honor, impartiality, integrity, justice, lawfulness, rectitude, right, righteousness, uprightness.*

INNOCENT

blameless	guileless	innoxious	sinless
clean	guiltless	inoffensive	spotless
clear	harmless	pure	stainless
exemplary	immaculate	right	upright
faultless	innocuous	righteous	virtuous

Innocent, in the full sense, signifies not tainted with sin; not having done wrong or violated legal or moral precept or duty; as, an *innocent* babe. *Innocent* is a negative word, expressing less than *righteous, upright,* or *virtuous,* which imply knowledge of good and evil, with free choice of the good. A little child or a lamb is *innocent*; a tried and faithful man is *righteous, upright, virtuous. Spotless, stainless,* and *immaculate* agree in denoting freedom from any kind of blemish. *Immaculate, pure,* and *sinless* may be used either of one who has never known the possibility of evil or of one who has perfectly and triumphantly resisted it. *Innocent* is used of inanimate substances in the sense of *harmless*; as, an *innocent* remedy, that is, one not dangerous, even if not helpful. *Innocent*, in a specific case, signifies free from the guilt of a particular act, even though the total character may be very evil; as, the thief was found to be *innocent* of the murder. *Innocuous* means non-poisonous, *harmless*; as, that snake is *innocuous*; *innoxious* also means *harmless* but in the sense of not likely to corrupt. *Exemplary*, as applied to conduct, signifies worthy to be used as an example, because free from wrong-doing. See **candid; pure.**

ANTONYMS: Compare synonyms for **criminal.**

INQUIRE

ask	inquire into	investigate	question
examine	interrogate	query	

To *inquire* is to *ask* information about or seek information by *asking* questions. To *ask* is to use some form of speech, short or direct command, for obtaining information from another. One may either *ask* or *inquire* one's way. In this sense *ask* and *inquire* are nearly interchangeable, chiefly differing in the fact that *ask* is the popular and *inquire* the more formal word, while *ask* has place in the best literary use. Also, *ask* has more reference to the presence of a second person; the solitary investigator *inquires* rather than *asks* the cause of some phenomenon; in this sense *ask* is often used reflexively; as, "I *asked* myself why this happened."

Inquire into thus becomes a natural synonym for *examine, investigate*, etc. To *interrogate* is to *ask* questions; to *query* is to *inquire into*, with an implication of doubt; to *question* is to make inquiries or to *examine* by queries. Compare **ask; question.**

> **PREPOSITIONS:** Inquire *into* any matter demanding investigation, *about, concerning,* or *in regard to* the transaction; inquire *of* one who can give information; inquire *at* a house *for* a person or thing, *after* one's health; inquire *out* items or individuals from a mass or aggregate.

INQUISITIVE

curious	meddlesome	prying	searching
inquiring	meddling	scrutinizing	snoopy
intrusive	peeping		

An *inquisitive* person is one who is bent on finding out all that can be found out by inquiry, especially of little and personal matters. The *meddlesome* or *prying* person is not only *inquisitive*, but also officious. *Inquisitive* may be used in a good sense, though in such connection *inquiring* is to be preferred; as, an *inquiring* mind. As applied to a state of mind, *curious* denotes a keen and rather pleasurable desire to know fully something to which one's attention has been called, but without the active tendency that *inquisitive* implies; a well-bred person may be *curious* to know, but will not be *inquisitive* or *snoopy* in trying to ascertain, what is of interest in the affairs of another.

> **ANTONYMS:** *apathetic, careless, heedless, inattentive, incurious, indifferent, unconcerned, uninterested.*

> **PREPOSITIONS:** Inquisitive *about, concerning, in regard to, regarding* trifles.

INSANITY

aberration	dementia	lunacy
craziness	derangement	madness
delirium	frenzy	mania

Of these terms *insanity*, although not technically used in medicine and psychiatry, is the most general, including in its loose sense almost any mental disorder; in legal use it is applied to those forms which deprive the afflicted person of capacity to distinguish between right and wrong, manage his personal affairs and discharge his social obligations. *Craziness* is a vague, popular term for any sort of disordered mental action, or for conduct suggesting it. *Lunacy* originally denoted intermittent *insanity*, supposed to be dependent on the changes of the moon. *Madness* is the old popular term for *insanity* in its widest sense, but with suggestion of excitement akin to *mania*. *Lunacy* denotes what is insanely foolish, *madness* what is insanely desperate.

Derangement is a common euphemism for *insanity*. *Delirium* is always temporary, and is specifically a mental disturbance caused by or associated with disease, as in acute fevers. *Dementia* is a general weakening of the mental powers; the word is especially used in psychiatry for mental disorders caused by organic brain diseases. *Aberration* is eccentricity of mental action due to an abnormal state of the perceptive faculties, and is manifested by error in perceptions and rambling thought. *Mania* is a mental disorder implying violence and excitability, often with fixation upon some definite object, emotion, or situation and accompanied by melancholy. *Frenzy* is a sudden outburst of emotion leading to excesses of behavior and action. See **delusion; idiocy.**

ANTONYMS: *clearness, good sense, lucidity, rationality, sanity.*

INTENSIFY

| aggravate | heighten | magnify |
| enhance | increase | make worse |

Intensify is to make greater in relative strength, degree, or force. *Aggravate* is always used in the bad sense, to *make worse* what is already bad; as, to *aggravate* a fever or a situation. *Enhance* and *magnify* are generally used in the lofty and good sense; as, to *enhance* the value; "I will *magnify* mine office," *Rom.* xi, 13. To *heighten* is to *increase* the height of; as, to *heighten* a bridge; to elevate; as, to *heighten* courage; or to augment; as, to *heighten* confusion.

ANTONYMS: *alleviate, assuage, attenuate, diminish, lessen, reduce.*

INTERPOSE

arbitrate	intercept	interrupt	**meddle**
insert	interfere	intervene	**mediate**
intercede	intermeddle	introduce	

To *interpose* is to place or come between other things or persons, usually as a means of obstruction or prevention of some effect or result that would otherwise occur, or be expected to take place. *Intercede* and *interpose* are used in a good sense; *intermeddle* always in a bad sense, and *interfere* frequently so. To *intercede* is to come between persons who are at variance, and plead with the stronger in behalf of the weaker. One may *interpose* with authority; he *intercedes* by petition. To *intermeddle* is to thrust oneself into the concerns of others with officiousness; *meddling* commonly arises from idle curiosity; to *interfere* is to intrude into others' affairs with more serious purpose, with or without acknowledged right or propriety.

Intercept is applied to an object that may be seized or stopped while in transit; as, to *intercept* a letter or a messenger; *interrupt* is applied to an action which might or should be continuous, but is broken in upon by some disturbing power; as, the conversation was *interrupted*. One who *arbitrates* or *mediates* must do so by the request or at least with the consent of the contending parties; the other words of the group imply that he steps in of his own accord. To *intervene* is to come between persons, things, actions, or periods of time; to *introduce*, in this comparison, is to bring or put in, *insert*; as, to *introduce* a probe into a wound.

> **ANTONYMS:** *avoid, hold aloof, hold off, keep aloof, keep away, keep clear, keep out, let alone, let be, retire, stand aside, stand away, stand back, stand off, withdraw.*

> **PREPOSITIONS:** Interpose *between* the combatants, *in* the matter.

INVOLVE

complicate	embarrass	entangle	imply
contain	embroil	implicate	include

To *involve* (from L. *in*, in, and *volvo*, roll) is to roll or wind up with or in so as to combine inextricably or inseparably, or nearly so; as, the nation is *involved* in war; the bookkeeper's accounts or the writer's sentences are *involved*. *Involve* is a stronger word than *implicate*, denoting more complete *entanglement* from which it is difficult to free oneself. As applied to persons, *implicate* is always used in an unfavorable sense, and *involve* ordinarily so; but *implicate* applies generally to that which is wrong, while *involve* is more commonly used of that which is unfortunate; one is *implicated* in a crime, *involved* in embarrassments, misfortunes, or perplexities.

As regards logical connection, that which is *included* is usually expressly stated; that which is *implied* is not stated, but is naturally to be inferred; that which is *involved* is necessarily to be inferred; as, a slate roof is *included* in the contract; that the roof shall be water-tight is *implied*; the contrary supposition *involves* an absurdity. To *complicate* is to *involve* in difficulty, to make intricate; to *embroil* is to *involve* in hostility, *entangle* in difficulties. Compare **complex.**

ANTONYMS: *disconnect, disentangle, distinguish, explicate, extricate, remove, separate.*

IRREGULAR

abnormal	disorderly	immoderate	unsystematic
anomalous	dissolute	inordinate	unusual
confused	eccentric	uneven	variable
crooked	erratic	unnatural	vicious
desultory	exceptional	unsettled	wandering
devious	fitful	unsymmetrical	wild

Irregular implies departing from the usual or proper form, order, course, method, proportion, etc., not conforming to rule or duty; as *irregular* verbs, *irregular* habits. *Abnormal* emphasizes excess, deformity, or strangeness; as, *abnormal* growth; *anomalous* stresses lack of conformity or fitness; as, Einstein's theory of relativity explained many *anomalous* facts. *Eccentric* implies peculiar in manner or character; *erratic* is *irregular* in habits, behavior, or opinions. *Desultory* and *fitful* imply passing abruptly and *irregularly* from one thing to another. In this comparison, *exceptional* denotes uncommon or *unusual*; *inordinate* and *immoderate* imply excessive; as, *inordinate* demands, *immoderate* indulgence. *Crooked* paths have many turns and twists; *devious* routes are indirect, rambling, and often circuitous. *Vicious*, in this connection, is rough and broken; as a *vicious* tract of land. *Unsymmetrical* structures are not well-balanced; that which is *variable* admits of change from the usual form.

ANTONYMS: *common, constant, established, fixed, formal, methodical, natural, normal, orderly, ordinary, periodical, punctual, regular, stated, steady, systematic, uniform, universal, unvarying, usual.*

J

JEALOUS

covetous	envious	suspicious

Jealous implies intolerance of rivalry and apprehension of being displaced. A *jealous* spirit may be good or bad, according to its object and tendency. A free people must be *jealous* of their liberties if they would retain them. A person is *jealous* of intrusion upon that which is his own, or to which he maintains a right or claim; he is *envious* of that which is another's and to which he himself has no right or claim. One is *envious* who begrudges another his superior success, endowments, possessions, or the like. An *envious* spirit is usually bad. One is *suspicious* of another from unfavorable indication or from a knowledge of wrong in his previous conduct, or even without reason; he is fearful of suffering something from another. One who is *covetous* has such deep envy of the possessions of another as to be avaricious. See **miserly.** Compare **doubt.**

> **ANTONYMS:** *indifferent, liberal, genial.*
>
> **PREPOSITIONS:** Jealous *of* a person or *of* rights.

JOURNEY

cruise	passage	transit	trip
excursion	pilgrimage	travel	voyage
expedition	tour		

A *journey* (from F. *journée*, from L. *diurnus*, daily) was primarily a day's work; hence, a movement from place to place within one day, which we now describe as "a day's *journey*"; in its extended modern use a *journey* is a direct going from a starting point to a destination, ordinarily over a considerable distance; we speak of a day's *journey*, or the *journey* of life. *Travel* is a passing from place to place, not necessarily in a direct line or with fixed destination; a *journey* through Europe would be a *passage* to some destination beyond or at the farther boundary; *travel* in Europe may be in no direct course, but may include many *journeys* in different directions. A *voyage*, which was formerly a *journey* of any kind, is now a going to a considerable distance by water, especially by sea; as, a *voyage* to India. A *trip* is a short and direct *journey*.

A *tour* is a *journey* that returns to the starting point, generally over a considerable distance; as, a bridal *tour* or business *tour*. An *excursion* is a brief *tour* or *journey*, taken for pleasure, often by many persons at once. *Passage* is a general word for a *journey* by any conveyance, especially by water; as, a rough *passage* across the Atlantic. *Transit*, literally the act of passing over or through, is used specifically of the conveyance of passengers or merchandise; rapid *transit* is demanded for suburban residents or perishable goods. *Pilgrimage,* once always of a sacred character, retains in derived uses something of that sense; as, a *pilgrimage* to Stratford-on-Avon. An *expedition* is a *journey* or *voyage* taken by a number of persons for a specific purpose; as, the Arctic *expedition.*

> **PREPOSITIONS:** A journey *from* Naples *to* Rome, *through* Mexico, *across* the continent, *over* the sea; a journey *into* Asia, *among* savages, *by* land, *by* rail, *for* health, *on* foot, *on* the cars, *by* car, etc.

JUDGE

| arbiter | arbitrator | justice | referee | umpire |

A *judge,* in the legal sense, is a judicial officer appointed or elected to preside in courts of law, and to decide legal questions duly brought before him; the name is sometimes given to other legally constituted officers; as, the *judges* of election; in other relations, any person duly appointed to pass upon the merits of contestants or of competing articles may be called a *judge;* as, the *judges* at an agricultural fair or at a racetrack; in the widest sense, any person who has good capacity for judging is called a *judge;* as, a person is said to be a *judge* of pictures, or a good *judge* of a horse, etc.

In most games the *judge* is called an *umpire;* as, the *umpire* of a game of ball or cricket. In some games and contests, a *referee* is the chief official and is in charge of the scoring and progress. In law, a *referee* is appointed by a court to decide disputed matters between litigants; an *arbitrator* is chosen by the contending parties to decide matters in dispute without action by a court. In certain cases an *umpire* is appointed by a court to decide where *arbitrators* disagree. *Arbiter,* with its suggestion of final and absolute decision has come to be used only in a high or sacred sense; as, war must now be the *arbiter;* the Supreme *Arbiter* of our destinies. The *judges* of certain courts, as the United States Supreme Court, are technically known as *justices.*

JUSTICE

equity	impartiality	legality	rightfulness
fairness	integrity	rectitude	truth
fair play	justness	right	uprightness
faithfulness	law	righteousness	virtue
honor	lawfulness		

In its governmental relations, human or divine, *justice* is the giving to every person exactly what he deserves, not necessarily involving any consideration of what any other may deserve; *equity* (the quality of being equal) is giving everyone as much advantage, privilege, or consideration as is given to any other; it is that which is equally right or just to all concerned; *equity* is equal *justice* and is thus a close synonym for *fairness* and *impartiality*, but it has a philosophical and legal precision that those words have not.

In legal proceedings cases arise for which the law has not adequately provided, or in which general provisions, just in the main, would work individual hardship. The system of *equity*, devised to supply the insufficiencies of *law*, deals with cases "to which the *law* by reason of its universality cannot apply." "*Equity*, then, . . . is the soul and spirit of all *law*; positive *law* is construed and rational *law* is made by it." BLACKSTONE. In personal and social relations *justice* is the rendering to everyone what is due or merited, whether in act, word, or thought; in matters of reasoning, or literary work of any kind, *justice* is close, faithful, unprejudiced, and unbiased adherence to essential truth or fact; we speak of the *justice* of a statement, or of doing *justice* to a subject.

Integrity, rectitude, right, righteousness and *virtue* denote conformity of personal conduct to the moral law, and thus necessarily include *justice*, which is giving others that which is their due. *Lawfulness* is an ambiguous word, meaning in its narrower sense mere *legality*, which may be very far from *justice*, but in its higher sense signifying accordance with the supreme *law* of *right*, and thus including perfect *justice*. *Justness* refers rather to logical relations than to practical matters; as, we speak of the *justness* of a statement of a criticism. See **virtue.** Compare **judge; law; right.**

ANTONYMS: *dishonesty, favoritism, inequity, injustice, partiality, unfairness, unlawfulness. unreasonableness, untruth, wrong.*

PREPOSITIONS: The justice *of* the king, *to* or *for* the oppressed.

K

KEEP

carry	defend	maintain	protect	solemnize
carry on	detain	obey	refrain	support
celebrate	fulfil	observe	restrain	sustain
conduct	guard	preserve	retain	withhold
conserve	hold			

Keep, signifying generally to have and retain in possession, is the terse, strong Saxon term for many acts which are more exactly discriminated by other words. We *keep, observe,* or *celebrate* a festival, *solemnize* a ceremony; we *keep* or *hold* a prisoner in custody; we *keep* or *preserve* silence, *keep* the peace, *preserve* order—*preserve* being the more formal word; a man *supports* or *maintains* his family; we *keep* or *obey* a commandment; *keep* or *fulfil* a promise. To *conserve* anything is to *keep* or *preserve* it in its present state; as, to *conserve* the interests of employers or of workingmen. In the expressions to *keep* a secret, *keep* one's own council, *keep* faith, or *keep* the faith, such words as *preserve* or *maintain* could not be substituted without loss.

A person *keeps* a shop or store, *conducts* or *carries on* a business; he *keeps* or *carries* a certain line of goods; we may *keep* or *restrain* one from folly, crime, or violence; we *keep* from or *refrain* from evil, ourselves. *Keep* in the sense of *guard* or *defend* implies that the defense is effectual. We *detain* a messenger while we write an answer; *protect* a child, *keeping* it safe from harm. We *retain* or *keep* possession of our rights; *retain* a lawyer by paying an advance fee to secure his services; some metals *retain* or *keep* heat a long time. Senators often *keep* up or *sustain* lengthy arguments. See **celebrate; restrain.**

> **PREPOSITIONS:** Keep *in* hand, *in* mind, *in* or *within* the house, *from* evil, *out of* mischief; keep *to* the subject; keep *for* a person, an occasion, etc.

KILL

assassinate	dispatch	massacre	put to death	slay
butcher	execute	murder	slaughter	

To *kill* is simply to deprive of life, human, animal, or vegetable, with no suggestion of how or why. *Assassinate, execute, murder* apply only to the taking of human life; to *murder* is to *kill* with premeditation and malicious intent; to *execute* is to *kill* in fulfilment of a legal sentence; to *assassinate* is to *kill* by assault; this word is chiefly applied to the *killing* of public or eminent persons through alleged political motives, whether secretly or openly. To *slay* is to *kill* by a blow, or by a weapon. *Butcher* and *slaughter* apply primarily to the *killing* of cattle; *massacre* is applied primarily and almost exclusively to human beings, signifying to *kill* them indiscriminately in large numbers; *massacre* implies that there is no chance of successful resistance; *butcher*, that the *killing* is especially brutal; soldiers mown down in a hopeless charge are said to be *slaughtered* when no brutality on the enemy's part is implied. To *dispatch* is to *kill* swiftly and in general quietly, always with intention, with or without right. See **massacre.**

PREPOSITIONS: To kill *with* or *by* sword, care, grief, etc.; killed *for* his money, *by* a robber, *with* a dagger.

KIN

affinity	blood	family	race
alliance	consanguinity	kind	relationship
birth	descent	kindred	relatives

Kin and *kindred* denote direct *relationship* that can be traced through either *blood* or marriage, preferably the former; either of these words may signify collectively all persons of the same *blood* or members of the same *family, relatives* or relations. *Kind* is broader than *kin,* denoting the most general *relationship,* as of the whole human species in man*kind,* human*kind,* etc. *Birth* and *descent* refer to parentage; *race,* to the major subdivisions of man*kind. Affinity* is *relationship* by marriage; *consanguinity* is *relationship* by blood. There are no true antonyms of *kin* or *kindred,* except those made by negatives, since strangers, aliens, foreigners, and foes may still be *kin* or *kindred.* Compare **alliance.**

KNOWLEDGE

acquaintance	erudition	learning	recognition
apprehension	experience	light	scholarship
cognition	information	lore	science
cognizance	intelligence	perception	wisdom
comprehension	intuition		

Knowledge is all that the mind knows, from whatever source derived or obtained, or by whatever process; the aggregate of facts, truths, or principles acquired or retained by the mind, including alike the *intuitions* native to the mind and all that has been learned respecting phenomena, causes, laws, principles, literature, etc. There is a tendency to regard *knowledge* as accurate and systematic, and to a certain degree complete; and in this it approaches the meaning of *science. Information* is *knowledge* of fact, real or supposed, derived from persons, books, or observation, and is regarded as casual and haphazard. We say of a studious man that he has a great store of *knowledge,* or of an intelligent man of the world, that he has a fund of varied *information.*

Lore is used in poetic or elevated style, for accumulated *knowledge,* as of a people or age, or in a more limited sense for *learning* or *erudition.* We speak of *perception* of external objects, *apprehension* of intellectual truth. Simple *perception* gives a limited *knowledge* of external objects, merely as such; the *cognition* of the same objects is a *knowledge* of them in some relation; *cognizance* is the formal or official *recognition* of something as an object of *knowledge*; we take *cognizance* of it. *Intuition* is primary *knowledge* antecedent to all teaching or reasoning; *experience* is *knowledge* that has entered directly into one's own life; as, a child's *experience* that fire will burn.

Learning is much higher than *information*, being preeminently wide and systematic *knowledge*, the result of long, assiduous study; *erudition* is recondite *learning* secured only by extraordinary industry, opportunity, and ability. *Wisdom* is the power of using *knowledge* and *experience* in the best way; *comprehension* is the act of understanding; *intelligence*, readiness of *comprehension*. *Scholarship* refers to proficiency in *knowledge*. See **science; wisdom.** Compare **acquaintance; education; light.**

ANTONYMS: *ignorance, illiteracy, inexperience, misapprehension, misconception, misunderstanding, unfamiliarity.*

L

LANGUAGE

barbarism	expression	patois	vernacular
dialect	idiom	speech	vocabulary
diction	mother tongue	tongue	

Language (from F. *langage*, from L. *lingua*, the tongue) signified originally *expression* of thought by spoken words, but now in its widest sense it signifies *expression* of thought by any means; as, the *language* of the eyes, the *language* of flowers. As regards the use of words, *language* in its broadest sense denotes all the uttered sounds and their combinations into words and sentences that human beings employ for the communication of thought, and, in a more limited sense, the words or combinations forming a means of communication among the members of a single nation, people, or race.

Speech involves always the power of articulate utterance; we can speak of the *language* of animals, but not of their *speech*. A *tongue* is the *speech* or *language* of some one people, country, or race. A *dialect* is a special mode of speaking a *language* peculiar to some locality or class, a provincial form of *language*; as a technical philological term, however, a *dialect* is one of several branches of a root *language*, markedly different from the original and from others derived from that original; as, any of the Romance *languages* are *dialects* of Latin.

A *barbarism* is a perversion of a *language* by ignorant foreigners, or some usage akin to that. *Idiom* refers to the construction of phrases and sentences, and the way of forming or using words; it is the peculiar mold in which each *language* casts thought. The great difficulty of translation is to give the thought expressed in one *language* in the *idiom* of another. *Vocabulary* is the sum of words used in a *language* or by a person; *diction,* the choice and arrangement of words with regard to clearness and beauty of sound.

A *dialect* may be used by the highest as well as the lowest within its range; a *patois* is a provincial *dialect* in a general sense, but is specifically applied to the illiterate *speech* of a bilingual group. *Vernacular* has two related meanings; *vernacular* is the native *language* of a region or country as, the Scriptures were translated into the *vernacular*; and also the *language* of the people, the crowd, as contrasted with the literary *language* of the same place or group. See **diction; speech.**

LARGE

abundant	coarse	gigantic	long
ample	colossal	grand	massive
big	commodious	great	spacious
broad	considerable	huge	vast
bulky	enormous	immense	wide
capacious	extensive		

Large denotes extension in more than one direction, and beyond the average of the class to which the object belongs; we speak of a *large* surface or a *large* solid, but of a *long* line; a *large* field, a *large* room, a *large* apple, etc. A *large* man is a man of more than ordinary size; a *great* man is a man of remarkable mental power. *Big* is a more emphatic word than *large*, but of less digni、 r. We do not say that George Washington was a *big* man. *Abundant* refers to an unusually *large* supply; *ample* and *spacious* denote of *large* size, extent, volume, etc. *Gigantic* is exceedingly *large* in size; *enormous*, *large* in size, amount, and degree. *Colossal*, like a Colossus, is used for something of extraordinary size and height, or greatness; *extensive* and *vast* refer to extent; *huge*, to bulk. *Capacious* is roomy, *large* enough to hold a lot. *Commodious* implies roomy and comfortable; *massive* is large and heavy.

ANTONYMS: *bric'. diminutive, inconsiderable, infinitesimal, insignificant, limit、 little, mean, microscopic, minute, narrow, paltry, petty, s. nty, short, slender, slight, small, tiny, trifling, trivial.*

LATENT

abeyant	implied	potential	undeveloped
concealed	included	quiescent	unknown
dormant	inherent	recondite	unobserved
hidden	invisible	secret	unperceived
imperceptible	involved	torpid	unseen
implicit	occult	uncomprehended	

That which is *latent* (from L. *lateo*, lie hidden) is *hidden* from ordinary observation; as, *latent* powers; a *latent* motive; a disease is said to be *latent* between the time of its contraction and its manifestation. *Dormant* (from L. *dormio*, sleep) applies to the winter condition of hibernating animals, when they seem asleep, or are even apparently lifeless; we speak of *dormant* energies (which have acted, and may yet again be aroused); a *dormant* volcano; *torpid* (from L. *torpeo*, be numb) is practically equivalent to *dormant* as applied to a hibernating animal; *torpid* merely denotes the insensibility, which *dormant* accounts for as a form of sleep; hence, *torpid* applies to whatever is sluggish, dull, and lethargic, without the same suggestion of possible arousal as in *dormant*; we should not speak of *torpid* energy. *Abeyant* is in a state of suspension, but liable to revival; *quiescent* is motionless, or in a state of inaction.

Potential applies to that which is possible; a *potential* poet or orator has the *latent* qualities, *inherent* though yet *undeveloped*, that may make a poet or an orator; *potential* energy or force is energy or force that under certain conditions is sure to come into action; *potential* has not the same suggestion as *dormant* of power that has been previously active. That is *recondite* which is *hidden* from ordinary and easy perception and intelligence, and only to be known (if at all) by unusual and difficult research.

Occult always carries the sense of mystery; originally applied to the *unknown* or ill-understood forces or facts of physical science, the word is now extended to whatever is *recondite* and mysterious, not to be discovered or understood by the ordinary action of the human faculties, or not to be l own by any action of the material senses, but only by an '''minated spiritual perception. That which is *invisible* cannot be seen; that which is *imperceptible* cannot be apprehended by the senses. *Included* means contained in something; *implied* is *included* by inference, although not stated; *implicit*, as compared here, is essentially contained or *included*, although not expressed. The *implicit* humor of a pun is based on the *implied* suggestion of another word. Compare **hide**; **mysterious.**

> **ANTONYMS:** *active, apparent, conspicu* ., *developed, evident, explicit, exposed, manifest, per* .tible, *unconcealea, visible.*

LAW

canon	economy	legislation	precept
code	edict	mandate	principle
command	enactment	order	regulation
commandment	formula	ordinance	rule
decree	jurisprudence	polity	statute

Law, in its ideal, is the statement of a *principle* of right in mandatory form, by competent authority, with adequate penalty for disobedience; in common use, the term is applied to any legislative *enactment* to enforce justice and prescribe duty. *Command* and *commandment* are personal and particular; as, the *commands* of a parent; the Ten *Commandments*. An *edict* is the proclamation of a *law* by an absolute sovereign or other authority; we speak of the *edict* of an emperor, the *decree* of a court. A *mandate* is specific, for an occasion or a purpose; a superior court issues its *mandate* to an inferior court to send up its records, and a nation is given a *mandate* over conquered territory.

Statute is the recognized legal term for a specific *law; enactment* is the more vague and general expression. We speak of algebraic or chemical *formulas*, municipal *ordinances*, military *orders*, army *regulations*, ecclesiastical *canons*, the *rules* of a business house; the *precepts* of the Sermon on the Mount. *Law* is often used, also, for a recognized *principle*, whose violation is attended with injury or loss that acts like a penalty; as, the *laws* of business; the *laws* of nature. As used in the natural sciences, *law* is a formal statement of uniformities and relations considered as established and invariable.

A *code* is a system of *laws; jurisprudence* is the science of *law*, or a system of *laws* scientifically considered, classed, and interpreted; *legislation,* primarily the act of legislating, denotes also the body of *statutes* enacted by a legislative body. An *economy* (from Gr. *oikonomia,* primarily the management of a house) is any comprehensive management or system of administration of total resources; as, domestic *economy;* but the word is extended to the administration or government of a state or people, signifying a body of *laws* and *regulations,* with the entire system, political or religious, especially the latter, of which they form a part; as, the *code* of Draco, Roman *jurisprudence,* British *legislation,* the Mosaic *economy.* *Law* is also used as a collective noun for a system of *laws* or recognized *rules* or *regulations,* including not only all special *laws,* but the *principles* on which they are based. The Mosaic *economy* is known also as the Mosaic *law,* and we speak of the English common *law,* or the *law* of nations.

Polity (from Gr. *politeia,* from *polis,* a city) signifies the form, constitution, or method of government of a nation, state, church, or other institution; in usage it differs from *economy* as applying rather to the *principles,* while *economy* applies especially to method, or to the system as administered; an *economy* might be termed a *polity* considered with especial reference to its practical administration, hence commonly with special reference to details or particulars, while *polity* has more reference to broad *principles.*

LIBERTY

emancipation   freedom   independence   license   permission

In general terms, it may be said that *freedom* is absolute, *liberty* relative; *freedom* is the absence of restraint, or of the awareness of it; *liberty* is the removal or avoidance of restraint; in its broadest sense, it is the state of being exempt from the domination of others or from restricting circumstances. *Freedom* and *liberty* are constantly interchanged: the slave is set at *liberty,* or gains his *freedom;* but *freedom* is the nobler word. *Independence* is said of states or nations, *freedom* and *liberty* of individuals; the *independence* of the United States did not secure *liberty* or *freedom* to its slaves.

Liberty keeps quite strictly to the thought of being clear of restraint or compulsion; *freedom* takes a wider range, applying to other oppressive influences; thus we speak of *freedom* from annoyance or intrusion. *License* is, in its limited sense, a *permission* or privilege granted by adequate authority, a bounded *liberty;* in the wider sense, *license* is an ignoring and defiance of all that should restrain, and a reckless doing of all that individual caprice or passion may choose to do—a dangerous counterfeit of *freedom.* Compare **allow; permission.**

ANTONYMS: *captivity, compulsion, constraint, imprisonment, necessity, obligation, oppression, serfdom, servitude, slavery, superstition, thraldom.*

LIGHT

beam	glare	glow	shimmer
blaze	gleam	illumination	shine
brilliancy	gleaming	incandescence	shining
effulgence	glimmer	luster	sparkle
flame	glistening	radiance	splendor
flare	glistering	scintillation	twinkle
flash	glitter	sheen	twinkling
flicker			

Light, strictly denoting a form of radiant energy, is used as a general term for any luminous effect discernible by the eye, from the faintest phosphorescence to the *blaze* of the noonday sun. A *flame* is both hot and luminous; if it contains few solid particles it will yield little *light* in proportion to its heat, as in the case of a hydrogen *flame*. A *blaze* is an extensive, brilliant *flame*. A *flare* is a wavering *flame* or *blaze*; a *flash* is a *light* that appears and disappears in an instant; as, a *flash* of lightning; the *flash* of gunpowder. The *glare* and *glow* are steady; the *glare* painfully bright, the *glow* subdued; as, the *glare* of headlights; the *glow* of dying embers. *Shine* and *shining* refer to a steady or continuous emission of *light*; *sheen* is a faint *shining*, usually by reflection.

Glimmer, *glitter*, and *shimmer* denote wavering *light*. We speak of the *glimmer* of distant lamps through the mist; of the *shimmer* of waves in sunlight or moonlight. A *glitter* is a hard *light*; as, the *glitter* of burnished arms. A *gleam* is not wavering, but transient or intermittent; a sudden *gleam* of light came through the half-open door. *Glistening* is a *shining* as from a wet surface. *Luster* denotes commonly a reflection from a polished surface, as of silk or gems. A *sparkle* is a sudden *light*, as of sparks thrown out; *scintillation* is the more exact and scientific term for the actual emission of sparks, also the figurative term for what suggests such emission; as, *scintillations* of wit or of genius.

Twinkle and *twinkling* are used of the intermittent *light* of the fixed stars. *Splendor* denotes an especial abundance and glory of *light* that may be beautiful, dazzling, or overwhelming; as the *splendor* of sunrise or sunset; the *splendor* of the Great White Throne. *Effulgence* is radiant *splendor*. *Illumination* is a wide-spread, brilliant *light*, as when all the windows of a house or of a street are lighted. The *light* of *incandescence* is intense and white like that from metal at a white heat. A *beam* is a ray of *light*; a *flicker* fluctuates for a brief interval. Compare **bright**.

ANTONYMS: *blackness, dark, darkness, dimness, dusk, gloom, gloominess, obscurity, shade, shadow.*

LIKELY

apt	credible	possible	probable
conceivable	liable	presumable	reasonable
conjectural	plausible		

Likely refers to a contingent event regarded as very *probable*; as, an industrious worker is *likely* to succeed. *Credible* signifies worthy of belief; as, a *credible* narrative; *likely* in such connection is used ironically to signify the reverse; as, a *likely* story! *Plausible* is often used colloquially for *credible*; as, a *plausible* excuse. *Apt* implies a natural fitness or tendency and applies to persons and things. An impetuous person is *apt* to speak hastily. *Liable* refers to a contingency regarded as unfavorable; or to exposure to damage or risk; as, the ship was *liable* to founder at any moment.

A thing is *conceivable* of which the mind can entertain the possibility; a thing is *conjectural* which is conjectured as *possible* or *probable* without other support than a conjecture, or tentative judgment; a thing is *presumable* which, from what is antecedently known, may be taken for granted in advance of proof. *Reasonable* in this connection signifies such as the reason can be satisfied with, independently of external grounds for belief or disbelief; as, that seems a *reasonable* supposition. Compare **apparent.**

ANTONYMS: *doubtful, dubious, improbable, incredible, questionable, unlikely, unreasonable.*

LIKENESS

affinity	image	resemblance	similarity
analogy	picture	sameness	similitude

Likeness is the state or quality of being alike or nearly identical in appearance or characteristics. The *likeness* of things is closer than the word *similarity* would imply; *similarity* implies merely that they are something alike in some respects. *Resemblance* applies to a certain *sameness* of external appearance. A portrait may be a good *likeness* or *picture* of a man, even be the *image* of him, and yet bear some *resemblance* to his father.

Analogy calls attention to specific parallels or relation between things that are unlike; as, the word "rime" is often spelled "rhyme" by *analogy* with "rhythm." *Affinity* carries the idea of close relationship plus an external resemblance or *similarity*.

ANTONYMS: *difference, dissimilarity, unlikeness.*

LISTEN

attend	hark	harken	hear	heed	list

To *listen* is to make a conscious effort or endeavor to *hear*. We may *hear* without *listening*, as words suddenly uttered in an adjoining room; or we may *listen* without *hearing*, as to a distant speaker. In *listening* the ear is intent upon the sound; in *attending* the mind is intent upon the thought, though *listening* implies some attention to the meaning or import of the sound. Between *listen* and *hear* is a difference like that between the words "look" and "see." To *hear* is simply to become conscious of sound. To *heed* is not only to attend, but remember and observe. *Harken* is nearly obsolete; *list* is poetic

ANTONYMS: *be deaf to, ignore, neglect, scorn, slight.*

PREPOSITIONS: We listen *for* what we expect or desire to hear; we listen *to* what we actually do hear; listen *for* a step, a signal, a train; listen *to* the debate.

LITERATURE

belles-lettres	letters	literary works	the humanitie
books	literary productions	publications	writings

Literature is collective, including in the most general sense all the written or printed productions of the human mind in all lands and ages, or in a more limited sense, referring to all that has been published in some land or age or in some department of human knowledge; as, the *literature* of Greece; the *literature* of the Augustan age; the *literature* of politics or of art. *Literature* meaning what has been called "polite *literature*" or *belles-lettres, i.e.,* work of literary art, esthetic rather than informational, as poetry, essays, fiction and dramatic compositions, includes also many philosophical writings, ora torical productions, and criticism.

In the broad sense, we can speak of the *literature* of science; in the narrower sense, we speak of *literature* and science as distinct departments of knowledge *Literature* is also used to signify literary pursuits or occupations; as, to devote one's life to *literature*. *The humanities* now primarily designates the study o the classical *literatures* of Greece and Rome, and the various sciences which deal with them, such as grammar, classical philology, etc., but sometimes sec ondarily includes all "culture studies" in contrast to professional studies *Letters* is another term for learning; as, a man of *letters*. Compare **knowl edge; science.**

LOAD

burden	charge	encumbrance	incubus	pack
cargo	clog	freight	lading	weight

A *load* (from the Old English *lād,* a way, course, carrying, or carriage) i what is laid upon a person, animal, or vehicle for conveyance, or what is cus tomarily so imposed; as, a two-horse *load*. *Weight* measures the pressure du to gravity; the same *weight* that one finds a moderate load when in his ful strength becomes a heavy *burden* in weariness or weakness. A *load* to b fastened upon a horse or mule is called a *pack*. and the animal is known as packhorse or *pack*mule.

A ship's *load* is called a *cargo*, or it may be known as *freight* or *lading*; we speak of a bill of *lading*. *Freight* denotes merchandise in or for transportation and is used largely of transportation or of merchandise transported by rail, although in commercial language it is said to be "shipped." A *burden* (from the Old English *byrthen*, from the verb *beran*, bear) is what one has to bear, and the word is used always of that which is borne by a living agent. An *incubus* is something that oppresses or weighs down; a *clog* is a *weight* that hinders progress. The child she carried was an *encumbrance* that slowed her pace but it was a *burden* willingly borne.

LOCK

| bar | catch | fastening | hook |
| bolt | clasp | hasp | latch |

A *lock* is an arrangement by which an enclosed *bolt* is shot forward or backward by a key, or other device; the *bolt* is the essential part of the *lock*. A *bolt* is a movable rod or pin of metal, sliding in a socket and adapted for securing a door or window. A *latch* or *catch* is an accessible *fastening* designed to be easily movable, and used to secure against accidental opening of the door, cover, etc. A *hasp* is a hinged metallic strap that fits over a staple, and is secured by a padlock or pin. A simple *hook* that fits into a staple is also called a *hasp*. A *clasp* is a *fastening* that can be sprung into place, to interlock or draw and hold the parts of some object firmly together, as the *clasp* of a book. A *bar* is a piece of wood or metal, usually of considerable size, by which an opening is obstructed, a door held fast, etc. A *bar* may be movable or permanent.

LOOK

behold	espy	observe	stare
contemplate	gaze	regard	survey
descry	glance	scan	view
discern	inspect	see	watch

To *look* is to make a conscious and direct endeavor to *see*. To *see* is simply to become conscious of an object of vision. We may *look* without *seeing*, as in pitch-darkness, and we may *see* without *looking*, as in case of a flash of lightning. To *gaze* is to *look* intently, long, and steadily upon an object. To *glance* is to *look* casually or momentarily. To *stare* is to *look* with a fixed intensity, often in surprise, alarm, or rudeness. To *scan* is to *look* at minutely, to note every visible feature. To *inspect* is to go below the surface, uncover, study item by item.

To *behold* is to fix the sight and the mind upon something that has come to be clearly before the eyes. *View* and *survey* are comprehensive, *survey* expressing the greater exactness of measurement or estimate. *Watch* brings ir the element of time and often of wariness; we *watch* for a movement o change, a signal, the approach of an enemy, etc. *Descry* is to *see* as in the dis tance or through obscurity; *discern* is to *descry* or make out something, bu also to discriminate; to *espy* implies to catch sight of. *Contemplate* means to *gaze* upon with thoughtful attention; *observe* is to *look* at attentively, bu connotes less thought than *contemplate*. Compare **appear; discern.**

LOVE

affection	charity	friendship	regard
attachment	devotion	liking	tenderness
attraction	fondness		

Affection is kindly feeling, deep, tender, and constant, going out to some person or object, being less fervent and ardent than *love*, whether applies to persons or things. *Love* is an intense and absorbing emotion, drawing one toward a person or object and causing one to appreciate, delight in, and crave the presence or possession of the person or object loved, and to desire to please and benefit the person, or to advance the cause, truth, or other object of *affection*; it is the yearning or outgoing of soul toward something that is regarded as excellent, beautiful, or desirable; *love* may be briefly defined as strong and absorbing *affection* for and *attraction* toward a person or object.

Love is more intense, absorbing, and tender than *friendship*, more intense impulsive, and perhaps passionate than *affection*; we speak of fervent *love*, but of deep or tender *affection*, or of close, firm, strong *friendship*. *Love* is used specifically for personal *affection* between the sexes in the highest sense, the *love* that normally leads to marriage, and subsists throughout all happy wedded life. *Love* can never properly denote mere animal passion, which is expressed by such words as "appetite," "desire," "lust." One may properly be said to have *love* for animals, for inanimate objects, or for abstract qualities that enlist the *affections*, as we speak of *love* for a horse or a dog, for mountains woods, ocean, or of *love* of nature, and *love* of virtue. *Love* of articles of food is better expressed as *liking*. See **attachment; friendship.**

ANTONYMS: See synonyms for **antipathy; enmity; hatred.**

PREPOSITIONS: Love *of* country, *for* humanity.

M

MAKE

assemble	construct	fashion	originate
become	create	forge	perform
build	do	form	produce
cause	effect	frame	reach
compel	establish	get	render
compose	execute	manufacture	require
constitute	fabricate	occasion	shape
constrain			

Make is essentially causative; to the idea of *cause*, all its various senses may be traced. To *make* is to *cause* to exist, or to *cause* to exist in a certain form or in certain relations; the word thus includes the idea of *create*. *Make* includes also the idea of *compose, constitute*; as, the parts *make* up the whole. Similarly, to *cause* a voluntary agent to do a certain act is to *make* him do it, or *compel* him to do it, *compel* fixing the attention more on the process, *make* on the accomplished fact.

To *form* is to *make* something in a definite shape, pattern, outline, or the like; as, to *form* a statue, or a plan; the author *formed* his novel from this incoherent narrative. *Fashion* stresses the idea of imaginativeness and ingenuity; as, he *fashioned* a beautiful box out of the cedar wood.

Fabricate meants to *make* a whole out of many parts; it connotes adherence to a standardized pattern; as, to *fabricate* the parts of a building. *Manufacture* means to *make* something by labor, now usually by rachinery rather than by hand. The individual parts of an automobile, as the axles, fenders, and tires, are *manufactured* separately from raw materials; they are fitted together, or *assembled*, to *fabricate* the finished product. Compare **cause; compel; do; influence;** (make better) **amend;** (make haste) **quicken;** (make known) **announce; confess; state;** (make prisoner) **arrest;** (make up) **add;** (make void) **cancel.**

ANTONYMS: See synonyms for **abolish; break; demolish.**

PREPOSITIONS: Make *of, out of,* or *from* certain materials, *into* a certain form, *for* a certain purpose or person; made *with* hands, *by* hand; made *by* a prisoner, *with* a jackknife.

MALICIOUS

bitter	ill-disposed	malign	resentful
evil-disposed	ill-natured	malignant	spiteful
evil-minded	invidious	mischievous	venomous
hostile	malevolent	rancorous	virulent

The *malicious* person has the desire and intent to do evil, if possible, to another; the *malevolent* person wishes evil to another, or has a very bad influence; he is *evil-disposed* and *evil-minded*. The *malign* or *malignant* spirit

277

has a deep, intense, and insatiable hostility, such as is indicated by *rancorous* or *venomous*, with or without active desire or intent to injure. *Malign* is used of secret or mysterious evil influence, such as astrology attributes to certain aspects or conjunctions of stars or planets. *Spiteful* is a feeble word indicating the desire or intent to inflict petty, exasperating annoyance or injury. A *hostile* attitude connotes a disposition to thwart; a *resentful* mood expresses indignant displeasure. *Invidious* remarks are prompted by, and often provoke, envy and ill will; *virulent* accusations show *bitter* enmity and are *venomous*. Compare **acrimony; bitter; enmity; hatred.**

> ANTONYMS: *amiable, amicable, beneficent, benevolent, benign, benignant, friendly, good-natured, kind, kind-hearted, kindly, sympathetic, tender, well-disposed.*

MARINE

maritime	nautical	naval	ocean	oceanic	sea-going

Marine denotes that which is found or produced by the sea, or that which is made for use at sea; as, *marine* growths, a *marine* compass. It also describes anything associated with vessels that cross the ocean or any large body of water; as, *marine* insurance. The word specifically means *sea-going*; as, the United States *Marine* Corps is composed of soldiers who serve on the sea.

Maritime refers to people, regions, etc., bordered by the sea; as, New Brunswick, Nova Scotia, and Prince Edward Island are the *Maritime* Provinces of Canada. *Maritime* also applies to salt-water navigation or commerce. With reference to law, insurance, etc., *marine* and *maritime* may be used interchangeably.

Nautical, in accordance with its etymology, denotes primarily anything connected with sailors, hence, with ships or navigation; *naval* describes the armed force of a nation on the sea, and, by extension, the similar forces on lakes and rivers. *Naval* refers not only to the ships themselves, but also to their personnel, equipment, and armament; *naval* stores include tar, pitch, turpentine, etc.

Ocean, used adjectivally, is applied to that which belongs to or is part of the ocean; we speak of *ocean* currents; an *ocean* liner is a ship that crosses the ocean. *Oceanic* means of, pertaining to, or like the ocean; an *oceanic* fish lives in the ocean; in the sense of vast, like the ocean, one could say, "He carries on an *oceanic* correspondence."

MARRIAGE

espousal	nuptials	spousals	wedding
espousals	spousal	union	wedlock
matrimony			

Marriage is applied either to the ceremony or to the rite whereby a man and woman are made husband and wife; or, more commonly, to the state of being husband and wife. *Matrimony* is used in legal and religious terminology; in the Roman Catholic, Eastern, and Anglican Churches it denotes one of the seven sacraments. Strictly speaking, therefore, *matrimony* can be used instead of *marriage* only when a religious ceremony is meant.

Wedding is the popular and literary term to denote the ceremony of uniting two persons as husband and wife. *Nuptials* is the more formal and stately term to express the same idea; it also implies an elaborate religious ritual. *Wedlock*, in its legal application, denotes *marriage* as a state or relationship sanctioned by law; as, children born in *wedlock*.

Spousal, espousal, or, more commonly, *spousals, espousals,* are archaic terms applying rather to the exchange of marriage vows rather than to any ceremony.

ANTONYMS: *bachelorhood, celibacy, divorce, maidenhood, spinsterhood, virginity, widowhood.*

PREPOSITIONS: Marriage *of* or *between* two persons, *of* one person *to* or *with* another, *among* the Greeks.

MASCULINE

male   manful   manlike   manly   mannish   virile

We apply *male* to the sex, *masculine* to the qualities, as strength, courage, size, etc., that distinguish the male sex; as applied to women, *masculine* has often the depreciatory sense of unwomanly, rude, or harsh; as, a *masculine* face or voice, or the like; though one may say in a commendatory way, she acted with *masculine* decision. *Manlike* may mean only having the outward appearance or semblance of a man, or may be closely equivalent to *manly*. *Manly* refers to all the qualities and traits worthy of a man; *manful,* especially to the valor and prowess that become a man; we speak of a *manful* struggle, *manly* decision; we say *manly* gentleness or tenderness; we could not say *manful* tenderness. *Mannish* is a depreciatory word referring to the mimicry or parade of some superficial qualities of manhood; as a *mannish* boy or woman. In its specifically sexual meaning, *virile* denotes procreative power in the male, and is opposed to "impotent." *Masculine* may apply to the distinctive qualities of the *male* sex at any age; *virile* applies to the distinctive qualities of mature manhood only, such qualities as vigor, aggressiveness, forcefulness, etc., and is opposed to such words as "puerile" and "childish."

ANTONYMS: See synonyms for **feminine.**

MASSACRE

bloodshed   butchery   carnage   pogrom   slaughter

A *massacre* is the indiscriminate killing in numbers of the unresisting or defenseless: *slaughter,* formerly and still a butcher's term, is the killing of men rudely and ruthlessly as cattle are killed in the shambles. *Butchery* adds to this the idea of wanton and cold-blooded cruelty. *Pogrom*, a Russian word, is an organized, often official, *massacre* of a certain class or group of people unable to resist; the word is specifically and historically applied to the *massacre* of Jews in Europe.

Carnage refers to widely scattered or heaped up corpses of the slain; *slaughter* is similar in meaning, but refers more to the process, as *carnage* does to the result; these two words only of the group may be used of great destruction of life in open and honorable battle, as when we say the enemy was repulsed with great *slaughter*, or the *carnage* was terrible.

MECHANIC

artificer	artist	laborer	workman
artisan	craftsman	operative	

The man who constructs anything by mere routine is a *mechanic*. The man whose work involves thought, skill, and constructive power is an *artificer*. *Artist, artificer*, and *artisan* are all from the root of "art," but *artist* holds to the esthetic sense, while *artificer* and *artisan* follow the mechanical or industrial sense of the word. *Artist* thus comes only into accidental association with the other words of this group. The work of the *artist* is creative; that of the *artisan*, mechanical. The man who paints a beautiful picture is an *artist*; the man who makes pin heads all day is an *artisan*.

The *artificer* is between the two, putting more thought, intelligence, and taste into his work than the *artisan*, but less of the idealizing, creative power than the *artist*. The sculptor, shaping his model in clay, is *artificer* as well as *artist*; patient *artisans*, working simply by rule and scale, chisel and polish the stone. The hod-carrier is a *laborer*; the bricklayer is a *mechanic*; the master mason is an *artificer*. Those who operate machinery nearly self-acting are *operatives*.

MEDDLESOME

impertinent	intrusive	meddling	obtrusive	officious

The *meddlesome* person interferes unasked in the affairs of others; the *intrusive* person thrusts himself uninvited into their company or conversation; the *obtrusive* person thrusts himself or his opinions conceitedly and undesirably upon their notice; the *officious* person thrusts his services, unasked and undesired, upon others. The *impertinent* person concerns himself with things which are none of his business. *Obtrusive* is oftener applied to words, qualities, actions, etc., than to persons; *intrusive* is used chiefly of persons, as is *officious*, though we speak of *officious* attentions, *intrusive* remarks; *meddl-*

some is used indifferently of persons, or of words, qualities, actions, etc. See **inquisitive.** Compare **impertinence; interpose; mix.**

ANTONYMS: *modest, reserved, retiring, shy, unassuming, unobtrusive.*

MELODY

air	harmony	symphony	unison
aria	music	tune	

A *melody* is a succession or series of single notes or tones usually in the same mode or key, constituting a consecutive musical whole. It is sometimes synonymous with *air* and *tune*. Specifically, an *air* is the chief voice part, or *melody*, in a simple harmonic composition, such as a hymn, a choral, or other song; a *tune* is the entire *melody* by which such a composition is recognized; we speak of the *tune* of a ballad; a dance *tune*; or say, "Can you remember the *tune*?" An *aria* is *melody* having an accompaniment, sung by one voice in one opera, oratorio, etc.; as contrasted with the *air* or *tune* of a simpler composition.

Harmony is simultaneous, the pleasing correspondence of two or more notes sounded at once. A *melody* may be wholly in one part; *harmony* must be of two or more parts. Accordant notes of different pitch sounded simultaneously produce *harmony*; *unison* is the simultaneous sounding of two or more notes of the same pitch. When the pitch is the same there may be *unison* between sounds of very different volume and quality, as a voice and a bell may sound in *unison*. Tones sounded at the interval of an octave are also said to be in *unison*, although this is not literally exact; this usage arises from the fact that bass and tenor voices in attempting to sound the same note as the soprano and alto will in fact sound a note an octave below. Speaking in terms of physics, two notes an octave apart are in *unison* because their overtones are the same. *Music* may denote the simplest *melody* or the most complex and perfect *harmony*. A *symphony* (apart from its technical orchestral sense) is any pleasing consonance of musical sounds, vocal or instrumental, as of many accordant voices or instruments.

ANTONYMS: *discord, recitative.*

MEMORY

mind	remembrance	retrospect
recollection	reminiscence	retrospection

Memory is the faculty by which knowledge is retained or recalled; in a more general sense, *memory* is a retention of knowledge within the grasp of the mind, while *remembrance* is having what is known consciously before the mind. *Remembrance* is the act of calling to *mind* rather than the power or faculty of so doing; it may be voluntary or involuntary; a thing is brought to *remembrance* or we call it to *remembrance*; the same is true of *memory*. *Recollection* involves volition, the mind making a distinct effort to recall something, or fixing the attention actively upon it when recalled. *Reminiscence* is a half-dreamy *memory* of scenes or events long past; *retrospection* is a distinct turning of the mind back upon the past, bringing long periods under survey. *Retrospection* is to *reminiscence* much what *recollection* is to *remembrance*. *Mind* is used in several idiomatic phrases to denote the function or power of remembering; as, to call a thing to *mind*; out of sight, out of *mind*

ANTONYMS: *forgetfulness, oblivion, obliviousness, oversight, unconsciousness.*

MERCY

benevolence	compassion	grace	mildness
benignity	favor	kindness	pardon
blessing	forbearance	lenience	pity
charity	forgiveness	leniency	tenderness
clemency	gentleness	lenity	

Mercy is the exercise of less severity than one deserves, or in a more extended sense, the granting of *kindness* or *favor* beyond what one may rightly claim. *Grace*, as here compared, is a rather archaic word suggesting a benignant attitude toward those situated beneath one, and a condescension in granting them *favors*. *Forgiveness, mercy,* and *pardon* are excercised toward the ill-deserving. *Pardon* remits the outward penalty which the offender deserves; *forgiveness* dismisses resentment or displeasure from the heart of the one offended; *mercy* seeks the highest possible good for the offender. There may be *mercy* without *pardon*, as in the mitigation of sentence, or in all possible alleviation of necessary severity; there may be cases where *pardon* would not be *mercy*, since it would encourage repetition of the offense, from which timely punishment might have saved. *Mercy* is also used in the wider sense of refraining from harshness or cruelty toward those who are in one's power without fault of their own; as, they besought the robber to have *mercy*.

Clemency is a colder word than *mercy*, and without its religious associations, signifying *mildness* and moderation in the use of power where severity would have legal or military, rather than moral sanction; it often denotes a habitual *mildness* of disposition on the part of the powerful, and is a matter rather of good nature or policy than of principle. *Leniency* or *lenity* denotes an easy-going avoidance of severity; these words are more general and less magisterial than *clemency*; we should speak of the *leniency* of a parent, the *clemency* of a conqueror. Compare **pity.**

ANTONYMS: *cruelty, hardness, harshness, implacability, justice, penalty, punishment, revenge, rigor, severity, sternness,
vengeance.*

PREPOSITIONS: The mercy *of* God *to* or *toward* sinners; have
mercy *on* or *upon* one.

MIGRATE

emigrate   immigrate

To *migrate* is to come and go with the seasons; to change one's dwelling-
place, usually with the idea of repeated change, or of periodical return; it
applies to wandering tribes of men, and to many birds and animals. *Emigrate*
(L. *e,* out, + *migrare,* to migrate or transfer) is to go out from one country in
order to settle in another. *Immigrate* (L. *in,* into, + *migrare,* to migrate) is to
come into another country of which one is not a native in order to settle there.
A person *emigrates from* the land he leaves, and *immigrates to* the land where
he takes up his abode.

MIND

awareness	instinct	reason	thought
brain	intellect	sense	understanding
consciousness	intelligence	soul	wit
disposition	psyche	spirit	wits

Mind, in a general sense, includes all the powers of sentient being apart
from the physical factors in bodily faculties and activities; in a limited sense,
mind is nearly synonymous with *intellect,* but includes *disposition,* or the
tendency toward action, as appears in the phrase "to have a *mind* to work."
As the seat of mental activity, *brain* (colloquially *brains*) is often used as a
synonym for *mind, intellect, intelligence. Thought,* the act, process, or power
of thinking, is often used to denote the thinking faculty, and especially the
reason. The *instinct* of animals is now held by many philosophers to be of
the same nature as the *intellect* of man, but inferior and limited; yet the
apparent difference is very great.

Human *instincts* denote tendencies independent of reasoning or instruction.
Soul is the term used for that immaterial human entity which thinks, feels, and
wills; it includes *intellect,* emotion, and will. In order to avoid the philosophical and religious connotations of the word *soul,* many modern psychologists
use the word *psyche* instead, with the meaning of subconscious self added to
the other meanings. *Spirit* is used especially in contradistinction from matter;
it may in many cases be substituted for *soul,* but *soul* has commonly a fuller
and more determinate meaning; fairies, elves, and brownies might be termed
spirits, but not *souls.* In the figurative sense, *spirit* denotes animation, ardor

enthusiasm, courage, spunk, etc.; as, a lad of *spirit*; he sang with *spirit*; he replied with *spirit*. Soul denotes energy and depth of feeling; or it may denote the very life of anything; as, "the hidden *soul* of harmony."

Sense may be an antonym of *intellect*, as when we speak of the physical *sense* of hearing; but *sense* is used also as denoting clear mental action, good judgment, acumen; as, he is a man of *sense*, or, he showed good *sense*; *sense*, even in its material signification, must be reckoned among the activities of *mind*, though dependent on bodily functions; the *mind*, not the eye, really sees; the *mind*, not the ear, really hears. *Wit* and *wits* are colloquial words for *mind*; as, he has lost his *wits*. *Consciousness* includes all that a sentient being perceives, knows, thinks, or feels, from whatever source arising and of whatever character, kind, or degree, whether with or without distinct thinking, feeling, or willing; we speak of the *consciousness* of the brute, of the savage, or of the sage. The *intellect* is that assemblage of faculties which is concerned with knowledge, as distinguished from emotion and volition. *Understanding* is the Saxon word of the same general import, but is chiefly used of the reasoning powers.

ANTONYMS: *body, brawn, brute force, material substance, matter.*

MINUTE

circumstantial	diminutive	little	slender
comminuted	exact	particular	small
critical	fine	precise	tiny
detailed			

That is *minute* which is exceedingly *small*, as a grain of dust, or which is of very little importance, or is of exceedingly slight amount. That which is broken up into *minute* particles is said to be *comminuted*; things may be termed *fine* which would not be termed *comminuted*; as, *fine* sand; *fine* gravel; but, in using the adverb, we say a substance is finely *comminuted*, *comminuted* referring more to the process, *fine* to the result. An account containing very *minute* particulars is *circumstantial, detailed, particular*; an examination is *critical, exact, precise*, when it delves into *minute* details. *Slender* refers to *small* girth; *tiny*, to anything unusually *small*. See **fine.**

ANTONYMS: See synonyms for **large.**

MISCELLANEOUS

assorted	dissimilar	motley	unlike
confused	heterogeneous	non-homogeneous	variant
conglomerate	mixed	promiscuous	various
discordant	mingled	unhomogeneous	

A *miscellaneous* collection is one which is brought together largely by chance. It may or may not be *heterogeneous*; if the objects are alike in kind, but different in size, form, quality, use, etc., and without special order or relation, the collection is *miscellaneous*; if the objects differ in kind, such a mixture is also, and more strictly, *heterogeneous*. A pile of unassorted lumber is *miscellaneous*; the contents of a schoolboy's pocket are commonly *miscellaneous* and might usually be termed *heterogeneous* as well.

Assorted also connotes a mixture, but a carefully chosen rather than a fortuitous one, including every known variety or calculated to suit every taste or need; as, a box of *assorted* nuts; a library of *assorted* books. *Motley* literally means variegated in color; as here considered, it adds to *heterogeneous* the suggestion of discordance or contrast of the component elements; as, a *motley* crowd of people. The implications of *promiscuous* are distinctly bad; the word suggests the absence of judgment or taste. Thus, while a *miscellaneous* collection of books might reveal a discriminating mind, a *promiscuous* collection would be evidence merely of a random, unorganized choice. See **complex.**

ANTONYMS: *alike, homogeneous, identical, like, pure, same, similar, uniform.*

MISERLY

acquisitive	covetous	parsimonious	sordid
avaricious	greedy	penurious	stingy
close	niggardly	rapacious	

Miserly and *niggardly* persons seek to gain by mean and petty savings; the *miserly* by stinting themselves, the *niggardly* by stinting others. *Parsimonious* and *penurious* may apply to one's outlay either for himself or for others; in the latter use, they are somewhat less harsh and reproachful terms than *niggardly.* The *close* man holds like a vise all that he gets.

Avaricious and *covetous* refer especially to acquisition, *miserly, niggardly, parsimonious* and *penurious,* to expenditure. The *avaricious* man has an eager craving for money; he is *stingy* and desires both to get and to keep; the *covetous* man longs to get something away from its possessor; though one may be made *avaricious* by the pressure of great expenditures. The *rapacious* have the robber instinct, and put it in practice in some form, as far as they dare. The *avaricious* and *rapacious* are ready to reach out for gain; the *parsimonious, miserly,* and *niggardly* prefer the safer and less adventurous way of avoiding expenditure. *Greedy* and *stingy* are used not only of money, but often of other things, as food, etc. The *greedy* child wishes to enjoy everything himself; the *stingy* child, to keep others from getting it. An *acquisitive* person is eager to have and to hold, and is generally able to get what he wants.

ANTONYMS: *bountiful, free, generous, liberal, munificent, prodigal, wasteful.*

MISFORTUNE

adversity	disappointment	ill fortune	ruin
affliction	disaster	ill luck	sorrow
bereavement	distress	misadventure	stroke
blow	failure	mischance	trial
calamity	hardship	misery	tribulation
catastrophe	harm	mishap	trouble
chastening	ill	reverse	visitation
chastisement			

Misfortune is adverse fortune or any instance thereof, any untoward event, usually of lingering character or consequences, and such as the sufferer is not deemed directly responsible for; as, he had the *misfortune* to be born blind. Any considerable *disappointment, failure,* or *misfortune,* as regards outward circumstances, as loss of fortune, position, and the like, when long continued constitutes *adversity.* For the loss of friends by death we commonly use *bereavement.* *Calamity* and *disaster* are used of sudden and severe *misfortunes,* often overwhelming; *ill fortune* and *ill luck,* of lighter troubles and failures. *Catastrophe* or *dènouement,* as here compared, is a disastrous end.

We speak of the *misery* of the poor, the *hardships* of the soldier. *Affliction, visitation, chastening, trial,* and *tribulation* have a somewhat religious bearing, suggesting some disciplinary purpose of God with beneficent design. *Affliction* may be keen and bitter, and it may refer to bodily suffering; *tribulation* is long and wearing. We speak of an *affliction,* but rarely of a *tribulation,* since *tribulation* is viewed as a continuous process, which may endure for years or for a lifetime; but we speak of our daily *trials.* *Chastisement* is the infliction of punishment; *mischance* implies bad luck in something; *mishap,* an unlucky incident. *Distress* can be mental or bodily, or be used of things. See **catastrophe.** Compare **blow.**

ANTONYMS: *blessing, boon, comfort, consolation, good fortune, good luck, gratification, happiness, joy, pleasure, prosperity, relief, success, triumph.*

MIX

amalgamate	commix	fuse	meddle
associate	compound	incorporate	merge
blend	confound	intermingle	mingle
combine	confuse	join	unite
commingle			

To *mix* is to put together promiscuously and indiscriminately, so that the parts or elements become, for the time at least, one mass, assemblage, or mixture; we may *mix* milk and water, but water and oil cannot be *mixed*. *Mingle* is almost equivalent to *mix*, but in *mingling* there is often more consideration of the separate units; *mingled* races may live together in the same city or country, and yet preserve their racial individuality so as not to become *mixed* races; we may speak of a descendant as of the *mingled* blood of distinct races; *mingle* is everywhere a word of more dignity than *mix*. *Mingle* is commonly preferred to *mix* in figurative use; we speak of *mingled* emotions, rather than of *mixed* emotions; in fact, the use of *mix* outside the material realm is rare.

Combine denotes a closer union than *mingle* or *mix*; this is especially noticeable in chemistry, where substances chemically *combined* form a compound, with properties different from those of either constitutent; oxygen and nitrogen are mechanically *mingled* or *mixed* in the atmosphere, which supports life; if they were chemically *combined,* the earth would be overflowed with nitric acid, destroying the possibility of life. To *compound* is to *mix* in definite proportions, so as to form a composite product; as, to *compound* an ointment; to *compound* two or more words so as to produce another of extended, diminished, or otherwise different meaning.

To *blend* is to *mix* or *mingle* in such a way as to retain some of the properties of each of the things *blended* but obscure the individuality of the parts. *Blend* is used especially of colors and tones, implying gradual and harmonious union, one shading off almost or quite imperceptibly into the other, as the bands of color in the rainbow *blend* at their edges, so that the eye can fix no definite dividing line. Different races, languages, qualities, or feelings may be said to be *blended*. To *confuse* is to *mix* in a disorderly or irrational way; a *confused* statement, argument, or composition has the different parts so out of order or relation that the mind cannot follow them to any clear result. To *confound* in this connection is to *confuse* identity, to take one thing for another that is in some way similar; as, to *confound* means with ends. When something *merges* with another it is absorbed in it.

Intransitively, *mingle* or *mix* signifies to take part, be, act, or move with, in, or among; as, a man *mingles* in a crowd, or *mixes* with politicians or in politics; *mingle*, so used, denotes less closeness of association than *mix*; both words, so used, are often close synonyms for *associate*. To *meddle* is to *mix* or *mingle* unnecessarily, officiously, or impertinently in or with the affairs of others; one may *mingle* with a company, but not *meddle* with their affairs. Things which are *mixed* or *mingled* may become *joined,* as the different materials in conglomerate rock; but distinct pieces of wood may be so perfectly *joined* in cabinetwork that neither eye nor hand can detect the juncture except by tracing the grain, and yet be neither *mixed* nor *mingled*. See **associate** *verb*. Compare **attach.**

ANTONYMS: *analyze, assort, classify, detach, disconnect, discriminate, disengage, disjoin, dissever, dissociate, disunite, divide, eliminate, part, remove, segregate, separate, sever, sift, sort, sunder, unravel, untangle, untwine.*

MOB

canaille	lower classes	multitude	rabble
crowd	masses	populace	throng
horde			

A *mob* is disorderly and lawless, but may be rich and influential. The *rabble* is despicable, worthless, purposeless; a *mob* may have effective, desperate purpose. A *crowd* may be drawn by mere curiosity; some strong, pervading excitement is needed to make it a *mob*. A government depends on the *populace* or the *masses*, even if poor or ignorant, for the observance of its laws. *Horde* suggests a rough crowd; *throng* often implies that the *crowd* is moving about, jostling and pushing. *Canaille* is a word borrowed from the French and means the lowest class, the *rabble*.

MODEL

archetype	facsimile	mold	prototype
copy	ideal	original	representation
design	image	paradigm	standard
example	imitation	pattern	type
exemplar			

A *model* may be either the thing to be copied or the *copy* that has been made from it; as, the *models* in the Patent Office. A sculptor may idealize his living *model*; his workmen must exactly *copy* in marble or metal the *model* he has made in clay. A *pattern* is always, in modern use, that from which a *copy* is to be made. A *pattern* is commonly superficial; a *model* is usually in relief. A *pattern* must be closely followed in its minutest particulars by a faithful copyist.

An *archetype* is the primal form, actual or imaginary, which serves as a *model* or *pattern* according to which things of the same kind are created or constructed. A *prototype* has or has had actual existence, and if not an original it must have equal authority with that as a *standard* from which to make reproductions with or without changes. A *facsimile* is an exact reproduction; an *imitation* is a *copy* that resembles the *original*. A *type* represents the characteristics of a group; a *standard* is an authorized measure or definite rule that stands as a *model*. A *design* is a *pattern* more or less in outline. A *paradigm* is a *model* or *pattern* for the inflection of words; an *exemplar* is an example that is worthy to be copied; an *ideal* is a perfect *type*, one's highest conception of something. See **example; idea; ideal.**

MODESTY

backwardness	constraint	reserve	timidity
bashfulness	coyness	shyness	unobtrusiveness
coldness	diffidence		

Modesty is an unconceited estimate of oneself in comparison with others, or with the demands of some undertaking. *Modesty* has also the specific meaning of a sensitive shrinking from anything indelicate. *Bashfulness* is a shrinking from notice without assignable reason; *unobtrusiveness* shrinks from intruding. *Coyness* is a half encouragement, half avoidance of offered attention, and is usually affected. *Diffidence* is self-distrust. *Shyness* is a tendency to shrink from observation; *timidity*, a distinct fear of criticism, error, or failure. *Reserve* is the holding oneself aloof from others, or holding back one's feelings from expression, or one's affairs from communication to others. *Reserve* may be the retreat of *shyness*, or, on the other hand, the contemptuous withdrawal of pride and haughtiness. Compare **embarrass; taciturn.**

ANTONYMS: *abandon, arrogance, assumption, assurance, boldness, conceit, confidence, egotism, forwardness, frankness, freedom, haughtiness, impudence, indiscretion, loquaciousness, loquacity, pertness, sauciness, self-conceit, self-sufficiency, sociability.*

MONEY

bills	cash	currency	notes	specie
bullion	coin	funds	property	wealth
capital	coinage	gold	silver	

Money is the authorized medium of exchange; coined *money* is called *coin* or *specie*. What are termed in England bank*notes* are in the United States commonly called *bills*; as, a five-dollar *bill*. The *notes* of responsible men are readily transferable in commercial circles, but they are not *money*; as, the stock was sold for $500 in *money* and the balance in negotiable paper. *Cash* is *specie* or *money* in hand, or paid in hand; as, the *cash* account; the *cash* price. In the legal sense, *property* is not *money*, and *money* is not *property*; for *property* is that which has inherent value, while *money*, as such, has but representative value, and may or may not have intrinsic value. *Bullion* is either *gold* or *silver* uncoined, or the coined metal considered without reference to its coinage, but simply as merchandise, when its value as *bullion* may be very different from its value as *money*. The word *capital* is used chiefly of accumulated *property* or *money* invested in productive enterprises or available for such investment. *Currency* applies to *money* in actual use or circulation in a country; *coinage*, to coined *money* as opposed to paper *money*. *Wealth* includes *property, money,* and other possessions. See **wealth.**

MOROSE

acrimonious	dour	ill-natured	splenetic
churlish	gloomy	severe	sulky
crabbed	glum	snappish	sullen
crusty	gruff	sour	surly
dogged	ill-humored		

Morose people are bitterly dissatisfied with the world in general, and disposed to vent their ill nature upon others. *Sullen* and *sulky* individuals are for the most part silent; the *morose* growl out bitter speeches. A *surly* person is in a state of latent anger, resenting approach as intrusion, and ready to take offense at anything; thus we speak of a *surly* dog. *Sullen* and *sulky* moods may be transitory; one who is *morose* or *sulky* is commonly so by disposition or habit. *Sullen* and *sulky* people are discontented and resentful in regard to that against which they are too proud to protest, or consider all protest vain; *sullen* denotes more of pride, *sulky* more of resentful obstinacy.

A *gloomy* person or outlook is dismal; a *glum* person is moody and silent. An *acrimonious* retort is bitter and stinging; a *churlish* remark is rough and impolite; a *dour* person is *severe* and grim. *Crabbed* implies *sour*-tempered; *crusty* refers to a harsh, forbidding manner; *gruff*, to a rough voice or manner. *Splenetic* applies to those who are fretfully spiteful or peevish.

> ANTONYMS: *amiable, benignant, bland, complaisant, friendly, genial, gentle, good-natured, indulgent, kind, loving, mild, pleasant, sympathetic, tender.*

MOTION

act	change	movement	process	transition
action	move	passage	transit	

Motion is *change* of place or position in space; *transition* is passing from one point or position in space to another. *Motion* may be either abstract or concrete, more frequently the former. *Movement* usually implies a certain regularity or rate of speed; as, the *movement* of the clouds; the *movement* of Whitman's poetry. *Movement* is always concrete, that is, considered in connection with the thing that moves or is moved; thus, we speak of the *movements* of the planets, but of the laws of planetary *motion*; of military *movements*, but of perpetual *motion*. *Move* is used chiefly of contests or competition, as in chess or politics; as, it is your *move*; a shrewd *move* of the opposition. It is also used to express a *change* in one's location toward a definite goal or objective; as, don't make a *move* for your gun. *Action* is a more comprehensive word than *motion*. We now rarely speak of mental or spiritual *motions*, but rather of mental or spiritual *acts* or *processes*, or of the laws of mental *action*, but a formal proposal of *action* in a deliberative assembly is termed a *motion*. See **act.**

> ANTONYMS: *immobility, quiescence, quiet, repose, rest, stillness.*

MOURN

bemoan	deplore	lament	rue
bewail	grieve	regret	sorrow

To *mourn* is to feel or express sadness or distress because of some loss, affliction, or misfortune, and carries a strong suggestion of the outward expression of grief, as in the wearing of black clothing; *mourning* is thought of as prolonged, but grief or regret may be transient. To *grieve* is to experience great mental suffering, whether it is expressed outwardly or not. *Sorrow* is closely akin in meaning to both *grieve* and *mourn*, but distinctively carries a stronger suggestion of sadness or regret. One may *grieve* or *mourn*, *regret*, *rue*, or *sorrow* without a sound; he *bemoans* with suppressed and often inarticulate sounds of grief; he *bewails* with passionate utterance, whether of inarticulate cries or of spoken words. He *laments* in plaintive or pathetic words, as the prophet Jeremiah in his "Lamentations." One *deplores* with settled sorrow which may or may not find relief in words. One is made to *rue* an act by some misfortune resulting, or by some penalty or vengeance inflicted because of it. One *regrets* a slight misfortune or a hasty word; he *sorrows* over the death of a friend.

ANTONYMS: *be joyful, exult, joy, make merry, rejoice, triumph.*

MUTUAL

common   **joint**   **reciprocal**   **shared**   **united**

That is *common* to which two or more persons have the same or equal claims, or in which they have equal interest or participation; in the strictest sense, that is *mutual* which is freely interchanged; that is *reciprocal* in respect to which one act or movement is met by a corresponding act or movement in return; we speak of our *common* country, *mutual* affection, *reciprocal* obligations, the *reciprocal* action of cause and effect, where the effect becomes in turn a cause. Many good writers hold it incorrect to say "a *mutual* friend," and insist that "a *common* friend" would be more accurate; but *"common* friend" is practically never used, because of the disagreeable suggestion of ordinary or inferior that attaches to *common*. *"Mutual* friend" has high literary authority (of Burke, Scott, Dickens, and others), and a considerable usage of good society in its favor, the expression being quite naturally derived from the thoroughly correct phrase *mutual* friendship.

ANTONYMS: *detached, disconnected, dissociated, distinct, disunited, separate, separated, severed, sundered, unconnected, unreciprocated, unrequited, unshared.*

MYSTERIOUS

abstruse	incomprehensible	obscure	transcendental
cabalistic	inexplicable	occult	unfathomable
dark	inscrutable	recondite	unfathomed
enigmatical	mystic	secret	unknown
hidden	mystical		

A *mysterious* thing arouses one's wonder or curiosity, and yet one is unable to understand it. *Inscrutable* connotes an inability to examine or scrutinize something; an *inscrutable* face reveals no emotion or feeling; an *inscrutable* person conceals his thoughts, motives, etc., so well as to discourage or repel attempts at closer acquaintance. *Recondite* is remote from ordinary perception; profound. That is *mystic* or *mystical* which has associated with it some *hidden* or *recondite* meaning, especially of a religious kind; as, the *mystic* Babylon of the Apocalypse. That is *dark* which we cannot personally see through, especially if sadly perplexing; as, a *dark* providence. That is *secret* which is intentionally *hidden*.

Abstruse applies to what is so remote from experience and so deep or abstract that it is extremely difficult to understand. *Occult* refers to secret knowledge, always involving the supernatural; *cabalistic* primarily referred to a *secret* interpretation of the Scriptures; in modern usage it cannotes *occult, secret, mysterious. Transcendental,* in this comparison, implies beyond human experience. *Enigmatical* is *obscure* and puzzling. Compare **dark; latent; obscure.**

ANTONYMS: See synonyms for **clear.**

N

NAME

agnomen	denomination	nickname	surname
appellation	designation	prenomen	title
cognomen	epithet	style	

Name in the most general sense, signifying the word by which a person or thing is called or known, includes all other words of this group; in this sense every noun is a *name*; in the more limited sense a *name* is personal, an *appellation* is descriptive, a *title* is official. In the phrase, William the Conqueror, king of England, William is the man's *name*, which belongs to him personally, independently of any rank or achievement; Conqueror is the *appellation* which he won by his acquisition of England; king is the *title* denoting his royal rank. An *epithet* is etymologically something placed upon a person or thing; the *epithet* does not strictly belong to an object like a *name*, but is given to mark some assumed characteristic, good or bad; an *epithet* is always an adjective, or a word or phrase used as an adjective, and is properly used to emphasize a characteristic but not to add information, as in the significant *appellations*, Harry "Hotspur," "Stonewall" Jackson. The idea that an *epithet* is always opprobrious, and that any word used opprobriously is an *epithet* is an error. A *nickname* is a popular *appellation* given to a person, place, or thing, often expressing derision, affection, hatred, or mere description; as Red, Lefty, etc.

Designation may be used much in the sense of *appellation*, but is more distinctive or specific in meaning; a *designation* properly so-called rests upon some inherent quality, while an *appellation* may be fanciful. Among the Romans the *prenomen* was the individual part of a man's *name*, the "nomen" designated the gens to which he belonged, the *cognomen* showed his family and was borne by all patricians, and the *agnomen* was added to refer to his achievements or character. For instance, Marcus Licinius Crassus Dives was called Marcus by his family and friends, belonged to the celebrated Licinia gens and to the Crassus family, and was nicknamed Dives (the Rich) in reference to his great wealth.

When scientists name an animal or a plant, they give it a binary or binomial technical *name* comprising a generic and a specific *appellation*. Frequently a third *name* designates the subspecies to which the animal or plant belongs. The Bohemian waxwing is called *Bombycilla garrula pallidiceps*. In modern use, a personal *name*, as John or Mary, is given in infancy, and is often called the given *name* or Christian *name*, or simply the first *name* (rarely the *prenomen*); the *cognomen* or *surname* is the family *name* which belongs to one by right of birth or marriage. *Style* is the legal *designation* by which a person or house is known in official or business relations; as, the *name* and *style* of Baring Brothers. The term *denomination* is applied to a separate religious organization, without the opprobrious meaning attaching to the word "sect"; also, to designate any class of like objects collectively, especially money or notes of a certain value; as, the sum was in notes of the *denomination* of one thousand dollars. Compare **term.**

NATIVE

aboriginal	**indigenous**	**natal**	**original**
endemic	**innate**	**natural**	

Native denotes that which belongs to one by birth, and stresses the contrast with that which is acquired or artificial; *natal* denotes that which pertains to the event of birth; *natural* denotes that which rests upon inherent qualities of character or being. We speak of one's *native* country, or of his *natal* day; of *natural* ability, *native* genius. *Indigenous* is used to describe that which is *native* to a country, climate, or soil; as, an *indigenous* plant. An *endemic* plant is one that is *native* to, peculiar to, and restricted to a certain typical geographical area. An *aboriginal* race of men is one which has no known or recorded ancestors. *Aboriginal* refers to the earliest inhabitants of a place, or to *indigenous* plants.

NEAT

clean	**natty**	**prim**	**tidy**
cleanly	**nice**	**spick-and-span**	**trim**
dapper	**orderly**	**spruce**	

That which is *clean* is simply free from soil or defilement of any kind. Things are *orderly* when in due relation to other things; a room or desk is *orderly* when every article is in place; a person is *orderly* who habitually keeps things so. *Tidy* denotes that which conforms to propriety in general; an unlaced shoe may be perfectly *clean,* but is not *tidy.* *Neat* refers to that which is *clean* and *tidy* with nothing superfluous, conspicuous, or showy, as when we speak of plain but *neat* attire; the same idea of freedom from the superfluous appears in the phrases "a *neat* speech," or "a *neat* turn," "a *neat* reply," etc. A *clean* cut has no ragged edges; a *neat* stroke does just what is intended. *Nice* is stronger than *neat,* implying value and beauty; a cheap, coarse dress may be perfectly *neat,* but would not be termed *nice.*

Spruce is applied to the show and affectation of neatness with a touch of smartness. *Trim* denotes a certain shapely and elegant neatness, often with suppleness and grace; as, a *trim* suit; a *trim* figure. *Prim* applies to a precise, formal, affected nicety. *Dapper* is *spruce* with the suggestion of smallness and slightness; *natty,* a diminutive of *neat,* suggests minute elegance, with a tendency toward the exquisite; as, a *dapper* little fellow in a *natty* business suit. *Spick-and-span* denotes anything which is fresh and bright with newness, or which is kept looking new by constant care.

ANTONYMS: *dirty, disorderly, dowdy, negligent, rough, rude, slouchy, slovenly, soiled, uncared for, unkempt, untidy.*

NECESSARY

essential	infallible	required	unavoidable
indispensable	needed	requisite	undeniable
inevitable	needful		

That is *necessary* which must exist, occur, or be true, which in the nature of things cannot be otherwise. That which is *essential* belongs to the essence of a thing, so that the thing cannot exist in its completeness without it; that which is *indispensable* may be only an adjunct, but it is one that cannot be spared; vigorous health is *essential* to an arctic explorer; warm clothing is *indispensable*. That which is *requisite* (or *required*) is so in the judgment of the person requiring it, but may not be so absolutely; thus, the *requisite* is more a matter of personal feeling than the *indispensable*. *Inevitable* is primarily the exact equivalent of *unavoidable*; both words are applied to things which some at least would prefer to escape or prevent, while that which is *necessary* may meet with no objection; food is *necessary*, death is *inevitable*; a *necessary* conclusion satisfies a thinker; an *inevitable* conclusion silences opposition. An *infallible* proof is one that necessarily leads the mind to a sound conclusion. *Needed* and *needful* are more concrete than *necessary*, and refer to an end to be attained; we speak of a *necessary* inference; *necessary* food is what one cannot live without, while *needful* food is that without which one cannot enjoy comfort, health, and strength.

ANTONYMS: *casual, contingent, needless, non-essential, optional, unnecessary, useless, worthless.*

PREPOSITIONS: Necessary *to* a sequence or a total, *for* or *to* a result or a person; unity is necessary *to* (to constitute) completeness; decision is necessary *for* command, or *for* a commander.

NECESSITY

compulsion	extremity	indispensableness	sine qua non
destiny	fatality	need	unavoidableness
emergency	fate	requirement	urgency
essential	indispensability	requisite	want
exigency			

Necessity is the quality of being necessary, or the quality of that which cannot but be, become, or be true, or be accepted as true. *Need* and *want* always imply a lack; *necessity* may be used in this sense, but in the higher philosophical sense *necessity* simply denotes the exclusion of any alternative either in thought or fact; righteousness is a *necessity* (not a *need*) of the divine nature. *Need* suggests the possibility of supplying the deficiency which *want* expresses: to speak of a person's *want* of decision merely points out a weakness in his character; to say that he has *need* of decision implies that he can exercise or attain it.

As applied to a deficiency, *necessity* is more imperative than *need*; a weary person is in *need* of rest; when rest becomes a *necessity* he has no choice but to stop work. An *essential* is something, as a quality, or element, that belongs to the essence of something else so as to be inseparable from it in its normal condition, or in any complete idea or statement of it. An *exigency* is an urgent, compelling *necessity*, especially one brought on by an accident or crisis; as, we are forced by the *exigencies* of time to foreclose the mortgage. *Sine qua non* is a Latin phrase for an indispensable *necessity*; literally, "without which not." Compare **necessary; predestination.**

> **ANTONYMS:** *choice, contingency, doubt, doubtfulness, dubiousness, fortuity, freedom, option, possibility, uncertainty.*

> **PREPOSITIONS:** The necessity *of* surrender; a necessity *for* action; this is a necessity *to* me.

NEGLECT

carelessness	heedlessness	negligence	scorn
default	inadvertence	omission	slackness
disregard	inattention	oversight	slight
disrespect	indifference	remissness	thoughtlessness
failure	neglectfulness		

Neglect (from L. *nec,* not, and *lego,* gather) is the failing to take such care, show such attention, pay such courtesy, etc., as may be rightfully or reasonably expected. *Negligence,* which is the same in origin, may be used in almost the same sense, but with a slighter force, as when Whittier speaks of "the *negligence* which friendship loves"; but *negligence* is often used to denote the quality or trait of character of which the act is a manifestation, or to denote the habit of neglecting that which ought to be done. We speak of *neglect* of books, friends, or duties, in which cases we could not use *negligence*; *negligence* in dress implies want of care as to its arrangement, tidiness, etc.; *neglect* of one's garments would imply leaving them exposed to defacement or injury, as by dust, moths, etc.

Neglect has a passive sense which *negligence* has not; the child was suffering from *neglect, i.e.,* from being neglected by others; the child was suffering from *negligence* would imply that he himself was neglectful. The distinction sometimes made that *neglect* denotes the act, and *negligence* the habit, is but partially true; one may be guilty of habitual *neglect* of duty; the wife may suffer from her husband's constant *neglect*, while the *negligence* which causes a railroad accident may be that of a moment, and on the part of one ordinarily careful and attentive; in such cases the law provides punishment for criminal *negligence*.

Disregard implies *neglect* that is usually intentional; *disrespect* is *neglect* of courtesy; *default* is *neglect* of duty, or *failure* to pay or to fulfil a contract. *Heedlessness* and *inattention* stress lack of attention; *carelessness* and *indifference*, want of due care; *remissness, negligence* in duty. An *inadvertence* is an *oversight* resulting from *negligence*. A *slight* is an intentional omission of kindness, courtesy, or attention.

ANTONYMS: See synonyms for **care.**

PREPOSITIONS: Neglect *of* duty, *of* the child *by* the parent; there was neglect *on the part of* the teacher.

NEW

fresh	new-fangled	novel	upstart
late	new-fashioned	original	young
modern	new-made	recent	youthful

That which is *new* has lately come into existence, possession, or use; a *new* house is just built, or in a more general sense is one that has just come into the possession of the present owner or occupant. *Modern* denotes that which has begun to exist in the present age, and is still existing; *recent* denotes that which has come into existence within a comparatively brief period, and may or may not be existing still. *Modern* history pertains to any period since the middle ages; *modern* literature, *modern* architecture, etc., are not strikingly remote from the styles and types prevalent today. That which is *late*, in this comparison, is very *recent* or just previous; as, the *late* storms ruined the crops. That which is *recent* is not quite so sharply distinguished from the past as that which is *new*; *recent* publications range over a longer time than *new* books.

That which is *novel* is either absolutely or relatively unprecedented in kind; a *novel* contrivance is one that has never before been known; a *novel* experience is one that has never before occurred to the same person; that which is *new* may be of a familiar or even of an ancient sort, as a *new* copy of an old book. *Young* and *youthful* are applied to that which has life; that which is *young* is possessed of a comparatively *new* existence as a living thing, possessing actual youth; that which is *youthful* manifests the attributes of youth. *Fresh* applies to that which has the characteristics of newness or youth, while capable of deterioration by lapse of time, that which is unworn, unspoiled, or unfaded; as, a *fresh* countenance, *fresh* eggs, *fresh* flowers. *New* is opposed to old, *modern* to ancient, *recent* to remote, *young* to old or aged, etc. Compare **youthful.**

ANTONYMS: See synonyms for **old.**

NEWS

advice	information	intelligence	tidings

News is the most general of these words, signifying simply the telling of something that has either just happened or just become known. *Advices* are communications of fact by a trusted informant with the design of guiding or influencing the action of the recipient; the word signifies *news* with a practical purpose and value. *Intelligence* is *news* that makes us more intelligent regarding something of interest. *Information* includes valuable or timely details, whereas *news* may be a mere announcement. We say, "What is the *news* in the headlines?" but "That columnist gives more *information* about the crisis." *Tidings*, often used poetically for *news*, usually refers to oral messages or *news*.

NIMBLE

active	bustling	quick	spry
agile	flexible	speedy	supple
alert	lively	sprightly	swift
brisk	prompt		

Nimble refers to lightness, freedom, and quickness of motion within a somewhat narrow range, with readiness to turn suddenly to any point; *swift* applies commonly to sustained and rapid motion over greater distances; a pickpocket is *nimble*-fingered, a dancer *nimble*-footed; an arrow, a race horse, or an ocean steamer is *swift*. *Supple* and *flexible* are almost pure synonyms, but *supple* applies especially to muscular movement that not only is *flexible* but is characterized by ease and grace. An acrobat has to be *supple*; we notice the *supple* slinking movements of a cat. *Flexible*, on the other hand, applies to anything having a pliable or resilient quality; both a rubber band and a steel spring are *flexible*.

Figuratively, we speak of a *nimble* wit, *swift* intelligence, *swift* destruction. *Alert*, which is strictly a synonym for *watchful*, comes sometimes near the meaning of *nimble* or *quick*, from the fact that the ready, wide-awake person is likely to be *lively, quick, speedy*. *Active*, as compared here, refers to energy in movement; *agile*, to ease and quickness in using one's limbs; *brisk*, to *lively* movement. *Spry* stresses alacrity, often unexpected; *sprightly* is full of vigor, vivacious; an old man may be *spry*, but a young one should be *sprightly*. Compare **active; alert.**

ANTONYMS: *clumsy, dilatory, dull, heavy, inactive, inert, slow, sluggish, unready.*

NORMAL

common	natural	regular	usual
general	ordinary	typical	

That which is *normal* conforms to the standard or rule which is observed or claimed to prevail in nature; that which is *natural* is according to nature. Symmetry is *normal*; the *normal* color of the crow is black, while the *normal* color of the sparrow is gray, but one is as *natural* as the other. *Typical* refers to such an assemblage of qualities as makes the specimen, genus, etc., a type of some more comprehensive group, while *normal* is more commonly applied to the parts of a single object; the specimen was *typical*; color, size, and other characteristics, *normal*.

The *regular* is etymologically that which is according to rule, hence that which is steady and constant, as opposed to that which is fitful and changeable; the *normal* action of the heart is *regular*. That which is *common* is shared by a great number of persons or things; disease is *common*. *Usual* refers to that which is customary, according to what commonly occurs; *ordinary* is commonplace, not distinguished from others, and often connotes inferiority. *General* may refer to all members of a class, etc., or to the greater number. See **general; usual.**

> **ANTONYMS:** *abnormal, exceptional, irregular, monstrous, peculiar, rare, singular, uncommon, unprecedented, unusual.*

NOTWITHSTANDING *conj.*

although	howbeit	nevertheless	though
but	however	still	yet

Notwithstanding marshals the two statements face to face, admits the one and its seeming contradiction to the other, while insisting that it cannot, after all, withstand the other; as, *notwithstanding* the force of the enemy is superior, we shall conquer. *Yet* and *still* are weaker than *notwithstanding*, while stronger than *but*; as, he was weak *yet* he succeeded; he was ill *but* he came. *Though* and *although* make as little as possible of the concession, dropping it, as it were, incidentally; as, "*though* we are guilty, you are good"; to say "we are guilty, *but* you are good," would make the concession of guilt more emphatic.

However simply waives discussion, and (like the archaic *howbeit*) says "be that as it may, this is true"; *nevertheless* concedes the truth of what precedes, but claims that what follows is none the less true; as, whatever the opposition, *nevertheless* he will win. See **but; yet.**

NOTWITHSTANDING *prep.*

despite	in spite of

Notwithstanding simply states that circumstances and difficulties shall not be or have not been allowed to withstand; *in spite of* is a much stronger phrase and is used when the opposition is great or seems impossible to overcome; as, he failed *notwithstanding* his good intentions; but he persevered *in spite of* the most bitter hostility. *Despite* is feebler than *in spite of*; as, *despite* his prejudices, he ate the foreign food.

O

OATH

adjuration	blasphemy	imprecation	reprobation
affidavit	curse	malediction	swearing
anathema	cursing	profane swearing	sworn statement
ban	denunciation	profanity	vow
blaspheming	execration		

In the highest sense, as in a court of justice, "an *oath* is a reverent appeal to God in corroboration of what one says," Abbott *Law Dict.*; an *affidavit* is a *sworn statement* made in writing in the presence of a competent officer; an *adjuration* is a solemn charge, entreaty, or command, as under an oath or curse. An *oath* is made to man in the name of God; a *vow* is a binding promise, especially when made to God. In the lower sense, an *oath* may be mere *blasphemy* or *profane swearing*.

Anathema, curse, execration, and *imprecation* are modes of invoking vengeance or retribution from a superhuman power upon the person against whom they are uttered. *Anathema* is a solemn authoritative, often ecclesiastical, condemnation of a person or of a proposition. *Curse* consigns a person or thing to injury or destruction; it may be wanton and powerless; "so the *curse* causeless shall not come," *Prov.* xxvi, 2. *Execration* expresses most of personal bitterness and abhorrence; *imprecation* refers especially to anger and a keen desire for revenge. *Malediction* implies *denunciation* and a general proclaiming or expression of evil against someone. Compare **testimony.**

ANTONYMS: *benediction, benison, blessing.*

OBJECT

contravene	disapprove	hesitate	scruple
demur	gainsay	oppose	take exception

To *object* (from L. *ob,* before, against, + *jacio,* throw) is, as it were, to throw something across the way of what is advanced or proposed, to bring, offer, or urge (something) in opposition, usually followed by *to* (sometimes by *against*) before the thing opposed; as, to *object to* suspension of the rules; to *object to* the introduction of personalities. *Object* may be used transitively; as, we *object* the cancellation of the order; or in the passive, especially with a clause for the subject; as, that we cannot help all should not be *objected as* a reason against helping any. To *take exception,* in this connection, is to *object* at or to a single point or item: followed by *to* or *against*; as, I favor the purpose of the resolution, but *take exception* to the closing words. To *hesitate* is to pause on account of indecision. To *demur* is to *object* irresolutely, as one who delays in hope of preventing: followed by *at* or *to;*

300

as, *at* that he *demurred*; to *demur to* a view or proposal; also, frequently used without a preposition;

> If he accepts it, why should you *demur*? BROWNING.

To *demur* is to *hesitate* in the spirit of doubt or opposition; to *scruple* is to *hesitate* on conscientious grounds. To *contravene* is to conflict with in word or act; to *gainsay* is to speak against. Compare **hesitate** under **fluctuate; oppose** under **hinder.**

ANTONYMS: *accede, accept, admire, admit, applaud, approve, assent, comply, concur, consent.*

OBSCURE

abstruse	darksome	dusky	involved
ambiguous	deep	enigmatical	muddy
cloudy	dense	hidden	mysterious
complex	difficult	incomprehensible	profound
complicated	dim	indistinct	turbid
cryptic	doubtful	intricate	unintelligible
dark			

That is *obscure* which the eye or the mind cannot clearly discern or see through, whether because of its own want of transparency, its depth or intricacy, or because of mere defect of light. That which is *complicated* is likely to be *obscure*, but that may be *obscure* which is not at all *complicated* and scarcely *complex*, as a *muddy* pool. In that which is *abstruse* (from L. *abs*, from, and *trudo*, push) as if removed from the usual course of thought or out of the way of apprehension or discovery, the thought is remote, *hidden*; in that which is *obscure* there may be nothing to hide; it is hard to see the bottom of the *profound*, because of its depth, but the most shallow turbidness is *obscure*. *Ambiguous* words or statements are capable of being interpreted in two or more ways; *enigmatical* words are puzzling; *cryptic* words have a *hidden* meaning or are *mysterious*. *Intricate* implies entangled and hence *difficult* to follow; *dark*, as here compared, implies *mysterious*, not understandable. See **complex; dark; difficult; mysterious.**

ANTONYMS: See synonyms for **clear.**

OBSOLETE

ancient	archaic	obsolescent	out-of-date
antiquated	disused	old	rare

A word is *obsolete* which has quite gone out of use; some of the most *ancient* words are not *obsolete*. A word is *archaic* or *obsolescent* which is falling out of use; *archaic* is also applied to a word that is *obsolete* in general usage but which survives in special texts, as in the Bible, hymnals, poetry, and legal documents. A word is *rare* if there are few modern instances of its use. Compare **old**.

ANTONYMS: See synonyms for **new**.

OBSTINATE

contumacious	heady	opinionated	resolute
decided	immovable	persistent	resolved
determined	indomitable	pertinacious	stubborn
dogged	inflexible	perverse	unconquerable
firm	intractable	pig-headed	unflinching
fixed	mulish	refractory	unyielding
headstrong	obdurate		

The *headstrong* person is not to be stopped in his own course of action, while the *obstinate* and *stubborn* is not to be driven to another's way. The *headstrong* person acts; the *obstinate* and *stubborn* may simply refuse to stir; the *dogged* person persists tenaciously, perhaps sullenly. The most amiable person may be *obstinate* on some one point; the *stubborn* person is for the most part habitually so; we speak of *obstinate* determination, *stubborn* resistance. *Stubborn* is the term most frequently applied to animals and inanimate things. *Refractory* implies more activity of resistance; the *stubborn* horse balks; the *refractory* animal plunges, rears, and kicks; metals that resist ordinary processes of reduction are termed *refractory*. He who is *perverse* acts counter to what is normal, customary, or expected.

One is *obdurate* who adheres to his purpose in spite of appeals that would move any tender-hearted or right-minded person. *Contumacious* refers to a proud and insolent defiance of authority, as of the summons of a court. *Pertinacious* demand is contrasted with *obstinate* refusal. The *unyielding* conduct which we approve we call *decided, firm, inflexible, resolute*; that which we condemn we are apt to term *headstrong, mulish, obstinate, pig-headed, stubborn*. See **perverse**.

ANTONYMS: *amenable, complaisant, compliant, docile, dutiful, gentle, irresolute, obedient, pliable, pliant, submissive, teachable, tractable, undecided, wavering, yielding.*

OFFER

adduce	exhibit	make a proposal	propose
allege	extend	make an offering	tender
attempt	hold out	present	volunteer
bid	make an offer	proffer	

What one *offers* he brings before another for acceptance or rejection; one may *offer* a gift, a suggestion, or a sacrifice; one may even *offer* an insult, leaving the other party, in common phrase, to "take it up" or not. *Proffer* is a more formal and deferential word, with a suggestion of contingency; as, to *proffer* one's services; the worshiper *offers*, but does not *proffer* sacrifice. We *allege* what we formally state to be true or capable of proof; we *adduce* what we bring forward for consideration. When we *bid* we *make an offer* of a price; what we *exhibit* we *present* to view. We *propose* a candidate when we *present* him for acceptance; we *make a proposal* about something that we *present* for consideration; we *tender* what we *offer* or *present* for acceptance or rejection. The possibility of advancement is often *held out* as an inducement to *volunteer* or *offer* oneself for special service. See **allege.**

ANTONYMS: *alienate, divert, refuse, retain, retract, withdraw, withhold.*

OLD

aged	decrepit	moldering	senile
ancient	elderly	olden	time-honored
antediluvian	gray	patriarchal	time-worn
antiquated	hoary	remote	venerable
antique	immemorial		

That is termed *old* which has existed long, or which existed long ago. *Ancient* is the more stately, *old,* the more familiar word. Familiarity, on one side, is near to contempt; thus we say, an *old* coat, an *old* hat. On the other hand, familiarity is akin to tenderness, and thus *old* is a word of endearment; as, "the *old* homestead," "the *old* oaken bucket." *Olden* is a statelier form of *old,* and is applied almost exclusively to time, not to places, buildings, persons, etc. As regards periods of time, the familiar are also the near; thus, the *old* times are not too far away for familiar thought and reference; the *olden* times are more remote, *ancient* times still further removed.

Antediluvian refers literally to that which existed before the Deluge; figuratively, and always scornfully, it describes anything extremely *antiquated.* *Gray, hoary,* and *moldering* refer to outward and visible tokens of age. *Aged* applies chiefly to long-extended human life. *Decrepit, gray,* and *hoary* refer to the effects of age on the body exclusively; *senile,* upon the mind also; as, a *decrepit* frame, *senile* garrulousness. One may be *aged* and neither *decrepit* nor *senile.* *Elderly* is applied to those who have passed middle life, but scarcely reached *old* age. *Remote* primarily refers to space, but is extended to that which is far off in time; as, at some *remote* period. *Venerable* expresses the involuntary reverence that we yield to the majestic and long-enduring, whether in the material world or in human life and character. See **antique; obsolete; primeval.**

ANTONYMS: Compare synonyms for **new; youthful.**

OPERATION

action	effect	force	performance	result
agency	execution	influence	procedure	

Operation is *action* considered with reference to the thing acted upon, and may apply to the *action* of an intelligent agent or of a material substance or *force*; as, the *operation* of a medicine. *Performance* and *execution* denote intelligent *action*, considered with reference to the actor or to that which he accomplishes, *performance* accomplishing the will of the actor, *execution* often the will of another; we speak of the *performance* of a duty, the *execution* of a sentence. *Agency* is active power or *operation*; as, through the *agency* of the press. To take *effect* is to make operative. See **act**.

ANTONYMS: *failure, inaction, ineffectiveness, inefficiency, inutility, powerlessness, uselessness.*

ORDER

behest	direction	instruction	prohibition
bidding	injunction	mandate	requirement
command			

Instruction implies superiority of knowledge, *direction* of authority on the part of the giver; a teacher gives *instructions* to his pupils, an employer gives *directions* to his workmen. *Order* is still more authoritative than *direction;* soldiers, sailors, and railroad employees have simply to obey the *orders* of their superiors, without explanation or question; an *order* in the commercial sense has the authority of the money which the one *ordering* the goods pays or is to pay. *Command* is a loftier word, as well as highly authoritative, less frequent in common life; we speak of the *commands* of God, or sometimes, by polite hyperbole, ask of a friend, "Have you any *commands* for me?"

A parent or master issues a *bidding*, and the word implies the expectation of obedience. *Mandate* stresses heavily the idea of the highest authority; as, the President must obey the *mandate* of the people. *Behest* is a literary word, equivalent in meaning to *bidding*. A *requirement* is imperative, but not always formal, nor made by a personal agent; it may be in the nature of things; as, the *requirements* of the position. *Prohibition* is wholly negative; it is a *command* not to do; *injunction* is generally so used, especially as the *requirement* by legal authority that certain action be suspended or refrained from, pending final legal decision. Compare **arrange; class; law; prohibit; system.**

ANTONYMS: *allowance, consent, leave, liberty, license, permission, permit.*

OSTENTATION

boast	display	parade	show
boasting	flourish	pomp	vaunt
brag	pageant	pomposity	vaunting
bravado	pageantry	pompousness	

Ostentation is an ambitious showing forth of whatever is thought adapted to win admiration or praise; *ostentation* may be without words; as, the *ostentation* of wealth in fine residences, rich clothing, costly equipage, or the like; when in words, *ostentation* is rather in manner than in direct statement; as, the *ostentation* of learning. *Boasting* is in direct statement, and is louder and more vulgar than *ostentation*. A *brag* or *bravado* is a *boast* or *ostentation* of courage, which may, perhaps, be real, but is often false and pretentious. There may be great *display* or *show* with little substance; *ostentation* suggests something substantial to be shown.

Pageant, pageantry, parade, and *pomp* refer principally to affairs of arms or state; as, a royal *pageant*; a military *parade*. *Pomp* is some material demonstration of wealth and power, as in grand and stately ceremonial, rich furnishings, processions, etc., considered as worthy of the person or occasion in whose behalf it is manifested; *pomp* is the noble side of that which as *ostentation* is considered as arrogant and vain. *Pageant* and *pageantry* are inferior to *pomp,* denoting spectacular *display* designed to impress the public mind, and since the multitude is often ignorant and thoughtless, the words *pageant* and *pageantry* have a suggestion of the transient and unsubstantial. *Parade* is an exhibition as of troops in camp going through the evolutions that are to be used in battle, and suggests a lack of earnestness and direct or immediate occasion or demand; hence, in the more general sense, a *parade* is an uncalled-for exhibition, and so used is a more disparaging word than *ostentation*; *ostentation* may spring merely from undue self-gratulation, *parade* implies a desire to impress others with a sense of one's abilities or resources, and is always offensive and somewhat contemptible; as, a *parade* of wealth or learning. *Pomposity* and *pompousness* are the affectation of *pomp.*

> **ANTONYMS:** *diffidence, modesty, quietness, reserve, retirement, shrinking, timidity, unobtrusiveness.*

OUGHT

have	have got	must	should

One *ought* to do that which he is under moral obligation or in duty bound to do. *Ought* is a stronger word than *should*, holding most closely to the sense of moral obligation, or sometimes of imperative logical necessity; *should* may have the sense of moral obligation or may apply merely to propriety or expediency, as in the proverb, "The liar *should* have a good memory," *i.e.,* he will need it. *Ought* is sometimes used of abstractions or inanimate things as indicating what the mind deems to be imperative or logically necessary in view of all the conditions; as, these goods *ought* to go into that space; these arguments *ought* to convince him. *Should* in such connections would be correct, but less emphatic. *Must* carries the idea of absolute necessity with no freedom of choice left to the individual; as, murderers *must* hang; in order to graduate you *must* pass your exams. *Have* and *have got* are colloquial synonyms used when duty or need are behind the compulsion; as, I *have* to write five letters; he *has got* to take his medicine. Compare **duty.**

OVERSIGHT

care	control	management	surveillance
charge	direction	superintendence	watch
command	inspection	supervision	watchfulness

A person may look over a matter in order to survey it carefully in its entirety, or he may look over it with no attention to the thing itself because his gaze and thought are concentrated on something beyond; *oversight* has thus two contrasted senses, in the latter sense denoting inadvertent error or omission, and in the former denoting watchful *supervision,* commonly implying constant personal presence; *superintendence* requires only so much of presence or communication as to know that the superintendent's wishes are carried out; the superintendent of a railroad will personally oversee very few of its operations; the railroad company has supreme *direction* of all its affairs without *superintendence* or *oversight. Control* is used chiefly with reference to restraint or the power of restraint; a good horseman has a restless horse under perfect *control;* there is no high character without self-*control. Surveillance* is an invidious term signifying watching with something of suspicion; as, the prison guards kept the inmates under strict *surveillance.* Compare **care; neglect.**

OVERTHROW

abolish	overturn	subvert	supplant
destroy	ruin	supersede	suppress
extinguish			

To *overthrow* is to upset or throw over and bring to a state of destruction; *overturn* is usually less violent than *overthrow.* To *subvert* is to *overthrow* from or as from the very foundation; utterly *destroy;* bring to ruin by undermining. The word is now generally figurative, as of moral or political ruin. To *supersede* implies the putting of something that is wisely or unwisely preferred in the place of that which is removed; to *subvert* does not imply substitution. To *upplant* is more often personal, signifying to take the place of another, usually by underhanded means; one is *superseded* by authority, *supplanted* by a rival. We *extinguish* a fire, *abolish* tyranny, *suppress* rebellion, and *overthrow* a government. See **abolish.**

ANTONYMS: *conserve, keep, perpetuate, preserve, sustain, uphold.*

P

PAIN

ache	distress	suffering	torture
agony	pang	throe	twinge
anguish	paroxysm	torment	woe

Pain is the most general term of this group, including all the others; *pain* is a disturbing sensation from which nature revolts, resulting from some injurious external interference (as from a wound, bruise, a harsh word, etc.), or from some lack of what one needs, craves, or cherishes (as, the *pain* of hunger or bereavement), or from some abnormal action of bodily or mental functions (as, the *pains* of disease, envy, or discontent). *Suffering* is one of the severer forms of *pain*. The prick of a needle causes *pain*, but we should scarcely speak of it as *suffering*.

Distress is too strong a word for little hurts, too feeble for the intensest *suffering*, but commonly applied to some continuous or prolonged trouble or need; as, the *distress* of a shipwrecked crew, or of a destitute family. *Ache* is lingering *pain*, more or less severe; *pang*, a *pain* short, sharp, intense, and perhaps repeated. We speak of the *pangs* of hunger or of remorse. A *twinge* is less severe than a *pang*, and may connote compunction; as, he felt a *twinge* of regret at leaving her. *Throe* is a violent and thrilling *pain*. *Paroxysm* applies to an alternately recurring and receding *pain*, which comes, as it were, in waves; the *paroxysm* is the rising of the wave. *Torment* and *torture* are intense and terrible *sufferings*. *Agony* and *anguish* express the utmost *pain* or *suffering* of body or mind. *Agony* of body is that with which the system struggles; *anguish*, that by which it is crushed.

> **ANTONYMS:** *comfort, delight, ease, enjoyment, peace, rapture, relief, solace.*

PALLIATE

apologize for	cover	gloze	screen
cloak (cloke)	extenuate	hide	veil
conceal	gloss over	mitigate	

Cloak, from the French, and *palliate,* from the Latin, are the same in original signification, but have diverged in meaning; a *cloak* may be used to *hide* completely the person or some object carried about the person, or it may but partly *veil* the figure, making the outlines less distinct; *cloak* is used in the former, *palliate* in the latter sense; to *cloak* a sin is to *hide* it from discovery; to *palliate* it is to attempt to *hide* some part of its blameworthiness. "When we *palliate* our own or others' faults we do not seek to *cloke* them altogether, but only to *extenuate* the guilt of them in part." TRENCH *Study of Words.* Either to *palliate* or to *extenuate* is to admit the fault; but to *extenuate* is rather to *apologize* for the offender, while to *palliate* is to disguise the

308

fault; hence, we speak of *extenuating* but not of *palliating* circumstances, since circumstances can not change the inherent wrong of an act, though they may lessen the blameworthiness of him who does it; *palliating* a bad thing by giving it a mild name does not make it less evil. In reference to diseases, to *palliate* is really to diminish their violence, or partly to relieve the sufferer. To *gloss over* a fault is to attempt to excuse it by dissembling or *hiding* its true disagreeableness. *Gloze*, more condemnatory than *gloss*, means the same thing. See **alleviate; hide.**

PARDON *noun*

absolution	amnesty	forgiveness	oblivion
acquittal	forbearance	mercy	remission

Pardon affects individuals; *amnesty* and *oblivion* apply to great numbers. *Pardon* is oftenest applied to the ordinary administration of law; *amnesty*, to national and military affairs. An *amnesty* is issued after war, insurrection, or rebellion; it is often granted by "an act of *oblivion*," and includes a full *pardon* of all offenders who come within its provisions. *Absolution* is a religious word. *Remission* is a discharge from penalty; as, the *remission* of a fine.

Acquittal is a release from a charge, after trial, as not guilty. *Pardon* is a removal of penalty from one who has been adjudged guilty. *Acquittal* is by the decision of a court, commonly of a jury; *pardon* is the act of the executive. An innocent man may demand *acquittal*, and need not plead for *pardon*. *Pardon* supposes an offense; yet, as our laws stand, to grant a *pardon* is sometimes the only way to release one who has been wrongly convicted. *Oblivion*, from the Latin, signifies overlooking and virtually forgetting an offense, so that the offender stands before the law in all respects as if it had never been committed. *Amnesty* brings the same idea through the Greek. Compare synonyms for **absolve.**

> **ANTONYMS:** *penalty, punishment, retaliation, retribution, vengeance.*

> **PREPOSITIONS:** A pardon *to* or *for* the offenders, *for* all offenses; the pardon *of* offenders or offenses.

PARDON *verb*

absolve	excuse	overlook	pass over
acquit	forgive	pass by	remit
condone			

To *pardon* is to let pass, as a fault or sin, without resentment, blame, or punishment. *Forgive* has reference to feelings, *pardon* to consequences; hence, the executive may *pardon*, but has nothing to do officially with *forgiving*. Personal injury may be *forgiven* by the person wronged; thus, God at once *forgives* and *pardons*; the *pardoned* sinner is exempt from punishment; the *forgiven* sinner is restored to the divine favor. To *pardon* is the act of a superior, implying the right to punish; to *forgive* is the privilege of the humblest person who has been wronged or offended. In law, to *remit* the whole penalty is equivalent to *pardoning* the offender; but a part of the penalty may be *remitted* and the remainder inflicted, as where the penalty includes both fine and imprisonment. To *condone* is to put aside a recognized offense by some act which restores the offender to forfeited right or privilege, and is the act of a private individual, without legal formalities. To *excuse* is to *overlook* some slight offense, error, or breach of etiquette; *pardon* is often used by courtesy in nearly the same sense. A person may speak of *excusing* or *forgiving* himself, but not of *pardoning* himself. Compare **absolve; pardon** *noun*.

> **ANTONYMS**: *castigate, chasten, chastise, condemn, convict, correct, doom, punish, recompense, scourge, sentence, visit.*

PART

atom	fraction	particle	section
component	fragment	partition	segment
constituent	ingredient	piece	share
division	instalment	portion	subdivision
element	member		

Part, a substance, quantity, or amount that is the result of the division of something greater, is the general word, including all the others of this group. A *fragment* is the result of breaking, rending, or disruption of some kind, while a *piece* may be smoothly or evenly separated and have a certain completeness in itself. A *piece* is often taken for a sample; a *fragment* scarcely would be. *Division* and *fraction* are always regarded as in connection with the total; *divisions* may be equal or unequal; *fraction*, by virtue of its mathematical connotations, usually means a very tiny or minute *part*.

A *portion* is a *part* viewed with reference to someone who is to receive it or some special purpose to which it is to be applied; in a restaurant one *portion* (*i.e.*, the amount designed for one person) is sometimes, by special order, served to two; a *share* is a *part* to which one has or may acquire a right in connection with others; an *instalment* is one of a series of proportionate payments that are to be continued till the entire claim is discharged; a *particle* is an exceedingly small *part*. A *component, constituent, ingredient,* or *element* is a *part* of some compound or mixture; an *element* is necessary to existence, as a *component* or *constituent* is necessary to the completeness of that which it helps to compose; an *ingredient* may be foreign or accidental. A *subdivision* is a *division* of a *division*. *Division* and *section* are frequently used to denote a distinct *part* formed by cutting or dividing. *Segment* is sometimes preferred to *section* in order to denote a *part* which separates along natural lines of cleavage; as, a *segment* of an orange; we also speak of a *segment* of a circle. See **particle; portion.**

PARTICLE

atom	grain	molecule	shred
bit	iota	scintilla	tittle
corpuscle	jot	scrap	whit
element	mite		

A *particle* is a very small part of any material substance; as, a *particle* of sand or dust; it is a general term, not accurately determinate in meaning. A *bit* is primarily a bite, and applies to solids. One may say, "a *bit* of bread," "a *bit* of money," but not "a little *bit* of water." *Mite* may connote either extreme diminutiveness, from its meaning of the smallest of insects, or small-ness in amount, from the Biblical reference to the widow's *mite*; as, he's a wee *mite* of a lad; not a *mite* of intelligence. *Iota,* and its Anglicized form, *jot,* name the smallest letter in the Greek alphabet (ι); *tittle* refers to any insig-nificant diacritical mark, as a cedilla or an accent mark. The terms are used together to mean the smallest possible amount or part, and in that meaning are indistinguishable; as, I refuse to yield one *jot* or *tittle* of my land to the usurper. *Scintilla* is a word meaning spark or, figuratively, a barely perceptible manifestation; as, he doesn't exhibit a *scintilla* of understanding.

Atom etymologically signifies that which cannot be cut or divided, but in physics and chemistry is regarded as a fundamental unit of matter, although itself composed of smaller *particles,* as the electron, proton, etc. A *molecule* is made up of *atoms,* and is regarded as separable into its constituent parts; as used by physicists, a *molecule* is the smallest conceivable part which retains all the characteristics of the substance; thus, a *molecule* of water is made up of two *atoms* of hydrogen and one *atom* of oxygen. *Element* in chemistry denotes, without reference to quantity, a substance regarded as simple, that is, composed of only one kind of *atom.* The *element* gold may be represented by an ingot or by a *particle* of gold dust. In popular language, an *element* is any essential constituent; the ancients believed that the universe was made up of the four *elements,* earth, air, fire, and water; a storm is spoken of as a manifestation of the fury of the *elements.* A *corpuscle* is one of the protoplasmic cells floating free in blood and lymph; figuratively the word means any minute *particle.* See also **part.**

ANTONYMS: *aggregate, entirety, mass, quantity, sum, total, whole.*

PATIENCE

calmness	forbearance	passiveness	submission
composure	fortitude	resignation	sufferance
endurance	long-suffering		

Patience is the quality of habit of mind shown in bearing passively and un-complainingly any pain, evil, or hardship that may fall to one's lot. *Endurance* hardens itself against suffering, and may be merely stubborn; *fortitude* is en-durance animated by courage; *endurance* may by modifiers be made to have a passive force, as we speak of "passive *endurance*"; *patience* is not so hard as *endurance* nor so self-effacing as *submission*. *Submission* is ordinarily and *resignation* always applied to matters of great moment, while *patience* may apply to slight worries and annoyances. As regards our relations to our fellow men, *forbearance* is abstaining from retaliation or revenge; *patience* is keeping kindliness of heart under vexatious conduct; *long-suffering* is continued *patience*. *Patience* may also have an active force denoting uncomplaining steadiness in doing, as in tilling the soil. Compare **apathy; industry.**

ANTONYMS: See synonyms for **anger.**

PREPOSITIONS: Patience *in* or *amid* sufferings; patience *with* (rarely *toward*) opposers or offenders; patience *under* afflictions; (rarely) patience *of* heat or cold, etc.

PAY

allowance	fee	recompense	salary
compensation	hire	remuneration	stipend
earnings	honorarium	requital	wages
emolument	payment		

Pay is commercial and strictly signifies an exact pecuniary equivalent for a thing or service, except when the contrary is expressly stated, as when we speak of "high *pay*" or "poor *pay*." *Wages* denotes what a worker receives. *Earnings* is often used as exactly equivalent to *wages*, but may be used with reference to the real value of work done or service rendered, and even applied to inanimate things; as, the *earnings* of capital. *Hire* is distinctly mercenary or menial. *Salary* is for literary or professional work, *wages* for handicraft or other comparatively inferior service; a *salary* is regarded as more permanent than *wages*; an editor receives a *salary*, a compositor receives *wages*. *Stipend* has become exclusively a literary word. A *fee* is given for a single service or privilege, and is sometimes in the nature of a gratuity. *Emolument* is a lofty term, signifying in the plural the reward for one's work.

An *allowance* is a stipulated amount furnished at regular intervals as a matter of discretion or gratuity, as of food to besieged solders, or of money to a child or ward. *Compensation* is a comprehensive word signifying a return for a service done. *Remuneration* is applied to matters of great amount or importance *Recompense* is a still wider and loftier word, with less suggestion of calcula-tion and market value; there are services for which affection and gratitude are the sole and sufficient *recompense*; *earnings, fees, hire, pay, salary,* and *wages* are forms of *compensation* and may be included in *compensation, remuneration,* or *recompense.* Compare **requite.**

PERCEIVE

apprehend   **comprehend**   **conceive**   **understand**

We *perceive* what is presented through the senses. We *apprehend* what is presented to the mind, whether through the senses or by any other means. Yet *perceive* is used in the figurative sense of seeing through to a conclusion, in a way for which usage would not allow us to substitute *apprehend.* That which we *apprehend* we catch, as with the hand; that which we *conceive* we are able to analyze and recompose in our mind; that which we *comprehend* we, as it were, grasp around, take together, seize, embrace wholly within the mind. Many things may be *apprehended* which cannot be *comprehended*; a child can *apprehend* the distinction between right and wrong, yet the philosopher cannot *comprehend* it in its fullness. We can *apprehend* the will of God as revealed in conscience or the Scriptures; we can *conceive* of certain attributes of Deity, as His truth and justice; but no finite intelligence can *comprehend* the Divine Nature, in its majesty, power, and perfection. *Understand* refers to an exact idea or notion, or to full knowledge; *comprehend* implies the mental process of arriving at such a result. Compare **anticipate; arrest; catch; knowledge.**

ANTONYMS: *fail of, ignore, lose, misapprehend, misconceive, miss, overlook.*

PERFECT

entire   **intact**   **whole**

That is *perfect* which has no faults, defects, or deficiencies; all its parts, qualities, and elements are present, and all are in sound and excellent condition. Nothing can be added to that which is *perfect,* and nothing can be taken away from it, without impairing its excellence, marring its symmetry, or detracting from its value. We speak of a *perfect* copy of "Moby Dick"; a *perfect* diamond; a *perfect* body. The word is also applied to some things for which there exists no fixed criterion other than a high standard of excellence; as, she is a *perfect* lady. Theoretically, from the nature of its meaning, *perfect* does not permit of comparison, and it is illogical to speak of anything as being "more *perfect*" or "most *perfect.*" However, as it is commonly used, the word does not imply absolute perfection as a philosophic idea, but rather perfection as it occurs in the world, that is, perfection of a greater or lesser degree. The framers of the Constitution, therefore, were justified in writing, "We, the people of the United States, in order to form a *more perfect* Union . . ."

Whole suggests a moral or physical perfection that can be lost or recovered, as by the regaining of health. We speak of someone's being made *whole* through faith. That which is *entire* possesses a spiritual, moral, or physical integrity or perfection. *Intact* is said of something which retains its original or its natural character. It often applies to something which has passed through an experience which might have destroyed or marred its beauty, completeness, or integrity; as, few buildings of Berlin remain *intact.*

ANTONYMS: *bad, blemished, corrupt, corrupted, defaced, defective, deficient, deformed, fallible, faulty, imperfect, incomplete, inferior, insufficient, marred, meager, perverted, poor, ruined, scant, short, spoiled, worthless.*

PERMANENT

abiding	fixed	invariable	stable
changeless	immutable	lasting	steadfast
constant	imperishable	perpetual	unchangeable
durable	indelible	persistent	unchanging
enduring	indestructible		

That which is *permanent* is not liable to change, or continues in the same state without essential change; as, a *permanent* color; buildings upon a farm are called *permanent* improvements. *Enduring* is a higher word, applied to that which resists both time and change; as, *enduring* fame. *Durable* (from L. *durus,* hard) is said almost wholly of material substances that resist wear; *lasting* is said of either material or immaterial things; *stable* applies to what is *lasting* or *durable* because firmly established.

Abiding is continuing; *perpetual* is continuing unlimited in time. *Imperishable* refers to that which endures *permanently. Changeless, unchangeable, unchanging, immutable, constant, invariable* are all used to mean not subject to change or that cannot change. *Indelible* ink cannot be erased; *persistent* efforts are long-continued.

ANTONYMS: See synonyms for **transient.**

PERMISSION

allowance	authorization	leave	license
authority	consent	liberty	permit

Permission justifies another in acting without interference or censure, and usually implies some degree of approval. *Authority* gives a certain right of control over all that may be affected by the action; *authorization* is the act of conferring *authority.* There may be a failure to object, which constitutes an implied *permission,* though this is more properly expressed by *allowance;* we *allow* what we do not oppose, *permit* what we expressly *authorize.* The noun *permit* implies a formal written *permission*. *Authority* unites the right and power of control; age, wisdom, and character give *authority* to their possessor; a book of learned research has *authority*, and is even called an *authority*

License is a formal *permission* granted by competent *authority* to an individual to do some act or pursue some business which would be or is made to be unlawful without such *permission*; as, a *license* to preach, to solemnize marriages, or to sell intoxicating liquors. A *license* is *permission* granted rather than *authority* conferred; the sheriff has *authority* (not *permission* nor *license*) to make an arrest. *Liberty* implies freedom from restraint or constraint. *Leave* is *permission* to do something otherwise forbidden; or *permission* to be absent from duty; as, on *leave* from the army. *Consent* is *permission* by the concurrence of wills in two or more persons, a mutual approval or acceptance of something proposed. See **liberty.** Compare **allow.**

ANTONYMS: *denial, hindrance, objection, opposition, prevention, prohibition, refusal, resistance.*

PERNICIOUS

bad	detrimental	insalubrious	pestilential
baleful	evil	mischievous	poisonous
baneful	foul	noisome	ruinous
deadly	harmful	noxious	unhealthful
deleterious	hurtful	pestiferous	unwholesome
destructive	injurious		

Pernicious (from L. *per*, through, and *neco*, kill) signifies having the power of destroying or injuring, tending to hurt or kill. *Pernicious* is stronger than *injurious*; that which is *injurious* is capable of doing harm; that which is *pernicious* is likely to be *destructive*. *Noxious* (from L. *noceo*, hurt) is a stronger word than *noisome*, as referring to that which is *injurious* or *destructive*. *Noisome* now always denotes that which is extremely disagreeable or disgusting, especially to the sense of smell; as, the *noisome* stench proclaimed the presence of *noxious* gases.

Baneful influences often cause irreparable harm; *baleful* applies to what is actively evil, malign. *Deleterious* is physically or morally *injurious*; *detrimental* implies causing loss, impairment, or damage. *Insalubrious* and *unwholesome* conditions are not conducive to health; *unhealthful*, often cause ill-health *Pestiferous* and *pestilential* imply carrying and spreading infection or vice.

ANTONYMS: *advantageous, beneficent, beneficial, favorable, good, healthful, helpful, innocuous, invigorating, life-giving, profitable, rejuvenating, salutary, serviceable. useful, wholesome.*

PERPLEXITY

amazement	confusion	doubt	perturbation
astonishment	distraction	embarrassment	surprise
bewilderment	disturbance		

Perplexity is the state of being not only puzzled but worried as to how to act or decide; *confusion* is a state in which the mental faculties are thrown into chaos, so that the clear and distinct action of the different powers, as of perception, memory, reason, and will is lost; *bewilderment* is akin to *confusion*, but is less overwhelming, and more readily recovered from.

The dividing of a woodland path may cause the traveler the greatest *perplexity*, which may become *bewilderment* when he has tried one path after another and lost his bearings completely. With an excitable person *bewilderment* may deepen into *confusion* that will make him unable to think clearly or even to see or hear distinctly. *Amazement* results from the sudden and unimagined occurrence of great good or evil, or the sudden awakening of the mind to unthought-of truth. *Astonishment* often produces *bewilderment*, which the word was formerly understood to imply. *Distraction* is the mental upset arising when faced with conflicting problems or merely differing interests, each of which in itself can be called a *distraction*. See **amazement; doubt.** Compare **anxiety; predicament.**

PERSIST

continue	insist	persevere	stay
endure	last	remain	

To *persist* is to *continue* in or adhere firmly or obstinately to a course, opinion, etc.; to *insist* is to assert emphatically and persistently. A man *insists* upon his demand; *persists* in his refusal; *perseveres* in his work. As applied to duration. *endure* is the nobler word; *last* is applied chiefly to things, *endure* to either persons or things. That *remains* or *stays* which is simply let alone; that which *endures* or *persists* does so against opposing forces. We speak of a *persistent* force.

ANTONYMS: See synonyms for **stop.**

PREPOSITIONS: Persist *in* a course, *against* remonstrance.

PERSUADE

allure	dispose	incline	move
bring over	entice	induce	prevail on or upon
coax	impel	influence	urge
convince	incite	lead	win over

To *persuade* is to bring the will of another to a desired decision by some influence exerted upon it short of compulsion; one may be *convinced* that the earth is round; he may be *persuaded* to travel round it; but persuasion is so largely dependent upon conviction that it is commonly held to be the orator's work first to *convince* in order that he may *persuade*. *Coax* seeks the same end as *persuade*, but by shallower methods, largely by appeal to personal feeling, with or without success; as, a child *coaxes* a parent to buy him a toy.

Of these synonyms *convince* alone has no direct reference to moving the will, denoting an effect upon the understanding only; one may be *convinced* of his duty without doing it, or he may be *convinced* of truth that has no manifest connection with duty or action, as of a mathematical proposition. One may be *brought over, induced,* or *prevailed upon* by means not properly included in persuasion, as by bribery or intimidation; he is *won over* chiefly by personal influence. The powerful speech *influenced* the boys and they were *enticed* to enter the contest, *allured* by the prospect of riches. See **influence.**

ANTONYMS: *deter, discourage, dissuade, hinder, hold back, repel, restrain.*

PERTNESS

| boldness | flippancy | impertinence | sauciness |
| briskness | forwardness | impudence | smartness |

Pertness and *sauciness* imply a lively *boldness* in speech and manner combined with lack of respect. *Impertinence* and *impudence* may be gross and stupid; *pertness* and *sauciness* are always vivid and keen. *Smartness* is a limited and showy acuteness or shrewdness, usually with unfavorable suggestion. *Flippancy* treats even serious matters with levity. Compare **impertinence.**

ANTONYMS: *bashfulness, demureness, diffidence, humility, modesty, shyness.*

PERVERSE

contrary	froward	petulant	untoward
factious	intractable	stubborn	wayward
fractious	obstinate	ungovernable	wilful

Perverse (from L. *perversus*, turned the wrong way) signifies wilfully wrong or erring, unreasonably set against right, reason, or authority. The *stubborn* or *obstinate* person will not do what another desires or requires; the *perverse* person will do anything contrary to what is desired or required of him. The *petulant* person frets, but may comply; the *perverse* individual may be smooth or silent, but is wilfully *intractable. Wayward* refers to a *perverse* disregard of morality and duty; *froward* is practically obsolete; *untoward* is rarely heard except in certain phrases; as, *untoward* circumstances. A *contrary* person is self-willed and *wayward*; a *fractious* child is unruly and irritable; *factious* people stir up dissension. See **obstinate**.

> **ANTONYMS:** *accommodating, amenable, complaisant, compliant, genial, governable, kind, obliging.*

PHYSICAL

bodily	material	sensible	tangible
corporal	natural	somatic	visible
corporeal			

Physical (from Gr. *physis*, nature) applies to *material* things considered as parts of a system or organic whole; hence, we speak of *material* substances, *physical* forces, *physical* laws. Whatever is composed of or pertains to matter may be termed *material*. *Bodily, corporal,* and *corporeal* apply primarily to the human body; *bodily* and *corporal* both denote pertaining or relating to the body; *corporeal* signifies of the nature of or like the body; *corporal* is now almost wholly restricted to signify applied to or inflicted upon the body; we speak of *bodily* sufferings, *bodily* presence, *corporal* punishment, the *corporeal* frame. *Natural*, in this comparison, implies characteristic of the *physical* world; *sensible* here means liable to be affected by the *material* world; *somatic* is pertaining to the *physical* body.

> **ANTONYMS:** *hyperphysical, immaterial, intangible, intellectual, invisible, mental, moral, spiritual, unreal, unsubstantial.*

PIQUE

displeasure	irritation	resentment	umbrage
grudge	offense		

Pique, from the French, signifies primarily a prick or a sting, as of a nettle; the word denotes a sudden feeling of mingled pain and anger, but slight and usually transient, arising from some neglect or *offense*, real or imaginary. *Umbrage* is a deeper and more persistent *displeasure* at being overshadowed (from L. *umbra*, a shadow) or subjected to any treatment that one deems unworthy of him. It may be said, as a general statement, that *pique* arises from wounded vanity or sensitiveness, *umbrage* from wounded pride or sometimes from suspicion. *Resentment* rests on more solid grounds, and is deep and persistent. *Grudge* is a feeling of *resentment* and ill will resulting from a grievance; *irritation* is momentary *displeasure* or anger. Compare **anger**.

> **ANTONYMS:** *approval, complacency, contentment, delight, gratification, pleasure, satisfaction.*

PITIFUL

abject	mean	paltry	sorrowful
base	miserable	pathetic	touching
contemptible	mournful	piteous	woeful
despicable	moving	pitiable	wretched
lamentable			

Pitiful originally signified full of pity; as, "the Lord is very *pitiful* and of tender mercy," *James* v, 11, but this usage is now archaic, and the meaning in question is appropriated by such words as merciful and compassionate. *Pitiful* and *pitiable* now refer to what may be deserving of pity, *pitiful* being used chiefly for that which is merely an object of thought, *pitiable* for that which is brought directly before the senses; as, a *pitiful* story; a *pitiable* object; a *pitiable* condition. Since pity, however, always implies weakness or inferiority in that which is pitied, *pitiable* is often used, by an easy transition, for what might awaken pity, but does awaken contempt; as, he presented a *pitiable* appearance.

Piteous is now rarely used in its earlier sense of feeling pity, but in its derived sense applies to what really excites the emotion; as, a *piteous* cry. *Abject* and *mean* refer to a low and sometimes *wretched* condition; *base, contemptible,* and *despicable,* to that which excites scorn or contempt. *Mournful, sorrowful,* and *woeful* include sorrow as the chief cause of being or looking *miserable. Lamentable* is *pitiable* and deplorable. Compare **humane; mercy; pity.**

> ANTONYMS: *august, beneficent, commanding, dignified, exalted, glorious, grand, great, helpful, lofty, mighty, noble, sublime, superb, superior.*

PITY

commiseration	condolence	sympathy
compassion	mercy	tenderness

Pity is a feeling of grief or pain aroused by the weakness, misfortunes, or distresses of others, joined with a desire to help or relieve. *Sympathy* (feeling or suffering with) implies some degree of equality, kindred, or union; *pity* is for what is weak or unfortunate, and so far, at least, detached from ourselves; hence, *pity* is often resented where *sympathy* would be welcome. We have *sympathy* with one in joy or grief, in pleasure or pain, *pity* only for those in suffering or need; we may have *sympathy* with the struggles of a giant or the triumphs of a conqueror; we are moved with *pity* for the captive or the slave. *Pity* may be only in the mind, but *mercy* does something for those who are its objects.

Compassion, like *pity,* is exercised only with respect to the suffering or unfortunate, but combines with the tenderness of *pity* the dignity of *sympathy* and the active quality of *mercy. Commiseration* is as tender as *compassion,* but more remote and hopeless; we have *commiseration* for sufferers whom we cannot reach or cannot relieve. It also implies the outward expression of *pity,* as in words, tears, or the like. *Condolence* is the expression of *sympathy* with one who has suffered a great misfortune. Compare **mercy.**

ANTONYMS: *barbarity, brutality, cruelty, ferocity, hard-heartedness, hardness, harshness, inhumanity, mercilessness, pitilessness, rigor, ruthlessness, severity, sternness, truculence.*

PREPOSITIONS: Pity *on* or *upon* that which we help or spare; pity *for* that which we merely contemplate.

PLANT

seed	seed down	set	set out	sow

We *set* or *set out* slips, cuttings, young trees, etc., though we may also be said to *plant* them; we *plant* corn, potatoes, etc., which we put in definite places, as in hills, with some care; we *sow* wheat or other small grains and seeds which are scattered in the process. Though by modern agricultural machinery the smaller grains are almost as precisely *planted* as corn, the old word for broadcast scattering is retained. Land is *seeded* or *seeded down* to grass.

ANTONYMS: *eradicate, extirpate, root up, uproot, weed out.*

PLEAD

advocate	ask	beseech	implore	solicit
argue	beg	entreat	press	urge

To *plead* for one is to employ argument or persuasion, or both, in his behalf, usually with earnestness or importunity; similarly one may be said to *plead* for himself or for a cause, etc., or with direct object, to *plead* a case; in legal usage, *pleading* is argumentative, but in popular usage, *pleading* always implies some appeal to the feelings. One *argues* a case solely on rational grounds and supposably with fair consideration of both sides; he *advocates* one side for the purpose of carrying it, and under the influence of motives that may range all the way from cold self-interest to the highest and noblest impulses; he *pleads* a cause, or *pleads* for a person with still more intense feeling. *Beseech, entreat,* and *implore* imply impassioned earnestness, with direct and tender appeal to personal considerations. *Press* and *urge* imply more determined or perhaps authoritative insistence. *Solicit* is a weak word denoting merely an attempt to secure consent or cooperation, sometimes by sordid or corrupt motives.

PREPOSITIONS: Plead *with* the tyrant, *for* the captive; plead *against* the oppression or the oppressor; plead *to* the indictment, *at* the bar, *before* the court, *in* open court.

PLEASANT

acceptable	delicious	kind	pleasurable
agreeable	delightful	kindly	refreshing
attractive	good-natured	obliging	satisfying
charming	grateful	pleasing	welcome
congenial	gratifying		

Whatever has active qualities adapted to give pleasure is *pleasant*; as, a *pleasant* breeze; a *pleasant* day. As applied to persons, *pleasant* always refers to a disposition ready and desirous to please; one is *pleasant*, or in a *pleasant* mood, when inclined to make happy those with whom one is dealing, or to show kindness and do any reasonable favor. In this sense *pleasant* is nearly akin to *kind*, but *kind* refers to act or intent, while *pleasant* stops with the disposition; many persons are no longer in a *pleasant* mood if asked to do a troublesome kindness. *Pleasant* keeps always something of the sense of actually giving pleasure, and thus surpasses the meaning of *good-natured*; there are *good-natured* people who by reason of rudeness and ill-breeding are not *pleasant* companions.

That is *pleasing* from which pleasure is received, or may readily be received, without reference to any action or intent in that which confers it. *Pleasant* imputes to the object which it modifies the quality of high acceptability; as, a *pleasant* smile; *pleasing* refers to the effect produced by such an object. A *pleasant* face and *pleasing* manners arouse *pleasurable* sensations, and make the possessor an *agreeable* companion. Such a person, if possessed of intelligence, wit, and goodness, will be a *delightful* companion.

That is *agreeable* which harmonizes with one's tastes or feelings; as, an *agreeable* flavor. That which is *grateful* is both *pleasing* and *agreeable*; the word connotes gratification of the senses; as, he came out of the dark, cold night into the *grateful* warmth of the kitchen. *Acceptable* indicates a thing to be worthy of acceptance; as, an *acceptable* offering. *Welcome*, even more than *pleasing*, suggests satisfaction given by the thing it describes, and usually implies a prior desire for that thing; as, a *welcome* breeze sprang up and drove the boat forward. Criminals may find each other's company *congenial*, but perhaps not *delightful*. *Satisfying* denotes anything that is received with calm acquiescence, as substantial food or established truth. See **amiable; beautiful; charming; comfortable; delicious.**

ANTONYMS: *arrogant, austere, crabbed, depressing, disagreeable, disappointing, displeasing, distressing, dreary, forbidding, gloomy, glum, grim, harsh, hateful, horrible, ill-humored, ill-natured, melancholy, miserable, mournful, offensive, painful, repellent, repelling, repulsive, saddening, unkind, unpleasant, woeful, wretched.*

PREPOSITIONS: Pleasant *to, with,* or *toward* persons, *about* a matter.

PLENTIFUL

abounding	bountiful	generous	plenteous
abundant	complete	large	profuse
adequate	copious	lavish	replete
affluent	enough	liberal	rich
ample	exuberant	luxuriant	sufficient
bounteous	full	overflowing	teeming

Plentiful is used of supplies, as of food, water, etc.; as, a *plentiful* rain. We may also say a *copious* rain; but *copious* can be applied to thought, language, etc., where *plentiful* cannot well be used. *Enough* is relative, denoting a supply equal to a given demand. A temperature of 70° Fahrenheit is *enough* for a living-room; of 212°, *enough* to boil water; neither is *enough* to melt iron. *Sufficient*, from the Latin, is an equivalent of the Saxon *enough*, with no perceptible difference of meaning, but only of usage, *enough* being the more blunt, homely, and forcible word, while *sufficient* is in many cases the more elegant or polite. *Sufficient* usually precedes its noun; *enough* usually and preferably follows. That is *ample* which gives a safe, but not a large, margin beyond a given demand; that is *abundant, affluent, bountiful, liberal, plentiful,* which is largely in excess of manifest need. Neither *copious* nor *plentiful* can be used of time or space; a field is sometimes called *plentiful*, not with reference to its extent, but to its productiveness.

Complete expresses not excess or overplus, and yet not mere sufficiency, but harmony, proportion, fitness to a design or ideal. *Ample* and *abundant* may be applied to any subject. We have time *enough*, means that we can reach our destination without haste, but also without delay; if we have *ample* time, we may move leisurely, and note what is by the way; if we have *abundant* time, we may pause to converse with a friend, to view the scenery, or to rest when weary. *Lavish* and *profuse* imply a decided excess. We rejoice in *abundant* resources, and honor *generous* hospitality; *lavish* or *profuse* expenditure suggests extravagance and wastefulness. *Luxuriant* is used especially of that which is *abundant* in growth; as, a *luxuriant* crop.

ANTONYMS: *deficient, drained, exhausted, impoverished, inadequate, insufficient, mean, miserly, narrow, niggardly, poor, scant, scanty, scarce, scrimped, short, small, sparing, stingy, straitened.*

PREPOSITION: Plentiful *in* resources.

POET

bard	**poetaster**	**rimester**	**troubadour**
minnesinger	**rimer**	**singer**	**versifier**
minstrel			

A *poet* expresses elevated and imaginative feelings in metrical or rhythmic form. A *versifier* is a composer of verses, but not always a *poet*. A *rimer* or *rimester* is a maker of rimes which do not necessarily express creative thought; hence, an inferior *poet*. In the Middle Ages, *minstrels* strolled through Europe singing or reciting poetry (sometimes their own), to the accompaniment of some instrument. *Bard* originally meant a Welsh or Irish *poet* who composed heroic or historical poems and often sang them; it has since come to mean the *poet* of a certain locality; as, Shakespeare, the *Bard* of Avon. *Minnesinger* applies only to a lyrical *poet* of medieval Germany; *troubadour*, to a lyric *poet* and musician who composed love songs in the Provençal tongue. A *poetaster* is a mere *rimer*, a composer of inferior verse. See **poetry.**

POETRY

meter	**poem**	**rime**	**verse**
numbers	**poesy**	**song**	

Poetry is that form of literature that embodies beautiful thought, feeling, or action in melodious, rhythmical, and (usually) metrical language, in imaginative and artistic constructions. *Poetry* in a very wide sense may be anything that pleasingly addresses the imagination; as, the *poetry* of motion. In ordinary usage, *poetry* is both imaginative and metrical. There may be *poetry* without *rime*, but hardly without *meter*, or what in some languages takes its place, as the Hebrew parallelism; but *poetry* involves, besides the artistic form, the exercise of the fancy or imagination in a way always beautiful, often lofty or even sublime. Failing this, there may be *verse, rime,* and *meter,* but not *poetry.* There is much in literature that is beautiful and sublime in thought and artistic in construction, which is yet not *poetry,* because quite devoid of the element of *song,* whereby *poetry* differs from the most lofty, beautiful, or impassioned prose. See **rhythm.**

ANTONYM: *prose.*

POLITE

accomplished	courteous	gallant	urbane
ceremonious	courtly	genteel	well-behaved
chivalrous	cultivated	gracious	well-bred
civil	cultured	obliging	well-mannered
complaisant	elegant	polished	

A *civil* person observes such propriety of speech and manner as to avoid being rude; one who is *polite* (literally *polished*) observes more than the necessary proprieties, conforming to all that is graceful, becoming, and thoughtful in the intercourse of refined society. A man may be *civil* with no consideration for others, simply because self-respect forbids him to be rude; but one who is *polite* has at least some care for the opinions of others, and if *polite* in the highest and truest sense, which is coming to be the prevailing one, he cares for the comfort and happiness of others in the smallest matters. *Civil* is a colder and more distant word than *polite*; *courteous* implies consideration of others in all social intercourse. *Courtly* suggests that which befits a royal court, and is used of external grace and stateliness without reference to the prompting feeling; as, the *courtly* manners of the ambassador.

Genteel refers to an external elegance, which may be showy and superficial, and the word is thus inferior to *polite* or *courteous*. *Urbane* refers to a politeness that is genial and successful in giving others a sense of ease and cheer. *Polished* refers to external elegancies of speech and manner without reference to spirit or purpose; as, a *polished* gentleman or a *polished* scoundrel; *cultured* refers to a real and high development of mind and soul, of which the external manifestation is the smallest part. *Complaisant* denotes a disposition to please or favor beyond what politeness would necessarily require. *Gallant* and *chivalrous*, as here compared, denote *courtly* attention to women. However, *gallant* implies a dashing, flamboyant attitude, while *chivalrous* suggests a more high-minded, self-effacing attention.

ANTONYMS: *awkward, bluff, blunt, boorish, brusk, clownish, coarse, discourteous, ill-behaved, ill-bred, ill-mannered, impertinent, impolite, impudent, insolent, insulting, raw, rude, rustic, uncivil, uncouth, unmannerly, unpolished, untaught, untutored.*

POLITY

constitution	policy

Polity is the permanent system of government of a state, a church, or a society; *policy* is the method of management with reference to the attainment of certain ends; the national *polity* of the United States is republican; each administration has a *policy* of its own. *Policy* is often used as equivalent to expediency; as, many think honesty to be good *policy*. *Polity,* when in ecclesiastical use, serves a valuable purpose in distinguishing that which relates to administration and government from that which relates to faith and doctrine; two churches identical in faith may differ in *polity*, or those agreeing in *polity* may differ in faith. Compare **law.**

PORTION

| lot | parcel | part | proportion | share |

When any whole is divided into *parts*, any *part* that is allotted to some person, thing, subject, or purpose is called a *portion*, though the division may be by no fixed rule or relation; a father may divide his estate by will among his children so as to make their several *portions* great or small, according to his arbitrary and unreasonable caprice. When we speak of a *part* as a *proportion*, we think of the whole as divided according to some rule or scale, so that the different *parts* bear an intended relation or ratio to one another; thus, the *portion* allotted to a child by will may not be a fair *proportion* of the estate. *Proportion* is often used where *part* or *portion* would be more appropriate. A *share* is one individual's *portion*; the word often implies that it is his fair or lawful *portion*. See **part.**

POSTURE

| attitude | pose | position |

Posture is a disposition of the limbs of the body in a particular way, or a person's bearing or carriage; as, a reclining *posture*, an erect *posture*. *Position*, as applied to the arrangement or situation of the human body or limbs, may denote that which is conscious or unconscious, of the living or the dead; but we do not speak of the *attitude, pose,* or *posture* of a corpse; unless, in some rare case, we might say the body was found in a sitting *posture*, where the *posture* is thought of as assumed in life, or as, at first glance, suggesting life.

Attitude is the *position* appropriate to the expression of some feeling; the *attitude* may be unconsciously taken through the strength of the feeling; as, an *attitude* of defiance; or it may be consciously assumed in the attempt to express the feeling; as, he assumed an *attitude* of humility. A *pose* is a *position* studied for artistic effect, or considered with reference to such effect; the unconscious *posture* of a spectator or listener may be an admirable *pose* from an artist's standpoint.

POVERTY

beggary	indigence	pauperism	privation
destitution	mendicancy	penury	want
distress	need		

All of these words express the condition of one who does not have enough to live on. *Poverty* is the most comprehensive, denoting either a total lack of material possessions or a state in which one must forego many of the necessities and all of the luxuries of life; as, the monk took the threefold vow of *poverty*, chastity, and obedience; during the last years of his life, Mozart lived in the uttermost *poverty*.

Indigence is less severe than *poverty*, implying straightened circumstances and the lack of material comforts; as, the old gentleman endured a life of genteel *indigence*. *Want* and *destitution* both connote a state of extreme *poverty*, in which one lacks the bare means of subsistence, and suggest dependence on charity to provide food and shelter; as, war has left the inhabitants of this region in a state of utter *destitution*; thrift is a good safeguard against *want* in one's old age. *Pauperism* is such *destitution* as throws one upon organized public charity for support; *beggary* and *mendicancy* denote *poverty* that solicits indiscriminate private charity.

Penury denotes a cramping or oppressing *need*, especially of money, which may not be so severe as actual *destitution*. On the other hand, *penury* may imply the mere pretense of *poverty*, such as is caused by miserliness or stinginess. *Privation*, though it may or may not denote *poverty*, always implies a going without the necessities of existence; the Western emigrants of 1849 suffered many hardships and *privations*, even though a great number of them were well-to-do.

POWER

ability	command	expertness	qualification
aptitude	competency	faculty	readiness
authority	dexterity	force	rule
capability	dominion	might	skill
capacity	efficacy	potency	strength
cleverness	efficiency	potentiality	sway
cogency	energy	puissance	talent

Power is the most general term of this group, including every quality, property, or *faculty* by which any physical, mental, natural, or mechanical change, effect, or result is, or may be, produced; as, the *power* of the legislature to enact laws, or of the executive to enforce them; the *power* of an acid to corrode a metal; the *power* of a polished surface to reflect light. *Ability* does not reach the positiveness and vigor that may be included in the meaning of *power*, *ability* often implying latent, as distinguished from active, *power*; we speak of an exertion of *power*, but not of an exertion of *ability*. *Power* and *ability* include *capacity*, which is *power* to receive; but *ability* is often distinguished from *capacity*; one may have great *capacity* for acquiring knowledge, and yet not possess *ability* to teach.

Efficiency is active *power* to effect a definite result, the *power* that actually

oes, as distinguished from that which may do. *Competency* is equal to the
occasion; *readiness,* prompt for the occasion. *Faculty* is an inherent quality of
mind or body; *talent,* some special *ability. Dexterity* and *skill* are *readiness*
and facility in action, having a special end; *talent* is innate, *dexterity* and
skill are largely acquired. Our *abilities* include our natural *capacity, faculties,*
and *talents,* with all the *dexterity, skill,* and *readiness* that can be acquired.

Efficacy is the *power* to produce an intended effect as shown in the production of it; as, the *efficacy* of a drug. *Efficiency* is effectual agency, competent
power; *efficiency* is applied in mechanics as denoting the ratio of the work
produced to the *energy* expended in producing it; but this word is chiefly used
of intelligent agents as denoting the quality that brings all one's *power* to
bear promptly and to the best purpose on the thing to be done. *Aptitude* signifies quickness and *readiness* in learning as well as *capacity, ability,* or *talent.
Authority, command, dominion, rule,* and *sway* refer to *power* over others.
Potentiality is possible, as opposed to evident, *power;* it is the *capacity* for
development or accomplishment; *potency* also is latent *power. Cogency* is the
power of convincing. See **address** *noun;* **dexterity.** Compare **skilful.**

ANTONYMS: *awkwardness, dulness, feebleness, helplessness,
imbecility, impotence, inability, inaptitude, incapacity, incompetence, inefficiency, maladroitness, stupidity, unskilfulness,
weakness.*

PRAISE

acclaim	approval	compliment	laudation
acclamation	blandishment	encomium	panegyric
adulation	cheering	eulogy	plaudit
applause	cheers	flattery	sycophancy
approbation	commendation		

Praise is the hearty *approval* of an individual, or of a number or multitude
considered individually, and is expressed by spoken or written words; *applause,*
the spontaneous outburst of many at once. *Applause* is expressed in any way,
by stamping of feet, clapping of hands, waving of handkerchiefs, etc., as well
as by voice; *acclamation* is the spontaneous and hearty *approval* of many at
once, and strictly by the voice alone. Thus one is chosen moderator by *acclamation* when he receives a unanimous viva voce vote; we could not say he
was nominated by *applause. Acclaim* is the more poetic term for *acclamation,*
commonly understood in a loftier sense; as, a nation's *acclaim. Plaudit* is a
shout of *applause,* and is commonly used in the plural; as, the *plaudits* of a
throng. *Applause* is also used in the general sense of *praise.*

Approbation is a milder and more qualified word than *praise;* while *praise*
is always uttered and is personal, *approbation* may be silent and speaks of the
thing or action. *Laudation* is the act of *praising. Approval* always supposes a

testing or careful examination, and frequently implies official sanction; *appro* *bation* may be upon a general view. The industry and intelligence of a cler win his employer's *approbation*; his decision in a special instance receive his *approval*. *Commendation* is *approbation* or *approval* formally expresse

Praise is always understood as genuine and sincere, unless the contrary expressly stated; *compliment* is a light form of *praise* that may or may not b sincere; *flattery* is insincere, fulsome *praise*; *blandishment* is one of the smooth cajoling arts of the flatterer in speech or action; *sycophancy* is servile *flattery* *Encomium* denotes warm but formal *praise* of persons or things; *eulogy*, th written or spoken *praise* of a person's life or character; *panegyric*, a forma public *eulogy*, unstinted *praise*.

ANTONYMS: *abuse, animadversion, blame, censure, condem-* *nation, contempt, denunciation, disapprobation, disapproval,* *disparagement, hissing, ignominy, obloquy, reproach, reproof,* *repudiation, scorn, slander, vilification, vituperation.*

PRAY

adjure	beseech	entreat	petition
appeal	bid	implore	plead
ask	call upon	importune	request
beg	conjure	invoke	supplicate

To *pray*, in the religious sense, is to talk to God, asking for divine grac or any favor or blessing, and in the fullest sense with thanksgiving and prais for the divine goodness and mercy; to *pray* also means to commune with God silently; to realize God's presence. The once common use of the word to express any earnest *request*, as "I *pray* you to come in," is now rare, unless in writings molded on older literature, or in certain phrases, as "Pray si down"; even in these "please" is more common; "I *beg* you" is also fre quently used as expressing a polite humility of *request*. *Beseech* and *entrea* express great earnestness of *petition*; *implore* and *supplicate* denote the utmos urgency and intensity, *supplicate* implying also humility. *Bid* and *conjure* are now rare terms for *entreat*; *conjure*, as formerly used, always added the idea of *adjure* or enjoin to the idea of *plead*. *Importune* is to *beg* pertinaciously A prisoner *pleads* for mercy and may *appeal* to friends for help. See **ask**; **plead.**

PRECARIOUS

dangerous	hazardous	risky	unsettled
doubtful	insecure	unassured	unstable
dubious	jeopardous	uncertain	unsteady
equivocal	perilous		

Precarious originally meant *insecure* or *uncertain* without any implication of danger; one held office by *precarious* tenure because his position depended on the will, the vote, or the pleasure of others; popularity is a *precarious* thing. Today the word retains this original sense with the added implication that the uncertainty may arise from danger; as, the icy walks give but *precarious* footing. The use of *precarious* as a pure and simple synonym, however, for *dangerous, perilous,* or *hazardous* is still unacceptable to many strict linguists.

Dangerous implies that a certain person, thing, act, or place is to be avoided because injury, death, or evil will befall him who comes in contact with it; *hazardous* stresses the idea of chance, the fact that there is a likely chance of harm, evil, or death befalling; *jeopardous* gives one a fifty-fifty chance of having either good or ill befall. The tightrope walker is in a *precarious* position on the rope; he follows a *dangerous* calling; his situation is indeed *jeopardous*, but if he is an expert he may cross the rope with success.

Risky implies that the uncertainty involves a known risk or danger. *Equivocal* is *uncertain* because able to be interpreted in more than one way; *dubious* is questionable, open to doubt. We speak of *unstable* markets, *unsettled* conditions, an *unsteady* rise in prices, *insecure* positions.

ANTONYMS: *actual, assured, certain, firm, immutable, incontestable, infallible, real, settled, stable, steady, strong, sure, undeniable, undoubted, unquestionable.*

PRECEDENT

| antecedent | case | instance | pattern |
| authority | example | obiter dictum | warrant |

A *precedent* is an authoritative *case, example,* or *instance.* The communism of the early Christians in Jerusalem is a wonderful *example* or *instance* of Christian liberality, but not a *precedent* for the universal church through all time. *Cases* decided by irregular or unauthorized tribunals are not *precedents* for the regular administration of law. An *obiter dictum* is an opinion outside of the case in hand, which cannot be quoted as an authoritative *precedent.* An *antecedent* is one who or that which precedes; *authority,* as compared here, signifies a previous decision which serves as a *pattern*; *warrant,* a reason for something. See **cause; example.**

PRECISE

accurate	distinct	identical	punctilious
careful	exact	minute	rigid
ceremonious	explicit	nice	right
correct	faultless	particular	scrupulous
definite	flawless	perfect	strict

Precise is clearly determined; no more or no less than; scrupulously *exact;* as, a *precise* reckoning, the *precise* instant. *Accurate, correct, definite, exact, precise,* all denote absolute conformity to some external standard. *Accurate* (L. *ad,* to, + *cura,* care) indicates conformity secured by scrupulous care. An *accurate* measurement or account can be verified and found true in all particulars. The native English word *careful* carries less sharp certainty; *careful* stupidity may blunder, *accurate* stupidity is almost unthinkable. *Exact* (L. *ex,* out, + *ago,* drive) indicates that which is worked out to the utmost limit of requirement in every respect; *precise* (L. *precido,* cut off) refers to a like conformity secured by cutting off all excess. *Exact* and *precise* are often interchangeable; but, as filling out is a greater achievement than cutting off, *exact* is the higher word; we speak of the *exact* sciences, not of the *precise* sciences. Hence, *precise* has often an invidious meaning, denoting excessive care of petty details; we speak of the martinet as insufferably *precise,* not insufferably *exact.* Something intricately *exact* and requiring precision and care is *nice;* as, a *nice* balance, a *nice* point in the discussion.

Correct (L. *con-,* together, + *rego,* rule) applies to a required or enforced correspondence with a standard. This is especially seen in the use of the verb; the printer *corrects* the proof. That is *correct* which is free from fault or mistake. Thus *correct* is lower in the scale than *accurate, exact,* or *precise,* which are positive, indicating attainment of the right, while *correct* is negative, denoting avoidance of the wrong; a composition may be *correct,* but intolerably dull; to speak of a *correct* statement or discrimination is to give very mild approval; an *accurate* statement or an *exact* discrimination is felt to have some noticeable excellence.

Definite implies that the limits of scope or meaning are clearly fixed or declared beyond all doubt; as, a *definite* time, a *definite* answer. *Explicit* refers to what is so plainly stated that no mistake as to meaning is possible; as, *explicit* directions. *Faultless* is without fault or error; *flawless,* without flaw or blemish. *Punctilious* people pay great attention to details; *scrupulous* people are extra *careful* to obey their sense of right; *ceremonious* people pay strict attention to etiquette and outward forms. *Identical,* as here compared, implies noting a certain thing, *particular;* as, the *identical* or *precise* moment. Compare **minute.**

> **ANTONYMS:** *careless, doubtful, erroneous, false, faulty, inaccurate, inexact, loose, mistaken, misty, nebulous, untrue, vague, wrong.*

PREDESTINATION

fate　　　　foreknowledge　　　　foreordination　　　　necessity

Predestination is a previous determination or decision; in theology, the doctrine that all events are determined beforehand by God. *Fate* is an irre-

istible, irrational power that is thought to determine one's future success or
ailure, with no manifest connection with reason or righteousness; *necessity* is
hilosophical, a blind something in the nature of things binding the slightest
ction or motion in the chain of inevitable, eternal sequence. *Foreknowledge* is
imply antecedent knowledge of events.

> **ANTONYMS:** *accident, chance, choice, free agency, freedom,*
> *free will, independence, uncertainty.*

> **PREPOSITIONS:** Predestination *of* believers *to* eternal life.

PREDICAMENT

difficulty	jam	puzzle	scrape
dilemma	perplexity	quandary	strait
fix	plight		

A *predicament* or *plight* is a situation or condition that is unfavorable or
disagreeable, trying, puzzling, or embarrassing; it may be shocking or even
dangerous, or on the contrary may be merely comical; a *predicament* may be
mental or social, as well as physical; *plight* is restricted almost wholly to some
physical condition; one who falls into a ditch emerges in sorry, shocking, or
wretched *plight*. *Scrape* is a colloquial term for any difficult or embarrassing
situation, a *predicament* or *plight,* resulting from one's own acts; *fix* and *jam*
are used colloquially in nearly the same sense, but *jam* stresses the discomfort
of the *plight*, while *fix* stresses the difficulties of getting out of the *difficulty.*

Dilemma, perplexity, puzzle, quandary, and *strait,* as applied to practical
matters, denote some *difficulty* of choice. The *dilemma* was originally a form
of argument driving the disputant to a choice between two (later extended to
more than two) conclusions equally unfavorable, called "the horns of the
dilemma"; the *dilemma* has also been called "horned syllogism." Hence, in
practical affairs, a *dilemma* is a situation in which one must choose between
opposite ends or courses of action that seem equally undesirable. A *quandary*
is a situation of *perplexity* where one must study anxiously to avoid a disagreeable outcome; a *quandary* has been defined as "a puzzling *predicament.*" A
trait, in this connection, is a perplexing situation commonly involving some
difficult but necessary choice, while the alternatives may be favorable or unfavorable. Compare **doubt** *noun*; **perplexity; riddle.**

> **ANTONYMS:** *assurance, calmness, certainty, comfort, confi-*
> *dence, content, contentment, decision, ease, firmness, fixity,*
> *resolution, rest, satisfaction, self-reliance, self-confidence, self-*
> *satisfaction.*

PREJUDICE

bias	preconception	presumption
partiality	prepossession	unfairness

A *prejudice* or *prepossession* is a judgment or opinion grounded often on feeling, fancy, association, etc., without due examination. A *prejudice* against foreigners is very common in some communities. A *presumption* (literally, a taking beforehand) is a partial decision formed in advance of argument or evidence, usually grounded on some general principle, and always held subject to revision upon fuller information. There is always a *presumption* in favor of what exists, so that the burden of proof is upon one who advocates a change. A *prepossession* is always favorable, a *prejudice* always unfavorable, unless the contrary is expressly stated. *Partiality* and *unfairness* favor one side; *bias* connotes a one-sided tendency that prevents fair judgment. Compare **injury.**

ANTONYMS: *certainty, conclusion, conviction, demonstration, evidence, proof, reason, reasoning.*

PREPOSITIONS: *Against,* rarely *in favor of, in one's favor.*

PRETENSE

affectation	dissimulation	ruse	simulation
assumption	excuse	seeming	subterfuge
cloak	mask	semblance	trick
color	pretension	show	wile
disguise	pretext		

A *pretense,* in the unfavorable, which is also the usual sense, is something advanced or displayed for the purpose of concealing the reality. A person makes a *pretense* of something for the credit or advantage to be gained by it; he makes what is allowed or approved a *pretext* for doing what would be opposed or condemned; a tricky schoolboy makes a *pretense* of doing an errand which he does not do, or he makes the actual doing of an errand a *pretext* for playing truant. A *trick* is a device to gain an advantage by deception. A *ruse* is something (especially something slight or petty) employed to blind or deceive so as to mask an ulterior design, and enable a person to gain some end that he might not be allowed to approach directly.

A *pretension* is a claim that is or may be contested; the word is now commonly used in an unfavorable sense. *Affectation* is a studied *pretense; assumption* implies a false or deceptive appearance. A *cloak,* as compared here, is something that hides; a *mask.* A *semblance* here refers to a mere *seeming* or *pretense.* A *subterfuge* is resorted to in order to conceal or escape. See **trick.** Compare **hypocrisy.**

ANTONYMS: *actuality, candor, fact, frankness, guilelessness, honesty, ingenuousness, openness, reality, simplicity, sincerity, truth.*

PREVENT

anticipate	forestall	obviate	preclude

The original sense of *prevent*, to come before, act in advance of, which is
ow practically obsolete, was still in good use when the Authorized Version
the Bible was made, as appears in such passages as, "Thou *preventest* him
ith the blessings of goodness" (*i.e.*, by sending the blessings before the desire
formulated or expressed), *Ps.* xxi, 3. *Prevent*, which at first had only the
nticipatory meaning, has come to apply to the stopping of an action at any
age, the completion or conclusion only being thought of as negatived by
nticipation; the enemy passed the outworks and were barely *prevented* from
pturing the fortress.

To *forestall* is to take or act in advance in one's own behalf and to the
rejudice of another or others, as in the phrase "to *forestall* the market." But
anticipate is very frequently used in the favorable sense; as, his thoughtful
ndness *anticipated* my wish (*i.e.*, met the wish before it was expressed): or
e say, "I was about to accost him when he *anticipated* me" (by speaking
st); or one *anticipates* a payment (by making it before the time); in neither
these cases could we use *forestall* or *prevent*.

To *obviate* (literally, to stop the way of or remove from the way), is to
revent by interception, so that something that would naturally withstand or
isturb may be kept from doing so; to *preclude* (literally, to close or shut in
dvance) is to *prevent* by anticipation or by logical necessity; walls and bars
recluded the possibility of escape; a supposition is *precluded*; a necessity or
ifficulty is *obviated*. See **hinder, prohibit.**

PREPOSITION: He was prevented *by* illness *from* joining the
expedition.

REVIOUS

| aforesaid | anterior | former | preceding |
| antecedent | foregoing | precedent | prior |

Previous and *prior* are often used interchangeably; however, *prior* may
enote greater importance than *previous*, describing something that is first
right as well as first in time. Hence, a *previous* engagement suggests merely
n engagement made earlier in time, whereas a *prior* engagement is one which
urpasses another in importance, and must be kept before or to the exclusion
f the other.

Preceding means coming before in space or time, and is limited to that
hich is immediately or next before; a *previous* statement or chapter may
e in any part of the book that has gone before; the *preceding* statement or
hapter comes next before without an interval. *Antecedent* usually denotes
imple priority in time, but, unlike *preceding,* it often implies an indefinite in-
erval; as, most of Hardy's works were written at a time *antecedent* to World
Var I. Very often *antecedent* implies a direct causal or logical connection
etween that which goes before and that which follows, as well as the mere

temporal relation; as, to understand fully the Civil War, one must stu the *antecedent* political and economic developments.

Precedent often describes one thing which must precede another if t latter is to become valid; in law, a condition *precedent* is a condition th must happen or be performed before the estate or right to which it is annex can vest or take effect. *Foregoing* is used only of that which is spoken written; as, the *foregoing* statements. *Anterior*, while it may be used of tim is employed chiefly with reference to space; as, the *anterior* lobes of the bra

Former is used of time, or of position in written or printed matter, not space in general; we speak of *former* times, a *former* chapter, etc. *Form* has a close relation, or sharp contrast, with something following; the *form* always implies the latter, even when not fully expressed; there can be a *form* obligation only when there is a later one, whereas a *prior* or *previous* obligati may preclude the making of a second one.

ANTONYMS: *after, concluding, consequent, following, hind, hinder, hindmost, later, latter, posterior, subsequent, succeeding.*

PREPOSITION: Such was the state of things previous *to* the revolution.

PRICE

| charge | expenditure | outgo | val |
| cost | expense | outlay | wor |

The *cost* of a thing is all that has been expended upon it, whether in d covery, production, refinement, decoration, transportation, or otherwise, bring it to its present condition in the hands of its present possessor; t *price* of a thing is what the seller asks for it. In regular business, as a ru the seller's *price* on his wares must be more than their *cost* to him; wh goods are sold, the *price* the buyer has paid becomes their *cost* to himse In exceptional cases, when goods are sold at *cost*, the seller's *price* is ma the same as the *cost* of the goods to him, the *cost* to the seller and the c to the buyer then becoming identical. *Price* always implies that an article for sale; what a man will not sell he declines to put a *price* on; hence t significance of the taunting proverb that "every man has his *price*."

Value is the estimated equivalent for an article, whether the article is f sale or not; the market *value* is what it would bring if exposed for sale in t open market; the intrinsic *value* is the inherent utility or *worth* of t article considered by itself alone; the market *value* of an old and rare volum may be very great, while its intrinsic *value* may be practically nothing. *Val* has always more reference to others' estimation (literally, what the thing w avail with others) than *worth*, which regards the thing in and by itself; th intrinsic *value* is a weaker expression than intrinsic *worth*. *Charge* has especi reference to services, *expense* to minor outlays; as, the *charges* of a lawyer or physician; traveling *expenses*; household *expenses*.

The *cost* of a thing is whatever one surrenders or gives up for it, intentionally or unintentionally, or even unconsciously; *expense* is what is laid out by calculation or intention. We say, "He won his fame at the *cost* of his life"; we speak of a joke at another's *expense*; at another's *cost* would seem to make it a more serious matter. *Outlay* is used of some definite *expenditure*, as for the purchase of supplies; *outgo*, of a steady drain or of incidental *expenses*.

PRIDE

arrogance	insolence	self-complacency	self-respect
assumption	ostentation	self-conceit	superciliousness
conceit	presumption	self-esteem	vainglory
disdain	reserve	self-exaltation	vanity
haughtiness			

Pride is an absorbing sense of one's own greatness; *haughtiness* feels one's own superiority to others; *disdain* sees contemptuously the inferiority of others to oneself. *Haughtiness* thinks highly of itself and poorly of others. *Arrogance* claims much for itself and concedes little to others. *Presumption* claims place or privilege above one's right; *pride* deems nothing too high. *Insolence* is open and rude expression of contempt and hostility, generally from an inferior to a superior, as from a servant to a master or mistress. In the presence of superiors overweening *pride* manifests itself in *presumption* or *insolence*; in the presence of inferiors, or those supposed to be inferior, *pride* manifests itself by *arrogance, disdain, haughtiness, superciliousness,* or in either case often by cold *reserve*. *Pride* is too self-satisfied to care for praise; *vanity* intensely craves admiration and applause.

Superciliousness, as if by the uplifted eyebrow, as its etymology suggests, evidently manifests mingled *haughtiness* and *disdain*. *Assumption* quietly takes for granted superiority and privilege which others would be slow to concede. *Conceit* and *vanity* are associated with weakness, *pride* with strength. *Conceit* may be founded upon nothing; *pride* is founded upon something that one is, or has, or has done; *vanity*, too, is commonly founded on something real, though far slighter than would afford foundation for *pride*. *Vanity* is eager for admiration and praise, is elated if they are rendered, and pained if they are withheld, and seeks them; *pride* could never solicit admiration or praise. *Conceit* is somewhat stronger than *self-conceit*. *Self-conceit* is ridiculous; *conceit* is offensive. *Self-respect* is a thoroughly worthy feeling; *self-esteem* is a more generous estimate of one's own character and abilities than the rest of the world are ready to allow. *Vainglory* is more pompous and boastful than *vanity*. See **egotism; ostentation.**

ANTONYMS: *humility, cowtiness, meekness, modesty, self-abasement, self-distrust.*

PRIMEVAL

aboriginal	indigenous	patriarchal	primitive
ancient	native	primal	primordia
autochthonic	old	primary	pristine
immemorial	original	prime	uncreated

Primeval signifies strictly belonging to the first ages, earliest in time, bu often only the earliest of which man knows or conceives, *immemorial*. *Aborig nal* signifies pertaining to the aborigines or earliest known inhabitants of country in the widest sense, including not merely human beings but anima and plants as well. *Autochthonic* signifies sprung from the earth, especial from the soil of one's native land. *Aboriginal, autochthonic,* and *primeval* com bine the meanings of *ancient* and *original; aboriginal* inhabitants, *autochthon* races, *primeval* forests. *Prime* and *primary* may signify either first in time o more frequently first in importance; *primary* has also the sense of elementar or preparatory; we speak of a *prime* minister, a *primary* school. *Primal* chiefly poetic, in the sense of *prime*; as, the *primal* curse. *Primordial* is first i an order of succession or development; as, a *primordial* leaf.

Primitive frequently signifies having the *original* characteristics of tha which it represents, as well as standing first in time; as, the *primitive* churc *Primitive* also very frequently signifies having the *original* or early characte istics without remoteness in time. *Primeval* simplicity is the simplicity of th earliest ages; *primitive* simplicity may be found in isolated villages. *Pris tine* is an elegant word, used almost exclusively in a good sense of tha which is *original* and perhaps *ancient*; as, *pristine* purity, innocence, vigo That which is both an *original* and natural product of a soil or country is sai to be *indigenous*; that which is actually produced there is said to be *nativ* though it may be of foreign extraction; hummingbirds are *indigenous* t America; canaries may be *native*, but are not *indigenous*. *Immemorial* refe solely to time, independently of quality, denoting, in legal phrase, "tha whereof the memory of man runneth not to the contrary"; as, an *immemoric* custom; an *immemorial* abuse. Compare **old.**

ANTONYMS: *adventitious, exotic, fresh, foreign, late, modern, new, novel, recent.*

PRINCIPAL

capital	foremost	predominant	prominent
cardinal	greatest	predominating	supereminen
chief	highest	preeminent	superior
controlling	leading	prevailing	supreme
dominant	main	prime	surpassing
first			

Principal signifies *first*, *chief*, or *highest* in rank, character, authority, value, or importance; *principal* is largely interchangeable with *chief* and *main*, but with various differences of usage; we speak of the *principal* street or the *main* street, but not the *chief* street; of the *principal* citizens or the *chief* citizens, but not of the *main* citizens. *Principal*, which is both adjective and noun, cannot be too carefully distinguished from principle (a source, general truth or law, etc.); principle is never an adjective and as a noun differs wholly in meaning from the noun *principal*. *Prominent* signifies literally jutting out; *predominant*, ruling, having mastery, excelling in power, influence, number, degree, etc.; *surpassing*, reaching beyond or over, overpassing, or overtopping. *Supreme* applies to that than which no greater can exist in fact or thought; as, the *Supreme* Being. Compare **chief** *noun*.

Capital signifies standing at the head, being of the first rank or importance; *chief* is often nearly equivalent to *capital*, but differs much in usage; *chief* lays more emphasis on the idea of importance than of rank; a *capital* city may not be the *chief* city; a *capital* letter stands foremost in a word or sentence, but is not called the *chief* letter. *Cardinal* denotes that on which something else turns or hinges, hence signifying of fundamental or vital importance; as the *cardinal* virtues; the *cardinal* points (north, south, east, and west) of the compass. *Main* is often interchangeable with *chief*, but in most exact usage *main* denotes what is more deeply essential and pervading; as, the *main* point, the *main* chance; we say "by *main* force" or "*main* strength," where "*chief* force" or "*chief* strength" could not be substituted; one may assume as the *chief* point of debate what is not the *main* question at issue.

ANTONYMS: *accessory, added, additional, assistant, auxiliary, contributory, helping, inconsiderable, inferior, minor, negligible, secondary, subject, subordinate, subsidiary, supplemental.*

PROFIT

advantage	expediency	proceeds	service
avail	gain	receipts	usefulness
benefit	good	return	utility
emolument	improvement	returns	value

The *returns* or *receipts* include all that is received from an outlay or investment; the *profit* is the excess (if any) of the *receipts* over the outlay; hence, in government, morals, etc., the *profit* is what is really good, helpful, useful, valuable. *Utility* is chiefly used in the sense of some immediate or personal *usefulness*, and generally some material *good*. *Advantage* is that which gives one a vantage ground, either for coping with competitors or with difficulties, needs, or demands; as, to have the *advantage* of a good education; is frequently used of what one has beyond another or secures at the expense of another; as, to have the *advantage* of another in an argument, or take *advantage* of another in a bargain. *Avail* stresses the idea of effectiveness an effectualness. *Gain* is what one secures beyond what he previously possesse *Benefit* is anything that does one *good*. *Emolument* is *profit, return,* or *valu* accruing through official position. *Expediency* has respect to *profit* or *advar tage,* real or supposed, considered apart from or perhaps in opposition to righ in actions having a moral character. Compare **utility.**

> **ANTONYMS:** *damage, destruction, detriment, disadvantage, harm, hurt, injury, loss, ruin, waste.*
>
> **PREPOSITIONS:** The profit *of* labor, *on* capital, *in* business.

PROGRESS

advance	development	improvement	proficienc
advancement	growth	increase	progressio
attainment			

Progress is a moving onward or forward, whether in space or in the ment or moral realm, and may be either mechanical, individual, or social. *Attai ment, development,* and *proficiency* are more absolute than the other wor of the group, denoting some point of advantage or of comparative perfectic reached by forward or onward movement; we speak of *attainments* in schola ship, *proficiency* in music or languages, the *development* of new powers organs; *proficiency* includes the idea of skill. *Advance* may denote either forward movement or the point gained by forward movement, but alwa relatively with reference to the point from which the movement started; this is a great *advance*. *Advance* admits the possibility of retreat; *progress* steady and constant forward movement, admitting of pause, but not of retre *advance* suggests more clearly a point to be reached, while *progress* lays t emphasis upon the forward movement; we may speak of slow or rapid *progre* but more naturally of swift *advance*. *Progress* is more frequently used in a stractions; as, the *progress* of ideas; *progression* fixes the attention chie upon the act of moving forward. In a thing good in itself all *advance progress* is *improvement*; there is a growing tendency to restrict the words this favorable sense, using *increase* indifferently of good or evil; one may s without limitation, "I am an advocate of *progress*."

> **ANTONYMS:** *check, decline, delay, falling back, falling off, relapse, retrogression, stay, stop, stoppage.*
>
> **PREPOSITIONS:** The progress *of* truth; progress *in* virtue, *to-ward* perfection, *from* a lower *to* a higher state.

PROHIBIT

ban	forbid	inhibit	preclu
debar	hinder	interdict	preve
disallow			

To *prohibit* is to give some formal command against, and especially to make some authoritative legal enactment against. *Debar* is said of persons, *disallow* of acts; one is *debarred* from anything when shut off, as by some irresistible authority or necessity; one is *prohibited* from an act in express terms; he may be *debarred* by silent necessity. An act is *disallowed* by the authority that might have allowed it; the word is especially applied to acts which are done before they are pronounced upon; thus, a government may *disallow* the act of its commander in the field or its admiral on the high seas.

Interdict is chiefly known for its ecclesiastical use; as, to *interdict* the administration of the sacrament. *Inhibit* carries the idea of restraint or prohibition not only officially imposed but also imposed by the situation or one's own reaction to the situation. The word is much used in modern psychiatry for the suppression of certain acts, thoughts, emotions, etc., that should be normally expressed or recognized; as, certain childhood fears *inhibit* him from attaining the fulfilment of his dearest ambitions.

As between *forbid* and *prohibit*, *forbid* is less formal and more personal, *prohibit* more official and judicial, with the implication of readiness to use such force as may be needed to give effect to the enactment; a parent *forbids* a child to take part in some game or to associate with certain companions; the slave trade is now *prohibited* by the leading nations of the world. Many things are *prohibited* by law which cannot be wholly *prevented*, as gambling and prostitution; on the other hand, things may be *prevented* which are not *prohibited*, as the services of religion, the payment of debts, or military conquest. That which is *precluded* need not be *prohibited*. *Ban* suggests not only civil or ecclesiastical prohibition, but also moral condemnation or disapproval. Compare **abolish; hinder; prevent.**

ANTONYMS: *allow, authorize, command, consent to, direct, empower, enjoin, give consent, give leave, give permission, let, license, order, permit, put up with, require, sanction, suffer, tolerate, warrant.*

PREPOSITIONS: An act is prohibited *by* law; a person is prohibited *by* law *from* doing a certain act. *Prohibit* was formerly construed, as *forbid* still is, with the infinitive, but the construction with *from* and the verbal noun has now entirely superseded the older usage.

PROJECT

contrivance	device	plan	scheme
design	invention	purpose	

A *project* is something mapped out in the mind, as a course of action; something thrown forth, as it were, and hence tentative or experimental; as, an irrigation or works *project*. A *plan* is something drawn out on a flat surface, as the ground-*plan* of a house. A *design* is a pattern or *plan*. A *scheme* is something only pictured in the mind—airy, visionary. *Contrivance* is the finding how to do something, especially how to get over or around a difficulty; *device* has much the same meaning, especially in mechanical art, but in other uses with more suggestion of trick or subterfuge. *Invention* is the coming to a method or process that has been sought by study and endeavor, and is a nobler and more complete word than *contrivance*. Compare **design.**

ANTONYMS: *accomplishment, achievement, act, deed, doing, execution, performance, production, work.*

PREPOSITIONS: The project *of* a promoter *for* a new company.

PROMOTE

advance	encourage	forward	prefer	raise
aid	exalt	foster	push	urge forward
assist	excite	further	push on	urge on
elevate	foment	help		

To *promote* is to cause to move forward toward some desired end or to *raise* to some higher position, rank, or dignity. We *promote* a person by *advancing, elevating,* or *exalting* him to a higher position or dignity. A person *promotes* a scheme or an enterprise which others have projected or begun, and which he *encourages, forwards, furthers, pushes,* or *urges on,* especially when he acts as the agent of the prime movers and supporters of the enterprise. One who *excites* a quarrel originates it; to *promote* a quarrel is strictly to *foment* and *urge* it *on,* the one who *promotes* keeping himself in the background. *Advance,* in its transitive meanings, may signify to move or put forward in space or time; as, the date of the party was *advanced* one week; or, to give effective assistance to; as, to *advance* the cause of freedom. Compare **abet; quicken.**

ANTONYMS: See synonyms for **allay; debase.**

PROPAGATE

beget	generate	originate	sire
breed	increase	procreate	spread
engender	multiply	reproduce	

Propagate is to have offspring; to be produced or multiplied by generation or other process or means. *Beget* and *sire* refer to the act of a male but *beget* also emphasizes any calling into being; as, one good idea *begets* another. To *breed* is to produce offspring, or to bring into being and to rear; as, to *breed* cattle. *Procreate* refers to the sexual act of producing offspring; *reproduce* has a wider meaning and refers to the bringing into existence of any living

ing. To *engender* is to bring about a birth or condition; as, discontent
engenders strikes. *Multiply* stresses increase in number or quantity; *spread*
emphasizes wider range of distribution. New species *propagated* by scientists
often *multiply* and *spread*.

ANTONYMS: *annihilate, destroy, eradicate, exterminate, extirpate, root out, root up, uproot.*

ROPITIATION

atonement   **expiation**   **reconciliation**   **satisfaction**

Propitiation is an offering, action, or sacrifice that makes the governing
power propitious toward the offender. *Satisfaction,* in this connection, denotes
rendering a full legal equivalent for the wrong done. *Propitiation* appeases
the lawgiver; *satisfaction* meets the requirements of the law.

Atonement (at-one-ment), originally denoting *reconciliation,* or the bringing into agreement of those who have been estranged, is now chiefly used, as
in theology, in the sense of some offering, sacrifice, or suffering sufficient to
win forgiveness or make up for an offense; especially and distinctively of the
sacrificial work of Christ in His humiliation, suffering, and death. *Expiation*
is the enduring of the full penalty of a wrong or crime in order to undo it or
make it as if it had not been, or to make some kind of reparation for it.

ANTONYMS: *alienation, chastisement, condemnation, curse,
estrangement, offense, penalty, punishment, reprobation, retribution, vengeance, wrath.*

ROPITIOUS

auspicious	favorable	gracious	lucky
benign	fortunate	kind	merciful
benignant	friendly	kindly	suitable
clement			

Propitious, when applied to persons, implies *kind* disposition and *favorable*
inclinations, especially toward the suppliant; *auspicious* is not used of persons.
That which is *auspicious* is of *favorable* omen, with the implication that supernatural forces are at work to make a person *fortunate* or *lucky,* or to bring
some undertaking to a *favorable* outcome; as, an *auspicious* morning. *Propitious* means *suitable* for and *favorable* to, without the supernatural implication; it is a stronger word than *favorable,* however; one says the fates were
propitious, or they sent a *propitious* breeze.

Gracious implies *kindly* and *courteous*; *benign* stresses a *kind* and *favorable*
attitude; *benignant* is condescendingly *gracious.* In this comparison, *clement*
is *merciful,* lenient; *friendly* is favorably inclined.

ANTONYMS: *adverse, antagonistic, forbidding, hostile, ill-disposed, inauspicious, repellent, unfavorable, unfriendly, unpropitious.*

PREPOSITION: May heaven be propitious *to* the enterprise.

PROPOSAL

bid	offer	propositic
motion	overture	suggestio

An *offer* or *proposal* puts something before one for acceptance or rejectio *proposal* being the more formal word; a *proposition* sets forth truth (or what claimed to be truth) in formal statement. The *proposition* is for consideratio the *proposal* for action; as, a *proposition* in geometry, a *proposal* of marriag but *proposition* is often used nearly in the sense of *proposal* when it concer a matter for deliberation; as, a *proposition* for the surrender of a fort. A *b* is commercial and often verbal; as, a *bid* at an auction; *proposal* is used nearly the same sense, but is more formal. An *overture* opens; it is a begi ning or a signal of willingness to begin; and the word is especially used some movement toward some kind of relationship; an *overture* to friendshi marriage, etc.; as, *overtures* of peace. A *suggestion* offers an idea or plan f consideration or action; a *motion* is a formal *proposition* in a meeting assembly.

ANTONYMS: *acceptance, denial, disapproval, refusal, rejection, repulse.*

PROPOSE

design	intend	mean	purpos

In its most frequent use, *propose* differs from *purpose* in that what we *pu* pose lies in our own mind, as a decisive act of will, a determination or purpos what we *propose* is offered or stated to others. In this use of the word, wh we *propose* is open to deliberation, as what we *purpose* is not. In another u of the word, one *proposes* something to or by himself which may or may n be stated to others. In this latter sense *propose* is nearly identical with *pu* pose, and the two words have often been used interchangeably. But in th majority of cases what we *purpose* is more general, what we *propose* mo formal and definite; I *purpose* to do right; (*i.e.*, my purpose is to do it right I *propose* to do this specific thing because it is right.

Intend implies a determination to effect an end; as, I *intend* to becom an author; *mean* refers to a wish or intention; as, he *meant* to be on tim *design* lays the emphasis on planning beforehand for a purpose; as, that is *d* signed for service.

PROTRACT

adjourn	delay	extend	procrastinate
continue	draw out	lengthen	prolong
defer	elongate	postpone	

To *protract* is to cause to occupy a longer time than is usual, expected, or desired. We *defer* a negotiation which we are slow to enter upon; we *protract* a negotiation which we are slow to conclude. We *adjourn* or *defer* a meeting to another day. *Delay* may be used of any stage in the proceedings; we may *delay* a person as well as an action, but *defer* and *protract* are not used of persons. *Elongate* is not used of actions or abstractions, but only of material objects or extension in space; *protract* is very rarely used of concrete objects or extension in space; we *elongate* a line, *protract, lengthen,* or *prolong* a discussion.

Protract has usually an unfavorable sense, implying that the matter referred to is already unduly long, or would be so if longer *continued; continue* is neutral, applying equally to the desirable or the undesirable. *Postpone* implies a definite intention to resume, as *defer* also does, though less decidedly; both are often used with some definite limitation of time; as to *postpone* till, until, or to a certain day or hour. One may *defer, delay,* or *postpone* a matter intelligently and for good reason; but we *procrastinate* through indolence and irresolution. See **adjourn.** Compare **hinder.**

ANTONYMS: *abbreviate, abridge, conclude, contract, curtail, hasten, hurry, limit, reduce, shorten.*

PREPOSITIONS: To protract a speech *by* verbosity, *through* an unreasonable time, *to, till* or *until* a late hour.

PROVERB

adage	byword	maxim	saw
aphorism	dictum	motto	saying
apothegm	epigram	precept	truism
axiom			

The *proverb* or *adage* gives homely truth in condensed, practical, and vivid language; the *adage* is a *saying* having the authority of ancient truth. Both the *proverb* and the *adage,* but especially the latter, are thought of as ancient and widely known. An *epigram* is a pointed and witty *saying;* an *aphorism* is a thought-provoking *epigram;* an *apothegm* is a terser, more pungent *aphorism.* The *aphorism* is philosophical, the *apothegm* practical. A *dictum* is a statement of some person or school, on whom it depends for authority; as, a *dictum* of Aristotle.

A *saying* is impersonal, current among the common people, deriving its authority from its manifest truth or good sense; as, it is an old *saying,* "The more haste, the worse speed." A *saw* is a *saying* that is old, but somewhat worn and tiresome. *Precept* is a rule, a direct injunction; *motto* or *maxim* is a brief statement of cherished truth, a guiding principle or rule of conduct, the *maxim* being more uniformly and directly practical; "God is love" may be a *motto*, "Fear God and fear naught," a *maxim*. The *precepts* of the Sermon on the Mount will furnish the Christian with invaluable *maxims* or *mottoes*. A *byword* is a phrase or *saying* used often for emphasis, a catchword; when a person or thing is said to be a *byword*, that person or thing is considered typically an object of scorn or reproach. An *axiom* is a self-evident truth that serves as a basis for future reasoning; a *truism* is too obvious to need proof. See **axiom.**

PROWESS

bravery   **courage**   **gallantry**   **heroism**   **intrepidity**   **valor**

Prowess and *valor* imply both daring and doing; we do not speak of the *prowess* of a martyr, a child, or a passive sufferer. *Valor* meets odds or perils with courageous action, doing its utmost to conquer at any risk or cost; *prowess* has skill and power adapted to the need. *Prowess* is also sometimes used to stress skill, irrespective of *bravery*; as, dauntless *valor* is often vain again superior *prowess*. *Courage* is a nobler word than *bravery*, involving more of the deep, spiritual, and enduring elements of character; such an appreciation of peril as would extinguish *bravery* may only intensify *courage*, which is resistant and self-conquering; *courage* applies to matters in regard to which *valor* and *prowess* can have no place, as submission to a surgical operation, or the facing of censure or detraction for conscience' sake. *Bravery, courage, heroism,* and *intrepidity* may be silent, spiritual, or passive; they may be exhibited by a martyr at the stake. *Gallantry* is dashing, chivalrous *bravery*; *intrepidity* emphasizes lack of fear. Compare **brave; fortitude.**

> **ANTONYMS:** *cowardice, cowardliness, effeminacy, fear, pusillanimity, timidity.*

PRUDENCE

care	consideration	forethought	judiciousness
carefulness	discretion	frugality	providence
caution	forecast	judgment	wisdom
circumspection	foresight		

Prudence may be briefly defined as good *judgment* and *foresight*, inclining to *caution* and *frugality* in practical affairs. *Care* and *carefulness* may respect only the present; *prudence* and *providence* look far ahead and sacrifice the present to the future, *prudence* watching, saving, guarding, *providence* planning, doing, preparing, and perhaps expending largely to meet the future demand. *Frugality* is in many cases one form of *prudence*. In a besieged city *prudence* will reduce the rations, *providence* will strain every nerve to intro- duce supplies and to raise the siege.

Discretion is an instinctive perception of what is wise or proper, with *caution* and resolution to act accordingly; in a different sense *discretion* may mean freedom to act according to one's personal *judgment*; as, in face of an express provision of law, a judge has no *discretion*. *Foresight* merely sees the future, and may even lead to the recklessness and desperation to which *pru- dence* and *providence* are so strongly opposed. *Forethought* is thinking in accordance with wise views of the future, and is nearly equivalent to *provi- dence,* but it is a more popular and less comprehensive term; we speak of man's *forethought,* God's *providence. Caution* is *forethought* exercised in planning to avoid future harm or failure; *circumspection* views matters from all sides so as to make a prudent decision; *wisdom* is the power of true and just discernment. See **care; frugality; wisdom.**

> ANTONYMS: *folly, heedlessness, improvidence, imprudence, indiscretion, prodigality, rashness, recklessness, thoughtless- ness, wastefulness.*

PUNISH

| afflict | chasten | correct | humble |
| castigate | chastise | discipline | subdue |

To *punish* is to inflict pain or loss upon someone as a penalty for dis- obedience or for breaking a law. *Chastise* always suggests corporal punish- ment, generally in order to reform; *castigate,* once used interchangeably with *chastise,* now implies bitter rebuke, an oral or written tongue-lashing. *Chasten* suggests purifying by trial or punishment. *Punish* is distinctly retributive in sense; *chastise,* partly retributive and partly corrective; *chasten,* wholly cor- rective. *Afflict* is to distress physically or mentally; *discipline* is to *punish* in order to *subdue.*

PURCHASE

| acquire | barter for | get | procure |
| bargain for | buy | obtain | secure |

Buy and *purchase* are close synonyms, signifying to *obtain* or *secure* as one's own by paying or promising to pay a price; in numerous cases the two words are freely interchangeable, but with the difference usually found be- tween words of Saxon and those of French or Latin origin. The Saxon *buy* is used for all the homely and petty concerns of common life, the French *pur- chase* is often restricted to transactions of more dignity; yet the Saxon word *buy* is commonly more emphatic, and in the higher ranges of thought appeals more strongly to the feelings. One may either *buy* or *purchase* fame, favor, honor, pleasure, etc., but when our feelings are stirred we speak of victory or freedom as dearly *bought*.

To *acquire* is to *get* as one's own, to *obtain* or gain by any means; to *procure* is to come into possession of, often only temporarily, by some effort or means; to *secure* is to get safe possession of or to insure payment of. We *barter for* or *bargain for* what we hope to *obtain* on better terms than those offered. Compare **business; get; price; sale.**

ANTONYMS: *barter, dispose of, exchange, put to sale, sell.*

PREPOSITIONS: Purchase *at* a price, *at* a public sale, *of* or *from* a person, *for* cash, *with* money, *on* time.

PURE

absolute	guiltless	simple	unmixed
chaste	holy	spotless	unpolluted
classic	immaculate	stainless	unspotted
classical	incorrupt	true	unstained
clean	innocent	unadulterated	unsullied
clear	mere	unblemished	untainted
continent	perfect	uncorrupted	untarnished
genuine	real	undefiled	upright
guileless	sheer	unmingled	virtuous

That is *pure* which is free from mixture or contact with anything that weakens, impairs, or pollutes. Material substances are called *pure* in the strict sense when free from admixture of any kind; as, *pure* oxygen; the word is often used to signify free from any defiling or objectionable admixture (the original sense); we speak of water as *pure* when it is bright, *clear,* and refreshing, though it may contain mineral salts in solution; in the medical and chemical sense, only distilled water (*aqua pura*) is *pure.*

In moral and religious use *pure* is a strong word, denoting positive excellence of a high order; one is *innocent* who knows nothing of evil, is sinless; one is *pure* who, with knowledge of evil and exposure to temptation, keeps heart and soul *unstained. Virtuous* refers primarily to right action; *pure,* to right feeling and motives; as, "Blessed are the *pure* in heart: for they shall see God," *Matt.* v. 8.

Classic and *classical,* as compared here, refer to styles of art or literature that are considered *pure* and *perfect. Chaste* emphasizes purity of thought and action, especially with regard to sex; *continent* is sexually self-restrained. *Immaculate* is *untainted, untarnished, unstained* in any way. *Absolute, simple, sheer,* in this comparison, refer to freedom from any dependence, reduction, or complexity respectively; hence, *pure* as used in arts and sciences. *Guileless* actions are free from deceit and trickery. *Genuine* articles are not counterfeit. are *unadulterated*. Compare **fine; innocent; perfect; real.**

> **ANTONYMS:** *adulterated, defiled, dirty, filthy, foul, gross, immodest, impure, indecent, indelicate, lewd, mixed, obscene, polluted, stained, sullied, tainted, tarnished, unchaste, unclean.*

PUT

| deposit | lay | place | set |

Put is the most general term for bringing an object to some point or within some space, however exactly or loosely; we may *put* a horse in a pasture, or *put* a bullet in a rifle or into an enemy. *Place* denotes more careful movement and more exact location; as, to *place* a crown on one's head, or a garrison in a city. To *lay* is to *place* in a horizontal position; we *lay* a cloth, or *lay* a book on a table. To *set* is to *place* in a definite position with the added inference of definite purpose; as, we *set* food before a guest; *set* milk to sour; *set* a trap for a mouse, etc. To *deposit* is to *put* in a certain place; as, to *deposit* money in a bank; the original sense, to *lay* down or let down (quietly), is equally common; as, the stream *deposits* sediment.

Q

QUARREL

affray	contention	feud	riot
animosity	contest	fight	row
bitterness	controversy	fracas	squabble
brawl	dispute	fray	strife
broil	dissension	hostility	wrangle
conflict	enmity		

A *quarrel* may be in word or act, or both; it may be, and commonly is, slight and transient, as we speak of childish *quarrels*; it may be fierce, noisy, and violent, or quiet, courteous, and deadly. *Contention* and *strife* may be in word or deed; *contest* ordinarily involves some form of action. *Contest* is often used in a good sense, *contention* and *strife* very rarely so. *Controversy* is commonly in words; *strife* is angry discord which often extends from verbal *controversy* to the *contests* of armies.

While all the other words of the group may refer to that which is transient, a *feud* is a long-enduring and often hereditary *quarrel*; it is *enmity* between families, clans, or parties, with acts of *hostility* mutually retaliated and avenged. *Feud* is rarely used of individuals, never of nations. *Dissension* is used of a number of persons, of a party or other organization. *Bitterness* is in feeling only; *enmity* and *hostility* involve will and purpose to oppose or injure. *Animosity* is active and often bitter *enmity*.

Affray, brawl, broil, and *row,* like *quarrel,* are words of inferior dignity; the *affray* always involves physical force; the *brawl, broil,* or *row* may be confined to violent language. *Fray,* an irregular *conflict,* generally of armed opponents, is a word that holds place in literature, but is not now in common use, except in the familiar phrase, "the thick of the *fray.*" A *fracas* is a disorderly and indiscriminate *fight,* usually involving a number of combatants. A *riot* is a serious disturbance of the peace, which may reach the wildest extremes of mob violence, and of which the law takes special cognizance. A *wrangle* is a noisy *quarrel*; a *squabble,* just a petty *wrangle.* See **enmity.** Compare **argument.**

QUEER

anomalous	erratic	odd	strange
bizarre	extraordinary	outlandish	uncommon
comical	fantastic	peculiar	unique
crotchety	funny	preposterous	unmatched
curious	grotesque	quaint	unusual
droll	laughable	ridiculous	whimsical
eccentric	ludicrous	singular	

Queer is *unusual,* aside from the common in a way that is *comical* or perhaps slightly *ridiculous,* or questionable. *Odd* is not matched; as, *odd* sizes;

348

also *strange*; as, an *odd* remark. *Singular* is alone of its kind; as, the *singular* number. What is *singular* is *odd*, but what is *odd* may not be *singular*; as, a drawerful of *odd* gloves. A *strange* thing is something hitherto unknown in fact or in cause. A *singular* coincidence is one the happening of which is *unusual*; a *strange* coincidence is one the cause of which is hard to explain.

That which is *peculiar* belongs especially to a person as his own; as, Israel was called Jehovah's "*peculiar* people," *i.e.*, especially chosen and cherished by Him; in its ordinary use *peculiar* refers to that which is not common to the majority nor quite approved by them, though it may be shared by many; as, the Shakers are *peculiar*. *Eccentric* is off or aside from the center, and so off or aside from the ordinary and what is considered the normal course; as, genius is usually *eccentric*. *Eccentric* is a higher and more respectful word than *odd* or *queer*. *Erratic* signifies wandering, a stronger and more censorious term than *eccentric*.

Quaint denotes that which is pleasingly *odd* and fanciful, often with something of the antique; as, the *quaint* architecture of medieval towns. That which is *funny* is calculated to provoke laughter because it is *strange*; that which is *droll* is more quietly amusing; that is *comical* which induces laughter. *Ludicrous* is laughable because absurd or *ridiculous*. That which is *grotesque* in the material sense is irregular or misshapen in form or outline, or ill-proportioned so as to be somewhat *ridiculous*; the French *bizarre* is practically equivalent to *grotesque*. *Anomalous* is lacking conformity to a standard or class; inconsistent; contradictory. *Curious* applies to what is surprisingly *strange*; *fantastic* and *whimsical* ideas are humorous and fanciful; *fantastic* shapes are extravagantly different; *grotesque* always carries the idea of misshapen or distorted. *Preposterous* is contrary to nature or reason.

ANTONYMS: *common, customary, familiar, natural, normal, ordinary, regular, usual.*

QUESTION

doubt	inquisition	interrogatory	query
inquiry	interrogation	investigation	

A *question* is an interrogative sentence or thought calling for an answer; a debatable topic; a subject of dispute. An *inquiry* seeks information for the benefit of the inquirer; a *question* may do the same, or may have the intent to perplex, confuse, or entrap the one of whom it is asked; one makes *inquiry* as to his way; we speak of idle or frivolous *questions* rather than of idle or frivolous *inquiries*. A *query* is a *question* more or less vaguely formulated and indefinite in purpose, often amounting to no more than a suspense of judgment, and a suggestion of future consideration; as, a proofreader's *query*, which is often but an interrogation point in the margin; a *doubt* may be termed a silent *question*, as a *question* is in many cases simply an expressed *doubt*.

An *interrogation* or *interrogatory* is a formal *inquiry*. *Interrogatory* has a special legal use, denoting an *inquiry* in writing by order of a court, to be answered under oath. An *investigation* is an elaborate search for truth or fact, not only by *questions*, but by every other means of procuring information; an *inquisition* is an *investigation* which is either unwarranted, unduly minute, or in some other way offensive and harsh. See **doubt** *noun*; **topic.**

QUICKEN

accelerate	drive on	hasten	promote
advance	expedite	hurry	speed
dispatch	facilitate	make haste	urge
drive	further	press forward	urge on

To *quicken*, in the sense here considered, is to increase speed, move or cause to move more rapidly, as through more space or with a greater number of motions in the same time. To *accelerate* is to increase the speed of action or of motion. A motion whose speed increases upon itself is said to be *accelerated*, as the motion of a falling body, which becomes swifter with every second of time. To *accelerate* any work is to *hasten* it toward a finish, commonly by *quickening* all its operations in orderly unity toward the result. To *dispatch* is to do and be done with quickly, to get a thing off one's hands. To *dispatch* an enemy is to kill him outright and at once; to *dispatch* a messenger is to send him in haste to a destination; to *dispatch* a business is to bring it quickly to an end. *Dispatch* is commonly used of single items. To *promote* a cause is in any way to bring it forward, *advance* it in power, prominence, etc.

To *speed* is to move swiftly; to *hasten* is to attempt swiftness, whether successfully or unsuccessfully. *Hurry* always indicates something of confusion. The *hurried* man forgets dignity, appearance, comfort, courtesy, everything but speed; he may forget something vital to the matter in hand; yet, *hurry* has come to be the colloquial and popular word for acting quickly. To *facilitate* is to *quicken* by making easy; to *expedite* is to *quicken* by removing hindrances. A good general will improve roads to *facilitate* the movements of troops, *hasten* supplies and perfect discipline to *promote* the general efficiency of the force, *dispatch* details of business, *expedite* all preparations, in order to *accelerate* the advance and victory of his army. Compare **drive; promote.**

ANTONYMS: *check, clog, delay, drag, hinder, impede, ob-struct, retard.*

QUOTE

cite	extract	plagiarize	repeat
excerpt	paraphrase	recite	

To *quote* is to give another's words, either exactly, as in direct quotation, or in substance, as in indirect quotation; to *cite* is to *quote* a passage as evidence or proof, as if calling a witness. In *citing* a passage its exact location by chapter, page, or otherwise, must be given, so that it can be promptly called into evidence; in *quoting*, the location may or may not be given, but the words or substance of the passage must be given. In *citing*, neither the author's words nor his thought may be given, but simply the reference to the location where they may be found. To *quote*, in the proper sense, is to give credit to the author whose words are employed.

To *paraphrase* is to state an author's thought more freely than in indirect quotation, keeping the substance of thought and the order of statement, but changing the language, and commonly interweaving more or less explanatory matter as if part of the original writing. One may *paraphrase* a work with worthy motive (as in the metrical versions of the Psalms), or he may *plagiarize* atrociously in the form of *paraphrase*, appropriating all that is valuable in another's thought, with the hope of escaping detection by change of phrase. To *plagiarize* is to *quote* without credit, appropriating another's words or thought as one's own. To *recite* or *repeat* is usually to *quote* orally, though *recite* is applied in legal phrase and sometimes in ordinary speech to a particular statement of facts which is not a quotation; as, to *recite* one's misfortunes. To *extract* is to select for citation; to *excerpt* is to take out or select a passage from a book or speech.

R

RACE

folk   **nation**   **people**   **population**   **state**   **tribe**

Race is an anthropological and ethnological term, denoting any of the major subdivisions of mankind regarded as having a common origin and exhibiting a relatively constant set of physical traits. On the basis of the more commonly used criteria, such as stature, cephalic index, texture of the hair, color of the skin, etc., mankind has been divided into primary stocks or *races*, each of which is regarded as including a varying number of ethnic groups. According to some authorities, the primary *races* are the Caucasian, Mongoloid, and Negroid.

A *people* is the aggregate of any public community, either in distinction from their rulers or as including them; a *race* is a division of mankind in the line of origin and ancestry; the *people* of the United States includes members of almost every *race*. The term *people* is used ethnologically to mean *folk* having the same linguistic and cultural origins, the same customs, traditions, and beliefs, and usually the same geographical distribution, as distinguished from political affiliations or physical origins.

A *nation* is an organized political community considered with reference to the persons composing it as having certain definite boundaries, a definite number of citizens, etc. The members of a *people* are referred to as persons or individuals; the individual members of a *state* or *nation* are called citizens or subjects. *Tribe* is now almost wholly applied to primitive *peoples* with very imperfect political organization; as, the Indian *tribes*; nomadic *tribes*.

RACY

flavorous	piquant	pungent	spicy
forcible	poignant	rich	spirited
lively			

Racy applies in the first instance to the pleasing flavor characteristic of certain wines, often attributed to the soil from which they come. *Pungent* denotes something sharply irritating to the organs of taste or smell, as pepper, vinegar, ammonia; *piquant* denotes a quality similar in kind to *pungent* but less in degree, stimulating and agreeable; *pungent* spices may be deftly compounded into a *piquant* sauce. *Poignant* is sharp or stimulating to the taste; keenly piercing. *Flavorous* implies savory; well-flavored; imparting a characteristic quality. As applied to literary products, *racy* refers to that which has a striking, vigorous, pleasing originality; *spicy*, to that which is stimulating to the mental taste, as spice is to the physical; *piquant*, *poignant*, and *pungent* in their figurative use keep very close to their literal sense.

ANTONYMS: *cold, dull, flat, flavorless, insipid, prosy, stale, stupid, tasteless, vapid.*

RADICAL

basal	extreme	natural	primitive
basic	fundamental	organic	thorough
complete	ingrained	original	thoroughgoing
constitutional	innate	perfect	total
entire	native	positive	underlying
essential			

The widely divergent senses in which the word *radical* is used, by which it can be at some time interchanged with any word in the above list, are all formed upon the one primary sense of having to do with or proceeding from the root (from L. *radix*); a *radical* difference is one that springs from the root, and is thus *constitutional, essential, fundamental, organic, original*; a *radical* change is one that does not stop at the surface, but reaches down to the very root, and is *entire, thorough, total*; *radical* measures, which strike at the root of evil or need, are apt to be looked upon as *extreme*. *Basic* and *basal*, as compared here, refer to a base, foundation, or starting point; *primitive*, to a beginning or origin. *Innate* means inborn; *native* means born or produced in. *Perfect, entire,* and *complete,* in this comparison, imply *thoroughgoing* from the root or origin through every part; as, a *radical, complete,* or *perfect* reorganization.

ANTONYMS: *conservative, inadequate, incomplete, moderate, palliative, partial, slight, superficial, tentative, trial.*

RARE

curious	odd	scarce	unique
extraordinary	peculiar	singular	unparalleled
incomparable	precious	strange	unprecedented
infrequent	remarkable	uncommon	unusual

To say of a thing that it is *rare* is simply to affirm that it is now seldom found, whether previously common or not; as, a *rare* old book, a *rare* word; to call a thing *scarce* implies that it was at some time more plentiful, as when we say food or money is *scarce*. A particular fruit or coin may be *rare*; *scarce* applies to demand and use, and almost always to concrete things; to speak of virtue, genius, or heroism as *scarce* would be somewhat ludicrous. *Rare* has the added sense of *precious*, which is sometimes, but not necessarily, blended with the above meanings; as, a *rare* gem. *Unique* is alone of its kind; *rare* is *infrequent* of its kind; great poems are *rare*; "Paradise Lost" is *unique*.

Extraordinary, signifying greatly beyond the ordinary, is a neutral word, capable of a high and good sense or of an invidious, opprobrious, or contemptuous signification; as, *extraordinary* genius; *extraordinary* wickedness; an *extraordinary* assumption of power; *extraordinary* antics; an *extraordinary* statement is incredible without overwhelming proof. *Incomparable* is *rare* in the sense that it is peerless and cannot be compared; *unparalleled* is *rare* because unequaled; an *odd* piece of pottery is *rare* because *strange* and *unusual.*

ANTONYMS: See synonyms for **general; normal; usual.**

RATIONAL

reasonable

A *rational* mind is one that is capable of the ordinary and normal processes of thought; a *reasonable* mood is one at the time susceptible to the influence of reasons. A *rational* man is capable of using his reasoning powers; a *reasonable* man has them habitually in exercise. *Rational* is opposed to insane, *reasonable* to fanatical, misguided, obstinate, unreasonable, visionary. Compare **sagacious.**

REACH

arrive   attain   come (to)   enter   gain   get (to)   land

To *reach,* in the sense here considered, is to *come to* by motion or progress. *Attain* is now most often used of abstract relations; as, to *attain* success. When applied to concrete matters, it commonly signifies the overcoming of hindrance and difficulty; as, the storm-beaten ship at length *attained* the harbor. *Come* is the general word for moving to or toward the place where the speaker or writer is or supposes himself to be. To *reach* is to *come to* from a distance that is actually or relatively considerable; to stretch the journey, so to speak, across the distance, as, in its original meaning, one *reaches* an object by stretching out the hand.

To *gain* is to *reach* or *attain* something eagerly sought; the wearied swimmer *reaches* or *gains* the shore. One *comes* in from his garden; he *reaches* home from a journey. To *arrive* is to *come to* a destination, to *reach* a point intended or proposed. The European steamer *arrives* in port, or *reaches* the harbor; the dismantled wreck drifts ashore, or *comes to* land. A plane or ship that lands passengers in Australia has caused them to *reach* Australia; a traveler who *reaches* or *comes to* a country can only *enter* or *come* into it if permitted. Compare **attain.**

ANTONYMS: *depart, embark, go, go away, leave, set out, set sail, start, weigh anchor.*

REAL

actual	demonstrable	genuine	true
authentic	developed	positive	unquestionable
certain	essential	substantial	veritable

Real (from L. *res,* a thing) signifies having existence, not merely in thought, but in fact, or being in fact according to appearance or claim; denoting the thing as distinguished from the name, the *genuine* as opposed to the imitation, or the existent as opposed to the non-existent. *Actual* has respect to a thing accomplished by doing; *real,* to a thing as existing by whatever means or from whatever cause; *positive,* to that which is fixed or established; *developed,* to that which has reached completion by a natural process of unfolding. *Actual* is in opposition to the supposed, conceived, or reported, and furnishes the proof of its existence in itself; *real* is opposed to feigned or imaginary, and is capable of demonstration; *positive,* to the uncertain or doubtful; *developed,* to that which is undeveloped or incomplete. The *developed* is susceptible of proof; the *positive* precludes the necessity for proof.

The present condition of a thing is its *actual* condition; ills are *real* that have a substantial reason; proofs are *positive* when they give the mind certainty; a plant is *developed* when it has reached its completed stage. *Real* estate is land, together with trees, water, minerals, or other natural accompaniments, and any permanent structure that man has built upon it. *True, authentic, veritable,* and *genuine,* all connote reliability as to the reality; we speak of *true* worth, *authentic* marks, *veritable* genius, and *genuine* diamonds. *Essential* is having *real* existence or substance; *substantial* is *real* because not imaginary. See **authentic.**

ANTONYMS: *conceived, fabulous, fanciful, feigned, fictitious, hypothetical, illusory, imaginary, reported, supposed, supposititious, theoretical, unreal, untrue, visionary.*

REASON *noun*

account	consideration	ground	principle
aim	design	motive	purpose
argument	end	object	reasoning
cause			

The *reason* of or for any event, act, or fact is the explanation given by the human mind, while the *cause,* as commonly understood, is the power that makes it to be; but *reason* is, in popular language, often used as equivalent to *cause,* especially in the sense of *final cause.* In the statement of any reasoning, the *argument* may be an entire syllogism, or the premises considered together apart from the conclusion, or in logical strictness the middle term only by which the particular conclusion is connected wtih the general statement. But when the *reasoning* is not in strict logical form, the middle term following the conclusion is called the *reason;* thus in the statement "All tyrants deserve death; Cæsar was a tyrant; therefore Cæsar deserved death," "Cæsar was a tyrant" would in the strictest sense be called the *argument;* but if we say "Cæsar deserved death because he was a tyrant," the latter clause would be termed the *reason*. We speak of *grounds* for divorce, the *object* of a special session, the *motives* for quick action, the *principle* or fundamental truth that serves as a basis for *reasoning*. See **cause; reason** *verb*; **reasoning.** Compare **aim; design; end.**

> **PREPOSITIONS:** The reason *of* a thing that is to be explained; the reason *for* a thing that is to be done.

REASON *verb*

argue	debate	dispute	question
contend	demonstrate	establish	wrangle
controvert	discuss	prove	

To *reason* is to examine by means of the reason, to *prove* by reasoning, or to influence or seek to influence others by reasoning or reasons. Persons may *contend* either from mere ill will or self-interest, or from the highest motives. To *argue* (from L. *arguo*, show) is to make a matter clear by reasoning; to *discuss* (from L. *dis*, apart, and *quatio*, shake) is, etymologically, to shake it apart for examination and analysis. *Reason* is a neutral word, not, like *argue, debate, discuss,* etc., naturally or necessarily implying contest. We *reason* about a matter by bringing up all that reason can give us on any side. We may *dispute* in a personal, fractious, and petty way, or *debate* in a formal and orderly manner; a *dispute* or *debate* may develop into a *wrangle* if tempers are frayed and details *questioned*.

Demonstrate strictly applies to mathematical or exact reasoning; *prove* may be used in the same sense, but is often applied to reasoning upon matters of fact by what is called probable evidence, which can give only moral and not absolute or mathematical certainty. To *demonstrate* is to force the mind to a conclusion by irresistible reasoning; to *prove* is rather to *establish* a fact by evidence; as, to *prove* one innocent or guilty. That which has been either *demonstrated* or *proved* so as to secure general acceptance is said to be *established*.

> **PREPOSITIONS:** We reason *with* a person *about* a subject, *for* or *against* an opinion; we reason a person *into* or *out of* a course of action; or we may reason *down* an opponent or opposition; one reasons *from* a cause *to* an effect.

REASONING

argument	argumentation	debate	ratiocination

Reasoning may be the act of one alone, as it is simply the orderly setting forth of reasons, to instruct inquirers, confute opponents, or establish truth. *Reasoning* may be either deductive or inductive. *Argument* or *argumentation* was formerly used of deductive *reasoning* only. With the rise of the inductive philosophy these words have come to be applied to inductive processes also; but while *reasoning* may be informal or even (as far as tracing its processes is concerned) unconscious, *argument* and *argumentation* strictly imply logical form. *Reasoning,* as denoting process, is a broader term than *reason* or *argument*; many *arguments* or *reasons* may be included in a single chain of *reasoning.*

Argumentation and *debate,* in the ordinary use of the words, suppose two parties alleging reasons for and against a proposition; the same idea appears figuratively when we speak of a *debate* or an *argument* with oneself, or of a *debate* between reason and conscience. *Ratiocination* refers to the process of formal or correct *reasoning.*

REBELLIOUS

contumacious	intractable	seditious	ungovernable
disobedient	mutinous	uncontrollable	unmanageable
insubordinate	refractory		

Rebellious signifies being in a state of rebellion, and is even extended to inanimate things that resist control or adaptation to human use. *Ungovernable* applies to that which successfully defies authority and power; *unmanageable,* to that which resists the utmost exercise of skill or of skill and power combined; *rebellious,* to that which is defiant of authority, whether successfully or unsuccessfully; *seditious,* to that which partakes of or tends to excite a *rebellious* spirit, *seditious* suggesting more of covert plan, scheming, or conspiracy, *rebellious* more of overt act or open violence.

While that which is *unmanageable* or *ungovernable* defies control, that which is *rebellious* or *seditious* may be forced to submission; as, the man has an *ungovernable* temper; the horses became *unmanageable;* he tamed his *rebellious* spirit. *Insubordinate* applies to the disposition to resist and resent control as such; *mutinous,* to open defiance of authority, especially in the army, navy, or merchant marine. A *contumacious* act or spirit is contemptuous as well as defiant. *Intractable* and *refractory* refer to unruliness and resistance to restraint. Compare **obstinate; revolution.**

> **ANTONYMS:** *compliant, controllable, deferential, docile, dutiful, gentle, manageable, obedient, submissive, subservient, tractable, yielding.*

> **PREPOSITIONS:** Rebellious *to* or *against* lawful authority.

RECORD

account	enrolment	instrument	register
archive	entry	inventory	roll
catalog(ue)	enumeration	memorandum	schedule
chronicle	history	memorial	scroll
document	inscription	muniment	story

Record is a word of wide signification, applying to any writing, mark, or trace that serves as a *memorial* giving enduring attestation of an event or fact;

an extended *account, chronicle,* or *history* is a *record*; the *inscription* on a tombstone is a *record* of the dead; the striæ on a rock surface are the *record* of a glacier's passage. An *account* is a detailed *record*; a *chronicle* gives details in order of time. The *story* of a person's career states the facts as known. A *schedule* is a detailed or tabulated statement or list, as of trains, directions, etc. A *roll* is a list of names; a *scroll* is a parchment, paper, or other material containing writing, especially one that can be rolled up. A *catalog* is an alphabetical and descriptive list of articles.

A *memorial* is any object, whether a writing, a monument, or other permanent thing, that is designed or adapted to keep something in remembrance.

A *register* is a formal or official written *record,* especially a series of entries made for preservation or reference; as, a *register* of births and deaths. *Archives,* in the sense here considered, are *documents* or *records,* often legal *records,* preserved in a public or official depository; the word *archives* is also applied to the place where such *documents* are regularly deposited and preserved. *Muniments* (from L. *munio,* fortify) are *records* that enable one to defend his title. See **history; story.**

RECOVER

be cured or healed	heal	recuperate	restore
be restored	reanimate	regain	resume
cure	recruit	repossess	retrieve

The chief transitive use of *recover* is in the sense of to obtain again after losing, *regain, repossess,* etc.; as, to *recover* stolen goods, to *recover* health. The intransitive sense, *be cured, be restored,* etc., is very common; as, to *recover* from sickness, terror, or misfortune.

The transitive use of *recover* in the sense of *cure, heal,* etc., as in *2 Kings* v, 6, "That thou mayest *recover* him of his leprosy," is now archaic. *Restore* is to put back into or bring back to a former state or position; to *reanimate* is to *restore* to life or strength; to *recuperate* is to *recover* health or *regain* something lost. *Retrieve* is to *recover* by an effort; bring back from a state of loss or impairment; as, to *retrieve* a fortune.

ANTONYMS: *die, fail, grow worse, relapse, sink.*

PREPOSITIONS: *From*; rarely *of*; (*Law*) to recover judgment *against,* to recover damages *of* or *from* a person.

REFINEMENT

breeding	cultivation	elegance	politeness
civilization	culture	poise	urbanity

Refinement applies either to nations or individuals, denoting the removal of what is coarse and rude, and a corresponding attainment of fineness in thought, tastes, and language. *Cultivation*, denoting primarily the process of cultivating the soil or growing crops, then the improved condition of either which is the result, is applied in similar sense to the human mind and character, but in this usage is now largely superseded by the term *culture*, which denotes a high development of the best qualities of man's mental and spiritual nature. *Culture* in the usual sense denotes that degree of *refinement* and development which results from continued *cultivation* and association with what is best through successive generations; a man's faculties may be brought to a high degree of *cultivation* in some specialty, while he himself remains uncultured even to the extent of coarseness and rudeness.

Civilization applies to nations, denoting the sum of those civil, social, economic, and political attainments by which a community is removed from barbarism; a people may be civilized while still far from *refinement*, for *civilization* is susceptible of various degrees and of continued progress. *Breeding* includes the *refinement*, *poise*, and good manners that result from careful training; *urbanity*, originally implying the manners of the city, now applies to that *refinement* and *poise* which only a person of wide social intercourse attains. *Elegance* suggests the *refinement* and polish that come from *breeding*; *politeness* refers chiefly to manners and language. Compare **humane; polite.**

ANTONYMS: *barbarism, boorishness, brutality, clownishness, coarseness, grossness, rudeness, rusticity, savagery, vulgarity.*

REFUTE

confute	controvert	disprove	rebut	repel

To *refute* and to *confute* are to answer so as to admit of no reply. To *refute* a statement is to demonstrate its falsity by argument or countervailing proof; *confute* is substantially the same in meaning, though differing in usage. *Refute* applies either to arguments and opinions or to accusations; *confute* is applied only to arguments or opinions. *Refute* is not now applied to persons, but *confute* is in good use in this application; a person is *confuted* when his arguments are *refuted*. To *disprove* is to *refute* generally what is false, erroneous, fraudulent, or illegal; to *controvert* is to try to *disprove* by denials and contradictions; to *rebut* is also to aim to *disprove* but by offering counter arguments. To *repel* is to refuse to accept or receive as valid; as, to *repel* an idea or a suggestion.

RELIABLE

dependable	tried	trustworthy	trusty

Reliable denotes the possession of such qualities as are needed for safe reliance; as, a *reliable* pledge, *reliable* information. A man is said to be *reliable* with reference not only to moral qualities, but to judgment, knowledge, skill, habit, or perhaps pecuniary ability. *Trusty* and *trustworthy* refer to inherent qualities of a high order, *trustworthy* being especially applied to persons, and denoting moral integrity and truthfulness; we speak of a *trusty* sword, a *trusty* servant; we say the man is thoroughly *trustworthy*.

A thoroughly *trustworthy* person might not be *reliable* as a witness on account of unconscious sympathy, or as a security by reason of insufficient means. A *reliable* messenger is one who may be depended on to do his errand correctly and promptly; a *trusty* or *trustworthy* messenger is one who may be admitted to knowledge of the views and purposes of those who employ him, and who will be faithful beyond the mere letter of his commission. We can speak of a railroad train as *reliable* when it can be depended on to arrive on time; but to speak of a *reliable* friend would be cold, and to speak of a warrior girding on his *reliable* sword would be ludicrous. A *dependable* person or thing can be relied on to help whenever a need arises; a *tried* person or thing has given proof of reliability on other occasions.

RELIGION

church	cult	faith	sect
communion	denomination	persuasion	theology
creed			

Religion applies to any system of religious belief and worship and to the conscientious devotion to it. *Denomination,* in this comparison, refers to a body of people having a name and set of beliefs that distinguish them from the larger body of which they are a part; as, the Baptist *denomination. Sect* is a group of people who follow a particular leader or teacher; also the doctrines of this group.

Faith and *creed,* in this comparison, refer to a formula or system of religious belief; *communion,* to a religious group perhaps comprising several bodies or *churches,* having a common essential *faith. Theology* is the science of *religion.* A *cult* may be a religious system or merely devotion to some idea or leader; *persuasion* also applies either to a religious *sect* or to a secular group.

ANTONYMS: *atheism, blasphemy, godlessness, impiety, irreligion, profanity, sacrilege, unbelief, ungodliness, wickedness.*

RELUCTANT

averse	disinclined	loath	slow
backward	indisposed	opposed	unwilling

Reluctant (from L. *re,* back, and *lucto,* strive, struggle) signifies struggling against what one is urged or impelled to do, or is actually doing; *averse* (from

L. *a*, from, and *verto*, turn) signifies turned away as with dislike or repugnance; *loath* (from OE. *lath*, evil, hateful) signifies having a repugnance, disgust, or loathing for, though the adjective *loath* is not so strong as the verb "loathe." A dunce is always *averse* to study; a good student is *disinclined* to work when a fine morning tempts him out; he is *indisposed* to start new work when weary.

A man may be *slow* or *backward* in entering upon that to which he is by no means *averse*. A man is *loath* to believe evil of his friend, *reluctant* to speak of it, absolutely *unwilling* to use it to his injury. A legislator may be *opposed* to a certain measure, while not *averse* to what it aims to accomplish. See **slow.** Compare **antipathy.**

> ANTONYMS: *desirous, disposed, eager, favorable, inclined, willing.*

REMARK

annotation   comment   note   observation   utterance

A *remark* is a saying or brief statement, oral or written, commonly made without much premeditation; a *comment* is an explanatory or critical *remark*, as upon some passage in a literary work or some act or speech in common life. A *note* is something to call attention, hence a brief written statement; in correspondence, a *note* is briefer than a letter. A *note* upon some passage in a book is briefer and less elaborate than a *comment*. *Annotations* are especially brief *notes*, commonly marginal, and closely following the text. *Comments*, *observations*, or *remarks* may be oral or written, *comments* being more often written, and *remarks* generally oral. An *observation* is properly the result of fixed attention and reflection; a *remark* may be the suggestion of the instant. *Remarks* are more informal than a speech. An *utterance* is spoken or published.

REND

break	divide	rip	sever	sunder
burst	lacerate	rive	slit	tear
cleave	mangle	rupture	split	

Rend and *tear* are applied to the separating of textile substances into parts by force violently applied (*rend* also to frangible substances), *tear* being the milder, *rend* the stronger word. *Rive* is a woodworkers' word for parting wood in the grain without a clean cut. *Split* and *cleave* both suggest a breaking apart through the entire length; *cleave* is the stronger, more rhetorical word. To *lacerate* is to *tear* roughly the flesh or animal tissue, as by the teeth of a wild beast; a *lacerated* wound is distinguished from a wound made by a clean cut or incision. *Mangle* is a stronger word than *lacerate*; *lacerate* is more superficial, *mangle* more complete. To *burst* or *rupture* is to *tear* or *rend* by force from within, *burst* denoting the greater violence; as, to *burst* a gun; to *rupture* a blood vessel; a steam boiler may be *ruptured* when its substance is made to *divide* by internal pressure without explosion. To *rip*, as usually applied to garments or other articles made by sewing or stitching, is to *divide* along the line of a seam by cutting or *breaking* the stitches; the other senses bear some resemblance or analogy to this; as, to *rip* open a wound. Compare **break.**

ANTONYMS: *heal, join, mend, reunite, secure, sew, solder, stitch, unite, weld.*

RENOUNCE

abandon	disavow	disown	recant	repudiate
abjure	discard	forswear	refuse	retract
deny	disclaim	recall	reject	revoke

Abjure, discard, forswear, recall, recant, renounce, retract, and *revoke,* like *abandon,* imply some previous connection. *Renounce* is to declare against and give up formally and definitively; as, to *renounce* the pomps and vanities of the world. *Recant* is to take back or *deny* formally and publicly, as a belief that one has held or professed. *Retract* is to take back something that one has said as not true or as what one is not ready to maintain; as, to *retract* a charge or accusation; one *recants* what was especially his own, he *retracts* what was directed against another. *Repudiate* is primarily to *renounce* as shameful; thus in general to put away with emphatic and determined repulsion; as, to *repudiate* a debt or a friend.

To *deny* is to affirm to be not true or not binding; as, to *deny* a statement or a relationship; or to *refuse* to grant as something requested; as, his mother could not *deny* him what he desired. To *discard* is to cast away as useless or worthless; thus, one *discards* a worn garment; a coquette *discards* a lover. *Revoke,* etymologically the exact equivalent of the English *recall,* is to take back something given or granted; as, to *revoke* a command, a will, or a grant; *recall* may be used in the exact sense of *revoke,* but is often applied to persons, as *revoke* is not; we *recall* a messenger and *revoke* the order with which he was charged.

Abjure is etymologically the exact equivalent of the Saxon *forswear,* signifying to put away formally and under oath, as an error, heresy, or evil practice, or a condemned and detested person. A man *abjures* his religion, *recants* his belief, *abjures* or *renounces* his allegiance, *repudiates* his wife, *renounces* old habits, *retracts* a false statement. A person may *deny, disavow, disclaim, disown* what has been truly or falsely imputed to him or supposed to be his. He may *deny* his signature, *disavow* the act of his agent, *disown* his child; he may *repudiate* a just claim or a base suggestion. A native of the

United States cannot *abjure* or *renounce* allegiance to the King of England, but will promptly *deny* it. Compare **abandon.**

ANTONYMS: *acknowledge, adopt, assert, avow, cherish, claim, defend, hold, maintain, own, proclaim, retain, uphold, vindicate.*

REPENTANCE

attrition	contrition	regret	self-condemnation
compunction	penitence	remorse	sorrow
contriteness			

Repentance is *sorrow* for sin with *self-condemnation*, and complete turning from the sin. *Regret* is *sorrow* for any painful or annoying matter. One is moved with *penitence* for wrong-doing. To speak of *regret* for a fault of our own marks it as slighter than one regarding which we should express *penitence.* *Penitence* is transient, and may involve no change of character or conduct. There may be *sorrow* without *repentance*, as for consequences only, but not *repentance* without *sorrow.* *Compunction* suggests a painful twinge of conscience, but only a momentary one, whereas *remorse* implies an abiding, prolonged suffering. *Remorse* is, as its derivation indicates, a biting or gnawing back of guilt upon the heart, with no turning of heart from the sin, and no suggestion of divine forgiveness.

Contrition and *attrition* are both theological terms. *Contrition* is sincere *sorrow* for sin, wrong-doing, or offense, especially as arising from a sense of the baseness of sin and of God's loving mercy; *attrition* is *sorrow* or *repentance* for sin arising from fear of punishment.

ANTONYMS: *approval, comfort, complacency, content, hardness, impenitence, obduracy, obstinacy, self-approval, self-complacency, self-congratulation, stubbornness.*

PREPOSITIONS: Repentance *of* or *in* heart, or *from* the heart; repentance *for* sins, *before* or *toward* God, *unto* life.

REPORT

account	narrative	relation	story
chronicle	recital	rumor	tale
description	record	statement	version
narration	rehearsal		

A *report*, as its etymology implies, is something brought back, as by one sent to obtain information, and may be concise and formal or highly descriptive and dramatic. *Account* is a detailed *report* or *record.* A *statement* is definite, confined to essentials and properly to matters within the personal knowledge of the one who states them; as, an ante-mortem *statement*. A *narrative* is a somewhat extended and embellished *account* of events in order of time, ordinarily with a view to please or entertain. A *description* gives especial scope to the pictorial element.

A *chronicle* is a detailed *account* of events in the order of their occurrence. *Version* and *story* stress the personal aspect of a *statement,* with the implication of a contrast with another *statement.* One man's *version* of some occurrence may differ greatly from another's. A *story* may be an untrue *report,* perhaps falsified in order to amuse rather than deceive; as, a "tall" *story.* Compare **allegory; history; record.**

REPROOF

admonition	chiding	disapproval	reprimand
animadversion	comment	objurgation	reproach
blame	condemnation	rebuke	reproval
censure	criticism	reflection	upbraiding
check	denunciation	reprehension	

Blame, censure, and *disapproval* may either be felt or uttered; *comment, criticism, rebuke, reflection, reprehension,* and *reproof* are always expressed. The same is true of *admonition* and *animadversion. Comment* and *criticism* may be favorable as well as censorious; they imply no superiority or authority on the part of him who utters them; nor do *reflection* or *reprehension,* which are simply turning the mind back upon what is disapproved. *Reprehension* is supposed to be calm and just, and with good intent; it is therefore a serious matter, however mild, and is capable of great force, as expressed in the phrase "severe *reprehension.*" *Reflection* is often from mere ill feeling, and is likely to be more personal and less impartial than *reprehension;* we often speak of unkind or unjust *reflections.*

Rebuke, literally a stopping of the mouth, is administered to a forward or hasty person; *reproof* is administered to one intentionally or deliberately wrong; both words imply authority in the reprover, and direct expression of *disapproval* to the face of the person *rebuked* or *reproved. Reprimand* is official *censure* formally administered by a superior to one under his command. *Animadversion* partakes of ill will expressed in petty *criticism. Rebuke* may be given at the outset, or in the midst of an action; *reflection, reprehension, reproof* always follow the act; *admonition* is anticipatory, and meant to be preventive. *Check* is allied to *rebuke,* and given before or during action; *chiding* is nearer to *reproof,* but with more of personal bitterness and less of authority. *Admonition* stresses the suggestion of counsel or warning. *Reproach* suggests *criticism* or fault-finding. Compare **condemn; reprove.**

ANTONYMS: *applause, approbation, approval, commendation, encomium, eulogy, panegyric, praise.*

REPROVE

admonish	check	rebuke	reproach
blame	chide	remonstrate with	take to task
censure	condemn	reprehend	upbraid
chasten	expostulate with	reprimand	warn

To *censure* is to pronounce an adverse judgment that may or may not be expressed to the person *censured*; to *reprove* is to *censure* authoritatively, openly, and directly to the face of the person *reproved*; to *rebuke* is to *reprove* with sharpness, and often with abruptness, usually in the midst of some action or course of action deemed censurable; to *reprimand* is to *reprove* officially; to *blame* is a familiar word signifying to pass *censure* upon, make answerable, as for a fault; *blame* and *censure* apply either to persons or acts; *reprove* and *rebuke* are applied chiefly, and *reprimand* exclusively, to persons. To *reproach* is to criticize, usually with intense personal feeling as of grief or anger; as, to *reproach* one for ingratitude; *reproach* knows no distinction of rank or character; a subject may *reproach* a king or a criminal judge.

To *expostulate* or *remonstrate with* is to mingle reasoning and appeal with *censure* in the hope of winning one from his evil way, *expostulate* being the more exclamatory, *remonstrate* the severer word. *Admonish* is the mildest of *reproving* words, and may even be used of giving a caution or warning where no wrong is implied, or of simply reminding of duty which might be forgotten. *Censure*, *rebuke*, and *reprove* apply to wrong that has been done; *warn* and *admonish* refer to anticipated error or fault. When one is *admonished* because of wrong already done, the view is still future, that he may not repeat or continue in the wrong. Compare **condemn; reproof.**

ANTONYMS: *abet, applaud, approve, cheer, countenance, encourage, impel, incite, instigate, urge on.*

REQUITE

avenge	punish	remunerate	revenge
compensate	quit	repay	reward
pay	reciprocate	retaliate	satisfy
pay off	recompense	return	settle with

To *repay* or to *retaliate*, to *punish* or to *reward*, may be to make some return very inadequate to the benefit or injury received, or the right or wrong done; but to *requite* (according to its etymology) is to make so full and adequate a return as to *quit* oneself of all obligation of favor or hostility, of punishment or reward. *Requite* is often used in the more general sense of *recompense* or *repay*, but always with the suggestion, at least, of the original idea of full equivalent: when one speaks of *requiting* kindness with ingratitude, the expression gains force from the comparison of the actual with the proper and appropriate return. Compare **pay.**

ANTONYMS: *absolve, acquit, excuse, forget, forgive, neglect, overlook, pardon, pass over, slight.*

PREPOSITION: To requite injury *with* injury is human, but not Christian.

RESPONSIBLE

accountable   amenable   answerable   liable

Accountable, answerable, and *responsible* are so close to each other in meaning that it is difficult to separate them except along fine lines of usage; a steward or agent is *accountable* to the extent of his trust; he is *answerable* for money or goods misappropriated; *answerable* has more suggestion of challenge, implying that one may be formally or legally cited to answer; *accountable* has more of commercial suggestion, as of one balancing a trust committed against return or service rendered; one is *accountable* to some superior, *answerable* to some law or tribunal; *responsible* is the more general term, including both *accountable* and *answerable,* but carrying a more diffused and less technical sense of obligation; when we say, "Every man is *responsible* for his own actions," we do not think definitely of any authority, law, or tribunal before which he must answer, but rather of the general law of right, the moral constitution of the universe; *responsible* may be said with reference to some specific authority, as the British government is said to be by a *responsible* ministry— *responsible,* that is, to the people through the parliament; we do not speak of an *accountable* or *answerable* ministry.

Amenable is almost exactly equivalent to *answerable,* but more rarely used, denoting subjection to authority or jurisdiction, so that one may be called to make formal answer. *Liable* signifies subject to some action or effect; as, metals are *liable* to be corroded by acids; hence *liable* refers to some legal obligation which may or may not come into exercise; one may be *liable* for the debts of another (who may, however, pay them himself); a person may be *liable* for damages (which no legal action may be taken to collect); because of this element of contingency, we do not say that a steward or agent is *liable* for the amount of his trust, but *accountable, answerable,* or *responsible.* In a derived sense, a *responsible* man, a *responsible* citizen is one able and ready to meet any reasonable responsibility, pecuniary or other, that may devolve upon him.

ANTONYMS: *absolute, arbitrary, free, irresponsible, lawless, supreme, unconditioned, uncontrolled, unfettered, unlimited, unrestrained.*

REST

calm	leisure	quiet	repose
calmness	peace	quietness	stillness
comfort	peacefulness	relaxation	tranquillity
ease			

Rest is the most general of the terms listed here, all of which denote freedom from toil or effort. *Rest* is a cessation of activity, and while it does not suggest any special way of passing time, it always implies recuperation from mental or physical fatigue as its aim or result. *Repose* is complete freedom from movement, either of the mind or of the body, and often specifically denotes the state of sleep. Hence its most common connotation is of the utter *relaxation* of mind and body that comes after a deep and refreshing sleep.

Relaxation is a loosening or releasing of mental or physical tension, and is brought about either by a complete cessation of activity or by a turning of one's efforts into channels of diversion or recreation. *Leisure* is freedom from the duties or labors of one's job or profession. It may apply to the time when one is not engaged in his daily work, or to a vacation period, or to the life of one who is not compelled to work for a living; as, he spent his *leisure* hours reading; she led a life of *leisure*.

Ease may imply exemption from all worries and disturbances, as well as from toil and activity. A life of *leisure* may be spent in doing whatever one is inclined to do, as in following a hobby; a life of *ease* is spent in doing nothing at all. *Peace, peacefulness,* and *tranquillity* suggest a settled composure and freedom from all annoyances and disturbances and agitations of any sort.

ANTONYMS: *agitation, commotion, disquiet, disturbance, excitement, motion, movement, restlessness; rush, stir, strain, toil, tumult, unrest, work.*

RESTIVE

balky	impatient	rebellious	skittish
fidgety	intractable	recalcitrant	stubborn
fractious	mulish	refractory	unruly
fretful	mutinous	resentful	vicious
frisky	obstinate	restless	

Balky, mulish, obstinate, and *stubborn* are synonyms of *restive* only in an infrequent use; the supposed sense of "tending to rest," "standing stubbornly still," is scarcely supported by any examples, and those cited to support that meaning often fail to do so. The disposition to offer active resistance to control by any means whatever is what is commonly indicated by *restive* in the best English speech and literature. A horse may be made *restless* by flies or by martial music, but with no refractoriness: the *restive* animal impatiently resists or struggles to break from control, as by bolting, flinging his rider, or otherwise. With this the metaphorical use of the word agrees, which is always in the sense of such terms as *impatient, intractable, rebellious,* and the like; a people *restive* under despotism are not disposed to "rest" under it, but to resist it and fling it off. *Fidgety* refers to nervous, *restless* movements; *frisky,* to lively, playful movements. *Skittish* can be lively, coy, or easily frightened; as a *skittish* woman, a *skittish* horse. *Unruly* is ungovernable.

ANTONYMS: *docile, gentle, manageable, obedient, passive, peaceable, quiet, submissive, tractable, yielding.*

RESTRAIN

abridge	constrain	hold in	keep under
arrest	curb	keep	repress
bridle	hinder	keep back	restrict
check	hold	keep down	suppress
circumscribe	hold back	keep in	withhold
confine			

To *restrain* is to *hold back* from acting, proceeding, or advancing, either by physical or moral force; it may carry the idea of control from excess, or it may carry the idea of complete prevention. *Constrain,* which is more of an antonym than a synonym, refers exclusively to a force arising either from outward circumstances or inner obligations. *Restrain* frequently refers to physical force, as when we speak of putting one under restraint. To *restrain* an action is to hold it partially or wholly in check, so that it is under pressure even while it acts; to *restrict* an action is to fix a limit or boundary which it may not pass, but within which it is free. To *repress,* literally to press back, is to hold in *check,* and perhaps only temporarily, that which is still very active; it is a feebler word than *restrain*; to *suppress* is finally and effectually to put down; *suppress* is a much stronger word than *restrain*; as, to *suppress* a rebellion.

To *abridge,* in this connection, is to reduce by restricting, as liberty or a privilege; to *arrest* means to interrupt some action in the process of being done. *Bridle* and *curb* are used figuratively to connote control as well as restraint; as, to *bridle* passion, *curb* appetites. To *circumscribe* implies encircling in order to *restrain.* When we *withhold* consent we *keep back* from giving it; when we *suppress* news we *withhold* it from publication. See **arrest.** Compare **bind; keep.**

ANTONYMS: *aid, animate, arouse, emancipate, encourage, excite, free, impel, incite, let loose, release, set free.*

RETIREMENT

loneliness	privacy	seclusion	solitude	withdrawal

In *retirement* one withdraws from association he has had with others; we speak of the *retirement* of a public man to private life, though he may still be much in company. In *seclusion* one shuts himself away from the society of all except intimate friends or attendants; in *solitude* no other person is present. While *seclusion* is ordinarily voluntary, *solitude* may be enforced; we speak of the *solitude* rather than the *seclusion* of a prisoner. As "private" denotes what concerns ourselves individually, *privacy* denotes freedom from the presence or observation of those not concerned or whom we desire not to have concerned in our affairs; *privacy* is more commonly temporary than *seclusion*; we speak of a moment's *privacy*. There may be *loneliness* without *solitude*, as amid an unsympathizing crowd, and *solitude* without *loneliness*, as when one is glad to be alone. *Withdrawal* is a voluntary *retirement*; a man's *withdrawal* from the world may be based on rebellion against society.

> **ANTONYMS:** *association, companionship, company, converse, fellowship, society.*

REVELATION

apocalypse	disclosure	manifestation	prophecy	vision

Revelation (from L. *re*, back, and *velum*, veil), literally an unveiling, is the act or process of making known what was before secret or hidden, or what may still be future. *Apocalypse* (from Gr. *apo*, from, and *kalypto*, cover), literally an uncovering, comes into English as the name of the closing book of the Bible, the *Revelation*. *Apocalypse* is also used to mean any writing that unveils the future, as if to the very gaze of the seer; the whole Gospel is a *disclosure* of the mercy of God; the character of Christ is a *manifestation* of the divine holiness and love; all Scripture is a *revelation* of the divine will. Or we might say that nature is a *manifestation* of the divine character and will, of which Scripture is the fuller and more express *revelation*.

A *vision* is something seen by the mind when either asleep or awake; it may be a supernatural representation of something not true or an inspired *revelation*. *Prophecy* in the Bible sense refers to the divine communications transmitted to the people by prophets; as these were often *revelations* or predictions, the word has come to mean any prediction.

> **ANTONYMS:** *cloud, cloudiness, concealment, hiding, mystery, obscuration, shrouding, veiling.*

REVENGE

avenging	reprisal	retaliation	vengeance
hatred	requital	retribution	

Revenge is the act of returning injury for injury vindictively, or the desire for *vengeance*. *Retaliation* returns like for like, not necessarily evil for evil.

Reprisal is an act of *retaliation* to force an opponent to amend his ways; often a seizure of goods or land as indemnity. *Hatred* which includes vindictiveness often desires *revenge*. *Retaliation* and *revenge* are personal and often bitter. *Retaliation* may be partial; *revenge* is meant to be complete, and may be excessive. *Vengeance,* which once meant an indignant vindication of justice, now signifies the most furious and unsparing *revenge,* the *avenging* of wrong by inflicting suffering equal to the injury.

A *requital* is strictly an even return, such as to quit one of obligation for what has been received, and even if poor and unworthy is given as complete and adequate. *Avenging* and *retribution* give a solemn sense of exact justice, *avenging* being more personal in its infliction, whether by God or man, and *retribution* the impersonal visitation of the doom of righteous law. See **hatred.** Compare **avenge; requite.**

> **ANTONYMS:** *compassion, excuse, forgiveness, grace, mercy, pardon, pity, reconciliation.*

> **PREPOSITIONS:** To take revenge *upon* the enemy, *for* the injury.

REVOLUTION

anarchy	insubordination	outbreak	riot
confusion	insurrection	Putsch	sedition
disintegration	lawlessness	rebellion	tumult
disorder	mutiny	revolt	uprising

The essential idea of *revolution* is a radical change in the form of government or constitution, or a change of rulers, otherwise than as provided by the laws of succession, election, etc.; while such change is apt to involve armed hostilities, these make no necessary part of the *revolution*. The *revolution* by which Dom Pedro was dethroned, and Brazil changed from an empire to a republic, was accomplished without a battle, and almost without a shot. *Anarchy* refers to the condition of a state when government is superseded or destroyed by factions or other causes. *Lawlessness* is a temper of mind or condition of the community which may result in *anarchy.*

Confusion, disorder, riot, and *tumult* are incidental and temporary outbreaks of *lawlessness,* but may not be *anarchy. Insubordination* is individual disobedience. *Sedition* is the plotting, *rebellion* the fighting, against the existing government, but always with the purpose of establishing some other government in its place. When *rebellion* is successful it is called *revolution;* but there may be *revolution* without *rebellion;* as, the English *Revolution* of 1688. A *revolt* is an *uprising* against existing authority without the comprehensive views of change in the form or administration of government that are involved in *revolution.*

Anarchy, when more than temporary *disorder,* is a proposed *disintegration* of society, in which it is imagined that social order might exist without government. Slaves may rise in mass and organize an *insurrection*; soldiers or sailors break out in *mutiny*; subject provinces rise in *revolt*. An *uprising* is a *revolt* against authority by a group of insurgents; a *Putsch* is a small, unsuccessful *uprising*. Compare **socialism.**

> ANTONYMS: *authority, command, control, domination, dominion, empire, government, law, loyalty, obedience, order, rule, sovereignty, submission, supremacy.*

REVOLVE

| circle | roll | spin | twirl | **wind** |
| gyrate | rotate | turn | whirl | |

To *revolve* is said of a body that moves in a curving path, as a circle or an ellipse, about a center outside of itself, so as to return periodically to the same relative position that it held at some previous time. A *revolving* body may also either *rotate* or *roll* at the same time; the earth *revolves* around the sun, and *rotates* on its own axis; in popular usage, the earth is often said to *revolve* about its own axis, or to have a daily "revolution," but *rotate* and "rotation" are the more accurate terms. A cylinder over which an endless belt is drawn is said to *roll* as regards the belt, though it *rotates* as regards its own axis.

Any round body *rolls* which continuously touches with successive portions of its surface successive portions of another surface; a wagon wheel *rolls* along the ground. To *rotate* is said of a body that has a circular motion or *circles* about its own center or axis. Any object that is in contact with or connected with a rolling body is often said to *roll*; as, the car *rolls* smoothly along the track. Objects whose motion approximates or suggests a rotary motion along a supporting surface are also said to *roll*; as, ocean waves *roll* in upon the shore, or the ship *rolls* in the trough of the sea.

Turn is a conversational and popular word often used vaguely for *rotate* or *revolve*, or for any motion about a fixed point, especially for a motion less than a complete "rotation" or "revolution"; a man *turns* his head or *turns* on his heel; the gate *turns* on its hinges. *Gyrate* is to *revolve* about a point or to have a spiral movement, as a tornado. To *twirl* is to *spin* something round, sometimes rapidly and with the fingers; to *whirl* is to *spin* round energetically and rapidly. *Wind* is to twine or be twined around a fixed object.

REWARD

amends	guerdon	recompense	requital
award	meed	remuneration	retribution
compensation	prize	reparation	satisfaction

Reward denotes something given in return for good or evil done or received. *Reward*, without any limiting word or phrase, is now commonly understood in the favorable sense of some desirable return for service rendered, as when a *reward* is offered for the return of lost property or the capture of a criminal; a *reward* may not be a material object, nor of value except to the recipient; a parent's grateful smile may be a child's sufficient *reward* for service rendered; a nation's gratitude may be a patriot's *reward*; an old and often repeated saying has described "virtue as its own *reward*."

A *prize* is a *reward* won in competition or contest. *Meed* and *guerdon* are somewhat archaic words, *guerdon* denoting a *reward* given as an honor or favor and *meed* a *reward* of merit. *Compensation, recompense,* and *remuneration* denote return recognized as adequate for something given or given up; these three words are especially used of return for service done or loss sustained; *recompense* and *remuneration* are personal, but *compensation* is extended to inanimate things, as the counterbalancing effects of physical or chemical forces, mechanical devices in machinery, etc.

Amends, reparation, and *satisfaction* are used specifically of some return that is designed to make good some loss sustained or injury suffered. *Requital* is an exact word, denoting complete and full return for either good or evil, and thus extending all the way from favor to retaliation or *retribution*. *Reward* is as wide in range as *requital*, but does not carry the same sense of full equivalence. *Retribution*, a word of high and solemn import, signifies the just *requital* of any act or course of moral wrong by the infliction of loss or suffering as a punishment. An *award* is both the decision, often judicial, that grants a *reward* and the *reward* itself. Compare **requite; revenge; subsidy.**

RHYTHM

| cadence | euphony | measure | meter | verse |

Rhythm, meter, and *measure* denote agreeable succession of sounds in the utterance of connected words; *euphony* may apply to a single word or even a single syllable; the other words apply to lines, sentences, paragraphs, etc.; *rhythm* and *meter* may be produced by accent only, as in English, or by accent and quantity combined, as in Greek or Italian; *rhythm* or *measure* may apply either to prose or to poetry, or to music, dancing, etc.; *meter* is more precise than *rhythm*, applies only to poetry and music, and denotes a measured *rhythm* with regular divisions into *verses*, stanzas, *measures*, etc.

Euphony is agreeable linguistic sound, however produced. A *verse* is strictly a metrical line, but the word is often used as synonymous with stanza. *Verse*, in the general sense, denotes metrical writing without reference to the thought involved; as, prose and *verse*. *Cadence* is a rhythmic flow and movement. We establish the *cadence* of a line of poetry by scanning, but the *rhythm* must be felt. *Cadence* is also used to determine uniform pace and time in marching. Compare **melody; poetry.**

RIDDLE

conundrum	mystery	problem
enigma	paradox	puzzle

A *riddle* is an ambiguous or paradoxical statement with a hidden meaning to be guessed by the mental acuteness of the one to whom it is proposed. *Conundrum*, a word of unknown origin, signifies some question or statement in which some hidden and fanciful resemblance is involved, the answer often depending upon a pun; an *enigma* is a dark saying, or one with a hidden meaning, clear only to one who understands the allusion or allusions therein; a *paradox* is a true statement that at first appears absurd or contradictory; a *problem* is something thrown out for solution; *puzzle* (from "oppose") referred originally to the intricate arguments by which disputants opposed each other in the old philosophic schools.

The *riddle* is not so petty as the *conundrum*, and may require much acuteness for its answer; a *problem* may require simply study and scholarship, as a *problem* in mathematics; a *puzzle* may be in something other than verbal statement, as a dissected map or any perplexing mechanical contrivance; the location of a missing object is often a *puzzle*. A *mystery* is something that is incomprehensible to human understanding.

ANTONYMS: *answer, axiom, explanation, proposition, solution.*

RIGHT *adj.*

appropriate	fitting	lawful	straight
correct	good	perpendicular	true
direct	honest	proper	unswerving
equitable	just	rightful	upright
fair			

Right implies done in accordance with or conformable to the moral law or to a standard of rightness; conformable to truth. We say, "He did the *right* thing," or "Those deductions are not *right*." A *correct* statement contains no errors; an *equitable* claim is *just* and *fair* to all. *Appropriate, fitting,* and *proper* refer to the *right* thing in the *right* place. *Perpendicular* lines are at *right* angles; one stands *upright* on the other. *Upright* in the figurative sense implies strictly *honest,* honorable. The *rightful* owner is *lawfully* entitled to his possessions. An *unswerving* course does not diverge from a *straight* direction. Compare **innocent; precise.**

ANTONYMS: *bad, crooked, evil, false, improper, incorrect, indirect, iniquitous, unfair, unjust, unrighteous, wrong.*

RIGHT *noun*

birthright	franchise	license	prerogative
claim	immunity	perquisite	privilege
exemption	liberty		

A *right* is that which one may properly demand or claim as just, moral, or legal, that to which one is entitled. A *right* may be either general or special, natural or artificial. "Life, liberty, and the pursuit of happiness" are the natural and inalienable *rights* of all men; *rights* of property, inheritance, etc., are individual and special, and often artificial, as the *right* of inheritance by primogeniture. A *privilege* is always special, exceptional, and artificial; it is something not enjoyed by all, or only to be enjoyed on certain special conditions, a peculiar benefit, favor, advantage, etc.

A *privilege* may be of doing or avoiding; in the latter case it is an *exemption* or *immunity*; we say a *privilege* of hunting or fishing; *exemption* from military service; *immunity* from arrest. A *franchise* is a specific *right* or *privilege* granted by the government or established as such by governmental authority; as, the elective *franchise*; a railroad *franchise*. A *prerogative* is an official *right* or *privilege*; in a wider sense it is an exclusive and peculiar *privilege* which one possesses by reason of being what he is; as, reason is the *prerogative* of man; kings and nobles have often claimed *prerogatives* and *privileges* opposed to the inherent *rights* of the people. *Perquisite* refers to a *privilege*, benefit, or profit considered as a *right* in addition to salary. *Birthright*, originally applying to possessions and lands only, connotes all to which one is entitled by *right* of birth, descent, or nationality. Compare **duty; justice.**

RISE

arise	emanate	issue	spring
ascend	flow	proceed	

To *rise* is to move up or upward whether slowly or quickly, whether through the least or greatest distance; the waves *rise*; the mists *rise*; the river *rises* after heavy rains; as said of persons, to *rise* is to come to an erect position after kneeling, sitting, reclining, or lying down; as, to *rise* from a sickbed; my friend *rose* as I entered; the guests *rose* to depart; so a deliberate assembly or a committee is said to *rise* when it breaks up a session; a sun or star *rises* when to our apprehension it comes above the horizon and begins to go up the sky. To *ascend* is to go far upward, and is often used in a stately sense; as, Christ *ascended* to heaven.

The shorter form *rise* is now generally preferred to the longer form *arise*, except in poetic or elevated style, or to stress the cause; as, the mistakes *arise* from blurred typing. The sun *rises*; the river *springs* from the foot of the glacier and *flows* through the lands to the ocean. Smoke *issues* from a chimney and *ascends* toward the sky. Light and heat *emanate* from the sun; *proceed* carries the idea of the source from which something *arises* "Laughter, *proceeding* from slight cause, is folly," CERVANTES.

> **ANTONYMS:** *decline, descend, drop, fall, go down, set, settle, sink.*

> **PREPOSITIONS:** Rise *from* slumber; rise *to* duty; rise *at* the summons; we rose *with* the lark.

ROBBER

bandit	depredator	freebooter	pirate
brigand	despoiler	highwayman	plunderer
buccaneer	footpad	marauder	raider
burglar	forager	pillager	thief

A *robber* seeks to obtain the property of others by force or intimidation; a *thief*, by stealth and secrecy. A *burglar*, in legal use, is one who break and enters the house of another, usually at night, with felonious intent. A *brigand*, formerly an armed soldier who plundered, now connotes a person who robs travelers, also anyone who robs defenseless people; a *bandit* generally belongs to a band of outlaws; a *pirate* is a sea-robber; *buccaneer* applies especially to the *pirate* bands who formerly infested the Spanish-American coasts. *Depredator* connotes anyone who robs or plunders; *despoilers* and *pillagers* use force and usually strip their victims of all belongings. *Highwaymen* and *footpads* rob on the highways, the former on horseback. A *freebooter* is an adventurous *robber*; a *forager* seeks or commands food for horses and cattle. *Raiders* and *marauders* rove about and invade districts to rob and plunder.

ROYAL

august	kingly	majestic	princely
imperial	magnificent	munificent	regal
kinglike			

Royal denotes that which actually belongs or pertains to a monarch, but does not necessarily imply splendor or magnificence; the *royal* residence is that which the king occupies, *royal* raiment that which the king wears. *Regal* denotes that which in outward state is appropriate for a king; a subject may assume *regal* magnificence in residence, dress, and equipage. *Kingly* denotes that which is worthy of a king in personal qualities, especially of character and conduct; as, a *kingly* bearing; a *kingly* resolve. *Princely* applies to the ruler of a principality, the eldest son of a king or emperor, or to any male member of a reigning family; in extended use, *princely* is especially used of treasure, expenditure, gifts, etc , as *princely* munificence, a *princely* fortune, where *regal* could not so well be used and *royal* would change the subject. The distinctions between these words are not absolute, but the tendency of the best usage is as here suggested.

Imperial is applied to a monarch who is called an emperor or an empress. In its extended use, *imperial* connotes a more awe-inspiring quality than *kingly*, a more magnificent appearance than *regal* or *royal*; as, an *imperial* mien; an *imperial* palace.

> ANTONYMS: *beggarly, contemptible, mean, poor, servile, slavish, vile.*

RUSTIC

agricultural	clownish	outlandish	uncouth
Arcadian	coarse	pastoral	unpolished
artless	countrified	plain	unsophisticated
awkward	country	rude	untaught
boorish	hoydenish	rural	verdant
bucolic	inelegant	sylvan	

Rural and *rustic* are alike derived from the Latin *rus*, country, and may be alike defined as pertaining to, characteristic of, or dwelling in the country; but in usage *rural* refers especially to scenes or objects in the country, considered as the work of nature; *rustic* refers to their effect upon man or to their condition as effected by human agency; as, a *rural* scene; a *rustic* lass. We speak, however, of the *rural* population, *rural* simplicity, etc. *Rustic* often implies a contrast between the crudities of the country and the refinements of the city. *Rural* has always a favorable sense; *rustic*, frequently an unfavorable one, or one denoting a lack of culture and refinement, as suggested by a *rustic* feast, *rustic* garb, etc. *Rustic* is, however, often used of a studied simplicity, an artistic rudeness, which is pleasing and perhaps beautiful; as, a *rustic* cottage; a *rustic* chair. *Pastoral* refers to the care of flocks, and to the shepherd's life with the pleasing associations suggested by the old poetic ideal of that life; as, *pastoral* poetry. *Bucolic* is kindred to *pastoral*, but is a less elevated term, and sometimes slightly contemptuous, often implying boorishness. *Arcadian*, with a greater literary flavor than *pastoral*, refers to any region of ideal *rustic* simplicity and contentment.

> ANTONYMS: *accomplished, citylike, cultured, elegant, polished, polite, refined, urban, urbane, well-bred.*

S

SACRAMENT

ceremony	Lord's Supper	ordinance	service
communion	observance	rite	solemnity
eucharist			

The terms *sacrament* and *ordinance*, in the religious sense, are often used interchangeably; the *ordinance* derives its sacredness from the authority that ordained it, while the *sacrament* possesses a sacredness due to something in itself, even when viewed simply as a representation or memorial. The *Lord's Supper* is the Scriptural name for the *observance* commemorating the death of Christ; the word *communion* is once applied to it (*1 Cor.* x, 16), but not as a distinctive name; at an early period, however, the name *communion* was so applied, as denoting the communing of Christians with their Lord, or with one another. The term *eucharist* describes the *Lord's Supper* as a thanksgiving *service*; it is also called by preeminence *the sacrament*, as the ratifying of a solemn vow of consecration to Christ.

Any religious act, especially a public act, viewed as a means of serving God is called a *service*; the word commonly includes the entire series of exercises of a single occasion of public worship. A religious *service* ordained as an outward and visible sign of an inward and spiritual grace is called a *sacrament*. *Ceremony* is a form expressing reverence, or at least respect; we may speak of religious *ceremonies*, the *ceremonies* of polite society, the *ceremonies* of a coronation, an inauguration, etc. An *observance* has more than a formal obligation, reaching or approaching a religious sacredness; a stated religious *observance*, viewed as established by authority, is called an *ordinance*; viewed as an established custom, it is a *rite*.

SAD

afflicted	distressed	grave	somber
dejected	distressing	heavy	sorrowful
depressed	doleful	lugubrious	sorry
desolate	downcast	melancholy	unhappy
despondent	dreary	miserable	woebegone
disconsolate	dull	mournful	woeful
dismal	gloomy	sober	

Sad, melancholy, unhappy, and many similar words may be used either of the personal experience of grief, sorrow, mental depression, etc., or of that which causes grief or pain; a person is *sad* on account of a *sad* event. A *distressing* experience causes pain or suffering; a *distressed* nation is suffering and *miserable*, and excites pity; an *afflicted* person is mentally or physically *distressed*. *Dejected, depressed,* and *downcast* refer to a state of discouragement, or to disheartened spirits; *melancholy, mournful,* and *doleful* stress sorrow rather than pain. When *desolate* implies forlorn or forsaken, it can be used of places as well as persons; but when it connotes *afflicted* it refers to a mental condition. We speak of a *dreary* outlook, *somber* tints, *dismal* surroundings, a *gloomy* man, a *dull* day, a *lugubrious* sight, and these synonyms all refer to the depressing lack of light or brightness. *Sober,* in this comparison implies subdued or *sad* in color.

ANTONYMS: See synonyms for **happy.**

SAGACIOUS

able	intelligent	perspicacious	sensible
acute	judicious	quick of scent	sharp
apt	keen	quick-scented	sharp-witted
clear-sighted	keen-sighted	rational	shrewd
discerning	keen-witted	sage	wise

Sagacious refers to a power of tracing the hidden or recondite by slight indications; the word was formerly applied to mere keenness of sense perception, as of a hound in following a trail. *Sagacious* is now restricted to acuteness of mental discernment, or to a swift certainty of judgment, or to a readiness to foresee the results of any action, especially upon human motives or conduct—a kind of prophetic common sense. *Sagacious* is a broader and nobler word than *shrewd,* and not capable of the invidious sense which the latter word often bears; on the other hand, *sagacious* is less lofty and comprehensive than *wise* in its full sense, and more limited to matters of direct practical moment. *Perspicacious* originally referred to sight, and signified unusually *keen-sighted;* in modern use it refers to mental insight. A person who is able to see through and comprehend that which is dark or obscure is called *perspicacious.* Compare **shrewd; wisdom.**

ANTONYMS: *absurd, dull, foolish, futile, ignorant, irrational, obtuse, senseless, silly, simple, sottish, stupid, undiscerning, unintelligent.*

SAILOR

bluejacket	mariner	seafaring man	tar
marine	seafarer	seaman	

In nautical language *sailors* and *seamen* are exclusive of officers, but in literary use all whose vocation is navigation are figuratively termed *sailors* or *seamen. Mariner* is a poetic and also a legal term for any *seafaring man;* in the United States statutes *mariner* denotes any person, from captain to cook, who is engaged in the merchant service. A *bluejacket* denotes an enlisted man in the United States or British Navy; a *marine* is a soldier who serves either at sea or on shore; a *tar* is a familiar name for a *sailor* and is often used in poetry.

ANTONYM: *landsman.*

SALE

bargain	change	exchange
barter	deal	trade

Sale is commonly, and with increasing strictness, limited to the transfer of property for money, or for something estimated at a money value or considered as equivalent to so much money in hand or to be paid. A *deal* in the political sense is a *bargain,* substitution, or transfer for the benefit of certain persons or parties against all others; as, the nomination was the result of a *deal;* in business it may have a similar meaning, but it frequently signifies simply a *sale* or *exchange,* a dealing; as, a heavy *deal* in stocks.

A *bargain* is strictly an agreement or contract to buy and sell, though the word is often used to denote the entire transaction and also as a designation for the thing sold or purchased. *Change* and *exchange* are words of wider signification, applying only incidentally to the transfer of property or value; a *change* secures something different in any way or by any means; an *exchange* secures something as an equivalent or return, though not necessarily as payment for what is given. *Barter* is the *exchange* of one commodity for another, the word being used generally with reference to portable commodities.

Trade in the broad sense may apply to vast businesses (as the book *trade*), but as denoting a single transaction is used chiefly in regard to things of moderate value, when it becomes nearly synonymous with *barter.*

SAMPLE

case	exemplification	instance
example	illustration	specimen

A *sample* is a portion taken at random out of a quantity supposed to be homogeneous, so that the qualities found in the *sample* may reasonably be expected to be found in the whole; as, a *sample* of sugar, a *sample* of cloth. A *specimen* is one unit of a series, or a fragment of a mass, all of which is supposed to possess the same essential qualities; as, a *specimen* of coinage, or of architecture, or a *specimen* of quartz. No other unit or portion may be exactly like the *specimen,* while all the rest is supposed to be exactly like the *sample.* An *instance* is a person or thing offered to prove or disprove a statement; as, he cited several *instances* of John's faithlessness. Compare **example.**

ANTONYMS: *abnormality, aggregate, exception, monstrosity, total, whole.*

SANGUINARY

bloodthirsty	cruel	inhuman	sanguine
bloody	gory	murderous	savage

Sanguinary applies either to the act of shedding blood or to the spirit that delights in bloodshed; *bloody* applies more directly to the actual staining with blood; we may say either a *sanguinary* or a *bloody* battle, but a *bloody* (not a *sanguinary*) field; we speak of a *sanguinary* rather than of a *bloody* threat, disposition, etc. *Sanguine* is sometimes used in poetic or elevated style in the sense of *bloody*; as, a *sanguine* stain; but, as it originally referred to qualities or temperament supposedly arising from an active blood stream, it more generally refers to a light-hearted or optimistic disposition. *Inhuman* applies to conduct and persons unlike human beings; hence, *cruel*. *Murderous* implies loving, causing, or planning murder or bloodshed; as, a *murderous* attack. *Gory* refers to a blood-stained, *bloody* state or condition; as, his hair was a *gory* mass but the injury was not great. *Savage* and *bloodthirsty* animals and men are *cruel*, and eager and prone to shed blood.

SATISFY

cloy	glut	sate	suffice
content	pall	satiate	surfeit
fill			

To *satisfy* is to furnish enough to meet physical, mental, or spiritual desire. To *sate* or *satiate* is to gratify desire so fully as for a time to extinguish it. To *cloy* or *surfeit* is to gratify to the point of revulsion or disgust. *Glut* is a strong but somewhat coarse word applied to the utmost filling of vehement appetites and passions; as, to *glut* a vengeful spirit with slaughter; we speak of *glutting* the market with a supply so excessive as to extinguish the demand. Much less than is needed to *satisfy* may *suffice* a frugal or abstemious person; less than a sufficiency may *content* one of a patient and submissive spirit. *Pall* is identical in meaning with *cloy* in so far as it denotes satisfaction of one's desires to the point at which one loses all interest in that with which one is *surfeited*; it is used chiefly of things which tend to *satiate*, rather than of people whose appetites or desires are *sated*. Compare **pay; requite.**

> **ANTONYMS:** *check, deny, disappoint, refuse, restrain, restrict, starve, stint, straiten, tantalize.*

> **PREPOSITIONS:** Satisfy *with* food, *with* gifts, etc., satisfy one (in the sense of make satisfaction) *for* labors and sacrifices; satisfy oneself *by* or *upon* inquiry.

SCHOLAR

disciple	learner	pupfl	student
fellow	pedant	savant	

The primary sense of a *scholar* is one who is being schooled; thence the word passes to denote one who is apt in school work, and finally one who is thoroughly schooled, master of what the schools can teach, an erudite, accomplished person; when used without qualification, the word is generally understood in this latter sense; as, he is manifestly a *scholar*. *Scholar* is also specifically applied to the recipient of a sum of money (a scholarship) to aid him in the pursuit of his studies at a college or university; as, the Rhodes *scholars* at Oxford. In this sense, *fellow*, denoting the recipient of a fellowship, is closely allied to *scholar*; the difference lies in the fact that scholarships are granted for undergraduate, fellowships for graduate study.

Pupil signifies one under the close personal supervision or instruction of a teacher or tutor. Those under instruction in schools below the academic grade are technically and officially termed *pupils*. The word *pupil* is uniformly so used in the Reports of the Commissioner of Education of the United States, but popular American usage prefers *scholar* in the original sense; as, teachers and *scholars* enjoyed a holiday. Those under instruction in Sunday schools are uniformly designated as Sunday-school *scholars*. *Student* is applied to those in the higher grades or courses of study, as the academic, collegiate, scientific, etc. *Student* suggests less proficiency than *scholar* in the highest sense, the *student* being one who is learning, the *scholar* one who has learned. On the other hand, *student* suggests less of personal supervision than *pupil*; thus, the college *student* often becomes the private *pupil* of some instructor in special studies. A *disciple* is one who follows devotedly the teachings of his master. A *pedant* insists on strict adherence to details, and makes a needless display of his learning. A *savant* is a man of learning.

ANTONYMS: *dunce, fool, idiot, idler, ignoramus, illiterate person.*

SCIENCE

erudition	knowledge	learning	lore

Knowledge of a single fact, not known as related to any other, or of many facts not known as having any mutual relations or as comprehended under any general law, does not reach the meaning of *science*; *science* is *knowledge* reduced to law and embodied in system. Any great body of *knowledge* or collection of facts, amassed by observation and experiment, and tested for adherence to some general truth or law, is called a *science*. Man's accumulated knowledge of the behavior of the physical world comprises the *science* of physics. *Learning* is *knowledge* learned, attained by much reading or other investigation. *Erudition* is bookishness. *Lore*, apart from its poetic usage, is used of particularized knowledge; we speak of the *lore* of the hunter, plant *lore*, etc.; it also applies to all the age-old traditional *knowledge* accumulated by a specific group; as, folk*lore*. See **knowledge, literature.**

SECURE

assured	defended	protected	undisturbed
carelesss	guarded	safe	unmolested
certain	impregnable	sure	unsuspecting
confident	insured	unassailable	untroubled

Secure is *guarded* against, or not likely to be exposed to, danger; free from fear, apprehension, etc. *Safe* implies that a danger has been passed through or is no longer to be feared; as, *safe* in the harbor, a *safe* place. An *assured* position is unquestioned and one from which a person is not likely to be ousted; an *impregnable* position is *safe* because it is not vulnerable to attack; it is *unassailable*. *Confident* refers to freedom from fear and usually implies belief in oneself or in what one can do. *Untroubled, unmolested,* and *undisturbed* stress freedom from outside interference, either mental or physical. *Unsuspecting* implies freedom from misgivings, or from suspicion that danger may be near. *Sure* is one of the strongest of these words and connotes the freedom from fear or uncertainty that comes from self-confidence and conviction. *Certain* is even stronger, and indicates absolutely convinced, *sure* to happen; as, he is *certain* that the report is true; rain is *certain* before nightfall.

ANTONYMS: *dangerous, dubious, exposed, hazardous, imperfect, insecure, perilous, risky.*

PREPOSITIONS: Secure *of* advantage; secure *from* loss; secure *in* the fastness; secure *against* attack.

SECURITY

bail	earnest	guarantee	pledge
bond	gage	guaranty	surety

Most of these words agree in denoting something given or deposited as an assurance of something to be given, paid, or done. *Security* may be of real or personal property—anything of sufficient value to make the creditor secure; a *pledge* is always of personal property or chattels. Every pawnshop contains unredeemed *pledges*; land, merchandise, bonds, etc., are frequently offered and accepted as *security*. An *earnest* is of the same kind as that to be given, a portion of it delivered in advance, as when part of the purchase-money is paid, according to the common expression, "to bind the bargain." A *pledge* or *security* may be wholly different in kind from that to be given or paid, and may greatly exceed it in value.

A person may become *security* or *surety* for another's payment of a debt, appearance in court, etc.; in the latter case, he is said to become *bail* for that person; the person accused gives *bail* for himself. *Gage* survives only as a literary word, chiefly in certain phrases; as, "the *gage* of battle." *Guaranty,* in this comparison, refers to that which is given or received to secure the pay-

ment of a debt or the performance of an obligation; also the guarantor, if he
is himself this *security*, is called the *guaranty*. *Guarantee* is the obligation of
the guarantor, and also the person to whom a *guaranty* is given: in this sense
the correlative of guarantor. *Bond* here implies either a *surety* or *bail*, or
the legal papers that constitute the *pledge*.

> **PREPOSITIONS:** Security *for* the payment of a debt; security
> *to* the state, *for* the prisoner, *in* the sum of a thousand dollars.

SEND

cast	discharge	emit	impel	propel
dart	dismiss	fling	lance	sling
delegate	dispatch	forward	launch	throw
depute	drive	hurl	project	transmit

To *send* is to cause to go or pass from one place to another, and always in
fact or thought away from the agent or agency that controls the act. *Send* in
its most common use involves personal agency without personal presence;
according to the adage, "If you want your business done, go; if not, *send*";
one *sends* a letter or a bullet, a messenger or a message. In all the derived
uses this same idea controls; if one *sends* a ball into his own heart, the action
is away from the directing hand. In an approach to personification we speak
of the bow *sending* the arrow, or the gun the shot.

To *dispatch* is to *send* hastily or very promptly, ordinarily with a destination in view; to *dismiss* is to *send* away from oneself without reference to a
destination; as, to *dismiss* a clerk, an application, or an annoying subject. To
discharge is to *send* away so as to relieve a person or thing of a load; we *discharge* a gun or *discharge* the contents; as applied to persons, *discharge* is a
harsher term than *dismiss*.

To *emit* is to *send* forth from within, with no reference to a destination; as
the sun *emits* light and heat. *Transmit*, from the Latin, is a dignified term,
often less vigorous than the Saxon *send*, but preferable at times in literary or
scientific use; as, to *transmit* the crown, or the feud, from generation to generation; to *transmit* a charge of electricity. *Transmit* fixes the attention more
on the intervening agency; *send* fixes it on the points of departure and
destination.

Cast, fling, hurl, and *sling* imply different ways of *throwing*; we *cast* a
store or a net; *fling* a door open or *fling* ourselves down; *hurl* a stick or an
epithet; *sling* or *hurl* a snowball. We *depute* or *delegate* someone by *sending*
him as a representative or substitute to act for us. A vessel is *launched* when
it is set afloat; an enterprise or a person is *launched, sent* off, or started; and
we *launch* imprecations as well as darts. Steam *propels* or *drives* a vessel
forward. To *project* is to *throw* forward; to *lance* is a poetic term for *fling*.

ANTONYMS: *bring, carry, convey, get, give, hand, hold, keep, receive, retain.*

PREPOSITIONS: To send *from* the hand *to* or *toward* (rarely *at*) a mark; send *to* a friend *by* a messenger or *by* mail; send a person *into* banishment; send a shell *among* the enemy.

SENSATION

emotion   feeling   image   percept   perception   sense

Sensation is the mind's consciousness due to a bodily affection, as of heat or cold; *perception* is the recognition of some external object which is the cause or occasion of the *sensation*; the *sensation* of heat may be connected with the *perception* of a fire. While *sensations* are connected with the body, *emotions*, as joy, grief, etc., are wholly of the mind. *Sensation* is the physical impression received from any outside stimulus, sometimes entering consciousness, sometimes not; technically it is the reaction between any organ of *sense* (eye, ear, nose, taste organs, tactile nerves, etc.) and the physical world; we have *sensations* of heat, cold, roughness, smoothness, pain, smells, tastes, etc.; when such a *sensation* enters consciousness to the point that the object producing the *sensation* is recognized, it is called a *percept.* When a child burns his finger and recognizes fire as the source, he has had a *percept.* The *sensation* that enters consciousness to the point beyond recognition (which is representation plus memory) is called an *image.* An *image* can be called up out of memory at will although the *sensation* will not be experienced without repetition of the physical stimulus. *Feeling* is a general term popularly denoting what is felt, whether through the body or by the mind alone, a full consciousness that includes both *sensation* and *emotion.* Compare **sensibility.**

SENSIBILITY

feeling   impressibility   sensitiveness   susceptibility

Sensibility, in the philosophical sense, denotes the capacity of emotion or *feeling,* as distinguished from the intellect and the will. In popular use *sensibility* denotes sometimes capacity of *feeling* of any kind; as, *sensibility* to heat or cold; sometimes, a peculiar readiness to be the subject of *feeling,* especially of the higher *feelings*; as, the *sensibility* of the artist or the poet; a person of great or fine *sensibility.* *Sensitiveness* denotes a special delicacy of *sensibility,* ready to be excited by the slightest cause, as displayed, for instance, in the "sensitive-plant."

Susceptibility is rather a capacity to take up, receive, and, as it were, to contain feeling, so that a person of great *susceptibility* is capable of being not only readily but deeply moved; *sensitiveness* is more superficial, *susceptibility* more pervading. Thus, in physics, the *sensitiveness* of a magnetic needle is the ease with which it may be deflected, as by another magnet; its *susceptibility* is the degree to which it can be magnetized by a given magnetic force or the amount of magnetism it will hold. So a person of great *sensitiveness* is quickly and keenly affected by any external influence, as by music, pathos, or ridicule, while a person of great *susceptibility* is not only touched, but moved to his inmost soul. Compare **sensation.**

> **ANTONYMS:** *coldness, deadness, hardness, insensibility, numbness, unconsciousness.*
>
> **PREPOSITIONS:** The sensibility *of* the organism *to* atmospheric changes.

SERIOUS

dangerous	grave	momentous	solemn
demure	great	sedate	staid
earnest	important	sober	

Serious connotes that which is of great concern to someone or something and that cannot be trifled with, and always includes gravity in one sense or another. *Demure, sedate, staid,* and *sober* refer to seriousness and modesty in manner or speech; *sedate* emphasizes composure, *demure* sometimes implies affected modesty, sometimes coyness; *staid* includes primness; *sober* emphasizes the seriousness of an aim or purpose. *Grave* applies to situations as well as to people; we speak of *grave* difficulties or of a *grave* look. *Momentous* is of great importance or weight, very important; as, a *momentous* decision. *Earnest* undertakings require *serious* consideration; an *earnest* person is intent on a purpose. *Solemn* is characterized by *serious* thought and is often awe-inspiring. A *serious* person is *demure, sedate, sober, solemn*; a *serious* purpose is *earnest*; a *serious* illness is *dangerous*; a *serious* business is *important,* and may be *momentous.* Compare **important.**

> **ANTONYMS:** *careless, gay, insignificant, jocose, jolly, light, slight, thoughtless, trifling, trivial, volatile.*

SEVERE

austere	inflexible	stern	unmitigated
hard	relentless	stiff	unrelenting
harsh	rigid	strict	unyielding
inexorable	rigorous	uncompromising	

That is *severe* which is devoid of all softness, mildness, tenderness, indulgence, or levity, or (in literature and art) devoid of unnecessary ornament, amplification, or embellishment of any kind; as, a *severe* style; as said of anything painful, *severe* signifies such as heavily taxes endurance or resisting power; as, a *severe* pain, fever, or winter. *Rigid* signifies primarily *stiff*, resisting any effort to change its shape; a corpse is said to be *rigid* in death; hence, in metaphorical sense, a *rigid* person or character is one that resists all efforts to change the will or course of conduct; a *rigid* rule or statement is one that admits of no deviation. *Rigorous* is nearly akin to *rigid*, but is a stronger word, having reference to action or active qualities, as *rigid* has to state or character; a *rigid* rule may be *rigorously* enforced.

Strict (from L. *stringo*, bind) signifies bound or stretched tight, tense, strenuously exact. *Stern* unites harshness and authority with strictness or severity; *stern*, as said even of inanimate objects, suggests something authoritative or forbidding. *Austere* signifies severely simple or temperate, *strict* in self-restraint or discipline, and similarly *unrelenting* toward others. We speak of *austere* morality, *rigid* rules, *rigorous* discipline, *stern* commands, *severe* punishment, *harsh* speech or a *harsh* voice, *hard* requirements, *strict* injunctions, and *strict* obedience. *Strict* discipline holds one exactly and unflinchingly to the rule; *rigorous* discipline punishes severely any infraction of it. The *austere* character is seldom lovely, but it is always strong and may be grand, commanding, and estimable.

Inexorable, inflexible, relentless, unrelenting, and *unyielding,* all refer to refusal to give way; *inexorable* implies not to be moved by entreaty or prayer; *inflexible* is unbendable, that cannot be modified; a *relentless* person refuses to yield to compassion; *unrelenting* and *unyielding* imply refusal to surrender or yield a position or point. *Unmitigated* means unmodified and unsoftened in any way.

> **ANTONYMS:** *affable, bland, easy, genial, gentle, indulgent, lenient, mild, pliable, soft, sweet, tender, tractable, yielding.*

SHAKE

agitate	jolt	reel	thrill
brandish	jounce	rock	totter
flap	oscillate	shiver	tremble
fluctuate	quake	shudder	vibrate
flutter	quaver	sway	wave
jar	quiver	swing	waver
joggle			

A thing is *shaken* which is subjected to short and abruptly checked movements, as forward and backward, up and down, from side to side, etc. A tree is *"shaken* with a mighty wind"; a man slowly *shakes* his head. A thing *rocks* that is sustained from below; it *swings* if suspended from above, as a pendulum, or pivoted at the side, as a crane or a bridge-draw; to *oscillate* is to *swing* with a smooth and regular returning motion. A *vibrating* motion may be tremulous or *jarring*. The pendulum of a clock may be said to *swing*, *vibrate*, or *oscillate*; a steel bridge *vibrates* under the passage of a heavy train; the term *vibrate* is also applied to molecular movements. To *jolt* is to move with jerky risings and fallings upon an unyielding surface; as, a carriage *jolts* over a rough road. A motion that *jars* is abruptly and very rapidly repeated through an exceedingly limited space; the *jolting* of the carriage *jars* the windows. To *rattle* refers directly to the sound produced by *shaking*; as, to *rattle* the handle of the door. To *joggle* is to *shake* slightly; as, a passing toucl *joggles* the desk on which one is writing.

A thing *trembles* that *shakes* perceptibly and with an appearance of uncertainty and instability, as a person under the influence of fear; a thing *shivers* when all its particles are stirred with a slight but pervading tremulous motion, as a human body under the influence of cold; to *shudder* applies to a more pronounced movement of a similar kind, in human beings often the effect of emotional or moral recoil; hence the word is used even when there is no such outward manifestation; as, one says, "I *shudder* at the thought."

To *quiver* is to have slight and often spasmodic contractile motions, as the flesh under the surgeon's knife. *Thrill* is applied to a pervasive movement felt rather than seen; as, the nerves *thrill* with delight; *quiver* is similarly used, but suggests somewhat more of outward manifestation. To *agitate* in its literal use is nearly the same as to *shake*, though we speak of the sea as *agitated* when we could not say it is *shaken*; the Latin *agitate* is preferred in scientific or technical use to the Saxon *shake*, and especially as applied to the action of mechanical contrivances; in the metaphorical use *agitate* is more transitory and superficial, *shake* more fundamental and enduring; a person's feelings are *agitated* by distressing news; his courage, his faith, his credit, or his testimony is *shaken*.

Sway applies to the movement of a body suspended from above or not firmly sustained from below, and the motion of which is less pronounced than *swinging*, smoother than *vibrating*, and not necessarily constant as *oscillating*; as, a reed *sways* in the wind. *Sway* used transitively especially applies to motions of grace or dignity; *brandish* denotes a threatening or hostile motion; *wave* is to move to and fro in the air; a monarch *sways* the scepter; the ruffian *brandishes* a club; the child *waves* a flag. To *reel* or *totter* always implies liability to fall; *reeling* is more violent than *swaying*, *tottering* more irregular; a drunken man *reels*; a child or an old man *totters*.

An extended mass which seems to lack solidity or cohesion is said to *quake*; as, a bog *quakes* when trodden on. A violent internal convulsion causes the earth to *quake*. *Quaver* is applied almost exclusively to tremulous sounds of the human voice. *Flap, flutter,* and *fluctuate* refer to wavelike movements, *flap* generally to such as produce a sharp sound; a cock *flaps* his wings; *flutter* applies to a less pronounced and more irregular motion; a captive bird or a feeble pulse *flutters*. To *waver*, in this comparison, is to falter, become ansteady; as, the ranks *wavered*. Compare **fluctuate.**

SHELTER

cover	guard	protect	shield
defend	harbor	screen	ward

To *shelter* is to *cover* so as to *protect* from injury or annoyance; as, the roof *shelters* from the storm; woods *shelter* from the heat. To *defend* implies the actual, *protect* implies the possible use of force or resisting power; *guard* implies sustained vigilance with readiness for conflict; we *defend* a person or thing against actual attack; we *guard* or *protect* against possible assault or injury. A powerful person may *protect* one who is weak by simply declaring himself his friend; he *defends* him by some form of active championship. An inanimate object may *protect*, as a garment from cold; *defend* is used but rarely in such connection. *Protect* is more complete than *guard* or *defend*; an object may be faithfully *guarded* or bravely *defended* in vain, but that which is *protected* is secure.

To *cover* is to extend completely over; a vessel is *covered* with a lid; a house is *covered* with a roof. That which *covers* may also *defend* or *protect*; thus, troops interposed between some portion of their own army and the enemy are often called a *covering* party. To *shield* is to interpose something over or in front of that which is assailed, so as to save from harm. One may *guard* another by standing armed at his side, *defend* him by fighting for him, or *shield* him from a missile or a blow by interposing his own person. *Harbor* is generally used in an unfavorable sense; confederates or sympathizers *harbor* a criminal; a person *harbors* evil thoughts or designs. *Ward* is to *protect* or to *defend* against a blow; *screen* is to *shelter* or *protect* as with a partition or curtain. See **cherish.** Compare **defense; hide.**

> **ANTONYMS:** *betray, cast out, expel, expose, give up, refuse, reject, surrender.*

> **PREPOSITIONS:** Shelter *under* a roof *from* the storm, *in* the fortress, *behind* or *within* the walls, *from* attack.

SHREWD

acute	cunning	knowing	sagacious
artful	discerning	penetrating	sharp
astute	discriminating	penetrative	subtile
clear-sighted	keen	perspicacious	subtle
crafty			

Shrewd means *keen* in perception and judgment, with the implications of inherent cleverness, the ability to penetrate beyond superficial appearances, and a hard-headed practicality in business affairs. One has a *shrewd* wit, makes a *shrewd* remark, or drives a *shrewd* bargain. An *astute* person is not merely *shrewd* but is extremely hard to deceive, especially in matters concerning himself. The *astute* debater leads his opponents into a snare by getting them to make admissions, or urge arguments, of which he sees a result that they do not perceive. *Perspicacious* originally meant very sharp-sighted, and is now used to denote *keen* mental sight. A *perspicacious* reader can see through and understand an obscure or difficult poem.

A *knowing* look, air, etc., in general indicates practical knowledge with a touch of shrewdness, and perhaps of cunning; in regard to some special matter, it indicates the possession of reserved knowledge which the person could impart if he chose. *Knowing* has often a slightly invidious sense. We speak of a *knowing* rascal, meaning *cunning* or *shrewd* within a narrow range, but of a *knowing* horse or dog, in the sense of *sagacious*, implying that he knows more than could be expected of such an animal. A *knowing* child has more knowledge than would be looked for at his years, perhaps more than is quite desirable, while to speak of a child as intelligent is altogether complimentary. See **sagacious.**

ANTONYMS: *blind, dull, idiotic, imbecile, shallow, shortsighted, stolid, stupid, undiscerning, unintelligent.*

SHUT

bar	close up	exclude	preclude
beleaguer	confine	imprison	prohibit
block	coop up	intercept	seal
blockade	enclose	lock up	stop
close			

To *shut* is to move something into position so as to *close* an opening or to prevent ingress or egress; as, to *shut* an eye or a gate. *Bar* and *block* refer to placing an obstacle across an opening to *close* up a passage. *Beleaguer* is to surround with an armed force so as to *imprison* within an area. To *confine,* *coop up,* and *enclose* connote restriction within fixed boundaries; we *confine* criminals in prison, *coop up* birds and small animals in enclosures, and *enclose* cattle in fields. To *exclude* is to *shut* out, usually for a purpose; to *preclude* is to prevent or *shut* out in advance. We *exclude* undesirable persons or things from entrance; we *preclude* the possibility of escape. To *intercept* is to *stop* en route; as, to *intercept* a message or a messenger. *Prohibit* implies debarring from or preventing entrance; *seal* connotes closing securely with a seal.

ANTONYMS: *expand, let loose, liberate, open, set free, unbar, unclose, undo, unfasten.*

PREPOSITIONS: Shut *into* or shut *up* in a dungeon, *out* of the house, *out* of society, *out from* social life; shut one's eyes *to* facts; shut one *up* to a single course; shut the door *against* intrusion.

SIGN

augury	manifestation	portent	symbol
badge	mark	presage	symptom
emblem	note	prognostic	token
indication	omen	signal	type

A *sign* is any distinctive *mark* by which a thing may be recognized or its presence known, and may be intentional or accidental, natural or artificial, suggestive, descriptive, or wholly arbitrary; thus, a blush may be a *sign* of shame; the footprint of an animal is a *sign* that it has passed; the *sign* of a business house now usually declares what is done or kept within, but formerly might be an object having no connection with the business, as "the *sign* of the trout"; the letters of the alphabet are *signs* of certain sounds.

While a *sign* may be involuntary, and even unconscious, a *signal* is always voluntary, and is usually concerted; a ship may show *signs* of distress to the casual observer, but *signals* of distress are a distinct appeal for aid. A *symptom* is a vital phenomenon resulting from a diseased condition; in medical language a *sign* is an *indication* of any physical condition, whether morbid or healthy; thus, a hot skin and rapid pulse are *symptoms* of pneumonia; dulness of some portion of the lungs under percussion is one of the physical *signs*.

Augury, omen, presage, prognostic, and *portent,* all connote prophetic *signs*; *augury* applies to the general discernment of future events; to superstitious people an *omen* is a definite *sign* foretelling good or evil; a *presage* is a presentiment or foretoken about the future; *prognostic* is some *symptom* that is predictive of a future course; *portents* are forewarnings of momentous or calamitous events. We offer something as a *token* of good will; a dove is the *emblem* of peace; a cornucopia is the *symbol* of plenty. A *badge* is something worn as a *token* or *sign* of membership in a society or class, or a characteristic *mark*. See **emblem.** Compare **characteristic; foretell.**

SIMILARITY

affinity	comparison	proportion	semblance
analogy	likeness	relation	simile
coincidence	parity	resemblance	similitude

Similarity, the most general of these terms, applies to things or persons somewhat alike; as, there is great *similarity* between the French and the Italian languages. *Likeness* connotes a closer agreement; one may speak of the *likeness* of a pair of twins. *Resemblance* is external and superficial, and may involve no deeper *relation*; as, the *resemblance* of a cloud to a distant mountain. *Similitude,* an uncommon and rather literary term, expresses the abstract idea of *resemblance* or *similarity.*

Analogy is specifically a *resemblance* of relations, and implies *comparison* between things essentially or substantially unlike. One may argue *analogy,* for instance, on the grounds that what holds true in one place or time must necessarily hold true in another; as, some scholars see an *analogy* between social conditions of today and those existing at the time of the Roman Empire. *Affinity* carries the idea of *resemblance,* with the additional connotation of some common relationship to which the *likeness* is attributable; as, the *affinity* between John's story and Joe's can be explained by the *resemblance* of their respective experiences. *Coincidence* is complete agreement in one or more respects; there may be *coincidence* in time of many dissimilar events.

ANTONYMS: *disagreement, disproportion, dissimilarity, incongruity, unlikeness.*

PREPOSITIONS: The similarity *between* (or *of*) nature and revelation; the similarity *of* sound *to* light; a family has some similarity *to* a state.

SIN

crime	fault	misdeed	vice
criminality	guilt	offense	viciousness
delinquency	ill-doing	transgression	wickedness
depravity	immorality	ungodliness	wrong
evil	iniquity	unrighteousness	wrong-doing

Sin is any lack of holiness, any defect of moral purity and truth, whether in heart or life, whether of commission or omission. "All *unrighteousness* is *sin,*" 1 John v, 17. *Transgression,* as its etymology indicates, is the stepping over a specific divine or human law, ordinarily by overt act, but, in the broadest sense, in volition or desire. *Sin* may be either act or state; *transgression* is always an act, mental or physical. *Crime* is often used for a flagrant violation of right, but in the technical sense denotes specific violation of human law. *Guilt* is desert of and exposure to punishment because of *sin.*

Depravity denotes not any action, but a perverted moral condition from which any act of *sin* may proceed. *Sin* in the generic sense, as denoting a state of heart, is synonymous with *depravity*; in the specific sense, as in the expression a *sin,* the term may be synonymous with *transgression, crime, offense, misdeed,* etc., or may denote some moral activity less positive than these. *Immorality* denotes outward violation of the moral law. *Sin* is thus the broadest word, and *immorality* next in scope; all *crimes,* properly so called, and all *immoralities,* are *sins*; but there may be *sin,* as ingratitude, which is neither *crime, transgression,* nor *immorality*; and there may be *immorality* which is not *crime,* as falsehood.

Criminality implies guiltiness of *offense* against public law; a *misdeed* is an improper, or gravely wrong, act; *delinquency* can apply to failure or neglect of duty, or to a *misdeed. Depravity* indicates a very corrupt moral condition; *wickedness* is *depravity* of heart, sinfulness; *iniquity* may be *wicked-*

ness or gross injustice; *vice* connotes *depravity* or a particular form of it; *viciousness* is an addiction to *vice* and includes ugly temper, cruelty, and malice. Compare **criminal.**

ANTONYMS: *blamelessness, excellence, godliness, goodness, holiness, innocence, integrity, morality, purity, rectitude, right, righteousness, sinlessness, uprightness, virtue.*

SING

| carol | chant | chirp | chirrup | hum | warble |

To *sing* is primarily and ordinarily to utter a succession of articulate musical sounds, especially with the human voice. The word has come to include any succession of musical sounds; we say the bird or the rivulet *sings*; we speak of "the *singing* quality" of an instrument, and by still wider extension of meaning we say the teakettle or the cricket *sings*. To *chant* is to *sing* in solemn and somewhat uniform cadence; *chant* is ordinarily applied to non-metrical religious compositions.

To *carol* is to *sing* joyously, and to *warble* (kindred with "whirl") is to *sing* with trills or quavers, usually also with joy. *Carol* and *warble* are especially applied to the singing of birds. To *chirp* is to utter a brief musical sound, perhaps repeated in the same key, as by certain small birds, insects, etc. To *chirrup* is to utter a series of somewhat similar sounds; the word is often used of a brief, sharp sound uttered as a signal to animate or rouse a horse or other animal. To *hum* is to utter murmuring sounds with somewhat monotonous musical cadence, usually with closed lips; we speak also of the *hum* of machinery, etc.

SKEPTIC

| agnostic | deist | doubter | infidel |
| atheist | disbeliever | freethinker | unbeliever |

The *skeptic* doubts divine revelation; the *disbeliever* and the *unbeliever* reject it, the *disbeliever* with more of intellectual dissent, the *unbeliever* (in the common acceptation) with indifference or with opposition of heart as well as of intellect. *Infidel* is a term that might once almost have been said to be geographical in its range. The Crusaders called all Mohammedans *infidels,* and were so called by them in return; the word is commonly applied to any decided opponent of an accepted religion. The *atheist* denies that there is a God; the *deist* admits the existence of God, but denies that the Christian Scriptures are a revelation from Him; the *agnostic* denies either that we do know or that we can know whether there is a God. A *freethinker* rejects authority especially about religious matters and is sometimes an *agnostic.*

ANTONYMS: *believer, Christian.*

SKETCH

brief	draft	painting	portrayal
delineation	drawing	picture	representation
design	outline	plan	skeleton

A *sketch* is a rough, suggestive presentation of anything, whether graphic or literary, commonly intended to be preliminary to a more complete or extended treatment. An *outline* gives only the bounding or determining lines of a figure or a scene; a *sketch* may give not only lines, but shading and color, but is hasty and incomplete. The lines of a *sketch* are seldom so full and continuous as those of an *outline*, being, like the shading or color, little more than indications or suggestions according to which a finished *picture* or *painting* may be made; the artist's first *representation* of a sunset, the hues of which change so rapidly, must of necessity be a *sketch*.

Draft and *plan* apply especially to mechanical *drawing*, of which *outline*, *sketch*, and *drawing* are also used; a *plan* is strictly a view from above, as of a building or machine, giving the lines of a horizontal section, originally at the level of the ground, now in a wider sense at any height; as, a *plan* of the cellar; a *plan* of the attic. A mechanical *drawing* is always understood to be in full detail; a *draft* is an incomplete or unfinished *drawing*; a *design* is such a preliminary *sketch* as indicates the object to be accomplished or the result to be attained, and is understood to be original. One may make a *drawing* of any well-known mechanism, or a *drawing* from another man's *design*; but if he says, "The *design* is mine," he claims it as his own invention or composition.

In written composition, an *outline* gives simply the main divisions, and in the case of a sermon is often called a *skeleton*; a somewhat fuller suggestion of illustration, treatment, and style is given in a *sketch*. A lawyer's *brief* is a succinct statement of the main facts involved in a case, and of the main heads of his argument on points of law, with reference to authorities cited; the *brief* has none of the vagueness of a *sketch*, being sufficiently exact and complete to form, on occasion, the basis for the decision of the court without oral argument, when the case is said to be "submitted on *brief*." A *portrayal* refers to the act of depicting, or a depiction by drawing, painting, etc., or by verbal description. *Delineation* also connotes *portrayal*, but stresses *representation* by lines rather than colors or shades. Compare **design.**

SKILFUL

accomplished	clever	handy	proficient
adept	deft	happy	skilled
adroit	dexterous	ingenious	trained
apt	expert	practiced	

Skilful signifies possessing and using practical knowledge and ability readily, having alert and well-trained faculties with reference to a given work. One is *adept* in that for which he has a natural gift improved by practice; he is *expert* in that of which training, experience, and study have given him a thorough mastery; he is *dexterous* in that which he can do effectively, with or without training, especially in work of the hand or bodily activities. In the case of the noun, "an expert" denotes one who is "experienced" in the fullest sense, a master of his branch of knowledge. A *skilled* workman is one who thoroughly learned his trade, though he may be naturally quite dull; a *skilful* workman has natural brightness, ability, and power of adaptation, in addition to his acquired knowledge and dexterity.

We like to listen to an *accomplished* musician; we admire *adroit* handling of a dangerous situation, praise an *apt* pupil, applaud a *clever* remark. *Deft* refers to actions that are *skilful*, neat, and quick; *handy* is *skilful* with the hands. A *proficient* person is thoroughly qualified or well-versed, as in art or other work; an *ingenious* man has inventive skill. See **clever.** Compare **dexterity; power.**

> **ANTONYMS:** *awkward, bungling, clumsy, helpless, inexpert, maladroit, shiftless, unhandy, unskilled, untaught, untrained.*

> **PREPOSITIONS:** Skilful *at* or *in* a work, *with* a pen or tool of any kind.

SLANDER

asperse	defame	disparage	revile
backbite	depreciate	libel	traduce
calumniate	detract	malign	vilify
decry			

To *slander* a person is to utter a false and injurious report concerning him; to *defame* is specifically and directly to attack one's reputation; to *defame* by spoken words is to *slander*, by written words, to *libel*. To *asperse* is, as it were, to bespatter with injurious charges; to *malign* is to circulate studied and malicious attacks upon character; to *traduce* is to exhibit one's real or assumed traits in an odious light; to *revile* or *vilify* is to attack with vile abuse. To *disparage* is to represent one's admitted good traits or acts as less praiseworthy than they would naturally be thought to be, as for instance, by ascribing a man's benevolence to a desire for popularity or display.

To *libel* or *slander* is to make an assault upon character and repute that comes within the scope of law; the *slander* is uttered, the *libel* written, printed, or pictured. To *backbite* is to speak something secretly to one's injury; to *calumniate* is to invent as well as utter the injurious charge. One may "abuse," "assail," or *vilify* another to his face; he *asperses, calumniates, slanders,* or *traduces* him behind his back. To *depreciate* is to *detract* from or belittle; to *decry* is to censure, discredit, or underrate publicly; to *detract* is to lessen or take away part of, as of reputation. Compare **disparage.**

> **ANTONYMS:** *defend, eulogize, extol, laud, praise, vindicate.*

SLANG

argot	cant	colloquialism	vulgarism

Slang, in the original sense, consisted of the *argot* or jargon of thieves and vagrants. In the modern sense, *slang* consists of certain words and phrases, either altered from their meanings in standard language or invented, which achieve wide popular currency. They are not acceptable in formal, standard usage, but are common in colloquial speech. They are the transitory by-words of a language; but in the evolution of language, many words called *slang* are constantly being adopted by good writers and speakers because of their vividness, color, or vitality, and these ultimately take their place as accepted English to permanently enrich the tongue.

The special vocabulary or *cant* of a certain trade, craft, or profession is also called *slang*; as, sailors' *slang*, racing *slang*; as well as the special speech of a certain class or group; as, college *slang*.

A *colloquialism* is an expression, not incorrect but below the literary grade, in standard usage in spoken, informal language. *Cant* denotes technical or professional phraseology; *argot* is the barbarous jargon used as a secret language by thieves, tramps, etc.

Vulgarisms are words or expressions in common, unrefined usage; the term does not imply coarseness, but rather applies to those expressions used by "the crowd" that have not received the sanction of cultured speakers; as "ain't" is considered by many to be a *vulgarism*.

SLOW

dawdling	dull	laggard	procrastinating
delaying	gradual	leisurely	slack
deliberate	inactive	lingering	sluggish
dilatory	inert	moderate	tardy
drowsy			

Slow signifies moving through a relatively short distance, or with a relatively small number of motions in a given time; *slow* also applies to that which is a relatively long while in beginning or accomplishing something; a watch or a clock is said to be *slow* when its indications are behind those of the standard time. *Tardy* is applied to that which is behind the proper or desired time, especially in doing a work or arriving at a place. *Deliberate* and *dilatory* are used of persons, though the latter may be used also of things, as of a stream; a person is *deliberate* who takes a noticeably long time to consider and decide before acting, or who acts or speaks as if he were deliberating at every point; a person is *dilatory* who lays aside, or puts off as long as possible, necessary or required action; both words may be applied either to undertaking or to doing.

Gradual (from L. *gradus,* a step) signifies advancing by steps, and refers to *slow* but regular and sure progression. *Slack* refers to action that seems to indicate a lack of tension, as of muscle or of will; *sluggish*, to action that seems as if reluctant to move or advance. *Dawdling* and *laggard* suggest wasting time in trifling or loitering; *lingering* refers to that which is *slow* and long-drawn-out. A *delaying* action slows down progress; a *leisurely* movement is unhurried. *Procrastinating* habits often postpone important business; a *sluggish* stream flows slowly; that which is *inert* is either *inactive* or disinclined to move.

ANTONYMS: See synonyms for **nimble.**

SMELL

aroma	odor	savor	stench
bouquet	perfume	scent	stink
fragrance			

Smell is the generic word including all the rest. *Aroma, fragrance*, and *perfume* are ordinarily pleasing; *odor, savor*, and *scent* may be so. *Odor* is nearly synonymous with *smell*, but is susceptible of more delicate use; as, the *odor* of incense. An *aroma* is a delicate and spicy *odor*, as of fine coffee; *bouquet* is said chiefly of the delicate *odor* of certain wines. We speak of the *fragrance* or *perfume* of flowers, but *fragrance* is more delicate; a *perfume* may be so strong and rich as to be repulsive by excess. There is a tendency to restrict the application of *perfume* to the artificial preparations called collectively "perfumery."

Scent is chiefly used for the characteristic *odor* of an animal by which it is tracked or avoided by other animals; the word is also applied to any *odor*, natural or artificial, especially when faintly diffused through the air; as, the *scent* of mignonette or of new-mown hay. *Savor* is chiefly said of the appetizing *odor* evolved from articles of food by the processes of cooking. Any *smell* that is at once foul, strong, and pervasive may be called a *stench*. *Smell* and *scent* denote also the sense to which *odors* appeal; as, man has the sense of *smell*; the keen *scent* of the foxhound.

SNEER

fling	gibe	jeer	mock	scoff	taunt

A *sneer* may be simply a contemptuous facial contortion, or it may be some brief satirical or derisive utterance that throws a contemptuous sidelight on what it attacks without attempting to prove or disprove; a depreciatory implication may be given in a *sneer*. A *fling* is a careless, scornful remark, commonly pettish; a *taunt* is intentionally insulting and provoking; the *sneer* is supercilious; the *taunt* is defiant. The *jeer* and *gibe* are uttered; the *gibe* is bitter, and often sly or covert; the *jeer* is rude and open. A *scoff* may be in act or word, and is commonly directed against that which claims honor, reverence, or worship. Compare **banter.**

> **PREPOSITION:** Only an essentially vicious mind is capable of a sneer *at* virtue.

SOCIALISM

anarchism   Bolshevism   collectivism   communism   nihilism

Socialism is a theory of political and economic organization advocating public ownership of the means of production, public management of all industries, and production for need and use instead of for profit. *Collectivism* is the doctrine that the people as a whole should own or control the material and means of production, distribution, etc. There is little difference between *socialism* and *collectivism,* except that *socialism* through the centuries has undergone many designations and ramifications. State *socialism* advocates state control of industries, public utilities, etc., and more equal distribution of the products, profits, and opportunities of labor, through existing government channels. Marxian *socialism* is *communism*: a theory of government and social order according to which property and the means of production belong to the people, are held as a common trust, and the profits arising therefrom devoted to the common good. The term *communism* is also applied to any social theory that calls for the abolition of private property and control by the community over economic affairs. *Bolshevism* is an old term for the variety of Marxian *communism* upheld by the left wing of the Social Democratic party in Russia prior to 1918.

Anarchism holds that all forms of government are wrong and unnecessary, that the individual should be a law unto himself, producing his best and receiving his deserts; in other words, the whole theory is based on the natural goodness of the individual. The word frequently connotes, however, violent resistance to law and order. *Nihilism* is a political doctrine holding that the existing structure of society should be destroyed; hence, the term is applied loosely to any revolutionary propaganda involving violence. Both *anarchism* and *nihilism* are basically antonyms of *socialism,* although commonly considered as its synonyms.

SOUND

noise   note   tone

Sound is the sensation produced through the organs of hearing or the physical cause of this sensation. *Sound* is the most comprehensive word of this group, applying to anything that is audible. *Tone* is *sound* considered as having some musical quality or as expressive of some feeling; *noise* is *sound* considered without reference to musical quality or as distinctly unmusical or discordant. Thus, in the most general sense *noise* and *sound* scarcely differ, and we say almost indifferently, "I heard a *sound*," or "I heard a *noise*." We speak of a fine, musical, or pleasing *sound*, but never thus of a *noise*. In music, *tone* may denote either a musical *sound* or the interval between two such *sounds*, but in the most careful usage the latter is now distinguished as the "interval," leaving *tone* to stand only for the *sound*.

Note in music strictly denotes the character representing a *sound*, but in loose popular usage it denotes the *sound* also, and becomes practically equivalent to *tone*. Aside from its musical use, *tone* is chiefly applied to that quality of the human voice by which feeling is expressed; as, he speaks in a cheery *tone*; the word is similarly applied to the voices of birds and other animals, and sometimes to inanimate objects. As used of a musical instrument, *tone* denotes the general quality of its *sounds* collectively considered.

SPEAK

announce	converse	discourse	say
articulate	declaim	enunciate	talk
chat	declare	express	tell
chatter	deliver	pronounce	utter

Speak, the most general of the words denoting articulate enunciation of one's thoughts, may refer to utterances of any kind; the word does not necessarily imply a listener. *Talk*, on the other hand, usually suggests the presence of a hearer or hearers and a certain amount of connection or coherence of speech. *Converse* always implies an exchange of thoughts or ideas between two or more persons.

To *utter* is to give forth as an audible sound, articulate or not. To *talk* is to *utter* a succession of connected words, ordinarily with the expectation of being listened to. To *speak* is to give articulate utterance even to a single word; the officer *speaks* the word of command, but does not *talk* it. To *speak* is also to *utter* words with the ordinary intonation, as distinguished from singing. To *chat* is ordinarily to *utter* in a familiar, conversational way; to *chatter* is to *talk* in an empty, ceaseless way like a magpie.

> **PREPOSITIONS:** Speak *to* (address) a person; speak *with* a person (converse with him); speak *of* or *about* a thing (make it the subject of remark); speak *on* or *upon* a subject; in parliamentary language, speak *to* the question.

SPECTACLE

display	pageant	representation	show
exhibition	parade	scene	sight

A *spectacle* is a grand *display* or *show* presented to public view, or an object of public attention; an opera is a dramatic *spectacle*, and a drunken man often makes a *spectacle* of himself. A *display* may be just a bringing into view or to notice; as, a *display* of courage; or it may connote an ostentatious *show*; as, a *display* of crude statuary. *Exhibition* refers to a public *display* of articles or works of art; or, in the figurative sense, to a showing forth; as, an *exhibition* of temper. A *pageant* is a brilliant, stately, or theatrical *spectacle*, an elaborate *exhibition* or procession for public amusement and often in celebration of a special event. A *parade* is a formal procession; as, a Memorial Day *parade*; or, figuratively, a flaunting *display*. A *sight* is something worth seeing, or something unusual or displeasing. Meteors are a grand *sight*; quarreling is an unpleasant *sight*.

SPEECH

address	harangue	oration	speaking
discourse	homily	oratory	talk
disquisition	language	sermon	utterance
dissertation	lecture		

Speech is the general word for *utterance* of thought in *language*. A *speech* may be the delivering of one's sentiments in the simplest way, often without previous preparation; an *oration* is a carefully prepared, elaborate, and eloquent *speech*; a *harangue* is a vehement appeal to passion, or a *speech* that has something disputatious and combative in it, and is usually delivered without preparation. A *discourse* is a set *speech* on a definite subject, intended to convey instruction.

An *address* is a carefully prepared, formal *speech*, delivered by a distinguished speaker, or upon a significant occasion; as, the Gettysburg *Address*; a commencement *address*. As its etymology suggests, a *lecture* is usually read aloud; it is a prepared *dissertation* on a special topic, designed to enlighten and instruct a group of students or some similar audience. *Sermon* and *homily* both commonly suggest religious instruction given by a minister or preacher to a congregation. A *sermon* is usually based on a Scriptural passage; a *homily* is a discourse on a moral problem. Compare **conversation; diction; language.**

> **ANTONYMS:** *hush, silence, speechlessness, stillness, taciturnity.*

SPONTANEOUS

automatic	impulsive	involuntary	voluntary
free	instinctive	unbidden	willing

That is *spontaneous* which is freely done, with no external compulsion and, in human actions, without special premeditation or distinct determination of the will; that is *voluntary* which is freely done with distinct act of will; that is *involuntary* which is independent of the will, and perhaps in opposition to it; a *willing* act is not only in accordance with will, but with desire. Thus *voluntary* and *involuntary*, which are antonyms of each other, are both partial synonyms of *spontaneous*. We speak of *spontaneous* generation, *spontaneous* combustion, *spontaneous* sympathy, an *involuntary* start, an *unbidden* tear, *voluntary* agreement, *willing* submission. A babe's smile in answer to that of its mother is *spontaneous*; the smile of a pouting child wheedled into good humor is *involuntary*.

In physiology, the action of the heart and lungs is called *involuntary*; the growth of the hair and nails is *spontaneous*; the action of swallowing is *voluntary* up to a certain point, beyond which it becomes *involuntary* or *automatic*. In the fullest sense of that which is not only without the will but distinctly in opposition to it, or compulsory, *involuntary* becomes an antonym, not only of *voluntary* but of *spontaneous*; as, *involuntary* servitude. A *spontaneous* outburst of applause is of necessity an act of volition, but so completely dependent on sympathetic impulse that it would seem frigid to call it *voluntary*, while to call it *involuntary* would imply some previous purpose or inclination not to applaud. That is *impulsive* which occurs impetuously and on the spur of the moment; an *impulsive* act is actuated by the emotions, and is *involuntary*, rather than *spontaneous* or natural.

SPY

detective	emissary	scout

The *scout* and the *spy* are both employed to obtain information of the numbers, movements, etc., of an enemy. The *scout* lurks on the outskirts of the hostile army with such concealment as the case admits of, but without disguise; a *spy* enters in disguise within the enemy's lines. A *scout*, if captured, has the rights of a prisoner of war; a *spy* is held to have forfeited all rights, and is liable, in case of capture, to capital punishment. An *emissary* is rather political than military; sent rather to influence opponents secretly than to bring information concerning them; so far as he does the latter, he is not only an *emissary*, but a *spy*.

STAIN

blot	discolor	dishonor	soil	sully	tinge
color	disgrace	dye	spot	tarnish	tint

To *stain* is primarily to *discolor*, to impart a color undesired and perhaps unintended, and which may or may not be permanent. To *color* is to impart a color desired or undesired, temporary or permanent, or, in the intransitive use, to assume a color in any way; as, he *colored* with shame and vexation. To *dye* is to impart a color intentionally and with a view to permanence, and especially so as to pervade the substance or fiber of that to which it is applied.

Thus, a character *"dyed* in the wool" is one that has received some early, permanent, and pervading influence; a character *stained* with crime or guilt is debased and perverted. *Stain* is, however, used of giving an intended color to wood, glass, etc., by an application of coloring matter which enters the substance a little below the surface, in distinction from painting, in which coloring matter is spread upon the surface; *dyeing* is generally said of wool, yarn, cloth, or similar materials which are dipped into the *coloring* liquid. Figuratively, a standard or a garment may be *dyed* with blood in honorable warfare; an assassin's weapon is *stained* with the blood of his victim. To *tinge* is to *color* slightly, and may also be used of giving a slight flavor, or of the admixture of one ingredient or quality with another that is more pronounced.

STAND

abide	halt	pause	stay
continue	hold out	remain	stop
endure	keep up		

To *stand,* in this comparison, is to place so as to *stay* in an upright position, or to *remain* upright or firmly at rest, or to *endure.* To *abide* is to *stay* for a period or dwell, as, "Today I must *abide* at thy house," *Luke* xix, 5; or to *stand* firm, as, "I *abide* by the decision." To *continue* is to *endure* or to *remain;* to *halt* is to bring to a complete stop. A small force may *hold out* or make a stand against superior numbers for a time, but find it impossible to *stand* or to *keep up* resistance indefinitely. To *pause* is to stop temporarily.

ANTONYMS: *decline, droop, drop, fail, faint, fall, falter, flee, fly, sink, succumb, yield.*

PREPOSITIONS: Stand *on* or *upon* the shore; stand *by* or *to* a pledge; stand *by* a friend, *with* the minority, *for* the right, *against* the wrong; stand *over* a fallen foe; to stand *upon* one's rights.

STATE

affirm	avow	maintain	set forth
allege	certify	predicate	specify
assert	claim	pronounce	swear
asseverate	declare	propound	tell
assure	depose	protest	testify
aver	express	say	vindicate
avouch	inform		

To *state* is to *set forth* explicitly, formally, or particularly, in speech or writing. *Assert* is strongly personal, signifying to *state* boldly and positively what the one making the statement has not attempted and may not attempt to prove. To *declare* is to make a public statement. *Affirm* has less of egotism than *assert* (as seen in the word *self-assertion*), coming nearer to *aver*. It has more solemnity than *declare*, and more composure and dignity than *asseverate*, which is to *assert* excitedly. In legal usage, *affirm* has a general agreement with *depose* and *testify*; it differs from *swear* in not invoking the name of God. To *assure* is to *state* with such authority and confidence as the speaker feels ought to make the hearer sure.

Certify is more formal, and applies rather to written documents or legal processes. *Assure, certify, inform* apply to the person; *affirm*, etc., to the thing. *Assert* is combative; *assure* is conciliatory. I *assert* my right to cross the river; I *assure* my friend it is perfectly safe. To *aver* is to *state* positively something of whose truth one is completely confident. One may *assert* himself, or *assert* his right to what he is willing to contend for; or he may *assert* in discussion what he is ready to maintain by argument or evidence. To *assert* without proof is always to lay oneself open to the suspicion of having no proof to offer, and seems to arrogate too much to one's personal authority, and hence in such cases both the verb *assert* and its noun assertion have an unfavorable sense; we say a mere assertion, a bare assertion, his unsupported assertion; he *asserted* his innocence, has less force than he *affirmed* or *maintained* his innocence. *Affirm, state,* and *tell* have not the controversial sense of *assert*, but are simply declarative.

To *protest* is to emphasize the truth of one's statement, especially in the face of doubt or contradiction. One who *avouches* has personal knowledge of, or authority for, his statement. To *vindicate* is to defend successfully what is assailed. Almost every criminal will *assert* his innocence; the honest man will seldom lack means to *vindicate* his integrity.

> **ANTONYMS:** *contradict, contravene, controvert, deny, disprove, dispute, gainsay, oppose, refute, repudiate, retract, waive.*

STEAL

abstract	embezzle	pilfer	purloin
commit larceny	extort	pillage	rob
commit theft	filch	plunder	swindle

To *steal* is to take away from another's possession, without right, authority, or permission, and usually in a secret manner and for one's own use or advantage. To *commit theft* (more commonly with the indefinite article, to *commit a theft*) has the same general meaning, but is not a common phrase in legal use. To *steal* is, in law, to *commit* simple *larceny*; but the word may be applied to any furtive, covert, or surreptitious taking of anything, whether material or immaterial. To *pilfer* is to *steal* petty articles. The word *filch* especially emphasizes the secrecy and slyness of the act; *filch* is ordinarily applied to things of little value, but may apply to the most precious, as in Shakespeare "he that *filches* from me my good name." To *purloin* is etymologically to carry far away, and is commonly applied to the dishonest removal of articles of value or importance.

To *rob* is, in law, to take feloniously from the person by force or fear, as in highway robbery; in a more extended use it is applied to the felonious taking of articles of value from places as well as persons, generally with suggestion of force and violence. To *abstract* is to take secretly and feloniously from among other things belonging to another. To *embezzle* is to appropriate fraudulently to oneself funds received and held in trust. To *swindle* is to cheat grossly, commonly by false pretenses, but is not a recognized legal offense under that name; one form of *swindling*, the "obtaining money by false pretenses," is an indictable offense, but much *swindling* may be carried on under the forms of law. To *plunder* is to take property from an enemy in time of war, and is not a crime at law. Compare **abstract.**

> ANTONYMS: *give back, give up, make good, refund, repay, restore, return, surrender.*

STEEP

| abrupt | high | precipitous | sharp | sheer |

High is used of simple elevation; *steep* is said only of an incline where the vertical measurement is sufficiently great in proportion to the horizontal to make it difficult of ascent. *Steep* is relative; an ascent of 100 feet to the mile on a railway is a *steep* grade; a rise of 500 feet to the mile makes a *steep* wagon-road; a roof is *steep* when it makes with the horizontal line an angle of more than 45°. A *high* mountain may be climbed by a winding road nowhere *steep*, while a little hill may be accessible only by a *steep* path. A *sharp* ascent or descent is one that makes a sudden, decided angle with the plane from which it starts; a *sheer* ascent or descent is perpendicular, or nearly so; *precipitous* applies to that which is of the nature of a precipice, and is used especially of a descent. *Abrupt* suggests not only a sharper angle of ascent or descent than that connoted by *steep*, but also a sudden change or break in a level surface. Compare **high.**

> ANTONYMS: *easy, flat, gentle, gradual, horizontal, level, low, slight.*

STOP

abstain	conclude	finish	pause
bring to an end	desist	give over	quit
cease	discontinue	intermit	refrain
come to an end	end	leave off	terminate

To *stop* is to suspend or cause to suspend the movement or progress of something. *Cease* is applied to states or conditions, or to that which is regarded as having existence. *Stop* connotes a sudden or abrupt, *cease* a gradual suspension or halting of activity. A clock may *stop*; but it *ceases* to run. When one *stops* work on a building it *ceases* to rise.

Quit, in the sense of *stop* or *cease*, is colloquial; as, he *quit* work at five o'clock. To *discontinue* is to suspend some habitual or customary activity or practice; as, to *discontinue* a correspondence or a subscription to a newspaper. To *desist*, now almost exclusively intransitive in use, is to *refrain* from further efforts, especially when such efforts will obviously be futile; as the enemy *desisted* from further assaults on the town.

Strains of music may gradually or suddenly *cease*. A man *quits* work on the instant; he may *discontinue* a practice gradually; he *quits* suddenly and completely; he *stops* short in what he may or may not resume; he *pauses* in what he will probably resume. What *intermits* or is *intermitted* returns again as a fever that *intermits*. Compare **abandon; die; end; rest.**

> **ANTONYMS:** *begin, commence, enter upon, inaugurate, initiate, institute, originate, set about, set going, set in operation, set on foot, start.*

STORM

agitation   disturbance   tempest

A *storm* is properly a *disturbance* of the atmosphere, with or without rain, snow, hail, or thunder and lightning. Thus we have rain*storm*, snow*storm*, etc., and by extension, magnetic *storm*. A *tempest* is a *storm* of extreme violence always attended with some precipitation, as of rain, from the atmosphere. In the moral and figurative use, *storm* and *tempest* are not closely discriminated except that *tempest* commonly implies greater intensity. We speak of *agitation* of feeling, *disturbance* of mind, a *storm* of passion, a *tempest* of rage.

> **ANTONYMS:** *calm, fair weather, hush, peace, serenity, stillness, tranquillity.*

STORY

account	myth	novel	relation
anecdote	narration	recital	tale
legend	narrative	record	yarn

A *story* is the telling of some series of connected incidents or events whether real or fictitious, in prose or verse, orally or in writing; or the series of incidents or events thus related may be termed a *story*. In children's talk a *story* is a common euphemism for a falsehood. *Narrative* is a more formal ord than *story*; commonly it connotes fact rather than fiction; as, a *narrative* of Indian captivity. As a literary composition, a *narrative* usually has a plot; hence, a chronicle or diary could not be termed a *narrative*.

Tale is nearly synonymous with *story*, but is somewhat archaic; it is used for an imaginative, legendary, or fictitious *recital*, especially if of ancient date; as, a fairy *tale*; also, for an idle or malicious report; as, do not tell *tales*. An *anecdote* tells briefly some incident, assumed to be fact. If it passes close limits of brevity, it ceases to be an *anecdote*, and becomes a *narrative* or *narration*. A traditional or mythical *story* of ancient times is a *legend*. A history is often somewhat poetically called a *story*; as, the *story* of the American Civil War. *Yarn* was originally nautical slang, and is now used colloquially to denote a long, rambling *tale* of travel or adventure, frequently of doubtful truthfulness, and seldom having a clear plot. Compare **allegory; fiction; history.**

ANTONYMS: *annals, biography, chronicle, history, memoir.*

STREAM

brook	eddy	race	runlet
channel	flood	rill	runnel
course	flow	river	streamlet
creek	flume	rivulet	tide
current	flux	run	watercourse
drift			

A *stream* is a *flow* of water or other fluid; or anything that moves along or seems to *flow* from a source; as, a *stream* of people issued from the theater. A *river* is a large *stream* of water that discharges into a larger body of water as the ocean, a lake, or another *stream*. A *brook, rivulet, run, runnel,* or *runlet* is a small natural *stream*; a *creek* is larger than a *brook* but smaller than a *river*, and usually flows through a valley. A *channel* is the bed of a *stream* or the deep part of a *river*; also an artificial *flow* of water joining two larger pieces. The *course* of a *stream* is the *channel* or bed in which it flows; a *watercourse* is the bed of a *stream* or a natural or artificial *channel*. A *current* is the swift part of a *stream*; a *race* is a swift *current*; a *flood* is a copious *stream* overflowing its banks and the adjoining land. A *flume* is an artificial *channel* or a ravine through which a *stream* flows. *Tide* is the periodic rise and fall of ocean water, *flux* indicates the inflow of the *tide* or suggests constant movement or change. A *rill* is a tiny *stream*.

STRETCH

distend	expand	reach	strain
elongate	extend	spread	tighten
exaggerate	lengthen		

To *stretch* is to draw out to full length, width, or size; as, to *stretch* wet shoes. To *elongate* is to increase the length in space; to *lengthen* or *extend* is to make longer in either time or space. *Extend* can also be used figuratively; as, to *extend* a courtesy; or in the sense of *reach* out or *stretch* out; as, he *extended* his hand. To *expand* is to increase the bulk, *stretch* the size; or, to give more details; as, he *expanded* his views. Some substances *expand* rapidly when heated; business *expands* in times of peace. To *distend* is to swell or become inflated, as a bladder. We *exaggerate* the truth when we *stretch* it; and when we *stretch* every nerve we *strain* or exert ourselves to the utmost.

ANTONYMS: *loosen, relax, slacken.*

STUPID

crass	dense	dull	dumb

A *stupid* person exhibits a state of mind that is either congenitally sluggish and deadened, or that is temporarily benumbed or dazed, as by narcotics, a blow on the head, or the like; as, the Indians had drunk themselves *stupid*; he was always a *stupid* person in school. The word is often used to denote mere carelessness or forgetfulness; as, it was *stupid* of the professor to forget his rubbers. Those exhibiting mental deficiency—the moron, the imbecile, and the idiot—are not commonly called *stupid*.

Dull implies a slow or sluggish mentality; the *dull* student lacks alertness of mind or perception. A *dull* speaker is so lacking in interest or liveliness that he bores his listeners; a *stupid* speaker, on the other hand, makes such inane or fatuous remarks that his audience is driven to the point of exasperation. *Dense* connotes the imperviousness to new ideas or thoughts that is suggested by such words as thickhead, blockhead, etc. It may imply stolidity, obtuseness, or any other quality which reveals lack of subtlety or perception. The *crass* mind is so cloddish or gross that it is incapable of the finer mental or esthetic processes, such as analysis or discrimination; we speak of *crass* materialism, *crass* ignorance. *Dumb* is a colloquial Americanism; it is used contemptuously in place of any of the other words discussed here, but chiefly to describe anyone who combines inarticulateness with stupidity.

STUPOR

apathy	insensibility	stupefaction	syncope
asphyxia	languor	swoon	torpor
coma	lassitude	swooning	unconsciousness
fainting	lethargy		

Stupor is a condition of the body in which the action of the senses and faculties is suspended or greatly dulled—weakness or loss of sensibility. The *apathy* of disease is a mental affection, a state of morbid indifference; *lethargy* is a state of antipathy to activity, a morbid tendency to heavy sleep, from which the patient may perhaps be momentarily aroused. *Coma* is a deep, abnormal sleep, from which the patient cannot be aroused, or is aroused only with difficulty. a state of profound *insensibility*, perhaps with full pulse and deep stertorous breathing.

Syncope or *swooning* is a sudden loss of sensation and of power of motion, with suspension of pulse and of respiration, and is due to failure of heart action, as from sudden nervous shock or intense mental emotion. *Insensibility* is a general term, denoting loss of feeling from any cause, as from cold, intoxication, or injury. *Stupor* is especially profound and confirmed *insensibility*, properly comatose. *Asphyxia* is a special form of *syncope* resulting from partial or total suspension of respiration, as in strangulation, drowning, or inhalation of noxious gases.

Torpor is partially or completely suspended animation, as of a hibernating animal; *lassitude* is listlessness, weariness or inertia of mind and body; *languor* is weakness or depression, often the result of illness, whereas *lassitude* is more often caused by worry or overwork. *Stupefaction* is the act of deadening or dulling the senses, or the state of being stupefied. Compare **apathy.**

SUBLIME

beautiful	grand	majestic	splendid
exalted	lofty	noble	stately
glorious	magnificent	resplendent	superb
gorgeous			

Sublime implies of such vast nobility, grandeur, power, beauty, etc., that it inspires awe, wonder, and reverence. *Majestic* applies to that which makes upon the mind an impression, as of the presence and bearing of a mighty sovereign. *Magnificent* denotes the possession at once of greatness, splendor, and richness; as, *magnificent* array. *Grand* stresses handsomeness and impressiveness; *glorious* is intensely delightful; *resplendent* implies dazzlingly bright; *gorgeous* usually refers to sumptuously brilliant in color. We speak of *grand* scenery and a *grand* speech, a *glorious* opportunity, a *gorgeous* sunset, *resplendent* attire.

Exalted refers to raised in position, thought, dignity, etc.; that which is *superb* has reached the highest point of excellence and grandeur; as, a *superb* performance, a *superb* view. A *noble* edifice impresses us by its imposing appearance; the *noble* effort to rescue the captain saved the ship. *Lofty*, in this comparison, implies of very high character; as, a *lofty* purpose. *Stately* refers to impressive dignity of bearing, style, or appearance; we speak of *stately* manners and *stately* mansions.

ANTONYMS: *base, contemptible, insignificant, little, mean, petty, ridiculous.*

SUBSIDY

aid	bounty	pension	subvention
allowance	gift	premium	support
appropriation	grant	reward	tribute
bonus	indemnity		

A *subsidy* is pecuniary *aid* directly granted by government to an individual or commercial enterprise to carry on work for the public welfare; as, a *subsidy* to a steamship company; or money furnished by one nation to another to aid it in carrying on war against a common enemy. A nation grants a *subsidy* to an ally, pays a *tribute* to a conqueror. An *indemnity,* or compensation for loss or injury, is often limited and temporary, while a *tribute* might be exacted indefinitely.

The somewhat rare term *subvention* is especially applied to a *grant* of governmental *aid* to a literary, artistic, or scientific enterprise. Governmental *aid* to a commercial or industrial enterprise other than a transportation company is more frequently called a *bounty* than a *subsidy*; as, the sugar *bounty*. The word *bounty* may be applied to almost any regular or stipulated *allowance* by a government to a citizen or citizens; as, a *bounty* for enlisting in the army; a *bounty* for killing wolves. A *bounty* is offered for something to be done; a *pension* is granted for something that has been done. An *appropriation* is money set apart in advance, as by a business or government, for a particular use in the future. A *premium*, in this comparison, is an additional *gift, reward,* or payment used as an incentive; a *bonus* is money or its equivalent given in excess of usual or stipulated payment.

SUCCEED

achieve	flourish	prosper	win
attain	prevail	thrive	

A person *succeeds* when he accomplishes what he attempts, or *attains* a desired object or result; an enterprise or undertaking *succeeds* when it has a prosperous result. To *win* implies that someone loses, but one may *succeed* where no one fails. A solitary swimmer *succeeds* in reaching the shore; if we say he *wins* the shore we contrast him with himself as a possible loser. Many students may *succeed* in study; a few *win* the special prizes, for which all compete. To *achieve* is to accomplish by overcoming difficulties by the use of skill, perseverance, etc. To *prosper* is to be or render successful; to *thrive* is to *succeed* by industry, economy, or other means; to *flourish* is to be successful or prosperous. To *prevail* is to be victorious or prove superior. Compare **follow.**

ANTONYMS: *be defeated, come short, fail, fall short, lose, miss, miscarry.*

SUGGESTION

hint	**innuendo**	**intimation**	**proposition**
implication	**insinuation**	**proposal**	

A *suggestion* (from L. *sub*, under, and *gero*, bring) brings something before the mind less directly than by formal or explicit statement, as by a partial statement, an incidental allusion, an illustration, a question, or the like. *Suggestion* is often used of an unobtrusive statement of one's views or wishes to another, leaving consideration and any consequent action entirely to his judgment, and is hence, in many cases, the most respectful way in which one can convey his views to a superior or a stranger. A *suggestion* may be given unintentionally, and even unconsciously.

An *intimation* is a *suggestion* in brief utterance, or sometimes by significant act, gesture, or token, of one's meaning or wishes; in the latter case it is often the act of a superior; as, God in His providence gives us *intimations* of His will. A *hint* is still more limited in expression, and is always covert, but frequently with good intent; as, to give one a *hint* of danger or of opportunity. *Insinuation* is a covert or partly veiled utterance, sometimes to the very person attacked; an *innuendo* is usually injurious to reputation, and secret as well as sly, as if pointing one out by a significant nod (from L. *in*, in, to, and *nuo*, nod). An *implication* is something that is expressed indirectly or implied as inference; a *proposal* suggests something for consideration or action; a *proposition* suggests something definite for consideration.

SUPERNATURAL

miraculous	**preternatural**	**superhuman**

The *supernatural* (*super*, above) is above or superior to the recognized powers of nature; the *preternatural* (*preter*, beyond) is aside from or beyond the recognized results or operations of natural law, often outside the ordinary course of nature, strange and inexplicable; as, a *preternatural* gloom. *Miraculous* is more emphatic and specific than *supernatural*, as referring to the direct intervention of divine power. Some hold that a miracle, as the raising of the dead, is a direct suspension and even violation of natural laws by the fiat of the Creator, and hence is, in the strictest sense, *supernatural*; others hold that the miracle is simply the calling forth of a power residing in the laws of nature, but not within their ordinary operation, so that the *miraculous* might be termed "extranatural," rather than *supernatural*. All that is beyond human power is *superhuman*; as, prophecy gives evidence of *superhuman* knowledge; the word is sometimes applied to remarkable manifestations of human power, surpassing all that is ordinary.

ANTONYMS: *common, commonplace, everyday, natural, ordinary, usual.*

SUPPORT

bear	cherish	keep	maintain	sustain
carry	hold up	keep up	prop	uphold

Support and *sustain* alike signify to *hold up* or *keep up*, to prevent from falling or sinking; but *sustain* has a special sense of continuous exertion or of great strength continuously exerted, as when we speak of *sustained* endeavor or a *sustained* note; a flower is *supported* by the stem or a temple roof by arches; the foundations of a great building *sustain* an enormous pressure; to *sustain* life implies a greater exigency and need than to *support* life; to say one is *sustained* under affliction is to say more both of the severity of the trial and the completeness of the *upholding* than if we say he is *supported*.

To *bear* is the most general word, denoting *holding up* or *keeping up* of any object, whether in rest or motion; in the derived senses it refers to something that is a tax upon strength or endurance; as, to *bear* a strain; to *bear* pain or grief. To *maintain* is to *keep* in a state or condition, especially in an excellent and desirable condition; as, to *maintain* health or reputation; to *maintain* one's position; to *maintain* a cause or proposition is to hold it against opposition or difficulty.

To *support* may be partial, to *maintain* is complete; *maintain* is a word of more dignity than *support*; a man *supports* his family; a state *maintains* an army or navy. To *prop* is always partial, signifying to add *support* to something that is insecure. In this comparison, *carry* implies to *hold up*, as a weight; as, the bridge will *carry* a weight of 100 tons; and *cherish* implies to *maintain* lovingly. Compare **abet; carry; cherish; endure; keep.**

> **ANTONYMS:** *abandon, betray, break down, cast down, demolish, desert, destroy, drop, let go, overthrow, throw down, wreck.*

> **PREPOSITIONS:** The roof is supported *by, on,* or *upon* pillars; the family was supported *on* or *upon* a pittance, or *by* charity.

SUPPOSE

conjecture	guess	surmise
deem	imagine	think

To *suppose* is temporarily to assume a thing as true, either with the expectation of finding it so or for the purpose of ascertaining what would follow if it were so. To *suppose* is also to think a thing to be true while aware or conceding that the belief does not rest upon any sure ground, and may not accord with fact; or yet again, to *suppose* is to imply as true or involved as a necessary inference; as, design *supposes* the existence of a designer. To *conjecture* is to put together the nearest available materials for a provisional opinion based on insufficient evidence, but always expecting to find the facts to be as *conjectured.* To *imagine* is to form a mental image of something as existing, though its actual existence may be unknown, or even impossible. To *think,* in this application, is to hold as the result of thought what is admitted not to be a matter of exact or certain knowledge; as, I do not know, but I *think* this to be the fact; a more conclusive statement than would be made by the use of *conjecture* or *suppose.* To *surmise* is to form opinions or *conjecture* from very slight evidence, to *guess* at or suspect something on the basis of probability rather than fact. To *deem* is to *think* or have an opinion; as, he *deemed* it wise to discontinue. Compare **doubt; hypothesis.**

> ANTONYMS: *ascertain, be sure, conclude, discover, know,* *prove.*

SURRENDER

abandon	give	leave	sacrifice
alienate	give oneself up	let go	waive
capitulate	give over	relinquish	yield
cede	give up	resign	

To *surrender* is to *give up* upon compulsion, as to an enemy in war, hence to *give up* to any person, passion, influence, or power. To *yield* is to give place or give way under pressure, and hence under compulsion. *Yield* implies more softness or concession than *surrender;* the most determined men may *surrender* to overwhelming force; when one *yields,* his spirit is at least somewhat subdued. A monarch or a state *cedes* territory, perhaps for a consideration; *surrenders* an army, a navy, or a fortified place to a conqueror; a military commander *abandons* an untenable position, unavailable stores, or former methods. We *sacrifice* something precious through error, friendship, or duty, *yield* to convincing reasons, a stronger will, winsome persuasion, or superior force.

An army *capitulates* when it *surrenders* on stipulated terms; we *relinquish* a claim when we *give* it *up, let* it *go;* we *resign* from an office, or *resign* ourselves and *give* ourselves *up* to the inevitable. A claim that is *waived* is *relinquished* voluntarily. To *alienate* in this connection is to *give over* to other ownership. See **abandon.**

SUSPEND

debar	discontinue	intermit	stop
defer	fall	interrupt	withhold
delay	hinder	stay	

To *suspend,* in this comparison, is to *stop* or cause to *stop* temporarily; to hold in a state of indecision. We *suspend* payment and *suspend* judgment. To *defer* is to put off to a later date; to *discontinue* is to bring or come to an

end altogether; to *delay* is to keep back or to postpone. Manufacturing operations are often *hindered* by incompetence of some of the workers, or because
electricity is *intermitted* or *withheld* for a time, and the work schedule is thus
interrupted. To *debar* implies to cause to *stop* from continuing. Compare
adjourn.

> **ANTONYMS:** *begin, continue, expedite, keep on, keep up,*
> *prolong, protract, urge on.*
>
> **PREPOSITIONS:** Suspend *on* or *upon* certain conditions; sus-
> pend *from* office.

SYNONYMOUS

alike	equivalent	like	similar
correspondent	identical	same	synonymic
corresponding	interchangeable		

Synonymous strictly signifies being *interchangeable* names for the same
thing, or being one of two or more *interchangeable* names for the same thing;
to say that two words are *synonymous* is strictly to say they are *alike, equivalent, identical,* or the *same* in meaning; but the use of *synonymous* in this
strict sense is somewhat rare, and rather with reference to statements than
to words.

In the strictest sense, *synonymous* words scarcely exist; rarely are any two
words in any language *equivalent* or *identical* in meaning; where a difference
in meaning cannot easily be shown, a difference in usage commonly exists, so
that the words are not *interchangeable.* By *synonymous* words (or synonyms)
we usually understand words that coincide or nearly coincide in some part of
their meaning, and may hence within certain limits be used interchangeably,
while outside of those limits they may differ very greatly in meaning and use.

It is the office of a work on synonyms to point out these correspondences
and differences, that language may have the flexibility that comes from freedom of selection within the common limits, with the perspicuity and precision
that result from exact choice of the fittest words to express each shade of
meaning outside of the common limits. To consider *synonymous* words *identical* is fatal to accuracy; to forget that they are *similar,* to some extent
equivalent, and sometimes *interchangeable,* is destructive of freedom and
variety.

SYSTEM

manner	method	mode	order	regularity	rule

System technically denotes the carefully formulated plan or procedure followed in doing a certain kind of work, but is also commonly used to denote

the actual way in which the work is done. *Order* in this connection denotes the fact or result of proper arrangement according to the due relation or sequence of the matters arranged; as, these papers are in *order*; in alphabetical *order*. *Method* denotes a process, a general or established way of doing or proceeding in anything; *rule,* an authoritative requirement or an established course of things; *system,* not merely a law of action or procedure, but a comprehensive plan in which all the parts are related to each other and to the whole; as, a *system* of theology; a railroad *system*; the digestive *system*; *manner* refers to the external qualities of actions, and to those often as settled and characteristic; we speak of a *system* of taxation, a *method* of collecting taxes, the *rules* by which assessments are made; or we say, as a *rule* the payments are heaviest at a certain time of year; a just tax may be made odious by the *manner* of its collection.

Regularity applies to the even disposition of objects or uniform recurrence of acts in a series. There may be *regularity* without *order,* as in the recurrence of paroxysms of disease or insanity; there may be *order* without *regularity,* as in the arrangement of furniture in a room, where the objects are placed at varying distances. *Order* commonly implies the design of an intelligent agent or the appearance or suggestion of such a design; *regularity* applies to an actual uniform disposition or recurrence with no suggestion of purpose, and as applied to human affairs is less intelligent and more mechanical than *order*. The most perfect *order* is often secured with least *regularity,* as in a fine essay or oration. The same may be said of *system*. There is a *regularity* of dividing a treatise into topics, paragraphs, and sentences that is destructive of true rhetorical *system*. Compare **habit; hypothesis.**

> **ANTONYMS:** *chaos, confusion, derangement, disarrangement, disorder, irregularity.*

T

TACITURN

close	mute	reticent	speechless
dumb	reserved	silent	uncommunicative

Taciturn refers to a temperamental disinclination to speak; *dumb, mute, silent,* and *speechless* denote a fact or state, an unwillingness or inability to speak. The talkative person may be stricken *dumb* with surprise or terror; the obstinate may remain *mute*; one may be *silent* through preoccupation of mind or of set purpose; but the *taciturn* person is averse to the utterance of thought or feeling and to communication with others, either from natural disposition or for the occasion.

Silent and *uncommunicative* both refer to one who habitually refrains from saying any more than is absolutely necessary. One who is *silent* does not speak at all; one who is *taciturn* speaks when compelled, but in a grudging way that repels further approach. *Reserved* suggests more of method and intention than *taciturn,* applying often to some special time or topic; one who is communicative regarding all else may be *reserved* about his business. *Reserved* is thus closely equivalent to *uncommunicative,* but is a somewhat stronger word, often suggesting pride or haughtiness, as when we say one is *reserved* toward inferiors. Compare **pride.**

ANTONYMS: *communicative, free, garrulous, loquacious, talkative, unreserved.*

TALKATIVE

chattering	garrulous	loquacious	prolix	verbose	voluble

The *talkative* person has a strong disposition to talk, with or without an abundance of words or many ideas; the *loquacious* person has an abundant and easy flow of language and much to say on any subject suggested; either may be lively and for a time entertaining. *Garrulous* signifies given to constant trivial talking; the *garrulous* person is tedious, repetitious, petty, and self-absorbed. *Chattering* signifies uttering rapid, noisy, and unintelligible, or scarcely intelligible, sounds, whether articulate words or such as resemble them; *chattering* is often used of vocal sounds that may be intelligible by themselves but are not easily understood owing to confusion of many voices or other cause.

Verbose is applied to utterances more formal than conversation, as to writings or public addresses using more words than necessary. It is difficult to stem the flow of *voluble* excuses, or to listen patiently to the long-winded address of a *prolix* speaker. We speak of a *chattering* monkey or a *chatteirng* idiot, a *talkative* child, a *talkative* or *loquacious* woman, a *garrulous* old man, a *verbose* commentator. Compare **circumlocution.**

ANTONYMS: *laconic, reserved, reticent, silent, speechless, taciturn.*

414

TAX

assessment	exaction	levy	tithe
customs	excise	rate	toll
demand	impost	tariff	tribute
duty			

A *tax* is a compulsory contribution levied upon persons, property, or business for the support of government; a sum levied on members of a society; hence, a heavy *demand* on one's powers or resources. A *levy* implies money or supplies collected, often by force, to meet a special emergency. An *assessment* is an amount, usually based on the value of property or investments, and levied on a person by an authority or a society; as, an *assessment* on a property for an improvement shared by neighboring properties. A *duty* or *impost* is levied on imports or exports; *customs* are collected on imports or exports at the frontiers of a country. *Duty* also implies a legal obligation.

An *excise* is *tax* levied on manufacture, trading transactions, or sports. A *toll* is paid for the right to pass over a bridge, through a tunnel, etc., to defray the cost of the structure. *Tribute* was formerly a *tax* levied by a ruler on his own people or on people he conquered; figuratively, *tribute* implies a voluntary contribution or a mark of respect; as floral *tribute*, a *tribute* to valor. A *tariff* is a *duty* or *tax* on some particular class of goods. A *tithe* is a *tax* or contribution of one-tenth.

TEACH

discipline	give instruction	inform	nurture
drill	give lessons	initiate	school
educate	inculcate	instil	train
enlighten	indoctrinate	instruct	tutor

The primary implication of *teach* is the communication of knowledge to another. However, the good teacher also aids the learner in mastering any difficulties that may arise, and in putting the newly acquired knowledge to practical use; as, his mother *taught* him to read. To *instruct* is to impart necessary knowledge or skill with special method and completeness; as, to *instruct* a class in the elements of Latin grammar.

Educate, while it usually presupposes formal teaching or instruction, stresses that these are merely the means of drawing out and developing harmoniously those mental and moral powers inherent in the individual which are regarded as essential for finding his proper place in society; as, experience, rather than books, *educated* this man. *School* is sometimes used as an equivalent of *educate;* as, he was *schooled* at Harvard; but its commonest use is in the sense of *train* or *discipline,* especially with the implication of hardships or difficulties to be endured; as, for many years he *schooled* himself to go without the luxuries of life.

To *train* is to direct to a certain result powers already existing. *Train* is used in preference to *educate* when the reference is to the inferior animals or to the physical powers of man; as, to *train* a horse; to *train* the hand or eye. To *discipline* is to bring into habitual and complete subjection to authority; *discipline* is a severe word, and is often used as a euphemism for punish; to be thoroughly effective in war, soldiers must be *disciplined* as well as *trained*. To *nurture* is to furnish the care and sustenance necessary for physical, mental, and moral growth; *nurture* is a more tender and homelike word than *educate*. Compare **education.**

TEMERITY

audacity	hastiness	precipitancy	rashness
brashness	heedlessness	precipitation	recklessness
foolhardiness	impetuosity	presumption	venturesomeness
hardihood	overconfidence		

Temerity denotes contempt of danger, and suggests a failure to estimate one's chances of success in a projected action. *Rashness* applies to the actual rushing into danger without counting the cost; *temerity* denotes the needless exposure of oneself to peril which is or might be clearly seen to be such. *Rashness* is used chiefly of bodily acts, *temerity* often of mental or social matters; there may be a noble *rashness*, but *temerity* is always used in a bad sense. We say it is amazing that one should have had the *temerity* to make a statement which could be readily proved a falsehood, or to make an unworthy proposal to one sure to resent it; in such use *temerity* is often closely allied to *hardihood, audacity,* or *presumption*.

Venturesomeness dallies on the edge of danger and experiments with it; *foolhardiness* rushes in for want of sense, *heedlessness* for want of attention, *rashness* for want of reflection, *recklessness* from disregard of consequences. *Impetuosity* is foolhardy, heedless, and rash, and is characterized by the impetus of its display; *brashness*, though equally impetuous, is marked by its tactlessness. *Audacity*, in the sense here considered, denotes a dashing and somewhat reckless courage, in defiance of conventionalities, or of other men's opinions, or of what would be deemed probable consequences; as, the *audacity* of a successful financier. See **effrontery.**

ANTONYMS: *care, caution, circumspection, cowardice, hesitation, timidity, wariness.*

TERM

article	denomination	member	phrase
condition	expression	name	word

Term in its figurative uses always retains something of its literal sense of a boundary or limit. The *articles* of a contract or other instrument are simply the portions into which it is divided for convenience; the *terms* are the essential statements on which its validity depends—as it were, the landmarks of its meaning or power; a *condition* is a contingent *term* which may become fixed upon the happening of some contemplated event. In logic, a *term* is one of the essential *members* of a proposition, the boundary of statement in some one direction. Thus, in general use, *term* is more restricted than *word, expression,* or *phrase*; a *term* is a *word* that limits meaning to a fixed point of statement or to a special class of subjects, as when we speak of the definition of *terms,* that is, of the key *words* in any discussion; or we say, that is a legal or scientific *term.* A *member* is part of a whole; the various propositions of a syllogism are called its *members.* Compare **boundary; diction.**

TERSE

brief	concise	neat	short
compact	condensed	pithy	succinct
compendious	laconic	sententious	summary

That which is *terse* has an elegant and finished completeness within the smallest possible compass, as if rubbed or polished down to the utmost. That which is *concise* is trimmed of all superfluities and elaborations; a person is *concise* who writes or speaks briefly. One who or that which is *succinct* compresses or is compressed into the smallest possible space; a *succinct* writer uses no more words than are absolutely necessary, and these he uses in a *brief, compact* manner.

Laconic, applied either to the writer or speaker or to that which is written or spoken, means using or consisting of few words, after the fashion of the Laconians. A *laconic* retort is so *short* as to be brusk or curt, perhaps even mystifying. A *pithy* utterance gives the gist of a matter effectively, whether in rude or elegant style; it is not merely *terse* or *succinct,* but also full of meaning and substance. That which is *compendious* gathers the substance of a matter into a few words, weighty and effective; the word is usually applied to the treatment that typifies a compendium; as, a *compendious* account of the Civil War.

Summary refers to a statement or announcement that is compacted to the utmost, often to the point of abruptness. A *summary* statement gives only the bare outlines or the chief points, with no details at all. That which is *condensed* is, as it were, pressed together, so as to include as much as possible within a small space. A *sententious* style is one abounding in sentences that are singly striking or memorable, apart from the context; the word may be used invidiously of that which is pretentiously oracular.

ANTONYMS: *diffuse, lengthy, long, prolix, tedious, verbose, wordy.*

TESTIMONY

affidavit	attestation	deposition	proof
affirmation	certification	evidence	witness

Testimony, in legal as well as in common use, signifies the statements of persons who are assumed to know the facts of a case, as experts or eye-witnesses. *Deposition* and *affidavit* denote *testimony* reduced to writing; the *deposition* differs from the *affidavit* in that the latter is voluntary and without cross-examination, while the former is made under interrogatories and subject to cross-examination. *Evidence* is a broader term, including the *testimony* of witnesses and all facts of every kind that tend to prove a thing true; we have the *testimony* of a traveler that a fugitive passed this way; his footprints in the sand are additional *evidence* of the fact. Compare **demonstration; oath.**

THEREFORE

accordingly	hence	then	whence
because	so	thence	wherefore
consequently			

Therefore, signifying for that (or this) reason, is the most precise and formal word for expressing the direct conclusion of a chain of reasoning; *then* carries a similar but slighter sense of inference, which it gives incidentally rather than formally; as, "All men are mortal; Cæsar is a man; *therefore* Cæsar is mortal"; or, "The contract is awarded; *then* there is no more to be said." *Consequently* denotes a direct result, but more frequently of a practical than a theoretic kind; as, "Important matters demand my attention; *consequently* I shall not sail today." *Consequently* is rarely used in the formal conclusions of logic or mathematics, but marks rather the freer and loser style of rhetorical argument.

Accordingly denotes correspondence, which may or may not be consequence; it is often used in narration; as, "The soldiers were eager and confident; *accordingly* they sprang forward at the word of command." *Thence* is a word of more sweeping inference than *therefore*, applying not merely to a single set of premises, but often to all that has gone before, including the reasonable inferences that have not been formally stated. *Wherefore* is the correlative of *therefore*, and *whence* of *hence* or *thence*, appending the inference or conclusion to the previous statement without a break. *So* is a colloquial connective, used indefinitely and loosely to indicate any kind of sequence; as, I felt bad, *so* I stopped working and went home. Compare synonyms for **because.**

THOUGHTFUL

attentive	circumspect	heedful	provident
careful	considerate	mindful	prudent

A *thoughtful* person provides in advance for needs and wishes not yet manifested. An *attentive* person waits upon another to supply what is needed or desired. A *considerate* person carefully spares another all that would harm, grieve, or annoy; one who is *circumspect* carefully avoids all that might compromise himself. A *careful* person pays great attention to work, duties, avoidance of waste or mistakes, and is watchful. A *heedful* person is cautious, discreet, and watchful. *Provident* implies *careful* about results or for the future; a *prudent* man is cautious and watchful as well as thrifty. *Mindful* indicates keeping someone or something in one's thoughts.

ANTONYMS: *careless, gay, giddy, heedless, inadvertent, inattentive, inconsiderate, neglectful, negligent, reckless, remiss.*

PREPOSITIONS: Thoughtful *of* one's reputation, *of* or *for* a friend, *to* lay up a store for winter.

THRONG

concourse	host	mass	press
crowd	jam	multitude	

Throng is a word of vastness and dignity, always implying that the persons are numerous as well as pressed or pressing closely together; there may be a dense *crowd* in a small room, but there cannot be a *throng*. A *crowd* is a company of persons filling to excess the space they occupy and pressing inconveniently upon one another; the total number in a *crowd* may be great or small. *Host* and *multitude* both imply vast numbers, but a *multitude* may be diffused over a great space so as to be nowhere a *crowd*; *host* is a military term, and properly denotes an assembly too orderly for crowding.

Concourse signifies a spontaneous gathering of many persons moved by a common impulse, and has a suggestion of stateliness not found in the word *crowd*, while suggesting less massing and pressure than is indicated by the word *throng*. *Mass* is used of a large assembly of people and of an aggregation of parts or things; *jam* refers to a number of persons or things very closely pressed together; *press* is an archaic word for a *crowd* or *throng*.

TIME

age	eon	period	succession
date	epoch	season	term
duration	era	sequence	while

Time and *duration* denote something conceived of as enduring while events take place and acts are done; continued existence. According to the necessary conditions of human thought, events are contained in *time* as objects are in space, *time* existing before the event, measuring it as it passes, and still existing when the event is past. *Duration* and *succession* are more general words than *time*; we can speak of infinite or eternal *duration* or *succession*, but *time* is commonly contrasted with eternity. *Time* usually means measured or measurable *duration*, but it may include infinity. *Sequence* and *succession* apply to events viewed as following one another.

A *period*, as ordinarily used, is a definite portion of *time* marked off by some recurring event or phenomenon; a series of days or years. An *age* is a great or distinct *period*; as, the *age* of Pericles; an *era* is a historical *period*; as, the Christian *era*. *Epoch* refers to the beginning of an *era*, often marked by drastic changes. In geological use, however, wherein the whole span of the formation of the earth is divided into distinct stages of development, the greater divisions are known as *eras*. These are subdivided into certain *periods* in rock systems, which are in turn further subdivided into certain *epochs* in rock series. Thus, the *age* of man, or *duration* of *time* in which some form of mankind is believed to have existed, is designated as the recent Pleistocene *epoch* of the Quaternary *period* in the Cenozoic *era*.

Eon refers to an incalculable, immeasurable *period of time*; *term*, to a prescribed *duration*, a fixed *period*. The *term* of a contract is the *period* of *time* between two specified *dates*. *Season* refers to *periods* of *time* into which the year is divided; as, the winter *season*; the hunting *season*. *While* indicates a short *time*; as, he can only stay a *while*.

TIP

| cant | dip | incline | list | slope |
| careen | heel over | lean | slant | tilt |

To *tilt* or *tip* is to throw out of a horizontal position by raising one side or end or lowering the other; the words are closely similar, but *tilt* suggests more of fluctuation or instability. *Slant* and *slope* are said of things somewhat fixed or permanent in a position out of the horizontal or perpendicular; either verb may indicate such condition, though *slope* is preferable with ground; thus, the roof *slants*, the hill *slopes*. *Incline* is a more formal word for *tip*, and also for *slant* or *slope*.

To *cant* is to set slantingly; in many cases *tip* and *cant* can be interchanged, but *tip* is more temporary, often momentary; one *tips* a pail so that the water flows over the edge; a mechanic *cants* a table by making or setting one side higher than the other. A vessel *careens* in the wind; *lists*, usually, from shifting of cargo, from water in the hold, etc. *Careening* is always toward one side or the other; *listing* may be forward or astern as well. To *heel over* is the same as to *careen*, and must be distinguished from "keel over," which is to capsize.

TIRE

| exhaust | fatigue | jade | weary |
| fag | harass | wear out | |

To *tire* is to reduce strength in any degree by exertion; one may be *tired* just enough to make rest pleasant, or even unconsciously *tired*, becoming aware of the fact only when he ceases the exertion; or, on the other hand, he may be, according to the common phrase, "too *tired* to stir"; but for this extreme condition the stronger words are commonly used. One who is *fatigued* suffers from a conscious and painful lack of strength as the result of some overtaxing; an invalid may be *fatigued* with very slight exertion; when one is *wearied*, the painful lack of strength is the result of long-continued demand or strain; and there is often an unwillingness to continue.

One is *exhausted* when the strain has been so severe and continuous as utterly to consume the strength, so that further exertion is for the time impossible. One is *fagged* by drudgery; he is *jaded* by incessant repetition of the same act until it becomes increasingly difficult or well-nigh impossible; as, a horse is *jaded* by a long and unbroken journey. To *harass* is to *weary* with continued or excessive burdens; to *wear out*, in this comparison, is to *exhaust*; as, he has at last *worn out* my patience.

> **ANTONYMS:** *invigorate, recreate, refresh, relax, relieve, repose, rest, restore.*

TOOL

apparatus	implement	machine	utensil
appliance	instrument	mechanism	weapon

A *tool* is something used in an occupation or pursuit, as by mechanics or craftsmen, to work, shape, move, or transform material. Those things by which pacific and industrial operations are performed are alone properly called *tools*, those designed for warlike purposes are *weapons*. An *instrument* is anything through which power is applied and a result produced; in general usage, the word is of considerably wider meaning than *tool*; as, a piano is a musical *instrument*. *Instrument* is the word usually applied to *tools* used in scientific pursuits; as, we speak of a surgeon's or an optician's *instruments*.

An *implement* is a mechanical contrivance or agency for use for some specific purpose to which it is adapted; as, an agricultural *implement*; *implements* of war. *Implement* is a less technical and artificial term than *tool*. The paw of a tiger might be termed a terrible *implement*, but not a *tool*. A *utensil* is that which may be used for some special purpose, and is especially applied to articles used for domestic or agricultural purposes; as, kitchen *utensils*; farming *utensils*. An *appliance* is that which is or may be applied to the accomplishment of a result, either independently or as subordinate to some power or to something more extensive or important; every mechanical *tool* is an *appliance*, but not every *appliance* is a *tool*; the traces of a harness are *appliances* for traction, but they are not *tools*.

Mechanism is a word of wide meaning, denoting any combination of mechanical devices for united action. A *machine* in the most general sense is any mechanical *instrument* for the conversion of motion; in this sense a lever is a *machine*; but in more commonly accepted usage a *machine* is distinguished from a *tool* by its complexity, and by the combination and coordination of powers and movements for the production of a result. A chisel by itself is a *tool*; when it is set so as to be operated by a crank and pitman, the entire *mechanism* is called a *machine*; as, a mortising *machine*.

An *apparatus* may be a *machine*, but the word is commonly used for a collection of distinct articles to be used in connection or combination for a certain purpose—a mechanical equipment; as, the *apparatus* of a gymnasium; especially, for a collection of *appliances* for some scientific purpose; as, a chemical or surgical *apparatus*; an *apparatus* may include many *tools, instruments,* or *implements*. *Implement* is for the most part and *utensil* is altogether restricted to the literal sense; *instrument, machine,* and *tool* have figurative use, *instrument* being used largely in a good, *tool* always in a bad sense; *machine* inclines to the unfavorable sense, as implying that human agents are made mechanically subservient to some controlling will; as, an *instrument* of Providence; the *tool* of a tyrant; a political *machine*.

TOPIC

division	issue	motion	proposition	subject
head	matter	point	question	theme

A *topic* is a *head* of discourse. Since a *topic* for discussion is often stated in the form of a *question, question* has come to be extensively used to denote a debatable *topic*, especially of a practical nature—an *issue*; as, the labor *question*; the temperance *question*. In deliberative assemblies a *proposition* presented or moved for acceptance is called a *motion*, and such a *motion* or other matter for consideration is known as the *question*, since it is or may be stated in interrogative form to be answered by each member with a vote of "aye" or "no"; a member is required to speak to the *question*; the chairman puts the *question*.

In speaking or writing the general *subject* or *theme* may be termed the *topic*, though it is more usual to apply *topic* to the subordinate *divisions, points,* or *heads* of discourse; as, to enlarge on this *topic* would carry me too far from my *subject*; a pleasant drive will suggest many *topics* for conversation. *Matter* can often be used interchangeably with *subject*; as, the *matter* (or *subject*) under discussion has been widely advertised.

TRACE

footmark	impression	remains	token	trail
footprint	mark	remnant	track	vestige
footstep	memorial	sign		

A *trace* may be merely the *mark* made by something that has been present or passed by, and that is still existing, or some slight evidence of its presence or of the effect it has produced; as, *traces* of game were observed by the hunter. An *impression* is a *mark* or series of *marks* produced by pressure; as, an *impression* or *footprint* in the snow, or the *impression* of a seal on paper. A *track*, in this comparison, is any *mark* or series of *marks* left by the passage of something, or a *footprint*, or a path beaten down by the feet. A *trail* is the *mark* or *marks* left by something being dragged along a surface; also a *track*.

A *memorial* is that which is intended or fitted to bring to remembrance something that has passed away; it may be vast and stately. On the other hand, a slight *token* of regard may be a cherished *memorial* of a friend; either a concrete object or an observance may be a *memorial*. A *vestige* is always slight compared with that whose existence it recalls; as, scattered mounds containing implements, weapons, etc., are *vestiges* of a former civilization. A *vestige* is always a part of that which has passed away. Explorers often find the *remains* of ancient temples, also the *remnants* or surviving *traces* of a former civilization.

TRANSACT

accomplish	**carry on**	**do**	**perform**
act	**conduct**	**negotiate**	**treat**

There are many acts that one may *do, accomplish,* or *perform* unaided; what he *transacts* is by means of or in association with others; one may *do* a duty, *perform* a vow, *accomplish* a task, but he *transacts* business, since that always involves the agency of others. To *negotiate* and to *treat* are likewise collective acts, but both these words lay stress upon deliberation, with adjustment of mutual claims and interests; *transact,* while it may depend upon previous deliberation, states execution only.

Notes, bills of exchange, loans, and treaties are said to be *negotiated,* the word so used covering not merely the preliminary consideration, but the final settlement. *Negotiate* has more reference to execution than *treat*; nations may *treat* for peace without result, but when a treaty is *negotiated,* peace is secured; the citizens of the two nations are then free to *transact* business with one another. To *act* is to *perform* actions or to function; as, the motor *acts* well; to *conduct* in this comparison means to *carry on*; as, he *conducted* his business without interference. See **do.**

TRANSACTION

act	**affair**	**deed**	**proceeding**
action	**business**	**doing**	

One's *acts* or *deeds* may be exclusively his own; his *transactions* involve the agency or participation of others. A *transaction* is something completed: a *proceeding* is or is viewed as something in progress; but since *transaction* is often used to include the steps leading to the conclusion, while *proceedings* may result in *action*, the dividing line between the two words becomes sometimes quite faint, though *transaction* often emphasizes the fact of something done, or brought to a conclusion. Both *transactions* and *proceedings* are used of the records of a deliberative body, especially when published; strictly used, the two are distinguished; as, the Philosophical *Transactions* of the Royal Society of London give in full the papers read; the *Proceedings* of the American Philological Association give in full the *business* done, with mere abstracts of or extracts from the papers read. See **act; business.**

TRANSCENDENTAL

a priori   intuitive   original   primordial   transcendent

All *intuitive* truths or beliefs are *transcendental*. But *transcendental* is a wider term than *intuitive*, including all within the limits of thought that is not derived from experience, as the ideas of space and time. *Transcendental,* according to Kant, means designed to make knowledge through experience possible, although preceding experience. *Transcendental* has been applied in the language of the Emersonian school to the soul's supposed *intuitive* knowledge of things divine and human, so far as they are capable of being known to man; the Cartesians use the word to mean pertaining to soul and body alike. *Transcendental* commonly implies wildly speculative, and sometimes connotes *transcendent*. In mathematics, that is *transcendental* which is not producible by a finite number of the five fundamental algebraic operations.

Intuitive truths are those which are in the mind independently of all experience, not being derived from experience nor limited by it, as that the whole is greater than a part, or that things which are equal to the same thing are equal to one another. *Transcendent* is superexcellent; of a very remarkable degree; or, according to Kant, lying beyond the bounds of all possible experience; hence, beyond knowledge. In theology, *transcendent* connotes pertaining to God; beyond limitation; hence, perfect. *A priori* signifies prior to experience; that can only be known by reason; presumptively. *Primordial* is pertaining to, or existing in, the beginning. Compare **mysterious.**

TRANSIENT

brief	flitting	momentary	short-lived
ephemeral	flying	passing	temporary
evanescent	fugitive	short	transitory
fleeting			

Transient and *transitory* are both derived from the same Latin source, denoting that which quickly passes or is passing away, but there is a fine shade of difference between them. A thing is *transient* which in fact is not lasting; a thing is *transitory* which by its very nature must soon pass away; a thing is *temporary* which is intended to last or be made use of but a little while; as, a *transient* joy; this *transitory* life; a *temporary* chairman.

Momentary suggests duration of only a moment or a very brief space of time; as, a *momentary* passion. *Ephemeral*, literally lasting but for a day, often marks more strongly than *transient* exceeding brevity of duration; it agrees with *transitory* in denoting that its object is destined to pass away, but is stronger, as denoting not only its certain but its speedy extinction; thus that which is *ephemeral* is looked upon as at once slight and perishable, and the word often carries a suggestion of contempt; man's life is *transitory*, a butterfly's existence is *ephemeral*; with no solid qualities or worthy achievements a pretender may sometimes gain an *ephemeral* popularity. That which is *fleeting* is viewed as in the act of *passing* swiftly by, and that which is *fugitive* as eluding attempts to detain it; that which is *evanescent* is in the act of vanishing even while we gaze. The hues of the sunset are *evanescent*. That which is *short-lived* has a very brief existence; as, his anger was *short-lived*.

ANTONYMS: *abiding, enduring, eternal, everlasting, immortal, imperishable, lasting, permanent, perpetual, persistent, undying, unfading.*

TRICK

art	cunning	guile	ruse
artifice	device	imposture	skill
blind	dodge	invention	stratagem
cheat	finesse	machination	subterfuge
contrivance	fraud	maneuver	wile
craft			

A *trick* implies using deceit to procure an advantage, and is often low, injurious, and malicious; we say a mean *trick*; the word is sometimes used playfully with less than its full meaning. A *ruse* or a *blind* may be quite innocent and harmless. A *contrivance*, as compared here, is a scheme or *device* which requires *skill*. An *artifice* is a carefully and delicately prepared *contrivance* for doing indirectly what one could not well do directly.

A *device* is something cleverly designed and studied out for promoting an end, as in a mechanism; the word is used of indirect action, often, but not necessarily, directed to an evil, selfish, or injurious end. *Finesse* is especially subtle *contrivance*, delicate *artifice*, whether for good or evil. A *cheat* is a mean advantage in a bargain; a *fraud*, any form of covert robbery or injury. *Imposture* is a deceitful *contrivance* for securing charity, credit, or consideration.

A *stratagem* outwits, and gains an end by trickery; a *maneuver* gains an advantage by skilful movements. *Wile* is the use of personal charm to beguile. See **fraud**.

ANTONYMS: *artlessness, candor, fairness, frankness, guilelessness, honesty, ingenuousness, innocence, openness, simplicity, sincerity, truth.*

TROUBLESOME

afflictive	harassing	laborious	tiresome
annoying	hard	painful	trying
arduous	importunate	perplexing	tumultuous
burdensome	intrusive	teasing	vexatious
difficult	irksome	tedious	wearisome
galling			

Troublesome means causing some kind of trouble, annoyance or distress; *afflictive* implies causing great trouble, pain, or misery. *Annoying, vexatious, irksome,* and *tiresome,* all refer to a causing of minor troubles; *annoying* people or conditions cause irritation; *vexatious* developments cause irritation and displeasure; *irksome* tasks fill us with distaste and impatience, and often with reluctance; *tiresome* people and journeys weary and bore us. *Wearisome* connotes greater fatigue than *tiresome.* A *tedious* wait is boresome and mentally tiring. An *arduous* task involves great labor, exertion, and, possibly, hardship; *burdensome* suggests a heavy burden hard to carry physically or mentally. *Intrusive* people thrust themselves uninvited into the company or conversation of others, and are very *troublesome. Importunate* people or demands are troublesomely insistent or urgent; *harassing* debts are *burdensome* and *importunate. Galling* sarcasm frets and irritates. *Tumultuous* waters or meetings are greatly agitated or disturbed.

ANTONYMS: *amusing, cheering, easy, entertaining, grateful, gratifying, helpful, light, pleasant.*

TRUTH

candor	honesty	reality	veracity
frankness	ingenuousness	truthfulness	verity

Truth is primarily and *verity* is always a quality of thought or speech, especially of speech, in exact conformity to fact or reality. *Veracity* is properly a quality of a person, the habit of speaking and the disposition to speak the *truth*; a habitual liar may on some occasion speak the *truth,* but that does not constitute him a man of *veracity*; on the other hand, a person of undoubted *veracity* may state (through ignorance or misinformation) what is not the *truth.*

Truthfulness is a quality that may inhere either in a person or in his statements or beliefs. *Candor, frankness, honesty,* and *ingenuousness* are allied with *veracity,* and *verity* with *truth,* while *truthfulness* may accord with either *Candor* emphasizes fairness and *honesty* in stating the *truth; frankness* expresses thoughts or feeling openly and freely; *ingenuousness* has an element of naïveté, and is guileless and artless. *Reality* is objective or inherent *truth.* *Truth* in a secondary sense may be applied to intellectual action or moral character, in the former case becoming a close synonym of *veracity;* as, I know him to be a man of *truth.*

ANTONYMS: *deceit, deception, delusion, duplicity, error, fabrication, falsehood, falseness, falsity, fiction, guile, imposture, lie, mendacity, untruth.*

TRY

| attempt | endeavor | essay | strive | undertake |

Try is the most comprehensive of these words. The original idea of testing or experimenting is not thought of when a man says "I will *try.*" To *try* implies using other means and studying out other ways if not at first successful. To *attempt* is to take action somewhat experimentally with the hope and purpose of accomplishing a certain result; to *endeavor* is to *attempt* strenuously and with firm and enduring purpose. To *attempt* expresses a single act; to *endeavor,* a continuous exertion; we say I will *endeavor* (not I will *attempt*) while I live. To *attempt* is with the view of accomplishing; to *essay,* with a view of testing our own powers. To *attempt* suggests giving up, if the thing is not accomplished at a stroke. *Endeavor* is more mild and formal; the pilot in the burning pilot house does not say "I will *endeavor*" or "I will *attempt* to hold the ship to her course," but "I'll *try,* sir!"

To *undertake* is to accept or take upon oneself as an obligation, as some business, labor, or trust; the word often implies complete assurance of success; as, I will *undertake* to produce the witness. To *strive* suggests little of the result, much of toil, strain, and contest in seeking it; I will *strive* to fulfill your wishes, *i.e.,* I will spare no labor and exertion to do it. *Essay* expresses something of the original meaning of *try,* to test one's powers, *try* out something; hence, sometimes, to test or *essay* metals.

ANTONYMS: *abandon, dismiss, drop, give up, let go, neglect, omit, overlook, pass by, throw away, throw over, throw up.*

U

UNION

coalition	conjunction	juncture	unification
combination	cooperation	oneness	unity
concert	junction	solidarity	

Union is a bringing together of things that have been distinct, so that they combine or coalesce to form a new whole, or the state or condition of things thus brought together; in a *union* the separate individuality of the things united is never lost sight of; we speak of the *union* of the parts of a fractured bone, or of the *union* of the thirteen colonies, or of the *union* of hearts in marriage. *Unity* is *oneness*, the state of being one, especially of that which never has been divided or of that which cannot be conceived of as resolved into parts; as, the *unity* of God or the *unity* of the human soul. But *unity* can be said of that which is manifestly or even conspicuously made up of parts, when a single purpose or ideal is so subserved by all that their possible separateness is lost sight of; as, we speak of the *unity* of the human body, or of the *unity* of the church. *Solidarity* denotes the *unity* of a group or class, by which it displays its strength or exerts its influence, either as a whole or through individuals; as, the *solidarity* of the working classes. Compare **alliance; association; attachment; harmony; marriage.**

> **ANTONYMS:** *analysis, contrariety, decomposition, disconnection, disjunction, dissociation, disunion, division, divorce, schism, separation, severance.*

UNITE

adjoin	associate	concatenate	connect
affix	attach	conjoin	join
append	combine		

To *unite* is to come together so as to form a larger or a stronger unit; as, the *United* States of America. *Combine* is the preferable term when a somewhat looser union is to be suggested. An object that *adjoins* another touches that other at one or more points or at one side or edge; a garden *adjoins* a house when lying beside or behind it; if we were to say that the garden is *connected* with the house, we should think of some path or passageway by which the one might be reached from the other.

To *conjoin* is to *join* with much completeness and permanence, as by adhesion, intergrowing, or fusing together at a point, edge, or surface; paint is at once *conjoined* with the surface to which it is applied; things that are *joined* may not be *conjoined*; friendly hands or meeting roads or streams are *joined*, but not *conjoined*. *Conjoin* is often interchangeable with *unite*, but *conjoin* directs attention to the original separateness, *unite* to the final *unity*. To *subjoin* is to add at the end, to *attach* or *affix* as something additional, to *append. Concatenate* (a somewhat rare or technical word) signifies to *join* in a chain or series, all the parts of which have neutral relations; as, in nature causes and effects are *concatenated.* See **add; append; apply; attach.**

ANTONYMS: See the antonyms for the words above referred to.

USUAL

accustomed	familiar	normal	public
common	frequent	ordinary	regular
customary	general	prevailing	wonted
everyday	habitual	prevalent	

Usual signifies such as regularly or often recurs in the *ordinary* course of events, or is habitually repeated in the life of the same person. *Ordinary* signifies according to an established order, hence of *everyday* occurrence. In strictness, *common* and *general* apply to the greater number of individuals in a class; but both words are in good use as applying to the greater number of instances in a series, so that it is possible to speak of one person's *common* practice or *general* custom, though *ordinary* or *usual* would in such case be preferable. *Habitual* denotes established practice, and is commonly applied to those acts or qualities which have become confirmed as habit; as, he wore his *habitual* frown. *Accustomed* and *wonted* are used interchangeably to denote that which is the result of habit, but *wonted* is a stilted and bookish term. Compare **general; normal.**

ANTONYMS: *exceptional, extraordinary, infrequent, out-of-the-way, rare. singular, strange, uncommon, unparalleled, unusual.*

UTILITY

advantage	expediency	service	use
avail	policy	serviceableness	usefulness
benefit	profit		

Utility signifies primarily the quality of being useful, but is somewhat more abstract and philosophical than *usefulness* or *use,* and is often employed to denote adaptation to produce a valuable result, while *usefulness* denotes the actual production of such result. We contrast beauty and *utility.* We say of an invention, its *utility* is questionable, or, on the other hand, its *usefulness* has been proved by ample trial, or I have found it of *use;* still, *utility* and *usefulness* are frequently interchanged.

Expediency refers primarily to escape from or avoidance of some difficulty or trouble; either *expediency* or *utility* may be used to signify *profit* or *advantage* considered apart from right as the ground of moral obligation, or of actions that have a moral character, *expediency* denoting immediate *advantage* on a contracted view, and especially with reference to avoiding danger, difficulty, or loss, while *utility* may be so broadened as to cover all existence through all time, as in the utilitarian theory of morals. *Policy* is often used in a kindred sense, more positive than *expediency* but narrower than *utility*, as in the proverb, "Honesty is the best *policy*." Compare **profit**.

ANTONYMS: *disadvantage, folly, futility, impolicy, inadequacy, inexpediency, inutility, unprofitableness, uselessness, worthlessness.*

V

VACANT

blank	leisure	unoccupied	void
devoid	unemployed	untenanted	waste
empty	unfilled	vacuous	

That is *empty* which contains nothing; that is *vacant* which is without that which has filled or might be expected to fill it; *vacant* has extensive reference to rights or possibilities of occupancy. A *vacant* room may not be *empty*, and an *empty* house may not be *vacant*. *Vacant*, as derived from the Latin, is applied to things of some dignity; *empty*, from the Saxon, is preferred in speaking of slight, common, or homely matters, though it may be applied with special force to the highest; we speak of *empty* space, a *vacant* lot, an *empty* dish, an *empty* sleeve, a *vacant* mind, an *empty* heart, an *empty* boast, a *vacant* office, a *vacant* or *leisure* hour.

Void and *devoid* are rarely used in the literal sense, but for the most part confined to abstract relations, *devoid* being followed by "of," and having with that addition the effect of a prepositional phrase; as, the article is *devoid* of sense; the contract is *void* for want of consideration. *Waste*, in this connection, applies to that which is made so by devastation or ruin, or gives an impression of desolation, especially as combined with vastness, probably from association of the words *waste* and vast; *waste* is applied also to uncultivated or unproductive land, if of considerable extent; we speak of a *waste* area or region, but not of a *waste* city lot. *Vacuous* refers to the condition of being *empty* or *vacant*, regarded as continuous or characteristic; specifically, *vacuous* describes that which encloses a vacuum. *Blank* refers to something, especially a surface, which has no writing on it, or which has *empty* spaces that are left to be filled in; as a *blank* slate; a *blank* check.

> **ANTONYMS:** *brimful, brimmed, brimming, busy, crammed, crowded, filled, full, gorged, inhabited, jammed, occupied, overflowing, packed, replete.*

VAIN

abortive	futile	trifling	unserviceable
baseless	idle	trivial	unsubstantial
bootless	inconstant	unavailing	useless
deceitful	ineffectual	unimportant	valueless
delusive	nugatory	unprofitable	vapid
empty	null	unreal	visionary
frivolous	profitless	unsatisfying	worthless
fruitless	shadowy		

Vain keeps the etymological idea through all changes of meaning; a *vain* endeavor is *empty* of result, or of adequate power to produce a result, a *vain*

431

pretension is *empty* or destitute of support, a *vain* person has a conceit that is *empty* or destitute of adequate cause or reason. *Futile* is equivalent to *vain* in denoting failure to achieve an immediate aim. Both may be applied to something contemplated but not yet attempted. *Vain*, however, suggests an opinion based on previous experience; as, it is *vain* to ask him for further help; while *futile* suggests reasoning from self-evident principles or facts; as, it would be *futile* to enumerate all his faults.

That which is *bootless, fruitless,* or *profitless* fails to accomplish any valuable result; that which is *abortive, ineffectual,* or *unavailing* fails to accomplish a result that it was, or was supposed to be, adapted to accomplish. That which is *useless, futile,* or *vain* is inherently incapable of accomplishing a specified result. *Useless,* in the widest sense, signifies not of use for any valuable purpose, and is thus closely similar to *valueless* and *worthless. Fruitless* is more final than *ineffectual,* as applying to the sum or harvest of endeavor. That which is *useless* lacks actual fitness for a purpose; that which is *vain* lacks imaginable fitness. Compare **ostentation; pride; vacant.**

> **ANTONYMS:** *adequate, advantageous, beneficial, competent, effective, efficient, expedient, potent, powerful, profitable, real, serviceable, solid, sound, substantial, sufficient, useful, valid, valuable, worthy.*

VENAL

| hack | hireling | purchasable |
| hackney | mercenary | salable |

Venal signifies ready to sell one's influence, vote, or efforts for money or other consideration; it frequently connotes the use of bribery, and with its implication of corruptibility is the most invidious of the words here considered. *Mercenary* signifies influenced chiefly or only by desire for gain or reward; thus, etymologically, the mercenary can be hired, while the venal are openly or actually for sale; *hireling* signifies serving for hire or pay, or having the spirit or character of one who works or of that which is done directly for hire or pay. *Mercenary* has especial application to character or disposition; as, a *mercenary* spirit; *mercenary* motives—*i.e.,* a spirit or motives of which money is the chief consideration or the moving principle. The hireling, the mercenary, and the venal are alike in making principle, conscience, and honor of less account than gold or sordid considerations; but the mercenary and venal may be simply open to the bargain and sale which the hireling has already consummated; a clergyman may be *mercenary* in making place and pay of undue importance while not *venal* enough to forsake his own communion for another for any reward that could be offered him The mercenary may retain much show of independence; *hireling* service sacrifices self-respect as well as principle; a public officer who makes his office tributary to private speculation in which he is interested is *mercenary*; if he receives a stipulated recompense for administering his office at the behest of some leader, faction, corporation, or the like, he is both *hireling* and *venal*; if he gives essential advantages for pay, without subjecting himself to any direct domination, his course is *venal*, but not *hireling*. *Hack* and *hackney* apply to a person who is willing to offer himself or his services for hire. The terms frequently suggest mediocre ability, willingness to drudge, or indifference to the quality of the work produced; as, a *hack* writer; a *hackney* sonneteer. Compare **pay; venial**.

ANTONYMS: *disinterested, generous, honest, honorable, incorruptible, patriotic, public-spirited, unpurchasable.*

VENERATE

adore   revere   reverence   worship

These verbs and their corresponding nouns, *adoration, reverence* (for both the verbs *revere* and *reverence*), *veneration*, and *worship*, agree in denoting a feeling of profound honor and respect for something or someone. Things or persons that are regarded as sacred or holy because of their age or character are *venerated*. To *venerate* is to hold in exalted honor without fear, and is applied to objects or persons less removed from us than those we *revere*, being said especially of aged persons, of places or objects having sacred associations, and of abstractions; we *venerate* an aged pastor, the dust of heroes or martyrs, lofty virtue or self-sacrifice, or some great cause, as that of civil or religious liberty; we do not *venerate* God, but *revere* or *reverence* Him.

To *revere* or *reverence* is to hold in mingled love and honor, with a feeling of tenderness and deference; one *reveres* or *reverences* that which, while lovely, is sublimely exalted and brings upon us by contrast a sense of our unworthiness or inferiority. One *reveres* persons deserving respect and honor, and things or qualities associated with those persons; one *reverences* things more often than persons.

In the strict sense of the word, one *worships* only God or a divine being, as by prayer or by ceremonial; as, a cathedral dedicated to the worship of God. In looser usage, *worship* suggests the offering of homage or deification, whether the object of such *veneration* is a divine being or not; as, he *worships* money and success; to *worship* at the shrine of Beauty. *Adore* also denotes the offering of homage and respect to a divine being; however, it connotes the act of an individual rather than a group, and therefore implies the performance of the single acts of worship, as prayer, obeisance, etc.

ANTONYMS: *contemn, despise, detest, disdain, dishonor, disregard, scoff at, scorn, slight, spurn.*

VENIAL

excusable   pardonable   slight   trivial

Venial signifies capable of being pardoned, and, in common use, capable of being readily pardoned, easily overlooked. Aside from its technical ecclesiastical use, *venial* is always understood as marking some fault comparatively *slight* or *trivial*. A *venial* offense is one readily overlooked; a *pardonable* offense requires more serious consideration, but on deliberation is found to be susceptible of pardon. *Excusable* is scarcely applied to offenses, but to matters open to doubt or criticism rather than direct censure; so used, it often falls little short of justifiable; as, I think, under those circumstances, his action was *excusable*. In theological use, *venial* applies to those sins which can be pardoned, as opposed to the unpardonable or mortal sins. Protestants do not recognize the distinction between *venial* and mortal sins. *Venial* must not be confounded with the very different word "venal." Compare **venal.**

> **ANTONYMS:** *inexcusable, inexpiable, mortal, unpardonable, unjustifiable.*

VERBAL

literal   oral   vocal

Verbal (from L. *verbum*, a word) signifies of, pertaining to, or connected with words, especially with words as distinguished from the ideas they convey; *vocal* (from L. *vox*, the voice) signifies of or pertaining to the voice, uttered or modulated by the voice, and especially uttered with or sounding with full, resonant voice; *literal* (from L. *litera*, a letter) signifies consisting of or expressed by letters, or according to the letter, in the broader sense of the exact meaning or requirement of the words used; what is called "the letter of the law" is its *literal* meaning without going behind what is expressed by the letters on the page.

Oral (from L. *os*, the mouth) signifies uttered through the mouth or (in common phrase) by word of mouth; thus *oral* applies to that which is given by spoken words in distinction from that which is written or printed; as, *oral* tradition; an *oral* examination. By this rule we should in strictness speak of an *oral* contract or an *oral* message, but *verbal* contract and *verbal* message, as indicating that which is by spoken rather than by written words, have become so fixed in the language that they can probably never be changed; this usage is also in line with other idioms of the language; as, "I give you my word," "by word of mouth," etc. A *verbal* translation may be *oral* or written, so that it is word for word; a *literal* translation follows the construction and idiom of the original as well as the words; a *literal* translation is more than one that is merely *verbal*; both *verbal* and *literal* are opposed to "free."

In the same sense, of attending to words only, we speak of *verbal* criticism, a *verbal* change. *Vocal* has primary reference to the human voice; as, *vocal* sounds, *vocal* music; *vocal* may be applied within certain limits to inarticulate sounds given forth by other animals than man; as, the woods were *vocal* with the songs of birds; *oral* is never so applied, but is limited to articulate utterance having a definite meaning; as, an *oral* statement.

VICTORY

achievement	ascendency	mastery	supremacy
advantage	conquest	success	triumph

Victory is the state resulting from the overcoming of an opponent or opponents in any contest, or from the overcoming of difficulties, obstacles, evils, etc., considered as opponents or enemies. In the latter sense any hard-won *achievement, advantage,* or *success* may be termed a *victory.* In *conquest* and *mastery* there is implied a permanence of state that is not implied in *victory.* *Triumph,* originally denoting the public rejoicing in honor of a *victory,* has come to signify also a peculiarly exultant, complete, and glorious *victory.* We speak of papal or royal *supremacy,* but of the *ascendancy* or dominating influence that a country gains by policy or war. Compare **conquer.**

ANTONYMS: *defeat, destruction, disappointment, disaster, failure, frustration, miscarriage, overthrow, retreat, rout.*

VIGILANT

alert	cautious	on the lookout	wary
awake	circumspect	sleepless	watchful
careful	on the alert	wakeful	wide-awake

Vigilant and its synonyms all connote *on the lookout* for good or evil, or sometimes for an opportunity. *Vigilant* implies more sustained activity and more intelligent volition than *alert;* one may be habitually *alert* by reason of native quickness of perception and thought, or one may be momentarily *alert* under some excitement or expectancy; one who is *vigilant* is so with thoughtful purpose. One is *vigilant* against danger or harm; he may be *alert* or *watchful* for good as well as against evil; he is *wary* in view of suspected stratagem, trickery, or treachery. A person may be *wakeful* or *sleepless* because of some merely physical excitement or excitability, as through insomnia; yet he may be utterly careless and negligent in his wakefulness, the reverse of *watchful;* a person who is truly *watchful* must keep himself *wide-awake* while on watch.

Watchful, from the Saxon, and *vigilant,* from the Latin, are almost exact equivalents; but *vigilant* has somewhat more of sharp definiteness and somewhat more suggestion of volition; one may be habitually *watchful;* one is *vigilant* of set purpose and for direct cause, as in the presence of an enemy.

Those who are *circumspect* are *watchful* in all directions and with regard to all possible consequences; a *cautious* person always tries to guard against contingencies. See **alert**.

> ANTONYMS: *careless, drowsy, dull, heedless, inattentive, incautious, inconsiderate, neglectful, negligent, oblivious, thoughtless, unwary.*

VIOLENT

acute	immoderate	outrageous	tumultuous
boisterous	impetuous	passionate	turbulent
fierce	infuriate	poignant	uncontrollable
frantic	intense	raging	ungovernable
frenzied	mad	raving	vehement
fuming	maniac	severe	wild
furious	maniacal	sharp	

Violent implies proceeding from, marked by, caused by, or resulting from great physical force or intensely excited feeling. *Boisterous* is rough and *violent* and applies to persons and things that are noisy and agitated. *Frenzied* and *frantic* apply to behavior and looks, and indicate violently distracted or excited. We speak of *frenzied* rage and *frantic* efforts. *Vehement* and *furious* connote very *violent*; as, *vehement* altercation, a *vehement* or *furious* storm. *Maniac* and *maniacal* imply characterized by *violent* madness; *raving* refers to a *frenzied*, excited condition or to madness that is accompanied by incoherent utterances. *Infuriate* is excessively angry; *passionate* is susceptible of *violent* emotion; *outrageous* is causing *violent* injury or offense. *Poignant* is intensely painful or affecting; as, *poignant* grief. See **fierce**.

VIRTUE

chastity	honesty	probity	truth
duty	honor	purity	uprightness
excellence	integrity	rectitude	virtuousness
faithfulness	justice	righteousness	worth
goodness	morality	rightness	worthiness

Virtue (from L. *virtus*, primarily manly strength or courage, from *vir*, a man, a hero) is, in its full sense, *goodness* that is victorious through trial, perhaps through temptation and conflict. *Goodness*, the being morally good, may be much less than *virtue*, as lacking the strength that comes from trial and conflict, or it may be very much more than *virtue*, as rising sublimely above the possibility of temptation and conflict. *Virtue* is distinctively human; we do not predicate it of God. *Morality* is conformity to the moral law in action, whether in matters concerning ourselves or others, whether with or without right principle.

Honesty and *probity* are used especially of one's relations to his fellow men; *probity* is *honesty* tried and proved, especially in those things that are beyond the reach of legal requirement; above the commercial sense, *honesty* may be applied to the highest truthfulness of the soul to and with itself and its Maker. *Integrity,* in the full sense, is moral wholeness without a flaw; when used, as it often is, of contracts and dealings, it has reference to inherent character and principle, and denotes much more than superficial or conventional *honesty.* *Honor* is a lofty *honesty* that scorns fraud or wrong as base and unworthy of itself. *Honor* rises far above thought of the motto that "*honesty* is the best policy."

Worth and *worthiness,* in this connection, both connote *honor* and *virtue;* *excellence* of character; we speak of an official of great *worth,* and the *worthiness* of a cause. *Purity* is freedom from all admixture, especially of that which debases; it is *chastity* both of heart and life, but of the life because from the heart. *Duty,* the rendering of what is due to any person or in any relation, is, in this connection, the fulfilment of moral obligations. *Rectitude* and *righteousness* denote conformity to the standard of right, whether in heart or act; *righteousness* is used especially in the religious sense. *Uprightness* refers especially to conduct. *Virtuousness* is a quality of the soul or of action; in the latter sense it is the essence of virtuous action. See **duty; justice.** Compare **innocent.**

ANTONYMS: *evil, vice, viciousness, wickedness, wrong.*

W

WANDER

deviate	go astray	range	stray
digress	meander	roam	swerve
diverge	ramble	rove	veer
err			

To *wander* (from AS. *windan,* wind) is to move in an indefinite or indeterminate way which may or may not be a departure from a prescribed way; to *deviate* (from L. *de,* from, and *via,* a way) is to turn from a prescribed or right way, physically, mentally, or morally, usually in an unfavorable sense; to *diverge* (from L. *di,* apart, and *vergo,* incline, tend) is to turn from a course previously followed or that something else follows, and has no unfavorable implication; to *digress* (from L. *di,* apart, aside, and *gradior,* step) is used only with reference to speaking or writing. To *err* is used of intellectual or moral action, and of the moral with primary reference to the intellectual, an error being viewed as in some degree due to ignorance.

Range, roam, and *rove* imply the traversing of considerable, often of vast, distances of land or sea; *range* commonly implies a purpose and defined territory; as, cattle *range* for food; a hunting dog *ranges* a field for game. *Roam* and *rove* are often purposeless, though both generally include the idea of zest. To *swerve* or *veer* is to turn suddenly from a prescribed or previous course, and often but momentarily; *veer* is more capricious and repetitious; the horse *swerves* at the flash of a sword; the wind *veers;* the ship *veers* with the wind.

To *stray* is to go in a somewhat purposeless way aside from the regular path or usual limits or abode, usually with unfavorable implication; cattle *stray* from their pastures; an author *strays* from his subject; one *strays* from the path of virtue. *Stray* is in most uses a lighter word than *wander. Ramble,* in its literal use, is always a word of pleasant suggestion, but in its figurative use always somewhat contemptuous; as, the speaker *rambled* on for half an hour. *Meander* may be used of persons or things that follow a winding course; as, the stream *meanders* through the woods.

WASHING

ablution	bathing	cleansing	laving
bath	cleaning	lavation	purification

Washing, bathing, laving, or *ablution* is effected by the use of water or some other liquid. The Old English word *washing* is most general in meaning, denoting the application of water or other liquid to cleanse any substance by any process; as, the *washing* of clothes, the *washing* of a roof by the rain, the *washing* of gases in the laboratory by passing them through water, the *washing* of ores in mining, or the like. In such use we do not employ *bathing. Washing* is also used of the sweep of water over a substance, with no reference to *cleansing;* as, the *washing* of waves upon the shore.

Bath and *bathing* apply primarily to the *washing* of the human body in whole or in part. *Bath* may also denote the place where, or the apparatus by which, such complete *bathing* may be performed; the *baths* of Caracalla had extensive facilities for complete immersion. *Bath* and *bathing* are sometimes limited to some specific application; as a mud *bath,* sun *bath,* sun *bathing,* sponge *bath,* foot *bath,* shower *bath,* etc. In science and the arts *bath* is employed to denote the partial or complete immersion of an object in some liquid or other substance for any one of various purposes, or the substance in which the object is immersed; as an oil *bath,* a sand *bath,* etc. *Bathing* is used of the free application of water or other liquid either to the whole body or to a part. Without some limitation *bathing* is understood to be complete; as, frequent *bathing* is essential to health; we speak of *bathing* the face or hands, though never of a face *bath* or hand *bath.* In science and the arts, though objects may be cleansed in various *baths* the process is spoken of, not as *bathing,* but as *washing.*

Lavation and *laving* (like the verb "lave") are literary or poetic words denoting the flowing or pouring of water over a substance. *Ablution,* a word not frequent in common speech, denotes a *washing,* partial or complete, or in many cases ceremonial; as, the *ablutions* required of Moslems before each of the five daily prayers. *Cleansing* and *purification* are more extensive in meaning than any of the above-mentioned words; they may be effected by *washing, ablution,* etc., but also by many other means, as, the *cleansing* of the system by medication, the *purification* of the air by ventilation, the *purification* of society by moral influences, the *cleansing* of the plague-smitten portion of London by the Great Fire.

Cleaning may be by sweeping, dusting, etc., as well as by *washing;* vacuum *cleaning* is for many purposes preferred to any other process. *Cleansing* implies some defilement to be removed, which may not be noticeably the case in *washing, bathing,* or *ablution;* a surgeon would not think that ordinary *washing* of his hands was sufficient *cleansing* after an operation. Compare **clean.**

ANTONYMS: *befouling, besmearing, besmirching, contaminating, contamination, defilement, defiling, polluting, pollution, smearing, smirching, soil, soiling, soilure, stain, staining, taint, tainting.*

WAY

alley	driveway	passage	route
artery	footpath	passageway	sidewalk
avenue	highroad	path	street
boulevard	highway	pathway	thoroughfare
bridlepath	lane	road	track
channel	mall	roadway	walk
course	pass		

Wherever there is room for one object to pass another there is a *way*. A *road* (originally a ride*way*) is a prepared *way* for traveling with horses or vehicles, always the latter unless the contrary is expressly stated; a *way* suitable to be traversed only by foot-passengers or by animals is called a *path, bridlepath,* or *track*; as, the *roads* through the hills are mere *bridle-paths.* A *footpath* is for pedestrians only; a *pathway* is either a beaten *track* or a *footpath*; a *sidewalk* is a *footpath* along the side of a *road* or *street*.

A *road* may be private; a *highway* or *highroad* is public, *highway* being a specific name for a *road* legally set apart for the use of the public forever; a *highway* may be over water as well as over land. A *route* is a line of travel, and may be over many *roads*. A *street* is in some center of habitation, as a city, town, or village; when it passes between rows of dwellings the country *road* becomes the village *street*. An *avenue* is a long, broad, and imposing or principal *street*. A *boulevard* is a broad *avenue*; a *mall* is a public promenade. *Track* is a word of wide significance; we speak of a goat *track* on a mountain-side, a railroad *track*, a race *track*, the *track* of a comet; on a traveled *road* the line worn by regular passing of hoofs and wheels in either direction is called the *track*.

An *alley* is a narrow *walk* in a garden, or a narrow *passageway* between buildings; a *lane* is a narrow, rural *road* often bordered by hedges, or a *passage-way* between rows of people. A *course* can mean a *track* for racing; a tract of ground, as a golf *course*; a *channel* for a stream; or progress from one point to another. An *artery*, primarily a blood vessel that carries blood from the heart, is also applied to any main *channel* which has a branching system; as, *arteries* of commerce. A *passage* is between any two objects or lines of enclosure, a *pass* commonly between mountains. A *driveway* is within enclosed grounds, as of a private residence. A *channel* is a water*way*. A *thoroughfare* is a *way* through; a *road* or *street* temporarily or permanently closed at any point ceases for such time to be a *thoroughfare*. Compare **direction.**

WEALTH

abundance	goods	money	profusion
affluence	lucre	opulence	property
assets	luxuriance	pelf	prosperity
competence	luxury	plenty	riches
competency	means	possessions	substance
fortune			

Wealth denotes a store or accumulation of those material things that men desire to possess, and that have exchangeable value; *riches* was originally a singular noun, used as a near equivalent of *wealth*; but *riches* has more of the relative and comparative meaning of the adjective "rich"; the "rich" man of a small rural town would commonly not be considered a man of *wealth* in New York or London; *wealth* is a broader, higher, and more substantial word than *riches*; we speak of the public *wealth*, the national *wealth*, rather than of the public or national *riches*; *riches* carries more of the idea of personal possession; *wealth* is distributive; a prosperous farming community may have great *wealth*, while few of its members possess *riches*, and none are in a condition of *affluence* or *opulence*.

Property is something of value that is, or may be, in personal possession of an owner; it may be of various kinds; as, personal *property* or real *property*; it may be of great or little value; as, a small or a large *property*, an unproductive *property*, etc.; but when used without qualification the word denotes *possessions* of considerable value; as, a man of *property*. *Substance* has similar use, but is less definite, vaguely denoting one's entire *possessions*, with the suggestion that these are considerable; as, a man of *substance*.

Money, in this connection, has more of the directly mercantile or mercenary suggestion than *riches* or *wealth*, and does not approach the meaning of *affluence* or *opulence*; the phrase "a man of *money*," carries less indication of membership in a substantial and respected class than the phrase "a man of *wealth*"; *money* may be all that the former man has. Financially, the public *wealth* denotes all the *possessions* of a community of whatever kind, including the means of production; the public *money* is in the treasury or on deposit, and is a very small part of the public *wealth*. *Means* denotes *money* or *property* considered as a procuring medium—available resources; when used without limitation, the phrase "a man of *means*" signifies one of considerable *possessions*, but various adjectives may modify the meaning of the word *means*; we may speak of small or limited *means*, ample or unlimited *means*; the owner of vast *property* may be of limited *means*, if he can neither utilize nor realize on his *property*.

A *fortune* is a considerable amount of *wealth* in the possession of a single owner, or of joint owners; as, to make or inherit a *fortune*; this, too, admits of degrees; as, a small, large, or ample *fortune*. A *competence* or *competency* is sufficient *property* for comfortable livelihood—and no more. *Plenty* denotes *abundance* of material supplies or resources, with especial reference to direct use or enjoyment; as, a land of *plenty*. *Lucre* and *pelf* are opprobrious terms, of inferior grade, *lucre* often denoting that the *money* or *wealth* is ill-gotten.

Affluence denotes *abundance* as freely flowing in; *opulence* denotes *abundance* in simple existence or possession; *affluence* is thus a more vivid term than *opulence*; an abundant income, as from a life estate, might enable one to live in *affluence*; only substantial possessions could fill the meaning of *opulence*. Both *affluence* and *opulence* have reference to condition, state, manifestation, or use, rather than to mere possession; both imply abundant resources accompanied by generous expenditure; we should not speak of a miser, however wealthy, as enjoying *affluence* or *opulence*, though we might refer to his hidden *wealth* or his useless *riches*. *Profusion* is *abundance* that pours forth or overflows, applying especially to extravagant or unchecked expenditure; *affluence* is a nobler word than *profusion*; *profusion* may characterize the mere spendthrift; *affluence*, the man of ample resources.

The secondary or figurative uses of these words closely follow the primary or literal; we may speak of *affluence* of thought or language; *opulence* of learning; *luxuriance* of style; *profusion* of epithets or imagery; *wealth* may figuratively denote an *abundance* of almost anything that is viewed as a valuable and desirable *possession.*

ANTONYMS: *beggary, destitution, impecuniosity, indigence, lack, mendicancy, misery, need, pauperism, penury, poverty, privation, scarcity, squalor, straitened circumstances, want, wretchedness.*

WILL

decision	disposition	resolution	volition
desire	inclination	resoluteness	wish
determination			

Will is a word of wide range of meaning, and, both as faculty and act, has been the subject of many and various theories. In popular language *will* is used for the power and process of choosing or deciding, and is often equivalent to *desire* or *inclination,* as when we speak of doing something against our *will. Volition* is a word of scientific precision, usually denoting the deliberate act of choosing or deciding. *Decision* is often the habit as well as the act of deciding something definitely. We speak of a man of *decision* or of an important *decision* by a court. *Determination* implies a fixed intention as the result of examination and choice; as, a *determination* to continue the search. *Disposition,* in this comparison, connotes a conscious *inclination* toward an end or course; as, a *disposition* to become overextended. *Resolution* always includes staying power to see something through; as, he faced the enemy with *resolution. Resoluteness* is the quality or character of remaining firm.

WISDOM

attainment	foresight	learning	reasonableness
depth	information	prescience	sagacity
discernment	insight	profundity	sense
discretion	judgment	prudence	skill
enlightenment	judiciousness	reason	understanding
erudition	knowledge		

Wisdom has been defined as "the right use of *knowledge,*" or "the use of the most important means for attaining the best ends," *wisdom* thus presupposing *knowledge* for its very existence and exercise. *Wisdom* is mental power acting upon the materials that fullest *knowledge* gives in the most effective way. There may be what is termed "practical *wisdom*" that looks only to material results; but, in its full sense, *wisdom* implies the highest and noblest exercise of all the faculties of the moral nature as well as of the intellect. *Prudence* is a lower and more negative form of the same virtue, respecting outward and practical matters, and largely with a view of avoiding loss and injury; *wisdom* transcends *prudence*, so that while the part of *prudence* is ordinarily also that of *wisdom*, cases arise, as in the exigencies of business or of war, when the highest *wisdom* is in the disregard of the maxims of *prudence*.

Enlightenment, erudition, information, knowledge, learning, and *skill* are acquired, as by study or practice. *Insight, judgment, profundity* or *depth, reason, sagacity, sense,* and *understanding* are native qualities of mind, though capable of increase by cultivation. The other qualities are on the borderline. *Judgment,* the power of forming decisions, especially correct decisions, is broader and more positive than *prudence,* leading one to do, as readily as to refrain from doing; but *judgment* is more limited in range and less exalted in character than *wisdom*; to say of one that he displayed good *judgment* is much less than to say that he manifested *wisdom*. *Skill* is far inferior to *wisdom,* consisting largely in the practical application of acquired *knowledge,* power, and habitual processes, or in the ingenious contrivance that makes such application possible. In the making of something perfectly useless there may be great *skill,* but no *wisdom*. Compare **acumen; knowledge; mind; prudence; sagacious; shrewd; skilful.**

ANTONYMS: *absurdity, error, fatuity, folly, foolishness, idiocy, imbecility, imprudence, indiscretion, miscalculation, misjudgment, nonsense, senselessness, silliness, stupidity.*

WIT

badinage	fun	joke	raillery
banter	humor	persiflage	waggery
burlesque	jest	playfulness	waggishness
drollery	jocularity	pleasantry	witticism
facetiousness			

Wit is the quick perception of unusual or commonly unperceived analogies or relations between things apparently unrelated, and has been said to depend upon a union of surprise and pleasure; it depends certainly on the production of a diverting, entertaining, or merrymaking surprise. The analogies with which *wit* plays are often superficial or artificial; *humor* deals with real analogies of an amusing or entertaining kind, or with traits of character that are seen to have a comical side as soon as brought to view. *Wit* is keen, sudden, brief, and sometimes severe; *humor* is deep, thoughtful, sustained, and always kindly. *Pleasantry* is lighter and less vivid than *wit*. *Fun* denotes the merry results produced by *wit* and *humor,* or by any fortuitous occasion of mirth, and is pronounced and often hilarious. *Badinage* denotes a delicate, often tender, *fun*-making or *banter*; *persiflage* is light and flippant conversation often mocking but not bitter; *raillery* is sharp, even sarcastic, ridicule.

ANTONYMS: *dulness, gravity, seriousness, sobriety, solemnity, stolidity, stupidity.*

WORK

achievement	doing	grind	product
action	drudgery	labor	production
business	employment	occupation	toil
deed	exertion	performance	

Work is the generic term for any continuous application of energy toward an end; it may imply activity of mind or body, or of a machine, and it may be hard or easy. *Labor* denotes only human *work*, and suggests usually physical or mental *exertion*. *Labor* is hard and wearying *work*; *toil* is prolonged and exhausting *work*, more severe than *labor*. *Work* is also used for any result of working, physical or mental, and has special senses, as in mechanics, which *labor* and *toil* do not share. *Drudgery* is plodding, irksome, and often menial *work*. *Grind* denotes *work* which one regards as *drudgery* or *toil*, and whose monotony is fatiguing to mind and body. Compare **act; business.**

ANTONYMS: *ease, idleness, leisure, recreation, relaxation, repose, rest, vacation.*

Y

YET

besides	hitherto	still
further	now	thus far

Yet and *still* have many closely related senses, and, with verbs of past time, are often interchangeable; we may say "while he was *yet* a child," or "while he was *still* a child." *Yet*, like *still*, often applies to past action or state extending to and including the present time, especially when joined with "as"; we can say "he is feeble as *yet*," or "he is *still* feeble," with scarcely appreciable difference of meaning, except that the former statement implies somewhat more of expectation than the latter. *Yet* with a negative applies to completed action, often replacing a positive statement with *still*; "he is not gone *yet*" is nearly the same as "he is here *still*." *Yet* has a reference to the future which *still* does not share; "we may be successful *yet*" implies that success may begin at some future time; "we may be successful *still*" implies that we may continue to enjoy in the future such success as we are winning now. *Further* may refer to either past or future; *hitherto* refers only to the past.

YOUTHFUL

adolescent	childish	immature	puerile
boyish	childlike	juvenile	virgin
callow	girlish	maiden	virginal

Youthful connotes the possession of youth or of the characteristics appropriate to the young; it may be used either in a favorable or in an extenuating sense; as, *youthful* good looks; he had atoned for his *youthful* misdeeds. *Youthful* in the sense of having the characteristics of youth may have a favorable meaning as applied to any age, as when we say the old man still retains his *youthful* ardor; *juvenile* in such use would belittle the statement. *Juvenile* denotes a mentally or physically immature person, or an inexperienced one; it is commonly applied to that which is suitable for or pertains to boys and girls in their teens; as *juvenile* clothes; *juvenile* literature; *juvenile* delinquency.

Puerile refers to acts or statements which are pardonable in a young person, but are unforgivable in an adult; in any case the word has unfavorable implications. *Boyish*, on the other hand, usually has entirely favorable implications; it describes the engaging or attractive qualities of normal, wholesome boys; as, a *boyish* laugh. *Boyish* may be said of girls, in reference to their clothes, looks, etc., and *girlish* of boys; the latter use connotes effeminacy.

Virgin and *virginal* are said especially of girls, but in an extended use they may apply also to boys because they suggest the innocence and purity associated with youth. *Maiden* is even more suggestive of *youthful* inexperience; its chief connotation is that one's ability, strength, virtue, etc., are still untried; as, a *maiden* effort, the *maiden* voyage of the "Queen Mary."

ANTONYMS: Compare synonyms for **old**.

445

INDEX OF SYNONYMS

Example:

pretty, Beautiful.......... 87

The discussion of the term "pretty" will be found under the key word "Beautiful" on page 87. Also see page ix.

Abandon 1
  Renounce 362
  Surrender 411
abandoned, Addicted 22
  Bad 80
abase, Debase 144
abash, Embarrass 174
Abate 1
  Abolish 5
  Alleviate 40
abbey, Cloister 126
Abbreviation 2
  Abridgment 7
abdicate, Abandon 1
aberration, Insanity ...259
Abet 2
  Help 231
abettor *or* abetter, Acces-
  sory 15
Abeyance 3
abeyant, Latent 269
Abhor 4
abhorrence, Abomination.. 6
  Antipathy 52
  Hatred 229
Abide 5
  Endure 179
  Stand 401
abiding, Permanent 314
ability, Power 326
abject, Base 85
  Pitiful 319
abjure, Abandon 1
  Renounce 362
able, Adequate 24
  Clever 125
  Good 221
  Sagacious 378
ablution, Washing 438
abnormal, Irregular ...261
abode, Home 239
Abolish 5
  Cancel 107
  Overthrow 306
abominable, Bad 80
  Criminal 141
abominate, Abhor 4
Abomination 5
aboriginal, Native 294
  Primeval 336
abortive, Vain 431
Abound 6
abounding, Plentiful 322
Above 7

aboveboard, Candid 108
abridge, Restrain 368
Abridgment 7
  Abbreviation 2
abrogate, Abolish 5
  Cancel 107
abrupt, Bluff 95
  Steep 403
Abscond 8
absent, Abstracted 12
absent-minded, Abstracted. 12
Absolute 9
  Infinite 253
  Pure 346
absolution, Pardon, *n.*....309
Absolve 9
  Pardon, *v.* 309
Absorb 10
absorbed, Abstracted 12
abstain, Stop 403
abstaining, Abstinence .. 11
abstemiousness, Abstinence 11
abstention, Abstinence ... 11
Abstinence 11
Abstract 11
  Abridgment 7
  Steal 402
Abstracted 12
abstruse, Complex 130
  Mysterious 291
  Obscure 301
Absurd 12
  Incongruous 251
abundance, Wealth 440
abundant, Large 268
  Plentiful 322
Abuse 13
  Abomination 6
abutting, Adjacent 25
abysm, Abyss 14
Abyss 14
Academic, Academical.... 14
accede, Agree 31
accelerate, Quicken 350
accept, Agree 31
  Assume 70
  Confess 133
acceptable, Pleasant 321
accepted, Authentic, ... 76
access, Entrance 182
accessible, Friendly 214
accession, Entrance 182
Accessory 15
  Appendage 58

Auxiliary 77
Accident 16
  Hazard 231
acclaim, Praise 327
acclamation, Praise 327
accommodate, Adapt 20
accommodation, Compro-
  mise 130
accompaniment, Appendage 58
  Circumstance 123
accompany, Follow 209
accomplice, Accessory ... 15
  Associate, *n.* 68
accomplish, Attain 75
  Do 161
  Transact 423
accomplished, Polite 324
  Skilful 393
accomplishment, Act 18
  Attainment 75
  End, *n.* 177
accord, Agree 31
  Harmony 228
accordance, Harmony ...228
accordingly, Therefore ...418
accost, Address, *v.* 23
account, *n.*, History 235
  Reason, *n.* 355
  Record 357
  Report 363
  Story 404
account, *v.*, Calculate....105
accountability, Duty 168
accountable, Responsible..366
accredited, Authentic ... 76
accumulate, Amass 44
accurate, Precise 329
accuse, Arraign 64
accustomed, Addicted 22
  Usual 429
acerb, Bitter 93
acerbity, Acrimony 18
acetous, Bitter 93
ache, Pain 308
achieve, Attain 75
  Do 161
  Get 219
  Succeed 408
achievement, Act 18
  End 177
  Victory 435
  Work 444
acid, Bitter 93
acidulated, Bitter 93

447

acidulous, Bitter 93
acknowledge, Confess 133
acknowledgment, Apology. 55
Acquaintance 17
   Knowledge 266
acquiesce, Agree 31
acquire, Attain 75
   Get 219
   Purchase 345
acquirement, Attainment.. 75
acquisition, Attainment... 75
acquisitive, Miserly 285
acquit, Absolve   9
   Pardon 309
acquittal, Pardon 309
acrid, Bitter 93
acrimonious, Bitter 93
   Morose 289
Acrimony 18
   Enmity 180
Act, n. 18
   Exercise 190
   Motion 290
   Transaction 423
act, v., Transact 423
action, Act 18
   Battle 86
   Behavior 90
   Exercise 190
   Motion 290
   Operation 304
   Transaction 423
   Work 444
Active 19
   Alert 35
   Alive 37
   Busy 103
   Nimble 298
activity, Alacrity 34
   Exercise 190
actor, Agent 30
   Cause 114
actual, Real 354
actualize, Do 161
actuate, Influence 254
Acumen 19
acute, Sagacious 378
   Shrewd 388
   Violent 436
acuteness, Acumen 19
   Ingenuity 254
adage, Proverb 343
Adapt 20
   Apply 60
adapted, Adequate 24
   Fit 205
Add 21
   Append 58
   Attach 71
addendum, Appendage ... 58
Addicted 22
addition, Appendage 58
addled, Drunk 167
Address, n. 22

Speech 399
Address, v. 23
   Appeal 57
adduce, Allege 38
   Offer 302
adept, Skilful 393
Adequate 24
   Fit 205
   Good 221
   Plentiful 322
adherence, Attachment .. 73
Adherent 24
adhesion, Attachment 73
Adhesive 25
adieu, Farewell 198
adit, Entrance 182
Adjacent 25
adjoin, Add 21
   Attach 71
   Unite 428
adjoining, Adjacent 25
Adjourn 26
   Protract 343
adjournment, Abeyance ..   3
adjunct, Appendage 58
adjuration, Oath 300
adjure, Ask 67
   Pray 328
adjust, Adapt 20
   Apply 60
   Arrange 65
adjustment, Compromise..130
administer, Execute 189
admirable, Fine 204
   Good 221
admiration, Amazement.. 45
   Esteem 184
Admire 26
   Esteem 184
Admissible 27
admission, Entrance 182
admit, Agree 31
   Allow 42
   Confess 133
admittance, Entrance 182
admixture, Alloy 42
admonish, Reprove 365
admonition, Counsel 140
   Reproof 364
adolescent, Youthful 445
adore, Admire 26
   Venerate 433
Adorn 27
adroit, Clever 125
   Skilful 393
adroitness, Address 22
   Dexterity 154
adulation, Praise 327
adulterant, Alloy 42
adulteration, Alloy 42
advance, Allege 38
   Amend 47
   Exalt 188
   Progress 338

Promote 340
Quicken 350
advancement, Progress ...338
advantage, Profit 337
   Utility ... .429
   Victory 435
advantageous, Good 221
adventure, Accident 16
adventurous, Brave 97
adversary, Enemy 179
Adverse 28
adversity, Misfortune ...286
advert, Allude 43
advertise, Announce ... 50
advice, Counsel 140
   News 297
advised, Conscious 135
advocate, Abet   2
   Plead 320
aerial, Airy 33
affable, Friendly 214
affair, Battle 86
   Business 102
   Transaction 423
affect, Assume 70
   Concern 131
affectation, Hypocrisy ...242
   Pretense 332
affection, Attachment 73
   Disease 159
   Friendship 215
   Love 276
affectionate, Friendly ...214
affidavit, Oath 300
   Testimony 418
affiliate, Associate, v. 68
affinity, Attachment 73
   Kin 266
   Likeness 273
   Similarity 390
affirm, Allege 38
   State 401
affirmation, Testimony ...418
affix, Add 21
   Append 58
   Apply 60
   Attach 71
   Unite 428
afflict, Punish 345
afflicted, Sad 377
affliction, Grief 223
   Misfortune 286
afflictive, Troublesome ..426
affluence, Wealth 440
affluent, Plentiful 322
afford, Endure 179
   Give 220
affray, Argument 62
   Quarrel 348
affright, Alarm 35
   Fear 199
   Frighten 215
Affront 29
aforesaid, Previous 333

Afraid 29
age, Time 419
aged, Old 303
agency, Operation 304
Agent 30
  Cause 114
agglomeration, Aggregate. 30
aggrandize, Exalt 188
aggravate, Affront 29
  Intensify 259
Aggregate 30
  Amass 44
aggregation, Aggregate... 30
aggression, Attack 73
aggrieve, Abuse 13
aghast, Afraid 29
agile, Active 19
  Nimble 298
agility, Alacrity 34
agitate, Shake 386
agitation, Storm 404
agnomen, Name 293
agnostic, Skeptic 392
agog, Eager 169
agony, Pain 308
Agree 31
agreeable, Amiable 47
  Comfortable 127
  Good 221
  Pleasant 321
agreement, Compromise..130
  Contract 137
  Harmony 228
agricultural, Rustic 376
Agriculture 31
agrology, Agriculture ... 31
agronomy, Agriculture ... 31
aid, n., Adherent 24
  Auxiliary 77
  Subsidy 408
aid, v., Abet 2
  Help 231
  Promote 340
aider, Adherent 24
ailment, Disease 159
Aim 32
  Design 152
  Direction 158
  Reason 355
Air 33
  Melody 281
Airy 33
akin, Alike 37
Alacrity 34
Alarm 35
  Fear 199
  Frighten 215
alarmed, Afraid 29
alarming, Awful 78
Alert 35
  Active 19
  Alarm 35
  Alive 37
  Nimble 298

Vigilant 435
alertness, Alacrity 34
alibi, Apology 55
Alien, adj. 36
Alien, n. 36
alienate, Surrender 411
Alike 37
  Synonymous 412
aliment, Food 209
Alive 37
  Active 19
  Alert 35
all, Every 186
Allay 38
  Alleviate 40
Allege 38
  Offer 302
  State 401
Allegiance 39
Allegory 39
  Fiction 202
Alleviate 40
  Abate 1
  Allay 38
alley, Way 439
Alliance 41
  Association 69
  Kin 266
allocate, Allot 41
Allot 41
  Apply 60
  Apportion 61
  Devote 154
Allow 42
  Confess 133
  Endure 179
allowable, Admissible ... 27
allowance, Pay 312
  Permission 314
  Subsidy 408
Alloy 42
Allude 43
Allure 43
  Draw 164
  Persuade 316
ally, n., Accessory 15
  Adherent 24
  Associate 68
  Auxiliary 77
ally, v., Associate 68
almsgiving, Benevolence . 91
Also 44
alter, Change, v. 117
alteration, Change, n. ...116
altercation, Argument... 62
alternative, Choice 121
although, Notwithstanding299
altruism, Benevolence.... 91
altruistic, Humane 240
amalgamate, Mix 286
Amass 44
Amateur 45
Amazement 45
  Perplexity 316

ambiguous, Equivocal ...183
  Obscure 301
Ambition 46
ameliorate, Amend 47
amenable, Docile 162
  Responsible 366
Amend 47
amends, Reward 371
Amiable 47
amicable, Friendly 214
Amid 48
amidst, Amid........... 48
amity, Friendship 215
  Harmony 228
amnesty, Pardon, n. 309
among, Amid 48
amongst, Amid 48
amount, Aggregate 30
ample, Large 268
  Plentiful 322
Amplify 48
  Add 21
amuse, Entertain 180
amusement, Entertainment181
analogous, Alike 37
analogy, Likeness 273
  Similarity 390
analysis, Abridgment ... 7
anarchism, Socialism ...397
anarchy, Revolution 370
anathema, Oath 300
ancient, Antique 53
  Obsolete 301
  Old 303
  Primeval 336
anecdote, Story 404
Anger 49
  Hatred 229
anguish, Anxiety 53
  Grief 223
  Pain 308
animadversion, Reproof..364
animal, Brutish 101
  Animate, Alive 37
  Encourage 176
animated, Airy 33
  Alive 37
  Eager 169
animation, Alacrity 34
animosity, Anger 49
  Enmity 180
  Hatred 229
  Quarrel 348
animus, Enmity 180
annals, History 235
annex, Add 21
  Append 58
  Attach 71
annihilate, Abolish 5
  Exterminate 191
annotation, Remark 361
Announce 50
  Speak 398
annoy, Affront.......... 29

annoyance, Abomination.. 6
annoying, Troublesome...426
annul, Abolish 5
   Cancel 107
anomalous, Absurd 12
   Irregular 261
   Queer 348
Answer 50
answerable, Responsible..366
antagonism, Antipathy... 52
   Enmity 180
antagonist, Enemy 179
antagonistic, Adverse 28
   Contrary 138
antagonize, Dispute 160
antecedent, Cause 114
   Precedent 329
   Previous, ...333
antediluvian, Old 303
antepast, Anticipation ... 52
anterior, Previous 333
Anticipate 51
   Prevent 322
Anticipation 52
Antipathy 52
   Enmity 180
   Hatred 229
antiquated, Antique 53
   Obsolete 301
   Old 303
Antique 53
   Old 303
Anxiety 53
   Care 110
anxious, Afraid 29
   Eager 169
any, Every 186
Apathy 54
   Stupor 406
aperture, Hole 236
aphorism, Proverb 343
Apiece 55
apocalypse, Revelation...369
apolog, Allegory 39
   Fiction 202
apologia, Apology 55
apologize for, Palliate .. 308
Apology 55
   Defense 146
apostate, Heretic 232
apostrophize, Address, v.. 23
apothegm, Proverb 343
appal, Frighten 215
appalling, Awful 78
apparatus, Tool 421
apparel, Dress 166
Apparent 56
   Clear 124
   Evident 187
Appeal 57
   Ask 67
   Pray 328
appeal to Address, v.... 23
Appear 57

appearance, Air 33
appease, Allay 38
appellation, Name 293
Append 58
   Add 21
   Attach 71
   Unite 428
Appendage 58
   Accessory 15
appendix, Appendage 58
appetence, Appetite 59
   Desire 152
Appetite 59
   Desire 152
applaud, Admire 26
applause, Praise 327
appliance, Tool 421
application, Exercise ...190
   Industry 252
Apply 60
   Adapt 20
   Allot 41
   Attach 71
   Devote 154
   Fix 206
apply (for or to), Appeal. 57
apply for, Ask.......... 67
apply to, Address........ 23
   Ask 67
appoint, Allot 41
   Apportion 61
Apportion 61
   Allot 41
   Devote 154
apposite, Fit 205
appreciate, Esteem, v.....184
apprehend, Anticipate.... 51
   Arrest 67
   Catch 113
   Perceive 313
apprehension, Alarm 35
   Anticipation 52
   Anxiety 53
   Fear 199
   Idea 244
   Knowledge 266
apprehensive, Afraid 29
apprised, Conscious 135
approach, Address, v.....23
   Approximation 61
   Entrance 182
approbation, Praise 327
appropriate, adj., Becom-
   ing 88
   Condign 132
   Fit 205
   Right 373
appropriate, v., Abstract.. 11
   Apply 60
   Apportion 61
   Assume 70
   Devote 154
appropriation, Subsidy ...408
approval, Praise 327

approve, Admire 26
   Agree 31
Approximation 61
appurtenance, Appendage. 58
a priori, Transcendental..424
apt, Clever 125
   Fit 205
   Likely 272
   Sagacious 378
   Skilful 393
aptitude, Dexterity 154
   Genius 218
   Power 326
arbiter, Judge 263
arbitrary, Absolute 9
arbitrate, Interpose 260
arbitration, Compromise. 130
arbitrator, Judge 263
Arcadian, Rustic 376
archaic, Antique 53
   Obsolete 301
archetype, Example 188
   Idea 244
   Ideal 244
   Model 288
archive, Record 357
archives, History 235
Ardent 62
   Eager 169
ardor, Enthusiasm 182
arduous, Difficult 157
   Troublesome 426
argot, Slang 395
argue, Dispute 160
   Plead 320
   Reason 356
Argument 62
   Reason 355
   Reasoning 356
argumentation, Reasoning.356
aria, Melody 281
arise, Rise 374
arising, Beginning 89
armament, Army 64
armor, Arms 64
Arms 64
Army 64
aroma, Smell 396
arouse, Encourage 176
Arraign 64
Arrange 65
   Adapt 20
arrangement, Compromise.130
   Contract 137
array, Arrange 65
   Dress 166
Arrest 67
   Check 119
   Hinder 234
   Restrain 368
arrive, Reach 354
arrive at Attain 75
arrogance, Assurance 70
   Pride 335

arrogant, Absolute 9
    Dogmatic 163
arrogate, Assume 70
art, Business 102
    Trick 425
artery, Way 439
artful, Shrewd 388
article, Term 416
article of belief, Doctrine.162
article of faith, Doctrine. 162
articulate, Speak 398
artifice, Fraud 213
    Trick 425
artificer, Mechanic 280
artisan, Mechanic 280
artist, Mechanic 280
artistic, Elegant 173
artless, Candid 108
    Rustic 376
as, Because 88
ascend, Rise 374
ascendancy, Victory 435
ascertain, Discover 158
ascribe, Attribute, v...... 76
ashes, Body 96
Ask 67
    Appeal 57
    Inquire 258
    Plead 320
    Pray 328
asperity, Acrimony 18
asperse, Slander 394
asphyxia, Stupor 406
aspiration, Aim 32
    Ambition 46
    Desire 152
assail, Attack, v......... 74
assassinate, Kill 265
assault, n., Attack....... 73
assault, v., Attack....... 74
assemblage, Company....128
assemble, Convoke 140
    Make 277
assembly, Company 128
assent, Agree 31
    Faith 193
assert, Allege 38
    State 401
assertion, Assurance 70
assessment, Tax 415
assets, Wealth 440
asseverate, Allege 38
    State 401
assiduity, Industry.....252
assiduous, Busy 103
assign, Allege 38
    Allot 41
    Apply 60
    Apportion 61
    Attribute 76
    Commit 127
    Devote 154
assimilate, Absorb 10
assist, Abet 2

Help 231
    Promote 340
assistant, Accessory 15
    Auxiliary 77
Associate, n. 68
    Accessory 15
Associate, v. 68
    Apply 60
    Attach 71
    Attribute 76
    Mix 286
    Unite 428
Association 69
    Acquaintance 17
    Class 123
assort, Arrange 65
assorted, Miscellaneous ..284
assuage, Allay 38
    Alleviate 40
Assume 70
assumption, Assurance.... 70
    Pretense 332
    Pride 335
Assurance 70
    Effrontery 171
    Faith 193
    Impertinence 249
assure, Confirm 133
    State 401
assured, Conscious 135
assured, Secure 382
astonishment, Amazement. 45
    Perplexity 316
astute, Shrewd 388
as well, Also 44
as well as, Also........ 44
at ease, Comfortable....127
atheist, Skeptic 392
athirst, Eager 169
atom, Part 310
    Particle 311
at once, Immediately....247
atonement, Propitiation.. 341
at rest, Comfortable......127
atrocious, Barbarous ... 84
Attach 71
    Add 21
    Append 58
    Apply 60
    Associate 68
    Fix 206
    Unite 428
attached, Addicted 22
    Adjacent 25
Attachment 73
    Acquaintance 17
    Appendage 58
    Friendship 215
    Love 276
Attack, n. 73
Attack, v. 74
Attain 75
    Get 219
    Reach 354

attain, Succeed 408
Attainment 75
    Progress 338
    Wisdom 442
attempt, Endeavor......178
    Offer 302
    Try 427
attend, Follow 209
    Listen 273
attendant, Accessory 15
attention, Care 110
    Industry 252
attentive, Thoughtful ...418
attestation, Testimony ...418
attire, Dress 166
attitude, Posture 325
attract, Allure 43
    Draw 164
attraction, Love 276
attractive, Amiable 47
    Beautiful 87
    Pleasant 321
Attribute, n. 75
    Characteristic 118
    Emblem 174
Attribute, v. 76
attrition, Repentance 363
audacity, Effrontery 171
    Temerity 416
auf Wiedersehen, Farewell198
augment, Add 21
    Amplify 48
    Exalt 188
augur, Foretell 210
augury, Sign 390
august, Awful 78
    Royal 375
au revoir, Farewell......198
auspicious, Propitious... 341
austere, Severe 385
Authentic 76
    Real 354
authenticate, Confirm ...133
author, Cause 114
authoritative, Absolute ... 9
    Authentic 76
    Dogmatic 163
authority, Permission ...314
    Power 326
    Precedent 329
authorization, Permission. 314
authorized, Authentic 76
autobiography, History ..235
autochthonic, Primeval ...336
autocratic, Absolute 9
automatic, Spontaneous ..399
Auxiliary 77
    Accessory 15
    Appendage 58
avail, Profit 337
    Utility 429
avaricious, Miserly 285
Avenge 77
    Requite 365

avenging, Revenge 369
avenue, Way 439
aver, Allege 38
   State 401
averse, Reluctant 360
aversion, Abomination ... 6
   Antipathy 52
   Hatred 229
avid, Eager 169
avocation, Business 102
avouch, State 401
avow, Confess 133
   State 401
await, Abide 4
awake, Vigilant 435
award, Allot 41
   Reward 371
aware, Conscious 135
awareness, Mind 283
awe, Amazement 45
   Fear 199
Awful 78
Awkward 78
   Rustic 376
Axiom 79
   Proverb 343

Babble 80
backbite, Slander 394
backbone, Fortitude 211
backer, Adherent 24
backward, Reluctant 360
backwardness, Modesty ..288
Bad 80
   Pernicious 315
badge, Sign 390
badinage, Banter 83
   Wit 443
Baffle 81
   Check 119
   Hinder 234
bail, Security 382
baleful, Bad 80
   Pernicious 315
balk, Baffle 81
   Hinder 234
balky, Restive 367
balmy, Calm 106
ban, Banish 82
   Oath 300
   Prohibit 338
band, Company 128
bandit, Robber 375
baneful, Bad 80
   Pernicious 315
Banish 82
   Exterminate 191
Bank 83
Bankruptcy 83
banquet, Feast 200
Banter 83
   Wit 443
bar, n., Barrier........... 84
   Impediment 248

Lock 275
bar, v., Hinder..........234
   Shut 389
barbarian, Barbarous 84
barbaric, Barbarous 84
barbarism, Language 268
Barbarous 84
bard, Poet 323
bare, Bleak 94
barely, But 103
bargain, Contract 137
   Sale 379
bargain for, Purchase....345
barren, Bleak 94
barricade, Barrier 84
Barrier 84
   Boundary 97
   Impediment 248
barter, Business 102
   Sale 379
barter for, Purchase.....345
basal, Radical 353
Base, adj. 85
   Bad 80
   Brutish 101
   Pitiful 319
base, n., Foundation.....212
baseless, Vain 431
bashfulness, Modesty 288
basic, Radical 353
basis, Foundation 212
bastinado, Beat 86
bath, Washing 428
bathing, Washing 438
batter, Beat 86
Battle 86
   Dispute 160
bawl, Call 106
beach, Bank 83
beam, Light 272
beaming, Bright 99
bear, Abide 4
   Carry 112
   Endure 179
   Support 410
bearing, Air 33
   Behavior 90
   Direction 158
bear up under, Endure...179
bear with, Endure.......179
beastly, Brutish........101
Beat 86
   Conquer 134
beauteous, Beautiful 87
Beautiful 87
   Fine 204
   Graceful 222
   Sublime 407
beautify, Adorn 27
Because 88
   Therefore 418
bechance, Happen 225
become, Make 277
Becoming 88

Fit 205
be cured, Recover 358
bedeck, Adorn 27
befall, Happen 225
befitting, Becoming 88
   Fit 205
befoul, Defile 147
befriend, Help 231
beg, Ask 67
   Plead 320
   Pray 328
beget, Propagate 340
beggarly, Base 85
beggary, Poverty 325
Beginning 89
beguile, Entertain 180
Behavior 90
   Air 33
be healed, Recover......358
behest, Order 304
behold, Discern 158
   Look 275
be in possession (of), have.230
belabor, Beat 86
beleaguer, Attack, v. 74
   Shut 389
belief, Doctrine 162
   Faith 193
   Fancy 197
   Idea 244
belittle, Disparage 159
belles-lettres, Literature ..274
bellow, Call 106
below, Beneath 91
bemoan, Mourn 290
Bend 90
Beneath 91
benefaction, Gift 219
beneficence, Benevolence.. 91
beneficial, Good 221
benefit, Favor 198
   Profit 337
   Utility 429
Benevolence 91
   Mercy 282
benevolent, Good 221
   Humane 240
benign, Propitious 341
benignant, Amiable 47
   Humane 240
   Propitious 341
benignity, Benevolence ... 91
   Mercy 282
bent, Genius 218
be possessed of, Have....230
bequest, Gift 219
bereavement, Misfortune..286
be restored, Recover.....358
beseech, Appeal 57
   Ask 67
   Plead 320
   Pray 328
beseeming, Becoming..... 88
beset, Attack, v..........74

beside, Adjacent 25
besides, Also 44
But 103
Yet 445
besiege, Attack, v........ 74
bestial, Brutish 101
bestow, Give 220
betide, Happen 225
betoken, Foretell 210
better, Amend 47
between, Amid 48
betwixt, Amid 48
bevy, Group 223
bewail, Mourn 290
bewilder, Embarrass 174
bewilderment, Amazement. 45
Perplexity 316
bewitching, Beautiful ... 87
Charming 118
bias, Bend 90
Prejudice 331
bid, Offer 302
Pray 328
Proposal 342
bidding, Order 304
bide, Abide 4
big, Large 268
bigotry, Fanaticism 196
bills, Money 289
Bind 92
Attach 71
Fix 206
bind up, Bind........... 92
biography, History 235
birth, Kin 266
birthright, Right, n.....374
bit, Particle 311
biting, Bitter 93
Bitter 93
Malicious 277
bitterness, Acrimony 18
Enmity 180
Quarrel 348
bizarre, Queer 348
blab, Babble 80
black, Dark 143
blame, n., Reproof......364
blame, v., Condemn......132
Reprove 365
blameless, Innocent 257
blanch, Bleach 93
bland, Calm 106
blandishment, Praise.....327
blank, Bleak 94
Vacant 431
blaspheming, Oath......300
blasphemy, Oath 300
blaze, Burn 101
Fire 204
Light 272
blazon, Announce 50
Bleach 93
Bleak 94
Blemish 94

Injury 256
blend, Mix 286
blessed, Happy 227
Holy 238
blessedness, Happiness ...226
blessing, Favor 198
Mercy 282
blind, Trick 425
bliss, Happiness 226
blissful, Happy 227
blithe, Happy 227
blithesome, Happy 227
block, Barrier 84
Hinder 234
Shut 389
blockade, Shut 389
blood, Kin 266
bloodshed, Massacre 279
bloodthirsty, Sanguinary..380
bloody, Sanguinary 380
blooming, Beautiful 87
blot, Blemish 94
Stain 400
blot out, Cancel 107
Blow 95
Misfortune 286
bluejacket, Sailor 378
Bluff 95
blunt, Bluff 95
blur, Blemish 94
blurt out, Babble 80
blustering, Bluff........ 95
bo, Hobo 236
boast, Ostentation 305
boasting, Ostentation 305
bode, Foretell 210
bodily, Physical 318
Body 96
boisterous, Violent 436
bold, Bluff 95
Brave 97
boldness, Assurance 70
Effrontery 171
Impertinence 249
Pertness 317
Bolshevism, Socialism ...397
bolt, Abscond 8
Lock 275
bombard, Attack, v...... 74
bond, Security 382
bondage, Fetter 201
bonds, Fetter 201
bonny, Beautiful 87
bonus, Subsidy 408
bon voyage, Farewell....198
bookish, Academic 14
books, Literature 274
boon, Favor 198
Gift 219
boorish, Awkward 78
Rustic 376
bootless, Vain 431
boozy, Drunk 167
border, Bank 83

Boundary 97
bordering, Adjacent 25
bore, Hole 236
Both 96
Every 186
bother, Care 110
bottom, Foundation 212
boulevard, Way 439
bound, n., Bank......... 83
Boundary 97
End 177
bound, v., Circumscribe...122
Boundary 97
boundary, Barrier....... 84
End 177
boundless, Infinite 253
bounteous, Plentiful ...322
bountiful, Generous 218
Plentiful 322
bounty, Benevolence 91
Gift 219
Subsidy 408
bouquet, Smell 396
bourn, Boundary 97
bourne, Boundary 97
bout, Battle 86
bow, Bend 90
box, Blow 95
boyish, Youthful.......445
brag, Ostentation 305
brain, Mind 283
brake, Check 119
brand, Blemish 94
Burn 101
brandish, Shake 386
brashness, Temerity 416
brass, Effrontery 171
bravado, Ostentation ...305
Brave 97
bravery, Prowess 344
brawl, Argument 62
Quarrel 348
breach, Hole 236
Break 98
Rend 361
break off, Adjourn...... 26
End 178
break up, Adjourn 26
breastwork, Barrier 84
Fortification 211
breathing, Alive 37
breed, Propagate 340
breeding, Behavior 90
Education 170
Refinement 358
bribe, Gift 219
bridle, Check 119
Restrain 368
bridlepath, Way 439
brief, adj., Terse........417
Transient 424
brief, n., Sketch........393
brigand, Robber 375
Bright 99

Bright (cont'd)
Clever 125
Happy 227
brilliancy, Light 272
brilliant, Bright 99
Clever 125
brim, Bank 83
bring, Carry 112
bring about, Do.........161
bring low, Debase.......144
bring over, Persuade.....316
bring to an end, Stop....403
bring to pass, Do........161
brink, Bank 83
brisk, Active 19
Alert 35
Alive 37
Nimble 298
briskness, Alacrity 34
Pertness 317
broad, Large 268
broil, Argument 62
Quarrel 348
brood, Group 223
brook, Endure 179
Stream 405
brotherly, Friendly 214
browbeat, Frighten 215
bruise, Beat 86
brush, Clean 124
brusk, Bluff 95
brutal, Barbarous 84
Brutish 101
brute, Brutish 101
Brutish 101
buccaneer, Robber 375
bucolic, Rustic 376
buffet, Beat 86
Blow 95
build, Make 277
bulky, Large 268
bullion, Money 289
bulwark, Barrier 84
Defense 146
bum, Hobo 236
bungling, Awkward 78
buoyant, Happy 227
burden, Load...........274
burdensome, Troublesome 426
burglar, Robber 375
burlesque, Caricature 111
Wit 443
Burn 101
burning, adj., Ardent.... 62
Eager 169
burning, n., Fire........204
burrow, Hole 236
bursal, Financial 203
burst, Break 98
Rend 361
bury, Dip 157
Hide 233
Business 102
Duty 168

Transaction 423
Work 444
bustling, Active 19
Alert 35
Nimble 298
Busy 103
Active 19
But 103
Notwithstanding 299
butcher, Kill 265
butchery, Massacre 279
buy, Purchase 345
by 104
by dint of, By 104
by means of, By 104
byword, Proverb........343

Cabal 105
cabalistic, Mysterious ...291
cackle, Babble 80
cadaver, Body 96
cadence, Rhythm 372
cajole, Allure 43
calamity, Accident 16
Blow 95
Catastrophe 113
Misfortune 286
Calculate 105
Esteem 184
calculated, Fit 205
Call 106
Convoke 140
Employ 176
calling, Business 102
call (out or upon), Appeal 57
callow, Youthful 445
call together, Convoke...140
call upon, Pray 328
Calm 106
Allay 38
Rest 367
calmness, Apathy 54
Patience 311
Rest 367
calumniate, Slander 394
canaille, Mob 288
Cancel 107
Abolish 5
Candid 108
Honest 239
candor, Truth 426
canon, Law 270
cant, Hypocrisy 242
Slang 395
Tip 420
capability, Power 326
capable, Adequate 24
Clever 125
capacious, Large 268
capacity, Power 326
Capital 108
Good 221
Money 289
Principal 336

capitulate, Surrender 411
caprice, Fancy 197
capricious, Fanciful ,....197
Fickle 201
captain, Chief 120
Captious 109
captivate, Allure 43
captivating, Charming...118
capture, Arrest 67
Catch 113
carcass, Body 96
cardinal, Principal 336
Care 110
Anxiety 53
Oversight 306
Prudence 344
careen, Tip 420
careful, Precise 329
Thoughtful 418
Vigilant 435
carefulness, Prudence ...344
careless, Imprudent 251
Secure 382
carelessness, Neglect 296
Caress 111
cargo, Load 274
Caricature 111
carnage, Massacre 279
carnal, Brutish 101
carnival, Carousal 111
carol, Sing 392
Carousal 111
carouse, Carousal 111
carp at, Disparage 159
carping, Captious 109
carriage, Air 33
Behavior 90
Carry 112
Convey 140
Keep 265
Support 410
carry on, Keep 265
Transact 423
carry out, Do 161
Execute 189
carry through, Do 161
cartel, Contract 137
case, Event 186
Precedent 329
Sample 379
cash, Money 289
cast, Calculate 105
Send 383
cast down, Debase 144
caste, Class 123
castigate, Beat 86
Punish 345
castle, Fortification 211
cast off, Abandon 1
cast up, Add 21
casualty, Accident 16
Hazard 231
casuistry, Fallacy 195
cataclysm, Catastrophe ...113

catalog(ue), Record 357
Catastrophe 113
   Misfortune 286
Catch 113
   Arrest 67
   Lock 275
catching, Contagious 137
categorical, Explicit 190
causality, Cause 114
causation, Cause 114
Cause 114
   Make 277
   Reason 355
caustic, Bitter 93
causticity, Acrimony 18
cauterize, Burn 101
caution, Care 110
   Counsel 140
   Prudence 344
cautious, Afraid 29
   Vigilant 435
cave, Hole 236
cavern, Hole 236
caviling, Captious 109
cavity, Hole 236
cease, Abandon 1
   Die 155
   End 178
   Stop 403
ceaseless, Continual 137
cede, Abandon 1
   Give 220
   Surrender 411
Celebrate 115
   Keep 265
celebrity, Fame 196
celerity, Alacrity 34
cell, Hole 236
censorious, Captious 109
censure, Arraign 64
   Condemn 132
   Reproof 364
   Reprove 365
Center 115
ceremonious, Polite 324
   Precise 329
ceremony, Sacrament ...377
certain, Authentic 76
   Conscious 135
   Real 354
   Secure 382
certainty, Demonstration..151
certification, Testimony ..418
certified, Conscious 135
certify, Confess 133
   State 401
cessation, End, n. 177
chaff, Banter 83
Chagrin 115
   Embarrass 174
chains, Fetter 201
challenge, Dispute 160
chance, Accident 16
   Event 186

Happen 225
Hazard 231
Change, n. 116
   Motion 290
   Sale 379
Change, v. 117
   Convey 140
changeable, Fickle 201
changeful, Fickle 201
changeless, Permanent ..314
channel, Stream 405
   Way 439
chant, Sing 392
char, Burn 101
Character 117
   Characteristic 118
Characteristic 118
charge, n., Care 110
   Load 274
   Oversight 306
   Price 334
charge, v., Arraign 64
   Attack 74
   Attribute 76
charitable, Humane 240
charity, Benevolence 91
   Love 276
   Mercy 282
Charming 118
   Amiable 47
   Beautiful 87
   Graceful 222
   Pleasant 321
chase, Follow 209
   Hunt 241
chasm, Abyss 14
   Hole 236
chaste, Elegant 173
   Pure 346
chasten, Punish 345
   Reprove 365
chastening, Misfortune ..286
chastise, Beat 86
   Punish 345
chastisement, Misfortune.286
chastity, Virtue 436
chat, Babble 80
   Conversation 139
   Speak 398
chatter, Babble 80
   Speak 398
chattering, Talkative 414
cheap, Base 85
cheat, Deceiver 145
   Fraud 213
   Trick 425
cheating, Fraud 213
check, n., Reproof.......364
Check, v. 119
   Hinder 234
   Reprove 365
   Restrain 368
checkmate, Check 119
   Conquer 134

cheek, Effrontery 171
cheer, n., Entertainment..181
   Happiness 226
cheer, v., Cherish 119
   Encourage 176
   Entertain 180
cheerful, Bright 99
   Comfortable 127
   Good 221
   Happy 227
cheering, Bright 99
   Good 221
   Happy 227
   Praise 327
cheerless, Bleak 94
cheers, Praise 327
cheery, Bright 99
   Comfortable 127
   Happy 227
Cherish 119
   Support 410
chicanery, Deception ...145
chide, Reprove 365
chiding, Reproof 364
Chief 120
   Principal 336
chief city, Capital 108
chieftain, Chief 120
childish, Youthful 445
childlike, Youthful 445
chill, Bleak 94
chilling, Bleak 94
chilly, Bleak 94
chimerical, Absurd 12
   Fanciful 197
chirp, Sing 392
chirrup, Sing 392
chivalric, Brave ... 97
chivalrous, Brave 97
   Polite 324
Choice 121
   Fine 204
choler, Anger 49
Choose 121
chronicle, History 235
   Record 357
   Report 363
chum, Associate 68
church, Religion 360
churlish, Morose 289
circle, n., Class 123
circle, v., Revolve 371
circulate, Announce 50
Circumlocution 122
Circumscribe 122
   Restrain 368
circumspect, Thoughtful..418
   Vigilant 435
circumspection, Care 110
   Prudence 344
Circumstance 123
   Event 186
circumstantial, Minute ..284
circumvent, Baffle 81

citadel, Fortification 211
cite, Allege 38
   Arraign 64
   Quote 350
civil, Polite 324
civility, Favor 198
civilization, Refinement...358
claim, n., Right 374
claim, v., Allege 38
   Assume 70
   State 401
clamor, Call 106
clan, Class 123
clarified, Fine 204
clash, Collision 126
clashing, Collision 126
clasp, Catch 113
   Lock 275
Class 123
classic, Pure 346
classical, Pure 346
classify, Arrange 65
clay, Body 96
Clean 124
   Innocent 257
   Neat 294
   Pure 346
cleaning, Washing 438
cleanly, Neat 294
cleanse, Amend 47
   Clean 124
cleansing, Washing 438
Clear, adj. 124
   Evident 187
   Explicit 190
   Fine 204
   Innocent 257
   Pure 346
clear, v., Absolve 9
clear-sighted, Sagacious..378
   Shrewd 388
cleave, Rend 361
cleft, Hole 236
clemency, Mercy 282
clement, Humane 240
   Propitious 341
Clever 125
   Skilful 393
cleverness, Acumen 19
   Dexterity 154
   Ingenuity 254
   Power 326
cling to, Cherish 119
clique, Class 123
cloak, Hide 233
   Palliate 308
   Pretense 332
clog, Hinder 234
   Impediment 248
   Load 274
Cloister 126
close, adj., Adjacent 25
   Miserly 285
   Taciturn 414

close, a., End 177
close, v., End 178
   Shut 389
close up, Shut 389
clothes, Dress 166
clothing, Dress 166
cloudy, Obscure 301
clownish, Awkward 78
   Rustic 376
cloy, Satisfy 380
club, Association 69
   Class 123
clumsy, Awkward 78
clutch, Catch 113
coadjutor, Accessory ... 15
   Associate 68
   Auxiliary 77
coalition, Alliance 41
   Union 428
coarse, Bluff 95
   Brutish 101
   Large 268
   Rustic 376
coast, Bank 83
coax, Allure 43
   Persuade 316
coddle, Caress 111
code, Law 270
coerce, Compel 129
coercive, Absolute 9
cogency, Power 326
cognition, Knowledge ...266
cognizance, Knowledge ..266
cognizant, Conscious ...135
cognomen, Name 293
cohesive, Adhesive 25
coin, Money 289
coinage, Money 289
coincide, Agree 31
coincidence, Similarity ..390
cold, Bleak............. 94
coldness, Modesty 288
colleague, Accessory 15
   Associate 68
collect, Amass 44
   Convoke 140
collected, Calm 106
collection, Aggregate 30
   Company 128
collectivism, Socialism ...397
collegiate, Academic 14
colligate, Arrange 65
Collision 126
collocate, Arrange 65
colloquialism, Slang 395
colloquy, Conversation ..139
color, Pretense 332
   Stain 400
colossal, Large 268
coma, Stupor 406
combat, n., Battle 86
combat, v., Attack 74
   Dispute 160
combination, Cabal 105

Union 428
combine, Agree 31
   Associate 68
   Attach 71
   Mix 286
   Unite 428
combustion, Fire 204
come after, Follow 209
comely, Beautiful 87
   Becoming 88
come (to), Reach 354
come to an end, Stop....403
come to pass, Happen...225
comfort, n., Happiness...226
   Rest 367
comfort, v., Cherish ...119
   Console 136
Comfortable 127
comical, Queer 348
comity, Friendship 215
command, n., Law 270
   Order 304
   Oversight 306
   Power 326
command, v., Govern ...222
commander, Chief 120
commander in chief, Chief.120
commandment, Law 270
commemorate, Celebrate..115
commencement, Beginning 89
commendation, Praise...327
commensurate, Adequate.. 24
comment, Definition ...148
   Remark 361
   Reproof 364
commentary, Definition ..148
commerce, Business 102
commingle, Mix 286
comminuted, Fine 204
   Minute 284
commiseration, Pity ...319
Commit 127
   Do 161
commit larceny, Steal ...402
commit theft, Steal 402
commix, Mix 286
commodious, Comfortable.127
   Large 268
common, General 217
   Mutual 291
   Normal 298
   Usual 429
commonplace, General ..217
communicable, Contagious.137
communicate, Announce.. 50
   Give 220
communication, Conversation 139
communion, Conversation.139
   Religion 360
   Sacrament 377
communism, Socialism ..397
community, Association .. 69
commute, Change 117

compact, *adj.*, Terse 417
compact, *n.*, Alliance 41
   Contract 137
companion, Accessory ... 15
   Associate 68
companionable, Friendly..214
   Good 221
companionship, Acquaint-
   ance 17
   Association 69
Company 128
   Association 69
   Class 123
compare, Contrast 138
comparison, Similarity...390
compass, Attain 75
compassion, Mercy 282
   Pity 319
compassionate, Humane..240
Compel 129
   Bind 92
   Drive 166
   Influence 254
   Make 277
compend, Abridgment ... 7
compendious, Terse......417
compendium, Abridgment 7
compensate, Requite.....365
compensation, Pay 312
   Reward 371
competence, Wealth 440
competency, Power 326
   Wealth 440
competent, Adequate..... 24
   Fit 205
   Good 221
competition, Ambition ... 46
competitor, Enemy 179
Complain 129
complaint, Disease 159
complaisant, Friendly ...214
   Polite 324
complete, *adj.*, Good ...221
   Plentiful 322
   Radical 353
complete, *v.*, Do 161
   End 178
completion, End 177
Complex 130
   Obscure 301
compliant, Docile 162
   Humble 240
complicate, Involve 260
complicated, Complex ...130
   Obscure 301
compliment, Praise 327
comply, Agree 31
component, Part 310
comport, Agree 31
compose, Allay 38
   Arrange 65
   Make 277
composed, Calm 106
composite, Complex 130

composition, Compromise.130
composure, Apathy 54
   Patience 311
compound, *adj.*, Complex.130
compound, *n.*, Alloy..... 42
compound, *v.*, Mix.......286
compounding, Compromise.130
comprehend, Catch 113
   Perceive 313
comprehension, Knowledge.266
Compromise 130
compulsion, Necessity ...295
compulsive, Absolute 9
compulsory, Absolute ... 9
compunction, Repentance.363
compute, Calculate 105
comrade, Associate 68
concatenate, Unite 428
concavity, Hole 236
conceal, Hide 233
   Palliate 308
concealed, Latent 269
conceal oneself, Abscond. 8
concede, Allow 42
   Confess 133
conceit, Egotism 172
   Fancy 197
   Idea 244
   Pride 335
conceivable, Likely 272
conceive, Perceive 313
concept, Idea 244
conception, Fancy 197
   Idea 244
Concern 131
   Anxiety 53
   Business 102
   Care 110
concert, Harmony 228
   Union 428
concession, Compromise..130
   Favor 198
conciliation, Composition.130
concise, Terse 417
conclave, Cabal 105
   Company 128
conclude, End 178
   Stop 403
conclusion, Demonstration.151
   End 177
   Inference 253
concomitant, Appendage. 58
   Circumstance 123
concord, Harmony 228
concordat, Contract.....137
concourse, Company ...128
   Throng 419
concupiscence, Desire ...152
concur, Agree 31
concurrence, Harmony...228
concussion, Blow 95
   Collision 126
Condemn 132
   Reprove 365

condemnation, Reproof ..364
condensed, Terse 417
condescension, Favor ...198
Condign 132
condition, Cause 114
   Term 416
conditional, Dependent .151
condolence, Pity 319
condole with, Console ...136
condone, Pardon, *v.* 309
conduct, *n.*, Behavior.... 90
conduct, *v.*, Keep 265
   Transact 423
confabulation, Conversa-
   tion 139
confederacy, Alliance 41
   Association 69
   Cabal 105
confederate, *n.*, Accessory 15
   Associate 68
   Auxiliary 77
confederate, *v.*, Associate. 68
confederation, Alliance... 41
   Association 69
confer, Deliberate 148
   Give 220
conference, Company ...128
   Conversation 139
Confess 133
confession, Apology 55
confide, Commit 127
confidence, Assurance ... 70
   Faith 193
confident, Secure 382
confine, Circumscribe ... 122
   Restrain 368
   Shut 389
confines, Boundary 97
Confirm 133
conflagration, Fire 204
conflict, Battle 86
   Collision 126
   Quarrel 348
conflicting, Adverse 28
   Alien 36
   Contrary 138
   Incongruous 251
conform, Adapt 20
   Agree 31
conformity, Harmony....228
confound, Embarrass 174
   Mix 286
confront, Abide 4
confuse, Displace 160
   Embarrass 174
   Mix 268
confused, Complex 130
   Irregular 261
   Miscellaneous 284
confusion, Amazement ... 45
   Chagrin 115
   Perplexity 316
   Revolution 370
confute, Refute 359

congé, Farewell 198
congenial, Pleasant 321
congenital, Inherent 255
conglomerate, Complex ..130
  Miscellaneous 284
Congratulate 134
congregation, Company ..128
congruent, Alike 37
congruity, Harmony 228
congruous, Becoming 88
  Fit 205
conjectural, Likely 272
conjecture, Hypothesis ..242
  Suppose 410
conjoin, Apply 60
  Associate 68
  Attach 71
  Unite 428
conjunction, Association . 69
  Union 428
conjure, Pray 328
connect, Apply 60
  Associate 68
  Attach 71
  Attribute 76
  Unite 428
connection, Association .. 69
connoisseur, Amateur 45
Conquer 134
  Beat 86
conquest, Victory 435
consanguinity, Kin 266
Conscious 135
consciousness, Mind 283
consecrate, Devote 154
consecrated, Holy 238
consent, Agree 31
  Harmony 228
  Permission 314
consent to, Allow 42
Consequence 136
  Demonstration 151
  Event 186
  Inference 253
consequent, Consequence..136
consequential, Important.249
consequently, Therefore..418
conserve, Keep 265
consider, Calculate 105
  Deliberate 148
  Esteem 184
considerable, Good 221
  Important 249
  Large 268
considerate, Thoughtful..418
consideration, Friendship.215
  Prudence 344
  Reason 355
consign, Commit 127
consistency, Harmony ..228
Console 136
consolidate, Fix 206
consonance, Harmony....228
consort, n., Associate.... 68

conspicuous, Eminent ...175
  Evident 187
conspiracy, Cabal 105
constancy, Industry 252
constant, Continual 137
  Faithful 194
  Permanent 314
consternation, Alarm ... 35
  Fear 199
constituent, Part 310
constitute, Make 277
constitution, Character ...117
  Polity 324
constitutional, Radical ...353
constrain, Compel 129
  Make 277
  Restrain 368
constraint, Modesty 288
construct, Make 277
consult, Deliberate 148
consume, Absorb 10
  Burn 101
consummate, Do 161
consummation, Act 18
  End 177
contact, Collision 126
Contagious 137
contain, Involve 260
contaminate, Defile 147
contemplate, Look 275
contemptible, Base 85
  Pitiful 319
contend, Dispute 160
  Reason 356
content, Satisfy 380
contented, Comfortable ..127
contention, Argument 62
  Quarrel 348
contentment, Happiness ..226
conterminous, Adjacent.. 25
contest, Battle 86
  Dispute 160
  Quarrel 348
contiguity, Approximation 61
contiguous, Adjacent 25
continence, Abstinence .. 11
continent, Pure 346
contingency, Accident ... 16
  Event 186
  Hazard 231
contingent, Dependent ..151
Continual 137
continue, Abide 4
  Persist 316
  Protract 343
  Stand 401
continuous, Continual ...137
Contract 137
contraction, Abbreviation. 2
contradictory, Alien 36
  Contrary 138
  Incongruous 251
contrariety, Difference ..156
Contrary 138

Adverse 28
Alien 36
  Incongruous 251
  Perverse 317
Contrast 138
  Difference 156
contrasted, Alien 36
  Contrary 138
contravene, Baffle 81
  Object 300
contriteness, Repentance.363
contrition, Repentance ...363
contrivance, Project 339
  Trick 425
contrived, Fit 205
control, Govern 222
  Oversight 306
controlling, Absolute 9
  Principal 336
controversy, Argument... 62
  Quarrel 348
controvert, Dispute 160
  Reason 356
  Refute 359
contumacious, Obstinate ..302
  Rebellious 357
conundrum, Riddle 373
convene, Convoke 140
convenient, Comfortable..127
  Good 221
convent, Cloister 126
convention, Company ..128
  Contract 137
conventional, Academic .. 14
Conversation 139
converse, Conversation ..139
  Speak 398
conversion, Change 116
Convert 139
  Change 117
Convey 140
  Carry 112
convict, Condemn 132
conviction, Faith 193
convince, Persuade 316
convocation, Company ..128
Convoke 140
cool, Calm 106
cooperate, Help 231
cooperation, Union 428
coop up, Shut 385
copious, Plentiful 322
copy, n., Duplicate.....167
  Model 285
copy, v., Follow 209
cordial, Friendly 214
core, Center 115
corporal, Physical 318
corporation, Association .. 69
corporeal, Physical 318
corpse, Body 96
corpuscle, Particle 311
correct, adj., Precise ...329
  Right 373

correct, v., Amend ... 47
Punish 345
correspondent, Synony-
mous 412
corresponding, Synony-
mous 412
corroborate, Confirm 133
corrupt, adj., Bad 80
corrupt, v., Decay.......144
Defile 147
corrupting, Bad 80
cost, Price 334
costume, Dress 166
coterie, Class 123
coterminous, Adjacent ... 25
Counsel 140
count, Calculate 105
countenance, Abet 2
Encourage 176
Favor 198
counteract, Baffle 81
Check 119
Hinder 234
counterfeit, Base 85
counterpart, Duplicate ...167
countless, Infinite 253
countrified, Rustic 376
country, Rustic 376
couple, v., Associate 68
courage, Fortitude.......211
Prowess 344
courageous, Brave 97
course, Direction 158
Stream 405
Way 439
court, v., Address 23
Caress 111
courteous, Polite 324
courtesy, Address 22
courtly, Polite 324
covenant, Contract 137
cover, Hide 233
Palliate 308
Shelter 388
coveting, Desire 152
covetous, Jealous 262
Miserly 285
covey, Group 223
cow, Frighten 215
cowardly, Afraid 29
coyness, Modesty 288
cozy, Comfortable 127
crabbed, Morose 289
crack, Blemish 94
Break 98
Hole 236
craft, Business 102
Deception 145
Trick 425
craftsman, Mechanic 280
crafty, Shrewd 388
crapulent, Drunk 167
crapulous, Drunk........167
crass, Stupid 406

crater, Hole 236
crave, Ask 67
craving, Appetite 59
Desire 152
craziness, Insanity 259
create, Make 277
creator, Cause 114
credence, Faith 193
credible, Likely 272
credit, Faith...........193
Fame 196
credulity, Fanaticism 196
creed, Faith 193
Religion 360
creek, Stream 405
cremate, Burn 101
crew, Cabal 105
crime, Abomination 6
Sin 391
Criminal 141
criminality, Sin 391
cringing, Base 85
Criterion 141
critic, Amateur 45
critical, Captious 109
Important 249
Minute 284
criticism, Reproof 364
croak, Complain 129
crook, Bend 90
crooked, Irregular 261
crop, Harvest 229
cross off, Cancel 107
cross out, Cancel 107
crotchety, Fickle 201
Queer 348
crowd, Company 128
Mob 288
Throng 419
crowd out, Displace 160
cruel, Barbarous........ 84
Sanguinary 380
cruise, Journey 262
crush, Break 98
Conquer 134
crusty, Bluff 95
Morose 289
cry out, Call 106
cryptic, Obscure 301
cuddle, Caress 111
cudgel, Beat 86
cuff, Blow 95
cull, Choose 121
culpable, Criminal 141
cult, Religion 360
cultivated, Polite 324
cultivation, Agriculture .. 31
Education 170
Refinement 358
culture, Agriculture 31
Education 170
Refinement 358
cultured, Polite 324
cunning, adj., Shrewd...388

cunning, n., Deception...145
Ingenuity 254
Trick 425
curb, Check 119
Govern 222
Restrain 368
cure, Recover 358
curious, Inquisitive 258
Queer 348
Rare 353
currency, Money 289
current, adj., Authentic.. 76
current, n., Stream......405
curse, Abomination 6
Oath 300
cursing, Oath 300
curt, Bluff 95
curtail, Abate 1
curve, Bend 90
custody, Fetter 201
custom, Habit 225
customary, General 217
Usual 429
customs, Tax 415
cut, Blow 95
cutting, Bitter.......... 93
Bleak 94
cynical, Captious 109

Daily 143
dainty, Delicious 149
Elegant 173
Fine 204
damage, Abuse 13
Injury 256
dandle, Caress 111
Danger 143
Hazard 231
dangerous, Formidable ..210
Precarious 328
Serious 385
dapper, Neat 294
daring, Brave 97
Dark 143
Mysterious 291
Obscure 301
darksome, Obscure 301
dart, Send 383
dashing, Brave 97
date, Time 419
daub, Blemish 94
daunt, Frighten 215
dauntless, Brave 97
dawdling, Slow 395
daydream, Dream 165
dazzling, Bright 99
deadly, Pernicious 315
deal, n., Sale...........379
deal, v., Apportion....... 61
deathless, Eternal 185
debacle, Catastrophe 113
debar, Prohibit 338
Suspend 411
Debase 144

debased, Base 85
debasement, Alloy 42
debate, *n.*, Argument..... 62
  Reasoning 356
debate, *v.*, Deliberate....148
  Dispute 160
  Reason 356
debauch, Carousal 111
decamp, Abscond 8
Decay 144
decayed, Bad 80
decaying, Bad 80
decease, Die 155
deceit, Deception 145
  Fraud 213
deceitful, Bad 80
  Deceptive 146
  Vain 431
deceitfulness, Deception..145
Deceiver 145
decent, Becoming 88
  Fit 205
Deception 145
  Fraud 213
Deceptive 146
  Bad 80
decide, Fix 206
decided, Obstinate......302
deciding, Important 249
decision, Determination...153
  Will 442
decisive, Important 249
deck, Adorn 27
declaim, Speak 398
declare, Allege 38
  Announce 50
  Speak 398
  State 401
decline, Abate 1
  Die 155
decompose, Decay 144
decorate, Adorn 27
decorous, Becoming 88
  Fit 205
decoy, Allure 43
decrease, Abate......... 1
decree, Law 270
decrepit, Old...........303
decry, Disparage 159
  Slander 394
dedicate, Apply 60
  Devote 154
deduction, Demonstration.151
  Inference 253
deed, Act 18
  Transaction 423
  Work 444
deem, Calculate 105
  Esteem 184
  Suppose 410
deep, *adj.*, Obscure 301
deep, *n.*, Abyss 14
defacement, Blemish 94
defame, Abuse 13

Slander 394
default, Neglect 296
defeat, Baffle 81
  Beat 86
  Conquer 134
defect, Blemish 94
defective, Bad 80
defend, Keep 265
  Shelter 388
defended, Secure 382
Defense 146
  Apology 55
defenses, Fortification ..211
defer, Adjourn 26
  Hinder 234
  Protract 343
  Suspend 411
deference, Esteem 184
deferential, Humble 240
deficient, Bad 80
defile, *n.*, Hole 236
Defile, *v.* 147
  Abuse 13
define, Circumscribe ...122
definite, Clear 124
  Explicit 190
  Precise 329
Definition 148
deflect, Bend 90
deformity, Blemish 94
deft, Skilful 393
degrade, Debase 144
degraded, Base 85
degrading, Base 85
deist, Skeptic 392
dejected, Sad 377
delay, Adjourn 26
  Hinder 234
  Protract 343
  Suspend 411
delaying, Slow 395
dele, Cancel 107
delectable, Delicious 149
Delegate 148
  Send 383
delete, Cancel 107
deleterious, Bad 80
  Pernicious 315
Deliberate 148
  Slow 395
delicate, Elegant 173
  Fine 204
Delicious 149
  Elegant 173
  Pleasant 321
delight, *n.*, Entertainment181
  Happiness 226
delight, *v.*, Entertain....180
delighted, Happy 227
delightful, Beautiful 87
  Charming 118
  Delicious 149
  Happy 227
  Pleasant 321

delight in, Admire 26
delineate, Circumscribe...122
delineation, Sketch 393
delinquency, Sin 391
delirium, Insanity 259
Deliver 149
  Give 220
  Speak 398
dell, Hole 236
Delusion 150
  Deception 145
delusive, Deceptive 146
  Vain 431
demand, *n.*, Tax.......415
demand, *v.*, Ask......67
demeanor, Air 33
  Behavior 90
dementia, Insanity 259
Demolish 150
  Break 98
demonstrable, Real 354
demonstrate, Reason....356
Demonstration 151
demur, Object 300
demure, Humble 240
  Serious 385
den, Hole 236
denomination, Name 293
  Religion 360
  Term 416
dénouement, Catastrophe.113
denounce, Condemn 132
dense, Obscure 301
  Stupid 406
dent, Blemish 94
  Hole 236
denunciation, Oath 300
  Reproof 364
deny, Renounce 362
depart, Abscond 8
  Die 155
depart from, Abandon 1
dependable, Reliable 359
Dependent 151
deplore, Mourn 290
deport, Banish 82
deportment, Behavior ... 90
depose, State 401
deposit, Put 347
deposition, Testimony ...418
depraved, Bad 80
depravity, Sin 391
depreciate, Disparage ...159
  Slander 394
depredator, Robber 375
depress, Debase 144
depressed, Sad 377
depression, Hole 236
depth, Abyss 14
  Hole 236
  Wisdom 442
depute, Send 383
deputy, Delegate 148
derange, Displace 160

derangement, Insanity ...259
derision, Banter 83
derogate from, Disparage.159
descent, Kin 266
describe, Circumscribe ..122
description, Definition ...148
    Report 363
descry, Discern 158
    Discover 158
    Look 275
desecrate, Abuse 13
desert, Abandon 1
deserter, Heretic 232
deserved, Condign 132
Design, *n.* 152
    Aim 32
    Idea 244
    Model 288
    Project 339
    Reason 355
    Sketch 393
design, *v.*, Propose 342
designate, Circumscribe ..122
designation, Name 293
designer, Cause 114
Desire 152
    Appetite 59
    Fancy 197
    Will 442
desirous, Eager 169
desist, End 178
    Stop 403
desolate, Bleak 94
    Sad 377
Despair 153
desperation, Despair 153
despicable, Base 85
    Pitiful 319
despise, Abhor 4
despite, Notwithstanding,
    prep. 299
despoiler, Robber 375
despondency, Despair 153
despondent, Sad 377
despotic, Absolute 9
destine, Allot 41
    Devote 154
destiny, Necessity 295
destitution, Poverty 325
destroy, Abolish 5
    Break 98
    Demolish 150
    Exterminate 191
    Overthrow 306
destructive, Pernicious ..315
desultory, Irregular 261
detach, Abstract 11
detail, Circumstance 123
detailed, Minute 284
detain, Arrest 67
    Keep 265
detect, Discover 158
detective, Spy 400
deter, Hinder 234

deterioration, Alloy 42
Determination 153
    Aim 32
    Will 442
determinative, Important.249
determine, Fix 206
determined, Obstinate ...302
determining, Important ..249
detest, Abhor 4
detestation, Abomination.. 6
    Antipathy 52
    Hatred 229
detract, Slander 394
detract from, Disparage ..159
detriment, Injury 256
detrimental, Bad 80
    Pernicious 315
develop, Amplify 48
developed, Real 354
development, Education..170
    Progress 338
deviate, Bend 90
    Wander 438
device, Design 152
    Project 339
    Trick 425
devious, Irregular 261
devoid, Vacant 431
Devote 154
    Apply 60
devoted, Addicted 22
    Faithful 194
    Friendly 214
    Holy 238
devotion, Allegiance..... 39
    Attachment 73
    Enthusiasm 182
    Friendship 215
    Love 276
Devout 154
Dexterity 154
    Address, *n.* 22
    Ingenuity 254
    Power 326
dexterous, Clever 125
    Good 221
    Happy 227
    Skilful 393
dialect, Language 268
dialogue, Conversation ...139
diaphanous, Clear 124
dictatorial, Absolute 9
    Dogmatic 163
Diction 155
    Language 268
dictum, Proverb 343
Die 155
diet, Food 209
Difference 156
    different, Contrary 138
differentiate, Contrast ..138
Difficult 157
    Obscure 301
    Troublesome 426

difficulty, Impediment ...248
    Predicament 331
diffidence, Modesty 288
diffuseness, Circumlocu-
    tion 122
digest, Abridgment 7
dignify, Exalt 188
digress, Wander 438
dilate, Amplify 48
dilatory, Slow 395
dilemma, Predicament....331
dilettante, Amateur 45
diligence, Industry 252
diligent, Active 19
    Busy 103
dim, Dark 143
    Faint 193
    Obscure 301
diminish, Abate 1
diminutive, Minute 284
Dip 157
    Tip 420
dire, Awful 78
direct, *adj.*, Right.......373
direct, *v.*, Govern 222
Direction 158
    Aim 32
    Care 110
    Order 304
    Oversight 306
directly, Immediately....247
direful, Awful 78
disability, Inability 251
disadvantage, Injury 256
disagreeable, Bad 80
disagreement, Difference..156
disallow, Prohibit 338
disappear, Abscond 8
disappointment, Chagrin..115
    Misfortune 286
disapproval, Reproof 364
disapprove, Object 300
disarrange, Displace 160
disaster, Accident 16
    Blow 95
    Catastrophe 113
    Misfortune 286
disavow, Renounce 362
disbelief, Doubt 163
disbeliever, Skeptic 392
discard, Renounce 362
Discern 158
    Discover 158
    Look 275
discernible, Evident 187
discerning, Sagacious 378
    Shrewd 388
discernment, Acumen 19
    Wisdom 442
discharge, Absolve 9
    Banish 82
    Cancel 107
    Deliver 149
    Do **161**

discharge (cont'd)
Send 383
disciple, Adherent 24
Convert 139
Scholar 380
discipline, n., Education..170
discipline, v., Punish....345
Teach 415
disclaim, Renounce 362
disclose, Confess 133
Discover 158
disclosure, Revelation....369
discolor, Stain 400
discomfit, Conquer 134
Embarrass 174
discomfiture, Chagrin 115
discompose, Embarrass ..174
discomposure, Chagrin ..115
disconcert, Embarrass ...174
disconsolate, Sad 377
discontinuance, Abeyance. 3
discontinue, Abandon 1
Stop 403
Suspend 411
discordant, Contrary 138
Incongruous 251
Miscellaneous 284
discouragement, Despair..153
discourse, Conversation...139
Speak 398
Speech 399
discourteous, Bluff 95
Discover 158
Catch 113
discredit, Debase 144
Disparage 159
discrepancy, Difference ..156
discrepant, Contrary 138
Incongruous 251
discretion, Address 22
Prudence 344
Wisdom 442
discriminate, Abstract ... 11
Contrast 138
Discern 158
discriminating, Shrewd ..388
discrimination, Difference.156
discuss, Dispute 160
Reason 356
discussion, Argument 62
disdain, Pride 335
Disease 159
disfigurement, Blemish .. 94
disgrace, Blemish 94
disgrace, Debase 144
Stain 400
disguise, Hide 233
Pretense 332
disgust, Abomination ... 6
Antipathy 52
dishearten, Embarrass ...174
dishonest, Bad 80
dishonesty, Fraud 213
dishonor, Blemish 94

Debase 144
Disparage 159
Stain 400
disinclined, Reluctant ...360
disinfect, Clean 124
disintegrate, Decay 144
disintegration, Revolution.370
disinterested, Generous ..218
dislike, n., antipathy 52
Hatred 229
dislike, v., Abhor........ 4
dislodge, Banish 82
dismal, Bleak 94
Dark 143
Sad 377
dismay, n., Alarm 35
Chagrin 115
Fear 199
dismay, v., Frighten.....215
dismiss, Banish 82
Send 383
disobedient, Rebellious ..357
disorder, Disease 159
Revolution 370
disorderly, Irregular 261
disown, Renounce 362
Disparage 159
Abuse 13
Slander 394
disparity, Difference 156
dispassionate, Calm 106
dispatch, Kill 265
Quicken 350
Send 383
dispense, Apportion 61
Execute 189
Displace 160
display, Ostentation 305
Spectacle 398
displease, Abhor 4
Affront 29
displeasure, Anger 49
Pique 318
disport, Entertain 180
dispose, Arrange 65
Influence 254
Persuade 316
disposed, Addicted 22
disposition, Appetite 59
Character 117
Mind 283
Will 442
disprove, Refute 359
disputation, Argument .. 62
dispute, n., Argument .. 62
Quarrel 348
Dispute, v. 160
Reason 356
disquiet, Anxiety 53
disquietude, Alarm 35
Fear 199
disquisition, Speech 399
disregard, Neglect 296
disrespect, Neglect 296

dissemble, Hide 233
dissembler, Deceiver 145
dissension, Argument ... 62
Quarrel 348
dissenter, Heretic 232
dissertation, Speech 399
dissimilar, Contrary 138
Miscellaneous 284
dissimilarity, Difference..156
dissimilitude, Difference..156
dissimulation, Deception..145
Hypocrisy 242
Pretense 332
dissipation, Excess 189
dissolute, Irregular 261
dissolve, Adjourn 26
dissuasion, Counsel 140
distant, Alien, a. 36
distaste, Antipathy 52
distemper, Disease 159
distend, Stretch 405
distinct, Clear 124
Evident 187
Precise 329
distinction, Characteristic.118
Difference 156
Fame 196
distinguish, Abstract 11
Contrast 138
Discern 158
distinguished, Eminent...175
distract, Abstract 11
distraction, Perplexity ...316
distrait, Abstracted 12
distraught, Abstracted ... 12
distress, Grief 223
Misfortune 286
Pain 308
Poverty 325
distressed, Sad 377
distressing, Bad 80
Sad 377
distribute, Allot 41
Apportion 61
distributively, Apiece 55
distrust, n., Doubt 163
distrust, v., Doubt 164
disturb, Displace 160
disturbance, Anxiety.... 53
Argument 62
Perplexity 316
Storm 404
disused, Obsolete 301
diurnal, Daily 143
diverge, Bend 90
Wander 438
divergence, Difference ...156
diversify, Change, v. ...117
diversion, Entertainment.181
diversity, Change, n......116
Difference 156
divert, Abstract 11
Entertain 180
divide, Allot 41

divide (*cont'd*)
  Apportion 61
  Rend 361
divine, *adj.*, Holy 238
divine, *v.*, Anticipate..... 51
  Foretell 210
division, Part 310
  Topic 422
Do 161
  Execute ...., ...189
  Make ...., ...277
  Transact 423
Docile 162
doctrinal, Dogmatic 163
Doctrine 162
  Faith 193
document, Record 357
dodge, Trick 425
doer, Agent 30
dogged, Morose 289
  Obstinate 302
dogma, Doctrine 162
Dogmatic 163
  Absolute 9
doing, Act 18
  Transaction 423
  Work ....,...........444
doleful, Sad 377
domicile, Home 239
dominant, Principal 336
domineering, Absolute ... 9
  Dogmatic 163
dominion, Power 326
donate, Give 220
donation, Gift 219
doom, Condemn 132
door, Entrance 182
doorway, Entrance 182
dormancy, Abeyance 3
dormant, Latent 269
double-dealing, Deception.145
Doubt, *n.* 163
  Perplexity 316
  Question 349
Doubt, *v.* 164
doubter, Skeptic 392
doubtful, Equivocal 183
  Obscure 301
  Precarious 328
doughty, Brave 97
dour, Morose...........289
douse, Dip 157
down, Conquer 134
downcast, Sad 377
draft, Sketch 393
drag, Draw 164
Draw 164
  Allure 43
  Influence 254
drawing, Sketch 393
draw out, Protract 343
dread, *adj.*, Awful 78
dread, *n.*, Alarm 35
  Anxiety 53

Fear 199
dreadful, Awful 78
Dream 165
dreary, Bleak 94
  Sad 377
Dress 166
drift, Stream 405
drifter, Hobo 236
drill, Exercise 190
  Teach 415
drink in, Absorb 10
drinking-bout, Carousal ..111
drink up, Absorb 10
Drive 166
  Compel 129
  Influence 254
  Quicken 350
  Send 383
drive on, Quicken 350
drive out, Banish 82
driveway, Way 439
droll, Queer 348
drollery, Wit 443
drove, Group 223
drowsy, Slow 395
drudgery, Work 444
Drunk 167
drunken, Drunk 167
dubiety, Doubt, *n.* 163
dubious, Equivocal 183
  Precarious 328
duck, Dip 157
due, Condign 132
dull, Bleak 94
  Sad 377
  Slow 395
  Stupid 406
dumb, Stupid 406
  Taciturn 414
Duplicate 167
duplicity, Deception 145
  Fraud 213
durable, Permanent 314
durance, Fetter 201
duration, Time 419
duress, Fetter 201
dusky, Dark 143
  Obscure 301
dust, *n.*, Body 96
dust, *v.*, Clean 124
dutiful, Good 221
Duty 168
  Business 102
  Tax 415
  Virtue 436
dwell, Abide 4
dwelling, Home 239
dwindle, Abate 1
dye, Stain 400

each, Apiece........... 55
Every 186
Eager 169
  Ardent ...., 62

eagerness, Alacrity 34
  Enthusiasm 182
earn, Attain 75
  Get 219
earnest, Eager 169
  Security 382
  Serious 385
earnestness, Enthusiasm..182
earnings, Pay 312
Ease 169
  Rest 367
easiness, Ease 169
easy, Comfortable 127
ebb, Abate 1
eccentric, Irregular 261
  Queer 348
economy, Frugality 216
  Law 270
ecstasy, Enthusiasm ...182
  Happiness 226
eddy, Stream 405
edge, Bank 83
  Boundary 97
edict, Law 270
educate, Teach 415
Education 170
efface, Cancel 107
effect, *n.*, Act 18
  Consequence 136
effect. *n.*, Operation......304
effect, *v.*, Do 161
  Make 277
effective, Efficient 171
effectual, Efficient 171
effeminate, Feminine 200
efficacious, Efficient 171
efficacy, Power 326
efficiency, Power 326
Efficient 171
effort, Endeavor 173
  Industry 252
Effrontery 171
  Assurance 70
  Impertinence 249
effulgence, Light 272
effulgent, Bright 99
egoism, Egotism 172
Egotism 172
either, Every 186
ejaculate, Call 106
eject, Banish 82
elderly, Old 303
elect, Choose 121
election, Choice 121
elegance, Refinement 358
Elegant 173
  Beautiful 87
  Fine 204
  Polite 324
element, Part 310
  Particle 311
elevate, Exalt 188
  Promote 340
elevated, High **234**

eliminate, Abstract 11
elongate, Protract 343
　Stretch 405
emanate, Rise 374
emancipate, Deliver 149
emancipation, Liberty ...271
Embarrass 174
　Hinder 234
　Involve 260
embarrassment, Perplexity.316
embellish, Adorn 27
embezzle, Steal 402
Emblem 174
　Sign 390
embolden, Abet 2
　Encourage 176
embrace, Caress 111
embroil, Involve 260
emend, Amend 47
emergency, Necessity ...295
emigrant, Alien, *n.* 36
emigrate, Migrate 283
émigré, Alien, *n.* 36
eminence, Fame 196
Eminent 175
　High 234
emissary, Spy 400
emit, Send 383
emolument, Pay 312
　Profit 337
emotion, Sensation 384
Employ 176
　Apply 60
employed, Busy 103
employment, Business ...102
　Exercise 190
　Work 444
empty, Vacant 431
　Vain 431
emulation, Ambition 46
enactment, Law 270
enchanting, Charming ...118
enclose, Circumscribe ...122
　Shut 389
enclosure, Boundary 97
encomium, Praise 327
encounter, *n.*, Battle ... 86
　Collision 126
encounter, *v.*, Attack 74
Encourage 176
　Abet 2
　Check 119
　Console 136
　Help 231
　Promote 340
encroachment, Attack ... 73
encumber, Hinder 234
encumbrance, Impediment.248
　Load 274
End, *n.* 177
　Aim 32
　Consequence 136
　Design 152
　Event 186

Reason 355
End, *v.* 178
　Abolish 5
　Stop 403
Endeavor 178
　Aim 32
　Try 427
endemic, Native 294
endless, Eternal 185
endorse, Confess 133
endowment, Gift 219
endurance, Fortitude 211
　Patience 311
Endure 179
　Abide 4
　Persist 316
　Stand 401
enduring, Permanent 314
Enemy 179
energetic, Active 19
energy, Power 326
enforce, Execute 189
engage, Bind 92
　Employ 176
engaged, Busy 103
engagement, Battle 86
　Contract 137
engaging, Amiable 47
engender, Propagate ...340
engross, Absorb 10
enhance, Intensify 259
enigma, Riddle 373
enigmatic, Equivocal 183
enigmatical, Equivocal ...183
　Mysterious 291
　Obscure 301
enjoy, Admire 26
enjoyment, Entertainment.181
　Happiness 226
enlarge, Add 21
　Amplify 48
enlighten, Teach 415
enlightenment, Wisdom..442
enliven, Entertain 180
Enmity 180
　Acrimony 18
　Hatred 229
　Quarrel 348
ennoble, Exalt 188
enormous, Large 268
enough, Adequate 24
　Plentiful 322
enrapturing, Charming ...118
enrich, Exalt 188
enrolment, Record 357
ensample, Example 188
ensconce, Hide 233
ensnare, Catch 113
ensue, Follow 209
entangle, Involve 260
entangled, Complex 130
entente, Contract 137
enter, Reach 354
Entertain 180

Cherish 119
Entertainment 181
　Feast 200
Enthusiasm 182
enthusiastic, Eager 169
entice, Allure 43
　Draw 164
　Persuade 316
entire, Perfect 313
　Radical 353
entirety, Aggregate 30
entomb, Hide 233
Entrance 182
entrancing, Charming ...118
entrap, Catch 113
entreat, Appeal 57
　Ask 67
　Plead 320
　Pray 328
entrée, Entrance 182
entrenchment, Fortifica-
　　tion 211
entrust, Commit 127
entry, Entrance 182
　Record 357
enumerate, Calculate ...105
enumeration, Record 357
enunciate, Announce 50
　Speak 398
envious, Jealous 262
eon. Time 419
eonian, Eternal 185
ephemeral, Transient 424
epigram, Proverb 343
episode. Circumstance....123
　Event 186
epithet, Name 293
epitome, Abridgment 7
epoch, Time 419
equal, Adequate 24
　Alike 37
equitable, Honest 239
　Right 373
equity, Justice 263
equivalent, Alike 37
　Synonymous 412
Equivocal 183
　Precarious 328
equivocation, Deception ..145
　Fallacy 195
era, Time...............419
eradicate, Abolish 5
　Cancel 107
　Exterminate 191
erase, Cancel 107
err, Wander 438
erratic, Irregular 261
　Queer 348
erroneous, Absurd 12
error, Delusion 150
erudition, Knowledge 266
　Science 381
　Wisdom 442
espousal, Marriage 278

espousals, Marriage 278
espy, Discern 158
   Look 275
essay, Endeavor 178
   Try 427
essential, *adj.,* Important.249
   Inherent 255
   Necessary 295
   Radical 353
   Real 354
essential, *n.,* Necessity..295
establish, Confirm 133
   Fix 206
   Make 277
   Reason 356
Esteem, *n.* 184
   Attachment 73
   Friendship 215
Esteem, *v.* 184
   Admire 26
esthetic, Elegant 173
esthetical, Elegant 173
estimate, *n.,* Esteem 184
estimate, *v.,* Calculate ...105
   Esteem 184
estimation, Attachment... 73
   Esteem 184
Eternal 185
   Infinite 253
ethereal, Airy 33
etiolate, Bleach 93
eucharist, Sacrament 377
eulogy, Praise 327
euphony, Rhythm 372
evanescent, Transient 424
evasion, Fallacy 195
even, Flat 207
Event 186
   Circumstance 123
   Consequence 136
everlasting, Eternal 185
ever-living, Eternal 185
Every 186
everyday, General 217
   Usual 429
evict, Banish 82
evidence, Demonstration..151
   Testimony 418
Evident 187
   Clear 124
evil, *adj.,* Bad 80
   Pernicious 315
evil, *n.,* Abomination.... 6
   Injury 256
   Sin 391
evil-disposed, Malicious ..277
evil-minded, Malicious ..277
exact, *adj.,* Minute 284
   Precise 329
exact, *v.,* Compel.......129
exacting, Absolute 9
exaction, Tax 415
exaggerate, Stretch 405
exaggeration, Caricature.111

Exalt 188
   Promote 340
exalted, Awful 78
   High 234
   Sublime 407
examine, Inquire 258
Example 188
   Ideal 244
   Model 288
   Precedent 329
   Sample 379
exasperate, Affront 29
exasperation, Anger 49
excavation, Hole 236
excellence, Virtue 436
excellent, Fine 204
   Good 221
except, But 103
excepting, But 103
exceptional, Irregular ...261
excerpt, Quote 350
Excess 189
exchange, *n.,* Sale......379
exchange, *v.,* Change...117
excise, Tax 415
excitable, Ardent 62
excite, Encourage 176
   Influence 254
   Promote 340
excitement, Enthusiasm..182
exclaim, Call 106
exclude, Shut 389
exculpate, Absolve 9
exculpation, Apology 55
excursion, Journey 262
excusable, Venial 434
excuse, *n.,* Apology 55
   Pretense 322
excuse, *v.,* Pardon 309
execration, Abomination.. 6
   Oath 300
Execute 189
   Do 161
   Kill 265
   Make 277
execution, Act 18
   Operation 304
exemplar, Example 188
   Model 288
exemplary, Condign 132
   Innocent 257
exemplification, Example.188
   Sample 279
exempt, Absolve 9
exemption, Right 374
Exercise, *n.* 190
   Act 18
exercise, *v.,* Apply 60
exertion, Act 18
   Endeavor 178
   Exercise 190
   Industry 252
   Work 444
exhaust, Absorb......... 10

Tire 420
exhausted, Faint 193
exhausting, Difficult ...157
exhibit, Offer 302
exhibition, Spectacle 398
exhilarated, Drunk 167
exhortation, Counsel 140
exigency, Necessity 295
exile, Banish 82
existent, Alive 37
existing, Alive 37
exonerate, Absolve 9
exorbitance, Excess 189
exotic, Alien 36
expand, Amplify 48
   Stretch 405
expatiate, Amplify 48
expatriate, Banish 82
expect, Abide 4
   Anticipate 51
expectancy, Abeyance 3
   Anticipation 52
expectation, Abeyance .. 3
   Anticipation 52
expediency, Profit 337
   Utility 429
expedite, Quicken 350
expedition, Journey 262
expeditious, Active 19
expel, Banish 82
   Exterminate 191
expenditure, Price 334
expense, Price 334
experience, Acquaintance. 17
   Knowledge 266
expert, Clever 125
   Good 221
   Skilful 393
expertness, Dexterity ...154
   Ease 169
   Power 326
expiation, Propitiation ...341
expiration, End 177
expire, Die 155
   End 178
explanation, Definition...148
Explicit 190
   Clear 124
   Precise 329
exploit, Act 18
expose, Discover 158
exposed, Bleak 94
exposition, Definition...148
expostulate with, Reprove.365
express, Explicit 190
   Speak 398
   State 401
expression, Air 33
   Diction 155
   Language 268
   Term 416
expunge, Cancel 107
exquisite, Beautiful 87
   Delicious 149

exquisite (cont'd)
Elegant 173
Fine 204
Extemporaneous 191
extemporary, Extempo-
raneous 191
extempore, Extempora-
neous 191
extend, Add 21
Amplify 48
Offer 302
Protract 343
Stretch 405
extension, Appendage ... 58
extensive, Large 268
extent, End 177
extenuate, Palliate 308
exterminate 191
Abolish 5
extinguish, Overthrow ..306
extirpate, Abolish 5
Exterminate 191
extol, Admire 26
extort, Steal 402
extract, Quote 350
extradite, Banish 82
extraneous, Alien, a. 36
extraordinary, Queer ...348
Rare 353
extravagance, Enthusiasm.182
Excess 189
extravaganza, Caricature.111
extreme, Radical 353
extremity, End, n. 177
Necessity 295
extrinsic, Alien, a. 36
exuberant, Plentiful 322

fable, Allegory 39
Fiction 202
fabricate, Make 277
fabrication, Deception ...145
Fiction 202
facetiousness, Wit 443
facilitate, Quicken 350
facility, Ease 169
facsimile, Duplicate 167
Model 288
fact, Circumstance 123
Event 186
faction, Cabal 105
factious, Perverse 317
factor, Agent 30
faculty, Genius 218
Power 326
fade, Die 155
faded, Faint 193
fadeless, Eternal 185
fag, Tire 420
failure, Bankruptcy 83
Misfortune 286
Neglect 296
Faint 193
faint-hearted, Afraid 29

Faint 193
fainting, Stupor 406
fair, Admissible 27
Beautiful 87
Candid 108
Good 221
Honest 239
Right 373
fairness, Justice 263
fair play, Justice 263
fairylike, Airy 33
Faith 193
Religion 360
Faithful 194
Honest 239
faithfulness, Allegiance.. 39
Justice 263
Virtue 436
fall, Happen 225
Suspend 411
Fallacy 195
Delusion 150
fall out, Happen 225
fall upon, Attack 74
false, Absurd 12
Bad 80
falsehood, Deception 145
Fiction 202
faltering, Faint 193
Fame 196
familiar, General 217
Usual 429
familiarity, Acquaintance. 17
Association 69
family, Kin 266
famous, Eminent 175
Fanaticism 196
Enthusiasm 182
Fanciful 197
Fickle 201
Fancy 197
Dream 165
Idea 244
Imagination 246
fantasm, Dream 165
fantastic, Fanciful 197
Queer 348
fantasy, Dream 165
Idea 244
Imagination 246
fare, Food 209
Farewell 198
farming, Agriculture 31
fascinating, Charming ..118
fashion, n., Air 33
Habit 225
fashion, v., Make.......277
fasten, Append 58
Attach 71
Bind 92
Fix 206
fastening, Lock 275
fastidious, Elegant 173
fasting, Abstinence 11

fastness, Fortification ...211
fatality, Necessity 295
fate, Necessity 295
Predestination 330
fatigue, Tire 420
fatigued, Faint 193
fatuity, Idiocy 245
fault, Blemish 94
Sin 391
faultfinding, Captious ...109
faultless, Innocent 257
Precise 329
Favor 198
Esteem 184
Friendship 215
Gift 219
Mercy 282
favorable, Friendly 214
Good 221
Propitious 341
favored, Fortunate 212
fealty, Allegiance 39
Fear 199
Alarm 35
Anxiety 53
fearful, Afraid 29
Awful 78
fearless, Brave 97
Feast 200
Entertainment 181
feat, Act 18
feature, Characteristic ..118
Circumstance 123
federation, Alliance 41
Association 69
fee, Pay 312
feeble, Faint 193
feed, Food 209
feeling, Sensation 384
Sensibility 384
feign, Assume 70
felicitate, Congratulate ..134
felicitous, Happy 227
felicity, Happiness 226
fellow, Associate, n...... 68
Scholar 380
fellowship, Acquaintance.. 17
Association 69
felonious, Criminal 141
female, Feminine 200
Feminine 200
fence, Circumscribe 122
ferocious, Fierce 203
ferret out, Discover 158
fervency, Enthusiasm ...182
fervent, Ardent 62
Eager 169
fervid, Ardent 62
fervor, Enthusiasm 182
festival, Feast 200
festivity, Feast 200
fête, Feast 200
Fetter 201
Bind 92

feud, Enmity 180
  Quarrel 348
Fickle 201
Fiction 202
  Allegory 39
fidgety, Restive 367
field-works, Fortification..211
Fierce 203
  Ardent 62
  Violent 436
fiery, Ardent 62
  Fierce 203
fight, Battle 86
  Quarrel 348
figment, Fiction 202
figure, Emblem 174
filch, Steal 402
fill, Satisfy 380
final cause, Design.......142
finale, End 177
Financial 203
find, Discover 158
find fault, Complain.....129
find out, Discover.......158
Fine 204
  Beautiful 87
  Elegant 173
  Minute 284
finesse, Deception 145
  Trick 425
finis, End 177
finish, n., End 177
finish, v., Do...........161
  End 178
  Stop 403
Fire 204
fireside, Home 239
firm, Faithful 194
  Obstinate 302
first, Principal 336
fiscal, Financial 203
fissure, Hole 236
Fit, adj. 205
  Adequate 24
  Becoming 88
  Condign 132
  Good 221
fit, v., Apply 60
fit (fix), Adapt 20
fitful, Fickle 201
  Irregular 261
fitted, Adequate 24
  Fit 205
fitting, Adequate 24
  Becoming 88
  Fit 205
  Right 373
fix, n., Predicament......331
fix, v. 206
  Append 58
  Attach 71
  Bind 92
  Confirm 133
fixed, Obstinate 302

Permanent 314
flagitious, Criminal 141
flame, n., Fire..........204
  Light 272
flame, v., Burn 101
flap, Shake 386
flare, Light 272
flash, n., Light 272
flash, v., Burn..........101
flashing, Bright 99
Flat 207
flatter, Caress 111
flattery, Praise 327
flavorous, Racy 352
flaw, Blemish 94
flawless, Precise 329
flee, Abscond 8
fleeting, Transient 424
flexible, Nimble 298
flicker, Light 272
flight, Group 223
fling, Send 383
  Sneer 396
flippancy, Pertness 317
flitting, Transient 424
floater, Hobo 236
flock, Group 223
flog, Beat 86
flood, Stream 405
floriculture, Agriculture.. 31
flourish, n., Ostentation.305
flourish, v., Abound..... 6
  Succeed 408
flow, Abound 6
  Rise 374
  Stream 405
Fluctuate 208
  Shake 386
fluctuating, Fickle 201
Fluid 208
flume, Stream 405
fluster, Embarrass 174
flutter, Shake 386
flux, Stream 405
fly, Abscond 8
flying, Transient 424
fodder, Food 209
foe, Enemy 179
foil, Baffle 81
  Check 119
  Hinder 234
folk, Race 352
Follow 209
follower, Accessory 16
  Adherent 24
folly, Idiocy 245
foment, Promote 340
fond, Friendly 214
fondle, Caress 111
fondness, Love 276
Food 209
foolhardiness, Temerity ..416
foolhardy, Imprudent 251
foolish, Absurd 12

foolishness, Idiocy 245
foot, Foundation 212
footmark, Trace 422
footpad, Robber 375
footpath, Way 439
footprint, Trace 422
footstep, Trace 422
for, Because 88
forage, Food 209
forager, Robber 375
forbearance, Mercy 282
  Pardon 309
  Patience 311
forbid, Prohibit 338
force, n., Army 64
  Operation 304
  Power 326
force, v., Compel 129
  Drive 166
forces, Army 64
forcible, Racy 352
forebode, Foretell 210
foreboding, Anticipation... 52
  Anxiety 53
forecast, n., Anticipation. 52
  Prudence 344
forecast, v., Anticipate... 51
  Foretell 210
foregoing, Previous 333
foreign, Alien 36
foreigner, Alien 36
foreknowledge, Predestination 330
foremost, Principal 336
foreordination, Predestination 330
foresight, Anticipation.... 52
  Prudence 344
  Wisdom 442
forestall, Prevent 332
foretaste, n., Anticipation. 52
foretaste, v., Anticipate... 51
Foretell 210
  Anticipate 51
forethought, Anticipation. 52
  Care 110
  Prudence 344
forge, Make 277
forgive, Absolve 9
  Pardon, v. 309
forgiveness, Mercy 282
  Pardon 309
forgiving, Humane 240
forgo, Abandon 1
form, n., Body 96
form, v., Arrange 65
  Make 277
formal, Academic 14
formalism, Hypocrisy ...242
former, adj., Previous...333
former, n., Cause.......114
Formidable 210
formula, Law 279
forsake, Abandon 1

forswear, Abandon 1
Renounce 362
fort, Fortification 211
forthwith, Immediately ..247
Fortification 211
Fortitude 211
Patience 311
fortress, Defense 146
Fortification 211
fortuity, Accident 16
Hazard 231
Fortunate 212
Happy 227
Propitious 341
fortune, Accident 16
Event 186
Wealth 440
forward, Encourage 176
Promote 340
Send 383
forwardness, Impertinence249
Pertness 317
foster, Cherish 119
Help 231
Promote 340
foul, Bad 80
Pernicious 315
Foundation 212
fount, Beginning 89
fountain, Beginning..... 89
Cause 114
fox-hole, Fortification ..211
fracas, Argument 62
Quarrel 348
fraction, Part 310
fractious, Perverse 317
Restive 367
fracture, Break 98
fragment, Part 310
fragrance, Smell 396
frame, n., Body 96
frame, v., Make 277
franchise, Right 374
frank, Bluff 95
Candid 108
Honest 239
frankness, Truth 426
frantic, Violent 436
fraternity, Association .. 69
Fraud 213
Deception 145
Trick 425
fraudulent, Bad 80
fray, Quarrel 348
free, adj., Generous.....218
Spontaneous 399
free, v., Absolve 9
Deliver 149
freebooter, Robber 375
freedom, Liberty 271
free-handed, Generous ...218
free-hearted, Generous ...218
freethinker, Skeptic 392

freight, Load 274
frenzied, Violent 436
frenzy, Enthusiasm 182
Insanity 259
frequent, General 217
Usual 429
fresh, New 297
fretful, Captious........109
Restive 367
fretfulness, Anger 49
Anxiety 53
Impatience 248
fretting, Anxiety 53
friary, Cloister 126
friend, Associate 68
friendliness, Friendship ..215
Friendly 214
Good 221
Propitious 341
Friendship 215
Acquaintance 17
Association 69
Attachment 73
Love 276
fright, Alarm 35
Fear 199
Frighten 215
frightened, Afraid 29
frightful, Awful 78
frisky, Restive 367
frivolous, Vain 431
frolic, Entertainment 181
frolicsome, Airy 33
frontier, Boundary 97
froward, Perverse 317
Frugality 216
Abstinence 11
Prudence 344
fruit, Harvest 229
fruitless, Vain 431
frustrate, Baffle 81
Hinder 234
fuddled, Drunk 167
fugitive, Transient 424
fulfil, Do 161
Keep 265
fulfilment, End 177
full, Drunk 167
Plentiful 322
fuming, Violent 436
fun, Entertainment 181
Wit 443
function, Duty 168
fundamental, Radical ...353
funds, Money 289
funny, Queer 348
furious, Fierce 203
Violent 436
furnish, Give 220
further, conj., But......103
Yet 445
further, v., Promote....340
Quicken 350
fury, Anger 49

fuse, Mix 286
fusion, Alliance 41
futile, Vain 431

gabble, Babble 80
gage, Criterion 141
Security 382
gaggle, Group 223
gaiety, Happiness 226
gain, Attain 75
Get 219
Profit 337
Reach 354
gainsay, Object 300
gall, Effrontery 171
gallant, Brave 97
Polite 324
gallantry, Prowess 344
galling, Troublesome 426
gam, Group 223
gang, Cabal 105
gap, Hole 236
garb, Dress 166
gardening, Agriculture... 31
garments, Dress 166
garnish, Adorn 27
garrulous, Talkative 414
gas, Fluid 208
gate, Entrance 182
gateway, Entrance 182
gather, Amass 44
Convoke 146
gathering, Company 128
gauche, Awkward 78
gawky, Awkward 78
gay, Airy 33
Happy 227
gaze, Look 275
Gender 217
General 217
Normal 298
Usual 429
generate, Propagate 340
generic, General 217
generosity, Benevolence... 91
Generous 218
Plentiful 322
genial, Comfortable 127
Friendly 214
Good 221
Genius 218
Character 117
Ingenuity 254
genteel, Polite 324
gentle, Amiable 47
Calm 106
Docile 162
Humane 240
Humble 240
gentleness, Mercy 282
genuine, Authentic 76
Good 221
Honest 239
Pure 346

genuine (cont'd)
Real 354
Get 219
   Attain 75
   Make 277
   Purchase 345
get (to), Reach 354
gibber, Babble 80
gibe, Sneer 396
Gift 219
   Favor 198
   Genius 218
   Subsidy 408
gifted, Clever 123
gigantic, Large 268
gild, Adorn 27
girlish, Youthful 445
Give 220
   Allot 41
   Convey 140
   Surrender 411
give instruction, Teach...415
give lessons, Teach......415
given, Addicted 22
give notice (of), Announce 50
given over, Addicted..... 22
given up, Addicted..... 22
give oneself up, Surren-
   der 411
give out, Announce...... 50
give over, Stop 403
   Surrender 411
give up, Abandon........ 1
   Surrender 411
glad, Happy 227
gladness, Happiness 226
glance, Look 275
glare, Light 272
glaring, Bright 99
   Evident 187
gleam, Light 272
gleaming, adj., Bright.... 99
gleaming, n., Light......272
glee, Happiness 226
glimmer, Light 272
glimmering, Bright 99
glistening, adj., Bright... 99
glistening, n., Light......272
glistering, Light 272
glitter, Light 272
glittering, Bright 99
gloomy, Bleak 94
   Dark 143
   Morose 289
   Sad 377
glorious, Bright 99
   Sublime 407
glory, Fame 196
gloss over, Palliate......308
glow, Light 272
glowing, Ardent 62
   Bright 99
   Eager 169
gloze, Palliate 308

gluey, Adhesive 25
glum, Morose 289
glut, Satisfy 380
glutinous, Adhesive 25
go after, Follow........209
goal, Aim 32
   End 177
go astray, Wander......438
godly, Devout 154
   Good 221
Godspeed, Farewell 198
gold, Money 289
Good, adj. 221
   Honest 239
   Right 373
good, n., Profit........337
good-by, Farewell 198
good-natured, Amiable ... 47
   Pleasant 321
goodness, Virtue 436
goods, Wealth 440
good-will, Benevolence ... 91
   Favor 198
   Friendship 215
gorge, Hole 236
gorgeous, Sublime 407
gory, Sanguinary 380
gossip, Babble 80
Govern 222
grace, Favor 198
   Mercy 282
Graceful 222
   Beautiful 87
   Becoming 88
gracious, Good 221
   Humane 240
   Polite 324
   Propitious 341
grade, Class 123
gradual, Slow 395
grain, Particle 311
grand, Awful 78
   Large 268
   Sublime 407
grant, n., Gift 219
   Subsidy 408
grant, v., Allot 41
   Allow 42
   Apportion 61
   Confess 133
   Give 220
grasp, Attain 75
   Catch 113
grateful, Pleasant 321
gratification, Happiness ..226
gratify, Entertain 180
gratifying, Good 221
   Pleasant 321
gratuity, Gift 219
grave, Important 249
   Sad 377
   Serious 385
gray, Old 303
great, Important 249

Large 268
   Serious 385
greatest, Principal 336
greedy, Miserly 285
greet, Address, v......... 23
Grief 223
grievance, Injustice 256
grieve, Mourn 290
grind, Work 444
grip, Catch 113
gripe, Catch 113
grit, Fortitude 211
groggy, Drunk 167
grotesque, Fanciful 197
   Queer 348
ground, Foundation 212
   Reason 355
groundwork, Foundation..212
Group, n. 223
   Company 128
group, v., Arrange 65
groveling, Base 85
growl, Complain 129
growth, Harvest 229
   Progress 338
grudge, Hatred 229
   Pique 318
gruff, Morose 289
grumble, Complain 129
grunt, Complain 129
guarantee, Security 382
guaranty, Security 382
guard, Defense 146
   Keep 265
   Shelter 388
guarded, Secure 382
guerdon, Reward 371
guess, Hypothesis 242
   Suppose 410
guile, Deception 145
   Trick 425
guileless, Candid 108
   Innocent 257
   Pure 346
guilt, Sin 391
guiltless, Innocent 257
   Pure 346
guilty, Criminal 141
gulf, Abyss 14
gummy, Adhesive 25
guts, Fortitude 211
gyrate, Revolve 371
gyves, Fetter 201

habiliments, Dress 166
Habit 225
   Dress 166
habitation, Home 239
habitual, General 217
   Usual 429
habituated, Addicted 22
habitude, Habit 225
hack, Venal 432
hackney, Venal 432

hail, Address, *v.* 23
hairsplitting, Fallacy 195
hale, *adj.,* Healthy.......231
hale, *v.,* Draw 164
half-hearted, Faint 193
half-seas-over, Drunk 167
hallow, Devote 154
hallowed, Holy 238
hallucination, Delusion ..150
    Dream 165
halt, Stand 401
hamper, Embarrass 174
    Hinder 234
handcuffs, Fetter 201
handicraft, Business 102
handsome, Beautiful 87
    Fine 204
    Generous 218
handy, Skilful 393
hankering, Desire 152
hap, Accident 16
Happen 225
happening, Accident 16
Happiness 226
Happy 227
    Clever 125
    Fortunate 212
    Skilful 393
harangue, Speech 399
harass, Tire 420
harassing, Troublesome ..426
harbor, Cherish 119
    Shelter 388
hard, Bad 80
    Difficult 157
    Severe 385
    Troublesome 426
hardihood, Effrontery 171
    Temerity 416
hardship, Misfortune 286
hark, Listen 273
harken, Listen 273
harm, Abuse 13
    Injury 256
    Misfortune 286
harmful, Pernicious 315
harmless, Innocent 257
harmonize, Agree 31
    Arrange 65
harmony 228
    Melody 281
harsh, Bitter 93
    Severe 385
harshness, Acrimony 18
Harvest 229
harvesting, Harvest 229
hasp, Lock 275
hasten, Quicken 350
hastiness, Temerity 416
hatch, Group 223
hate, *n.,* Hatred 229
hate, *v.,* Abhor 4
Hatred 229
    Abomination 6

Antipathy 52
Enmity 180
    Revenge 369
haughtiness, Pride 335
haughty, Absolute 9
haul, Draw 164
Have 230
    Ought 305
have got, Ought 305
Hazard 231
    Accident 16
    Danger 143
hazardous, Precarious ..328
head, Chief 120
    Topic 422
headman, Chief 120
headstrong, Obstinate ..302
heady, Obstinate 302
heal, Recover 358
healthful, Healthy 231
Healthy 231
heap, Aggregate 30
heap up, Amass 44
hear, Listen 273
heart, Center 115
hearten, Encourage 176
hearth, Home 239
hearthstone, Home 239
hearty, Friendly 214
    Healthy 231
heavy, Sad 377
heed, Care 110
    Follow 209
    Listen 273
heedful, Thoughtful 418
heedless, Abstracted 12
    Imprudent 251
heedlessness, Neglect 296
    Temerity 416
heel over, Tip...........420
heighten, Intensify 259
Help 231
    Abet 2
    Promote 340
helper, Accessory 15
    Auxiliary 77
helpmate, Associate, *n....* 68
hence, Therefore 418
henchman, Accessory 15
herald, Announce 50
herd, Group 223
heresiarch, Heretic 232
Heretic 232
hermitage, Cloister 126
heroic, Brave 97
heroism, Fortitude 211
    Prowess 344
hesitancy, Doubt, *n.*.....163
hesitate, Fluctuate 208
    Object 300
hesitation, Doubt, *n.*.....163
heterogeneous, Complex ..130
    Miscellaneous 284
hidden, Latent 269

Mysterious 291
Obscure 301
Hide 233
    Abscond 8
    Palliate 308
High 234
    Steep 403
highest, Principal 336
highroad, Way 439
highway, Way 439
highwayman, Robber 375
Hinder 234
    Check 119
    Embarrass 174
    Prohibit 338
    Restrain 368
    Suspend 411
hindrance, Barrier 84
    Impediment 248
hint, Allude 43
    Suggestion 409
hire, Employ 176
    Pay 312
hireling, Venal 432
History 235
history, Record 357
hit, Beat 86
    Blow 95
hitch, Attach 71
    Bind 92
hitherto, Yet 445
hoard, Amass 44
hoard up, Amass.... 44
hoary, Old 303
Hobo 236
hold, *n.,* Hole 236
hold, *v.,* Arrest 67
    Esteem 184
    Have 230
    Keep 265
    Restrain 368
hold back, Restrain.....368
hold dear, Cherish.......119
hold in, Restrain 368
hold out, Offer 302
    Stand 401
hold up, Support 410
Hole 236
hollow, Hole 236
Holy 238
    Devout 154
    Good 221
    Pure 346
homage, Allegiance 39
Home 239
homily, Speech 399
homogeneous, Alike 37
Honest 239
    Candid 108
    Right 373
honesty, Truth 426
    Virtue 436
honor, Admire 26
    Fame 196

honor (cont'd)
   Justice 263
   Virtue 436
honorable, Good 221
   Honest 239
honorarium, Pay 312
hook, Lock 275
hope, n., Anticipation.... 52
hope, v., Anticipate...... 51
hopelessness, Despair 153
horde, Mob 288
horizontal, Flat 207
horrible, Awful 78
horror, Abomination 6
   Fear 199
horticulture, Agriculture.. 31
host, Army 64
   Company 128
   Throng 419
hostile, Adverse 28
   Alien 36
   Malicious 277
hostility, Antipathy 52
   Enmity 180
   Hatred 229
   Quarrel 348
hot, Ardent 62
   Eager 169
house, Home 239
howbeit, Notwithstanding,
   conj. 299
however, But 103
   Notwithstanding 299
hoydenish, Rustic 376
hub, Center 115
huge, Large 268
hum, Sing 392
human, Humane 240
Humane 240
   Good 221
humanitarian, Humane ..240
humanity, Benevolence ... 91
Humble 240
   Conquer 134
   Debase 144
   Embarrass 174
   Punish 345
humiliate, Debase 144
   Embarrass 174
humiliation, Chagrin 115
humor, Fancy 197
   Wit 443
Hunt 241
hunting, Hunt 241
hurl, Send 385
hurt, Injury 256
hurtful, Bad 80
   Pernicious 315
hurry, Quicken 350
husbandry, Agriculture .. 31
hygienic, Healthy 231
hypercritical, Captious ..109
Hypocrisy 242
   Deception 145

hypocrite, Deceiver 145
Hypothesis 242

Idea 244
   Fancy 197
Ideal 244
   Example 188
   Idea 244
   Model 288
identical, Alike 37
   Precise 329
   Synonymous 412
Idiocy 245
idiom, Language 268
Idle 245
   Vain 431
ignite, Burn 101
ignoble, Base 85
Ignorant 246
   Brutish 101
ill, Bad 80
   Misfortune 286
ill-advised, Absurd 12
   Imprudent 251
ill-considered, Absurd 12
ill-defined, Faint 193
ill-disposed, Malicious .. 277
ill-doing, Sin 391
illegal, Criminal 141
ill fortune, Misfortune...286
ill-humored, Morose 289
illimitable, Infinite 253
ill-informed, Ignorant ...246
illiterate, Ignorant 246
ill-judged, Absurd 12
   Imprudent 251
ill luck, Misfortune......286
ill-matched, Incongruous..251
ill-natured, Malicious ...277
   Morose 289
illness, Disease 159
ill-treat, Abuse 13
illuminated, Bright 99
illumination, Light 272
illumined, Bright 99
ill-use, Abuse 13
illusion, Delusion 150
illusive, Deceptive 146
illusory, Apparent 56
   Deceptive 146
illustrate, Adorn 27
illustration, Allegory 39
   Sample 379
illustrious, Eminent 175
ill will, Enmity 180
   Hatred 229
image, Emblem 174
   Fancy 197
   Idea 244
   Likeness 273
   Model 288
   Sensation 384
Imagination 246
   Fancy 197

Idea 244
imaginative, Fanciful 197
imagine, Suppose 410
imbecility, Idiocy 245
imbibe, Absorb 10
imbruted, Brutish 101
imitate, Follow 209
imitation, Caricature 111
   Duplicate 167
   Model 288
immaculate, Good 221
   Innocent 257
   Pure 346
immanent, Inherent 255
immature, Youthful 445
immeasurable, Infinite ...253
Immediately 247
immemorial, Old 303
   Primeval 336
immense, Large 268
immerge, Dip 157
immerse, Dip 157
immigrant, Alien, n...... 36
immigrate, Migrate 283
Imminent 247
immobility, Apathy 54
immoderate, Irregular ...261
   Violent 436
immoral, Bad 80
   Criminal 141
immorality, Sin 391
immortal, Eternal 185
immovable, Obstinate ...302
immunity, Right, n......374
immutable, Permanent ..314
impact, Collision 126
impairment, Injury 256
impart, Give 220
impartial, Candid 108
impartiality, Justice 263
impassibility, Apathy 54
impassioned, Ardent 62
Impatience 248
   Anger 49
impatient, Eager 169
   Restive 367
impeach, Arraign 64
impede, Check 119
   Embarrass 174
   Hinder 234
Impediment 248
   Barrier 84
impel, Drive 166
   Encourage 176
   Influence 254
   Persuade 316
   Send 383
impending, Imminent....247
imperative, Absolute 9
imperceptible, Latent ...269
imperfect, Bad 80
imperfection, Blemish ... 94
imperial, Royal 375
imperious, Absolute 9

imperious (*cont'd*)
Dogmatic 163
imperishable, Eternal 185
Permanent 314
Impertinence 249
Pertness 317
impertinent, Alien 36
Meddlesome 280
imperturbable, Calm 106
impetuosity, Temerity ...416
impetuous, Eager 169
Fierce 203
Violent 436
impingement, Collision ...126
implement, Tool 421
implicate, Involve 260
implication, Suggestion ..409
implicit, Latent 269
implied, Latent 269
implore, Ask 67
Plead 320
Pray 328
imply, Allude 43
Involve 260
impolite, Bluff 95
impolitic, Imprudent 251
Important 249
Serious 385
importunate, Eager 169
Troublesome 426
importune, Pray 328
impose on, Abuse........ 13
impose upon, Abuse...... 13
imposing, Awful 78
imposition, Deception 145
Fraud 213
impossible, Impracticable..250
impost, Tax 415
impostor, Deceiver 145
imposture, Fraud 213
Trick 425
impotence, Inability 251
Impracticable 250
impractical, Impracticable.250
imprecation, Oath 300
impregnable, Secure 382
impress, Concern 131
impressibility, Sensibility.384
impression, Idea 244
Trace 422
imprison, Shut 389
imprisonment, Fetter ...201
impromptu, Extemporaneous 191
improve, Amend 47
improvement, Profit 337
Progress 338
improvident, Imprudent ...251
improvised, Extemporaneous 191
imprudent 251
impudence, Assurance ... 70
Effrontery 171
Impertinence 249

Pertness 317
impulse, Appetite 59
impulsive, Spontaneous ..399
impute, Attribute, *v*...... 76
Inability 251
inaction, Abeyance 3
inactive, Idle 245
Slow 395
in addition, Also 44
inadvertence, Neglect ...296
inapplicable, Alien....... 36
inapposite, Incongruous ..251
inappropriate, Alien...... 36
Incongruous 251
inasmuch as, Because.... 88
inattention, Neglect 296
inattentive, Abstracted .. 12
inauguration, Beginning... 89
inborn, Inherent 255
inbred, Inherent 255
incandescence, Light ...272
incandescent, Bright 99
incapability, Inability ...251
incapacity, Idiocy 245
incautious, Imprudent ...251
inception, Beginning 89
incessant, Continual 137
incident, Accident 16
Circumstance 123
Event 186
Story 404
incinerate, Burn 101
incite, Abet 2
Influence 254
Persuade 316
incivility, Impertinence ..249
inclination, Aim 32
Appetite 59
Attachment 73
Desire 152
Direction 158
Fancy 197
Will 442
incline, Bend 90
Draw 164
Influence 254
Persuade 316
Tip 420
inclined, Addicted 22
include, Involve 260
included, Latent 269
incoherent, Incongruous ..251
incommensurable, Incongruous 251
incomparable, Rare 353
incompatible, Adverse ... 28
Contrary 138
Incongruous 251
incompetent, Bad 80
incomprehensible, mysterious 291
Obscure 301
inconclusive, Absurd 12
Incongruous 251

Contrary 138
inconsiderate, Bluff 95
Imprudent 251
inconsistency, Difference...156
inconsistent, Contrary ...138
Incongruous 251
inconstant, Fickle 201
Vain 431
incorporate, Mix 286
incorrect, Absurd 12
Bad 80
incorrupt, Pure 346
incorruptible, Faithful ...194
increase, Add 21
Amplify 48
Harvest 229
Intensify 259
Progress 338
Propagate 340
incredulity, Doubt, *n*...163
incubus, Load 274
inculcate, Teach 415
incursion, Attack, *n*....73
indecision, Doubt, *n*......163
indefinite, Equivocal 183
indelible, Permanent 314
indemnity, Subsidy 408
indentation, Hole 236
indenture, Contract 137
independence, Liberty ...271
indestructible, Permanent.314
indeterminate, Equivocal..183
indicate, Allude 43
indication, Characteristic..118
Sign 390
indict, Arraign 64
indifference, Apathy 54
Neglect 296
indifferent, Abstracted ...12
indigence, Poverty 325
indigenous, Native 294
Primeval 336
indignation, Anger 49
indiscreet, Imprudent 251
indispensability, Necessity295
indispensable, Inherent ..255
Necessary 295
indispensableness, Necessity 295
indisposed, Reluctant 360
indisposition, Disease ...159
indistinct, Equivocal 183
Faint 193
Obscure 301
individuality, Character ..217
individually, Apiece 55
indoctrinate, Teach 415
indolent, Idle 245
indomitable, Obstinate ...302
indubitable, Evident 187
induce, Draw 164
Influence 254
Persuade 316

Induction, Demonstration..151
Inference 253
Industrious, Active 19
Busy 103
Industry 252
indwelling, Inherent ...255
inebriated, Drunk 167
ineffectual, Vain 431
inelegant, Rustic 376
inept, Awkward 78
inequality, Difference 156
inert, Idle 245
Slow 395
inevitable, Necessary ...295
inexorable, Severe 385
inexplicable, Mysterious..291
infallible, Necessary 295
infamous, Base 85
infatuated, Absurd 12
infect, Defile 147
infectious, Contagious ...137
Inference 253
Demonstration 151
inferior, Bad 80
infidel, Skeptic 392
Infinite 253
Eternal 185
infirmity, Disease 159
infixed, Inherent 255
inflammable, Ardent 62
inflexible, Obstinate 302
Severe 385
inflict, Execute 189
influence, n., Operation..304
Influence, v. 254
Bend 90
Drive 166
Govern 222
Persuade 316
influential, Important ...249
inform, State 401
Teach 415
information, Education ..170
Knowledge 266
News 297
Wisdom 442
informed, Conscious 135
infrequent, Rare 353
infringement, Attack, n... 73
infuriate, Violent 436
ingathering, Harvest ...229
ingenious, Clever 125
Skilful 393
ingeniousness, Ingenuity..254
Ingenuity 254
Address 22
ingenuous, Candid 108
Honest 239
ingenuousness, Truth 426
ingleside, Home 239
ingrained, Inherent 255
Radical 353
ingredient, Part 310
ingress, Entrance 182

inhabit, Abide 4
inharmonious, Incongru-
  ous 251
Inherent 255
Latent 269
inhering, Inherent 255
inhibit, Check 119
Prohibit 338
inhuman, Barbarous 84
Sanguinary 380
inimical, Adverse 28
iniquitous, Criminal 141
iniquity, Abomination ... 6
Injustice 256
Sin 391
initiate, Teach 415
initiation, Beginning 89
injudicious, Imprudent ..251
injunction, Order 304
injure, Abuse 13
injurious, Bad 80
Pernicious 315
Injury 256
Blemish 94
Injustice 256
Injustice 256
Injury 256
inlet, Entrance 182
in like manner, Also.... 44
innate, Inherent 255
Native 294
Radical 353
Innocent 257
Candid 108
Pure 346
innocuous, Innocent 257
innovation, Change 116
innoxious, Innocent.....257
innuendo, Suggestion...409
innumerable, Infinite ...253
inoffensive, Innocent....257
inordinate, Inquire 258
Irregular 261
inquire into, Inquire....258
inquiring, Inquisitive ...258
inquiry, Question 349
inquisition, Hunt.......241
Question 349
Inquisitive 258
insalubrious, Pernicious..315
Insanity 259
inscription, Record 357
inscrutable, Mysterious...291
insecure, Precarious 328
insecurity, Danger......143
insensibility, Apathy..... 54
Stupor 406
insensible, Brutish......101
inseparable, Inherent....255
insert, Interpose 260
insight, Acumen......... 19
Wisdom 442
insinuate, Allude 43
insinuation, Suggestion...409

insist, Persist 316
insolence, Effrontery.....171
Impertinence 249
Pride 335
insolvency, Bankruptcy... 83
inspect, Look...........275
inspection, Oversight....306
inspiration, Enthusiasm..182
inspire, Encourage 176
inspirit, Encourage 176
in spite of, Notwithstanding, prep. 299
instalment, Part 310
instance, Precedent......329
Sample 379
instanter, Immediately ...247
instantly, Immediately...247
instigate, Abet.......... 2
Encourage 176
Influence 254
instil, Teach 415
instinct, Mind 283
instinctive, Spontaneous..399
instruct, Teach 415
instruction, Education ...170
Order 304
instrument, Agent 30
Record 357
Tool 421
insubordinate, Rebellious.357
insubordination, Revolu-
  tion 370
insult, Affront 29
insured, Secure 382
insurrection, Revolution..370
intact, Perfect 313
integrity, Justice 263
Virtue 436
intellect, Mind 283
intellectual, Clever 125
intelligence, Knowledge..266
Mind 283
News 297
intelligent, Clever 125
Sagacious 378
intelligible, Clear........124
intemperance, Excess ...189
intend, Propose 342
intense, Ardent 62
Eager 169
Violent 436
Intensify 259
intensity, Enthusiasm....182
intent, adj., Eager......169
intent, n., Aim 32
Design 152
intention, Aim 32
Design 152
intentness, Industry 252
inter, Hide 233
intercede, Interpose 260
intercept, Interpose......260
Shut 389

interchangeable, Synony-
mous 412
intercourse, Conversation.139
interdict, Prohibit......338
interest, Concern........131
  Entertain 180
interfere, Interpose......260
intermeddle, Interpose....260
interminable, Eternal.....185
  Infinite 253
intermingle, Mix........286
intermission, Abeyance .. 3
intermit, Stop...........403
  Suspend 411
internal, Inherent.......255
Interpose 260
interpretation, Definition.148
interrogate, Inquire......258
interrogation, Question...349
interrogatory, Question...349
interrupt, Hinder........234
  Interpose 260
  Suspend 411
interruption, Abeyance .. 3
intervene, Interpose......260
in the midst of, Amid... 48
intimacy, Acquaintance... 17
intimate, Allude 43
intimation, Suggestion ...409
intimidate, Frighten 215
intolerance, Fanaticism...196
intoxicated, Drunk.......167
intractable, Impracticable.250
  Obstinate 302
  Perverse 317
  Rebellious 357
  Restive 367
intrenchment, Fortifica-
tion 211
intrepid, Brave 97
intrepidity, Prowess.....344
intricate, Complex.......130
  Obscure 301
intrinsic, Inherent 255
introduce, Allege 38
  Interpose 260
introduction, Entrance...182
intrusion, Attack........ 73
intrusive, Inquisitive....258
  Meddlesome 280
  Troublesome 426
intrusiveness, Imperti-
nence 249
intuition, Knowledge.....266
intuitive, Transcendental.424
invade, Attack 74
invariable, Continual....137
  Permanent 314
invasion, Attack 73
inveigle, Allure 43
invent, Discover 158
invention, Fiction 202
  Ingenuity 254
  Trick 425

Project 339
inventiveness, Ingenuity..254
inventory, Record 357
investigate, Inquire 258
investigation, Question ..349
invidious, Malicious......277
invisible, Latent 269
invoke, Appeal 57
  Pray 328
involuntary, Spontaneous.399
Involve 260
involved, Complex.......130
  Latent 269
  Obscure 301
inwrought, Inherent 255
iota, Particle 311
irate, Bitter 93
ire, Anger 49
irksome, Troublesome....426
irons, Fetter 201
irony, Banter 83
irrational, Absurd 12
irreconcilable, Incongru-
ous 251
Irregular 261
irrelevant, Alien......... 36
irresolute, Faint.........193
  Fickle 201
irresolution, Doubt, n....163
irresponsible, Absolute... 9
irritable, Captious 109
irritate, Affront 29
irritation, Anger 49
  Impatience 248
  Pique 318
issue, n., Consequence...136
  Event 186
  Topic 422
issue, v., Rise 374
item, Circumstance 123

jabber, Babble 80
jade, Tire 420
jagged, Drunk 167
jam, Predicament 331
  Throng 419
jar, Shake 386
Jealous 262
jeer, Sneer 396
jeering, Banter 83
jeopardy, Danger 143
  Hazard 231
jeopardous, Precarious ..328
jest, Wit 443
jiggered, Drunk 167
jingled, Drunk 167
job, Business 102
jocularity, Wit 443
jocund, Happy 227
joggle, Shake 386
join, Agree 31
  Associate 68
  Attach 71
  Mix 286

Unite 428
join on, Add 21
joint, Mutual 291
joke, Wit 443
jollification, Carousal....111
jolly, Happy 227
jolt, Shake 386
jot, Particle 311
jounce, Shake 386
Journey 262
jovial, Happy 227
joy, Happiness 226
joyful, Happy 227
joyous, Airy 33
  Happy 227
Judge 263
judgment, Idea 244
  Inference 253
  Prudence 344
  Wisdom 442
judicious, Sagacious ...378
judiciousness, Prudence..344
  Wisdom 442
jumble, Displace 160
junction, Union 428
juncture, Union 428
junto, Cabal 105
jurisprudence, Law 270
just, adj., Admissible.... 27
  Condign 132
  Honest 239
  Right 373
just, conj., But 103
Justice 263
  Judge 263
  Virtue 436
justification, Apology.... 55
  Defense 146
justness, Justice 263
juvenile, Youthful 445
juxtaposed, Adjacent..... 25

keen, Ardent 62
  Clever 125
  Eager 169
  Fine 204
  Sagacious 378
  Shrewd 388
keenness, Acumen....... 19
keen-sighted, Sagacious ..378
keen-witted, Sagacious ..378
Keep 265
  Celebrate 115
  Restrain 368
  Support 410
keep back, Restrain 368
keep down, Restrain 368
keep in, Restrain 368
keep under, Restrain ...368
keep up, Stand 401
  Support 410
Kill 265
Kin 266
kind, adj., Amiable...... 47

kind (cont'd)
Friendly 214
Good 221
Humane 240
Pleasant 321
Propitious 341
kind, n. Kin 266
kind-heartedness, Benevo-
lence 91
Humane 240
kindle, Burn 101
kindliness, Benevolence.. 91
kindly, Friendly 214
Pleasant 321
Propitious 341
kindness, Benevolence.... 91
Favor 198
Mercy 282
kindred, adj., Alike 37
kindred, n., Kin 266
king, Chief 120
kinglike, Royal 375
kingly, Royal 375
kiss, Caress 111
kitchen-gardening, Agri-
culture 31
knack, Ease 169
Genius 218
knock, Blow 95
knowing, Clever 125
Shrewd 388
Knowledge 266
Acquaintance 17
Education 170
Science 381
Wisdom 442
known, Eminent 175

labor, Industry 252
Work 444
laborer, Mechanic........280
laborious, Difficult 157
Troublesome 426
lacerate, Rend 361
lacking, Bad 80
laconic, Terse 417
lading, Load 274
ladylike, Feminine.......200
laggard, Slow 395
lament, Mourn 290
lamentable, Pitiful......319
lance, Send 383
land, Reach 354
landmark, Boundary..... 97
lane, Way 439
Language 268
Diction 155
Speech 399
languid, Faint 193
languor, Stupor 406
Large 268
Plentiful 322
largess, Gift 219
lascivious, Brutish 101

lash, Blow 95
lassitude, Stupor 406
last, Persist 316
lasting, Permanent 314
latch, Lock 275
late, New 297
Latent 269
laudation, Praise 327
laughable, Queer 348
launch, Send 383
laurels, Fame 196
lavation, Washing 438
lave, Clean 124
laving, Washing 438
lavish, Plentiful 322
lavishness, Excess 189
Law 270
Hypothesis 242
Justice 263
lawful, Right 373
lawfulness, Justice 263
lawlessness. Revolution..370
lay, Put 347
lay hold of, Catch......113
lay hold on (upon), Catch113
lazy, Idle 245
lead, Draw 164
Influence 254
Persuade 316
leader, Chief 120
leading, Principal 336
league, n., Alliance 41
league, v., Associate.... 68
lean, Tip 420
learned, Academic 14
learner, Scholar 380
learning, Education 170
Knowledge 266
Science 381
Wisdom 442
leave, n., Permission 314
leave, v., Abandon 1
Abscond 8
Surrender 411
leave off, Stop 403
leave-taking. Farewell....198
lecture, Speech 399
legality, Justice 263
legate, Delegate 148
legend, Fiction 202
Story 404
legions, Army 64
legislation, Law 270
legitimate, Authentic 76
leisure, adj., Idle.......245
Vacant 431
leisure, n., Rest 367
leisurely, Slow 395
lengthen, Protract 343
Stretch 405
lenience, Mercy 282
leniency, Mercy 282
lenity, Mercy 282
lessen, Abate 1

Alleviate 40
let, Allow 42
let go, Surrender........411
lethargy, Apathy 54
Stupor 406
lettered, Academic 14
letters, Literature 274
level, Flat 207
levy, Tax 415
liable, Likely 272
Responsible 366
libel, Slander 394
liberal, generous 218
Plentiful 322
liberality, Benevolence... 91
liberate, Absolve 9
Deliver 149
Liberty 271
Permission 314
Right 374
license, Liberty 271
Permission 314
Right 374
lie, Deception 145
life, Behavior 90
lift, Carry 112
light, adj., Airy 33
Light, n. 272
Knowledge 266
lighten, Allay 38
Alleviate 40
like, Alike 37
Synonymous 412
Likely 272
Apparent 56
likeness 273
Approximation 61
Duplicate 167
Similarity 390
likewise, Also 44
liking, Appetite 59
Fancy 197
Love 276
limit, n., Boundary 97
End 177
limit, v., Circumscribe...122
limitless, Infinite 253
limpid, Clear 124
line, Boundary 97
lingering, Slow 395
link, v., Associate 68
liquid, Fluid 208
list, Listen 273
Tip 420
Listen 273
listless, Abstracted 12
Faint 193
literal, Verbal 434
literary, Academic 14
literary productions, Literature 274
literary works, Literature.274
Literature 274
lithe, Graceful 222

litter, Group 223
little, Minute 284
live, *adj.*, Alive 37
live, *v.*, Abide 4
liveliness, Alacrity...... 34
lively, Active 19
  Airy 33
  Alert 35
  Alive 37
  Good 221
  Nimble 298
  Racy 352
living, Alive 37
Load 274
loath, Reluctant 360
loathe, Abhor 4
loathing, Abomination.... 6
locate, Fix 206
Lock 275
lock up, Shut 389
lodge, *n.*, Association 69
lodge, *v.*, Abide 4
lofty, Eminent 175
  High 234
  Sublime 407
loneliness, Retirement....368
lonely, Bleak 94
long, Large 268
longing, *adj.*, Ardent..... 62
  Eager 169
longing, *n.*, Appetite 59
  Desire 152
long-suffering, Patience..311
look, *n.*, Air 33
Look, *v.* 275
  Appear 57
look forward to, Anticipate 51
loquacious, Talkative 414
lordly, Absolute 9
Lord's Supper, Sacrament377
lore, Knowledge 266
  Science 381
loss, Injury 256
lot, Group 223
  Portion 325
lovable, Amiable 47
Love, *n.*, ...276
  Attachment 73
  Friendship 215
love, *v.*, Admire 26
lovely, Amiable 47
  Beautiful 87
loving, Amiable 47
  Friendly 214
low, Base 85
lower, Abate 1
  Debase
  Disparage 159
lower classes, Mob.....288
lowly, Humble 240
low-minded, Base 85
loyal, Faithful 194
loyalty, Allegiance 39
lucid, Clear 124

lucky, Fortunate 212
  Happy 227
  Propitious 341
lucre, Wealth 440
ludicrous, Absurd 12
  Queer 348
lugubrious, Sad 377
luminous, Bright 99
lunacy, Insanity 259
lure, Allure 43
  Draw 164
luscious, Delicious 149
lush, Drunk 167
lust, Appetite 59
luster, Light 272
lustrous, Bright 99
luxuriance, Excess 189
  Wealth 440
luxuriant, Plentiful 322
luxuriate, Abound 6
luxury, Wealth 440
lying, Deception 145

machination, Trick 425
machine, Tool 421
mad, Violent 436
madness, Insanity 259
magisterial, Dogmatic...163
magnanimous, Generous..218
magnificent, Royal 375
  Sublime 407
magnify, Exalt 188
  Intensify 259
maiden, Youthful 445
mail, Arms 64
main, Principal 336
maintain, Allege 38
  Keep 265
  State 401
  Support 410
majestic, Awful 78
  Royal 375
  Sublime 407
Make 277
  Compel 129
make an offer, Offer....302
make an offering, Offer..302
make a proposal, Offer...302
make better, Amend 47
make haste, Quicken....350
make known, Announce.. 50
make prisoner, Arrest.... 67
make-up, Add 21
make use of, Employ....176
make void, Cancel.......107
make white, Bleach 93
make worse, Intensify...259
maladroit, Awkward..... 78
malady, Disease 159
male, Masculine 279
malediction, Oath 300
malevolence, Enmity 180
  Hatred 229
malevolent, Malicious....277

malice, Enmity 180
  Hatred 229
Malicious 277
malign, *adj.*, Malicious..277
malign, *v.*, Abuse 13
  Slander 394
malignant, Malicious....277
malignity, Acrimony..... 18
  Enmity 180
  Hatred 229
mall, Way 439
maltreat, Abuse 13
manacles, Fetter 201
manage, Govern 222
manageable, Docile 162
management, Care 110
  Oversight 306
mandate, Law 270
  Order 304
maneuver, Trick 425
manful, Masculine 279
mangle, Rend 361
mania, Insanity 259
maniac, Violent 436
maniacal, Violent 436
manifest, Clear 124
  Evident 187
manifestation, Revelation.369
  Sign 390
manifold, Complex 130
manlike, Masculine 279
manly, Masculine 279
manner, Air 33
  Behavior 90
  System 412
manners, Address...... 22
  Behavior 90
mannish, Masculine 279
manufacture, Make 277
marauder, Robber.....375
marches, Boundary 97
marge, Bank 83
  Boundary 97
margin, Bank 83
  Boundary 97
Marine 278
  Sailor 378
mariner, Sailor 378
maritime, Marine 278
mark, Aim 32
  Characteristic 118
  Sign 390
  Trace 422
market-gardening, Agriculture 31
mark off, Circumscribe..122
mark out, Circumscribe..122
Marriage 278
marshal, Arrange 65
Masculine 279
mask, *n.*, Pretense 322
mask, *v.*, Hide 233
mass, Aggregate 30
  Throng 419

Massacre 279
　Kill 265
masses, Mob 288
massive, Large 268
master, *n.*, Chief 120
master, *v.*, Attain 75
　Conquer 134
mastery, Victory 435
mate, *n.*, Associate 68
material, Important....249
　Physical 318
matrimony, Marriage....278
matter, Topic 422
maudlin, Drunk 167
maxim, Proverb 343
mean, *adj.*, Bad 80
　Base 85
　Pitiful 319
mean, *v.*, Propose 342
meander, Wander 438
means, Agent 30
　Wealth 440
mean-spirited, Base.... 85
measure, Criterion 141
　Rhythm 372
measureless, Infinite ...253
Mechanic 280
mechanism, Tool 421
meddle, Interpose 260
　Mix 286
Meddlesome 280
　Inquisitive 258
meddling, Inquisitive...258
　Meddlesome 280
mediate, Interpose......260
meditate, Deliberate.....148
meed, Reward 371
meek, Humble 240
meet, Becoming 88
　Condign 132
　Fit 205
meeting, Collision 126
　Company 128
melancholy, *adj.*, Sad...377
melancholy, *n.*, Grief....223
Melody 281
member, Part 310
　Term 416
memoir, History 235
memorandum, Record....357
memorial, History 235
　Record 357
　Trace 422
Memory 281
mend, Amend 47
mendicancy, Poverty 325
menial, Base 85
mention, Allude 43
mercenary, Auxiliary.... 77
　Venal 432
merciful, Good 221
　Humane 240
　Propitious 341

merciless, Barbarous 84
Mercy 282
　Pardon 309
　Pity 319
mere, Pure 346
merely, But 103
merge, Mix 286
merited, Condign........132
merriment, Entertainment.181
　Happiness 226
merry, Happy 227
metamorphose, Change, *v.*117
metaphor, Allegory...... 39
mete out, Allot......... 41
　Execute 189
meter, Poetry..........323
　Rhythm 372
method, System 412
métier, Business 102
metropolis, Capital 108
middle, Center 115
midst, Center 115
mien, Air 33
might, Power 326
Migrate 283
mild, Calm 106
　Humble 240
mildness, Mercy 282
military, Army 64
militia, Army 64
mimicry, Caricature....111
Mind 283
　Memory 281
mindful, Thoughtful....418
mine, Hole 236
mingle, Mix 286
mingled, Complex......130
　Miscellaneous 284
mingled with, Amid...... 48
minimize, Disparage 159
minimizer, Poet 323
minstrel, Poet 323
Minute 284
　Fine 204
　Precise 329
miraculous, Supernatural.409
mirth, Happiness 226
mirthful, Happy 227
misadventure, Accident... 16
　Misfortune 286
Miscellaneous 284
mischance, Catastrophe..113
　Misfortune 286
mischief, Injury 256
mischievous, Bad 80
　Malicious 277
　Pernicious 315
misdeed, Sin 393
misemploy, Abuse....... 13
miserable, Base 85
　Pitiful 319
　Sad 377
miserliness, Frugality....216
Miserly 285

misery, Misfortune......286
Misfortune 286
　Accident 16
　Catastrophe 113
misgiving, Alarm 35
　Anxiety 3
　Doubt 163
　Fear 199
mishap, Accident 16
　Catastrophe 113
　Misfortune 286
mislay, Displace 160
mismatched, Incongruous.251
mismated, Incongruous...251
misplace, Displace 160
mistaken, Absurd....... 12
mistrust, *v.*, Doubt 164
misuse, Abuse 13
mite, Particle 311
mitigate, Abate 1
　Allay 38
　Alleviate 40
　Amend 47
　Palliate 308
Mix 286
　mixed, Complex......130
　Miscellaneous 284
Mob 288
mobile, Active 19
mock, Sneer 396
mockery, Banter 83
mode, System 412
Model 288
　Example 188
　Idea 244
　Ideal 244
moderate, Abate 1
　Alleviate 40
　Check 119
　Slow 395
moderation, Abstinence... 11
modern, New 297
modest, Humble 240
Modesty 288
modify, Change 117
mold, Bend 90
　Govern 222
　Model 288
molder, Decay 144
moldering, Old 303
molecule, Particle 311
molest, Abuse 13
mollify, Allay 38
momentary, Transient....424
momentous, Important...249
　Serious 385
monastery, Cloister 126
monetary, Financial 203
Money 289
　Wealth 440
monstrous, Absurd 12
mood, Fancy 197
moor, Bind 92
mop, Clean 124

moral, Devout 154
morality, Virtue 436
moreover, But 103
moronity, Idiocy 245
Morose 289
moroseness, Acrimony.... 18
mortification, Chagrin....115
mortify, Embarrass......174
mother tongue, Language.268
Motion 290
   Act 18
   Proposal 342
   Topic 422
motive, Cause 114
   Reason 355
motley, Miscellaneous....284
motto, Proverb..........343
Mourn 290
mournful, Pitiful 319
   Sad 377
mourning, Grief 223
move, n., Motion 290
move, v., Carry 112
   Concern 131
   Convey 140
   Influence 254
   Persuade 316
movement, Act 18
   Motion 290
mover, Agent 30
moving, Pitiful 319
mucilaginous, Adhesive.. 25
muddled, Drunk 167
muddy, Obscure 301
mulish, Obstinate........302
   Restive 367
multiform, Complex.....130
multiply, Propagate.....340
multitude, Army 64
   Company 128
   Mob 288
   Throng 419
munificence, Benevolence. 91
munificent, Generous.....218
   Royal 375
muniment, History 235
   Record 357
murder, Kill 265
murderous, Sanguinary..380
murky, Dark 143
murmur, Babble 80
   Complain 129
muse, Deliberate........148
music, Melody 281
must, Ought 305
muster, Convoke 140
mutable, Fickle.........201
mutation, Change, n......116
mute, Taciturn 414
mutinous, Rebellious....357
   Restive 367
mutiny, Revolution 370
Mutual 291
Mysterious 291

Obscure 301
mystery, Riddle 373
mystic, Mysterious 291
mystical, Mysterious....291
myth, Allegory 39
   Fiction 202
   Story 404

naive, Candid 108
Name, n., ...293
   Term 416
name, v., Allude 43
narration, History 235
   Report 363
   Story 404
narrative, History 235
   Report 363
   Story 404
natal, Native 294
nation, Race 352
Native 294
   Inherent 255
   Primeval 336
   Radical 353
natty, Neat 294
natural, Inherent 255
   Native 294
   Normal 298
   Physical 318
   Radical 353
nature, Character 117
naughty, Bad 80
nauseate, Abhor 4
nautical, Marine 278
naval, Marine 278
near, Adjacent 25
nearness, Approximation.. 61
Neat 294
   Terse 417
Necessary 295
necessitate, Compel 129
Necessity 295
   Predestination 330
need, Necessity 295
   Poverty 325
needed, Necessary 295
needful, Necessary 295
nefarious, Criminal......141
Neglect 296
neglectfulness, Neglect...296
negligence, Neglect......296
negligent, Abstracted.... 12
negotiate, Transact......423
neighborhood, Approxima-
   tion 61
neighboring, Adjacent.... 25
neighborly, Friendly.....214
neophyte, Convert......139
nerve, Effrontery 171
never-ending, Eternal....185
never-failing, Eternal....185
nevertheless, But 103
   Notwithstanding 299
New 297

new-fangled, New 297
new-fashioned, New.....297
new-made, New.........297
News 297
next, Adjacent 25
nice, Elegant 173
   Fine 204
   Neat 294
   Precise 329
nickname, Name 293
niggardly, Miserly 285
nigh, Adjacent 25
nihilism, Socialism......397
Nimble 298
   Active 19
   Alert 35
noble, Awful 78
   Generous 218
   High 234
   Sublime 407
noise, Sound 397
noisome, Pernicious......315
nonconformist, Heretic...232
non-homogeneous, Miscel-
    laneous 284
nonsensical, Absurd 12
Normal 298
   General 217
   Usual 429
notable, Eminent 175
notch, Hole 236
note, Remark 361
   Sign 390
   Sound 397
noted, Eminent..........175
notes, Money 289
noticeable, Eminent......175
notify, Announce 50
notion, Idea 244
notoriety, Fame 196
Notwithstanding, conj. ..299
   But 103
Notwithstanding, prep...299
nourish, Cherish 119
nourishment, food.......209
novel, adj., New.........297
novel, n., Fiction 202
   Story 404
novelty, Change 116
novice, Amateur 45
now, Immediately 247
   Yet 445
noxious, Bad 80
   Pernicious 315
nugatory, Vain 431
nuisance, Abomination... 6
null, Vain 431
nullify, Abolish 5
   Cancel 107
number, Calculate 105
numberless, Infinite 253
numbers, Poetry 323
nunnery, Cloister 126
nuptials, Marriage 278

nurse, Cherish 119
nurture, *n.*, Education....170
nurture, *v.*, Cherish 119
   Teach 415
nutrients, Food 209
nutriment, Food 209
nutrition, Food 209

Oath 300
obdurate, Obstinate 302
obedience, Allegiance ... 39
obedient, Docile 162
obey, Follow 209
   Keep 265
obiter dictum, Precedent..329
Object 300
   Aim 32
   Design 152
   Reason 355
objurgation, Reproof....364
obligation, Contract.....137
   Duty 168
oblige, Bind 92
   Compel 129
obliging, Good 221
   Pleasant 321
   Polite 324
obliterate, Abolish 5
   Cancel 107
oblivion, Pardon, *n*.....309
oblivious, Abstracted 12
Obscure 301
   Complex 130
   Dark 143
   Equivocal 183
   Mysterious 291
obsequious, Base 85
observance, Sacrament...377
observation. Remark....361
observe, Celebrate......115
   Discern 158
   Follow 209
   Keep 265
   Look 275
obsolescent, Antique..... 53
   Obsolete 301
Obsolete 301
   Antique 53
obstacle, Barrier 84
   Impediment 248
Obstinate 302
   Perverse 317
   Restive 367
obstruct, Check 119
   Hinder 234
obstruction, Barrier 84
   Impediment 248
obtain, Attain 75
   Get 219
   Purchase 345
obtrusive, Meddlesome...280
obviate, Prevent 322
obvious, Clear 124
   Evident 187

occasion, Cause 114
   Make 277
occult, Latent 269
   Mysterious 291
occupation, Business 102
   Exercise 190
   Work 444
occupied, Busy 103
occupy, Have 230
occur, Happen 225
occurrence, Circumstance.123
   Event 186
ocean, Marine 278
oceanic, Marine 278
odd, Queer 348
   Rare 353
odor, Smell 396
offend, Affront 29
offense, Abomination 6
   Anger 49
   Pique 318
   Sin 391
offer, *n.*, Proposal 342
Offer, *v.* 302
   Allege 38
offhand, Extemporaneous.191
office, Duty 168
officious, Active 19
   Meddlesome 280
officiousness, Impertinence.249
Old 303
   Obsolete 301
   Primeval 336
olden, Old 303
old-fashioned, Antique... 53
omen, Sign 390
omission, Neglect 296
on, Above 7
on the alert, Vigilant....435
on the lookout, Vigilant..435
on the watch, Alert 35
opaque, Dark 143
open, Bluff............. 95
   Candid 108
   Evident 187
open-handed, Generous.. 218
open-hearted, Generous...218
opening, Beginning 89
   Entrance 182
   Hole 236
Operation 304
   Act 18
   Exercise 190
operative, Mechanic 280
operator, Agent 30
opinion, Faith 193
   Idea 244
opinionated, Dogmatic...163
   Obstinate 302

opponent, Enemy 179
oppose, Contrast 138
   Dispute 160
   Hinder 234
   Object 300
opposed, Adverse 28
   Alien 36
   Contrary 138
   Reluctant 360
opposing, Adverse 28
opposite, Adverse 28
   Contrary 138
opposition, Ambition.... 46
   Antipathy 52
   Collision 126
oppress, Abuse 13
opt, Choose 121
option, Choice 121
opulence, Wealth 440
oral, Verbal 434
oration, Speech 399
oratory, Speech 399
Order, *n.* 304
   Class 123
   Law 270
   System 412
order, *v.*, Arrange 65
orderly, Neat 294
ordinance, Law 270
   Sacrament 377
ordinary, General 217
   Normal 293
   Usual 429
organic, Radical 353
organize, Arrange 65
orgy, Carousal 111
orifice, Hole 236
origin, Beginning 89
   Cause 114
   Foundation 213
original, Authentic 76
   Ideal 244
   Model 288
   Native 294
   New 297
   Primeval 336
   Radical 353
   Transcendental 424
originate, Make 277
   Propagate 340
originator, Cause 114
ornament, Adorn 27
oscillate, Fluctuate 208
   Shake 386
ostensible, Apparent.....56
Ostentation 305
   Pride 335
ostracize, Banish 82
Ought 305
oust, Banish 82
outbreak, Revolution....370
outcome, Consequence ...136
   End 177
   Event 186

outgeneral, Baffle 81
outgo, Price 334
outgrowth, Consequence..136
outlandish, Queer........348
 Rustic 376
outlay, Price 334
outline, Abridgment...... 7
 Sketch 393
outmaneuver, Baffle 81
out-of-date, Obsolete....301
outrage, Abuse 13
 Injury 256
outrageous, Violent......436
outset, Beginning 89
outstanding, Eminent....175
outwit, Baffle 81
over, Above 7
overawe, Embarrass.....174
overbearing, Absolute.... 9
 Dogmatic 163
overcome, adj., Drunk...167
overcome, v., Beat....... 86
 Conquer 134
overconfidence, Temerity.416
overflow, Abound 6
overflowing, Plentiful....322
overlook, Pardon, v.....309
overmaster, Conquer 134
overmatch, Conquer 134
overplus, Excess 189
overpower, Conquer 134
Oversight 306
 Care 110
 Neglect 296
overt, Evident 187
overtake, Catch 113
Overthrow 306
 Abolish 5
 Conquer 134
 Demolish 150
 Exterminate 191
overture, Proposal 342
overturn, Demolish 150
 Overthrow 306
overwhelm, Hide 233
own, Confess 133
 Have 230

pabulum, Food 209
pacific, Calm 106
pacify, Allay 38
pack, Group 223
 Load 274
pact, Contract 137
pageant, Ostentation 305
 Spectacle 398
pageantry, Ostentation ...305
Pain 308
painful, Troublesome.....426
pains, Industry 252
painting, Sketch 393
palaver, Babble 80
pall, Satisfy 380
Palliate 308

palpable, Evident 187
paltry, Base 85
 Pitiful 319
pamper, Caress 111
panegyric, Praise 327
pang, Pain 308
panic, Alarm 35
 Fear 199
parable, Allegory 39
parade, Ostentation 305
 Spectacle 398
paradigm, Model 288
paradox, Riddle 373
paradoxical, Absurd 12
paralogism, Fallacy 195
paramount, Eminent 175
parapet, Barrier 84
paraphrase, Quote 350
parcel, Portion 325
parcel (out), Apportion.. 61
Pardon, n. 309
 Mercy 282
Pardon, v. 309
 Absolve 9
pardonable, Venial 434
parity, Similarity 390
parley, Conversation 139
parody, Caricature 111
paroxysm, Pain 308
parsimonious, Miserly....285
parsimoniousness, Frugal-
 ity 216
parsimony, Frugality ...216
Part 310
 Portion 325
partiality, Prejudice 331
participation, Association. 69
participator, Accessory .. 15
Particle 311
 Part 310
particular, Circumstance..123
 Minute 284
 Precise 329
parting salutation, Fare-
 well 198
partisan, Adherent 24
partition, Part 310
partner, Accessory 15
 Associate 68
partnership, Alliance ... 41
 Association 69
party, Company 128
pass, Way 439
passable, Admissible 27
passage, Journey 262
 Motion 290
 Way 439
passage of arms, Battle... 86
passageway, Way 439
pass by, Pardon, v.......309
passing, Transient 424
passion, Anger 49
 Appetite 59
 Enthusiasm 182

passionate, Ardent 62
 Violent 436
passiveness, Apathy 54
 Patience 311
pass over, Pardon.......309
pastime, Entertainment ..181
pastoral, Rustic 376
patent, Evident 187
path, Way 439
pathetic, Pitiful 319
pathway, Way 439
Patience 311
 Industry 252
patois, Language 268
patriarchal, Old 303
 Primeval 336
patronage, Favor 198
patter, Babble 80
pattern, Example 188
 Idea 244
 Ideal 244
 Model 288
 Precedent 329
pauperism, Poverty 325
pause, Stand 401
 Stop 403
Pay 312
 Requite 365
payment, Pay 312
pay off, Requite........365
peace, Rest 367
peaceful, Calm 106
peacefulness, Rest 367
peculiar, Queer 348
 Rare 353
peculiarity, Characteristic.118
pecuniary, Financial ...203
pedant, Scholar 380
pedantic, Academic 14
peeping, Inquisitive 258
peer, Associate 68
peevish, Captious 109
peevishness, Anger 49
 Impatience 248
pelf, Wealth 440
pellucid, Clear 124
penetrating, Shrewd 388
penetration, Acumen 19
 Entrance 182
penetrative, Shrewd 388
penitence, Repentance ...363
pension, Subsidy 408
penurious, Miserly 285
penury, Poverty 325
people, Race 352
Perceive 313
 Discern 158
percept, Sensation 384
perceptible, Evident 187
perception, Acumen 19
 Knowledge 266
 Sensation 384
percussion, Collision 126
peremptory, Absolute ... 9

perennial, Continual 137
  Eternal 185
r-erfect 313
  Good 221
  Precise 329
  Pure 346
  Radical 353
perforation, Hole 236
perform, Do 161
  Execute 189
  Make 277
  Transact 423
performance, Act 18
  Exercise 190
  Operation 304
  Work 444
performer, Agent 30
perfume, Smell 396
peril, Danger 143
  Hazard 231
perilous, Precarious 328
period, End 177
  Time 419
periphrasis, Circumlocu-
  tion 122
perish, Die 155
  Permanent 314
permissible, Admissible .. 27
Permission 314
  Liberty 271
permit, n., Permission...314
permit, v., Allow........ 42
  Endure 179
Pernicious 315
  Bad 80
perpendicular, Right, adj..373
perpetrate, Do 161
perpetual, Continual 137
  Eternal 185
  Permanent 314
perplexing, Equivocal ...183
  Troublesome 426
Perplexity 316
  Amazement 45
  Anxiety 53
  Care 110
  Doubt 163
  Predicament 331
perquisite, Right, n......374
persecute, Abuse 13
perseverance, Industry ..252
persevere, Persist 316
persiflage, Wit 443
Persist 316
persistence, Industry ...252
persistent, Obstinate 302
  Permanent 314
personality, Character ...117
perspicacious, Sagacious ..378
  Shrewd 388
perspicacity, Acumen 19
perspicuous, Clear 124
Persuade 316
  Bend 90

Influence 254
persuasion, Counsel 140
  Faith 193
  Religion 360
pertinaceous, Obstinate...302
pertinent, Fit...........205
Pertness 317
  Impertinence 249
perturbation, Perplexity..316
Perverse 317
  Obstinate 302
pervert, n., Heretic......232
pervert, v., Abuse....... 13
pest, Abomination 6
pestiferous, Pernicious...315
pestilential, Pernicious...315
pet, Caress 111
petition, Ask 67
  Pray 328
pettishness, Anger....... 49
  Impatience 248
petulance, Anger........ 49
  Impatience 248
petulant, Captious......109
  Perverse 317
phalanx, Army 64
phantasm, Delusion.....150
  Dream 165
phantasy, Dream........165
  Imagination 246
pharisaism, Hypocrisy....242
philanthropic, Humane...240
philanthropy, Benevolence. 91
phlegm, Apathy........ 54
phrase, Diction 155
  Term 416
phraseology, Diction....155
Physical 318
pick, n., Choice........121
pick, v., Choose........121
pick out, Choose.......121
picture, Likeness.......273
  Sketch 393
picturesque, Beautiful.... 87
piece, Part 310
pie-eyed, Drunk........167
piercing, Bleak.......... 94
pietism, Hypocrisy......242
pietistic, Devout 154
pig-headed, Obstinate....302
pile-up, Amass.......... 44
pilfer, Steal 402
pilgrimage, Journey....262
pillage, Steal 402
pillager, Robber 375
pious, Devout 154
  Good 221
pipe, Hole 236
piquant, Racy 352
Pique 318
pirate, Robber 375
pit, Abyss 14
piteous, Pitiful 319
pithy, Terse 417

pitiable, Pitiful 319
Pitiful 319
pitiless, Barbarous....... 84
Pity 319
  Mercy 282
pitying, Humane 240
place, Fix..............206
  Put 347
place in order, Arrange.. 65
placid, Calm............106
plagiarize, Quote........350
plague, Abomination..... 6
plain, Clear 124
  Evident 187
  Flat 207
  Rustic 376
plain-spoken, Bluff....... 95
plan, Design 152
  Idea 244
  Project 339
  Sketch 393
plane, Flat 207
Plant 320
  Fix 206
Platonic, Academic...... 14
Platonistic, Academic.... 14
plaudit, Praise 327
plausible, Likely........272
playfulness, Wit.........443
plea, Apology 55
Plead 320
  Allege 38
  Pray 328
Pleasant 321
  Amiable 47
  Comfortable 127
  Good 221
pleasantry, Wit 443
please, Entertain 180
pleased, Happy 227
pleasing, Amiable 47
  Pleasant 321
pleasurable, Pleasant....321
pleasure, Entertainment..181
  Happiness 226
pledge, Contract 137
  Security 382
plenteous, Plentiful 322
Plentiful 322
plenty, Wealth 440
pleonasm, Circumlocution.122
plethora, Excess 189
pliable, Docile 162
pliant, Docile 162
plight, Predicament 331
pluck, Fortitude 211
plunder, Steal 402
plunderer, Robber 375
plunge, Dip 157
poem, Poetry 323
poesy, Poetry 323
Poet 323
poetaster, Poet 323
Poetry 323

pogrom, Massacre 279
poignant, Racy 352
  Violent 436
point, n., Circumstance..123
  End 177
  Topic 422
point, v., Allude 43
poise, Refinement 358
poisonous, Pernicious....315
policy, Polity 324
  Utility 429
polished, Fine 204
  Polite 324
Polite 324
politeness, Address, n. .. 22
  Refinement 3 8
Polity 324
  Law 270
pollute, Defile 147
pommel, Beat 86
pomp, Ostentation 305
pomposity, Ostentation...305
pompousness, Ostentation.305
ponder, Deliberate 148
poor, Bad 80
  Base 85
poor-spirited, Base...... 85
populace, Mob 288
popular, General 217
population, Race 352
pore, Hole 236
port, Air 33
portal, Entrance 182
portend, Foretell 210
portent, Sign 390
Portion, n., ...325
  Part 310
portion, v., Apportion... 61
portion out, Allot....... 41
portrayal, Sketch 393
pose, Posture 325
position, Circumstance...123
  Posture 325
positive, Absolute 9
  Dogmatic 163
  Radical 353
  Real 354
possess, Have 230
possessions, Wealth 440
possibility, Accident 16
  Event 186
possible, Admissible 27
  Likely 272
postpone, Adjourn 26
  Hinder 234
  Protract 343
postulate, Assume 70
  Posture 325
potency, Power 326
potential, Latent 269
potentiality, Power 326
pound, Beat 86
Poverty 325
Power 326

Cause 114
powerful, Important 249
practice, n., Habit 225
practice, v., Exercise 190
  Follow 209
practiced, Skilful 393
Praise 327
prate, Babble 80
prattle, Babble 80
Pray 328
  Ask 67
Precarious 328
  Equivocal 183
precaution, Care 110
precedent, adj., Previous.333
Precedent, n. 329
  Cause 114
  Example 188
preceding, Previous 333
precept, Doctrine 162
  Law 270
  Proverb 343
precious, Good 221
  Rare 353
precipitancy, Temerity...416
precipitation, Temerity ..416
precipitous, Steep......403
précis, Abridgment 7
Precise 329
  Minute 284
preclude, Prevent 322
  Prohibit 338
  Shut 389
preconception, Prejudice.331
Predestination 330
Predicament 331
predicate, State 401
predict, Anticipate 51
  Foretell 210
predilection, Fancy 197
  Favor 198
predominant, Principal...336
predominating, Principal.336
preeminent, Principal ...336
prefer, Choose 121
  Promote 340
preference, Choice 121
  Favor 198
Prejudice 331
  Injury 256
premium, Subsidy 408
prenomen, Name 293
preoccupied, Abstracted .. 12
prepared, Alert 35
  Fit 205
prepossession, Prejudice..331
preposterous, Absurd .. 12
  Queer 348
prerogative, Right 374
presage, n., Sign 390
presage, v., Foretell.....210
prescience, Wisdom.....442
presence, Air 33
present, n., Gift 219

present, v., Give 220
  Offer 302
presentiment, Anticipation 52
presently, Immediately ..247
preserve, Keep 265
press, Plead 320
  Throng 419
press forward, Quicken...350
presumable, Apparent ... 56
  Likely 272
presume, Assume 70
presumption, Assurance.. 70
  Impertinence 249
  Prejudice 331
  Pride 335
  Temerity 416
pretend, Assume 70
pretender, Deceiver 145
Pretense 332
  Hypocrisy 242
pretension, Pretense ...322
preternatural, Supernatural 409
pretext, Apology 55
  Pretense 322
pretty, Beautiful 87
prevail, Abound 6
  Succeed 408
prevailing, Principal ...336
  Usual 429
prevail on, Persuade.....316
prevail over, Conquer...134
prevail upon, Persuade...316
prevalent, General 217
  Usual 429
prevarication, Deception..145
Prevent 322
  Hinder 234
  Prohibit 338
Previous 333
prevision, Anticipation... 52
Price 334
Pride 335
  Group 223
prim, Neat 294
primal, Primeval 336
primary, Primeval 336
prime, Primeval 336
  Principal 336
Primeval 336
primitive, Primeval 336
  Radical 353
primordial, Primeval ...336
  Transcendental 424
prince, Chief 120
princely, Royal 375
Principal 336
  Chief 120
principle, Doctrine 162
  Law 270
  Reason, n. 355
prior, Previous 333
priory, Cloister 126
pristine, Primeval 336

privacy, Retirement......368
privation, Poverty 325
privilege, Right, *n.* 374
prize, Esteem 184
 Reward 371
probable, Admissible 27
 Apparent 56
 Likely 272
probity, Virtue 436
problem, Riddle 373
procedure, Operation 304
proceed, Rise 374
proceeding, Act 18
 Transaction 423
proceeds, Harvest 229
 Profit 337
process, Motion 290
proclaim, Announce 50
proclivity, Appetite...... 59
 Desire 152
procrastinate, Adjourn... 26
 Protract 343
procrastinating, Slow....395
procreate, Propagate 340
procure, Attain 75
 Get 219
 Purchase 345
prodigality, Excess 189
produce, Allege 38
 Harvest 229
 Make 277
product, Harvest 229
 Work 444
production, Work 444
profane, Abuse 13
profane swearing, Oath..300
profanity, Oath 300
profession, Business 102
professional, Hobo 236
proffer, Offer 302
proficiency, Progress 338
proficient, Skilful.......393
Profit 337
 Utility 429
profitable, Good 221
profitless, Vain 431
profound, Obscure 301
profundity, Wisdom 442
profuse, Plentiful 322
profusion, Excess 189
 Wealth 440
prognostic, Sign........390
prognosticate, Foretell....210
Progress 338
progression, Progress 338
Prohibit 338
 Abolish 5
 Shut 389
prohibition, Barrier 84
 Order 304
Project, *n.* ... .339
 Design 152
project, *v.,* Send 383
prolix, Talkative 414

prolixity, Circumlocution.122
prolong, Hinder 234
 Protract 343
prominent, Eminent 175
 Important 249
 Principal 336
promiscuous, Miscellane-
 ous 284
promise, Contract 137
Promote 340
 Abet 2
 Encourage 176
 Exalt 188
 Quicken 350
promoter, Agent 30
 Auxiliary 77
prompt, *adj.,* Active 19
 Alert 35
 Nimble 298
prompt, *v.,* Encourage ..176
 Influence 254
promptitude, Alacrity.... 34
promptness, Alacrity.... 34
promulgate, Announce.... 50
prone, Addicted 22
proneness, Appetite 59
pronounce, Speak 398
 State 401
proof, Criterion 141
 Demonstration 151
 Testimony 418
prop, Support 410
Propagate 340
propel, Drive 166
 Send 383
propensity, Appetite 59
 Desire 152
proper, Admissible 27
 Becoming 88
 Fit 205
 Good 221
 Right 373
property, Attribute 75
 Characteristic 118
 Money 289
 Wealth 440
prophecy, Revelation ...369
prophesy, Foretell 210
propinquity, Approxima-
 tion 61
Propitiation 341
Propitious 341
proportion, Portion 325
 Similarity 390
Proposal 342
 Design 152
 Suggestion 409
Propose 342
 Offer 302
proposition, Proposal 342
 Suggestion 409
 Topic 422
propound, Announce 50
 State 401

prorate, Apportion 61
prorogue, Adjourn 26
prosecute, Arraign 64
proselyte, Convert 139
prosper, Succeed 408
prosperity, Wealth 440
prosperous, Fortunate ...212
 Happy 227
prostitute, Abuse 13
protect, Cherish 119
 Keep 265
 Shelter 388
protected, Secure 382
protection, Defense ...146
protest, State 401
prototype, Example 188
 Ideal 244
 Model 288
Protract 343
 Adjourn 26
proud, High 234
prove, Confirm 133
 Reason 356
provender, Food 209
Proverb 343
provided, But 103
providence, Frugality ...216
 Prudence 344
provident, Thoughtful ...418
providential, Fortunate ...212
provoke, Affront 29
Prowess 344
proxy, Delegate 148
Prudence 344
 Care 110
 Frugality 216
 Wisdom 442
prudent, Thoughtful 418
prying, Inquisitive 258
psyche, Mind 283
public, General 217
 Usual 429
publications, Literature ..274
publish, Announce 50
puerile, Youthful 445
puissance, Power 326
pull, Draw 164
punctilious, Precise ...329
pungent, Bitter 93
 Racy 352
Punish 345
 Avenge 77
 Requite 365
pupil, Scholar 380
purchasable, Venal......432
Purchase 345
Pure 346
 Fine 204
 Innocent 257
purification, Washing....438
purify, Amend 47
 Clean 124
 Punish 345
purity, Virtue 436

purloin, Abstract 11
   Steal 402
purpose, *n.*, Aim 32
   Design 152
   End 177
   Idea 244
   Project 339
   Reason 355
purpose, *v.*, Propose 342
purposeless, Faint 193
   Fickle 201
pursue, Follow 209
pursuit, Business 102
   Hunt 241
push, Drive 166
   Promote 340
push on, Promote 340
Put 347
put down, Conquer.....134
put in order, Adapt......20
   Arrange 65
put in place, Adapt 20
put off, Adjourn 26
put on, Assume 70
putrefy, Decay 144
putrid, Bad 80
put right, Adapt 20
Putsch, Revolution 370
put to death, Kill 265
put to rights, Adapt 20
put up with, Endure 179
puzzle, Predicament 331
   Riddle 373

quaint, Antique 53
   Queer 348
quake, Shake 386
qualification, Power 326
qualified, Adequate 24
   Fit 205
qualify, Change........117
quality, Attribute 75
   Characteristic 118
quandary, Predicament...331
Quarrel 348
   Argument 62
   Dispute 160
quash, Cancel 107
quaver, Shake 386
Queer 348
quell, Conquer 134
query, Inquire 258
   Question 349
Question, *n.* 349
   Doubt 163
   Topic 422
question, *v.*, Dispute ...160
   Inquire 258
   Reason 356
questionable, Equivocal...183
quibble, Fallacy 195
quibbling, Fallacy 195
quick, Active 19
   Alive 37

Clever 125
Nimble 298
Quicken 350
quickness, Alacrity 34
quick of scent, Sagacious.378
quick-scented, Sagacious..378
quick-witted, Clever.....125
quiescence, Abeyance 3
quiescent, Latent 269
quiet, Allay 38
   Calm 106
   Rest 367
quietness, Apathy 54
   Rest 367
quietude, Apathy 54
quit, Abandon 1
   End 179
   Requite 365
   Stop 403
quiver, Shake 386
Quote 350
quotidian, Daily 143

rabble, Mob 288
Race 352
   Kin 266
   Stream 405
Racy 352
radiance, Light 272
radiant, Bright 99
Radical 353
rage, Anger 49
raging, Fierce 203
   Violent 436
raider, Robber 375
rail at, Abuse 13
raillery, Banter 83
   Wit 443
raiment, Dress 166
raise, Promote 340
rally, Encourage 176
ramble, Wander 438
rampart, Barrier 84
   Defense 146
rancor, Enmity 180
   Hatred 229
rancorous, Malicious ...277
range, Arrange 65
   Wander 438
rank, Class 123
ransom, Deliver 149
rap, Blow 95
rapacious, Miserly 285
rapture, Enthusiasm....182
   Happiness 226
rapturous, Happy 227
Rare ....,..353
   Elegant 173
   Obsolete 301
rascally, Bad 80
rash, Imprudent 251
rashness, Temerity 416
rate, Calculate 105
   Tax 415

ratify, Confirm ...,....133
ratiocination, Reasoning..356
ration, Apportion 61
Rational 354
   Sagacious 378
rattle, Embarrass 174
ravine, Hole 236
raving, Violent 436
ravish, Abuse 13
raze, Demolish 150
Reach 354
   Attain 75
   Make 277
   Stretch 405
readiness, Address 22
   Alacrity 34
   Dexterity 154
   Ease 169
   Ingenuity 254
   Power 326
reading, Education 170
ready, Active 19
   Alert 35
   Good 221
Real 354
   Authentic 76
   Good 221
   Pure 346
reality, Truth 426
realize, Do 161
reanimate, Recover 358
reaping, Harvest 229
Reason, *n.* 355
   Cause 114
   Mind 283
   Wisdom 442
Reason, *v.* 356
   Dispute 160
reasonable, Admissible ... 27
   Likely 272
   Rational 354
reasonableness, Wisdom..442
Reasoning 356
   Reason 355
reassure, Encourage 176
rebellion, Revolution ...370
Rebellious 357
   Restive 367
rebuke, *n.*, Reproof....364
rebuke, *v.*, Reprove.....365
rebut, Refute 359
recalcitrant, Restive 367
recall, Renounce 362
recant, Abandon 1
   Renounce 362
receipts, Profit 337
receive, Get 219
received, Authentic 76
recent, New 297
recherché, Elegant 173
reciprocal, Mutual......291
reciprocate, Requite 365
recital, History 235
   Report 363

recital (*cont'd*)
  Story 404
recite, Quote 350
reckless, Imprudent 251
recklessness, Temerity ...416
reckon, Calculate 105
recognition, Knowledge...266
recognize, Confess 133
  Discern 158
recollection, Memory 281
recommendation, Counsel.140
recompense, Pay 312
  Requite 365
  Reward 371
reconciliation, Propitia-
  tion 341
recondite, Latent 269
  Mysterious 291
Record 357
  Character 117
  History 235
  Report 363
  Story 404
Recover 358
recreate, Entertain 180
recreation, Entertainment.181
recruit, Recover 358
rectify, Amend 47
rectitude, Justice 263
  Virtue 436
recuperate, Recover 358
redeem, Deliver 149
redoubtable, Formidable..210
reduce, Abate 1
  Alleviate 40
  Check 119
  Conquer 134
  Debase 144
redundance, Circumlocu-
  tion 122
  Excess 189
redundancy, Circumlocu-
  tion 122
  Excess 189
reel, Shake 386
refer, Allude 43
  Apply 60
  Attribute 76
refer (to), Appeal 57
referee, Judge 263
refine, Punish 345
refined, Fine 204
Refinement 358
  Fallacy 195
reflect, Deliberate 148
reflection, Reproof 364
reform, Amend 47
refractory, Obstinate 302
  Rebellious 357
  Restive 367
refrain, Keep 265
  Stop 403
refreshing, Pleasant 321
refulgent, Bright 99

refuse, Renounce 362
Refute 359
regain, Recover 358
regal, Royal 375
regard, *n.*, Attachment... 73
  Esteem 184
  Favor 198
  Friendship 215
  Love 276
regard, *v.*, Esteem 184
  Look 275
regeneration, Change ...116
regimen, Food 209
register, History 235
  Record 357
regret, *n.*, Grief 223
  Repentance 363
regret, *v.*, Mourn 290
regular, Continual 137
  Normal 298
  Usual 429
regularity, System 412
regulation, Law 270
rehearsal, Report 363
reign, Govern 222
reign over, Govern 222
reject, Renounce 362
rejoiced, Happy 227
rejoicing, Happiness 226
  Happy 227
rejoinder, Answer 50
relation, Report 363
  Similarity 390
  Story 404
relationship, Kin 266
relative, Dependent 151
relatives, Kin 266
relaxation, Rest 367
release, Absolve 9
  Deliver 149
relegate, Commit 127
relentless, Severe 385
relevant, Important 249
Reliable 359
  Authentic 76
reliance, Faith 193
relieve, Allay 38
  Alleviate 40
Religion 360
religious, Devout 154
  Good 221
  Holy 238
relinquish, Abandon 1
  Surrender 411
relish, Appetite 59
Reluctant 360
remain, Abide 4
  Persist 316
  Stand 401
remains, Body 96
  Trace 422
Remark 361
remarkable, Eminent ...175
  Rare 353

remembrance, Memory ...281
reminiscence, Memory...281
remission, Pardon 309
remissness, Neglect 296
remit, Pardon 309
remnant, Trace 422
remonstrate, Complain ...129
remonstrate with, Reprove.365
remorse, Repentance 363
remote, Alien 36
  Old 303
remove, Abolish 5
  Abstract 11
  Alleviate 40
  Cancel 107
  Carry 112
  Convey 140
  Displace 160
  Exterminate 191
remunerate, Requite 365
remuneration, Pay 312
  Reward 371
Rend 361
  Break 98
render, Make 277
rendering, Definition 148
renegade, Heretic 232
renewal, Change........116
renewing, Change 116
Renounce 362
  Abandon 1
renown, Fame 196
renowned, Eminent 175
rent, Hole 236
repair, Amend 47
reparation, Reward 371
repartee, Answer 50
repast, Feast 200
repay, Requite 365
repeal, Abolish 5
  Cancel 107
repeat, Quote 350
repel, Drive 166
  Refute 359
Repentance 363
repine, Complain 129
replete, Plentiful 322
replica, Duplicate 167
reply, Answer 50
Report 363
  Announce 50
repose, Rest 367
reposeful, Comfortable ...127
repossess, Recover 358
reprehend, Condemn 132
  Reprove 365
reprehension, Reproof 364
representation, Model ...288
  Sketch 395
  Spectacle 398
representative, Delegate..148
repress, Check 119
  Restrain 368
reprimand, *n.*, Reproof...364

reprimand, v., Reprove...365
reprisal, Revenge 369
reproach, n. Blemish..... 94
   Reproof 364
reproach, v., Abuse 13
   Reprove 365
reprobate, Condemn 132
reprobation, Oath 300
reproduce, Propagate 340
reproduction, Duplicate ..167
Reproof 364
reproval, Reproof 364
Reprove 365
   Condemn 132
repudiate, Abandon 1
   Renounce 362
repugnance, Antipathy .. 52
   Hatred 229
repugnant, Incongruous..251
repulse, Drive 166
repulsion, Antipathy 52
reputation, Character ...117
   Fame 196
repute, Character 117
   Fame 196
request, Appeal 57
   Ask 67
   Pray 328
require, Ask 67
   Make 277
required, Necessary 295
requirement, Necessity ..295
   Order 304
requisite, Necessary 295
   Necessity 295
requital, Pay 312
   Revenge 369
   Reward 371
Requite 365
rescind, Cancel 107
rescue, Deliver 149
resemblance, Approxima-
   tion 61
   Likeness 273
   Similarity 390
resembling, Alike 37
resentful, Malicious 277
   Restive 367
resentment, Anger 49
   Hatred 229
   Pique 318
reservation, Abeyance ... 3
reserve, Modesty 288
   Pride 335
reserved, Taciturn 414
reside, Abide 4
residence, Home 239
resign, Abandon 1
   Surrender 411
resignation, Patience 311
resist, Drive 166
   Hinder 234
resistance, Defense 146
resolute, Faithful 194

Obstinate 302
resoluteness, Will 442
resolution, Determination.153
   Fortitude 211
   Will 442
resolve, Determination ...153
resolved, Obstinate 302
resort (to), Appeal 57
resource, Choice 121
respect, n., Esteem......184
respect, v., Admire 26
   Esteem 184
respectively, Apiece 55
resplendent, Bright 99
   Sublime 407
response, Answer 50
responsibility, Duty 168
Responsible 366
Rest 367
   Abide 4
restful, Comfortable 127
Restive 367
restless, Active 19
   Fickle 201
   Restive 367
restore, Recover 358
Restrain 368
   Arrest 67
   Bind 92
   Check 119
   Govern 222
   Keep 265
restraint, Barrier 84
restrict, Bind 92
   Circumscribe 122
   Restrain 368
restriction, Barrier 84
result, n., Consequence...136
   End 177
   Event 186
   Harvest 229
   Operation 304
result, v., Follow 209
resume, Recover 358
retain, Keep 265
retainer, Accessory 15
retaliate, Avenge 77
   Requite 365
retaliation, Revenge 369
retard, Hinder 234
reticent, Taciturn 414
retire, Abscond 8
retire from, Abandon 1
Retirement 368
retort, Answer 50
retract, Abandon 1
   Renounce 362
retreat, Abscond 8
retribution, Revenge 369
   Reward 371
retrieve, Recover 358
retrospect, Memory 281
retrospection, Memory ...281
return, n., Harvest......229

Profit 337
return, v., Requite......365
returns, Profit 337
reveal, Announce 50
revel, Abound 6
   Carousal 111
Revelation 369
revelry, Carousal 111
revenge, n., Hatred 229
Revenge, v. 369
   Avenge 77
   Requite 365
revere, Admire 26
   Venerate 433
reverence, Admire...... 26
   Venerate 433
reverie, Dream 165
reverse, Abolish 5
   Misfortune 286
revile, Abuse 13
   Slander 394
revoke, Abolish 5
   Cancel 107
   Renounce 362
revolt, Revolution......370
Revolution 370
   Change 116
Revolve 371
Reward, n. 371
   Subsidy 408
reward, v., Requite 365
Rhythm 372
rich, Plentiful 322
   Racy 352
riches, Wealth 440
Riddle 373
ride, Drive 166
ridicule, Banter 83
ridiculous, Absurd 12
   Queer 348
rifle pit, Fortification ...211
Right, adj. 373
   Admissible 27
   Good 221
   Innocent 257
   Precise 329
Right, n. 374
   Duty 168
   Justice 263
right away, Immediately..247
righteous, Devout 154
   Good 221
   Innocent 257
righteousness, Duty 168
   Justice 263
   Virtue 436
rightful, Right 373
rightfulness, Justice 263
rightness, Virtue 436
right off, Immediately..247
rigid, Precise 329
   Severe 385
rigorous, Severe 385
rill, Stream 405

rim, Bank 83
rime, Poetry 323
rimer, Poet 323
rimester, Poet 323
rinse, Clean 124
riot, Quarrel 348
　Revolution 370
rip, Rend 361
Rise 374
　Beginning 89
risk, Danger 143
　Hazard 231
risky, Precarious 328
rite, Sacrament 377
rival, Enemy 179
rivalry, Ambition 46
rive, Break 98
　Rend 361
river, Stream 405
rivulet, Stream 405
road, Way 439
roadway, Way 439
roam, Wander 438
roar, Call 106
rob, Steal 402
Robber 375
robes, Dress 166
rock, Shake 386
roll, n. Record 357
roll, v., Revolve 371
romance, Dream 165
　Fiction 202
root, n., Foundation......212
root, v., Fix 206
root out, Exterminate ...191
rot, Decay 144
rotate, Revolve 371
rotten, Bad 80
rough, Awkward 78
　Bluff 95
rout, Carousal 111
　Conquer 134
route, Way 439
routine, Habit 225
rove, Wander 438
row, Argument 62
　Quarrel 348
Royal 375
rub off, Cancel 107
rub out, Cancel 107
rude, Barbarous 84
　Bluff 95
　Rustic 376
rudeness, Impertinence ..249
rue, Mourn 290
ruin, n., Misfortune 286
ruin, v., Abuse 13
　Demolish 150
　Overthrow 306
ruinous, Pernicious 315
rule, Criterion 141
　Govern 222
　Habit 225
　Law 270

Power 326
System 412
ruler, Chief 120
ruminate, Deliberate ...148
rumor, Report 363
run, Stream 405
run away, Abscond 8
runlet, Stream 405
runnel, Stream 405
run off, Abscond 8
rupture, Break 98
　Rend 361
rural, Rustic 376
ruse, Pretense 322
　Trick 425
Rustic 376

sable, Dark 143
sachem, Chief 120
Sacrament 377
sacred, Holy 238
sacrifice, Surrender 411
Sad 377
　Bad 80
saddening, Bad 80
sadness, Grief 223
safe, Secure 382
safeguard, Defense 146
Sagacious 378
　Shrewd 388
sagacity, Acumen 19
　Wisdom 442
sage, Sagacious 378
Sailor 378
saintly, Holy 238
salable, Venal 432
salary, Pay 312
Sale 379
salubrious, Healthy 231
salutary, Healthy 231
salute, Address, v. 23
same, Alike 37
　Synonymous 412
sameness, Likeness......273
Sample 379
　Example 188
sanctimonious, Devout...154
sanctimoniousness, Hypoc-
　risy 242
sanctimony, Hypocrisy...242
sanction, Abet 2
　Allow 42
　Confirm 133
Sanguinary 380
sanguine, Ardent 62
　Sanguinary 380
sanitary, Healthy 231
sarcasm, Banter 83
sate, Satisfy 380
satiate, Satisfy 380
satire, Banter 83
satisfaction, Happiness..226
　Propitiation 341
　Reward 371

satisfactory, Adequate ... 24
　Comfortable 127
　Good 221
satisfied, Comfortable 127
Satisfy 380
　Requite 365
satisfying, Pleasant 321
saturnalia, Carousal 111
sauciness, Impertinence..249
　Pertness 317
savage, Barbarous 84
　Bitter 93
　Fierce 203
　Sanguinary 380
savant, Scholar 380
save, conj., But 103
save, v., Deliver........149
saving, Frugality.......216
savoir faire, Address, n.. 22
savor, Smell...........396
savory, Delicious 149
saw, Proverb 343
say, Allege 38
　Announce 50
　Speak 398
　State 401
saying, Proverb 343
scan, Look 275
scarce, Rare 353
scare, Fear 199
　Frighten 215
scared, Afraid 29
scene, Argument 62
　Spectacle 398
scent, Smell 396
schedule, Record 357
scheme, Design 152
　Hypothesis 242
　Project 339
schismatic, Heretic 232
Scholar 380
scholarly, Academic 14
scholarship, Knowledge ..266
scholastic, Academic 14
school, Teach 415
schooling, Education 170
Science 381
　Knowledge 266
scintilla, Particle 311
scintillating, Bright 99
scintillation, Light.......272
scoff, Sneer 396
scorch, Burn 101
scorn, Abhor 4
　Neglect 296
scour, Clean 124
scourge, Beat 86
scout, Spy 400
scrap, Argument 62
　Particle 311
scrape, Predicament 331
scratch out, Cancel 107
scream, Call 106
screen, Hide 233

screen (cont'd)
Palliate 308
Shelter 388
scrimping, Frugality 216
scroll, Record 357
scrub, Clean 124
scruple, Doubt 163
Object 300
scrupulous, Honest 239
Precise 329
scrutinizing, Inquisitive..258
scurvy, Bad 80
Base 85
seafarer, Sailor 378
seafaring man, Sailor....378
sea-going, Marine 278
seal, Shut 389
seaman, Sailor 378
sear, Burn 101
search, Hunt 241
searching, Inquisitive....258
season, Time 419
seat of government, Capi-
tal 108
seclusion, Retirement....368
second, Help 231
secret, Latent 269
Mysterious 291
secrete, Hide 233
sect, Religion 360
sectarian, Heretic 232
section, Part 310
Secure 382
Arrest 67
Attach 71
Attain 75
Bind 92
Catch 113
Fix 206
Get 219
Purchase 345
Security 382
sedate, Calm 106
Serious 385
sedition, Revolution 370
seditious, Rebellious 357
seduce, Allure 43
sedulous, Busy 103
sedulousness, Industry...252
see, Discern 158
Look 275
seed, Plant 320
seed down, Plant 320
seem, Appear 57
seeming, Apparent 56
Pretense 322
seemly, Becoming 88
Fit 205
segment, Part 310
seize, Arrest 67
Catch 113
select, Allot 41
Choose 121
self-assertion, Assurance. 70

Egotism 172
self-complacency, Pride..335
self-conceit, Egotism.....172
Pride 335
self-condemnation, Repentance 363
self-confidence, Assurance. 70
Egotism 172
self-consciousness, Ego-
tism 172
self-control, Abstinence... 11
self-denial, Abstinence... 11
self-esteem, Egotism.....172
Pride 335
self-exaltation, Pride ...335
self-opinionated, Dogmatic.163
self-possessed, Calm 106
self-reliance, Assurance.. 70
self-respect, Pride 335
self-restraint, Abstinence. 11
sell, Convey 140
semblance, Pretense 322
Similarity 390
Send 383
senile, Old 303
Sensation 384
sense, Mind 283
Sensation 384
Wisdom 442
senseless, Absurd 12
senselessness, Idiocy 245
Sensibility 384
sensible, Conscious 135
Physical 318
Sagacious 378
sensitive, Fine 204
sensitiveness, Sensibility..384
sensual, Brutish 101
sentence, Condemn 132
sententious, Terse 417
sentiment, Idea 244
separate, Abstract 11
separately, Apiece 55
sequel, Consequence 136
Event 186
sequence, Time 419
serene, Calm 106
Serious 385
Bad 80
Good 221
Important 249
sermon, Speech 399
service, Profit 337
Sacrament 377
Utility 429
serviceable, Good 221
serviceableness, Utility ..429
servile, Base 85
set, n., Class 123
Group 223
set, v., Arrange 65
Fix 206
Plant 320
Put 347

set apart, Allot 41
Devote 154
set aside, Abolish 5
set fire to, Burn 101
set forth, State 401
set free, Absolve 9
Deliver 149
set in order, Arrange... 65
set on fire, Burn 101
set out, Plant 320
set right, Adapt 20
settle, Confirm 133
Fix 206
settlement, Compromise..130
settle with, Requite 365
set to rights, Adapt 20
set up, Arrange 65
set upon, Attack, v. 74
sever, Break 98
Rend 361
severally, Apiece 55
Severe 385
Bad 80
Difficult 157
Morose 289
Violent 436
severity, Acrimony 18
sex, Gender 217
shabby, Bad 80
Base 85
shackle, Bind 92
shackles, Fetter 201
shadowy, Dark 143
Vain 431
shady, Dark 143
Shake 386
sham, Assume 70
Hypocrisy 242
shame, n., Abomination.. 6
Chagrin 115
shame, v., Embarrass ...174
shamelessness, Effrontery.171
shape, Make 277
share, Apportion 61
Part 310
Portion 325
shared, Mutual 291
sharp, Bitter 93
Clever 125
Fine 204
Sagacious 378
Shrewd 388
Steep 403
Violent 436
sharpness, Acrimony 18
Acumen 19
sharp-witted, Sagacious..378
shatter, Break 98
sheen, Light 272
sheer, Pure 346
Steep 403
shelter, n., Defense 146
Shelter, v. 388
Cherish 119

shield, *n.*, Defense 146
shield, *v.*, Shelter 388
shift, *n.*, Fallacy 195
shift, *v.*, Change 117
   Convey 140
shifting, *adj.*, Fickle....201
shifting, *n.*, Fallacy 195
shimmer, Light 272
shimmering, Bright 99
shine, Light 272
shining, Bright 99
   Light 272
shiver, Break 98
shiver, Shake 386
shoal, Group 223
shock, Blow 95
   Collision 126
shocking, Awful 78
shore, Bank 83
short, Terse 417
   Transient 424
short-lived, Transient 424
short-sighted, Imprudent.251
should, Ought 305
shout, Call 106
show, Ostentation 305
   Pretense 322
   Spectacle 398
shred, Particle 311
Shrewd 388
   Sagacious 378
shrewdness, Acumen 19
shriek, Call 106
shudder, Shake 386
shun, Abhor 4
Shut 389
shyness, Modesty 288
sickness, Disease 159
sidewalk, Way 439
sight, Spectacle 398
Sign 390
   Characteristic 118
   Emblem 174
   Trace 422
signal, *adj.*, Eminent.....175
signal, *n.*, Sign........390
significant, Important ...249
signify, Allude 43
silent, Taciturn 414
silly, Absurd 12
silver, Money 289
similar, Alike 37
   Synonymous 412
Similarity 390
   Approximation 61
   Likeness 273
similarly, Also 44
simile, Allegory 39
   Similarity 390
similitude, Likeness 273
   Similarity 390
simple, Candid 108
   Pure 346
simulate, Assume 70

simulation, Pretense 132
Sin 391
since, Because 88
sincere, Candid 108
   Honest 239
sine qua non, Necessity..295
sinful, Bad 80
   Criminal 141
Sing 392
singe, Burn 101
singer, Poet 323
singular, Group 223
   Queer 348
   Rare 353
singularity, Characteristic.118
sink, Debase 144
   Dip 157
sinless, Innocent 257
sire, Propagate 340
situation, Circumstance...123
sizzled, Drunk 167
skeleton, Sketch 393
Skeptic 392
skepticism, Doubt, *n.* ...163
Sketch 393
Skilful 393
   Clever 125
   Good 221
skill, Dexterity 154
   Ingenuity 254
   Power 326
   Trick 425
   Wisdom 442
skilled, Skilful 393
skirmish, Battle 86
skittish, Restive 367
slack, Slow 395
slacken, Check 119
slackness, Neglect 296
Slander 394
   Abuse 13
Slang 395
slant, Tip 420
slap, Blow 95
slaughter, Kill 265
   Massacre 279
slavish, Base 85
slay, Kill 265
sleepless, Vigilant 435
slender, Fine 204
   Minute 284
slight, *adj.*, Fine 204
   Venial 434
slight, *v.*, Neglect 296
sling, Send 383
slip away, Abscond 8
slit, *n.*, Hole 236
slit, *v.*, Rend 361
slope, Tip 420
slothful, Idle 245
Slow 395
   Reluctant 360
sluggish, Idle 245
   Slow 395

sluggishness, Apathy ... 54
small, Fine 204
   Minute 284
smart, Clever 125
smartness, Pertness 317
smash, Break 98
Smell 396
smiling, Happy 227
smirch, Blemish 94
smite, Beat 86
smooth, Calm 106
   Fine 204
   Flat 207
snag, Impediment 248
snappish, Morose 289
snatch, Catch 113
sneaking, Base 85
Sneer 396
snoopy, Inquisitive 258
snug, Comfortable 127
so, Therefore 418
sober, Sad 377
   Serious 385
sobriety, Abstinence ... 11
sociable, Friendly 214
social, Friendly 214
   Good 221
Socialism 397
society, Association 69
soft, Humble 240
soften, Alleviate 40
soil, Blemish 94
   Defile 147
   Stain 400
sojourn, Abide 4
solace, Console 136
soldiers, Army 64
soldiery, Army 64
solemn, Awful 78
   Serious 385
solemnity, Sacrament ...377
solemnize, Celebrate 115
   Keep 265
solicit, Ask 67
   Plead 320
solicitude, Alarm 35
   Anxiety 53
   Care 110
solidarity, Union 428
solitude, Retirement 368
somatic, Physical 318
somber, Dark 143
   Sad 377
song, Poetry 323
soothe, Allay 38
sophism, Fallacy 195
sophistry, Fallacy 195
sordid, Base 85
   Miserly 285
sorrow, Grief 223
   Misfortune 286
   Mourn 290
   Repentance 363
sorrowful, Bad 80

sorrowful (*cont'd*)
　Pitiful 319
　Sad 377
sorry, Bad 80
　Sad 377
sort, Air 33
　Arrange 65
sort over, Arrange...... 65
sort out, Arrange........ 65
sottish, Brutish 101
　Drunk 167
soul, Mind 283
Sound 397
　Good 221
　Healthy 231
sour, Bitter 93
　Morose 289
source, Beginning 89
　Cause 114
sourness, Acrimony 18
sow, Plant 320
spacious, Large 268
spank, Beat 86
sparing, Frugality 216
sparkle, Light 272
sparkling, Bright 99
spasmodic, Fickle 201
Speak 398
speaking, Speech 399
speak to, Address, *v*..... 23
special pleading, Fallacy..195
specie, Money 289
specific, Explicit 190
specify, State 401
specimen, Example 188
　Sample 379
speck, Blemish 94
Spectacle 398
speculation, Hypothesis ..242
speculative, Academic ... 14
Speech 399
　Language 268
speechless, Taciturn 414
speed, Alacrity 34
　Quicken 350
speedy, Nimble 298
spick-and-span, Neat 294
spicy, Racy 352
spin, Revolve 371
spirit, Character 117
　Mind 283
spirited, Racy 352
spiritual, Holy 238
spite, Enmity 180
　Hatred 229
spiteful, Malicious 277
splendid, Bright 99
　Fine 204
　Sublime 407
splendor, Light 272
splenetic, Captious 109
　Morose 289
split, Break 98
　Rend 361

spoil, Decay 144
　Defile 147
sponge, Clean 124
Spontaneous 399
sport, Entertainment 181
spot, Blemish 94
　Stain 400
spotless, Innocent 257
　Pure 346
spousal, Marriage 278
spousals, Marriage 278
spread, Propagate 340
　Stretch 405
spread abroad, Announce. 50
spree, Carousal 111
sprightliness, Alacrity .. 34
sprightly, Active 19
　Airy 33
　Happy 227
　Nimble 298
spring, Beginning 89
　Cause 114
　Rise 374
spruce, Neat 294
spry, Active 19
　Nimble 298
Spy 400
squabble, Quarrel 348
squalid, Base 85
square, Agree 31
stable, Permanent 314
staid, Serious 385
stain, *n*., blemish........ 94
Stain, *v*. 400
　Defile 147
stainless, Innocent 257
　Pure 346
stamp out, Abolish....... 5
　Exterminate 191
Stand 401
standard, Criterion 141
　Example 188
　Ideal 244
　Model 288
stand by, Help 231
stare, Look 275
start, Beginning 89
startle, Frighten 215
state, *n*., Race 352
State, *v*. 401
　Allege 38
　Announce 50
stately, Awful 78
　Sublime 407
statement, Report 363
statute, Law 270
staunch, Good 221
stay, Abide 4
　Check 119
　Hinder 234
　Persist 316
　Stand 401
　Suspend 411
steadfast, Faithful 194

Permanent 314
Steal 402
　Abstract 11
steal away, Abscond 8
steal off, Abscond 8
Steep 403
　High 234
stench, Smell 396
sterling, Good 221
stern, Severe 385
stick, Attach 71
sticking, Adhesive 25
sticky, Adhesive 25
stiff, *adj*., Severe 385
stiff, *n*., Hobo 236
stigma, Blemish 94
still, *conj*., But 103
　Notwithstanding 299
　Yet 445
still, *v*., Allay 38
　Calm 106
stillness, Apathy 54
　Rest 367
stimulate, Encourage 176
stinging, Bitter 93
stingy, Miserly 285
stink, Smell 396
stipend. Pay 312
stipulation, Contract 137
stir, Influence 254
stoicism, Apathy 54
stolid, Brutish 101
stoop, Bend 90
Stop 403
　Abate 1
　Abide 4
　Arrest 67
　Check 119
　End 178
　Hinder 234
　Shut 389
　Stand 401
　Suspend 411
store up, Amass 44
Storm, *n*. 404
storm, *v*., Attack........ 74
stormy, Bleak 94
Story 404
　Fiction 202
　History 235
　Record 357
　Report 363
straight, Right 373
straightforward, Candid ..108
　Clear 124
　Honest 239
straightway, Immediately..247
strain, Stretch 405
strait, Predicament 331
strand, Bank 83
strange, Alien 36
　Queer 348
　Rare 353
stranger, Alien 36

stratagem, Trick 425
strategy, Design 152
stray, Wander 438
Stream 405
   Abound 6
streamlet, Stream 405
street, Way 439
strength, Power 326
strengthen, Confirm 133
Stretch 405
strict, Precise 329
   Severe 385
strife, Argument 62
   Battle 86
   Quarrel 348
strike, Beat 86
strike out, Cancel 107
stripe, Blow 95
strive, Try 427
striving, Endeavor 178
stroke, Blow 95
   Misfortune 286
strong, Healthy 231
stronghold, Fortification ..211
struggle, Endeavor 178
stubborn, Obstinate 302
   Perverse 317
   Restive 367
student, Scholar 380
study, Education 170
stupefaction, Stupor 406
Stupid 406
   Absurd 12
   Brutish 101
stupidity, Idiocy 245
Stupor 406
style, Air 33
   Diction 155
   Name 293
subdivision, Part 310
subdue, Conquer 134
   Punish 345
subject, n., Topic 422
subject, v., Conquer 134
subjection, Allegiance ... 39
subjective, Inherent 255
subjoin, Add 21
   Append 58
subjugate, Conquer 134
Sublime 407
submerge, Dip 157
submission, Patience 311
submissive, Docile 162
   Humble 240
submit, Bend 90
submit to, Endure 179
subordinate, Auxiliary ... 77
subscribe, Append 58
subservient, Base 85
subside, Abate 1
Subsidy 408
subsisting, Alive 37
substance, Wealth 440
substantial, Important ...249

Real 354
substantiate, Confirm 133
substitute, Change, v.....117
   Delegate 148
substratum, Foundation ..212
substructure, Foundation..212
subterfuge, Deception ...145
   Fallacy 195
   Pretense 322
   Trick 425
subtile, Fine 204
   Shrewd 388
subtle, Fine 204
   Shrewd 388
subvention, Subsidy 408
subvert, Abolish 5
   Overthrow 306
Succeed 408
   Follow 209
success, Victory 435
successful, Fortunate 212
   Happy 227
succession, Time 419
succinct, Terse 417
succor, Help 231
suck up, Absorb 10
suffer, Allow 42
   Endure 179
sufferance, Patience 311
suffering, Pain 308
suffice, Satisfy 380
sufficient, Adequate ... 24
   Plentiful 322
suggest, Allude 43
Suggestion 409
   Counsel 140
   Proposal 342
suit, Adapt 20
suitable, Adequate 24
   Admissible 27
   Becoming 88
   Condign 132
   Fit 205
   Good 221
   Propitious 341
suited, Adequate 24
   Fit 205
sulky, Morose 289
sullen, Morose 289
sully, Defile 147
   Stain 400
sum, Aggregate 30
summary, adj., Terse....417
summary, n., Abridgment. 7
summon, Arraign 64
   Convoke 140
sum up, Add 21
   Calculate 105
sunder, Break 98
   Rend 361
sundowner, Hobo 236
sunny, Bright 99
Happy 227
sunshiny, Bright 99

superabundance, Excess ..189
superannuated, Antique .. 53
superb, Sublime 407
superciliousness, Pride ...335
supereminent, Principal ..336
superfluity, Excess 189
superhuman, Supernatural409
superintendence, Oversight306
superior, Principal 336
Supernatural 409
supersede, Overthrow 306
superstition, Fanaticism ..196
supervene, Happen 225
supervision, Oversight ...306
supplant, Abolish 5
   Overthrow 306
supple, Active 19
   Graceful 222
   Nimble 298
supplement, Appendage .. 58
supplicate, Ask 67
   Pray 328
supply, Give 220
support, n., Subsidy......408
Support, v. 410
   Abet 2
   Carry 112
   Endure 179
   Help 231
   Keep 265
supporter, Adherent 24
Suppose 410
supposition, Fancy 197
   Hypothesis 242
   Idea 244
suppress, Abate 1
   Abolish 5
   Hide 233
   Overthrow 306
   Restrain 368
supremacy, Victory 435
supreme, Absolute 9
   Eminent 175
   Principal 336
sure, Authentic 76
   Conscious 135
   Faithful 194
   Secure 382
surety, Security 382
surfeit, Satisfy 380
surly, Morose 289
surmise, n., Hypothesis ..242
surmise, v., Doubt......164
   Suppose 410
surmount, Conquer 134
surname, Name 293
surpass, Beat 86
surpassing, Principal 336
surplus, Excess 189
surplusage, Circumlocu-
   tion 122
surprise, Amazement..... 45
   Perplexity 316
Surrender 411

Surrender (cont'd)
Abandon 1
surrounded by, Amid ... 48
surveillance, Oversight..306
survey, Look 275
susceptibility, Sensibility.384
suspect, v., Doubt.......164
Suspend 411
Adjourn 26
suspense, Abeyance 3
Doubt 163
suspension, Abeyance 3
suspension of payment,
Bankruptcy 83
suspicion, Doubt 163
suspicious, Equivocal....183
Jealous 262
sustain, Carry 112
Confirm 133
Endure 179
Help 231
Keep 265
Support 410
sustenance, Food 209
swagman, Hobo 236
swallow, Absorb 10
swallow up, Absorb 10
swarm, Abound 6
Group 223
swart, Dark 143
swarthy, Dark 143
sway, n., Power 326
sway, v., Govern 222
Influence 254
Shake 386
swear, State 401
swearing, Oath 300
sweep, Clean 124
sweet, Amiable 47
swell, Abound 6
swerve, Fluctuate 208
Wander 438
swift, Nimble 298
swiftness, Alacrity 34
swindle, Fraud 213
Steal 402
swindling, Fraud 213
swing, Shake 386
swinish, Brutish 101
switch, Beat 86
swoon, Stupor 406
swooning, Stupor 406
sworn statement, Oath ..300
sycophancy, Praise 327
sylvan, Rustic 376
symbol, Emblem 174
Sign 390
symmetry, Harmony 228
sympathetic, Humane ..240
sympathize with, Console.136
sympathy, Benevolence .. 91
Pity 319
symphony, Melody 281
symptom, Sign 390

syncope, Stupor 406
synonymic, Synonymous..412
Synonymous 412
synopsis, Abridgment 7
System 412
Body 96
Habit 225
Hypothesis 242
systematic, Dogmatic 163

Taciturn 414
tact, Address, n. 22
taint, n., Blemish....... 94
taint, v., Defile.........147
take, Assume 70
Carry 112
Catch 113
take away, Abstract 11
take exception, Object ...300
take hold of, Catch 113
take in, Absorb 10
take into custody, Arrest. 67
take-off, Caricature 111
take oneself off, Abscond. 8
take place, Happen 225
take prisoner, Arrest ... 67
take to task, Reprove ...365
take up, Absorb 10
tale, Report 363
Story 404
talent, Genius 218
Power 326
talented, Clever 125
talents, Genius 218
talk, n., Conversation ..139
Speech 399
talk, v., Speak 398
Talkative 414
tall, High 234
tally, Agree 31
tame, Docile 162
tangent, Adjacent 25
tangible, Evident 187
Physical 318
tangled, Complex 130
tar, Sailor 378
tardy, Slow 395
tariff, Tax 415
tarnish, Blemish 94
Defile 147
Stain 400
tarry, Abide 4
tart, Bitter 93
tartness, Acrimony 18
tasteful, Elegant 173
tattle, Babble 80
taunt, Sneer 396
tautology, Circumlocution.122
Tax 415
Teach 415
teachable, Docile 162
teaching, Doctrine 162
Education 170
tear, Rend 361

tease, Affront 29
teasing, Troublesome....426
tedious, Troublesome ...426
tediousness, Circumlocu-
tion 122
teem, Abound 6
teeming, Plentiful 322
tell, Announce 50
Speak 398
State 401
Temerity 416
Effrontery 171
temper, Anger 49
Character 117
temperament, Character..117
temperance, Abstinence.. 11
tempest, Storm 404
temporary, Transient ...424
tempt, Allure 43
tendency, Aim 32
Direction 158
tender, adj., Friendly....214
Humane 240
tender, v., Offer 302
tender-hearted, Humane .240
tenderness, Attachment.. 73
Benevolence 91
Love 276
Mercy 282
Pity 319
tenet, Doctrine 162
tenuous, Fine 204
Term 416
Boundary 97
Time 419
terminate, Abate 1
Abolish 5
End 178
Stop 403
termination, Boundary .. 97
End 177
terminus, End 177
terrible, Awful 78
Formidable 210
terrific, Awful 78
terrified, Afraid 29
terrify, Frighten 215
terror, Alarm 35
Fear 199
terrorize, Frighten 215
terror-stricken, Afraid... 29
Terse 417
test, Criterion 141
testify, State 401
Testimony 418
testy, Captious 109
tether, Bind 92
that, But 103
the humanities, Literature.274
theme, Topic 422
then, Therefore 418
thence, Therefore 418
theology, Religion 360
theoretic, Academic 14

theoretical, Academic ... 14
theory, Hypothesis 242
    Idea 244
Therefore 418
thief, Robber 375
thin, Fine 204
think, Esteem 184
    Suppose 410
thirst, Appetite 59
this instant, Immediately.247
thorough, Good 221
    Radical 353
thoroughfare, Way 439
thoroughgoing, Radical ..353
though, But 103
    Notwithstanding 299
thought, Idea 244
    Mind 283
Thoughtful 418
thoughtless, Abstracted .. 12
    Imprudent 251
thoughtlessness, Neglect..296
thrash, Beat 86
threatening, Imminent ...247
thrift, Frugality 216
thriftless, Imprudent 251
thrill, Shake 386
thrive, Succeed 408
throe, Pain 308
Throng 419
    Company 128
    Mob 288
through, By 104
throw, Send 383
thrust, Drive 166
thump, Blow 95
thus far, Yet 445
thwart, Baffle 81
    Hinder 234
tide, Stream 405
tidings, News 297
tidy, Neat 294
tie, Attach 71
    Bind 92
    Fix 206
tie up, Bind 92
tight, Drunk 167
tighten, Stretch 405
tillage, Agriculture 31
tilt, Tip 420
Time 419
time-honored, Old 303
timeless, Eternal 185
time-worn, Old 303
timid, Afraid 29
    Faint 193
timidity, Alarm 35
    Fear ...,.........199
    Modesty 288
timorous, Afraid 29
tinge, Stain 400
tint, Stain 400
tiny, Minute 284
tip, *n.*. End 177

Tip, *v.* 420
tipsy, Drunk 167
Tire 420
tiresome, Troublesome ..426
tithe, Tax 415
title, Name 293
tittle, Particle 311
tocsin, Alarm 35
toil, Work 444
toilsome, Difficult 157
token, Emblem 174
    Sign 390
    Trace 422
tolerable, Admissible ... 27
tolerate, Abide 4
    Allow 42
    Endure 179
toll, Tax 415
tone, Sound 397
tongue, Language 268
too, Also 44
Tool 421
    Agent 30
Topic 422
torment, Pain 308
torpid, Latent 269
torpor, Stupor 406
tort, Injustice 256
torture, Pain 308
total, Aggregate 30
    Radical 353
totality, Aggregate 30
totter, Shake 386
touch, Concern 131
touching, Pitiful 319
touchstone, Criterion ...141
touchy, Captious 109
tour, Journey 262
tourist, Hobo 236
tow, Draw 164
towering, High 234
Trace 422
    Characteristic 118
    track, Trace 422
    Way 439
tractable, Docile 162
trade, Business 102
    Sale 379
trading, Business 102
traduce, Slander 394
traffic, Business 102
trail, Trace 422
train, Teach 415
trained, Skilful 393
training, Education 170
trait, Characteristic 118
traitor, Heretic 232
tramp, Hobo 236
trance, Dream 165
tranquil, Calm 106
tranquilize, Allay 38
tranquillity, Apathy 54
    Rest 367
Transact 423

Do 161
Transaction 423
    Act 18
    Business 102
transcendent, Transcend-
    ental 424
Transcendental 424
    Mysterious 291
transcript, Duplicate 167
transfer, Convey 140
transfigure, Change, *v.*..117
transform, Change 117
transformation, Change, *n.*116
transgression, Sin 391
Transient 424
transit, Journey 262
    Motion 290
transition, Change, *n.* ...116
    Motion 290
transitory, Transient ...424
translation, Definition ...148
translucent, Clear 124
transmit, Carry 112
    Convey 140
    Send 383
transmutation, Change, *n.*116
transmute, Change, *v.* ..117
transparent, Candid 108
    Clear 124
    Evident 187
transport, *n.*, Enthusiasm.182
transport, *v.*, Banish 82
    Carry 112
    Convey 140
travel, Journey 262
travesty, Caricature 111
treachery, Fraud 213
treason, Fraud 213
treasure, Cherish 119
treat, Feast 200
    Transact 423
treaty, Contract 137
tremble, Shake 386
trembling, Fear 199
tremendous, Formidable..210
trench, Fortification 211
trepidation, Fear 199
trespass, Attack, *n.* 73
trial, Endeavor 178
    Misfortune 286
tribe, Race 352
tribulation, Grief 223
    Misfortune 286
tribute, Subsidy 408
    Tax 415
Trick 425
    Fraud 213
    Pretense 322
trickery, Deception 145
tried, Reliable 359
trifling, Idle 245
    Vain 431
trim, Neat 294
trip, Journey 262

triumph, Happiness 226
   Victory 435
trivial, Vain 431
   Venial 434
trombo, Hobo 236
troop, Company 128
troops, Army 64
troubadour, Poet 323
trouble, Anxiety 53
   Care 110
   Grief 223
   Misfortune 286
   Troublesome 426
   Bad 80
troupe, Company 128
true, Authentic 76
   Faithful 194
   Good 221
   Honest 239
   Pure 346
   Real 354
   Right 373
truism, Axiom 79
   Proverb 343
trunk, Body 96
trust, *n.*, Assurance 70
   Faith 193
trust, *v.*, Commit 127
trustworthy, Authentic .. 76
   Faithful 194
   Honest 239
   Reliable 359
trusty, Faithful 194
   Honest 239
   Reliable 359
Truth 426
   Justice 263
   Virtue 436
truthful, Candid 108
truthfulness, Truth 426
Try 427
   Endeavor 178
trying, Difficult 157
   Troublesome 426
tube, Hole 236
tug, Draw 164
tuition, Education 170
tumult, Revolution 370
tumultuous, Troublesome.426
   Violent 436
tune, Melody 281
tunnel, Hole 236
turbid, Obscure 301
turbulent, Violent 436
turn, Bend 90
   Change 117
   Revolve 371
tutor, Teach 415
twaddle, Babble 80
twain, Both 96
twine, Bend 90
twinge, Pain 308
twinkle, Light 272
twinkling, Bright 99

Light 272
twirl, Revolve 371
twist, Bend 90
two, Both 96
type, Emblem 174
   Example 188
   Model 288
   Sign 390
typical, Normal 298
tyrannical, Absolute 9
tyrannous, Absolute 9
tyro, Amateur 45

umbrage, Pique 318
umpire, Judge 263
unadorned, Clear 124
unadulterated, Pure 346
unambiguous, Clear 124
unanimity, Harmony ...228
unassailable, Secure 382
unassuming, Humble ...240
unassured, Precarious ..328
unavailing, Vain 431
unavoidable, Necessary ..295
unavoidableness, Necessity.295
unbelief, Doubt 163
unbeliever, Skeptic 392
unbiased, Candid 108
unbidden, Spontaneous ..399
unblemished, Good 221
   Pure 346
unbounded, Infinite 253
unbroken, Continual 137
unceasing, Continual ...137
   Eternal 185
uncertain, Equivocal ...183
   Fickle 201
   Precarious 328
uncertainty, Doubt, *n.* ..163
unchangeable, Permanent.314
unchanging, Permanent ..314
uncivil, Bluff 95
uncivilized, Barbarous .. 84
uncommon, Queer 348
   Rare 353
uncommunicative, Taci-
   turn 414
uncomprehended, Latent..269
uncompromising, Severe..385
unconcern, Apathy 54
unconditional, Absolute .. 9
unconditioned, Absolute.. 9
   Infinite 253
uncongeniality, Antipathy. 52
unconnected, Alien 36
unconquerable, Obstinate.302
unconsciousness, Stupor..406
uncontrollable, Rebellious.357
   Violent 436
uncorrupted, Pure 346
uncouth, Awkward 78
   Barbarous 84
   Rustic 376
uncreated, Primeval 336

uncultivated, Fierce......203
undaunted, Brave 97
undefiled, Pure 346
undeniable, Necessary ..295
under, Beneath 91
underestimate, Disparage.159
undergo, Endure 179
underlying, Radical 353
underneath, Beneath 91
underrate, Disparage 159
understand, Perceive ...313
understanding, Mind 283
   Wisdom 442
undertake, Try 427
undervalue, Disparage ..159
undeveloped, Latent 269
undismayed, Brave 97
undisturbed, Calm 106
   Secure 382
undulate, Fluctuate 208
undying, Eternal 185
unearth, Discover 158
uneducated, Ignorant ...246
unemployed, Idle 245
   Vacant 431
unending, Eternal 185
unenlightened, Ignorant..246
unequivocal, Absolute .. 9
   Clear 124
uneven, Irregular 261
unfading, Eternal 185
unfailing, Eternal 185
unfair, Bad 80
unfairness, Injustice ...256
   Prejudice 331
unfathomable, Infinite ...253
   Mysterious 291
unfathomed, Mysterious..291
unfavorable, Adverse .. 28
unfeelingness, Apathy ... 54
unfeigned, Good 221
unfilled, Vacant 431
unfixed, Fickle 201
unflinching, Obstinate ..302
unfold, Amplify 48
unfortunate, Bad 80
ungainly, Awkward 78
ungodliness, Sin 391
ungovernable, Perverse...317
   Rebellious 357
   Violent 436
unhandy, Awkward 78
unhappy, Bad 80
   Sad 377
unhealthful, Pernicious ..315
unhealthiness, Disease...159
unhomogeneous, Miscel-
   laneous 284
unification, Union 428
uniform, *adj.*, Alike 37
uniform, *n.*, Dress 166
uniformity, Harmony ...228
unimpeached, Good 221
unimportant, Vain 431

uninformed, Ignorant ...246
uninstructed, Ignorant ...246
unintellectual, Brutish ..101
unintelligible, Obscure ..301
uninterrupted, Continual.137
Union 428
  Alliance 41
  Association 69
  Attachment 73
  Harmony 228
  Marriage 278
unique, Queer 348
  Rare 353
unison, Harmony 228
  Melody 281
Unite 428
  Add 21
  Agree 31
  Associate 68
  Attach 71
  Mix 286
united, Mutual 291
unity, Harmony 228
  Union 428
universal, General 217
unkindness, Acrimony.... 18
unknown, Latent........269
  Mysterious 291
unlawful, Criminal 141
unlearned, Ignorant ...246
unless, But 103
unlettered, Ignorant ...246
unlike, Alien 36
  Contrary 138
  Miscellaneous 284
unlikeness, Difference ..156
unlimited, Absolute 9
  Infinite 253
unlucky, Adverse 28
  Bad 80
unmanageable, Rebellious.357
unmannerly, Bluff 95
unmatched, Queer 348
unmeasured, Infinite 253
unmingled, Pure 346
unmistakable, Clear 124
  Evident 187
unmitigated, Severe 385
unmixed, Pure 346
unmolested, Secure 382
unnatural, Irregular ...261
unobserved, Latent 269
unobtrusiveness, Modesty.288
unoccupied, Idle 245
  Vacant 431
unostentatious, Humble..240
unparalleled, Rare 353
unperceived, Latent 269
unpleasant, Bad 80
unpolished, Rustic 376
unpolluted, Pure 346
unprecedented, Rare ...353
unprejudiced, Candid ...108

unpremeditated, Extempo-
  raneous 191
unpretentious, Humble .240
unprincipled, Bad 80
unprofitable, Bad 80
  Vain 431
unpropitious, Adverse .. 28
unquestionable, Real ...354
unreal, Vain 431
unreasonable, Absurd ... 12
unrelenting, Severe 385
unreliable, Fickle 201
unremitting, Continual..137
unreserved, Candid 108
unrighteousness, Injustice.256
  Sin 391
unruffled, Calm 106
unruly, Restive 367
unsatisfying, Vain 431
unseen, Latent 269
unselfishness, Benevolence. 91
unserviceable, Vain 431
unsettle, Displace 160
unsettled, Fickle 201
  Irregular 261
  Precarious 328
unsheltered, Bleak 94
unskilful, Awkward 78
unskilled, Ignorant 246
unsophisticated, Candid..108
  Rustic 376
unsoundness, Disease ...376
unspiritual, Brutish 101
unspotted, Pure 346
unstable, Fickle 201
  Precarious 328
unstained, Pure 346
unsteady, Fickle 201
  Precarious 328
unsubstantial, Vain 431
unsuitable, Incongruous..251
unsullied, Good 221
  Pure 346
unsuspecting, Secure ...382
unswerving, Right 373
unsymmetrical, Irregular.261
unsystematic, Irregular ..261
untainted, Pure 346
untamed, Barbarous 84
untarnished, Good 221
  Pure 346
untaught, Ignorant 246
  Rustic 376
untenanted, Vacant 431
unthinking, Imprudent ..251
unthrifty, Imprudent ...251
untoward, Adverse 28
  Perverse 317
untrained, Fierce 203
untroubled, Secure 382
untrue, Bad 80
untrustworthy, Bad 80
untruth, Deception 145
untutored, Ignorant 246

unusual, Irregular 261
  Queer 348
unusual, Rare 353
unvarying, Continual ...137
unwavering, Faithful ...194
unwelcome, Bad 80
unwholesome, Bad 80
  Pernicious 315
unwilling, Reluctant ...360
unworthy, Bad 80
unyielding, Obstinate ...302
  Severe 385
upbraid, Reprove 365
upbraiding, Reproof ...364
uphold, Abet 2
  Confirm 133
  Help 231
  Support 410
uplifted, High 234
upon, Above 7
upright, Good 221
  Honest 239
  Innocent 257
  Pure 346
  Right 373
uprightness, Justice 263
  Virtue 436
uprising, Revolution 370
uproot, Exterminate 191
upshot, Consequence ...136
upstart, New 297
urbane, Polite 324
urbanity, Refinement ...358
urge, Desire 152
  Influence 254
  Persuade 316
  Plead 320
  Quicken 350
urge forward, Promote...340
urgency, Necessity 295
urge on, Drive 166
  Encourage 176
  Promote 340
  Quicken 350
usage, Habit...........225
use, n., Habit.........225
  Utility 429
use, v., Apply 60
  Employ 176
  Exercise 190
useful, Good 221
usefulness, Profit 337
  Utility 429
useless, Vain 431
use up, Employ 176
Usual 429
  General 217
  Normal 298
usurp, Assume 70
utensil, Tool 421
Utility 429
  Profit 337
utmost, End 177
utter, Speak 398

utterance, Remark 361
Speech 399
uttermost, End 177

Vacant 431
Idle 245
vacate, Abandon 1
Cancel 107
vacillate, Fluctuate......208
vacillating, Fickle........201
vacuous, Vacant 431
vagabond, Hobo........236
vagary, Fancy 197
vagrant, Hobo 236
Vain 431
Idle 245
vainglory, Pride 335
vale, Hole 236
valediction, Farewell 198
valedictory, Farewell....198
valiant, Brave 97
valid, Good 221
validate, Confirm 133
valley, Hole 236
valor, Prowess 344
valuable, Good 221
value, *n.*, Price 334
Profit 337
value, *v.*, Cherish.......119
Esteem 184
valueless, Vain 431
vanity, Egotism 172
Pride 335
vanquish, Beat 86
Conquer 134
vapid, Vain 431
variable, Fickle 201
Irregular 261
variant, Miscellaneous ..284
variation, Change 116
Difference 156
variety, Change 116
Difference 156
various, Miscellaneous ..284
vary, Change 117
Fluctuate 208
vast, Large 268
vaunt, Ostentation 305
vaunting, Ostentation ...305
veer, Change 117
Fluctuate 208
Wander 438
vehemence, Enthusiasm..182
vehement, Ardent.......62
Eager 169
Violent 436
veil, Hide 233
Palliate 308
Venal 432
venerable, Old 303
Venerate 433
Admire 26
vengeance, Revenge 369
Venial 434

venomous, Malicious 277
venture, Hazard 231
venturesome, Brave 97
Imprudent 251
venturesomeness, Temer-
ity 416
venturous, Imprudent....251
veracity, Truth 426
Verbal 434
verbiage, Circumlocution.122
Diction 155
verbose, Talkative 414
verbosity, Circumlocution.122
verdant, Rustic 376
verge, Boundary 97
verify, Confirm 133
veritable, Authentic 76
Real 354
verity, Truth 426
vernacular, Language....268
versatile, Fickle 201
verse, Poetry 323
Rhythm 372
versifier, Poet 323
version, Report 363
vestige, Trace 422
vestments, Dress 166
vesture, Dress 166
vex, Affront 29
vexation, Anger 49
Chagrin 115
Impatience 248
vexatious, Troublesome..426
viands, Food 209
vibrate, Shake 386
vice, Sin 391
vicious, Bad 80
Criminal 141
Irregular 261
Restive 367
viciousness, Sin 391
vicissitude, Change, *n.* ..116
victimize, Abuse 13
Victory 435
victuals, Food 209
view, Look 275
vigilance, Care 110
Vigilant 435
Alert 35
vigorous, Active 19
Healthy 231
vile, Bad 80
Base 85
Brutish 101
Criminal 141
vilify, Abuse 13
Slander 394
villainous, Bad 80
villainy, Abomination.... 6
vindicate, Avenge 77
State 401
vindication, Apology 55
Defense 146
vinegarish, Bitter 93

violate, Abuse 13
Violent 436
Fierce 203
virgin, Youthful 445
virginal, Youthful 445
virile, Masculine 279
Virtue 436
Justice 263
virtuous, Good 221
Innocent 257
Pure 346
virtuousness, Virtue 436
virulence, Acrimony..... 18
virulent, Bitter 93
Malicious 277
viscid, Adhesive 25
viscous, Adhesive........ 25
visible, Evident 187
Physical 318
vision, Dream 165
Revelation 369
visionary, Fanciful 197
Vain 431
visit, Avenge 77
visitation, Misfortune...286
vital, Alive 37
vitiate, Defile 147
vituperate, Abuse 13
vivacious, Alive 37
vivacity, Alacrity 34
vocabulary, Diction 155
Language 268
vocal, Verbal 434
vocation, Business 102
vociferate, Call 106
void, Abolish 5
Abyss 14
Vacant 431
volition, Will 442
voluble, Talkative 414
voluntary, Spontaneous..399
volunteer, Offer 302
vow, Oath 300
voyage, Journey 262
vulgarism, Slang 395

wages, Pay 312
waggery, Wit 443
waggishness, Wit 443
wait (for), Abide 4
waive, Surrender 411
wakeful, Vigilant 435
walk, Way 439
Wander 438
wandering, Irregular ...261
want, Necessity 295
Poverty 325
warble, Sing 392
ward, Shelter 388
wariness, Care 110
warmth, Enthusiasm....182
warn, Reprove 365
warning, Counsel 140
Example 188

warp, Bend 90
warrant, Precedent 329
wary, Vigilant 435
wash, Clean 124
Washing 438
wassail, Carousal 111
waste, adj., Bleak 94
  Vacant 431
waste, n., Excess 189
wastefulness, Excess 189
watch, n., Oversight.....306
watch, v., Abide 4
  Look 275
watchful, Alert 35
  Vigilant 435
watchfulness, Care 110
  Oversight 306
watercourse, Stream.....405
wave, Shake 386
waver, Fluctuate 208
  Shake 386
wavering, Fickle 201
Way 439
  Air 33
  Direction 158
wayward, Perverse 317
weak, Faint 193
Wealth 440
  Money 289
weapon, Tool 421
weapons, Arms 64
wearied, Faint 193
wearisome, Troublesome.426
wear out, Tire 420
weary, Tire 420
wedded, Addicted 22
wedding, Marriage 278
wedlock, Marriage 278
weigh, Deliberate 148
weight, Load 274
weighty, Important 249
welcome, Pleasant 321
well, Healthy 231
well-adapted, Good 221
well-behaved, Polite 324
well-bred, Polite 324
well-disposed, Friendly...214
  Good 221
well-mannered, Polite ...324
well-off, Comfortable 127
well-qualified, Good 221
well-to-do, Comfortable...127
whence, Therefore 418
wherefore, Therefore 418
while, Time 419
whim, Fancy 197
whimsical, Fanciful 197
  Fickle 201
  Queer 348
whip, Beat 86
whirl, Revolve 371
whit, Particle 311
whiten, Bleach 93
whitewash, Bleach 93

whole, Aggregate 30
  Perfect 313
wholesome, Good 221
  Healthy 231
wicked, Bad 80
  Criminal 141
wickedness, Abomination. 6
  Sin 391
wide, Large 268
wide-awake, Active 19
  Alert 35
  Vigilant 435
widen, Amplify 48
wild, Absurd 12
  Bleak 94
  Fierce 203
  Irregular 261
  Violent 436
wile, Pretense 322
  Trick 425
wilful, Perverse 317
Will 442
willie, Hobo 236
willing, Spontaneous.....399
win, Allure 43
  Attain 75
  Conquer 134
  Get 219
  Succeed 408
wind, Revolve 371
wind up, End 178
windy, Bleak 94
winning, Amiable 47
  Charming 118
win over, Persuade.....316
winsome, Amiable 47
wipe, Clean............124
wipe out, Exterminate...191
Wisdom 442
  Knowledge 266
  Prudence 344
wise, Sagacious 378
wish, Desire 152
  Will 442
Wit 443
  Mind 283
with, By 104
withal, Also 44
withdraw, Abscond 8
  Abstract 11
withdrawal, Retirement..368
withdraw from, Abandon. 1
wither, Die 155
withhold, Keep 265
  Restrain 368
  Suspend 411
without delay, Immedi-
  ately 247
without end, Eternal 185
witness, Testimony 418
wits, Mind 283
witticism, Wit 443
woe, Grief 223
  Pain 308

woebegone, Sad 377
woeful, Pitiful 319
  Sad 377
womanish, Feminine.....200
womanlike, Feminine ...200
womanly, Feminine 200
wonder, n., Amazement.. 45
wonder, v., Admire 26
wont, Habit 225
wonted, Usual 429
woo, Address 23
woozy, Drunk 167
word, Term 416
wordiness, Circumlocution.122
wording, Diction 155
Work 444
  Act 18
  Business 102
work(s), Fortification ...211
workman, Mechanic 280
work out, Do 161
worn, Faint 193
worn down, Faint 193
worn out, Faint 193
worry, Anxiety 53
  Care 110
worship, Venerate 433
worst, Beat 86
  Conquer 134
worth, Price 334
  Virtue 436
worthiness, Virtue 436
worthless, Bad 80
  Base 85
  Vain 431
worthy, Becoming 88
  Good 221
wound, Affront 29
wrangle, n., Argument... 62
  Quarrel 348
wrangle, v., Dispute.....160
  Reason 356
wrangling, Argument 63
wrath, Anger 49
wretched, Bad 80
  Base 85
  Pitiful 319
writings, Literature 274
wrong, adj., Criminal ...141
wrong, n., Injury 256
  Injustice 256
  Sin 391
wrong, v., Abuse 13
wrong-doing, Sin.......391

yardstick, Criterion 141
yarn, Story 404
yearning, Eager 169
yell, Call 106
Yet 445
  But 103
  Notwithstanding 299
yield, Allow 42
  Bend 90

yield (*cont'd*)
　Harvest 229
　Surrender 411
yielding, Docile 162

Humble 240
young, New 297
Youthful 445
　New 297

zeal, Enthusiasm 182
zealous, Eager 169
zest, Appetite 59

INDEX OF ANTONYMS

abandon, 5, 75, 289, 410, 427
abandonment, 147
abase, 188
abbreviate, 49, 343
abet, 82, 119, 365
abettor, 180
abhor, 27
abhorrence, 184
abide, 117, 208
abiding, 425
ability, 251
abjure, 57
abnormal, 299
abnormality, 379
abominable, 239
abominate, 27
above
    (see syn for Beneath), 91
abridge, 49, 343
abrogate, 134
absolute, 152, 366
absolve, 132, 366
abstemious, 167
abstemiousness, 112
abstinence, 112, 200
abstinent, 167
abstract, 22
absurd, 27, 378
absurdity, 79, 443
abundance, 216
abuse, *n.*, 328
abuse, *v.*, 154
accede, 301
accelerate, 119
accept, 301
acceptance, 342
accessory, 180, 337
accident, 331
accidental, 255
accommodating, 318
accomplice, 180
accomplished, 376
accomplishment, 245, 340
accordant, 252
accountable, 9
accumulatively, 55
accurate, 197
accusation, 56
accuse, 10
achievement, 245, 340
acknowledge, 363
acquit, 65, 132, 366
acrid, 149
acrimonious, 48
act, 26, 245, 340
action, 4, 245
active, 246, 270
act on, 20
actual, 329
actuality, 150, 198, 244, 332
acuteness, 245

add, 12
added, 337
additional, 337
adequate, 432
adhere, 208
adherent, 120
adjourn, 140
adjust, 160
admire, 4, 301
admit, 234, 301
admittance, 85
adopt, 1, 363
adroit, 79, 108
adulterated, 347
advance, 82, 144
advantage, 249, 256
advantageous, 28, 315, 432
adventitious, 336
adventurous, 30
adversary, 16, 25
adverse, 215, 342
advertise, 234
advocate, 1
afar from, 48
affable, 386
affection, 6
affectionate, 203
affinity, 53
affluence, 216
afraid, 98
after, 334
after a while, 247
aggrandize, 144
aggravate, 2, 40, 47
aggregate, 311, 379
agitate, 38
agitated, 107
agitation, 55, 367
agreeing, 252
agreement, 53, 63, 127, 156,
    180
aid, 74, 82, 249, 368
aiding, 28
aimlessness, 33
akin, 36
alarm, 55
alert, 12
alien, 27
alienate, 72, 154, 165, 303
alienated, 215
alienation, 73, 341
alike, 285
alleviate, 259
alliance, 180
allow, 119, 339
allowance, 304
ally, 180
altercation, 131
although, 88
ambiguous, 125, 191
amelioration, 256

amenable, 302, 319
amiability, 18, 50, 24
amiable, 278, 290
amicable, 278
amiss, 205
amity, 127, 180
amplify, 2
amputate, 49
amusing, 426
analysis, 428
analyze, 287
animadversion, 328
animate, 174
animosity, 73
annals, 405
annihilate, 341
annoy, 136, 181
annoyance, 170
annul, 134
answer, 373
antagonism, 41, 228
antagonist, 16, 25, 68, 77
antagonistic, 215, 342
anticipation, 46, 153
antipathy, 60, 73, 184
anxiety, 55
apathetic, 62, 169, 258
apathy, 34, 54
apocryphal, 77
apostate, 139
apparent, 270
appear, 8
applaud, 13, 129, 132, 301
    365
applause, 364
appointment, 17
appreciation, 6
appreciative, 109
approbation, 364
appropriate, 36, 42
approval, 6, 318, 363, 364
approve, 4, 108, 129, 132,
    301, 365
approving, 109
apropos, 36
arbitrary, 366
archetype, 168
argument, 196
armistice, 86
arouse, 38, 368
array, 160
arrive, 8
arrogance, 289
arrogant, 86, 241, 342
artful, 108
artlessness, 426
ascertain, 411
ascetic, 167
assent, 301
assert, 1, 363
assist, 82

499

assistance, 249
assistant, 337
assisting, 26
association, 369
assort, 160, 287
assuage, 259
assuming, 241
assumption, 289
assurance, 35, 54, 153, 164, 231, 289, 331
assure, 210
assured, 329
astonishment, 52
astuteness, 245
atheism, 360
attach, 99
attainment, 245
attendant, 120
attentive, 12
attenuate, 259
attraction, 53
audacious, 30
augment, 40, 192
august, 319
auspicious, 28
austere, 322
austerity, 112
authority, 371
authorize, 6, 339
auxiliary, 337
avaricious, 218
averse, 22
aversion, 34, 60, 73, 184
avoid, 5, 23, 69, 260
avoidance, 33
avow, 234, 363
away from, 48
awkward, 88, 89, 126, 171, 205, 324, 394
awkwardness, 23, 170, 255, 327
axiom, 196, 373

bachelorhood, 279
bad, 314, 373
    (see syn. for Good, 221)
baffle, 3, 162
balmy, 94
barbarism, 359
barbarity, 92, 320
bareness, 166
barter, 346
base, 78, 234, 407
baseless, 77
bashfulness, 71, 172, 173, 249, 317
battle, 131, 228
be, 58
be born, 156
be certain, 58
be deaf to, 274
be defeated, 408
be deficient, 7
be destitute, 7

befriend, 74
befoul, 124
befouling, 439
beget, 192
beggarly, 78, 376
beggary, 442
begin, 156, 178, 404, 412
beginning
    (see syn. for End, 177)
be immortal, 156
being, 76
be in subjection, 222
be joyful, 291
be lacking, 7
belief, 164
believe, 164
believer, 392
bellicose, 215
belligerent, 215
beneath
    (see syn. for Above, 7)
benediction, 300
beneficent, 278, 315, 319
beneficial, 315, 432
benefit, 6, 13, 113, 249, 256
benevolent, 278
benign, 28, 278
benignant, 278, 290
benignity, 248
benison, 300
be present, 8
be real, 58
be silent, 106
besmear, 124
besmearing, 439
besmirch, 124
besmirching, 439
bespatter, 124
be still, 106
be subject, 222
be sure, 411
be the fact, 58
betray, 150, 234, 388, 410
betrayal, 147
betrayer, 16, 25
be true, 58
be wanting, 7
beyond, 48
bide, 117
big, 204
bind, 10, 99
biography, 405
bitter, 149
blacken, 94
blackness, 272
blame, 328
blamelessness, 392
bland, 96, 290, 386
blasphemy, 360
blemish, 47
blemished, 314
blessing, 6, 113, 256, 286, 300
blind 389

bluff, 324
blunt, 204, 324
bluntness, 20
body, 284
"boil down," 49
boisterous, 107
bold, 30, 241
boldness, 289
boon, 113, 256, 286
boorish, 324
boorishness, 23, 359
bore, 181
bound, 115
boundary, 115
bounded, 254
bountiful, 285
bounty, 216
brave, 30
brawn, 284
break, 179
break down, 179, 410
break up, 140
breed, 192
brevity, 122
brief, 254, 269
bright, 94, 144, 193
    (see syn. for Dark, 143)
brilliancy, 245
brilliant, 144, 193
brimful, 431
brimmed, 431
brimming, 431
bring, 384
broken, 208, 212
brusk, 324
brutality, 92, 320, 359
brute force, 284
build, 151
build up, 192
bungling, 126, 394
buoy, 174
busy, 50, 181, 246, 431
    (see syn. for Idle, 245)
but, 44
by and by, 247

calculable, 197
calculate, 210
calculated, 197
calculation, 17, 182
calm, 30, 62, 169, 404
calmness, 35, 46, 54, 182, 231
cancel, 134
candor, 146, 242, 332, 426
canopy of heaven, 14
capability, 251
capacity, 245
capitulate, 135
capitulation, 147
capricious, 194
captivity, 271
capture, 150
care, 55, 416
care for, 13

careless, 109, 169, 258, 330, 385, 419, 436
carelessness, 33, 46, 54, 110
caress
  (see syn. for Affront), 29
carry, 384
cast away, 121
cast down, 410
castigate, 310
cast out, 10, 121, 388
casual, 255, 295
causal, 152
caution, 182, 416
cede, 135
celibacy, 279
censure, 56, 328
center, 97
certain, 13, 184, 329
certainty, 17, 150, 164, 165, 196, 198, 203, 231, 243, 331, 332
cessation, 19
chance, 142, 331
change, 207
changeableness, 253
changeless, 202
chaos, 413
charge, 10, 56
charity, 50
chasten, 310
chastise, 310
chastisement, 341
check, 338, 350, 380
cheer, 153, 174, 365
cheerful, 94
cheering, 426
cheerless, 127
cheery, 94
cherish, 1, 6, 13, 192, 363
  (see syn. for Abandon, 1)
chief, 16, 30
chill, 44
chimerical, 248
choice, 296, 331
choleric, 241
Christian, 392
chronicle, 40, 405
churlish, 48
churlishness, 92
circumference, 115
circumscribed, 254
circumspection, 416
citadel, 97
citizen, 36
citylike, 376
civilized, 84
claim, 1, 68, 363
classify, 160, 287
clean, 147
cleanse, 147
clear, 130, 144, 184, 193
clearness, 259
clever, 79
cling to, 61, 140

cloak, 133
clog, 350
close, 218
cloud, 369
cloudiness, 369
cloudy, 125
clownish, 324
clownishness, 23, 359
clumsiness, 23, 255
clumsy, 34, 88, 126, 173, 204, 298, 394
coarse, 173, 204, 324
coarseness, 359
coincidence, 127
cold, 62, 136, 169, 215, 352
coldness, 182, 385
collect, 61
collected, 30
collectively, 55
colonize, 192
color, 94
combine, 12
come into being, 156
come into view, 8
come short, 162, 408
come to life, 156
comfort, 113, 286, 308, 331, 363
command, 68, 339, 371
commander, 16
commanding, 319
commence, 178
commend, 129
commendation, 364
commendatory, 109
commerce, 404
common, 176, 239, 261, 349, 409
commonplace, 15, 78, 176, 197, 409
common-sense, 15
common sense, 245
commotion, 367
communicate, 414
compactness, 122
companionship, 369
company, 369
compassion, 370
compatible, 252
compel, 10
  (see syn. for Hinder), 234
compensation, 220
competent, 432
complacency, 318, 363
complaint, 56
complaisant, 9, 290, 302, 318
complete, 12
compliant, 9, 302, 318, 357
complimentary, 109
comply, 222, 301
composed, 30
composure, 46
compression, 122
compulsion, 121, 271

conceal, 50, 133
concealed, 188
concealment, 369
conceit, 289
conceited, 86
conceive, 178
conceived, 355
concert, 127
conciliate, 29
conciseness, 122
conclude, 343, 411
concluding, 334
conclusion, 332
concord, 63, 86, 127, 180
concur, 301
concurrence, 63, 127
condemn, 10, 310
condemnation, 56, 328, 341
condensation, 122
condense, 49
conditional, 9
condole with, 134
condone, 65
confess, 234
confide in, 164
confidence, 35, 54, 153, 164, 289, 331
confident, 30
confine, 150
confirm, 6, 108
confiscate, 42
conflict, 228
conformity, 63, 127
confound, 3, 21
confuse, 21, 66
confusedly, 55
confusion, 71, 413
congeniality, 53
conjecture, 142
conjoin, 12
consent, 301, 304
consent to, 339
consequence, 114
consequent, 334
conservative, 353
conserve, 13, 307
consider, 13
considerate, 109
consistent, 13, 252
consolation, 286
console, 134
consolidate, 61
consonance, 63, 156
conspicuous, 193, 276
constancy, 116
constant, 202, 261
consternation, 71
constitutional, 9
constraint, 170, 271
construct, 151
consummation, 52
contaminate, 124
contaminating, 439
contamination, 439

contemn, 27, 115, 433
contempt, 184, 196, 328
contemptible, 78, 211, 376, 407
contend, 31
content, 29, 331, 363
contention, 131, 228
contentious, 215, 241
contentment, 46, 318, 331
contest, 131, 228
contingency, 296
contingent, 9, 248, 295
continuance, 116
continue, 2, 6, 117, 412
contract, 343
contradict, 31, 402
contradiction, 79
contrariety, 428
contravene, 402
contributory, 28, 337
control, 371
controllable, 357
controversy, 131, 228
controvert, 402
contumely, 196
converse, 369
convexity, 238
convey, 384
convict, 10, 310
conviction, 164, 332
cool, 30, 62, 102, 169
coolness, 46, 73
cooperating, 28
cooperative, 28
correct, 310
corrupt, 47, 124, 314
corrupted, 314
countenance, 365
counteract, 3, 232
counterfeit, 77
countryman, 36
courage, 153
courageous, 30
court, 1
courteous, 96
courtesy, 18
courtly, 84
cover, 74, 133
covert, 188
cover (up), 50
covet, 4
covetous, 218
cowardice, 344, 416
cowardliness, 344
cowardly, 98
coyness, 172, 249
crabbed, 48, 322
crafty, 108
crammed, 431
crave, 4
create, 151
creation, 114
credit, 83
cringing, 98
crooked, 373

crowded, 431
cruel, 48
cruelty, 283, 320
crushed, 212
crusty, 48
crystalline, 144
cultured, 84, 376
cunning, 108
curse, 341
cursed, 239
curtail, 49, 343
customary, 349
cut, 23
cut down, 49
cynicism, 197

damage, 338
damp, 44
dangerous, 382
daring, 30, 193
dark, 188, 272
darken, 94
darkness, 272
dauntless, 30
dazzling, 144
dead, 38, 136
deadness, 182, 385
deaf, 136
dearth, 189
debase, 47, 124, 188
debate, 131
deceased, 38
deceit, 427
deceitful, 108, 240
deception, 427
decided, 202
decision, 164, 331
decline, 31, 121, 338, 375, 401
decomposition, 428
decree, 17
deduct, 22
deed, 340
deep, 234
deface, 28
defaced, 314
defeat, 162, 435
defect, 189
defective, 314
defend, 1, 74, 363, 394
defense, 74, 143
deference, 173
deferential, 357
deficiency, 189
deficient, 314, 323
defile, 124
defiled, 347
defilement, 439
defiling, 439
deform, 28
deformed, 88, 173, 314
defunct, 38
defy, 57
degrade, 188
degraded, 234

delay, 338, 350
deliberation, 19
delicate, 84, 231
delight, 6, 116, 308, 318
delusion, 427
demolish, 410
demonstrable, 13
demonstrate, 210
demonstrated, 13
demonstration, 79, 196, 246, 332
demur, 31
demureness, 317
denial, 194, 315, 342
denounce, 3
denunciation, 328
deny, 31, 42, 57, 68, 76, 133, 380, 402
depart, 5, 354
departure, 183
depend on, 164
depend upon, 164
deprave, 124
depress, 47, 188
depressed, 234
depressing, 322
derange, 21, 66
derangement, 413
descend, 375
desecrate, 154
desert, 410
deserter, 25
desertion, 147
designing, 108
desire, 4, 6
   (see syn. for Antipathy, 52)
desirous, 361
despair, 52, 179
despair of, 52
despatch, 26
despicable, 78, 211
despise, 27, 115, 433
destitution, 189, 200, 442
destroy, 134, 162, 341, 410
destruction, 338, 435
detach, 58, 72, 207, 287
detached, 26, 291
deter, 3, 44, 254, 317
deteriorate, 47
determination, 164
determine, 210
determined, 162, 202
detest, 27, 433
detestation, 60
detriment, 338
develop, 2, 192
developed, 270
development, 114, 245
dexterous, 79
die, 358
differ, 31
difference, 62, 228, 273
different, 37
difficulty, 170

diffidence, 172, 173, 249, 305, 317
diffuse, 417
dignified, 86, 319
dignify, 144
dilate, 122
dilatory, 298
diligent, 246
dim, 125
diminish, 22, 259
diminutive, 269
dimness, 272
diplomatic, 108
direct, 130, 339
directness, 122
dirty, 294, 347
disadvantage, 338, 430
disaffected, 215
disaffection, 39
disagree, 31
disagreeable, 48, 127, 322
disagreement, 228, 391
disallow, 42
disappoint, 380
disappointing, 322
disappointment, 435
disapprobation, 328
disapproval, 199, 328, 342
disapprove, 3, 42
disarrange, 21, 66, 207
disarrangement, 413
disarray, 166
disaster, 435
disavow, 57, 133
disband, 140
disbelief, 194
discard, 72
discharge, 65, 67, 140
disclaim, 57, 121
disclose, 234
discomfort, 170
discompose, 21
disconcert, 3
disconnect, 58, 69, 72, 76, 261, 287
disconnected, 26, 291
disconnection, 428
discontented, 127
discord, 41, 281, 228
discourage, 3, 232, 254, 317
discourteous, 324
discover, 234, 411
   (see syn. for Hide, 233)
discovery, 243
discredit, 196
discriminate, 287
discussion, 131
disdain, 433
diseased, 231
disengage, 58, 287
disentangle, 261
disfavor, 199
disfigure, 28
disgorge, 10

disgrace, 188, 196
disguise, 133
disgust, 60
disgusting, 88, 173
dishabille, 166
dishonest, 240
dishonesty, 264
dishonor, 115, 188, 196, 433
disinclination, 34
disinclined, 22
disinfect, 147
disingenuous, 240
disintegration, 70
disinter, 234
disinterested, 433
disjoin, 21, 69, 72, 287
disjoined, 26
disjoint, 21
disjunction, 428
dislike, 27, 34, 60, 73, 184, 199
dislocate, 21
disloyalty, 39
dismay, 71
dismember, 21
dismiss, 67, 121, 140, 427
disorder, 21, 66, 413
disorderly, 294
disown, 133
disparage
   (see syn. for Praise, 327)
disparagement, 328
dispassionate, 62, 169
disperse, 10, 45, 66, 140
dispersion, 128
dispirited, 38
displace, 21, 207
displeasing, 173, 322
dispose, 160
disposed, 361
dispose of, 346
disproportion, 228, 391
disprove, 402
disputation, 131
dispute, 31, 131, 402
disputed, 77
disqualified, 24
disquiet, 170, 181, 367
disregard, 110, 115, 433
disrelish, 60
disrepute, 196
disrupt, 69
dissatisfied, 127
dissemble, 133
dissension, 131, 228
dissent, 31, 194
dissever, 22, 287
dissimilar, 37
dissimilarity, 273, 391
dissimulate, 133
dissipate, 10, 45
dissociate, 69, 72, 76, 287
dissociated, 291
dissociation, 428

dissolve, 140
dissuade, 3, 44, 254, 317
distance, 62, 73
distant, 26, 215
distaste, 60
distasteful, 173
distend, 122
distinct, 37, 184, 291
distinguish, 261
distract, 10, 181
distress, 55, 136
distressed, 127
distressing, 322
distrust, 52, 71, 194
disturb, 21, 66, 136, 181, 207
disturbance, 55, 367
disturbed, 107
disunion, 41, 228, 428
disunite, 69, 72, 287
disunited, 291
diverge, 69
divert, 72, 303
divide, 45, 69, 287
division, 428
divorce, 41, 69, 72, 73, 279, 428
divulge, 234
docile, 9, 203, 302, 357 368
dogged, 48, 162
doing, 245, 340
dome of heaven, 14
domination, 371
dominion, 371
doom, 310
doubt, 52, 71, 153, 194, 296
doubtful, 56, 191, 248, 273, 330
doubtfulness, 296
dowdy, 294
drag, 350
drained, 323
dread, 52
dreary, 127, 322
drive
   (see syn. for Draw, 164)
drive away, 44
droop, 179, 401
drop, 112, 375, 401, 410, 427
drowsy, 35, 436
drunkenness, 11
dubious, 56, 125, 273, 382
dubiousness, 296
ductile, 9
dulcet, 93
dull, 19, 34, 35, 38, 126, 171, 298, 352, 378, 389, 436
dulness, 20, 34, 182, 219, 255, 327, 444
dunce, 381
duplicity, 427
dusk, 272
dutiful, 302, 357
dwarfed, 234
dye, 94

each, 96
eager, 361
eagerness, 55
earnings, 220
ease, 54, 308, 331, 444
easy, 109, 157, 250, 386, 403, 426
easy-going, 109
economy, 189
educated, 246
effect, 114
effective, 432
effeminacy, 344
efficient, 432
egotism, 289
egress, 183
either, 96
eject, 10
ejection, 183
elaborated, 191
elation, 153
elegant, 84, 376
elevate, 144
elevated, 101
elevation, 14, 238
eliminate, 287
elude, 23
emaciated, 231
emancipate, 368
embark, 354
embark in, 178
embitter, 40
embodiment, 245
embolden, 174
emerge, 8
eminence, 238
eminent, 86
emit, 10
emotion, 55
empire, 371
employed, 246
empower, 339
empyrean, 14
enact, 6, 108
encomium, 364
encourage, 82, 119, 174, 365, 368
encouragement, 153
encouraging, 109
end, 114
  (see syn. for Beginning, 89)
endurance, 19
endure, 117
enduring, 425
enemy, 16, 25, 68
energetic, 193
enfeeble, 188
enforce, 68, 108
enforcement, 4
enhance, 2, 40
enjoin, 339
enjoy, 4
enjoyment, 4, 6, 52, 308
enlarge, 2, 122

enlightened, 101
en masse, 55
enmity, 41, 73
ennui, 181
enslave, 150
entertaining, 426
enter upon, 178, 404
entirety, 311
entrance, 85
epitomize, 49
equity, 257
eradicate, 320, 341
erroneous, 330
error, 62, 427, 443
essence, 76
essential, 36
establish, 6, 108, 210
established, 13, 261
estate, 97
esteem, 4, 6
esteemed, 86
estrange, 69, 165
estranged, 215
estrangement, 73, 341
eternal, 425
eulogistic, 109
eulogize, 13, 129, 394
eulogy, 364
evanescent, 254
event, 114
everlasting, 425
every, 96
everyday, 15, 409
evidence, 196, 243, 332
evident, 184, 270
evil, 373, 437
exact, 68
exalt, 144
exalted, 86, 101, 319
excellence, 392
exception, 379
exceptional, 217, 299, 429
excess, 11
exchange, 346
excite, 38, 368
excited, 107
excitement, 55, 367
exclusion, 183
excrescence, 238
excuse, 65, 366, 370
execrate, 27
execution, 245, 340
exercise, 4
exhausted, 231, 323
exhibit, 234
exhume, 234
exist, 58, 156
exit, 183
exonerate, 65, 132
exotic, 336
expand, 122, 389
expectancy, 153
expectation, 46, 153
expedient, 432

expedite, 26, 119, 412
expel, 388
explanation, 373
explicate, 261
explicit, 270
exploded, 77
expose, 3, 234, 383
exposed, 270, 382
exposure, 166
expulsion, 183
extend, 2
exterminate, 341
external, 255
extinguish, 102
extirpate, 320, 341
extol, 13, 394
extort, 68
extraordinary, 429
extravagance, 216
extricate, 261
extrinsic, 255
exude, 10
exult, 291
exultation, 116

fabrication, 427
fabulous, 77, 355
facile, 157
fact, 40, 150, 165, 196, 198, 203, 243, 244, 245, 332
fail, 7, 75, 87, 135, 162, 179, 358, 401, 408
failing, 231
fail of, 114, 313
failure, 189, 304, 435
faint, 179, 401
faint-hearted, 98
fainting, 231
fair, 109, 146
fair dealing, 146
fairness, 214, 257, 426
fair play, 257
fair weather, 404
faithfulness, 257
faithless, 194, 240
fall, 87, 135, 179, 375, 401
fallen, 212
fallible, 314
falling back, 338
falling off, 338
fall short, 408
fall short of, 114
fall under, 112
false, 77, 194, 240, 330, 355
falsehood, 427
falseness, 427
falsity, 427
falter, 179, 401
faltering, 153
familiar, 349
famine, 200
fan, 38
fanciful, 355
fancy, 142

far from, 48
fashionable, 53
fast, 112, 200
fasten, 99
fasting, 200
fate, 17
fatigue, 181
fatuity, 23, 443
faulty, 314, 330
favor, 1, 13, 113
favorable, 28, 315, 361
favoritism, 264
fear, 52, 344
    (see syn. for Fortitude, 211)
fearful, 98
fearless, 30
feasible, 250
feckless, 171
feeble, 171, 211, 250
feebleness, 327
feeling, 55
feigned, 355
fellow-countryman, 36
fellow-feeling, 53
fellowship, 369
feminine
    (see syn. for Masculine, 279)
ferocity, 320
fickle, 194
fickleness, 153, 253
fiction, 427
fictitious, 77, 355
fierce, 107, 241
fiery, 241
filled, 431
fill up, 12
filthy, 347
finite, 254
firm, 162, 202, 329
firmament, 14
firmness, 116, 331
fixed, 202, 261
fixedness, 116
fixity, 116, 331
flat, 352, 403
flattering, 109
flavorless, 352
flee, 401
flight, 147
flimsy, 250
fling wide, 122
flourish, 156
fly, 135, 401
foe, 16, 68
foggy, 125
follower, 120
following, 334
folly, 23, 219, 345, 430, 443
foment, 2
fool, 381
foolish, 126, 378
foolishness, 443
forbearance, 50, 243

forbid, 42
forbidding, 322, 342
force, 4
foreign, 27, 336
foreordination, 17
forfeit, 5, 75, 135
forfend, 5
forget, 115, 366
forgetfulness, 282
forgive, 65, 366
forgiveness, 370
forlorn, 127
formal, 261
fortuitous, 255
fortuity, 296
forwardness, 289
foster, 192
foul, 347
foxy, 108
fragile, 231
frail, 231
frank, 146
frankness, 146, 242, 289, 332, 426
frantic, 107
fraudulent, 240
free, 25, 67, 92, 119, 207, 285, 366, 368, 414
free agency, 331
freedom, 289, 296, 331
free-thinking, 197
free will, 331
frenzied, 107
frenzy, 55
fresh, 53, 193, 336
friend, 180
friendly, 278, 290
friendship, 180
    (see syn. for Battle, 86; Enmity, 180; Hatred, 229; Quarrel, 348)
frightened, 98
frightful, 88
frigid, 62, 169, 215
frivolous, 250
frugality, 189
fruit, 114
fruitless, 171
frustrate, 3, 162
frustration, 435
full, 431
fulsome, 173
furious, 107, 241
fury, 55
futile, 378
futility, 430

gainsay, 402
gallant, 30
garrulous, 414
gather together, 61
gaudy, 173
gay, 385, 419
generous, 285, 433

genial, 94, 96, 109, 262, 290, 318, 386
gentle, 9, 133, 203, 290, 302, 357, 368, 386, 403
gentleness, 18, 50, 248
genuine, 146
genuineness, 242
germane, 36
get, 384
    (see syn. for Abandon, 1)
get the worst of, 87
ghastly, 88
giddy, 419
give, 384
give back, 403
give consent, 339
give leave, 339
give out, 179
give permission, 339
give up, 10, 75, 112, 114, 179, 388, 403, 427
gleaming, 144
gloom, 272
gloominess, 272
gloomy, 322
glorious, 319
glory, 116
glowing, 144
glum, 322
gluttony, 11
go, 354
go away, 354
godlessness, 360
godliness, 392
go down, 87, 375
good, 315
    (see syn. for Bad, 80)
good faith, 214
good fortune, 286
good luck, 286
good nature, 18
good-natured, 109, 278, 290
goodness, 392
good sense, 259
gorged, 431
go under, 87
governable, 318
government, 371
grace, 370
graceful, 84
    (see syn. for Awkward, 78)
gradual, 403
grand, 101, 319
grateful, 426
gratification, 6, 286, 318
gratify, 29
gratifying, 426
gravity, 444
great, 101, 204, 319
greed, 11
greediness, 92
greedy, 218
grief
    (see syn. for Happiness, 226)

grieve, 136
grim, 88, 322
grisly, 88
gross, 347
grossness, 359
grotesque, 88, **173**
group, 160
grow, 156
grow worse, **358**
gruff, 48
guerdon, 220
guess, 142
guile, 427
guilelessness, **146, 332, 426**

hallow, 147
hand, 384
handy, 79
happiness, 286
  (see syn. for Grief, 233)
happy
  (see syn. for Sad, 377)
hard-heartedness, 320
hardness, 283, 320, 363, 385
hark, 106
harmless, 47, 199, 203, 211, 338
harmonious, 252
harmony, 53, 63, 127, 156, 180
harsh, 173, 322
harshness, 92, 283, 320
hasten, 26, 119, 343
hate, 27
hateful, 48, 322
hater, 25
hatred, 60, 184
  (see syn. for Friendship, 215; Love, 276)
haughtiness, 289
haughty, 86, 241
haunt, 1
hazardous, 382
heal, 362
health, 159
healthful, 315
hearken, 106
hearty, 193
heated, 107
heavy, 19, 34, 35, 204, 298
heedless, 169, 258, 419, 436
heedlessness, 33, 110, 345
height, 14, 238
heighten, 40
help, 113, 249, 256
helper, 180
helpful, 28, 315, 319, 426
helping, 337
helpless, 211, 394
helplessness, 327
hereafter, 247
heroic, 30
hesitancy, 71, 153
hesitation, 153, 416
heterogeneous, 37

hidden, 188
hide, 50, 133
hideous, 88, 173
hiding, 369
high-spirited, 241
hill, 14, 238
hillock, 238
hilly, 208
hind, 334
hinder, 3, 232, 254, 317, 334, 350
  (see syn. for Quicken, 350)
hinderer, 16, 68, 77
hindmost, 334
hindrance, 315
hissing, 328
history, 40, 203, 405
  (see syn. for Fiction, 20·
hold, 1, 117, 140, 363, 384
hold aloof, 260
hold back, 317
hold fast, 208
hold off, 260
hold one's ground, 8
hold one's place, 8
holiness, 392
homelike, 94
homogeneous, 130, 285
honest, 146, 433
honesty, 146, 214, 242, 257, 332, 426
honeyed, 93
honor, 29, 144, 257
honorable, 86, 433
hope, 153
hopefulness, 153
horizontal, 403
horrible, 322
horrid, 88, 173
hostile, 215, 342
hostility, 41, 199, 228
however, 88
huge, 204
humane, 84, 101
  (see syn. for Barbarous, 84)
humble, 9, 78, 188
humiliation, 188, 196
humility, 46, 173, 249, 317, 335
hurry, 26, 119, 343
hurt, 136, 199, 338
hush, 50, 106, 399, 404
hypocritical, 240
hyperphysical, 318
hypothetical, 355

icy, 62
identical, 285
identity, 116, 156
idiocy, 443
idiot, 381
idiotic, 126, 389
idle, 19, 171, 250
idleness, 253, 444

idler, 381
ignoble, 218
ignominy, 196, 328
ignoramus, 381
ignorance, 17, 171, 267
ignorant, 15, 126, 136, 373
ignore, 23, 115, 274, 313
ignoring, 17
ill, 231
ill-becoming, 89
ill-behaved, 324
ill-bred, 324
ill-breeding, 23
ill-conditioned, 48
ill-contrived, 205
ill-disposed, 215, 342
illegitimate, 27
ill-fitted, 205
ill-fitting, 89, 205
ill-humored, 48, 322
illiberal, 218
illiberality, 92
illiteracy, 171, 267
illiterate, 15
illiterate person, 381
ill-mannered, 324
ill manners, 23
ill-natured, 48, 322
ill-starred, 212
ill-suited, 205
ill-tempered, 48
ill-timed, 205
illumined, 144
illusory, 355
illustrious, 86
ill will, 92
imaginary, 355
imagination, 142
imbecile, 389
imbecility, 219, 327, 443
immaterial, 250, 318
immense, 204
immobility, 19, 290
immodest, 347
immortal, 425
immunity, 143
immutable, 202, 329
impair, 47
impalpable, 188
impartiality, 257
impeach, 10
impecuniosity, 442
impede, 3, 254, 350
impel, 365, 368
impenetrable, 188
impenitence, 363
imperceptible, 188
imperfect, 314, 382
imperishable, 425
impertinent, 27, 241, 324
impiety, 360
implacability, 283
implicit, 191
implied, 191

impolicy, 430
impolite, 324
imposture, 427
impotence, 327
impoverish, 188
impoverished, 323
imprison, 150
imprisonment, 271
improbable, 56, 248, 273
improper, 89, 205, 373
improvement, 256
improvidence, 345
imprudence, 345, 443
imprudent
    (see syn. for Shrewd, 388)
impudence, 289
impudent, 241, 324
impure, 239, 347
imputation, 56
inability, 327
inaccurate, 330
inaction, 19, 304
inactive, 19, 35, 298
inactivity, 19
inadequacy, 189, 430
inadequate, 24, 133, 205, 323,
    353
inadhesive, 25
inadmissible, 27
inadvertent, 419
inanimate, 38
inapplicable, 27
inapposite, 27
inappropriate, 205
inaptitude, 327
inartistic, 173
inattention, 110, 253
inattentive, 258, 419, 436
inaugurate, 404
inauspicious, 342
incapacity, 327
incarcerate, 150
incarnation, 245
incautious, 436
incidental, 255
incite, 365, 368
inclined, 208, 361
incompetence, 327
incompetent, 24
incomplete, 314, 353
incongruity, 228, 391
inconsequential, 250
inconsiderable, 250, 269, 337
inconsiderate, 419, 436
inconsistency, 228
inconstancy, 253
incontestable, 13, 329
incontrovertible, 13
incorrect, 373
incorruptible, 433
increase, 2, 12, 40, 192
incredible, 273
incredulity, 194
inculpate, 10

incurious, 258
indecent, 89, 347
indecision, 153
indecorous, 89
indefinite, 191
indelicate, 347
independence, 70, 331
independent, 86, 152
indeterminate, 191
indifference, 34, 46, 60, 73,
    110, 182, 197
indifferent, 62, 169, 215, 250,
    258, 262
indigence, 442
indirect, 373
indiscretion, 289, 345, 443
indiscriminately, 55
indisposed. 22
indisputable, 13, 184
indistinct, 125
indolence, 34, 253
indolent, 19
indubitable, 13, 184
indulge, 119
indulgent, 290, 386
industrious, 246
ineffective, 171
ineffectiveness, 304
ineffectual, 171
inefficacious, 171
inefficiency. 304, 327
inefficient, 171
inequity, 264
inert, 19, 34, 298
inertia, 19
inertness, 34
inexact, 330
inexcusable, 434
inexpediency, 430
inexpedient, 205
inexperience, 17, 267
inexpert, 394
inexpiable, 434
infallible, 13, 329
infamy, 196
inferior, 24, 78, 176, 234, 314,
    337
infidelity, 194
infinite, 152
infinitesimal, 269
inflexible, 162
infrequent, 217, 429
ingenuousness, 242, 332, 426
inhabited, 431
inharmonious, 173
inhibit, 254
inhumanity, 92, 320
inimical, 215
iniquitous, 373
initiate, 178, 404
injure, 47
injury, 56, 199, 338
injustice, 264
innocence, 392, 426

innocent, 141
    (see syn. for Criminal, 141)
innocuous, 315
inoperative, 171
insecure, 382
insensibility, 385
insensible, 136
inside, 97
insignificant, 250, 269, 385,
    407
insincere, 108
insipid, 352
insist, 68
insolent, 86, 324
insolence, 324
inspirit, 174
in spite of, 44
instability, 153
instigate, 119, 365
instigator, 16
institute, 6, 404
instructed, 246
insufficiency, 189
insufficient, 24, 314, 323
insult, 56, 199
insulting. 324
insure, 210
intangible, 318
integrity, 214, 257, 392
intellectual, 96, 101, 318
intelligence, 96, 245
intelligent, 101
intemperance, 11
intensify, 40
intention, 17
interior, 97
in the future, 247
intoxication, 11
intractable, 162
intrepid, 30
intriguing, 108
introduce, 6
inutility, 304, 430
invariability, 116
invariable, 202
inventor, 30
invigorate, 421
invigorating, 315
invisible, 188, 318
irrational, 378
irregular, 208, 299
irregularity, 413
irrelevant, 27
irreligion, 360
irresolute, 302
irresolution. 153
irresponsible, 366
irritation, 170
isolation, 70
issue, 114

jammed, 431
jocose, 385
join, 99, 362
jolly, 385

journey, 5
joy, 6, 286, 291
jumble, 21, 66
just, 141
justice, 257, 283
justify, 132

keep, 1, 117, 140, 307, 384
keep aloof, 260
keep away, 260
keep back, 50
keep clear, 260
keep on, 412
keep out, 260
keep secret, 50
keep up, 412
kind, 203, 278, 290, 318
kind-hearted, 278
kindle, 38
kindliness, 53, 180
kindly, 278
kindness, 18, 180
knoll, 238
know, 411
knowing, 108

labor, 181
lack, 7, 189, 442
laconic, 414
land, 97
landsman, 379
large, 204
lassitude, 181
lasting, 425
late, 336
latent, 188
later, 334
latitudinarianism, 197
latter, 334
laud, 13, 129, 394
laudatory, 109
launch, 178
law, 17, 371
lawful, 141
lawfulness, 257
lawless, 366
lay bare, 234
lay open, 234
laziness, 34
lazy, 19
leader, 16
learned, 246
leave, 121, 304, 354
leave open, 122
legal, 141
legalize, 6
leisure, 444
lengthy, 417
leniency, 50, 248
lenient, 9, 133, 386
lenity, 50, 248
lessen, 22, 259
let, 339
let alone, 260

let be, 260
let go, 75, 112, 114, 119, 410,
    427
let loose, 368, 389
level, 403
lewd, 347
liberal, 262, 285
liberality, 216
liberate, 67, 119, 389
liberty, 304
license, 119, 304, 339
lie, 427
life-giving, 315
lifeless, 38
light, 144, 157, 250, 385, 426
light-heartedness, 54
like, 4, 285
likeness, 156
limit, 343
limited, 9, 254, 269
list, 106
listen, 106
listless, 62
literal, 197
literalness, 203
little, 254, 269, 407
live, 156
loathing, 60, 184
loathsome, 149
lofty, 86, 241, 319
logic, 196
logical, 13
loneliness, 128
long, 417
long-suffering, 50
loose, 25, 92, 119, 207, 330
loosen, 119, 207, 406
loquacious, 414
loquaciousness, 289
loquacity, 289
lose, 75, 114, 135, 313, 408
loss, 338
love, 4, 50
    (see syn. for Antipathy, 52;
    Enmity, 180; Hatred, 229)
loving, 290
low, 176, 234, 403
lower, 188
lowliness, 249, 335
lowly, 9, 78
loyalty, 371
lucid, 144, 184
lucidity, 259
lukewarmness, 182
luminous, 144
lump, 238
luscious, 93
luxury, 216
lying, 240

magnify, 2, 40
maidenhood, 279
main body, 59
maintain, 1, 108, 363

make, 151
    (see syn. for Abolish, 5;
    Break, 98; Demolish, 150)
make good, 403
make known, 234
make merry, 291
make sure, 210
make worse, 40
maladroit, 394
maladroitness, 327
malevolence, 92
malignity, 92
manageable, 357, 368
maneuvering, 108
manifest, 184, 234, 270
mar, 28, 47, 162
marred, 314
masculine
    (see syn. for Feminine, 200)
mask, 133
mass, 311
material substance, 284
matter, 284
matter-of-course, 15
matter-of-fact, 15
meager, 314
mean, 78, 176, 218, 234, 250,
    269, 323, 376, 407
measurable, 254
meek, 9
meekness, 249, 335
melancholy, 322
memoir, 405
mend, 99, 362
mendacious, 240
mendacity, 427
mendicancy, 442
mental, 318
mercilessness, 320
mercy, 370
meretricious, 173
meritorious, 141
methodical, 261
microscopic, 269
mighty, 319
migrate, 5
mild, 9, 94, 133, 203, 290, 386
mildness, 18, 50, 248
mind, 96
minion, 120
minor, 250, 337
minute, 269
    (see syn. for Large, 268)
misapplied, 205
misapply, 21, 154
misapprehend, 313
misapprehension, 267
misappropriate, 154
miscalculated, 205
miscalculation, 443
miscarriage, 435
miscarry, 162, 408
misconceive, 313
misconception, 267

miscontrived, 205
miserable, 127, 212, 322
miserly, 218, 323
misery, 442
misfit, 21
misfitted, 205
misfitting, 205
misgiving, 71, 194
misjoin, 21
misjudgment, 443
misplace, 21
miss, 75, 114, 162, 313, 408
mistaken, 330
misty, 330
misunderstanding, 267
misuse, 154
mixed, 347
model, 168
moderate, 133, 254, 353
modern, 53, 336
modest, 281
modesty, 172, 173, 249, 305, 317, 335
modish, 53
monstrosity, 379
monstrous, 299
moral, 141, 318
morality, 392
morose, 48
mortal, 434
motion, 367
mound, 238
mount, 14, 238
mountain, 14, 238
mournful, 322
move, 5
movement, 367
munificent, 285
mysterious, 125
   (see syn. for Clear, 124)
mystery, 369

nakedness, 166
narrow, 254, 269, 323
native, 36
native-born inhabitant, 36
natural, 261, 349, 409
naturalized person, 36
nature, 76
nauseous, 149
nebulous, 330
necessity, 17, 121, 231, 271
nectared, 93
need, 7, 189, 200, 442
needless, 250, 295
neglect, 33, 110, 115, 162, 253, 274, 366, 427
   (see syn. for Care, 110)
neglectful, 419, 436
negligence, 33, 110, 253
negligent, 109, 169, 171, 294, 419, 436
negligible, 250, 337
neither, 96

nevertheless, 44, 88
new, 53, 336
   (see syn. for Old, 303)
nice, 84
niggardliness, 92
niggardly, 218, 323
nightly, 143
noble, 86, 101, 319
nocturnal, 143
nonchalance, 54
none, 96
non-essential, 250, 295
nonsense, 79, 443
no one, 96
normal, 261, 349
not any, 96
notwithstanding, 44, 88
novel, 336
nudity, 166
numbness, 385

obduracy, 363
obedience, 371
obedient, 302, 357, 368
obey, 222
objection, 315
obligate, 10
obligation, 271
oblige, 10
obliging, 318
oblivion, 196, 282
oblivious, 436
obliviousness, 282
obloquy, 328
obscene, 347
obscuration, 369
obscure, 125, 188
   (see syn. for Clear, 124)
obscurity, 196, 272
obsolete
   (see syn. for New, 297)
obstinacy, 363
obstinate, 162, 241
obstruct, 3, 350
obtuse, 378
obtuseness, 20, 219
obvious, 15, 130, 184
occult, 188
occupied, 246, 431
occupy, 1
odious, 88
offense, 56, 341
offensive, 173, 322
old
   (see syn. for New, 297; Youthful, 445)
omission, 110
omit, 427
on hand, 12
on the contrary, 44
on the other hand, 44
opaque, 125
open, 122, 146, 389
opening, 85

openness, 146, 242, 332, **426**
operation, 4
opinionated, 162
opponent, 16, 25, 68, **77**
oppose, 31, 232, 402
opposer, 16, 68, **77**
opposition, 73, 228, **315**
oppress, 150
oppression, 271
option, 296
optional, 295
opulence, 216
ordainment, 17
order, 160, 339, **371**
orderly, 261
ordinance, 17
ordinary, 15, **76, 197, 261,** 349, 409
original, 59, 152, 168
originate, 178, 404
originator, 30
outcome, 114
outgrowth, 114
out of place, 27
out-of-the-way, 429
outside, 48
outward, 255
overflowing, 431
overlook, 23, 65, **115, 313,** 366, 427
oversight, 33, 110, 282
overthrow, 134, 410, **435**
own, 363

packed, 431
painful, 322
palliative, 353
paltry, 78, 250, **269**
panegyric, 364
panegyrize, 13
paradox, 79
parcel, 45
pardon, 65, 132, 366, **370**
parsimonious, 218
part, 69, 287
partial, 353
partiality, 264
particular, 217
pass, 23
passage, 85
pass by, 23, 427
passion, 55
passionate, 107
passive, 368
passivity, 19
pass over, 366
patience, 50, 248
   (see syn. for Anger, **49)**
patient, 203
patriotic, 433
pattern, 168
pauperism, 442
peace, 50, 86, 248, 308, **409**
peaceable, 368

peaceableness, 50, 248
peaceful, 203
peacefulness, 50, 248
peak, 238
peculiar, 299
penalty, 220, 283, 309, 341
penurious, 218
penury, 442
perceptible, 270
perfidious, 240
performance, 245, 340
perilous, 382
perimeter, 115
periodical, 261
permanence, 116
permanent, 425
  (see syn. for Transient, 424)
permission, 304
permit, 304, 339
perpetual, 425
perpetuate, 108, 307
perplexity, 170
persist, 117, 208
  (see syn. for Stop, 403)
persistence, 116
persistent, 425
perspicuous, 184
persuasion, 164
pertinent, 36
pertness, 289
pervert, 139, 154
perverted, 314
petty, 133, 218, 250, 269, 407
phlegmatic, 62, 169
pi *or* pie (print), 66
pitilessness, 320
pity, 370
place, 160
plain, 15, 130, 184
plainness, 122
plan, 17, 231
plant, 192
platonic, 62
pleasant, 157, 290, 426
please, 29
pleasure, 113, 286, 318
pliable, 302, 386
pliant, 302
policy, 182
polished, 96, 376
polite, 84, 96, 376
pollute, 124
polluted, 239, 347
polluting, 439
pollution, 439
pompous, 86
ponderous, 34
poor, 24, 314, 323, 376
populate, 192
portion, 45
possess, 140
possession, 4
possibility, 142, 296
possible, 250

posterior, 334
potent, 432
poverty, 189, 442
power, 251
powerful, 432
powerless, 171, 211
powerlessness, 304
practicable, 250
practical, 15
practice, 245
praise, 13, 129, 132, 364, 394
premeditated, 191
preparation, 17, 46
prepared, 191
present oneself, 8
preserve, 140, 307
presuming, 241
presumptuous, 241
prevent, 254
prevention, 315
princely, 86
principal, 16, 30
privacy, 128
privation, 112, 200, 442
privilege, 113
probability, 142
problematical, 248
proceed, 5
proclaim, 363
prodigal, 285
prodigality, 345
product, 114
production, 340
profane, 115, 239
profanity, 360
profitable, 315, 432
prohibition, 315
projection, 238
prolix, 417
prolong, 412
prominence, 238
promote, 6, 82, 144
  (see syn. for Allay, 38;
  Debase, 144)
prompt, 12
promulgate, 234
proof, 196, 243, 332
propagate, 192
proper, 36
propitious, 28
proposition, 373
prorogue, 140
prosaic, 197
prose, 323
prosecute, 1
prosper, 82
prosperity, 83, 113, 286
prosperous, 28
prosy, 352
protect, 1, 13, 74
protection, 143, 231
protest, 31, 42
prototype, 168
protract, 412

protuberance, 238
proud, 86, 241
prove, 210, 411
provision, 17
provoke, 38
prudence, 182
public-spirited, 433
publish, 234
punctual, 261
punish, 310
punishment, 283, 309, 341
pure, 285
purify, 147
purity, 392
purpose, 17
purposeless, 169
purposelessness, 33
pursue, 1
pusillanimity, 344
pusillanimous, 98
put forth, 10
put in an appearance, 8
put in order, 160
put in place, 160
put out, 102
put to sale, 346
put up with, 339

quantity, 311
quarrel, 131
questionable, 273
quicken, 26, 119
quiescence, 19, 290
quiet, 19, 290, 368
quietness, 305

radiant, 144
radiate, 10
raging, 107, 241
raise, 2, 144, 234
rally, 174
rampart, 238
rapacious, 218
rapture, 308
rare, 217, 299, 429
  (see syn. for General, 217;
  Normal, 298; Usual, 429)
rashness, 345
rational, 13
rationality, 259
raw, 324
read, 191
ready, 12
real, 146, 197, 329, 432
reality, 150, 165, 198, 203,
  244, 245, 332
realization, 52, 165, 245
reappear, 8
reason, 332
reasonable, 13, 109, 197
reasoning, 332
rebellion, 39
rebuff, 165
recall, 52

receive, 61, 384
recent, 53, 336
recitative, 281
recited, 191
reckless, 30, 419
recklessness, 110, 345
recollect, 52
recompense, 310
reconciliation, 370
record, 40, 108
recreate, 421
recreation, 444
rectitude, 257, 392
reduce, 22, 49, 188, 259, 343
reenact, 108
refined, 84, 96, 101, 376
refresh, 421
refund, 403
refusal, 183, 315, 342
refuse, 31, 42, 57, 68, 121, 303, 380, 388
refute, 402
regard, 13, 53, 180
regardless, 169
region, 97
regular, 197, 261, 349
reinstate, 6
reject, 5, 42, 68, 121, 165, 388
rejection, 183, 194, 342
rejoice, 291
rejoicing, 116
rejuvenating, 315
relapse, 338, 358
relax, 406, 421
relaxation, 444
release, 65, 67, 114, 368
relevant, 36
relief, 249, 286, 308
relieve, 421
relish, 4
reluctance, 34
rely on, 164
rely upon, 164
remain, 8, 117
remedy, 256
remember, 52
remiss, 171, 419
remissness, 110, 253
remote, 26
remoteness, 62
remove, 22, 72, 261, 287
renegade, 25, 139
renew, 6
renewal, 4
renumeration, 220
repair, 6, 151
repay, 403
repel, 44, 165, 317
repellent, 322, 342
repelling, 322
replenish, 192
replete, 431
reported, 355

repose, 19, 35, 290, 421, 444
reproach, 328
reprobation, 341
reproof, 328
repudiate, 57, 121, 133, 402
repudiation, 328
repugnance, 34, 60, 73, 184
repulse, 165, 199, 342
repulsion, 60, 74
repulsive, 88, 149, 322
require, 339
resemblance, 156
resentful, 241
reserve, 305
reserved, 96, 281, 414
resign, 135
resist, 5, 42, 74, 232
resistance, 74, 315
resolute, 162, 193, 202
resolution, 164, 331
resolve, 164
respect, 13
responsible, 9
rest, 19, 290, 331, 421, 444
restlessness, 367
restore, 6, 12, 114, 151, 403, 421
restrain, 254, 317, 380
restrict, 380
restricted, 254
result, 114
resume, 42
resuscitation, 4
retain, 1, 42, 61, 117, 140, 303, 363, 384
retainer, 120
retaliation, 309
retard, 254, 350
reticent, 414
retire, 135, 260
retirement, 128, 305
retiring, 281
retract, 303, 402
retreat, 74, 135, 435
retrench, 49
retribution, 309, 341
retrogression, 338
return, 403
reunite, 362
reveal, 234
reveling, 11
revelry, 11
revenge, 283
revengeful, 241
revival, 4
revive, 2, 6
riches, 216
ridicule, 27
ridiculous, 407
right, 141, 257, 392
righteousness, 257, 392
rigor, 283, 320
rim, 115
rise again, 156

rise from the dead, 156
rising, 238
risky, 382
rival, 16, 68
road, 85
robustness, 159
rolling, 208
root out, 341
root up, 320, 341
rough, 173, 208, 294
rouse, 38
roused, 107
rout, 435
rude, 173, 204, 294, 324
rudeness, 23, 359
ruffled, 107
rugged, 173, 208
ruin, 162, 338
ruined, 314
rule, 371
rush, 119, 367
rustic, 324
rusticity, 359
ruthlessness, 320

saccharine, 93
sacrilege, 360
sad
  (see syn. for Happy, 227)
sadden, 136
saddening, 322
safeguard, 143, 231
safety, 143, 231
sagacious, 13
sagacity, 245
sage, 246
salutary, 315
same, 285
sameness, 156
sanctify, 147
sanction, 339
sanity, 259
satellite, 120
satisfaction, 6, 46, 54, 318, 331
sauciness, 289
savagery, 359
scant, 133, 314, 323
scantiness, 189
scanty, 133, 269, 323
scarce, 323
scarcity, 442
scatter, 45, 66, 140
schism, 41, 228, 428
scoff at, 433
scorn, 27, 274, 328, 433
scourge, 310
screen, 133
scrimped, 323
secession, 41
seclusion, 128
secondary, 250, 337
secret, 188
secrete, 50, 133

secular, 239
secure, 99, 362
security, 35, 143, 231
sedition, 39
seek, 1
segregate, 287
seize, 42
self-abasement, 335
self-approval, 363
self-asserting, 241
self-assertive, 86
self-complacency, 363
self-conceit, 289
self-conceited, 86
self-confidence, 331
self-congratulation, 363
self-control, 50, 248
self-distrust, 173, 335
self-forgetfulness, 173
self-indulgence, 11
selfishness, 92
self-possession, 46
self-reliance, 331
self-reliant, 86
self-respectful, 86
self-restraint, 50, 248
self-satisfaction, 331
self-seeking, 92
self-sufficiency, 289
self-willed, 162
sell, 346
send out, 10
sense, 245
senseless, 126, 378
senselessness, 219, 443
sensibility, 55
sensible, 13, 197
sensitiveness, 55, 172
sensuality, 11
sentence, 310
separable, 25
separate, 26, 58, 69, 72, 76,
   140, 261, 287, 291
separated, 291
separation, 41, 70, 73, 228,
   428
serenity, 404
serfdom, 271
seriousness, 444
servant, 120
service, 256
serviceable, 315, 432
servile, 376
servitude, 271
set, 375
set about, 404
set free, 65, 67, 92, 207, 368,
   389
set going, 404
set in operation, 404
set in order, 160
set on foot, 404
set out, 354
set sail, 354

settle, 192, 210, 375
settled, 202, 329
set up, 6
sever, 69, 72, 76, 287
severance, 73, 428
severed, 291
severity, 283, 320
sew, 362
shade, 272
shadow, 272
shake, 134, 207
shake off, 112
shallow, 254, 389
shame, 188, 196
sharp, 108
shatter, 134
shelter, 74, 143
sheltered, 94
shield, 13, 74
shiftless, 394
shining, 144
shocking, 88
shoot forth, 10
short, 234, 254, 269, 314, 323
shortcoming, 189
shorten, 343
shortness, 122
short-sighted, 389
show, 234
shrewd, 108
shrinking, 98, 172, 305
shrouding, 369
shun, 5, 23
shy, 281
shyness, 71, 172, 173, 317
sick, 231
sift, 287
silence, 399
silent, 414
silliness, 443
silly, 378
similar, 285
similarity, 156
simple, 15, 130, 378
simplicity, 146, 332, 426
sincerity, 146, 242, 332, 426
singular, 217, 299, 429
sink, 179, 358, 375, 401
sinlessness, 392
skepticism, 194
skilful, 79
skilled, 246
slacken, 406
slander, 328
slanting, 208
slavery, 271
slavish, 376
slender, 269
slight, 110, 133, 157, 250, 269,
   274, 353, 366, 385, 403, 433
sloping, 208
sloth, 253
slouchy, 294
slovenly, 294

slow, 19, 34, **35, 126, 298**
   (see syn. for **Nimble, 298**)
slowness, 34
sluggish, 19, 34, **35, 298**
sluggishness, 34
sly, 108
small, 254, 269, **323**
smearing, 439
smirching, 439
smoothness, 18
smother, 102
sober, 167
sobriety, 112, **444**
sociability, 289
society, 369
soft, 386
soil, 94, 124, **439**
soiled, 294
soiling, 439
soilure, 439
solace, 308
solder, 99, 362
solemnity, **444**
solid, 197, 432
solitude, 70, 128
solution, 373
solvency, 83
sometime, 247
sophism, 79
sort, 160, 287
sottish, 378
soul, 96
sound, 13, 197, 432
soundness, 83, 159, **196, 243**
sour, 48
sovereignty, 371
sparing, **323**
special, 217
specific, 217
speechless, 414
speechlessness, **399**
speed, 119
spend, 45
spinsterhood, 279
spirit, 96
spiritless, 38
spiritual, 318
spoil, 28, 47, 124, **162**
spoiled, 314
spurious, 77
spurn, 433
squalor, 442
squander, 45, **154**
stable, 202, 329
stain, 94, 124, **439**
stained, 347
staining, 439
stale, 352
stand aside, 260
stand away, 260
stand back, 260
stand fast, **208**
standing, 83
stand off, 260

stand one's ground, 8
start, 178, 354, 404
starve, 380
stated, 261
stay, 8, 117, 208, 338
steadfast, 202
steadiness, 46, 116
steady, 202, 261, 329
sternness, 283, 320
stick, 208
stifle, 102
stillness, 290, 399, 404
stinginess, 92
stingy, 218, 323
stint, 380
stir, 38, 367
stir up, 38
stitch, 362
stoicism, 46
stolid, 62, 169, 389
stolidity, 444
stony, 34, 62, 169
stop, 338
stoppage, 338
storm, 55
stormy, 107
stout, 204
straightforward, 15
strain, 367
straiten, 380
straitened, 323
straitened circumstances, 442
strange, 429
stranger, 68
strength, 159
strengthen, 12
strife, 131
strong, 193, 329
stubborn, 162, 241
stubbornness, 363
studied, 191
stunted, 234
stupid, 19, 35, 126, 169, 352, 378, 389
stupidity, 20, 23, 34, 219, 255, 327, 443, 444
sturdiness, 159
sturdy, 193
stylish, 53
subaltern, 120
subdue, 102
subject, 337
sublime, 319
submission, 74, 371
submissive, 9, 203, 302, 357, 368
submissiveness, 249
submit, 135, 222
subordinate, 120, 337
subsequent, 334
subservient, 357
subsidiary, 255, 337
substance, 76, 165, 244
substantial, 13, 432

subtle, 108
subtract, 22
succeeding, 334
success, 113, 286
succinctness, 122
succor, 249
succumb, 135, 179, 401
suffer, 339
suffering, 19
sufficient, 432
suitable, 252
sullen, 48
sullied, 347
sully, 124
sum, 311
summarize, 49
summit, 14
sum up, 49
sunder, 69, 76, 287
sunny, 94
superadded, 255
superb, 319
supercilious, 86
superficial, 255, 353
superfluous, 255
superimposed, 255
superior, 86, 319
superstition, 271
supplemental, 255, 337
support, 1, 6, 74
supporter, 180
supporting, 28
supposed, 355
supposition, 142
suppositious, 355
suppress, 50
supremacy, 371
supreme, 86, 366
sure, 197, 202, 329
sureness, 196
surety, 196, 231
surly, 48
surprise, 52
surrender, 74, 87, 135, 147, 179, 388, 403
survive, 156
susceptibility, 55
suspension, 19
suspension of hostilities, 86
suspicion, 194
sustain, 6, 13, 74, 108, 307
sustaining, 28
sweet, 93, 203, 386
sweetness, 18
swelling, 238
sympathetic, 278, 290
sympathy, 53, 55, 180
synthetically, 55
systematic, 261

taciturn, 414
taciturnity, 399
taint, 124, 439
tainted, 347

tainting, 439
take up, 26
talkative, 414
tame, 203
tantalize, 380
tarnish, 47
tarnished, 347
tasteless, 352
tawdry, 173
teachable, 302
tedious, 417
tell, 234
temperance, 112
temperate, 167
tend, 13
tender, 84, 203, 278, **290, 386**
tentative, 353
territory, 97
terseness, 122
theoretical, 355
thick, 204
thick-headed, 126
thoroughfare, 85
thoughtful, 12, 109
thoughtless, 385, 436
thoughtlessness, 33, **345**
thraldom, 271
throw aside, 114, 121
throw away, 114, 427
throw down, 112, 410
throw off, 10, 112
throw open, 122
throw over, 427
throw up, 427
thwart, 232
timid, 98
timidity, 71, 172, 182, **305, 344, 416**
timorous, 98
tiny, 269
tire, 181
together, 55
toil, 181, 367
tolerate, 339
total, 59, 311, 379
tractable, 302, 357, 368, **386**
trained, 246
traitor, 25
traitorous, 240
tranquillity, 54, 404
transient, 254, 255
transit, 85
transitory, 254
transparency, 242
transparent, 144
treacherous, 240
treason, 39
treat, 6
trial, 353
tricky, 108
trifling, 133, 157, 250, **269, 385**
triumph, 116, 286, 291

trivial, 133, 157, 250, 269, 385
trouble, 136, 170
truce, 86
truculence, 320
true, 13, 197
trust, 153, 164
truth, 146, 150, 196, 198, 203, 214, 242, 332, 426
truthful, 146
truthfulness, 242
tumult, 367
turbid, 125
turbulence, 55
turbulent, 107

ugly, 88
unaccustomed, 22
unallowable, 27
unalterable, 202
unambiguous, 184
unamiable, 48
unanimity, 63
unassuming, 281
unattractive, 88
unauthorized, 77
unavailing, 171
unaware, 136
unbar, 389
unbecoming, 89
unbelief, 194, 360
unbind, 92
unbolt, 207
uncared for, 294
uncertain, 191
uncertainty, 296, 331
unchangeableness, 116
unchanging, 202
unchaste, 347
uncivil, 324
unclean, 347
unclose, 389
uncombined, 130
uncomfortable, 127
uncommon, 217, 299, 429
uncompounded, 130
unconcealed, 270
unconcerned, 169, 258
unconditioned, 366
unconnected, 27, 255, 291
unconscious, 136
unconsciousness, 282, 385
unconsecrated, 239
uncontrolled, 366
uncouth, 88, 324
uncover, 234
undaunted, 30
undecided, 302
undeniable, 13, 329
underling, 120
undertake, 1
undignified, 78
undiscerning, 378, 389
undiscovered, 188

undismayed, 30
undo, 389
undoubted, 329
undress, 166
undying, 425
uneasiness, 170
unequal, 24
unequivocal, 184
uneven, 208
unexpected, 248
unfading, 425
unfair, 27, 373
unfairness, 264
unfaithful, 194, 240
unfamiliarity, 17, 267
unfasten, 92, 207, 389
unfavorable, 342
unfettered, 366
unfit, 24, 89, 205
unfix, 207
unfortunate, 212
unfriendly, 215, 342
ungainly, 88, 205
ungodliness, 360
unhallowed, 239
unhandy, 394
unhappy, 212
unhealthy, 231
unholy, 239
uniform, 130, 261, 285
uniformity, 116, 156
unimaginable, 56
unimagined, 188
unimportant, 250
uninfluential, 250
uniform, 202
uninstructed, 15
unintelligent, 378, 389
unintelligible, 125
uninterested, 169, 258
union, 63
unison, 127
unite, 12, 99, 362
(see syn. for Add, 21; Append, 58; Apply, 60; Attach, 71)
unitedly, 55
unity, 63, 127, 156
universal, 261
unjust, 373
unjustifiable, 434
unkempt, 294
unkind, 215, 322
unkindness, 92
unknown, 188, 217
unlatch, 207
unlawfulness, 264
unlike, 37
unlikely, 56, 248, 273
unlikeness, 62, 273, 391
unlimited, 366
unlock, 207
unloose, 92
unlovely, 48, 88

unlucky, 212
unmannerliness, 23
unmannerly, 324
unmask, 234
unmindful, 169
unmoved, 169
unnecessary, 250, 295
unobtrusive, 281
unobtrusiveness, 173, 305
unostentatiousness, 173
unpalatable, 149
unparalleled, 429
unpardonable, 434
unpleasant, 88, 322
unpolished, 324
unprecedented, 299
unprofitableness, 430
unpropitious, 342
unpurchasable, 433
unqualified, 24
unquestionable, 13, 184, 329
unquestioned, 184
unravel, 287
unraveled, 130
unready, 298
unreal, 318, 355
unreasonable, 273
unreasonableness, 264
unreasoned, 15
unreciprocated, 291
unrequited, 291
unreserved, 414
unrest, 367
unrestrained, 366
unrighteous, 373
unsanctified, 239
unsatisfactory, 24
unsavory, 149
unscrupulous, 240
unseemly, 89, 205
unseen, 188
unsettle, 134, 207
unshared, 291
unskilfulness, 255, 327
unskilled, 394
unsound, 231
unstudied, 15
unsubstantial, 318
unsuitable, 24, 27, 89, 205
untangle, 287
untaught, 15, 324, 394
unthought of, 188
untidy, 294
untie, 92
untimely, 205
untrained, 394
untrue, 194, 240, 330, 355
untrustworthy, 194
untruth, 264, 427
untutored, 324
untwine, 287
unusual, 217, 299, 429
unvarying, 261
unveil, 234

unwarrantable, 27
unwarranted, 27
unwary, 436
unwavering, 202
unwillingness, 34
unwisdom, 23
unyielding, 162
uphold, 1, 13, 74, 108, 174, 307, 363
uplift, 144
uprightness, 214, 257, 392
uproot, 320, 341
upset, 134
urban, 376
urbane, 84, 96, 376
urge forward, 26, 119
urge on, 26, 119, 365, 412
useful, 315, 432
useless, 24, 171, 250, 295
uselessness, 304, 430
usual, 261, 349, 409
utility, 256

vacation, 444
vacillation, 153
vague, 125, 191, 330
vain, 86, 171
valiant, 30
valid, 432
valorous, 30
valuable, 432
vapid, 352
variance, 228
variation, 62
vassal, 120
vault of heaven, 14
vehemence, 55
veil, 133
veiling, 369
vengeance, 283, 309, 341
vengeful, 241
venturesome, 30
veracious, 146
veracity, 146
verbose, 417
verity, 150, 165, 196, 198, 203
vexation, 170
vice, 437
viciousness, 437
vigor, 159

vigorous, 193
vile, 376
vilification, 328
vindicate, 1, 13, 363, 394
vindictive, 241
violate, 115
violence, 55
violent, 107
virginity, 279
virtue, 392
virtuous, 141
visible, 270
visionary, 355
visit, 310
vitiate, 47, 124
vituperation, 328
volatile, 385
vomit, 10
vulgar, 78
vulgarity, 359

wages, 220
waive, 402
want, 7, 189, 200, 442
wantonness, 11
war, 41, 131
wariness, 182, 416
warlike, 215
warm, 94
warn, 44
warrant, 210, 339
wash, 147
waste, 45, 154, 216, 338
wasted, 231
wasteful, 285
wastefulness, 345
wavering, 153, 194, 302
way, 85
weak, 211, 231
weaken, 134, 207
weakness, 327
wealth, 216
weariness, 181
weary, 181
weed out, 320
weigh anchor, 354
weld, 99, 362
welfare, 228
well-bred, 376
well-disposed, 278
well-informed, 246

white, 144
whole, 59, 311, 379
wholesome, 315
wicked, 239
wickedness, 360, 437
wide-awake, 12
widowhood, 279
wild, 107
wilful, 162, 241
willing, 361
wily, 108
wisdom, 245
wise, 13, 246
withdraw, 22, 260, 303
withdrawal, 183
withhold, 42, 50, 303
without, 48
withstand, 42, 74, 232
witless, 126
woeful, 212, 322
wonder, 52
wooden, 34
wordy, 417
work, 181, 340, 367
working, 246
worldly, 239
worn, 231
worry, 170
worthless, 24, 250, 295, **314**
worthlessness, 430
worthy, 432
wound, 136
wrangle, 131
wrangling, 131
wrath, 341
wrathful, 107, 241
wreck, 410
wretched, 127, 212, 322
wretchedness, 442
write, 108
written, 191
wrong, 56, 264, 330, 373, **437**

yet, 44, 88
yield, 135, 179, 222, 401
yielding, 9, 302, 357, **368,** 386
youthful
  (see syn. for Old, **303**)

zenith, 14